BY RONEN BERGMAN

RISE AND KILL FIRST:
THE SECRET HISTORY OF ISRAEL'S TARGETED ASSASSINATIONS

OPERATION RED FALCON

THE SECRET WAR WITH IRAN:
THE 30-YEAR CLANDESTINE STRUGGLE AGAINST THE WORLD'S
MOST DANGEROUS TERRORIST POWER

# RISE
# AND
# KILL
# FIRST

# RISE AND KILL FIRST

THE SECRET HISTORY

OF ISRAEL'S

TARGETED ASSASSINATIONS

## RONEN BERGMAN

TRANSLATED BY RONNIE HOPE

RANDOM HOUSE NEW YORK

TO YANA,

*who appeared*

*at exactly the right moment*

*If someone comes to kill you,*

*rise up and kill him first.*

THE BABYLONIAN TALMUD, TRACTATE SANHEDRIN,
PORTION 72, VERSE 1

# CONTENTS

# A NOTE ON THE SOURCES

THE ISRAELI INTELLIGENCE COMMUNITY guards its secrets jealously. Its near-total opacity is protected by a complex array of laws and protocols, strict military censorship, and the intimidation, interrogation, and prosecution of journalists and their sources, as well as a natural solidarity and loyalty among the espionage agencies' personnel.

All glimpses behind the scenes have, to this day, been partial at best.

How then, it might reasonably be asked, to write a book about one of the most secretive organizations on earth?

Efforts to persuade the Israeli defense establishment to cooperate with the research for this project went nowhere. Requests to the intelligence community that it comply with the law by transferring its historical documents to the State Archive and allowing publication of materials fifty years old or more were met with stony silence. A petition to the Supreme Court for an order forcing compliance with the law was dragged out over years, with the complicity of the court, and ended with nothing but an amendment to the law itself: The secrecy provisions were extended from fifty to seventy years, longer than the history of the state.

The defense establishment did not merely sit with folded arms. As early as 2010, before the contract for this book was even signed, a special meeting was held in the Mossad's operations division, Caesarea, to discuss ways of disrupting my research. Letters were written to all former Mossad employees warning them against giving interviews, and individual conversations were held with certain ex-staffers who were considered the most problematic. Later in 2011, the chief of the General Staff of the IDF, Lieutenant General Gabi Ashkenazi, asked the Shin Bet to take aggressive steps against the author, claiming that I had perpetrated "aggravated espionage" by having in my possession classified secrets and "using classified material in order to disparage me [Ashkenazi] personally." Since then, several actions have been taken by various bodies to stop publication of the book, or at least large parts of it.

The military censor requires the Israeli media to add the words "according to foreign publications" whenever it mentions secret actions attributed to Israeli intelligence, primarily targeted assassinations. This is to make it clear that the existence of the publication does not constitute official acknowledgment of Israel's responsibility. In this sense, then, this book must be taken as a "foreign publication" whose contents do not have any official Israeli confirmation.

None of the thousand interviews upon which this book is based— with sources ranging from political leaders and chiefs of intelligence agencies to the operatives themselves—were approved by Israel's defense establishment. Most of the sources are identified by their names. Others understandably feared being identified and are therefore referred to by their initials or nicknames, in addition to any details about them I was able to provide while still keeping their identities secret.

I have also made use of thousands of documents given to me by these sources, all of which are referenced for the first time here. My sources never received permission to remove these documents from their places of employment, and certainly did not have permission to pass them on to me. This book is thus about as far as possible from an authorized history of Israeli intelligence.

So, why did these sources speak with me and supply me with these documents? Each had his own motive, and sometimes the story behind the scenes was only a little less interesting than the content of the interview itself. It is clear that some politicians and intelligence personnel—two professions highly skilled in manipulation and deception—were trying to use me as the conduit for their preferred version of events, or to shape history to suit themselves. I have tried to thwart such attempts by cross-checking with as many written and oral sources as I could.

But it seemed to me that there was often another motive, which had much to do with a particularly Israeli contradiction: On the one hand, nearly everything in the country related to intelligence and national security is classified as "top secret." On the other hand, everyone wants to speak about what they've done. Acts that people in other countries might be ashamed to admit to are instead a source of pride for Israelis, because they are collectively perceived as imperatives of national security, necessary to protect threatened Israeli lives, if not the very existence of the embattled state.

After a time, the Mossad did manage to block access to some of my sources (in most cases only after they had already spoken to me). Many more have died since I met them, most of natural causes. Thus, the firsthand accounts that these men and women have given for this book—men and women who witnessed and participated in significant historic events—are in fact the only ones that exist outside the vaults of the defense establishment's secret archives.

Occasionally, they are the only ones that exist at all.

# PROLOGUE

MEIR DAGAN, CHIEF OF the Israeli Mossad, legendary spy and assassin, walked into the room, leaning on his cane.

He'd been using it ever since he was wounded by a mine laid by Palestinian terrorists he was fighting in the Gaza Strip as a young special-ops officer in the 1970s. Dagan, who knew a thing or two about the power of myths and symbols, was careful not to deny the rumors that there was a blade concealed in the cane, which he could bare with a push of a button.

Dagan was a short man, so dark-skinned that people were always surprised to hear that he was from Polish origins, and he had a potbelly with a presence of its own. On this occasion he was wearing a simple open-necked shirt, light black pants, and black shoes, and it looked as if he'd not paid any special attention to his appearance. There was something about him that expressed a direct, terse self-confidence, and a quiet, sometimes menacing charisma.

The conference room that Dagan entered that afternoon, on January 8, 2011, was in the Mossad Academy, north of Tel Aviv. For the first time ever, the head of the espionage agency was meeting with journalists in the heart of one of Israel's most closely guarded and secret installations.

Dagan had no love for the media. "I've reached the conclusion that it is an insatiable monster," he would tell me later, "so there's no point in maintaining a relationship with it." Nevertheless, three days before the meeting, I and a number of other correspondents had received a confidential invitation. I was surprised. For an entire decade

I had been leveling some harsh criticism at the Mossad, and in particular at Dagan, making him very angry.

The Mossad did everything it could to give the affair a cloak-and-dagger atmosphere. We were told to come to the parking lot of Cinema City, a movie theater complex not far from Mossad HQ, and to leave everything in our cars except notebooks and writing implements. "You will be carefully searched, and we want to avoid any unpleasantness," our escorts told us. From there we were driven in a bus with dark tinted windows to the Mossad headquarters complex. We passed through a number of electric gates and electronic signs warning those entering what was permitted and what forbidden inside the perimeter. Then came a thorough scanning with metal detectors to make sure we hadn't brought any video or audio recording equipment. We entered the conference room, and Dagan came in a few minutes after us, walking around and shaking hands. When he got to me, he gripped my hand for a moment and said with a smile, "You really are some kind of a bandit."

Then he sat down. He was flanked by the spokesman of Prime Minister Benjamin Netanyahu and the chief military censor, a female brigadier general. (The Mossad is a unit of the prime minister's office, and, under national law, reporting on any of its activities is subject to censorship.) Both of these officials believed that Dagan had called the meeting merely to bid a formal farewell to the people who had covered his tenure, and that he would say nothing substantive.

They were wrong. The surprise was evident on the face of the prime minister's spokesperson, whose eyes got wider and wider as Dagan continued speaking.

"There are advantages to having a back injury," Dagan said, opening his address. "You get a doctor's certificate confirming that you're not spineless." Very quickly, we realized that this was no mere wisecrack, as Dagan launched into a vehement attack on the prime minister of Israel. Benjamin Netanyahu, Dagan claimed, was behaving irresponsibly and, for his own egotistical reasons, leading the country into disaster. "That someone is elected does not mean that he is smart" was one of his jibes.

This was the last day of Dagan's term as the Mossad's director.

Netanyahu was showing him the door, and Dagan, whose life's dream had been to hold the position of Israel's top spy, was not going to stand by with folded arms. The acute crisis of confidence between the two men had flared up around two issues, and both of them were intimately connected to Meir Dagan's weapon of choice: assassination.

Eight years earlier, Ariel Sharon had appointed Dagan to the Mossad post and put him in charge of disrupting the Iranian nuclear weapons project, which both men saw as an existential threat to Israel. Dagan acted in a number of ways to fulfill this task. The most difficult way, but also the most effective, Dagan believed, was to identify Iran's key nuclear and missile scientists, locate them, and kill them. The Mossad pinpointed fifteen such targets, of whom it eliminated six, mostly when they were on their way to work in the morning, by means of bombs with short time fuses, attached to their cars by a motorcyclist. In addition, a general of Iran's Islamic Revolutionary Guard Corps, who was in charge of the missile project, was blown up in his headquarters together with seventeen of his men.

These operations and many others initiated by the Mossad, some in collaboration with the United States, were all successful, but Netanyahu and his defense minister, Ehud Barak, had begun to feel that their utility was declining. They decided that clandestine measures could no longer effectively delay the Iranian nuclear project, and that only a massive aerial bombardment of the Iranians' nuclear facilities would successfully halt their progress toward acquiring such weapons.

Dagan strongly opposed this idea. Indeed, it flew in the face of everything he believed in: that open warfare should be waged only when "the sword is on our throat," or as a last resort, in situations in which there was no other choice. Everything else could and should be handled through clandestine means.

"Assassinations," he said, "have an effect on morale, as well as a practical effect. I don't think there were many who could have replaced Napoleon, or a president like Roosevelt or a prime minister like Churchill. The personal aspect certainly plays a role. It's true that anyone can be replaced, but there's a difference between a replacement with guts and some lifeless character."

Furthermore, the use of assassination, in Dagan's view, "is a lot more moral" than waging all-out war. Neutralizing a few major figures is enough to make the latter option unnecessary and save the lives of untold numbers of soldiers and civilians on both sides. A large-scale attack against Iran would lead to a large-scale conflict across the Middle East, and even then it likely would not cause enough damage to the Iranian installations.

Finally, from Dagan's point of view, if Israel started a war with Iran, it would be an indictment of his entire career. History books would show that he had not fulfilled the task that Sharon had given him: to put an end to Iranian nuclear acquisition using covert means, without recourse to an open assault.

Dagan's opposition, and similar heavy pressure from the top military and intelligence chiefs, forced the repeated postponement of the attack on Iran. Dagan even briefed CIA Director Leon Panetta about the Israeli plan (the prime minister alleges he did so without permission), and soon President Obama was also warning Netanyahu not to attack.

The tension between the two men escalated even higher in 2010, seven years into Dagan's tenure. Dagan had dispatched a hit team of twenty-seven Mossad operatives to Dubai to eliminate a senior official of the Palestinian terror group Hamas. They did the job: the assassins injected him with a paralyzing drug in his hotel room and made their getaway from the country before the body was discovered. But just a short while after their departure, due to a series of gross errors they made—forgetting to take into account Dubai's innumerable CCTV cameras; using the same phony passports that the operatives had previously used to enter Dubai in order to follow the target; and a phone setup that the local police had no trouble in cracking—the whole world was soon watching video footage of their faces and a complete record of their movements. The discovery that this was a Mossad operation caused serious operational damage to the agency, as well as profound embarrassment to the State of Israel, which had once again been caught using fake passports of friendly Western countries for its agents. "But you told me it would be easy and simple, that the risk of things going wrong was close to zero," Netanyahu fumed at Dagan, and ordered him to suspend many of the pending assassination plans and other operations until further notice.

The confrontation between Dagan and Netanyahu became more and more acute until Netanyahu (according to his version) decided not to extend Dagan's tenure, or (in Dagan's words) "I simply got sick of him and I decided to retire."

At that briefing in the Mossad Academy and in a number of later interviews for this book, Dagan displayed robust confidence that the Mossad, under his leadership, would have been able to stop the Iranians from making nuclear weapons by means of assassinations and other pinpoint measures—for instance, working with the United States to keep the Iranians from being able to import critical parts for their nuclear project that they could not manufacture themselves. "If we manage to prevent Iran from obtaining some of the components, this would seriously damage their project. In a car there are 25,000 parts on average. Imagine if one hundred of them are missing. It would be very hard to make it go."

"On the other hand," Dagan added with a smile, returning to his favorite modus operandi, "sometimes it's most effective to kill the driver, and that's that."

OF ALL THE MEANS that democracies use to protect their security, there is none more fraught and controversial than "killing the driver"—assassination.

Some, euphemistically, call it "liquidation." The American intelligence community calls it, for legal reasons, "targeted killings." In practice, these terms amount to the same thing: killing a specific individual in order to achieve a specific goal—saving the lives of people the target intends to kill, averting a dangerous act that he is about to perpetrate, and sometimes removing a leader in order to change the course of history.

The use of assassinations by a state touches two very difficult dilemmas. First, is it effective? Can the elimination of an individual, or a number of individuals, make the world a safer place? Second, is it morally and legally justified? Is it legitimate, both ethically and judicially, for a country to employ the gravest of all crimes in any code of ethics or law—the premeditated taking of a human life—in order to protect its own citizens?

This book deals mainly with the assassinations and targeted killings carried out by the Mossad and by other arms of the Israeli government, in both peacetime and wartime—as well as, in the early chapters, by the underground militias in the pre-state era, organizations that were to become the army and intelligence services of the state, once it was established.

Since World War II, Israel has assassinated more people than any other country in the Western world. On innumerable occasions, its leaders have weighed what would be the best way to defend its national security and, out of all the options, have time and again decided on clandestine operations, with assassination the method of choice. This, they believed, would solve difficult problems faced by the state, and sometimes change the course of history. In many cases, Israel's leaders have even determined that in order to kill the designated target, it is moral and legal to endanger the lives of innocent civilians who may happen to find themselves in the line of fire. Harming such people, they believe, is a necessary evil.

The numbers speak for themselves. Up until the start of the Second Palestinian Intifada, in September 2000, when Israel first began to respond to suicide bombings with the daily use of armed drones to perform assassinations, the state had conducted some 500 targeted killing operations. In these, at least 1,000 people were killed, both civilians and combatants. During the Second Intifada, Israel carried out some 1,000 more operations, of which 168 succeeded. Since then, up until the writing of this book, Israel has executed some 800 targeted killing operations, almost all of which were part of the rounds of warfare against Hamas in the Gaza Strip in 2008, 2012, and 2014 or Mossad operations across the Middle East against Palestinian, Syrian, and Iranian targets. By contrast, during the presidency of George W. Bush, the United States of America carried out 48 targeted killing operations, according to one estimate, and under President Barack Obama there were 353 such attacks.

Israel's reliance on assassination as a military tool did not happen by chance, but rather stems from the revolutionary and activist roots of the Zionist movement, from the trauma of the Holocaust, and from the sense among Israel's leaders and citizens that the country and its people are perpetually in danger of annihilation and that, as in the Holocaust, no one will come to their aid when that happens.

Because of Israel's tiny dimensions, the attempts by the Arab states to destroy it even before it was established, their continued threats to do so, and the perpetual menace of Arab terrorism, the country evolved a highly effective military and, arguably, the best intelligence community in the world. They, in turn, have developed the most robust, streamlined assassination machine in history.

The following pages will detail the secrets of that machine—the fruit of a mixed marriage between guerrilla warfare and the military might of a technological powerhouse—its operatives, leaders, methods, deliberations, successes, and failures, as well as the moral costs. They will illustrate how two separate legal systems have arisen in Israel—one for ordinary citizens and one for the intelligence community and defense establishment. The latter system has allowed, with a nod and a wink from the government, highly problematic acts of assassination, with no parliamentary or public scrutiny, resulting in the loss of many innocent lives.

On the other hand, the assassination weapon, based on intelligence that is "nothing less than exquisite"—to quote the former head of the NSA and the CIA, General Michael Hayden—is what made Israel's war on terror the most effective ever waged by a Western country. On numerous occasions, it was targeted killing that saved Israel from very grave crises.

The Mossad and Israel's other intelligence arms have done away with individuals who were identified as direct threats to national security, and killing them has also sent a bigger message: *If you are an enemy of Israel, we will find and kill you, wherever you are.* This message has indeed been heard around the world. Occasional blunders have only enhanced the Mossad's aggressive and merciless reputation—not a bad thing, when the goal of deterrence is as important as the goal of preempting specific hostile acts.

The assassinations were not all carried out by small, closed groups. The more complex they became, the more people took part—sometimes as many as hundreds, the majority of them below the age of twenty-five. Sometimes these young people will come with their commanders to meet the prime minister—the only one authorized to green-light an assassination—in order to explain the operation and get final approval. Such forums, in which most of the participants advocating for someone's death are under the age of thirty, are probably unique to Israel. Some of the low-ranking officers involved in these meetings have advanced over the years to become national leaders and even prime ministers themselves. What marks have remained imprinted on them from the times they took part in hit operations?

The United States has taken the intelligence-gathering and assassination techniques developed in Israel as a model, and after 9/11 and President Bush's decision to launch a campaign of targeted killings against Al Qaeda, it transplanted some of these methods into its own intelligence and war-on-terror systems. The command-and-control systems, the war rooms, the methods of information gathering, and the technology of the pilotless aircraft, or drones, that now serve the Americans and their allies were all in large part developed in Israel.

Nowadays, when the same kind of extrajudicial killing that Israel has used for decades is being used daily by America against its enemies, it is appropriate not only to admire the impressive operational capabilities that Israel has built, but also to study the high moral price that has been paid, and still is being paid, for the use of such power.

RONEN BERGMAN
Tel Aviv

# RISE
# AND
# KILL
# FIRST

# IN BLOOD AND FIRE

ON SEPTEMBER 29, 1944, David Shomron hid in the gloom of St. George Street, not far from the Romanian Church in Jerusalem. A church building was used as officers' lodgings by the British authorities governing Palestine, and Shomron was waiting for one of those officers, a man named Tom Wilkin, to leave.

Wilkin was the commander of the Jewish unit at the Criminal Investigation Department (CID) of the British Mandate for Palestine, and he was very good at his job, especially the part that involved infiltrating and disrupting the fractious Jewish underground. Aggressive, yet also exceptionally patient and calculating, Wilkin spoke fluent Hebrew, and after thirteen years of service in Palestine, he had an extensive network of informants. Thanks to the intelligence they provided, underground fighters were arrested, their weapons caches were seized, and their planned operations, aimed at forcing the British to leave Palestine, were foiled.

Which was why Shomron was going to kill him.

Shomron and his partner that night, Yaakov Banai (code-named Mazal—"Luck"), were operatives with Lehi, the most radical of the Zionist underground movements fighting the British in the early 1940s. Though Lehi was the acronym for the Hebrew phrase "fighters for the freedom of Israel," the British considered it a terrorist organization, referring to it dismissively as the Stern Gang, after its founder, the romantic ultra-nationalist Avraham Stern. Stern and his tiny band of followers employed a targeted mayhem of assassinations and bombings—a campaign of "personal terror," as Lehi's operations chief (and later Israeli prime minister), Yitzhak Shamir, called it.

Wilkin knew he was a target. Lehi already had tried to kill him and his boss, Geoffrey Morton, nearly three years earlier, in its first, clumsy operation. On January 20, 1942, assassins planted bombs on the roof and inside the building of 8 Yael Street, in Tel Aviv. Instead they ended up killing three police officers—two Jews and an Englishman—who arrived before Wilkin and Morton and tripped the charges. Later, Morton fled Palestine after being wounded in another attempt on his life—that one in retribution for Morton having shot Stern dead.

None of those details, the back-and-forth of who killed whom and in what order, mattered to Shomron. The British occupied the land the Zionists saw as rightfully theirs—that was what mattered, and Shamir had issued a death sentence against Wilkin.

For Shomron and his comrades, Wilkin was not a person but rather a target, prominent and high-value. "We were too busy and hungry to think about the British and their families," Shomron said decades later.

After discovering that Wilkin was residing in the Romanian Church annex, the assassins set out on their mission. Shomron and Banai had revolvers and hand grenades in their pockets. Additional Lehi operatives were in the vicinity, smartly dressed in suits and hats to look like Englishmen.

Wilkin left the officers' lodgings in the church and headed for the CID's facility in the Russian Compound, where underground suspects were held and interrogated. As always, he was wary, scanning the street as he walked and keeping one hand in his pocket all the time. As he passed the corner of St. George and Mea Shearim Streets, a youngster sitting outside the neighborhood grocery store got up and dropped his hat. This was the signal, and the two assassins began walking toward Wilkin, identifying him according to the photographs they'd studied. Shomron and Banai let him pass, gripping their revolvers with sweating palms.

Then they turned around and drew.

"Before we did it, Mazal [Banai] said, 'Let me shoot first,'" Shomron recalled. "But when we saw him, I guess I couldn't restrain my-self. I shot first."

Between them, Banai and Shomron fired fourteen times. Eleven of those bullets hit Wilkin. "He managed to turn around and draw his pistol," Shomron said, "but then he fell face first. A spurt of blood came out of his forehead, like a fountain. It was not such a pretty picture."

Shomron and Banai darted back into the shadows and made off in a taxi in which another Lehi man was waiting for them.

"The only thing that hurt me was that we forgot to take the brief-case in which he had all his documents," Shomron said. Other than that, "I didn't feel anything, not even a little twinge of guilt. We be-lieved the more coffins that reached London, the closer the day of freedom would be."

THE IDEA THAT THE return of the People of Israel to the Land of Israel could be achieved only by force was not born with Stern and his Lehi comrades.

The roots of that strategy can be traced to eight men who gath-ered in a stifling one-room apartment overlooking an orange grove in Jaffa on September 29, 1907, exactly thirty-seven years before a fountain of blood spurted from Wilkin's head, when Palestine was still part of the Turkish Ottoman Empire. The flat was rented by Yitzhak Ben-Zvi, a young Russian who'd immigrated to Ottoman Pal-estine earlier that year. Like the others in his apartment that night—all emigrants from the Russian empire, sitting on a straw mat spread on the floor of the candlelit room—he was a committed Zionist, al-beit part of a splinter sect that had once threatened to rend the move-ment.

Zionism as a political ideology had been founded in 1896 when Viennese Jewish journalist Theodor Herzl published *Der Judenstaat* (*The Jewish State*). He had been deeply affected while covering the trial in Paris of Alfred Dreyfus, a Jewish army officer unjustly accused and convicted of treason.

In his book, Herzl argued that anti-Semitism was so deeply ingrained in European culture that the Jewish people could achieve true freedom and safety only in a nation-state of their own. The Jewish elite of Western Europe, who'd managed to carve out comfortable lives for themselves, mostly rejected Herzl. But his ideas resonated with poor and working-class Jews of Eastern Europe, who suffered repeated pogroms and continual oppression and to which some of them responded by aligning themselves with leftist uprisings.

Herzl himself saw Palestine, the Jews' ancestral homeland, as the ideal location for a future Jewish state, but he maintained that any settlement there would have to be handled deliberately and delicately, through proper diplomatic channels and with international sanction, if a Jewish nation was to survive in peace. Herzl's view came to be known as *political* Zionism.

Ben-Zvi and his seven comrades, on the other hand, were—like most other Russian Jews—*practical* Zionists. Rather than wait for the rest of the world to give them a home, they believed in creating one themselves—in going to Palestine, working the land, making the desert bloom. They would take what they believed to be rightfully theirs, and they would defend what they had taken.

This put the practical Zionists in immediate conflict with most of the Jews already living in Palestine. As a tiny minority in an Arab land—many of them peddlers and religious scholars and functionaries under the Ottoman regime—they preferred to keep a low profile. Through subservience and compromise and bribery, these established Palestinian Jews had managed to buy themselves relative peace and a measure of security.

But Ben-Zvi and the other newcomers were appalled at the conditions their fellow Jews tolerated. Many were living in abject poverty and had no means of defending themselves, utterly at the mercy of the Arab majority and the venal officials of the corrupt Ottoman Empire. Arab mobs attacked and plundered Jewish settlements, rarely with any consequences. Worse, as Ben-Zvi and the others saw it, those same settlements had consigned their defense to Arab guards— who in turn would sometimes collaborate with attacking mobs.

Ben-Zvi and his friends found this situation to be unsustainable and intolerable. Some were former members of Russian left-wing revolutionary movements inspired by the People's Will (Narodnaya Volya), an aggressive anti-tsarist guerrilla movement that employed terrorist tactics, including assassinations.

Disappointed by the abortive 1905 revolution in Russia, which in the end produced only minimal constitutional reforms, some of these socialist revolutionaries, social democrats, and liberals moved to Ottoman Palestine to reestablish a Jewish state.

They all were desperately poor, barely scraping by, earning pennies at teaching jobs or manual labor in the fields and orange groves, often going hungry. But they were proud Zionists. If they were going to create a nation, they first had to defend themselves. So they slipped through the streets of Jaffa in pairs and alone, making their way to the secret meeting in Ben-Zvi's apartment. That night, those eight people formed the first Hebrew fighting force of the modern age. They decreed that, from then forward, everything would be different from the image of the weak and persecuted Jew all across the globe. Only Jews would defend Jews in Palestine.

They named their fledgling army Bar-Giora, after one of the leaders of the Great Jewish Revolt against the Roman Empire, in the first century. On their banner, they paid homage to that ancient rebellion and predicted their future. "In blood and fire Judea fell," it read. "In blood and fire Judea will rise."

Judea would indeed rise. Ben-Zvi would one day be the Jewish nation's second president. Yet first there would be much fire, and much blood.


BAR-GIORA WAS NOT, AT first, a popular movement. But more Jews arrived in Palestine from Russia and Eastern Europe every year—35,000 between 1905 and 1914—bringing with them that same determined philosophy of practical Zionism.

With more like-minded Jews flooding into the Yishuv, as the Jewish community in Palestine was called, Bar-Giora in 1909 was reconstituted into the larger and more aggressive Hashomer (Hebrew for "the Guard"). By 1912, Hashomer was defending fourteen settlements. Yet it was also developing offensive, albeit clandestine, capabilities, preparing for what practical Zionists saw as an inevitable eventual war to take control of Palestine. Hashomer therefore saw itself as the nucleus for a future Jewish army and intelligence service.

Mounted on their horses, Hashomer vigilantes raided a few Arab settlements to punish residents who had harmed Jews, sometimes beating them up, sometimes executing them. In one case, a special clandestine assembly of Hashomer members decided to eliminate a Bedouin policeman, Aref al-Arsan, who had assisted the Turks and tortured Jewish prisoners. He was shot dead by Hashomer in June 1916.

Hashomer did not recoil from using force to assert its authority over other Jews, either. During World War I, Hashomer was violently opposed to NILI, a Jewish spy network working for the British in Ottoman Palestine. Hashomer feared that the Turks would discover the spies and wreak vengeance against the entire Jewish community. When they failed to get NILI to cease operations or to hand over a stash of gold coins they'd received from the British, they made an attempt on the life of Yosef Lishansky, one of its members, managing only to wound him.

In 1920, Hashomer evolved again, now into the Haganah (Hebrew for "Defense"). Though it was not specifically legal, the British authorities, who had been ruling the country for about three years, tolerated the Haganah as the paramilitary defensive arm of the Yishuv. The Histadrut, the socialist labor union of the Jews in Israel that was founded in the same year, and the Jewish Agency, the Yishuv's autonomous governing authority, established a few years later, both headed by David Ben-Gurion, maintained command over the secret organization.

Ben-Gurion was born David Yosef Grün in Płońsk, Poland, in 1886. From an early age, he followed in his father's footsteps as a Zionist activist. In 1906, he migrated to Palestine and, thanks to his charisma and determination, soon became one of the leaders of the Yishuv, despite his youth. He then changed his name to Ben-Gurion, after another of the leaders of the revolt against the Romans.

Haganah in its early years was influenced by the spirit and aggressive attitude of Hashomer. On May 1, 1921, an Arab mob massacred fourteen Jews in an immigrants' hostel in Jaffa. After learning that an

Arab police officer by the name of Tewfik Bey had helped the mob get into the hostel, Haganah sent a hit squad to dispose of him, and on January 17, 1923, he was shot dead in the middle of a Tel Aviv street. "As a matter of honor," he was shot from the front and not in the back, according to one of those involved, and the intention was "to show the Arabs that their deeds are not forgotten and their day will come, even if belatedly."

The members of Hashomer who led the Haganah at the outset were even willing to commit acts of violence against fellow Jews. Jacob de Haan was a Dutch-born Haredi—an ultra-Orthodox Jew— living in Jerusalem in the early 1920s. He was a propagandist for the Haredi belief that only the Messiah could establish a Jewish state, that God alone would decide when to return the Jews to their ancestral homeland, and that humans trying to expedite the process were committing a grave sin. In other words, de Haan was a staunch anti-Zionist, and he was surprisingly adept at swaying international opinion. To Yitzhak Ben-Zvi, by now a prominent Haganah leader, that made de Haan dangerous. So he ordered his death.

On June 30, 1924—just a day before de Haan was to travel to London to ask the British government to reconsider its promise to establish a Jewish nation in Palestine—two assassins shot him three times as he emerged from a synagogue on Jaffa Road in Jerusalem.

Ben-Gurion, however, took a dim view of such acts. He realized that in order to win even partial recognition from the British for Zionist aims, he would have to enforce orderly and more moderate norms on the semi-underground militia under his command. Hashomer's brave and lethal lone riders were replaced after the de Haan murder by an organized, hierarchical armed force. Ben-Gurion ordered Haganah to desist from using targeted killings. "As to personal terror, Ben-Gurion's line was consistently and steadily against it," Haganah commander Yisrael Galili testified later, and he recounted a number of instances in which Ben-Gurion had refused to approve proposals for hits against individual Arabs. These included the Palestinian leader Hajj Amin al-Husseini and other members of the Arab Higher Committee, and British personnel, such as a senior official in the Mandate's lands authority who was obstructing Jewish settlement projects.

Not everyone was eager to acquiesce to Ben-Gurion. Avraham Tehomi, the man who shot de Haan, despised the moderate line Ben-Gurion took against the British and the Arabs, and, together with some other leading figures, he quit Haganah and in 1931 formed the Irgun Zvai Leumi, the "National Military Organization" whose Hebrew acronym is Etzel, usually referred to in English as IZL or the Irgun. This radical right-wing group was commanded in the 1940s by Menachem Begin, who in 1977 was to become prime minister of Israel. Inside the Irgun, too, there were clashes, personal and ideological. Opponents of Begin's agreement to cooperate with Britain in its war against the Nazis broke away and formed Lehi. For these men, any cooperation with Britain was anathema.

These two dissident groups both advocated, to different degrees, the use of targeted killings against the Arab and British enemy, and against Jews they considered dangerous to their cause. Ben-Gurion remained adamant that targeted killings would not be used as a weapon and even took aggressive measures against those who did not obey his orders.

But then World War II ended, and everything, even the views of the obstinate Ben-Gurion, changed.


DURING WORLD WAR II, some 38,000 Jews from Palestine volunteered to help and serve in the British Army in Europe. The British formed the so-called Jewish Brigade, albeit somewhat reluctantly and only after being pressured by the Yishuv's civilian leadership.

Unsure exactly what to do with the Brigade, the British first sent it to train in Egypt. It was there, in mid-1944, that its members first heard of the Nazi campaign of Jewish annihilation. When they were finally sent to Europe to fight in Italy and Austria, they witnessed the horrors of the Holocaust firsthand and were among the first to send detailed reports to Ben-Gurion and other leaders of the Yishuv.

One of those soldiers was Mordechai Gichon, who later would be one of the founders of Israeli military intelligence. Born in Berlin in 1922, Gichon had a father who was Russian and a mother who was the scion of a famous German-Jewish family, niece of Rabbi Leo Baeck, a leader of Germany's Liberal (Reform) Jews. Gichon's family moved to Palestine in 1933, after Mordechai had been required in his German school to give the Nazi salute and sing the party anthem.

He returned as a soldier to a Europe in ruins, his people nearly destroyed, their communities smoldering ruins. "The Jewish people had been humiliated, trampled, murdered," he said. "Now was the time to strike back, to take revenge. In my dreams, when I enlisted, revenge took the form of me arresting my best friend from Germany, whose name was Detlef, the son of a police major. That's how I would restore lost Jewish honor."

It was that sense of lost honor, of a people's humiliation, as much as rage at the Nazis, that drove men like Gichon. He first met the Jewish refugees on the border between Austria and Italy. The men of the Brigade fed them, took off their own uniforms to clothe them against the cold, tried to draw out of them details of the atrocities they had undergone. He remembers an encounter in June 1945 in which a female refugee came up to him.

"She broke away from her group and spoke to me in German," he said. "She said, 'You, the soldiers of the Brigade, are the sons of Bar Kokhba'"—the great hero of the Second Jewish Revolt against the Romans, in A.D. 132–135. "She said, 'I will always remember your insignia and what you did for us.'"

Gichon was flattered by the Bar Kokhba analogy, but for her praise and gratitude, Gichon felt only pity and shame. If the Jews in the Brigade were the sons of Bar Kokhba, who were these Jews? The soldiers from the Land of Israel, standing erect, tough, and strong, saw the Holocaust survivors as victims who needed help, but also as part of the European Jewry who had allowed themselves to be massacred. They embodied the cowardly, feeble stereotype of the Jews of the Diaspora—the Exile, in traditional Jewish and Zionist parlance—who surrendered rather than fought back, who did not know how to shoot or wield a weapon. It was that image—in its most extreme version, the Jew as a *Muselmann*, prisoners' slang for the emaciated, zombie-like inmates hovering near death in the Nazi camps—that the new Jews of the Yishuv rejected. "My brain could not grasp, not then and not today, how it could have been that there were tens of thousands of Jews in a camp with only a few German guards, but they did not rise up, they simply went like lambs to the slaughter,"

Gichon said more than sixty years later. "Why didn't they tear [the Germans] to shreds? I've always said that no such thing could happen in the Land of Israel. Had those communities had leaders worthy of the name, the entire business would have looked completely different."

In the years following the war, the Zionists of the Yishuv would prove, both to the world and, more important, to themselves, that Jews would never again go to such slaughter—and that Jewish blood would not come cheaply. The six million would be avenged.

"We thought we could not rest until we had exacted blood for blood, death for death," said Hanoch Bartov, a highly regarded Israeli novelist who enlisted in the Brigade a month before his seventeenth birthday.

Such vengeance, though—atrocity for atrocity—would violate the rules of war and likely be disastrous for the Zionist cause. Ben-Gurion, practical as always, publicly said as much: "Revenge now is an act of no national value. It cannot restore life to the millions who were murdered."

Still, the Haganah's leaders privately understood the need for some sort of retribution, both to satisfy the troops who had been exposed to the atrocities and also to achieve some degree of historical justice and deter future attempts to slaughter Jews. Thus, they sanctioned some types of reprisals against the Nazis and their accomplices. Immediately after the war, a secret unit, authorized and controlled by the Haganah high command and unknown to the British commanders, was set up within the Brigade. It was called Gmul, Hebrew for "Recompense." The unit's mission was "revenge, but not a robber's revenge," as a secret memo at the time put it. "Revenge against those SS men who themselves took part in the slaughter."

"We looked for big fish," Mordechai Gichon said, breaking a vow of silence among the Gmul commanders that he'd kept for more than sixty years. "The senior Nazis who had managed to shed their uniforms and return to their homes."

The Gmul agents worked undercover even as they performed their regular Brigade duties. Gichon himself assumed two fake identities—one as a German civilian, the other as a British major—as he hunted Nazis. In expeditions under his German cover, Gichon recovered the Gestapo archives in Tarvisio, Villach, and Klagenfurt, to which fleeing Nazis had set fire but only a small part of which actually burned. Operating as the British major, he gleaned more names from Yugoslavian Communists who were still afraid to carry out revenge attacks themselves. A few Jews in American intelligence also were willing to help by handing over information they had on escaped Nazis, which they thought the Palestinian Jews would use to better effect than the American military.

Coercion worked, too. In June 1945, Gmul agents found a Polish-born German couple who lived in Tarvisio. The wife had been involved in transferring stolen Jewish property from Austria and Italy to Germany, and her husband had helped run the regional Gestapo office. The Palestinian Jewish soldiers offered them a stark choice: cooperate or die.

"The goy broke and said he was willing to cooperate," said Yisrael Karmi, who interrogated the couple and later, after Israel was born, would become the commander of the Israeli Army's military police. "I assigned him to prepare lists of all the senior officials that he knew and who had worked with the Gestapo and the SS. Name, date of birth, education, and positions."

The result was a dramatic intelligence breakthrough, a list of dozens of names. Gmul's men tracked down each missing Nazi—finding some wounded in a local hospital, where they were being treated under stolen aliases—and then pressured those men to provide more information. They promised each German he would not be harmed if he cooperated, so most did. Then, when they were no longer useful, Gmul agents shot them and dumped the bodies. There was no sense in leaving them alive to tip the British command to Gmul's clandestine mission.

Once a particular name had been verified, the second phase began: locating the target and gathering information for the final killing mission. Gichon, who'd been born in Germany, often was assigned that job. "No one suspected me," he said. "My vocal cords were of Berlin stock. I'd go to the corner grocery store or pub or even just knock on a door to convey greetings from someone. Most of the time, the people would respond [to their real names] or recoil into vague silence, which was as good as a confirmation." Once the identification was confirmed, Gichon would track the German's movements and provide a detailed sketch of the house where he lived or the area that had been chosen for the abduction.

The killers themselves worked in teams of no more than five men. When meeting their target, they generally wore British military police uniforms, and they typically told their target they had come to take a man named so-and-so for interrogation. Most of the time, the German came without objection. As one of the unit's soldiers, Shalom Giladi, related in his testimony to the Haganah Archive, the Nazi was sometimes killed instantly, and other times transported to some remote spot before being killed. "In time we developed quiet, rapid, and efficient methods of taking care of the SS men who fell into our hands," he said.

As anyone who has ever gotten into a pickup truck knows, a person hoisting himself up into one braces his foot on the rear running board, leans forward under the canvas canopy, and sort of rolls in. The man lying in wait inside the truck would take advantage of this natural tilt of the body.

The minute the German's head protruded into the gloom, the ambusher would bend over him and wrap his arms under his chin—around his throat—in a kind of reverse choke hold, and, carrying that into a throttle embrace, the ambusher would fall back flat on the mattress, which absorbed every sound. The backward fall, while gripping the German's head, would suffocate the German and break his neck instantly.

One day, a female SS officer escaped from an English detention camp next to our base. After the British discovered that the officer had escaped, they sent out photographs of her taken during her imprisonment—front and side view—to all the military police stations. We went through the refugee camp and identified her. When we addressed her in German, she played the fool and said she only knew Hungarian. That wasn't a problem. A Hungarian kid went up to her and said: "A ship carrying illegal immigrants from Hungary is about to sail for Palestine. Pack up your belongings quietly and come with us." She had no choice but to take the bait and went with us in the truck. During this operation, I sat with Zaro [Meir

Zorea, later an IDF general] in the back while Karmi drove. The order Karmi gave us was: "When I get some distance to a suitable deserted place, I'll honk the horn. That will be the sign to get rid of her."

That's what happened. Her last scream in German was: *"Was ist los?"* ("What's going on?"). To make sure she was dead, Karmi shot her and we gave her body and the surroundings the appearance of a violent rape.

In most cases we brought the Nazis to a small line of fortifications in the mountains. There were fortified caves there, abandoned. Most of those facing their executions would lose their Nazi arrogance when they heard that we were Jews. "Have mercy on my wife and children!" We would ask him how many such screams the Nazis had heard in the extermination camps from their Jewish victims.

The operation lasted only three months, from May to July, during which time Gmul killed somewhere between one hundred and two hundred people. Several historians who've researched Gmul's operations maintain that the methods used to identify targets were insufficient, and that many innocents were killed. On many occasions, those critics argue, Gmul teams were exploited by their sources to carry out personal vendettas; in other cases, operatives simply identified the wrong person.

Gmul was closed down when the British, who'd heard complaints about disappearances from German families, grasped what was going on. They decided not to investigate further, but to transfer the Jewish Brigade to Belgium and the Netherlands, away from the Germans, and Haganah command issued a firm order to cease revenge operations. The Brigade's new priorities—according to the Haganah, not the British—were to look after Holocaust survivors, to help organize the immigration of refugees to Palestine in the face of British opposition, and to appropriate weapons for the Yishuv.

YET, THOUGH THEY ORDERED Gmul to stop killing Germans in Europe, the Haganah's leaders did not forsake retribution. The vengeance that had been halted in Europe, they decided, would be carried on in Palestine itself.

Members of the German Tempelgesellschaft (the Templer sect) had been expelled from Palestine by the British at the beginning of the war because of their nationality and Nazi sympathies. Many joined the German war effort and took an active part in the persecution and annihilation of the Jews. When the war ended, some of them returned to their former homes, in Sarona, in the heart of Tel Aviv, and other locations.

The leader of the Templers in Palestine was a man named Gotthilf Wagner, a wealthy industrialist who assisted the Wehrmacht and the Gestapo during the war. A Holocaust survivor by the name of Shalom Friedman, who was posing as a Hungarian priest, related that in 1944 he met Wagner, who "boasted that he was at Auschwitz and Buchenwald twice. When he was in Auschwitz, they brought out a large group of Jews, the youngest ones, and poured flammable liquid over them. 'I asked them if they knew there was a hell on earth, and when they ignited them I told them that this was the fate awaiting their brethren in Palestine.'" After the war, Wagner organized the attempts to allow the Templers to return to Palestine.

Rafi Eitan, the son of Jewish pioneers from Russia, was seventeen at the time. "Here come exultant Germans, who had been members of the Nazi Party, who enlisted to the Wehrmacht and SS, and they want to return to their property when all the Jewish property outside was destroyed," he said.

Eitan was a member of a seventeen-man force from the Haganah's "special company" sent to liquidate Wagner, under a direct order from the Haganah high command. The Haganah chief of staff, Yitzhak Sadeh, realized that this was not a regular military operation and summoned the two men who had been selected to squeeze the trigger. To encourage them, he told them about a man he had shot with his pistol in Russia as revenge for a pogrom.

On March 22, 1946, after painstaking intelligence gathering, the hit squad lay in wait for Wagner in Tel Aviv. They forced him off the road onto a sandy lot at 123 Levinsky Street and shot him. Haganah's underground radio station, Kol Yisrael (the Voice of Israel), announced the following day, "The well-known Nazi Gotthilf Wagner, head of the German community in Palestine, was executed yesterday by the Hebrew underground. Let it be known that no Nazi will place a foot on the soil of the Land of Israel."

Shortly thereafter, Haganah assassinated two other Templers in the Galilee and two more in Haifa, where the sect had also established communities.

"It had an immediate effect," Eitan said. "The Templers disappeared from the country, leaving everything behind, and were never seen again." The Templers' neighborhood in Tel Aviv, Sarona, would become the headquarters of Israel's armed forces and intelligence services. And Eitan, an assassin at seventeen, would help found the Mossad's targeted killing unit.

The killing of the Templers was not merely a continuation of the acts of revenge against the Nazis in Europe, but signified a major change in policy. The lessons that the new Jews of Palestine learned from the Holocaust were that the Jewish people would always be under the threat of destruction, that others could not be relied upon to protect the Jews, and that the only way to do so was to have an independent state. A people living with this sense of perpetual danger of annihilation is going to take any and all measures, however extreme, to obtain security, and will relate to international laws and norms in a marginal manner, if at all.

From now on, Ben-Gurion and the Haganah would adopt targeted killings, guerrilla warfare, and terrorist attacks as additional tools—above and beyond the propaganda and political measures that had always been used—in the effort to achieve the goal of a state and to preserve it. What had only a few years before been a means used only by the outcast extremists of Lehi and the Irgun was now seen by the mainstream as a viable weapon.

At first, Haganah units began assassinating Arabs who had murdered Jewish civilians. Then the militia's high command ordered a "special company" to begin "personal terror operations," a term used at the time for the targeted killings of officers of the British CID who had persecuted the Jewish underground and acted against the Jewish immigration to the Land of Israel. They were ordered to "blow up

British intelligence centers that acted against Jewish acquisition of weapons" and "to take retaliatory action in cases where British military courts sentence Haganah members to death."

Ben-Gurion foresaw that a Jewish state would soon be established in Palestine and that the new nation would immediately be forced to fight a war against Arabs in Palestine and repel invasions by the armies of neighboring Arab states. The Haganah command thus also began secretly preparing for this all-out war, and as part of the preparations, an order code-named Zarzir (or Starling) was issued, providing for the assassination of the heads of the Arab population of Palestine.

WHILE THE HAGANAH SLOWLY stepped up the use of targeted killings, the radical undergrounds had their killing campaign in full motion, trying to push the British out of Palestine.

Yitzhak Shamir, now in command of Lehi, resolved not only to eliminate key figures of the British Mandate locally—killing CID personnel and making numerous attempts to do the same to the Jerusalem police chief, Michael Joseph McConnell, and the high commissioner, Sir Harold MacMichael—but also Englishmen in other countries who posed a threat to his political objective. Walter Edward Guinness, more formally known as Lord Moyne, for example, was the British resident minister of state in Cairo, which was also under British rule. The Jews in Palestine considered Moyne a flagrant anti-Semite who had assiduously used his position to restrict the Yishuv's power by significantly reducing immigration quotas for Holocaust survivors.

Shamir ordered Moyne killed. He sent two Lehi operatives, Eliyahu Hakim and Eliyahu Bet-Zuri, to Cairo, where they waited at the door to Moyne's house. When Moyne pulled up, his secretary in the car with him, Hakim and Bet-Zuri sprinted to the car. One of them shoved a pistol through the window, aimed it at Moyne's head, and fired three times. Moyne gripped his throat. "Oh, they've shot us!" he cried, and then slumped forward in his seat. Still, it was an amateurish operation. Shamir had counseled his young killers to arrange to escape in a car, but instead they fled on slow-moving bicycles. Egyptian police quickly apprehended them, and Hakim and Bet-Zuri were tried, convicted, and, six months later, hanged.

The assassination had a decisive effect on British officials, though not the one Shamir had envisioned. As Israel would learn repeatedly in future years, it is very hard to predict how history will proceed after someone is shot in the head.

After the unmitigated evil of the Holocaust, the attempted extermination of an entire people in Europe, there was growing sympathy in the West for the Zionist cause. According to some accounts, up until the first week of November 1944, Britain's prime minister, Winston Churchill, had been pushing his cabinet to support the creation of a Jewish state in Palestine. He rallied several influential figures to back the initiative—including Lord Moyne. It is not a stretch to assume, then, that Churchill might well have arrived at the Yalta summit with Franklin Roosevelt and Joseph Stalin with a clear, positive policy regarding the future of a Jewish state, had Lehi not intervened. Instead, after the Cairo killing, Churchill labeled the attackers "a new group of gangsters" and announced that he was reconsidering his position.

And the killing continued. On July 22, 1946, members of Menachem Begin's Irgun planted 350 KG explosives in the south wing of the King David Hotel, in Jerusalem, where the British Mandate's administration and army and intelligence offices were housed. A warning call from the Irgun apparently was dismissed as a hoax; the building was not evacuated before a massive explosion ripped through it. Ninety-one people were killed, and forty-five wounded.

This was not the targeted killing of a despised British official or a guerrilla attack on a police station. Instead, it was plainly an act of terror, aimed at a target with numerous civilians inside. Most damningly, many Jews were among the casualties.

The King David Hotel bombing sparked a fierce dispute in the Yishuv. Ben-Gurion immediately denounced the Irgun and called it "an enemy of the Jewish people."

But the extremists were not deterred.

Three months after the King David attack, on October 31, a Lehi cell, again acting on their own, without Ben-Gurion's approval or knowledge, bombed the British embassy in Rome. The embassy building was severely damaged, but thanks to the fact that the operation took place at night, only a security guard and two Italian pedestrians were injured.

Almost immediately after that, Lehi mailed letter bombs to every senior British cabinet member in London. On one level, this effort was a spectacular failure—not a single letter exploded—but on another, Lehi had made its point, and its reach, clear. The files of MI5, Britain's security service, showed that Zionist terrorism was considered the most serious threat to British national security at the time— even more serious than the Soviet Union. Irgun cells in Britain were established, according to one MI5 memo, "to beat the dog in its own kennel." British intelligence sources warned of a wave of attacks on "selected VIPs," among them Foreign Secretary Ernest Bevin and even Prime Minister Clement Attlee himself. At the end of 1947, a report to the British high commissioner tallied the casualties of the previous two years: 176 British Mandate personnel and civilians killed.

"Only these actions, these executions, caused the British to leave," David Shomron said, decades after he shot Tom Wilkin dead on a Jerusalem street. "If [Avraham] Stern had not begun the war, the State of Israel would not have come into being."

One may argue with these statements. The shrinking British Empire ceded control of the majority of its colonies, including many countries where terror tactics had not been employed, due to economic reasons and increased demands for independence from the native populations. India, for instance, gained its independence right around the same time. Nevertheless, Shomron and his ilk were firmly convinced that their own bravery and their extreme methods had brought about the departure of the British.

And it was the men who fought that bloody underground war— guerrillas, assassins, terrorists—who would play a central role in the building of the new state of Israel's armed forces and intelligence community.

# A SECRET WORLD IS BORN

ON NOVEMBER 29, 1947, the United Nations General Assembly voted to divide Palestine, carving out a sovereign Jewish homeland. The partition wouldn't go into effect until six months later, but Arab attacks began the very next day. Hassan Salameh, the commander of the Palestinian forces in the southern part of the country, and his fighters ambushed two Israeli buses near the town of Petah-Tikva, murdering eight passengers and injuring many others. Civil war between Palestinian Arabs and Jews had begun. The day after the bus attacks, Salameh stood in the central square of the Arab port city of Jaffa. "Palestine will turn into a bloodbath," he promised his countrymen. He kept that promise: During the next two weeks, 48 Jews were killed and 155 wounded.

Salameh, who led a force of five hundred guerrillas and even directly attacked Tel Aviv, became a hero in the Arab world, lionized in the press. The Egyptian magazine *Al-Musawar* published an enormous photograph of Salameh briefing his forces in its January 12, 1948, issue, under the banner headline THE HERO HASSAN SALAMEH, COMMANDER OF THE SOUTHERN FRONT.

Ben-Gurion had prepared for such assaults. To his thinking, Palestine's Arabs were the enemy, and the British—who would continue to rule until the partition took formal effect in May 1948—were their abettors. The Jews could depend only on themselves and their rudimentary defenses. Most of the Haganah troops were poorly trained and poorly equipped, their arms hidden in secret caches to avoid confiscation by the British. They were men and women who had served in the British Army, bolstered by new immigrants who had survived the Holocaust (some of them Red Army veterans), but they were vastly outnumbered by the combined forces of the Arab states. Ben-Gurion was aware of the estimations of the CIA and other intelligence services that the Jews would collapse under Arab attack. Some of his own people weren't confident of victory. But Ben-Gurion, at least outwardly, displayed confidence in the Haganah's ability to win.

To bridge the numerical gap, the Haganah's plan, then, was to use selective force, picking targets for maximum effectiveness. As part of this conception, a month into the civil war, its high command launched Operation Starling, which named twenty-three leaders of the Palestinian Arabs who were to be targeted.

The mission, according to Haganah's commander in chief, Yaakov Dori, was threefold: "Elimination or capture of the leaders of the Arab political parties; strikes against political centers; strikes against Arab economic and manufacturing centers."

Hassan Salameh was at the top of the list of targets. Under the leadership of Hajj Amin al-Husseini, the grand mufti of Jerusalem and spiritual leader of the Palestinian Arabs, Salameh had helped lead the Arab Revolt of 1936, in which Arab guerrillas for three years attacked both British and Jewish targets.

Both al-Husseini and Salameh fled Palestine after they were put on the British Mandate's most-wanted list. In 1942, they joined forces with the SS and the Abwehr, the Nazis' military intelligence agency, to plot Operation Atlas. It was a grandiose plan in which German and Arab commandos would parachute into Palestine and poison Tel Aviv's water supply in order to kill as many Jews as possible, rousing the country's Arabs to fight a holy war against the British occupiers. It failed miserably when the British, having cracked the Nazis' Enigma code, captured Salameh and four others after they dropped into a desert ravine near Jericho on October 6, 1944.

After World War II, the British released al-Husseini and Salameh. The Jewish Agency's Political Department, which oversaw much of the Yishuv's covert activity in Europe, tried to locate the former and kill him several times between 1945 and 1948. The motive was partly revenge for the mufti's alliance with Hitler, but it was also defensive: Al-Husseini might have been out of the country, but he was still actively involved in organizing attacks on Jewish settlements in northern Palestine and in attempts to assassinate Jewish leaders. Due to a lack of intelligence and trained operational personnel, all those attempts failed.

The hunt for Salameh, the first Haganah operation to integrate human and electronic intelligence, began promisingly. A unit belonging to SHAI, the Haganah's intelligence branch, and commanded by Isser Harel, tapped into the central telephone trunk line that connected Jaffa with the rest of the country. Harel had a toolshed built on the grounds of the nearby Mikveh Israel agricultural school and filled it with pruning shears and lawn mowers. But hidden in a pit under the floor was a listening device clipped to the copper wires of Jaffa's phone system. "I'll never forget the face of the Arabic-speaking SHAI operative who put on a set of headphones and listened to the first conversation," Harel later wrote in his memoir. "His mouth gaped in astonishment and he waved his hand emotionally to silence the others who were tensely waiting. . . . The lines were bursting with conversations that political leaders and the chiefs of armed contingents were conducting with their colleagues." One of the speakers was Salameh. In one of the intercepted calls, SHAI learned he would be traveling to Jaffa. Haganah agents planned to ambush him by felling a tree to block the road on which his car would be traveling.

But the ambush failed, and it was not the last failure. Salameh survived multiple assassination attempts before falling in combat in June 1948, his killer unaware of his identity. Almost all of the other Operation Starling targeted killing bids also failed, because of faulty intelligence or flawed performances by the unskilled and inexperienced hit men.

THE ONLY OPERATIONS THAT did succeed were all carried out by two of the Haganah's elite units, both of which belonged to the Palmach, the militia's only well-trained and fairly well-armed corps. One of these units was the Palyam, the "marine company," and the other was "the Arab Platoon," a clandestine commando unit whose members operated disguised as Arabs.

Palyam, the naval company, was ordered to take over the port in Haifa, Palestine's most important maritime gateway, as soon as the British departed. Its task was to steal as much of the weaponry and equipment the British were beginning to ship out as possible, and to prevent the Arabs from doing likewise.

"We focused on the Arab arms acquirers in Haifa and the north. We searched for them and killed them," recalled Avraham Dar, one of the Palyam men.

Dar, who was a native English speaker, and two other Palyam men posed as British soldiers wanting to sell stolen gear to the Palestinians for a large amount of cash. A rendezvous was set up for the exchange near an abandoned flour mill on the outskirts of an Arab village. The three Jews, wearing British uniforms, were at the meeting place when the Palestinians arrived. Four others who were hiding nearby waited for the signal and then fell upon the Arabs, killing them with metal pipes. "We feared that gunshots would wake the neighbors, and we decided on a silent operation," said Dar.

The Arab Platoon was established when the Haganah decided it needed a nucleus of trained fighters who could operate deep inside enemy lines, gathering information and carrying out sabotage and targeted killing missions. The training of its men—most of them immigrants from Arab lands—included commando tactics and explosives, but also intensive study of Islam and Arab customs. They were nicknamed Mistaravim, the name by which Jewish communities went in some Arab countries, where they practiced the Jewish religion, but were similar to the Arabs in all other respects—dress, language, social customs, etc.

Cooperation between the two units produced an attempt on the life of Sheikh Nimr al-Khatib, a head of the Islamic organizations of Palestine, one of the original targets of Operation Starling, because of his considerable influence over the Palestinian street. The Mistaravim could move around without being stopped by either the British or the Arabs. In February 1948, they ambushed al-Khatib when he returned from a trip to Damascus with a carload of ammunition. He was badly wounded, left Palestine, and removed himself from any active political roles.

A few days later, Avraham Dar heard from one of his port worker informants that a group of Arabs in a café had been talking about their plan to detonate a vehicle packed with explosives in a crowded Jewish section of Haifa. The British ambulance that they had acquired for this purpose was being readied in a garage in Nazareth Road, in the Arab part of the city. The Mistaravim prepared a bomb of their own in a truck that they drove into the Arab district, posing as workers engaged in fixing a burst pipe, and parked next to the wall of the garage. "What are you doing here? No parking here! Move the truck!" the men in the garage yelled at them in Arabic.

"Right away, we're just getting a drink, and we need to take a leak" the Mistaravim replied in Arabic, adding a few juicy curses. They walked away to a waiting car, and minutes later their bomb went off, detonating the one in the ambulance as well, and killing the five Palestinians working on it.

ON MAY 14, 1948, Ben-Gurion declared the establishment of the new state of Israel and became its first prime minister and minister of defense. He knew what to expect next.

Years earlier, Ben-Gurion had ordered the formation of a deep network of sources in the Arab countries. Now, three days before the establishment of Israel, Reuven Shiloah, director of the Political Department of the Jewish Agency, the agency's intelligence division, had informed him that "the Arab states have decided finally to launch a simultaneous attack on May 15. . . . They are relying on the lack of heavy armaments and a Hebrew air force." Shiloah provided many details about the attack plan.

The information was accurate. At midnight, after the state was declared, seven armies attacked. They far outnumbered and were infinitely better equipped than the Jewish forces, and they achieved significant gains early on, conquering settlements and inflicting casualties. The secretary general of the Arab League, Abdul Rahman

Azzam Pasha, declared, "This will be a war of great destruction and slaughter that will be remembered like the massacres carried out by the Mongols and the Crusaders."

But the Jews—now officially "Israelis"—rapidly regrouped and even went on the offensive. After a month, a truce was mediated by the United Nations special envoy, Count Folke Bernadotte. Both sides were exhausted and in need of rest and resupply. When fighting resumed, the tables were turned and, with excellent intelligence and battle management, along with the help of many Holocaust survivors who had only just arrived from Europe, the Israelis drove the Arab forces back and eventually conquered far more territory than had been allocated to the Jewish state in the UN partition plan.

Though Israel had repelled superior armies, Ben-Gurion was not sanguine about the embryonic Israel Defense Forces' short-term victory. The Arabs might have lost the first battles, but they—both those who lived in Palestine and those in the Arab states surrounding Israel—refused to accept the legitimacy of the new nation. They vowed to destroy Israel and return the refugees to their homes.

Ben-Gurion knew the IDF couldn't hope to defend Israel's long, convoluted borders through sheer manpower. From the remnants of the Haganah's SHAI intelligence operations, he had to begin building a proper espionage system fit for a legitimate state.

On June 7, Ben-Gurion summoned his top aides, headed by Shiloah, to his office in the former Templer colony in Tel Aviv. "Intelligence is one of the military and political tools that we urgently need for this war," Shiloah wrote in a memo to Ben-Gurion. "It will have to become a permanent tool, including in our [peacetime] political apparatus."

Ben-Gurion did not need to be persuaded. After all, a large part of the surprising, against-all-odds establishment of the state, and its defense, was owed to the effective use of accurate intelligence.

That day, he ordered the establishment of three agencies. The first was the Intelligence Department of the Israel Defense Forces General Staff, later commonly referred to by its Hebrew acronym, AMAN. Second was the Shin Bet (acronym for the General Security Service), responsible for internal security and created as a sort of hybrid between the American FBI and the British MI5. (The organization later changed its name to the Israeli Security Agency, but most Israelis still refer to it by its acronym, Shabak, or, more commonly, as in this book, as Shin Bet.) And a third, the Political Department—now belonging to the new Foreign Ministry, instead of the Jewish Agency—would engage in foreign espionage and intelligence collection. Abandoned Templer homes in the Sarona neighborhood, near the Defense Ministry, were assigned to each outfit, putting Ben-Gurion's office at the center of an ostensibly organized force of security services.

But nothing in those first months and years was so tidy. Remnants of Haganah agencies were absorbed into various security services or spy rings, then shuffled and reabsorbed into another. Add to that the myriad turf battles and clashing egos of what were essentially revolutionaries, and much was chaos in the espionage underground. "They were hard years," said Isser Harel, one of the founding fathers of Israeli intelligence. "We had to establish a country and defend it. [But] the structure of the services and the division of labor was determined without any systematic judgment, without discussions with all the relevant people, in an almost dilettantish and conspiratorial way."

Under normal conditions, administrators would establish clear boundaries and procedures, and field agents would patiently cultivate sources of information over a period of years. But Israel did not have this luxury. Its intelligence operations had to be built on the fly and under siege, while the young country was fighting for its very existence.

THE FIRST CHALLENGE THAT Ben-Gurion's spies faced was an internal one: There were Jews who blatantly defied his authority, among them the remnants of the right-wing underground movements. An extreme example of this defiance was the Altalena affair, in June 1948. A ship by that name, dispatched from Europe by the Irgun, was due to arrive, carrying immigrants and arms. But the organization refused to hand all the weapons over to the army of the new state, insisting that some of them be given to still intact units of its own. Ben-Gurion, who had been informed of the plans by agents inside Irgun, ordered that the ship be taken over by force. In the ensuing fight, it was sunk, and sixteen Irgun fighters and three IDF soldiers were killed. Shortly afterward, security forces rounded up two hundred Irgun members all over the country, effectively ending its existence.

Yitzhak Shamir and the Lehi operatives under his command also refused to accept the more moderate Ben-Gurion's authority. Over the summer, during the truce, UN envoy Bernadotte crafted a tentative peace plan that would have ended the fighting. But the plan was unacceptable to Lehi and Shamir, who accused Bernadotte of collaborating with the Nazis during World War II and of drafting a proposal that would redraw Israeli borders in such a way—including giving most of the Negev and Jerusalem to the Arabs, and putting the Haifa port and Lydda airport under international control, as well as obliging the Jewish state to take back 300,000 Arab refugees—that the country would not survive.

Lehi issued several public warnings, in the form of notices posted in the streets of cities: ADVICE TO THE AGENT BERNADOTTE: CLEAR OUT OF OUR COUNTRY. The underground radio was even more outspoken, declaring, "The Count will end up like the Lord" (a reference to the assassinated Lord Moyne). Bernadotte ignored the warnings, and even ordered UN observers not to carry arms, saying, "The United Nations flag protects us."

Convinced that the envoy's plan would be accepted, Shamir ordered his assassination. On September 17, four months after statehood was declared, and the day after Bernadotte submitted his plan to the UN Security Council, he was traveling with his entourage in a convoy of three white DeSoto sedans from UN headquarters to the Rehavia neighborhood of Jewish Jerusalem, when a jeep blocked their way. Three young men wearing peaked caps jumped out. Two of them shot the tires of the UN vehicles, and the third, Yehoshua Cohen, opened the door of the car Bernadotte was traveling in and opened fire with his Schmeisser MP40 submachine gun. The first burst hit the man sitting next to Bernadotte, a French colonel by the name of André Serot, but the next, more accurate, hit the count in the chest. Both men were killed. The whole attack was over in seconds—"like thunder and lightning, the time it takes to fire fifty rounds," is the way the Israeli liaison officer, Captain Moshe Hillman, who was in the car with the victims, described it. The perpetrators were never caught.

The assassination infuriated and profoundly embarrassed the Jewish leadership. The Security Council condemned it as "a cowardly act which appears to have been committed by a criminal group of terrorists in Jerusalem," and *The New York Times* wrote the following day, "No Arab armies could have done so much harm [to the Jewish state] in so short a time."

Ben-Gurion saw Lehi's rogue operation as a serious challenge to his authority, one that could lead to a coup or even a civil war. He reacted immediately, outlawing both the Irgun and Lehi. He ordered Shin Bet chief Isser Harel to round up Lehi members. Topping the wanted list was Yitzhak Shamir. He wasn't captured, but many others were, and they were locked up under heavy guard. Lehi ceased to exist as an organization.

Ben-Gurion was grateful to Harel for his vigorous action against the underground and made him the number-one intelligence official in the country.

A short, solid, and driven man, Isser Harel was influenced by the Russian Bolshevik revolutionary movement and its use of sabotage, guerrilla warfare, and assassination, but he abhorred communism. Under his direction, the Shin Bet kept constant surveillance and conducted political espionage against Ben-Gurion's political opponents, the left-wing socialist and Communist parties, and the right-wing Herut party formed by veterans of Irgun and Lehi.

Meanwhile, Ben-Gurion and his foreign minister, Moshe Sharett, were at loggerheads over what policy should be adopted toward the Arabs. Sharett was the most prominent of Israel's early leaders who believed diplomacy was the best way to achieve regional peace and thus secure the country. Even before independence, he made secret overtures to Jordan's King Abdullah and Lebanon's prime minister, Riad al-Solh, who would be instrumental in forming the coalition of invading Arabs, and who already had been largely responsible for the Palestinian militias that exacted heavy losses on the pre-state Yishuv. Despite al-Solh's virulently anti-Jewish rhetoric and anti-Israel actions, he secretly met with Eliyahu Sasson, one of Sharett's deputies, several times in Paris in late 1948 to discuss a peace agreement. "If we want to establish contacts with the Arabs to end the war," said Sasson when Sharett, enthusiastic about his secret contacts, took him to report to the cabinet, "we have to be in contact with those people who are now in power. With those who have declared war on us . . . and who are having trouble continuing."

Those diplomatic overtures obviously were not effective, and Ben-Gurion, on December 12, 1948, ordered military intelligence agents to assassinate al-Solh.

"Sharett was vehemently opposed to the idea," recalled Asher (Arthur) Ben-Natan, a leading figure in the Foreign Ministry's Political Department, the arm responsible for covert activities abroad. "And when our department was asked to help military intelligence execute the order, through our contacts in Beirut, he countermanded the order, effectively killing it."

This incident, plus a number of other clashes between Harel and Sharett, made Ben-Gurion's blood boil. He considered diplomacy a weak substitute for a strong military and robust intelligence, and he viewed Sharett, personally, as a competitor who threatened the prime minister's control. In December 1949, Ben-Gurion removed the Political Department from the control of the Foreign Ministry and placed it under his direct command. He later gave the agency a new name: the Institute for Intelligence and Special Operations. More commonly, though, it was known simply as "the Institute"—the Mossad.

With the establishment of the Mossad, Israeli intelligence services coalesced into the three-pronged community that survives in more or less the same form today: AMAN, the military intelligence arm that supplies information to the IDF; the Shin Bet, responsible for internal intelligence, counterterror, and counterespionage; and the Mossad, which deals with covert activities beyond the country's borders.

More important, it was a victory for those who saw the future of the Israeli state as more dependent upon a strong army and intelligence community than upon diplomacy. That victory was embodied in real estate: The former Templer homes in Tel Aviv that the Political Department had occupied were handed over to the Mossad. It was also a personal victory for Isser Harel. Already in charge of the Shin Bet, he was installed as the chief of the Mossad as well, making him one of the most powerful—and secretive—figures in early Israeli history.

From that point on, Israeli foreign and security policy would be determined by jousting between Tel Aviv—where the military high command, the intelligence headquarters, and the Defense Ministry were located, and where Ben-Gurion spent most of his time—and Jerusalem, where the Foreign Ministry was housed in a cluster of prefabricated huts. Tel Aviv always had the upper hand.

Ben-Gurion kept all of the agencies under his direct control. The Mossad and the Shin Bet were under him in his capacity as prime minister, and military intelligence fell under his purview because he was also minister of defense. It was an enormous concentration of covert, and political, power. Yet from the beginning, it was kept officially hidden from the Israeli public. Ben-Gurion forbade anyone from acknowledging, let alone revealing, that this sprawling web of official institutions even existed. In fact, mentioning the name Shin Bet or Mossad in public was prohibited until the 1960s. Because their existence could not be acknowledged, Ben-Gurion prevented the creation of a legal basis for those same agencies' operations. No law laid out their goals, roles, missions, powers, or budgets or the relations between them.

In other words, Israeli intelligence from the outset occupied a shadow realm, one adjacent to yet separate from the country's democratic institutions. The activities of the intelligence community—most of it (Shin Bet and the Mossad) under the direct command of the prime minister—took place without any effective supervision by Israel's parliament, the Knesset, or by any other independent external body.

In this shadow realm, "state security" was used to justify a large number of actions and operations that, in the visible world, would have been subject to criminal prosecution and long prison terms: constant surveillance of citizens because of their ethnic or political affiliations; interrogation methods that included prolonged detention without judicial sanction, and torture; perjury in the courts and concealment of the truth from counsel and judges.

The most notable example was targeted killing. In Israeli law, there is no death penalty, but Ben-Gurion circumvented this by giving himself the authority to order extrajudicial executions.

The justification for maintaining that shadow realm was that anything other than complete secrecy could lead to situations that would threaten the very existence of Israel. Israel had inherited from the British Mandate a legal system that included state-of-emergency provisions to enforce order and suppress rebellions. Among those provisions was a requirement that all print and broadcast media submit any reports on intelligence and army activities to a military censor, who vetoed much of the material. The state of emergency has not been rescinded as of the time of this writing. But as a sop to the hungry media, Ben-Gurion was shrewd enough to establish an Editors Committee, which was composed of the editors in chief of the print and radio news outlets. From time to time, Ben-Gurion himself, or someone representing him, would appear before the committee to share covert tidbits while explaining why those tidbits could never, under any circumstances, be released to the public. The editors were thrilled because they had gained for themselves entrée to the twilight realm and its mysteries. In gratitude, they imposed on themselves a level of self-censorship that went beyond even that imposed by the actual censor.

IN JULY 1952, AN exhibit of paintings by the Franco-German artist Charles Duvall opened at the National Museum in Cairo. Duvall, a tall young man with a cigarette permanently dangling from his lip, had moved to Egypt from Paris two years earlier, announcing that he'd "fallen in love with the land of the Nile." The Cairo press published a number of fawning pieces about Duvall and his work—strongly influenced, the critics said, by Picasso—and he soon became a fixture in high society. Indeed, the Egyptian minister of culture attended the opening of Duvall's show and even purchased two of the paintings that he left on loan to the museum, where they would hang for the next twenty-three years.

Five months later, when his show had closed, Duvall said that his mother had fallen ill and he had to rush back to Paris to care for her.

After his return to France, he sent a few letters to old friends in Egypt, and then he was never heard from again.

Duvall's real name was Shlomo Cohen-Abarbanel, and he was an Israeli spy. He was the youngest of four sons born to a prominent rabbi in Hamburg in Germany. In the winter of 1933, as the Nazis rose to power and began enforcing race laws, the family fled to France and then Palestine. Fifteen years later, in 1947, Cohen-Abarbanel, whose artistic abilities had been apparent since he was a toddler, returned to Paris to study painting at the age of twenty-seven. A short time later, Haganah intelligence personnel heard about his talents and recruited him to forge passports and papers to be used by European and North African Jews being smuggled into Palestine in violation of British immigration laws. It was the beginning of a long career in espionage. Portraying himself as a bohemian artist, Cohen-Abarbanel operated networks of agents in Egypt and recruited new agents throughout the Arab world. He collected information about Nazi war criminals who had taken refuge in the Middle East, and he reported to his superiors on the initial attempts of German rocket scientists to sell their services to Arab armies. When he returned to Israel in 1952, he pushed his superiors in the young intelligence agency the Mossad to invest more resources into finding and killing Nazis.

A short time after taking command of the Mossad, Isser Harel asked Cohen-Abarbanel to design an official emblem for the agency. The artist shut himself in his room and emerged with a design, which he'd drawn by hand. At its center was a seven-branched menorah, the sacred lamp that stood in the Temple in Jerusalem that the Romans destroyed in A.D. 70. The seal also bore a legend—verse 6 from chapter 24 of the Book of Proverbs, authored, according to Jewish tradition, by King Solomon himself: "For by subterfuge you will make war." This was later changed to another line from Proverbs (chapter 11, verse 14), which reads, "Where there is no subterfuge—the nation falls, but in the multitude of counselors there is safety." Cohen-Abarbanel's meaning could not have been clearer: using covert stratagems, the Mossad would be the supreme shield of the new Jewish commonwealth, ensuring that never again would Jews be dishonored, that never again would Judea fall.

The Mossad's charter, written by Harel, was equally broad and ambitious. The organization's purpose, according to its official orders, was "secret collection of information (strategic, political, operational) outside the country's borders; carrying out special operations outside Israel's borders; thwarting the development and acquisition of unconventional weapons by hostile states; prevention of terror attacks against Israeli and Jewish targets outside Israel; development and maintenance of intelligence and political ties with countries that do not maintain diplomatic relations with Israel; bringing to Israel Jews from countries that refused to allow them to leave, and creating frameworks for the defense of the Jews still in those countries." In other words, it was charged with not only protecting Israel and its citizens but also standing as a sentinel for world Jewry.

ISRAEL'S YOUNG INTELLIGENCE SERVICES had to offer a response to a series of challenges presented by the ring of twenty-one hostile Arab nations that surrounded Israel and threatened to destroy it. There were those in the top echelons of the defense establishment who believed that these challenges would best be met by the use of pinpointed special operations far beyond enemy lines.

To this end, AMAN set up a unit called Intelligence Service 13 (which in Jewish tradition is considered a lucky number). Avraham Dar, now one of its prominent officers, went to Egypt in 1951 to set up a network of agents culled from local Zionist activists. On various pretexts, the recruits traveled to Europe, and then to Israel for training in espionage and sabotage. Outlining the goal of his network, Dar explained that "the central problem that made Egypt so antagonistic to Israel was the way King Farouk ran the government. If we could get rid of that obstacle many problems would be solved. In other words"—and here Dar turned to a Spanish proverb—"no dog, no rabies."

Getting rid of "the dog" proved to be unnecessary—Farouk soon was overthrown in a coup. And AMAN's assumption that things would be better when he was gone turned out to be totally groundless. However, the idea that this already established Egyptian network could be employed to change the course of history in the region was simply too tempting for Israel's leaders to let go. AMAN decided to use these local agents against the Free Officers Movement, which had just recently ousted Farouk, "aiming to undermine Western confidence in the [Egyptian] regime by causing public insecurity and provoking demonstrations, arrests, and retaliatory actions, with Israel's role remaining unexposed." But the whole operation ended in catastrophe.

Despite intensive training, AMAN's recruits were amateurish and sloppy, and all of their sabotage operations ended in failure. Eventually, eleven operatives were ferreted out by Egyptian authorities. Some were executed after short trials, and one killed himself after suffering gruesome torture. The lucky ones were sentenced to long prison terms and hard labor.

The ensuing turmoil gave rise to a major political dispute that raged in Israel for many years, over whether AMAN had received the approval of the political establishment for these abortive operations.

The main lesson drawn by Israel was that local Jews should never be recruited in hostile "target" countries. Their capture was almost certain to end in death, and send ripples throughout the entire Jewish community. Despite the temptation to use people who were already on the ground and didn't need to establish a cover story, Israel almost never again did.

However, the underlying conviction that Israel could act boldly and change history through special operations behind enemy lines remained, and was in fact cemented in place as the core principle of Israel's security doctrine. Indeed, this philosophy—that special ops behind enemy lines should be at least one of the country's primary methods of national defense—would predominate among Israel's political and intelligence establishment all the way up to the present day.

And while many of the world's established nations kept a separation between the intelligence outfits that gathered information and the operations units that utilized that information to conduct clandestine missions, from the very beginning Israel's special forces were an integral part of its intelligence agencies. In America, for instance, special-operations units Delta Force and SEAL Team Six are components of the Joint Special Operations Command, not the CIA or military intelligence. In Israel, however, special-operations units were under the direct control of the intelligence agencies Mossad and AMAN.

The goal was to continually translate gathered intelligence into operations. While other nations at the time were also gathering intelligence during peacetime, they did so only to be prepared in case war broke out, or to authorize the occasional special-ops attack. Israel, on the other hand, would constantly use its intelligence to develop special-ops attacks behind enemy lines, in the hope of avoiding all-out warfare entirely.

THE FASHIONING OF AN emblem, a charter, and a military philosophy was one thing. Implementation, as Harel was soon to learn, was another thing altogether, especially when it came to aggressive action.

The Mossad's first major operation ended badly. In November 1954, a captain in the Israeli Navy named Alexander Yisraeli—a philandering grifter deeply in debt—slipped out of the country on a bogus passport and tried to sell top-secret documents to the Egyptian embassy in Rome. A Mossad agent working in that embassy tipped off his superiors in Tel Aviv, who immediately began to develop a plan to kidnap Yisraeli and return him to Israel for trial as a traitor.

For Harel, this was a critical test, both for the security of the nation and his career. In those formative years, the heads of all the agencies jockeyed for power and prestige, and one significant failure could prove professionally fatal. He assembled a top-notch team of Mossad and Shin Bet operatives to grab Yisraeli in Europe. He put his second cousin, Rafi Eitan, who as a teenager had assassinated two German Templers, in charge.

Eitan says that "there were some who proposed finding Yisraeli and killing him as quickly as possible. But Harel squelched this immediately. 'We don't kill Jews,' he said, and declared this was to be an abduction operation." Harel himself said, "It never occurred to me to issue an order to kill one of our own. I wanted him to be brought to Israel and put on trial for treason."

This is an important point. There is a tradition of mutual responsibility in Judaism, and a deep connection among all Jews, as if they are one big family. These values are seen as having kept the Jewish people alive as a nation throughout the two thousand years of exile, and for a Jew to harm another Jew is considered intolerable. Back in the days of the Palestinian underground, when it was effectively impossible to hold trials, eliminating Jewish traitors was deemed legitimate to a certain extent, but not after the state was established. "We do not kill Jews"—even if they were believed to be a grave danger to national security—became an iron law of the Israeli intelligence community.

The plan unfolded perfectly at first. Eitan and three others pinched Yisraeli after he'd been stopped by another Mossad female asset at a Paris intersection. The captive was taken to a safe house, where a Mossad doctor injected him with a sedative and placed him in a crate typically used to transfer arms, before putting him on a long, multi-stop flight on an Israeli Air Force cargo plane. At every stop, Yisraeli was injected again until, just as the plane touched down in Athens, he suffered a massive seizure and died. Following Harel's orders, one of Eitan's men ended up dumping the body from the back of the plane into the sea.

Harel's people fed the Israeli press false information that Yisraeli, who left behind a pregnant wife, had stolen money and settled somewhere in South America. Harel, who was very embarrassed that an operation of his had ended in the death of a Jew, ordered that all the records on the case be secreted deep in one of the Mossad's safes. But Harel's rivals kept a copy of some of the documents, to be used against him someday if so required.

Harel also came to the conclusion that there was an urgent need for the formation of a special unit specifically designed to carry out sabotage and targeted killing missions. He began searching for "trained fighters, tough and loyal, who would not hesitate to squeeze the trigger when necessary." He found them in the last place he would have been expected to look: the veterans of the Irgun and Lehi, against whom he had once fought a bitter struggle.

Ben-Gurion had forbidden the employment of any former members of the right-wing underground in government departments, and many of them were jobless, frustrated, and hungry for action. The Shin Bet believed that some of them were dangerous and were liable to start underground movements against the regime.

Harel aimed to kill two birds: to set up his special-ops unit, and to get the underground fighters into action under his command, outside the borders of the state.

David Shomron, Yitzhak Shamir, and those of their comrades in the Irgun and Lehi who were deemed tough and daring enough were invited to Harel's home in north Tel Aviv and sworn in. This was the establishment of Mifratz, Hebrew for "Gulf" or "Bay," the Mossad's first hit team.

# THE BUREAU FOR ARRANGING
# MEETINGS WITH GOD

ISRAEL'S WAR OF INDEPENDENCE officially ended with armistice agreements in 1949. The unofficial fighting never stopped. Throughout the early 1950s, the country was constantly infiltrated by Arabs from the parts of Palestine that remained in Arab hands after the war—namely, the Gaza Strip, in the south, which was administered by Egypt, and the West Bank, in the east, which Jordan had annexed. The IDF estimated that in 1952, about sixteen thousand infiltrations occurred (eleven thousand from Jordan and the rest from Egypt). Some of those infiltrators were refugees who had fled during the War of Independence, either voluntarily or involuntarily, and were trying to return to their villages and salvage what was left of their property. But many others were militants whose objective was to kill Jews and spread terror. They called themselves fedayeen—"those who self-sacrifice."

The Egyptians, despite having signed an armistice, quickly realized that the fedayeen could fight a proxy war on their behalf. With proper training and supervision, those Palestinian militants could wreak substantial havoc on Israel while giving Egypt the cover of plausible deniability.

A young captain in Egyptian military intelligence, Mustafa Hafez, was put in charge of organizing the fedayeen. Beginning in mid-1953, Hafez (along with Salah Mustafa, the Egyptian military attaché in Jordan's capital, Amman) started recruiting and training guerrilla squads to be dispatched into Israel's south. For years, those squads, six hundred fedayeen in total, sneaked across the border from Gaza and laid waste to anything they could. They blew up water pipes, set fire to fields, bombed train tracks, mined roads; they murdered farmers in their fields and yeshiva students at study—altogether some one thousand civilians between 1951 and 1955. They spread panic and fear to the point that Israelis refrained from driving at night on main roads in the south.

The proxy squads were considered a huge success. The Israelis couldn't hold Egypt or Jordan directly responsible. They would respond instead by recruiting their own proxies, turning Arabs into informers, collecting intelligence on fedayeen targets, and then assassinating them. Those tasks were assigned, for the most part, to an IDF intelligence team known as Unit 504.

Some of the men of Unit 504 had been raised in Arab neighborhoods of Palestine and thus were intimately familiar with the language and customs of the locals. Unit 504 was under the command of Rehavia Vardi. Polish-born, Vardi had served as a senior Haganah intelligence officer prior to the establishment of the state, and he was known for his sharp wit and blunt statements. "Every Arab," he said, "can be recruited on the basis of one of the three Ps—praise, payment or pussy." Whether through those three Ps or other means, Vardi and his men recruited four hundred to five hundred agents, who passed on invaluable information in the period between 1948 and 1956. Those recruits, in turn, provided Unit 504 with information on a number of senior fedayeen dispatchers. Several were identified, located, and targeted, and in ten to fifteen of those cases, the Israelis persuaded their Arab agents to place a bomb near that target.

That was when they would call Unit 188. That was when they required the services of Natan Rotberg.

"IT WAS ALL VERY, very secret," Rotberg said. "We were not allowed to mention the names of units; we were not allowed to tell anyone where we were going or where we were serving or—it goes without saying—what we were doing."

Rotberg, a thick-necked and good-natured kibbutznik with a bushy mustache, was one of a small group, only a few hundred men, who took part in forming the original triumvirate of AMAN, Shin Bet, and the Mossad. In 1951, when Rotberg was assigned to a marine commando unit called Shayetet 13 (Flotilla 13), Israeli intelligence set up a secret facility north of Tel Aviv to teach "special demolitions" and manufacture sophisticated bombs. Rotberg, Flotilla 13's explosives officer, was appointed to run it.

Rotberg had a large vat installed in which he mixed TNT and pentaerythritol tetranitrate and other chemicals into deadly concoctions. But though his mixtures were designed to kill people, he claimed that he did not act with hatred in his heart. "You need to know how to forgive," he said. "You need to know how to forgive the enemy. However, we have no authority to forgive people like bin Laden. That, only God can do. Our job is to arrange a meeting between them. In my laboratory, I opened a matchmaker's office, a bureau that arranged such meetings. I orchestrated more than thirty such meetings."

When Rehavia Vardi and his men had identified a target, they would go to Rotberg for the bomb. "At first we worked with double-bottomed wicker baskets," Rotberg said. "I would cushion the bottom part of the basket with impermeable paper and pour the concoction in from the vat. Then we'd put on a cover and, above that, fill it up with fruits and vegetables. For the [triggering] mechanism, we used pencils into which we inserted ampoules filled with acid that ate away at the cover until it reached the detonator, activated it, and set off the charge. The problem with the acid was that weather conditions affected the time it took to eat away [the cover], producing nonuniform timing. A bomb in the Gaza Strip would go off at a different time than one in the West Bank, where it is generally colder. We then switched to clocks, which are much more accurate."

But Rotberg's bombs were hardly enough to solve the fedayeen problem. According to several sources, explosives killed only seven targets between mid-1951 and mid-1953, while in the process killing six civilians.

The attacks continued unabated, terrorizing Israeli civilians, humiliating the Israel Defense Forces. Vardi and his men, talented as they were at recruiting agents, managed to glean only sparse information about the identities of the fedayeen handlers, and even when the unit did ferret out specific targets, the IDF was unable to find or kill them. "We had our limitations," says Yigal Simon, a Unit 504 veteran and later on its commander. "We didn't always have intelligence, we couldn't send our agents everywhere, and they didn't appreciate us enough in the IDF. It was important to the high command to show that the IDF—Jewish hands—could execute these actions."

Regular IDF units did try several times to penetrate the Gaza Strip, Sinai, and Jordan to carry out retaliation attacks, but they repeatedly failed. Prime Minister Ben-Gurion accordingly decided to develop whatever capability the IDF lacked. At a secret meeting on June 11, 1953, the Israeli cabinet approved his recommendation that it "authorize the minister of defense"—Ben-Gurion himself—"to approve . . . acts of reprisal against the attacks and murders [committed by] those coming from beyond the Israel-Jordan armistice lines."

Ben-Gurion used the authority vested in him to act a short time afterward. Two guards at Even Sapir, a settlement near Jerusalem, were murdered on May 25, and he ordered that an ad hoc secret detail be set up in order to do away with a Palestinian arch-terrorist by the name of Mustafa Samweli, who had been behind the slaying of the guards.

Now Ben-Gurion just needed the right man to lead it.


ARIEL SCHEINERMAN—BETTER KNOWN AS Ariel Sharon—was a twenty-five-year-old student in the summer of 1953, but he already had extensive combat experience. He'd established himself as a leader from his days as a teenaged youth-movement counselor and had proven his courage during the War of Independence, during which he had been badly wounded. Arik, as he was also known, was charismatic and authoritative, a warrior in top physical condition, and he didn't hesitate when the IDF General Staff recruited him to eliminate Samweli. "My father immediately said yes," wrote Sharon's son Gilad, in a biography of Ariel. "He was confident that with seven or eight good men, friends who'd served with him in the war and afterward, and with the right kit, he could do it."

On the night of July 12–13, Sharon and a squad made up of reservists managed to get inside Samweli's village in the West Bank and blow his house up. But the intelligence they were given was flawed, and Samweli wasn't at home. The force got entangled in a firefight and made it out by the skin of their teeth.

The high command saw the operation as a success—deep penetration of enemy territory, demonstration of its ability to hit a target, and returning to base without casualties. Sharon, by contrast, came back exhausted and totally dissatisfied. His conclusion was that such operations have to be carried out by professionals, something completely different from the random group of buddies he had taken with him that night. He told his superiors that there was a need for an elite commando unit. On August 10, Unit 101 came into being.

"This unit was set up for the purpose of operations across the border, those non-standard missions that demand special training and high-level performance," according to the "101 Operations Procedures," written by Sharon himself.

Sharon was given free rein to select his own men, from reservist soldiers redrafted to the army as well as regular soldiers. He wanted to put them through a grueling, yearlong training program. His fighters learned how to handle explosives, how to navigate over long distances, and how to fire accurately and precisely while on the run over mountainous terrain, exercises that both developed their skills and instilled a sense of pride and confidence.

The young leader made sure his men stood apart from the IDF regulars, arming them with a different personal weapon from the outdated bolt-action Czechoslovak rifle in use at the time. Instead they were issued Carl Gustav submachine guns, and they were also the first to try out the new and still secret Israeli-made Uzi.

Sharon also relaxed the rules of both dress and conduct; at their secret base in the Jerusalem mountains, the men of Unit 101 often worked entirely in civilian attire. To Sharon, the outward trappings of military order were of marginal use; more important was that his men believed they were special, better, the best. And that they trusted their commander: Sharon's operational briefings were precise and unequivocal, and he fought at the front of his battalion, often in the most vulnerable position, embodying the well-known motto of IDF commanders: "Follow me!"

Sharon was imbued with a limitless and unrestrained motivation to go on operations, and he grasped that if he had to wait for precise intelligence from AMAN to carry out a targeted killing, he might never do anything.

Accordingly, Sharon and Moshe Dayan, chief of the general staff, shifted tactics, abandoning pinpoint precision for something more primal. Rather than kill prime Palestinian terrorists, they would avenge the killings of Israelis by attacking and terrorizing the Arab villages from which the terrorists had set forth to harm Jews, as well as the army camps and police stations.

"We cannot prevent the murder of workers in the orchards and of families in their beds," Dayan said in a lecture in 1955, "but we have the ability to set a high price for our blood."

Sharon, craving action, drew up plans for a series of punitive raids against Arab military and civilian targets, then lobbied for his superiors to approve them. Yet it is an open question how many of those raids were punitive as opposed to provocative. Sharon was fond of quoting Dayan's famous dictum "We do not initiate battles in times of peace." Uzi Eilam, who served as Sharon's intelligence officer, suggests that this was not an ironclad rule. "There were many cases in which we, at Arik's bidding, provoked the enemy over the border and incited war. In a real analysis of 'who started it' over the entire history of the IDF's retaliations, we will not come out squeaky clean."

Even in real time, as they were unfolding, there was an apparent downside to Sharon's tactics. In the fall of 1953, fedayeen murdered a young woman and her two children in Yehud, just southeast of Tel Aviv, brutal deaths that shocked the Israeli public. The government vowed to retaliate. The assumption was that Arab militants were using West Bank villages close to the border as bases to attack Israel. Sharon selected one of those villages—Qibya, which may or may not have been involved in the Yehud murders—as a target.

On October 15, before dawn, Sharon led a force of 130 men from Unit 101 and other outfits, carrying more than 1,500 pounds of explosives, into Qibya. Within hours, the village was destroyed. "In the Qibya operation," one of Sharon's lieutenants later testified, "we blew up forty-three houses. The IDF was equipped with small flashlights left over from the British Army, something you could barely see with. We went in with a megaphone, shining flashlights and shouting: 'If there's anyone here, come out, because we are about to blow it up.' Some got up and came out. Then we'd apply the explosives and blow up the house. When we returned, we reported eleven [Arabs] killed. It wasn't that we lied; we just didn't know."

The death toll was sixfold higher. At least sixty-nine were killed, most of them women and children. The world, including much of Israel and Jewish communities around the globe, was horrified. The UN Security Council condemned the raid, as did the U.S. State Department, which announced that it already had suspended aid to Israel for violating the armistice agreements of 1949.

Israel's official explanation for the massacre was that rogue Jewish civilians were responsible. "All IDF units were at their bases" on the night of the raid, Ben-Gurion said publicly. Abba Eban, Israel's ambassador to the UN, repeated Ben-Gurion's lie at a session of the Security Council.

Privately, Ben-Gurion gave Sharon his full support, because Unit 101—despite the worldwide outrage—boosted morale within an Israeli Army exhausted by unrelenting defensive operations. The unit represented dedication, daring, physical prowess, and mental stamina, ideals to which each IDF unit aspired. As Sharon later said, Unit 101 "proved, within a short period of time, that there was no mission it could not carry out," and that those missions helped secure Israel's borders. That claim is open to debate—there are serious questions about how successful those commando raids were in reducing attacks by infiltrators, and some didn't even achieve their immediate objectives—but Israeli soldiers believed it was true.

And that was enough. In early 1954, only five months after Unit 101 had been established, Dayan merged it with the Paratroopers Brigade, with Sharon as one of the battalion commanders. Dayan believed that Unit 101 had become a model—of training and discipline, of dedication and skill—that Sharon could replicate with the paratroops and then in the entire army.

Sharon's activity within the paratroops was more restrained, because he was no longer commander of an independent unit, but also because changes had taken place in the high command. Ben-Gurion had resigned and been replaced as prime minister by the dovish Moshe Sharett, who generally refrained from approving retaliation attacks.

But what Sharett did not approve, Sharon's men took upon themselves. The sister of the most renowned warrior in 101, Meir Har-Zion, was brutally murdered by Bedouins while on an illegal hike across the Jordanian border. Har-Zion and two comrades, with Sharon's moral encouragement and logistical assistance, went to the scene and killed four Bedouin shepherds in revenge. Sharett demanded that they be court-martialed, but Dayan and Sharon, with Ben-Gurion's backing, thwarted it.

Sharett wrote in his diary on January 11, 1955: "I wonder about the nature and the fate of this nation, capable of such fine spiritual sensitivity, of such profound love of humanity, of such honest yearning for the beautiful and the sublime, while at the same time it produces from amongst the ranks of its youth boys who are capable of murdering people with a clear mind and in cold blood by thrusting knives into the flesh of young, defenseless Bedouin. Which of the two souls that run around in the pages of the Bible will overcome its rival within this nation?"

MUSTAFA HAFEZ, MEANWHILE, WAS still alive. The Egyptian intelligence captain and his colleague in Jordan, Salah Mustafa, continued running squads of Palestinian infiltrators, and those infiltrators were still wreaking havoc in Israel.

On March 17, 1954, a gang of twelve Arab terrorists ambushed a civilian bus on its way from Eilat to Tel Aviv at Scorpion Pass, a winding stretch of road in the heart of the Negev Desert. Firing point-blank, they killed eleven passengers. A nine-year-old boy, Haim Furstenberg, hiding under a seat, got up after they had left the bus and asked, "Have they gone?" The terrorists heard him, returned to the bus, and shot him in the head. He survived but was paralyzed until his death, thirty-two years later. The Arabs mutilated and spat on the bodies of the dead. It turned out later that they were Palestinians and Bedouins who had come from Jordan and were supported by Salah Mustafa.

Sharett was under heavy pressure to retaliate, but he would not approve a revenge operation. "An act in reaction to the bloodbath would only blur the horrifying effect, and would place us on the same level as the mass murderers on the other side," he wrote in his diary.

Instead, AMAN's Unit 504 sent in a detail of three Bedouin assassins whom they employed as agents. They crossed into Jordan heavily armed and carrying two explosive devices prepared by Natan Rotberg. They discovered where one of the terrorists lived, in a village in southern Jordan, and, after deciding not to blow up his house, they waited until he was alone and shot him dead. "Our agents found the ID card of the bus driver among the things he'd looted and brought it back to us," Yigal Simon, a 504 senior veteran, recounts.

This pinpoint operation was considered a success by 504, but it didn't make much of a difference in the wider picture. Targeted killings, with their limited success, had failed to stop, or even noticeably stall, the cross-border attacks. Punitive raids had drawn global ire but hadn't slowed the carnage.

In the middle of the 1950s, Hafez was winning. The terrorists he trained carried out ever more deadly attacks in Israeli territory—collecting intelligence, sabotaging infrastructure, stealing property, and killing Israelis. Israel, lacking proper infrastructure, including high-resolution intelligence, experience, know-how, and large enough trained and equipped forces, could respond only with increasingly nonspecific retaliation operations and heavy bombing of the Gaza Strip.

Hafez's name appeared frequently in the reports that Unit 504 received from its sources in the south. Yet he was a vague figure, cloaked in shadows. "We never got a picture of him," said Yaakov Nimrodi, who commanded the unit's southern base. "But we knew that he was a young man of about thirty, fairly good-looking and very charismatic. Our prisoners and agents spoke of him with admiration and awe."

Hafez and Nimrodi, himself a young, charismatic officer, stood on either side of the Arab-Israeli conflict. "Hafez was considered one of the best minds in Egyptian intelligence," Nimrodi said. "Few were our agents who managed to slip through his fingers. Many were captured and liquidated, or became double agents after the treatment they received from him, and turned against us. In this war of minds, only the best won and survived."

Against the background of the security impotency and under heavy public pressure, Sharett was compelled first to accept Ben-Gurion as his defense minister, and then to give him back the premiership, in November 1955. Sharett went back to being just the foreign minister and later was forced to resign under pressure from Ben-Gurion.

Ben-Gurion's return encouraged AMAN to again plan more vigorous attacks against the fedayeen. One idea was to do away with Hafez. "He was the head of the snake," Nimrodi said, "that we had to cut off."

"But this was difficult, for three reasons," said Avraham Dar, who now, as a major in AMAN, was charged with gathering intelligence about Hafez. "First, collecting enough intelligence about him and about the places he frequented; secondly, getting to him and killing him; and third, the diplomatic problem. He was a senior officer in the army of a sovereign state. Hitting him might have been seen as crossing a red line in relations with Egypt, and lead to deterioration."

Attempts by the UN to mediate between Israel and Egypt failed, and Hafez's raids continued, through 1955 and into the spring of 1956.

On April 29, 1956, a squad of Palestinian guerrillas trained by Hafez opened fire on farmers working in the fields of Nahal Oz, a kibbutz on Israel's southern border. Roi Rotberg, a young first lieutenant in the IDF reserves, in charge of security for the kibbutz, rode out on horseback to repel them. The Palestinians killed him, gouged out his eyes, and dragged his body through the field and across the trench that marked the border, an effort to suggest that Rotberg had invaded foreign soil.

Moshe Dayan took Rotberg's death particularly hard. He had met the lieutenant only the day before, as he toured southern settlements. The next day, April 30, Dayan stood over Rotberg's open grave and read a eulogy that, in the intervening years, has come to be seen as the seminal formulation of Israeli militarism:

> Roi was murdered yesterday, in the early morning. The silence of the spring morning blinded him and he did not see those lying in wait at the edge of the furrow.

Let us not today cast blame on the murderers. Who are we to argue against their potent hatred for us? For eight years they have been sitting in the refugee camps in Gaza, and before their eyes we have been turning the land and villages in which they and their forefathers lived into our own inheritance . . .

We are the generation of settlement, and without steel helmets and the maw of the cannon we will not be able to plant a tree or build a home. Our children will not live if we do not dig shelters, and without barbed wire fences and machine guns we will not be able to pave roads or drill for water. Millions of Jews, annihilated because they had no country, gaze at us from the dust of Jewish history and command us to settle and raise up a land for our people.

. . . We must not flinch from seeing the hatred that accompanies and fills the lives of hundreds of thousands of Arabs who live around us and await the moment when they are strong enough to get our blood. We will not avert our gaze lest our hands grow weak. This is our generation's destiny.

In simple terms, Dayan meant that the Jews in the State of Israel may have arrived as settlers returning to their ancient homeland, but, from the perspective of the Arabs, they came as invaders. Therefore the Arabs—justifiably, from their point of view—hated the Jews. And the continued existence of the Jews depended, more than anything, on their ability to defend themselves against the Arabs who wished to kill them. All the rest—development, the economy, society, and culture—were subordinate and must bend to the needs of security and survival. This, in Dayan's view, was Israel's destiny, born of thousands of years of Jewish history.

Standing over the grave as Dayan spoke was Roi's cousin, Natan Rotberg, the bomb maker. After the funeral, Natan promised his uncle, Shmaryahu, that he would avenge Roi, his son.

As it happened, Dayan was determined to avenge Roi, too, and all the other Israelis killed and terrorized by Hafez's squads. This time, Dayan persuaded Ben-Gurion not only to launch a retaliation raid against a Palestinian village, but to allow him to instruct the intelligence community to kill the Egyptians running killers into Israel— the colonels Hafez and Salah. This was a significant escalation.

Avraham Dar wrote the operational order, which was code-named Eunuch (Saris). As far as can be ascertained, this was the first operational order for a targeted killing that was both written and carried out in the history of the State of Israel.

"In light of Egypt's organization of fedayeen activities in the Gaza Strip and Jordan," Dar wrote, "it has been decided to act against its organizers, Mustafa Hafez in the Gaza Strip and the Egyptian military attaché in Jordan. The goal: the physical elimination of the said two men with booby-trap bombs." In Hafez's case, Dar recalls, "it was clear to us that the bomb had to be given to him by someone he trusted."

They found their man in Muhammad al-Talalqa, a young Bedouin who lived in the Gaza Strip and was working for both Hafez and Unit 504. Al-Talalqa and Hafez were not aware that 504 knew he was a double agent, and the AMAN unit decided to exploit this and give him something in a package that would seem to him so important that he would immediately take it to Hafez.

What could that something be? A book that included all the ciphers in Morse code used by the Israelis, which Talalqa would be instructed by 504 to take to another Israeli agent in Gaza.

Once again, the services of Natan Rotberg were called for. He would indeed avenge his cousin.

"Zadok [Ofir, an officer at Unit 504's southern base] called me and told me about the plan," Rotberg said more than five decades later. "I understood who was involved and was very pleased. I told them that if they could deliver a thick book to Hafez, I would take care of the rest.

"I cut out the book's insides and poured in three hundred grams of my stuff. Was it enough? Of course. A detonator is twenty grams—if it explodes in your hand, you'll end up without any fingers. So three hundred grams that explodes in a person's face will kill him for sure.

"The apparatus was based on a metal arm, a marble, and a strong spring. When the book was closed, inside a wrapper reinforced by ribbons, the arm is under pressure and doesn't move. The minute you undo the ribbons and loosen the wrapper, the arm springs free and propels the marble forward, puncturing the detonator, which sets off the bomb and—*kaboom!*"

The plan and the booby trap worked perfectly. On July 11, 1956, al-Talalqa crossed the border, went straight to the Egyptian military intelligence HQ in Gaza, and excitedly handed the package to Hafez. "When he pulled the book out of the package," an eyewitness later told a secret Egyptian inquiry, "a piece of paper fell out. Colonel Mustafa Hafez bent down to pick it up from the floor, and at that moment the explosion occurred." Hafez was mortally wounded. Some of those present testified that, as he lay sprawled on the floor, he shouted, "You beat me, you dogs."

The next night, Natan Rotberg paid a visit to his uncle, Roi's father. He made a special point of putting on his dress uniform. "I told him, 'Shmaryahu, I took care of your account with Mustafa Hafez,'" Rotberg said. "Did it make him feel better? I'm not sure, but me it did. I was happy. Shmaryahu was silent. A tear formed in his eye and he thanked me for updating him."

The Egyptians were too embarrassed to acknowledge their security lapse publicly. The day after Hafez died, a notice appeared in the Egyptian newspaper *Al-Ahram:* "Col. Mustafa Hafez, stationed in the Gaza Strip, was killed when his vehicle hit a mine. . . . He was one of the heroes of the war in Palestine and fought for its liberation. History has recorded his heroic deeds. His name sowed fear and panic in Israel."

The same day Hafez was killed, Salah Mustafa, the Egyptian military attaché in Amman, received in the mail a copy of *Achtung Panzer!* by Heinz Guderian, the German army's tank warfare hero and one of the fathers of the concept of blitzkrieg. Avraham Dar, an aficionado of military history and strategy, chose the book because he was sure Salah would think it a suitable gift. Two Mistaravim had entered East Jerusalem, which was under Jordanian rule, and mailed the book from there so the postmark wouldn't arouse suspicion. Salah, who had not yet heard of the attack on his counterpart in Gaza, opened the book, and it blew up, wounding him mortally. He later died in the hospital.

Chief of staff Dayan grasped the significance of these two hits, and he held in his backyard a lavish party to celebrate the killings of Hafez and Salah. Avraham Dar put together the guest list.

# THE ENTIRE SUPREME COMMAND,
# WITH ONE BLOW

THE TARGETED KILLINGS OF Hafez and Salah jolted Egyptian military intelligence, and there was a certain reduction in the number of terrorist incursions into Israel. From the Israeli point of view, this was a success.

But then the skies over the region grew clouded for a different reason.

On July 26, 1956, Egypt's president, Gamal Abdel Nasser, acting on an anticolonialist agenda, nationalized the Suez Canal, the vital shipping link between the Mediterranean Sea and the Red Sea. The British and French governments, whose citizens were the major shareholders in the highly profitable company that operated the waterway, were furious. Israel, for its part, wished to regain passage through the canal, but at the same time, it also saw an opportunity to deliver a clear message to Egypt: namely, that Nasser would finally pay a heavy price for sending militants in the Gaza Strip to attack Israel, and that his explicit ambitions to destroy the country would be met with crushing force.

This convergence of interests begat a secret alliance between the three countries, with the energetic young director general of the Israeli Defense Ministry, Shimon Peres, playing a leading part in drawing up an ambitious war plan. Israel would invade the Sinai Peninsula, thus giving the French and the British a pretext—a crisis threatening the Suez—to also invade. France promised to provide Israel with an air umbrella against attacks by the Egyptian Air Force.

Shortly before D-Day, Israel's AMAN learned that a delegation that included the powerful Egyptian chief of staff, Field Marshal Abd al-Hakim Amer, and many other senior officials had left Cairo by plane for Damascus. An opportunity presented itself. With one precision strike, Israel could eliminate nearly the entire Egyptian military leadership.

The air force began conducting intensive training in night interception, a difficult operation, given the technological capabilities available at the time. Ben-Gurion and Dayan decided that Israel would do all it could to conceal its involvement, and try to make it look as if the plane had crashed because of a technical fault.

The mission was code-named Operation Rooster.

The Egyptians were expected to make the short flight from Damascus back to Cairo in two Ilyushin Il-14 aircraft. AMAN assigned the task of identifying and tracking the air convoy to its signals intelligence (SIGINT) unit. The unit (known nowadays as Unit 8200) had already racked up a number of prominent successes in the 1948–49 war, and afterward AMAN invested many resources in the development of the unit, which would eventually become the largest—and, some say, the most important—in the IDF.

The investment proved out. A few days before the delegation left Cairo for Damascus, SIGINT technicians managed to isolate the broadcast frequency the Egyptians were expected to use on the short flight back to Cairo. Twenty Israeli radio operators, all under the age of twenty-five, waited tensely at headquarters in Ramat Hasharon, north of Tel Aviv, manning round-the-clock shifts, waiting for the Egyptians to leave the tarmac in Damascus. The unit was under intense pressure from the high command, as the land invasion of the Sinai Peninsula was planned for October 29, and the demoralizing chaos of losing its entire senior military staff would put the Egyptians at a distinct disadvantage. Time was running out.

Days passed slowly, radio operators patiently waiting for a sound in their headsets. Dawn broke on October 28, the day before zero hour, and still the Egyptians hadn't left Syria. Finally, at two o'clock on the afternoon of October 28, the signal they were waiting for was picked up: the pilots of the Ilyushin Il-14s were getting ready to leave.

Mattias "Chatto" Birger, commander of the air force's 119 Squadron and one of the air force's best pilots at the time, was selected for the dramatic mission. At about 8 P.M., SIGINT informed the air force that only one of the two Egyptian Ilyushins had taken off. Still, SIGINT believed that all of the Egyptian officers were on board. Operation Rooster was a go.

Chatto climbed into the Meteor Mk. 13 jet and took off with his navigator, Elyashiv "Shivi" Brosh. It was a particularly dark night, so dark that even the horizon nearly vanished in the blackness.

Chatto climbed to ten thousand feet and leveled off. The radar pinged off an approaching plane. "Contact, contact, contact!" Shivi said over the intercom. "Two o'clock, our altitude, three miles head-on, moving to three o'clock. Four! Make a hard right! Slower! You're closing in too fast!"

Against the massive black sky, Chatto saw tiny orange flares, the flames from the Ilyushin's exhaust pipes. "Eye contact," he reported to ground control.

"I want a positive identification of the craft," said air force commander Dan Tolkowsky, who sat in the control center. "Positive, beyond all doubt. Understand?"

Chatto veered slightly to the left until he could see light in the windows of the passenger compartment. The windows of the cockpit were larger than the others. *That's a positive identification,* Chatto thought. *Only an Ilyushin has windows like that.* He also made out people in army uniforms walking among the seats.

"Identification confirmed!" he said.

"Cleared to open fire, only if you have no doubt," Tolkowsky responded.

"Roger."

Shells erupted from four twenty-millimeter cannons fitted on the nose of the airplane. Chatto was blinded by an unexpected brilliance: someone on the ground crew, trying to be helpful, had loaded tracer rounds into the cannons, but the bright flashes in the near-total darkness seared his eyes.

Chatto recovered his sight. He saw fire in the sky. "Got him!" Chatto told ground control. "The left engine is in flames, and it looks like there's a short circuit, because everything is dark."

Chatto squeezed the trigger again. The Ilyushin exploded, a fireball in the night, spewing flaming chunks of wreckage. It began to spin down toward the sea.

"Did you see it crash?" Tolkowsky asked as Chatto pulled his plane out of the spin.

"Affirmative, crashed," Chatto answered.

Chatto brought his plane in on fumes and was greeted on the tarmac by chief of staff Moshe Dayan and General Tolkowsky, who gave Chatto the news that, at the last minute, Amer had apparently decided to wait for the second plane.

"If there's time," Chatto said, "we'll fuel up and go out again."

"We've considered that but reached the conclusion that it would look too obvious and would be liable to reveal our intelligence source," Dayan responded. "We've decided to let Amer be. Even so, the minute you liquidated the Egyptian General Staff, you won half the war. Let's have a drink for the second half."

Operation Rooster was without doubt a superb intelligence and aerial warfare achievement. Indeed, the participants in Operation Rooster later began calling it "the downing of the Egyptian General Staff" and would claim that the chaos that prevailed in the high command in Cairo had contributed significantly to Israel's victory in the war that broke out the next day.

Whether or not the impact was quite as large as these men claimed, the IDF would go on to easily rout the Egyptian Army. It put the world on notice: The Jewish state was now a serious fighting force. Ben-Gurion, temporarily in a state of euphoria, sent a public letter to the officers and soldiers of the 9th Brigade talking about the "Third Kingdom of Israel."

TOGETHER WITH THE SINAI Peninsula, Israel had also conquered the Gaza Strip. After the IDF occupied the Strip, Rehavia Vardi sent some of his men from Unit 504 to search the Egyptian intelligence building in Gaza City, where Mustafa Hafez had been killed a few months before. In a cellar they found a hidden treasure, one that the desperately fleeing Egyptians had neglected to destroy: the intact card file of all the Palestinian terrorists that Hafez and his men had deployed against Israel in the five years preceding the Sinai Campaign.

It was as if the Egyptians had left a hit list. Vardi met with chief of staff Dayan and asked for his permission to begin killing the Palestinians named in the card file. Dayan, in turn, received Ben-Gurion's approval. Vardi then ordered Natan Rotberg—and his vat of explosives—to go into overdrive.

Rotberg's special formula was poured into wicker baskets, cigarette lighters, fruits, vegetables, even pieces of furniture. Unit 504's Arab agents concealed the bombs in appropriate places or passed them on as gifts to as many as thirty Palestinian fedayeen in Gaza. Between November 1957 and March 1958, Vardi's men worked through the file, eliminating men who'd terrorized Israelis for years. The targeted killing missions were largely a success, tactically speaking, but not necessarily strategically. "All these eliminations were of very limited importance," Rotberg said, "because others simply took their place."

Very quickly, the secret conspiracy by Britain, France, and Israel turned into a resounding international diplomatic disaster. The United States forced Israel to withdraw from Sinai and Gaza. France and Britain also caved in and finally lost control of the canal, and the leaders of both of those superpowers were forced to resign.

The Egyptian regime was now seen as having stood up to meddling Western colonialism, and having forced two great European powers and its sworn Jewish enemy to stand down. Nasser was cast as a hero and became, for all practical purposes, the leader of the Arab world.

Nasser did, however, agree to allow Israeli ships to use the canal, and to stop sponsoring fedayeen operations in Gaza. He grasped that the potential for a general military flare-up with Israel from these operations was greater than the advantages to be derived from them.

Finally, in 1957, it seemed that terror would stop streaming into Israel from across the border.

THE SINAI CAMPAIGN MADE it clear to the Arab states that destroying Israel would be very difficult, and it gave Israel eleven years of freedom from large-scale warfare, up until the Six-Day War of 1967. The IDF used this time to morph into a powerful, large, well-trained, technology-based military force, equipped with modern weapons and boasting an intelligence arm, AMAN, with extensive capabilities.

The years that followed were also good years for the Mossad. Isser Harel had nurtured it from a fledgling, sometimes stumbling organization into an agency of close to a thousand employees, renowned internationally for its toughness, tenacity, and enterprise.

Israel had begun to emerge as an intelligence power in 1956, after Nikita Khrushchev gave a secret speech to the Twentieth Communist Party Congress in which he spoke frankly about the crimes committed by his predecessor, Joseph Stalin. Every spy outfit in the Western world was anxious to obtain the text, to study it for clues to Khrushchev's mindset, but none of them could penetrate the Soviet Union's iron veil of secrecy. It was Israeli intelligence that succeeded, and Isser Harel ordered that a copy of the speech be handed to the CIA.

The agency's impressed and grateful director, Allen Dulles, passed it on to President Dwight Eisenhower, who then ordered that it be leaked to *The New York Times*. The publication stirred up a global storm and greatly embarrassed the Soviet Union.

The secret alliance between American and Israeli intelligence was born. On the American side, it was led by James Jesus Angleton, chief of the CIA's counterintelligence staff, a supporter of Israel who, like Harel, saw a Soviet spy under every bed. Through this channel, the CIA would obtain a great deal of Middle East intelligence, a practice that continues to this day.

Israel's Sinai Campaign of 1956, though a political disaster, further cemented the country's standing in intelligence operations. In the wake of that brief war, Harel began weaving a network of secret contacts within countries all over the Middle East, Asia, and Africa, including many that publicly sided with Arabs. This modus operandi was known in the Mossad as "the periphery doctrine," and it called for the establishment of covert links with countries and organizations that lay just outside the ring of hostile Arab states surrounding Israel, or with minorities inside those states who were at conflict with Israel's adversaries.

The outstanding achievement of the Mossad's periphery strategy was a tripartite intelligence alliance—code-named Trident—between Israel, the shah's Iran, and Turkey. The heads of the three countries' spy agencies would meet from time to time and exchange large amounts of intelligence material. The alliance also carried out joint operations against the Soviets and the Arabs. Ben-Gurion persuaded President Eisenhower that Trident was a top-class asset, and the CIA provided funds for its activities.

The biggest coup for the Mossad, however, came in 1960, when Israeli operatives tracked Adolf Eichmann—one of the main architects and facilitators of Hitler's Final Solution—to Buenos Aires, where he'd been living for ten years under the name Ricardo Klement.

A German Jewish prosecutor, Fritz Bauer, despaired of the chances of bringing Nazi war criminals to justice in Germany, so instead he leaked information that he had gathered about Eichmann to the Mossad. When a Mossad official came to see him, Bauer left him alone, with the classified documents lying on the desktop. The Israeli understood the hint and copied the relevant details.

Ben-Gurion authorized Harel to go to Buenos Aires, at the head of a large team. The premier was determined to settle accounts with Eichmann, who was given the code name Dybbuk, from the Hebrew word for an evil spirit that takes hold of a living person. But the aim of the operation was far greater than wreaking vengeance upon an individual, however egregious his transgressions may have been. Ben-Gurion ordered Harel and his team not to physically harm Eichmann, although killing him would have been the easiest option, but instead to kidnap him and bring him to face trial in Israel. The goal was to stir an internationally resonant awareness and ineradicable memory of the Holocaust, via exposure of the acts of one of its chief perpetrators.

Dozens of Mossad operatives and collaborators took part in the operation, some of them carrying and switching passports of up to five nations. They spread out into a number of safe houses all over the Argentinean capital.

On May 11, the team positioned itself near the stop where the man known as Klement got off the bus every evening at 7:40 and walked a short distance to his home. On this evening, the bus came, but Eichmann did not appear. The team's orders were to wait until no later than 8 P.M. and, if he did not appear by then, to abort, so as not to arouse suspicion.

At eight, they were preparing to pack it up, but Rafi Eitan, commander on the field, decided to wait a little longer. Five minutes later, when Eitan was about to give up for the night, another bus stopped. Klement descended and began walking, one hand in his pocket.

Zvi Malchin was the first to pounce. He feared that Klement suspected something and was about to draw a gun, so instead of grabbing him from behind and dragging him to the car, as planned, he pushed him from behind into a ditch and jumped on top of him, with Eitan and another operative close behind. Klement yelled, but there was no one around to hear him. Within seconds, he was overpowered and tossed into the backseat of a car. Zvi Aharoni, a Mossad operative, who was sitting there, told him in German that if he made trouble he would be shot on the spot.

Eitan began looking for marks that would indicate beyond doubt that he was indeed Eichmann. The scar under his arm, where the SS tattoo had been, was easily located. The scar of an appendectomy that he had undergone, meticulously documented in his SS file, was more of a problem. Eitan had to open his belt and shove his hand under Klement's trousers, all while the car was roaring ahead and the passengers were being jolted from side to side. But he eventually found it and exclaimed, *"Zeh hoo! Zeh hoo!"*—Hebrew for "It's him! It's him!"

In the dark, Eitan and Malchin's eyes were shining. They shook hands and hummed a few bars of the Partisans' Song, which had been written in honor of the Jews who had fought the Nazis in the forests, and ends with the line "Our march beats out the message: We are here."

Eichmann was sedated and smuggled to Israel in an El Al plane. His trial in Jerusalem attracted unprecedented international attention, and the procession of witnesses reminded the world of the atrocities of the Holocaust. Eichmann was sentenced to death and executed by hanging. His body was cremated and his ashes scattered at sea.

Meanwhile, the skimpy news release about Eichmann's discovery and abduction had given the Mossad the standing of a ruthless and capable espionage agency. By mid-1962, Harel was considered the strongman of the Israeli intelligence and defense establishments.

Ben-Gurion had gotten everything he'd hoped for.

But for all that glory, Harel's agency had completely missed a devastating threat developing right next door.

# "AS IF THE SKY WERE FALLING ON OUR HEADS"

ON THE MORNING OF July 21, 1962, Israelis woke up to their worst nightmare: Egypt's newspapers reported the successful test launch of four surface-to-surface missiles—two of the new Al-Zafer (the Victor) model and two of the Al-Qaher (the Conqueror) model. Two days later, the missiles—ten of each type, draped with the Egyptian flag—were paraded through Cairo along the Nile River. Some three hundred foreign diplomats were among the spectators, as were many of the residents of Cairo. President Nasser himself reviewed the parade from a special stand before a government building near the Nile. He proudly declared that the Egyptian military was now capable of hitting any point "south of Beirut." Given that the entire territory of Israel lay between Egypt, to its south, and Lebanon, with Beirut as its capital, to the north, the implication was clear.

The next day, a broadcast delivered in Hebrew from Egypt-based radio station "The Voice of Thunder from Cairo" was even more explicit. "These missiles are intended to open the gates of freedom for the Arabs, to retake the homeland that was stolen as part of imperialist and Zionist plots," the anchorman boasted.

The Israeli public's deep unease was only magnified when, just a few weeks later, it became clear that a team of German scientists had played an integral role in developing these missiles. World War II had ended only seventeen years earlier, and suddenly the traumas of the Holocaust, suffused as they were with images of German scientists in Wehrmacht uniforms, gave way to a new and different existential threat: weapons of mass destruction in the hands of Israel's new great enemy, Nasser, whom Israelis regarded as the Hitler of the Middle East. "Former German Nazis are now helping Nasser in his anti-Israeli genocide projects" was the news described by the Jewish press.

And the Mossad, despite its sweeping charter to monitor and protect Israel from external threats, had been caught unaware. The Jewish nation's intelligence services—to say nothing of its political and military leaders—had been stunned to learn of Egypt's missile project mere days before the test launch. It was a devastating reminder of the little country's vulnerability and a humiliating failure for Harel's Mossad.

Worse, the German scientists developing the Egyptian missiles that could destroy Israel weren't obscure technicians. They were some of the Nazi regime's most senior engineers, men who'd worked during the war at the research base at Peenemünde, a peninsula on the Baltic coast where the Third Reich's most advanced weaponry was developed. They helped build the V-1—the flying bomb that terrorized England—and the V-2 ballistic missile, which the Germans had used to destroy huge sections of Antwerp and London and which served as the prototype for today's long-range surface-to-surface missiles.

"I felt helpless," said Asher Ben-Natan, the director general of the Defense Ministry, "as if the sky were falling on our heads. Ben-Gurion again and again spoke of the nightmare that kept him awake at night—that he, the first prime minister, had brought the surviving Jews of Europe to the State of Israel, only for them here, in their own country, to undergo a second Holocaust."

The Mossad itself, in a top-secret internal inquiry into the affair conducted in 1982, summed it up like this: "It was one of the most important and traumatic events in the history of the Israeli intelligence community, of the type that leads to a chain reaction that engenders extreme actions."

And indeed, the reactions were extreme.

HAREL PLACED THE ENTIRE Mossad on emergency footing. An atmosphere of crisis swept through every corridor of the agency, reflected in the internal cables of those months. "We are interested in obtaining [intelligence] material, whatever may happen," the HQ in Tel Aviv cabled Mossad stations in Europe in August 1962. "If a German turns up who knows something about this and is not prepared to cooperate, we are ready to take him by force and to get him to talk. Please take note of this because we must get information at any cost."

Mossad operatives immediately began breaking into Egyptian diplomatic embassies and consulates in several European capitals to photograph documents. They were also able to recruit a Swiss employee at the Zurich office of EgyptAir—a company that occasionally served as cover for Nasser's intelligence agencies. The Swiss employee allowed Mossad operatives to take the mailbags at night, twice a week, to a safe house. They were opened, their contents were photocopied, and then they were closed again by experts who left no sign they'd been tampered with, then returned to the airline office. After a relatively short period, the Mossad had a preliminary understanding of the Egyptian missile project and its heads.

The project had been initiated by two internationally known scientists, Dr. Eugen Sänger and Wolfgang Pilz. During the war, they had played key roles at Peenemünde Army Research Center. In 1954, they joined the Research Institute of Jet Propulsion Physics, in Stuttgart. Sänger headed this prestigious body. Pilz and two other veteran Wehrmacht specialists, Dr. Paul Goercke and Dr. Hans Krug, were heads of departments. But this group, feeling underemployed and underutilized in postwar Germany, approached the Egyptian regime in 1959 and offered to recruit and lead a group of scientists to develop long-range surface-to-surface rockets. Nasser readily agreed and appointed one of his closest military advisers, General 'Isam al-Din Mahmoud Khalil, former director of air force intelligence and the chief of the Egyptian Army's R&D, to coordinate the program. Khalil set up a compartmentalized system, separate from the rest of the Egyptian Army, for the German scientists, who first arrived in Egypt for a visit in April 1960.

In late 1961, Sänger, Pilz, and Goercke relocated to Egypt and recruited about thirty-five highly experienced German scientists and technicians to join them. The facilities in Egypt contained test fields, laboratories, and luxurious living quarters for the German expats, who enjoyed excellent conditions and huge salaries. Krug, however, remained in Germany, where he set up a company called Intra Commercial, which was in fact the group's European front.

Almost as soon as the Mossad had gained a basic grasp of the situation, however, more bad news arrived. On August 16, 1962, a grave-faced Isser Harel came to see Ben-Gurion, bringing with him a document from the Egyptian intelligence mailbags that had been photocopied two days before in Zurich.

The Israelis were in shock. The document was an order written in 1962 by Pilz, to the project managers in Egypt, and it included itemization of the materials that needed to be acquired in Europe for the manufacture of nine hundred missiles. This was an enormous number. After its interception, according to a Mossad internal report, the organization was hit by "an atmosphere of near panic." Worse still, the document raised the fear among Israeli experts that the Egyptians' true aim was to arm the missiles with radioactive and chemical warheads.

Ben-Gurion summoned urgent conferences at the highest level.

Harel had a plan, of sorts.

The intelligence collected so far by the Mossad revealed an Achilles' heel in the missile project: The guidance systems were lagging so far behind as to be borderline nonfunctional, which meant that the missiles could not go into mass production. As long as this was the case, Egypt would need the German scientists. Without them, the project would collapse. Harel's plan, then, was to kidnap or to eliminate the Germans.

Toward the end of August, Harel went to Europe to put his plan into action. The weather was turning cold, heralding the coldest winter the area had known in many years. After all efforts to locate Pilz had failed, Harel decided to act against Krug.

On Monday, September 10, at 5:30 P.M., a man who introduced himself as Saleh Qaher phoned Krug's home in Munich. He said he was speaking on behalf of Colonel Said Nadim, chief aide to General Mahmoud Khalil, and that Nadim had to meet Krug "right away, on an important matter." Saleh added, in the friendliest of tones, that Nadim, whom Krug knew well, sent his regards and was waiting for

Krug at the Ambassador Hotel in Munich. The matter at hand, Saleh said, was a deal that would make a tidy profit for Krug. It was impossible to discuss it at the Intra office because of its special nature.

Krug didn't see this as unusual, and he accepted the invitation. Saleh was none other than an old Mossad hand, Oded. Born in Iraq, he had been active in the Zionist underground there, fleeing the country in 1949 after almost being caught. He'd gone to regular schools in Baghdad, with Muslims, and could easily pass for an Arab. For years, he served the Mossad in an operational capacity against Arab targets.

Krug met Oded in the lobby of the Ambassador Hotel. "We, Colonel Nadim and I, need you for an important job," he said.

The next day, Oded went to the Intra offices to pick Krug up and take him to meet Nadim at a villa outside the city. "I came in a taxi, and Krug was happy to see me and introduced me to the company's employees. He never suspected for a moment that I wasn't who I said I was. There was good chemistry between us. In the Mercedes, on the way to the address I'd given him, I flattered Krug and told him how we, in Egyptian intelligence, appreciate his services and contribution. He spoke mainly about the new Mercedes he just bought."

The two arrived at the house where Krug believed Nadim was waiting for him. They got out of the car. A woman opened the front door, and Krug went in. Oded was behind him, and the door closed, with Oded, as planned, remaining outside.

Three other operatives were waiting inside the room. They stunned Krug with a few blows, gagged him, and tied him up. When he came to, he was examined by a French Jewish doctor recruited by the team. He thought Krug was suffering from slight shock and therefore recommended not giving him sedation shots. A German-speaking Mossad operative told him, "You are a prisoner. Do exactly what we say or we'll finish you off." Krug promised to obey, and he was placed in a secret compartment built into one of the vehicles, a Volkswagen camper, and the whole squad, including Isser Harel himself, who was present throughout, set out for the French border in that car and two others. On the way they stopped in a forest, and Harel told Krug that they were about to cross the border and that if he made a sound, the driver of the car would activate a mechanism that would pump a lethal amount of poison gas into the compartment.

When they reached Marseille, a heavily sedated Krug was placed on an El Al plane flying Jewish North African immigrants to Israel. The Mossad handlers told the French authorities he was a sick immigrant.

At the same time, the Mossad launched a wide-ranging disinformation operation, with a man resembling Krug and carrying documents in his name traveling around South America, leaving a paper trail that indicated Krug had simply grabbed the money and run away from Egypt and his collaborators. Simultaneously, the Mossad leaked disinformation to the media saying that Krug had quarreled with General Khalil and his people and had apparently been abducted and murdered by them.

In Israel, Krug was imprisoned in a secret Mossad installation and subjected to harsh interrogation. At first he remained silent, but soon he began cooperating, and over the course of several months he "yielded much fruit," according to a Mossad report. "The man had a good memory and he knew all of the organizational-administrative details of the missile project." The documents that were in his briefcase were also useful. The report concluded, "This data made it possible to build up an intelligence encyclopedia."

Krug even volunteered to go back to Munich and work as a Mossad agent there. Eventually, though, after it seemed to the interrogators that Krug had told them everything he knew, the Mossad pondered what to do with him. It was clear that complying with his offer to go back to Munich would be very dangerous—Krug could betray his new controllers, go to the police, and tell them how the Israelis had abducted a German citizen on German soil. Harel chose the easier way out. He ordered S.G., one of his men, to take Krug to a deserted spot north of Tel Aviv and shoot him. An air force plane picked the body up and dumped it into the sea.

The success of the Krug operation spurred Ben-Gurion to give a green light to more and more targeted killing operations. He approved the use of Military Intelligence (AMAN) Unit 188, a secret operational outfit that put Israeli soldiers under false cover deep inside enemy countries. The unit's command was located in the Sarona compound in Tel Aviv, not far from Ben-Gurion's office, and it had a training facility on the beach in north Tel Aviv, adjoining Natan Rotberg's special demolitions lab.

Isser Harel resented Unit 188. Since the mid-1950s he had been trying to persuade Ben-Gurion to transfer it to the Mossad, or at least to put him in charge of it, but with the army vehemently opposed, Ben-Gurion turned him down.

The head of AMAN, Major General Meir Amit, didn't believe that the German scientists were as grave a threat to Israel as Harel did. However, because of the interorganizational rivalry with the Mossad, he demanded that his Unit 188 be permitted to act against them, because, as he put it, "We must not ignore it. We must nip this matter in the bud." Thus, intense competition over who would kill more Germans began between Unit 188 and the Mossad.

During that time, 188 had a veteran operative under deep cover in Egypt. Wolfgang Lotz was the perfect mole—the son of a gentile father and a Jewish mother, he was uncircumcised and looked like a typical German. He built up a cover story as a former Wehrmacht officer in Rommel's Afrika Korps who had become a horse breeder and returned to Egypt to start a stud farm.

Within a short time, Lotz, a gifted actor, had become an integral part of the growing German social circle in Cairo. He supplied 188 with many details about the missile projects and its personnel. He could not, however, take it upon himself to eliminate them in actions that would require his direct participation, for fear that he would be exposed. The head of Unit 188, Yosef Yariv, reached the conclusion that the best way to do away with the German scientists would be to use letter and parcel bombs.

Yariv ordered Natan Rotberg to start preparing the bombs. As it happened, Rotberg was working on a new type of explosive: thin, flexible Detasheet, "sheets of explosive material, developed for civilian purposes, which were meant to fuse two pieces of steel when they went off" and would allow him to make more compact charges. "We had to develop a system that could be kept unarmed and safe during all the shuffling that a letter goes through in the mail system, and then go off at the right time," Rotberg explained. "The envelope's mechanism thus worked in such a way that the bomb was armed not when it was opened, which would make the whole thing very explosive, but only when the contents were drawn out." The R&D was done in collaboration with French intelligence, in exchange for information conveyed by Lotz about the activities of the Algerian National Liberation Front (FLN) underground in Cairo. Unit 188 also helped the French smuggle explosives into Cairo to be used in assassinating FLN members there.

The first target to be sent one of the new letter bombs was Alois Brunner, an absconded Nazi war criminal who had been a deputy of Adolph Eichmann and served as commander of a concentration camp in France, sending 130,000 Jews to their deaths. Unit 188 located him in Damascus, where he'd been living for eight years under an assumed name. The Arab countries gave asylum to more than a few Nazi war criminals, and in exchange they received various services. Brunner helped train the interrogation and torture units of the Syrian secret services.

He was found with the help of Eli Cohen, one of the unit's top agents, who was active inside the higher echelons of the Syrian defense establishment. After Ben-Gurion gave his approval for the elimination of Brunner, Yariv decided to try out one of Rotberg's Detasheet devices on the Nazi. "We sent him a little gift," said Rotberg.

On September 13, 1962, Brunner received a large envelope in Damascus. It exploded after he opened it. He suffered severe facial injuries and lost his left eye, but survived.

Still, encouraged by having gotten the bomb delivered to the target, Unit 188 was eager to use the same method against the German scientists. The Mossad objected. As Rafi Eitan explained, "I oppose any action that I don't control. The mailman can open the envelope, a child can open the envelope. Who does things like that?"

And getting to the Germans in Egypt turned out to be a very complicated matter, because they didn't receive their mail directly. Egyptian intelligence collected all of the mail for the project and its personnel at the offices of EgyptAir, where it was then sent on to Cairo. Thus, it was decided to break into the airline office during the night and place the envelopes into the mailbags.

Using a new method for opening locks with a sophisticated master key developed in the Mossad's workshops, Mossad operatives who were assisting Unit 188 gained entry to the Frankfurt offices of EgyptAir on November 16.

The break-in specialist was half-hidden behind a woman operative as they leaned together against the door like a couple of lovers. The team entered the office but failed to find the mailbag. The next day, they tried again. While they were busy with the door, the janitor made an appearance, totally inebriated. There were no women with the team this time, so two of the men pretended to be homosexuals making out, and they managed to escape without arousing the suspicion of the drunken janitor. The next night, another attempt was made, and this time it went smoothly. The pouch of mail to be sent to Egypt was on one of the desks. The team inserted the booby-trapped envelopes into the bags.

Pilz had been selected as the prime target. The intelligence gathered about him indicated that he was divorcing his wife so he could wed his secretary, Hannelore Wende. The wife lived in Berlin, but she had hired a lawyer from Hamburg. The letter bomb targeting Pilz was thus designed to look as if it had come from that lawyer, with his logo and address appearing on the back. "The planners of the project assumed that such a personal item of mail wouldn't be opened by Wende, and that she would give it to Pilz himself," said the final report on the operation.

But the planners were wrong. Wende, who received the letter on November 27, presumably thought that it concerned her life as much as Pilz's. She opened it and it exploded in her hands, blowing off some of her fingers, blinding her in one eye, damaging the other, and blowing some of her teeth out of her gums. The Egyptian authorities immediately realized what was going on and located the other booby-trapped mail items with X-ray machines, then handed them over to be defused and probed by specialists from Soviet intelligence in Cairo. The Cairo blasts frightened the scientists and their families but didn't make any of them give up their cushy, well-paid jobs. Instead, Egyptian intelligence hired the services of an expert German security officer, a former SS man by the name of Hermann Adolf Vallentin. He visited the Intra offices and the project's various suppliers, advising them on security precautions, on replacing the locks on their doors, and on securing their mail deliveries. He also began probing the backgrounds of certain employees.

The next target on Harel's hit list was Dr. Hans Kleinwächter and his laboratory in the town of Lorch, which had been hired to develop a guidance system for the missiles. Harel sent the Birds (Tziporim)— the Shin Bet's operational unit, which was also used by the Mossad—to Europe with orders to start planning Operation Hedgehog against Kleinwächter. Harel's orders were straightforward: "Kleinwächter is to be abducted and brought to Israel, or if that doesn't work, kill him."

Harel himself set up his headquarters in the French city of Mulhouse, to his increasing chagrin.

Birds commander Rafi Eitan recalls: "It's the middle of the winter, horrible snow, bone-chilling cold, twenty-something degrees below zero outside. Isser is furious, sitting in some boarding house in France, beyond the Rhine. He shows me some pictures and says, 'This is the target—go kill him.'"

The Birds operatives were exhausted after the innumerable operations connected with the German scientists that they had been assigned to in the previous months and the support they had been giving to Unit 188. Eventually Eitan told Harel that in his opinion the circumstances were not ripe for a targeted killing. "We needed to wait a bit and create a trap of our own, not just shoot people in the street. 'Give me a month,' I told him. 'I'll carry out the mission and no one will know that I was even here.'"

But Harel wouldn't listen. On January 21, he dismissed the Birds and called in Mifratz, the Mossad targeted killing unit commanded by Yitzhak Shamir, in order to have Kleinwächter done away with. What Harel didn't know was that Vallentin had grasped that Kleinwächter would be the Mossad's next target. He gave him a series of briefings, made sure he was constantly accompanied by an escort, and gave him an Egyptian military pistol.

On February 20, a Mossad lookout saw Kleinwächter setting out alone on the road from Lorch to Basel. They decided to make the hit when he got back. Shamir, who, together with Harel, commanded the operation in the field, assigned the job of firing the shots to a trained former Irgun assassin by the name of Akiva Cohen. Harel sent the German-speaking Zvi Aharoni along with him. They waited for the target to get back in the evening. But he didn't show up, and it was decided to call the operation off. Then everything went wrong. Kleinwächter finally did appear, and the cancellation order was suddenly reversed, but the execution of the entire action was hasty and amateurish. The Mifratz operatives' car blocked Kleinwächter's, but the way both vehicles had stopped on the narrow road prevented the Mossad men from getting away after the operation.

Aharoni got out of the car and went up to Kleinwächter, as if to ask him for directions. The idea was to get him to open the window. He began doing so. Cohen, who approached Aharoni from behind, drew his gun, tried to aim it through the open window, and fired. But the bullet hit the glass and shattered it, and then hit Kleinwächter's scarf, but it missed his body. For some unknown reason, the pistol didn't fire again. One theory is that the spring snapped, another is that the bullet was a dud, and yet another is that the magazine got loose and fell out. Aharoni saw that the plan had failed and yelled at everyone to make a run for it. They couldn't use their car, so they ran off in different directions to try to get to waiting escape vehicles. Kleinwächter drew his pistol and began firing at the fleeing Israelis. He didn't hit anyone, but the entire operation was an embarrassing failure.

Harel then launched a number of actions aimed at intimidating the scientists and their families, including anonymous letters threatening their lives and containing much information about them, as well as actual visits in the middle of the night to give similar warnings.

These operations also failed dismally when the Swiss police arrested a Mossad operative by the name of Joseph Ben-Gal after he threatened Professor Goercke's daughter Heidi. He was extradited to Germany, convicted, and sentenced to a short term in prison. Mossad agents following the trial had the disagreeable experience of watching as the missile project's security officer, the hulky Hermann Vallentin, appeared at the proceedings with a smug smile, not even pretending to hide his pistol.

By the spring of 1963, Harel's Mossad hadn't slowed, let alone ended, the Egyptians' progress toward rockets that could annihilate Israel. So Harel then took to political subterfuge. He began leaking stories to the press—some true, some embellished, some outright lies (that the Germans were helping Egypt produce atom bombs and deadly lasers)—about Nazis building weapons for Arabs to kill Jews. Harel was totally convinced that the German scientists were Nazis still determined to complete the Final Solution, and that the German authorities were aware of their activities but were doing nothing to stop them. The truth was that they were people who had become accustomed to the good life under the Third Reich, had become unemployed when it fell, and now were simply trying to make some easy money off the Egyptians. But Harel dragged the entire organization, and in fact the whole country, behind this obsession of his.

In order to prove his claims, Harel presented information gathered in Cairo about a Dr. Hans Eisele, the Butcher of Buchenwald, who'd been involved in appalling experiments on Jewish inmates. He was designated a war criminal but escaped trial and found a comfortable refuge in Egypt, where he became the physician of the German scientists. Harel also fingered a number of other Nazis in Cairo, though none of them belonged to the group of missile scientists.

His goal was to publicly vilify Germany, with which Israel had a complicated relationship, a subject of much dispute internally. Relative moderates such as Ben-Gurion and his chief aide, Shimon Peres, maintained that, at a time when the United States was reluctant to provide Israel with all the military and economic aid it asked for, Israel could not afford to turn down assistance from the West German government, which came in the form of a reparations-and-compensation agreement and the sale of military equipment at a fraction of its real cost. Hardliners such as Golda Meir and Harel himself, on the other hand, rejected the notion that the Federal Republic of Germany was a "new" or "different" Germany. History, to their minds, had left a permanent stain.

Harel also called in the Editors Committee, that unique Israeli institution, then composed of the top editors of the print and electronic media, who self-censored items in their publications at the request of the government. Harel asked the Editors Committee to provide him with three journalists, whom he subsequently recruited into the Mossad. They were sent to Europe, at the Mossad's expense, to gather intelligence about the front companies that were buying equipment for the Egyptian project. Harel claimed he needed the journalists for operational reasons, but the truth was that he wanted to use their involvement and the materials they collected to launder information he already possessed; as such, it could be disseminated to the foreign and Israeli media for the purpose of manufacturing newspaper reports that would create a climate suited to his purposes.

Harel's stories generated a media frenzy and a growing sense of panic in Israel. Ben-Gurion tried to calm Harel down, to no avail. "He was not, in my opinion, quite sane," said Amos Manor, the Shin Bet chief at the time. "It was something much more profound than an obsession. You couldn't have a rational conversation about it with him."

It ended, as most obsessions do, in Harel's own destruction. His publicity campaign, the frenzied newspaper stories he'd planted of Hitler's minions rising again, badly wounded Ben-Gurion. The prime minister was attacked for not having done enough to end the threat posed by the German scientists working in Egypt—a threat Israeli citizens saw as a clear and present danger to their very existence—and for leading his country into a conciliation with West Germany, which now seemed to be at least indirectly responsible for a new version of the Final Solution.

On March 25, 1963, Ben-Gurion summoned Harel to his office and demanded an explanation for a number of actions Harel had carried out vis-à-vis the local and international media without Ben-Gurion's approval. The conversation degenerated into a bitter debate over the Israeli government's policy toward Germany. The prime minister reminded Harel that he was supposed to implement government policy, not set it. Offended by the rebuke, Harel offered his resignation, confident the Old Man couldn't manage without him and would beg him to stay.

Ben-Gurion thought otherwise. He accepted the resignation on the spot. Isser Harel's once brilliant career ended in a failed bluff and utter defeat. He was immediately replaced by Meir Amit, the chief of AMAN.

BUT IT WAS TOO late for Ben-Gurion, too. Harel's campaign against the scientists had played into the hands of opposition leader Begin, who never let up his attacks on Ben-Gurion. Even inside his own party, Mapai, things had reached a boiling point. Ben-Gurion squabbled ceaselessly with Golda Meir, Harel's main supporter.

Less than two months after replacing Harel, Ben-Gurion, convinced he'd lost the support of even his own party, resigned. He was replaced by Levi Eshkol.

Meanwhile, Egypt was still tinkering with the guidance systems for the missiles that could have caused grave harm to Israel.

Meir Amit, one of the IDF's brilliant young commanders—a planner of the 1956 Sinai Campaign who was responsible for advancing the Military Intelligence Directorate by several generations—took over a Mossad in disarray.

The agency was deeply demoralized. In the nine months since Egypt had announced its four missile tests, the Israelis had learned precious little about the program, and everything the Mossad and AMAN had tried thus far had failed to even slow the project, let alone dismantle it. Pressuring Germany—whether through Harel's self-immolating press campaign or Foreign Minister Golda Meir's fiery speeches to the Knesset—had made no difference. Later that summer, a strongly worded missive from Eshkol to Chancellor Konrad Adenauer, demanding immediate action to get the scientists back from Egypt, also failed to spur the Germans. As Israeli diplomats reported to the Foreign Ministry in Jerusalem, they could only assume that "Adenauer and the leadership are preoccupied with more important problems," such as "managing the Cold War in the post–Cuban missile crisis period."

Amit set about rebuilding the organization, reinforcing it with the best personnel he knew from AMAN. As soon as he took over, he ordered a halt to any matters that he considered extraneous, and a drastic reduction of the resources being devoted to the hunt for Nazi criminals, explaining that it was "a matter of priorities. Before all else, we have to produce information about the enemies of the State of Israel nowadays."

Amit knew he needed a tactical reset, and that the Mossad had to rethink its approach to the problem of Egyptian missiles. His first order, then, was for a shift away from targeted killing operations, and for the vast majority of his resources to be focused instead on trying to understand what precisely was going on inside the missile project.

Secretly, however, with most of the top officials of the organization out of the loop, he prepared a targeted killing project of his own against the scientists. Operations personnel were trying to find ways to send parcel bombs from inside Egypt, thereby significantly shortening the time between the sending and opening of the package. They tried out the method on a relatively easy target, the physician Hans Eisele. On September 25, there was a blast in the post office in the upscale Cairo neighborhood of Maadi, when a letter bomb that had been addressed to Dr. Carl Debouche, the false name Eisele was using, exploded and blinded a postal worker.

The failure of this operation convinced Amit that targeted killings should only be used very sparingly—if not as a last resort, then at the very least only after meticulous planning that would prevent embarrassing failures. Nevertheless, he ordered the Mossad to prepare plans to shoot, blow up, or poison the scientists, in the event that the effort to solve the matter peacefully didn't work.

Amit ordered that break-ins to all the offices connected to the missile project in Germany and Switzerland be stepped up, and as many documents as possible photographed. These operations were enormously complex. The sites were well guarded—both by Egyptian intelligence and by Hermann Vallentin's men—in the hearts of crowded European cities, in countries where the law was strictly enforced.

Mossad operatives burglarized the Egyptian embassies, the Egyptian purchasing mission in Cologne, and the Intra office in Munich. They broke into the EgyptAir office in Frankfurt no fewer than fifty-six times between August 1964 and December 1966.

The information obtained in the break-ins (some thirty thousand documents were photographed up to the end of 1964 alone) was important, but far from sufficient. The Mossad had to recruit someone on the inside of the missile project. This critical task was assigned to a division called Junction (Tsomet in Hebrew), which would become the Mossad's most important branch, responsible for bringing in the bulk of the organization's intelligence.

Unlike in Hollywood movies and pulp fiction, most of this information is not collected directly by Mossad employees darting about in the shadows. Rather, it is gleaned from foreign nationals in their home countries. The Mossad case officers responsible for recruiting and operating these sources are called "collection officers"—*katsa,* in the Hebrew acronym—and they are expert psychologists. They know how to persuade a person to betray everything and everyone he believes in: his friends and family, his organization, his nation.

Unfortunately, though, none of them had been able to work their psychology on anyone close to the Egyptian program. Recruiting agents in Arab countries became a long-term strategic priority, but in the short run, with the clock ticking, Junction would have to look elsewhere.

IN APRIL 1964, AMIT sent Rafi Eitan to Paris, which served as the European nerve center of Israeli intelligence, to run Junction's operations on the Continent. Up to this point, all of Junction's efforts to enlist one of the scientists had come to naught, mostly because of the rigid security precautions instituted by Vallentin. From day to day, he was becoming more of a problem.

The need to deal with Vallentin would lead to the netting of a much bigger fish. Avraham Ahituv, Junction coordinator in Bonn, had an idea, and he presented it to Eitan in Paris in May 1964. He'd identified a dubious character who'd sold arms and intelligence to the Nasser regime and who also was close to the German scientists. "There is just one small problem," Ahituv said. "The man's name is Otto Skorzeny, and he was a high-ranking Wehrmacht officer, Hitler's special-operations commander, and a favorite of the Führer."

"And you want to recruit this Otto?" Eitan asked sarcastically. "Wonderful."

"There's one more small matter," Ahituv added. "He was a devoted Nazi and a member of the SS."

In 1960, Ahituv told Eitan, Harel had ordered Amal, the unit that handled the hunt for Nazi war criminals, to gather as much information as possible about Skorzeny, with the goal of bringing him to justice or killing him. His file said he was an enthusiastic member of the

Austrian Nazi Party at the age of twenty-three, had enlisted in 1935 to a secret SS unit in Austria, and had taken part in the Anschluss (Hitler's annexation of Austria) and in Kristallnacht. He rose rapidly in rank in the Waffen-SS, becoming head of its special-operations units.

Sturmbannführer Skorzeny parachuted into Iran and trained local tribes to blow up oil pipelines serving the Allied armies, and he plotted to murder the Big Three—Churchill, Stalin, and Roosevelt. He also had a plan for abducting and killing General Dwight D. Eisenhower, who was forced to spend Christmas 1944 surrounded by a heavy guard. Most famously, Skorzeny was selected personally by Hitler to lead the Gran Sasso raid, which successfully extricated the Führer's friend and ally, the former Fascist dictator Benito Mussolini, from the Alpine villa where he was being held prisoner by the Italian government.

Allied intelligence called Skorzeny "the most dangerous man in Europe." He was not, however, convicted of war crimes. He was acquitted by one tribunal, and after he was rearrested on other charges, he escaped with the help of his SS friends. He took refuge in Franco's Spain, from where he established profitable commercial relations with fascist regimes around the world and also maintained contact with the German scientists in Egypt.

Skorzeny's acquaintance with the scientists in Egypt and the fact that he'd been a superior officer to Hermann Vallentin during the war were enough, in Eitan's view, to justify trying to recruit him, despite his Nazi past. Eitan was not a Holocaust survivor, and he dealt with the matter, as was his wont, without emotional involvement. If it helped Israel, he thought, that would make it worth forgiveness. "And we could offer him in exchange something that no one else could," he told his colleagues. "Life without fear."

Through a number of intermediaries the Mossad established contact with Countess Ilse von Finckenstein—Skorzeny's wife. She would serve as the Mossad's entrée. The Mossad file on the countess says that she was "a member of the aristocracy. She is a cousin of the German [prewar] Finance Minister Hjalmar Schacht. . . . She is 45, a fairly attractive woman, brimming over with energy."

"She was involved in everything," said Raphael (Raphi) Medan, the German-born Mossad operative who was assigned to the mission. "She sold titles of nobility, had ties with Vatican intelligence, and sold arms as well." She and her husband also had liberal ideas about their relationship. "They didn't have children," Medan said, "and they maintained an open marriage. Ilse always looked stunning. Every two years she underwent hormonal treatment in Switzerland in order to preserve her youth."

Medan "had had a reputation, because of his European good looks, for being able to influence women," according to the Mossad report on the affair. A meeting was set in late July 1964, in Dublin, Ireland. Medan introduced himself as an Israeli Defense Ministry employee on leave and looking for an opening in international tourism. He might be interested in taking part in the Bahamas development project that the countess was involved in, he said. The countess liked Medan, and their relationship warmed up. When their business talk was over, she invited him to a party at her farm. This was the start of a series of meetings, including some wild visits nightclubbing all over Europe.

According to a Mossad rumor that circulated for many years, and was gently hinted at in the reports but not explicitly stated, Medan "sacrificed" himself for his country—and took advantage of the German couple's open marriage—by wooing the countess and eventually taking her to bed. (Medan commented on this by saying, "There are things that gentlemen do not speak about," and described their encounter, with a smile, as "good and even gratifying.")

In Madrid, on the night of September 7, Medan told her that a friend of his from the Israeli Defense Ministry wanted to meet her husband "about a very important matter." The friend was already in Europe and waiting for a reply.

Convincing von Finckenstein to cooperate was not difficult. Only four years before, Israel had found, grabbed, tried, and executed Adolf Eichmann. There were powerful forces in the Jewish world, including Nazi hunter Simon Wiesenthal, engaged in worldwide campaigns to find and prosecute Nazis like Skorzeny. Medan, therefore, was able to offer the countess—and, by extension, her husband—that "life without fear."

In the morning, when they were still groggy from the alcohol and smoke in the clubs, von Finckenstein informed Medan happily that her husband was ready to meet his friend—that night, if possible.

Medan called Ahituv to Madrid. He set up a meeting in a hotel lobby that evening. The countess came first, glamorously accoutred. Fifteen minutes later, the colonel appeared. Medan introduced them to Ahituv. Then he took von Finckenstein aside, for a "business talk." Skorzeny stayed with Ahituv.

The Mossad's internal final report on the affair, though written in dry professional language, could not overlook the intensity of the meeting: "It is difficult to overstate Avraham Ahituv's emotional reluctance over this operation. Avraham is a scion of a religiously observant family, a native of Germany educated in a religious Jewish school. For him, the contact with a Nazi monster was a shocking emotional experience that went beyond the demands of the profession."

In the detailed report Ahituv himself submitted, on September 14, 1964, he described the talks he had that week with Skorzeny:

> Skorzeny was a giant. A hulk of a man. He was obviously remarkably strong physically. On his left cheek was the well known scar from his pictures, reaching his ear. He was partly deaf in that ear and asked me to sit on his right. Well dressed.
>
> Two moments gave me a shock. Skorzeny was looking for a number in his phone book to give me. All of a sudden, he took a monocle out of his pocket and stuck it into his right eye socket. His appearance then, what with his bodily dimensions, the scar, and his aggressive gaze, made him look like the complete Nazi.
>
> The second incident happened after our meeting, when we were dining together in a restaurant near his office. Suddenly someone came up to us, clicked his heels together loudly, and greeted him in German as "My General." Skorzeny told me that this was the owner of the restaurant and he used to be one of the top Nazis in those parts . . .
>
> I have no illusions about his original opinions. Even his wife didn't try to clear him. She only stressed that he played no part in the Holocaust. . . . Most of the conversation at the first meeting centered on political issues, on World War II and the Holocaust, East-West relations, and the Middle East situation.

Ahituv brought up the issue of Skorzeny's participation in the Kristallnacht pogroms. He pulled out a long list of people who had taken part in the attacks and presented it to Skorzeny. Skorzeny was familiar with the document, which had been stored in Yad Vashem, because the accusation had been raised and discussed during the war crimes trial from which he had managed to escape.

He pointed to an X inked next to his name. "That's proof that I did not participate," he said, though Nazi hunter Wiesenthal interpreted the mark as proof of just the opposite. Skorzeny complained that Wiesenthal was hunting him, and that more than once he had found himself in a situation where he "feared for his life." Ahituv decided not to stretch the point too far and did not argue.

At a certain stage, Skorzeny got tired of talking about the war. "He stopped me and asked me what my business was. It was clear that there was no point in playing hide-and-seek. I told him I was in the Israeli [intelligence] service. [Skorzeny said that] he wasn't surprised we had gotten to him. At different times, he had been linked to different countries, and with some of them he still maintained excellent relations. He was definitely prepared for an exchange of views with us as well."

"An exchange of views" was Skorzeny's delicate way of saying that he agreed to full and comprehensive cooperation with Israel. Skorzeny demanded a price for his help. He wanted a valid Austrian passport issued in his real name, a writ of lifetime immunity from prosecution, signed by Prime Minister Eshkol, and his immediate removal from Wiesenthal's list of wanted Nazis, as well as some money.

Skorzeny's conditions sparked a sharp argument in the Mossad. Ahituv and Eitan saw in them "an operational constraint and a requirement for the success of the operation." Other senior officials argued that they were "an attempt by a Nazi criminal to cleanse his name," and they demanded a new look at Skorzeny's past. This new investigation revealed further details about the role he played on Kristallnacht, "as the leader of one of the mobs that burned synagogues in Vienna," and that "until recently, he was an active supporter of neo-Nazi organizations."

Meir Amit, practical and unemotional as always, thought that Eitan and Ahituv were right, but he needed the moral support of the prime minister. Levi Eshkol listened to Amit and consulted some of the high-ranking Mossad members who were Holocaust survivors (unlike Amit, Eitan, and Ahituv, who were not), hearing their vehement objections. Nevertheless, he finally approved giving Skorzeny money, a passport, and immunity.

The prime minister also approved the request concerning Wiesenthal, but that wasn't his decision to make, nor the Mossad's. Wiesenthal was an opinionated and obstinate man, and although he had close links with the State of Israel and even the Mossad, which financed some of his operations, he wasn't an Israeli citizen, and he worked out of Vienna, outside of Israel's jurisdiction.

In October 1964, Raphi Medan met with Wiesenthal to discuss, without elaborating the details of the operation, why Skorzeny had to be removed from Wiesenthal's blacklist of Nazi criminals to be hunted down and prosecuted.

"To my astonishment," Medan recalled, "Wiesenthal said, 'Herr Medan, there is not a chance. This is a Nazi and a war criminal and we will never strike him from our list.' No matter what I said or how I tried, he simply refused categorically."

When told he would remain on Wiesenthal's list, Skorzeny was disappointed but agreed to the deal anyhow. Thus did the unbelievable come to pass—the Führer's favorite, wanted all over the world as a Nazi war criminal who had apparently burned synagogues and taken part in SS operations, became a key agent in the most important operation waged by Israeli intelligence at the time.

Skorzeny's first step was to send word to his friends among the scientists in Egypt that he was reviving a network of SS and Wehrmacht veterans "to build a new Germany"—in other words, to establish a Fourth Reich. To prepare the ground, he would tell them, his organization would have to gather information in secret. The German scientists working for Nasser would thus be required, under their Wehrmacht oaths, to provide Skorzeny's phantom organization with the details of their missile research so it could be used by the new German military force in the making.

At the same time, Skorzeny and Ahituv also masterminded a plan to get information out of the formidable security officer Hermann Vallentin, who knew everything about the Egyptian missile project.

Unlike with the recruitment of the sophisticated and experienced Skorzeny, who was aware he was dealing with a Mossad man, and whom Ahituv never tried to mislead, the two decided to use some subterfuge on Vallentin.

Skorzeny played his part perfectly. He summoned Hermann Vallentin to Madrid under the pretense that he was hosting a special gathering for his subordinates from the "glorious war." He put Vallentin up, at Mossad expense, in a luxurious hotel and presented him with his phony plan for reviving the Reich. Then he revealed that this was not his only reason for the invitation to Madrid, and that he wanted him to meet "a close friend," an officer of the British MI6 secret service. The British, he said, were interested in what was going on in Egypt, and he asked Vallentin to help his friend.

Vallentin was suspicious. "Are you sure the Israelis aren't involved?" he asked.

"Stand to attention when you're spoken to, and apologize!" Skorzeny fired back. "How dare you say something like that to your superior officer!"

Vallentin duly apologized, but he wasn't convinced. And he was, in fact, completely right. Skorzeny's "friend" was no Brit, but an Australian-born case officer in the Mossad by the name of Harry Barak.

Vallentin agreed to meet him, but not to cooperate, and the meeting between the two led nowhere.

The resourceful Skorzeny immediately came up with a solution. At his next meeting with Vallentin, he told him that his friend from MI6 had reminded him that a cable Skorzeny had sent close to the end of the war, in which he notified the general staff that he was promoting Vallentin, had not reached the general staff or Vallentin.

Vallentin's eyes lit up. Though this retroactive promotion was now purely symbolic, it clearly meant a lot to him. He stood up and gave the Heil Hitler salute and thanked Skorzeny profusely.

Skorzeny told Vallentin that he was ready to give him a written document confirming that he had been promoted. Vallentin was grateful to his new friend from British intelligence for the information he had provided, and agreed to help him as much as he wanted.

In time, Skorzeny invited other former Wehrmacht officers involved in the missile project to Madrid. They attended lavish parties at his home, billed as gatherings of Waffen-SS special forces veterans. His guests ate, drank, and enjoyed themselves late into the night, never knowing that the Israeli government was paying for their food and drinks and bugging their conversations.

The information provided by Skorzeny, Vallentin, and the scientists who came to Madrid solved most of the Mossad's information problem regarding Egypt's missile program. It identified precisely who was involved in the project and exactly what the current status of each component was.

Thanks to the new wealth of information from this operation, Meir Amit's Mossad managed to crumble Egypt's missile project from the inside, using a number of methods in parallel. One was the dispatch of threatening letters to many of the German scientists. They were very cleverly worded, based on top-grade intelligence provided by Vallentin, and included intimate details about the recipients.

"Remember that even if you are not to blame for the crimes of the German nation in the past, you will not be able to deny your responsibility for your deeds today. You had better consider very seriously the contents of this letter, for the sake of your future and the future of your young family." "The Gideons" was the name of the unknown organization that signed the letters.

Meanwhile, thanks to new intelligence from its sources, primarily Vallentin, the Mossad was able to identify a secret Egyptian plan to recruit scores of workers from the Hellige aircraft-and-rocket factory in Freiburg who were about to be dismissed. Amit decided to take advantage of the momentum to carry out a quick move aimed at preventing their departure for Egypt.

On the morning of December 9, Shimon Peres, then deputy defense minister, and Raphi Medan carried a locked case containing a number of documents in English that had been prepared by the Mossad director's office based on material supplied by Skorzeny, Vallentin, and the scientists who came to Madrid, and flew off for a hurriedly arranged meeting with one of West Germany's senior politicians, former defense minister Franz Josef Strauss. Peres and Strauss were architects of the restitution agreement between West Germany and Israel. Strauss rose from his seat to greet the two Israelis, and he and Peres embraced warmly.

"We sat for six hours," Peres said. "God, that man could drink. Wines from all over the world, and beer. I can also drink, but quantities like that? Six hours and we didn't stop drinking."

The information Peres presented to Strauss was far more detailed, cross-checked, authentic, and grave than anything that had been presented to the Germans previously. "It is inconceivable that German scientists would help our worst enemy in such a manner, while you stand idly by," Peres told Strauss, who must have grasped what the leakage of this material to the international press would have meant.

Strauss looked at the documents, and agreed to intervene. He called Ludwig Bölkow, a powerful figure in the German aerospace industry, and asked for his help. Bölkow sent his representatives to offer the Hellige scientists and engineers jobs under good conditions at his plants, as long as they'd promise not to help the Egyptians.

The plan worked. Most of the new group never went to Egypt, where the missile program urgently needed their assistance with the balky guidance systems—a development that fatally crippled the project.

The final blow came when a representative of Bölkow's arrived in Egypt to persuade the scientists already working there to come home. One by one they deserted the program, and by July 1965 even Pilz was gone, having returned to Germany to head one of Bölkow's airplane component divisions.

The German scientists affair was the first time the Mossad mobilized all of its forces to stop what it perceived as an existential threat from an adversary, and the first time Israel allowed itself to target civilians from countries with which it had diplomatic relations. Given the newly raised stakes, a 1982 top-secret internal report was written, analyzing whether it would have been possible to resolve the affair using "soft" methods—generous offers of money from the government of Germany to the scientists—without "the mysterious disappearance of Krug, or the bomb that maimed Hannelore Wende, or the other letter bombs and the intimidation."

The report concluded that it would not have been possible: The Mossad believed that, without the threat of violence directed at them, the German scientists would not have been willing to accept the money and give up on the project.

# A SERIES OF CATASTROPHES

AFTER THE GERMAN SCIENTISTS affair, the Mossad was on a roll. Meir Amit brought in more professionals from the military, introduced new technologies, and strengthened links with intelligence services abroad. He also continued to set in motion numerous organizational reforms.

Amit wanted to establish a single operations division in the Mossad, which would bring all of the units dealing with sabotage, targeted killings, and espionage in the Arab countries under one umbrella. In order to do this, Amit did what Harel had tried to do for years and he, Amit, had opposed: He transferred Unit 188 from AMAN to the Mossad and merged it with Shamir's Mifratz. Yosef Yariv was appointed head of the division, with Shamir as his deputy.

The Mossad chief named the division Caesarea, after the Roman city on the Mediterranean coast, another example of the Israeli intelligence community's penchant for code names taken from the country's ancient history. The network of Caesarea activities outside of Israel was code-named the Senate.

Amit also wanted his own intelligence division. Until recently, the same unit, the Birds, had served both the Shin Bet and the Mossad. Amit now decided that he wanted a separate unit that would work only outside of Israel and only for the Mossad. He co-opted some of the Birds unit's personnel for a new intelligence unit, which he named Colossus.

In addition to these bureaucratic changes, under Amit the agency carried out operations that garnered unprecedented amounts of information about the Arab states and their military services. One of the most outstanding of these was Operation Diamond, in which Junction recruited an Iraqi pilot, Munir Redfa, who defected to Israel with his brand-new MiG-21 fighter plane, the most advanced and threatening attack weapon in the hands of the Soviet bloc at the time. The Israeli Air Force was now able to prepare to cope with its most powerful adversary in future aerial combat. The Pentagon was very eager to learn the secrets of the plane, and Amit gave the Americans not just the blueprints for the MiG but the plane itself, fully equipped and with a trained pilot.

Amit had also assiduously cultivated Israel's secret relations with Morocco, in line with the "periphery doctrine." Though Morocco was an Arab country, in close contact with Israel's main enemies, it also was moderate and had no territorial dispute with Israel. Furthermore, its leader was the relatively pro-Western king Hassan II.

Morocco received valuable intelligence and technological assistance from Israel, and, in exchange, Hassan allowed Morocco's Jews to immigrate to Israel, and the Mossad received the right to establish a permanent station in the capital, Rabat, from which it could spy on Arab countries.

The height of the cooperation came in September 1965, when the king allowed a Mossad team led by Zvi Malchin and Rafi Eitan to bug all the meeting rooms and private suites of the leaders of the Arab states and their military commanders during an Arab summit in Casablanca. The purpose of the summit was to discuss the establishment of a joint common Arab command in future wars with Israel. But King Hassan's relations with some of the other Arab rulers were shaky, and he feared that some of them were acting to depose him, so he let the Mossad listen in.

This gave Israel an unprecedented glimpse of the military and intelligence secrets of its greatest enemies, and of the mindsets of those countries' leaders. At that summit, commanders of the Arab armies reported that their forces were not prepared for a new war against Israel, information that was the basis of the Israeli military's supreme confidence when they urged Prime Minister Eshkol to go to war two years later, in June 1967. "This sensational material," a

Mossad report stated, "was one of the highlights of the achievements of Israeli intelligence since its foundation."

These successful operations provided the IDF with the critical intelligence it needed to prepare for the next war. But then, at a dizzying pace, one catastrophe after another hit Amit and his organization.

THE TOP SPY FOR Unit 188, and now Caesarea, was Eli Cohen, who'd penetrated the ruling circles in Damascus and provided the information that enabled the Mossad to locate the Nazi Alois Brunner and send him a letter bomb.

Cohen was originally assigned to serve as a sleeper agent who, rather than collect and convey information, would become active only if he had to alert Israel that Syria was planning to launch a surprise attack against it.

However, under pressure from his operators, and having become deeply enmeshed with and overconfident in his own cover story, he started broadcasting messages to his Mossad handlers on a daily basis, using a telegraphic device he kept hidden at his apartment. He reported on secret military installations, Syria's plot to take control of the region's water sources (with the assistance of a Saudi contracting firm headed by Mohammed bin Laden, Osama's father), and Syria's relationship with the Soviet Union, but also on Nazis holed up in Damascus, parliamentary gossip, and accounts of government power struggles. Cohen's transmission of information of this nature and at this frequency was a serious and unprofessional error, on his own part but also, more important, on the part of his handlers.

"Eli Cohen was one of the people who went through life walking sideways," said Moti Kfir, who, among other Mossad jobs, served as head of its training program in the early 1960s. "When you are sideways, sometimes you think that no one sees you. But he was wrong. He became too prominent. I told him during training, 'Never be the life of the party.' But he did the opposite."

The letter bomb sent to Brunner and the lively interest that Cohen showed in other Nazis in talks with top Syrians—along with the fact that he was "in an unusual situation, an immigrant without a job . . .

who was giving parties, mixing with high society," and "providing his guests and friends entertainment of all kinds"—put the Syrian intelligence services on the alert and led one of his interlocutors to doubt the cover story of Kamal Amin Thabet, a wealthy Syrian merchant who'd returned to his homeland after long years of exile in Buenos Aires.

In a tragic coincidence for Cohen, during the same period, his transmitter caused interference with broadcasts from the Syrian General Staff HQ, across the street from the luxurious apartment he rented, and in which he held wild parties for Syrian high officials. Puzzled, the Syrians asked GRU, Soviet military intelligence, to investigate. The Russians sent in special prowl cars, which managed to lock into the signals emanating from Cohen's transmitter during one of his broadcasts.

Cohen was arrested, brutally tortured, quickly tried, and sentenced to death. He was hanged in public in the central square of Damascus on May 18. His body was left dangling on the gallows, draped in a white sheet bearing the text of his death sentence, as a message to the State of Israel.

The man who had recruited, trained, and operated Cohen, Gedaliah Khalaf, later said, "I looked at him, at my Eli, on Syrian television, and I saw in his face the diabolical torments he had undergone. I didn't know what to do with myself. I wanted to scream, to do something, to take a pistol and break into the Mezzeh prison, to bang my head against the wall until it broke, until we could save him. And they killed him and we could do nothing but stand there and watch."

Amit's Mossad, so freshly confident, was humiliated, impotent. Worse, the Mossad was exposed. The Syrians had tortured Cohen so severely—yanking out his fingernails, electrifying his testicles—that he'd broken. He revealed the secret communication codes and deciphered two hundred messages that he'd sent and the Syrians had picked up but hadn't been able to read, and he told them what he knew about Israeli intelligence's recruitment, training, and cover-building methods.

Shortly after Cohen was caught, Caesarea was hit by another disaster. Wolfgang Lotz, the Caesarea spy in Cairo's high society, a key element in the intelligence gathering for the attempts to kill the German scientists in Egypt, was also uncovered, on February 10, 1965. His downfall also came from excessive activity, overconfidence in his cover story, and a number of crude errors that he and his handlers made.

The only thing that saved Lotz from suffering the same fate as Eli Cohen was the intervention of the BND, the German espionage service, which responded to Israel's request and told the Egyptians that Lotz was also working for them. Lotz and his wife, Waltraud, were spared the gallows and sentenced to life in prison. (They were later released in a prisoner exchange following the Six-Day War, in 1967.) But this was another hard blow for the Mossad. For fear of further losses, Yosef Yariv ordered his other spies, whose training and cover stories had cost many years of effort, to come home. Caesarea, barely out of its infancy, was nearly in ruins.

Prime Minister Eshkol regarded the downfall of the two spies as a national disaster. But despite the bad state the Mossad was in, Eshkol decided to approve a special targeted killing mission by Caesarea in Uruguay anyway. Two months prior, a conference attended by representatives of the various intelligence agencies had been held to discuss the state of the hunt for Nazis, a matter that was not high on the list of priorities. Raphi Medan, deputy chief of the Amal unit, which handled the issue, surveyed the possible targets for assassination on the list from which the name of Otto Skorzeny had just been erased. When he came to the name of Herbert Cukurs, a Latvian Nazi war criminal who, as an aviator, had volunteered to assist the SS and the Gestapo, and began describing his horrific acts, a loud thud was heard. The head of AMAN, the Military Intelligence Directorate, Major General Aharon Yariv, had collapsed, and it took some time before he came to. Cukurs, it emerged, had burned alive some of Yariv's relatives and friends.

After the conference, Amit, who was very close to Yariv and deeply affected by the incident, went to see Prime Minister Eshkol and received permission to have Cukurs eliminated.

Cukurs had killed Jews for sport. He had gunned them down on city streets after telling them to run for their lives. He had locked Jews in synagogues he then set on fire, drinking whisky as he listened to the screams. Holocaust survivors called him the Butcher of Riga, and his name came up frequently at the Nuremberg war crimes trials as directly involved in the murder of some fifteen thousand Jews, and indirectly in the killing of twenty thousand more. But after the war, he had managed to escape and find refuge in Brazil, where he developed a tourism business, surrounding himself with security guards for fear of the same fate that befell Eichmann.

Yaakov Meidad, a Caesarea operative who spoke Spanish and German, posed as an Austrian businessman seeking openings in the tourism industry in South America and managed to persuade Cukurs to go to Uruguay to meet a group of developers at a luxurious mansion outside Montevideo. At the mansion, three assassins would lie in wait. The plan was for Meidad to enter first, followed by Cukurs. One of the assassins would shove him inside and close the door behind him. Then, when the Mossad team was out of the line of fire, he would shoot him.

The job, however, did not go as smoothly as planned. Cukurs was alert and feared a trap. The moment he entered, he grasped what was happening and made a break for it. Yariv tried to get a stranglehold on him as another Israeli dragged him inside. "The fact that Cukurs was frightened to death," said Meidad, "and had lived in dread of this moment for twenty years gave him superhuman strength. He managed to knock the guy down. He grabbed the doorknob and, had it not been for the three of us, including me, holding the door shut, he would have been able to get out."

Cukurs bit hard into one of Yariv's fingers, cutting off the tip, which remained in his mouth. Yariv screamed in pain and had to loosen his grip on Cukurs's neck. He almost broke free, but at the last moment one of the hit men, Ze'ev Amit (a cousin of the Mossad director), who had not been able to fire because of the danger to his comrades, picked up a hammer and smashed it into Cukurs's head again and again until he passed out. Then the third assassin, Eliezer Sodit-Sharon, formerly the chief hit man for the Irgun, fired two shots into the mass murderer, assuring that he was dead.

The operatives put the body into a suitcase, which they left in the mansion, and added on top a "verdict," a sheet of paper inscribed with the words "In consideration of his personal responsibility for the murder of 30,000 Jews with horrible brutality, the condemned man has been executed. [Signed] Those Who Will Never Forget."

Inside the Mossad, the operation was officially deemed a success, but the truth was that the unprofessional implementation could easily have led to disaster. Either way, Yariv was left with half a finger. The man who had crushed Cukurs's head with a hammer, Ze'ev Amit, suffered from horrific nightmares for the rest of his life, haunted by the trauma of the murder.

THE NEXT DISASTER ALMOST cost Prime Minister Eshkol and Director Amit their jobs. On September 30, 1965, one day after the Mossad received the vitally important tapes from the Arab summit, one of the commanders of the Moroccan intelligence service, Ahmed Dlimi, contacted the Mossad and made it clear that the Moroccans wanted the debt for this valuable information repaid as soon as possible. In the intelligence world, there are no free gifts.

Amit reported to Eshkol, "On the one hand they've given us these tapes, but on the other, they've said 'Give!' They want something very simple. There's this goy, Ben Barka, who's in the opposition to the king . . . and the king has given an order to wipe him out. They've come to us and said, 'You're great killers . . . Do it!'"

The opposition leader Mehdi Ben Barka had been exiled from Morocco at the beginning of the 1960s and later sentenced to death in absentia. Moroccan intelligence tried to locate him, but Ben Barka was careful to conceal his location, moving from place to place, using pseudonyms. The heads of the Moroccan secret services asked the Mossad to help find, trap, and kill him.

"We faced a dilemma," Amit recalled. "Either help and get drawn in, or refuse and endanger the national achievements of the highest order."

Years later, Amit tried to paint a picture of himself having chosen "to walk between the raindrops" and not to directly abet the killing but "to incorporate it [the aid to the Moroccans] into our regular joint activities with them." But a close look at Mossad internal cables and records shows that the organization was deeply involved.

Caesarea and Colossus helped the Moroccans pinpoint the kiosk in Geneva to which Ben Barka had his magazines mailed, enabling them to place him under surveillance. Later, they proposed a plan whereby Ben Barka would be lured to Paris by a man posing as a documentary filmmaker fascinated by the Moroccan exile's life story and interested in making a film about it. The Mossad supplied the Moroccans with safe houses in Paris, vehicles, fake passports, and two different kinds of poison with which to kill him, as well as shovels and "something to disguise the traces."

When Ben Barka came to Paris on October 29, 1965, the Moroccans kidnapped him, with the help of corrupt French police officers. He was taken to an empty Mossad safe house, where the Moroccans began brutally interrogating him. He died not long afterward from asphyxiation, after repeatedly being submerged in a bath of filthy water.

Mossad operatives were not involved or present when the killing took place, but they took it upon themselves to handle the corpse, a joint team from Caesarea and Colossus removing it to the nearby Saint-Germain forest. They dug a deep hole in the ground and buried the body, after which they scattered chemical powder, which was designed to consume the body and is particularly active when it comes into contact with water. Heavy rain fell almost immediately, so there was probably not much left of Ben Barka shortly afterward. What *was* left, according to some of the Israelis involved, was moved again and today lies beneath the road to the recently constructed ultramodern Louis Vuitton Foundation, or even under the building itself.

Amit had promised Eshkol, "I won't take any steps without telling you," but then told him about only part of the truth, and only after the fact. On November 25, 1965, Amit told Eshkol, "Everything is fine."

In truth, however, everything was not fine. The fact that Ben Barka had disappeared in Paris and that the heads of Moroccan intelligence and French mercenaries were involved exploded into the French media with a great bang, and stayed in the headlines for a long time. President Charles de Gaulle disbanded his intelligence services and prosecuted some of those involved. When King Hassan refused to hand over the heads of his spy agencies to stand trial, de Gaulle angrily cut off diplomatic relations with Morocco.

The fallout from the operation has lasted for decades and left a dark shadow on relations between Morocco and France, where there is still an investigating magistrate in charge of the case. The probes raised suspicions against Mossad personnel, too, and all those involved left Paris in a hurry. For many years they remained at risk of facing trial.

Isser Harel was serving at the time as Eshkol's adviser on intelligence. Bitter and frustrated over the way he had been ousted from the directorship of the Mossad, and envious of the successful Amit, Harel got hold of the pertinent documents on the Ben Barka affair and went to war against Amit.

In a lengthy report he submitted to the prime minister, he declared, "The Mossad, and through it the state, were engaged in various actions connected to a political assassination, in which Israel not only had no interest, but should not have, I believe, from a moral, public, and international perspective, been involved at all."

Harel demanded that Eshkol fire Amit and send a personal emissary to tell the truth to de Gaulle. Eshkol refused, and Harel accused the prime minister of becoming involved in the murder himself and demanded that he resign forthwith. He threatened Eshkol, saying that "the echoes of the affair will come to the attention of the public and the entire party [Labor] will be tainted with the shame."

When that didn't work, he leaked the gist of the story to a sensationalist yellow weekly, and when the censor blocked the publication, he informed high-ranking party members of the details and urged them to rebel against Eshkol's leadership. These members then tried to persuade Golda Meir to lead a coup against Eshkol. Meir agreed that Amit must go, but she drew the line at ousting the prime minister. "I should topple Eshkol, and take his place?" she asked the conspirators, with the pathos for which she was famous. "I would rather throw myself into the sea."

When Harel's vitriolic attacks did not subside, Eshkol and Amit decided to fight back, combating extortion with counter-extortion. Amit told his close associates, "Harel will not drop the subject of his own accord . . . unless it is hinted to him that in his past there is enough material to undermine his claim that he is 'the moral guardian' of the Mossad."

And, indeed, there was enough material. Amit had Alexander Yisraeli's file brought back up from the archives. Yisraeli was the naval officer who had sold secrets to Egypt in 1954 and then was abducted, with the intent of bringing him to trial, though he died in transit of an overdose of sedatives. Harel had ordered his body to be thrown into the sea and for his family to be told he'd settled in South America.

Amit gave Yisraeli's file to a veteran of the Mossad who despised Harel, was friendly with Amit, and knew about the affair. That person summoned Harel for a meeting. "What do you think would happen if this affair became public?" the man asked Harel. "Don't you think such a serious matter would require a thorough examination and an intense investigation? Of course, we will try to keep the story quiet, but we are not the only ones who know it, and it's outrageous what comes to the attention of journalists these days."

Harel understood the situation. Shortly afterward, he resigned.

For Amit, the main lesson of the affair was that "we must never get involved in carrying out sensitive tasks of others in which we do not have a direct interest, especially not assassinations. We must kill someone only if he is threatening Israel's interests, and the execution—only blue and white," a reference to the colors of the Israeli flag, by which he meant "only by Israelis."


ALL THESE CATASTROPHES LEFT the agency, and particularly Caesarea, its spearhead, bruised and confused. Amit set up a number of inquiry panels to try to analyze what had gone wrong.

The predominant figure conducting these inquiries was Michael "Mike" Harari. When their work was completed, Amit named Harari the deputy head of Caesarea. Harari served in this position for five years, first under Yosef Yariv and then under Zvi Aharoni, but in practice he was the living spirit of the division and, in effect, commanded it. In 1970, he was made head of Caesarea, a position he held for ten years. The fifteen years during which he led the division were the most important and turbulent in its history. Harari was nicknamed Caesar and became the figure with the most profound influence on the world of the Mossad's special operations.

Harari was born in Tel Aviv in 1927. "Two events shaped my life," he said. In 1936, while still a child, he witnessed the violent riots by Palestine's Arabs against the Jews and the British, which later became known as the Palestinian Revolt. "I saw the rioting mob and a burned-out British jeep with the charred body of the sergeant still gripping the steering wheel." When he saw Arabs and Jews fighting, he says, he did not hold back, but went into a nearby store and chose what looked like the best weapon—a hefty pick handle—and went to join the battle against the Arabs.

The second defining experience occurred in 1942, when he went down to play in the street and arrived on the scene a few minutes after officers of the British police's CID had shot dead Avraham Stern, the commander of the extremist Jewish underground group Lehi. "I saw them bringing the body down. Then I went upstairs. I was a boy, and no one stopped me. I went into the apartment and saw the closet he had hidden in. . . . These things affect you."

In 1943, he lied about his age to join the Palmach, the secret army of the Jewish Yishuv in Palestine. "It was underground. It was secret, it intrigued me." He took part in many actions, including the sabotage of railroad lines and bridges, attacks on British police stations, and intelligence collecting. He was arrested several times by the CID.

After World War II, when the Haganah command learned that Harari spoke a few languages, he was sent to Europe, to help with the transportation of the surviving Jewish refugees to Israel. He was involved in the secret acquisition of ships and the complicated logistics involved in moving these illegal immigrants through the ruins of Europe to the boats, then smuggling them into Palestine under the noses of the British. "That was the period during which I created for myself the criteria and the methods for covert activities abroad, the tools that I used later on in the Mossad."

After the establishment of the state, Isser Harel recruited Harari to the Shin Bet and then the Mossad, where he rose rapidly before being assigned to investigate Caesarea's operations. What he found was a unit in very bad shape, with a hodgepodge of personnel (former members of 188 Mifratz and the Birds, the operational unit of the

Shin Bet, among others), a fuzzy combat doctrine, and undefined goals.

Caesarea's string of failures led Harari to the conclusion that Caesarea must be rebuilt from the bottom up, with its objectives, tasks, and personnel redefined. After several months of work, he submitted his doctrine to the heads of the Mossad: "In my view of the world, I believe that any country that wants to live must have a Caesarea of its own, a clandestine, compartmentalized, and elite body that will be able to carry out, beyond the country's borders, the things that no other agency in the country is able to do. It is a unique tool our leadership can use to operate against the country's enemies."

Harari set Caesarea's primary objectives as targeted killings, sabotage, collecting intel in hostile "target" countries, and special ops, like smuggling abductees across borders.

Most of the Mifratz field operatives that Harari investigated were former members of the extremist anti-British underground groups who'd been recruited by Isser Harel and commanded by Yitzhak Shamir. Harari found them to be extremely tough, with a lot of experience in combat and covert ops, ready to pull the trigger when the moment came. In other ways, however, Harari found them to be very weak: "They always failed in the getaway stage. I ordered that in planning an operation, the same weight be given to the goal and the getaway, and if there's no way of getting out in one piece, don't execute."

Harari ordered the establishment of a "targets committee," which would make in-depth studies to decide who'd be on the hit list, and ruled that slayings should never be carried out in close contact, with knives or other "cold" weapons.

The field personnel in the two operational divisions, Caesarea and Colossus, disliked being called operatives, which sounded bland and perfunctory, lacking the appropriate heroic inflection. (Worse was "agent," an almost derisive term reserved for foreign nationals who'd been recruited to betray their own countries on Israel's behalf.) Rather, they considered themselves warriors (*lohamim*), dedicated to defending and preserving their young nation.

Warriors though they both might have been, there was an essential difference between the personnel of the two divisions. A Colossus spy arrested in a "base country"—one with full diplomatic relations with Israel, like France or Italy—might risk imprisonment. In a "target country," like Syria or Egypt, a Caesarea warrior would likely be subjected to horrific torture and interrogation and then executed. The exposure and capture of a Caesarea operative is perceived as a national disaster in Israel. This is why Harari insisted on iron discipline and zero errors.

And indeed, from the time that Harari rebuilt Caesarea, very few significant errors have occurred. In the entire history of the division, Eli Cohen is the only operative to have been caught and executed.

"This phenomenal record," says "Ethan," who was a top officer of the unit for many years, "was achieved mainly thanks to Harari's innovations and, above all, waterproof cover stories."

The recruitment process was also a key factor in their success. "The main weapon of a Caesarea operative is the ability to work under deep cover," Ethan explained. "This weapon has to be built in. All the rest, we can teach them."

The Mossad was given access to Israel's population database, which Caesarea's selection experts scoured for certain types of people. For Harari, the natural place to look first for his personnel was among those serving, or those who had formerly served, in combat roles in the Israel Defense Forces. But this was just the start of the screening process. After the downfall of Eli Cohen and the exposure of the Mossad's use of Jews from Arab countries as spies, he decided to rely mainly upon people who could pose as gentiles from Western countries.

The perfect candidate was of European appearance, one who could pass as a tourist or businessman from a country whose citizens were welcomed in the Arab world. One pool of possible recruits consisted of the children of Israeli scholars or members of the Israeli diplomatic corps who had spent considerable time overseas because of their parents' jobs. But most of Caesarea's recruits were immigrants who'd lived in their native countries until adulthood (in very rare cases, Caesarea will recruit a Jew still living outside Israel), because they offered an obvious advantage: They did not need to be trained to play the role of a non-Israeli.

On the other hand, former training chief Kfir explained, there was a corresponding complication with such recruits. All aspirants undergo a thorough security check by Shin Bet, of course. But if an immigrant has not been properly distilled by Israeli society—if he or she hasn't served in the IDF, hasn't developed a network of long-term friends, doesn't have relatives in the country—it's much more difficult to ascertain their loyalty to both Israel and the Mossad. It's even possible that they're already spies for another country. Consequently, the background checks following the initial polygraph tests for Caesarea recruits, already the most stringent in the Mossad, were made even tougher, with the investigators sometimes traveling abroad to scrutinize a candidate's past. A massive effort was invested in the recruitment of each candidate.

Once prospects were identified, they received calls from persons who identified themselves as "government employees" and suggested a meeting in a café, where they described in a very general manner what it was all about. Others received a somewhat cryptic letter from the prime minister's office or the Defense Ministry, with more or less the following language: "We offer you a chance to take part in an operation involving varied and unique activities, which will confront you with exciting challenges and give you an opportunity to contend with them while reaching your full potential and personal satisfaction." In addition to this direct approach, the Mossad has long run ambiguous want ads in Israeli newspapers referring to a "state organization" seeking candidates for "challenging work."

From those pools of potential recruits, the Mossad began winnowing down the group through a variety of tests, until they were left with only those psychologically fit for the job. The screening process for all operational jobs in the Mossad was and still is conducted by Mossad recruitment officers and psychologists. Harari insisted that the psychologists themselves undergo an exhausting training program, including the horrific "prisoner exercise," so they would realize what qualities were demanded from an operative and be better able to screen the candidates.

Finding candidate operatives with all the desired characteristics was, and is, a very difficult challenge. In the Mossad, they note with pride that the acceptance rate is 0.1 percent. Moti Kfir put it this way: "The desired warrior has to be a Zionist. He needs to identify with Israel and its objectives. Above all, he has to have a balance of contrary characteristics. He needs initiative without being aggressive. Brave but not fearless. Outgoing but reticent. They must be willing to take huge risks, but without putting the mission and the organization in jeopardy and without this turning into a death wish. They need to be able to live a life of lies and deception while transmitting reliable reports and not hiding anything from their commanders. They need to employ personal charm without creating personal connections."

And then there is always the question of motivation: Why would a man or woman want one of the most dangerous jobs in the world? "There are two groups of warriors," Kfir said. "One comes from the positive direction, people who are coming *to* something. The second group comes from the negative direction, people who are getting *away* from something. The ones from the positive direction don't have a problem making a living, and they don't have wives who don't understand them. They are people who come to serve Zionism and seek to satisfy their spirit of adventure; they want to see the world, to play because they like the game. The ones from the negative direction—they're people who are running away from something, who don't like their homes, who haven't been successful in a civilian career. They are people who are trying to create a better life for themselves."

The Mossad takes both kinds of warriors, the positive and the negative. Their reasons for leaving their old life matter less than the ability to function in complete isolation in an enemy country, under an entirely different identity. "You are both a soldier and a general," says Kfir. "It's a heavy emotional and intellectual burden."

Hoping to find a way to obviate or at least mitigate that burden, Harari also initiated one other particularly ambitious recruitment program. "I heard that the KGB used to identify orphans, who wouldn't have any restrictive commitments, at the age of thirteen or fourteen, took them under its wing, and trained them under the best possible conditions to be operatives functioning under cover. I thought it was a good idea." He got Caesarea's psychologist to find a fourteen-year-old Israeli boy without parents, and Caesarea took him under its wing, without his knowing who was now taking care of him. A psychologist and two tutors kept constant tabs on him, and he was given an excellent education, enrichment classes in art and culture, and time for sports and leisure. "We told him we wanted him to serve the nation when he grew up," says Harari.

All of the grooming and tuition was a success. The boy became a soldier and then a talented young officer, highly cultured and capable of functioning under cover as a foreigner. But the project as a whole failed. "It became clear to me that it may work in a totalitarian country like Russia, but not in Israel. The Israeli Jew doesn't have that kind of perseverance, and very soon he wanted a girlfriend, a civilian career, and a good salary. He would likely have aspirations in very different directions than what the intelligence world could offer. We had no alternative but to just let him go his own way."

Other recruitment policies proved more successful. For practical operational reasons, the Mossad actually became an early pioneer in gender equality. "It is a huge advantage having a woman on the team during an operation," says Ethan. "A team made up of members of both sexes . . . always provides for a better cover story and reduces suspicions."

If recruits manage to make it past the initial screening stage, they then begin the "operatives course." Most Caesarea cadets never visit Mossad headquarters during their training and have no contact with other trainees. They are exposed to as little information as possible so that they will have little to reveal if they are captured and tortured. During training, their home base is one of several apartments in Tel Aviv, so that they won't be exposed to regular Mossad employees who come to work at headquarters every day.

Cadets undergo training in a host of spycraft fields—encrypted Morse code transmission (until technological developments rendered that mode of communication obsolete), surveillance, losing tails, weaponry, and hand-to-hand combat. They also study the geography, politics, and history of the Arab countries.

Skills are honed in a series of practice missions, almost entirely on Israeli soil, and are usually mundane: slipping a listening device into a telephone in a bank lobby, recovering innocuous documents, breaking into homes or businesses just to prove a recruit has the skill.

The creation of an elaborate cover story goes well beyond a fake name. The recruit is expected to learn an entirely new, fictitious biography: where he was born and raised, who his parents were, the social, cultural, and economic background in which he was raised, his hobbies, and so forth. A passport issued by a friendly base country—or forged by the Mossad—will allow the warrior to travel freely, even to countries that don't admit Israelis. The counterfeit profession, meanwhile, typically is one that requires frequent international travel and lots of time spent working alone, without partners, offices, or regular hours. A newspaper reporter or photographer, for example, or a screenwriter doing research for a movie script both work well, because neither requires much explanation.

The cover story, molded over time, distances the recruit from his true self and endows him with a new life in a new country that arouses no suspicion. Next, recruits practice creating second-level covers specific to individual situations. A warrior needs to be able to plausibly account for why he was in a particular place at a particular time—lingering outside a government ministry, for instance, monitoring how many people come and go—if pestered by a curious police officer. In order to be believable, that explanation needs to be given quickly, calmly, and with as little detail as possible; offering too much information can arouse suspicion as easily as no explanation at all.

Trainers will ratchet up the pressure by simulating arrest and brutal interrogation. A Caesarea warrior code-named Kurtz said that this is the toughest part of the course. "They sent us in pairs to Jerusalem to shadow foreign diplomats. It seemed like a simple assignment—just to follow them and report, without establishing contact," he said. "We were equipped with foreign passports, and our instructions were that under no circumstances were we to reveal to anyone who we really were. Suddenly, from out of nowhere, three police cars pull up and a few other thugs in civilian clothes jump us, knock us down, handcuff us, and throw us into the wagon.

"They took us to the Shin Bet interrogation facility in the Russian Compound in Jerusalem. We spent three and a half horrible days there, without sleep, handcuffed, blindfolded. For part of the time, we were handcuffed to a chair with our arms behind us in a position that tensed our entire bodies; part of the time, they chained us to the ceiling, forcing us to stand on tiptoe. During the interrogations, policemen and Shin Bet agents beat us and spit on us. I heard that they even urinated on one guy. The goal was to see who would break and who would survive with his counterfeit cover." Kurtz did not break. If he had, he likely would have been cut from the program.

Upon completion of the course, successful cadets qualify as operatives and begin going on missions in target countries.

Harari introduced iron discipline into Caesarea and demanded absolute obedience. Anyone who didn't follow the path he laid down found himself immediately on the outside. The division's offices, on the eleventh floor of 2 Kaplan Street, Tel Aviv, were run quietly and with exemplary order. "Mike brought a European atmosphere with him to Caesarea," said Ethan. "The speech, the finesse, the manners, the way of behavior. His office was always clean and tidy, tip-top, and so was he, in his behavior and dress. He was always well groomed, clean-shaven, with the scent of his favorite French Macassar cologne following him around wherever he went. This was important, because he got the whole unit accustomed to working in the atmosphere of the countries from which we ostensibly came."

"Good intelligence and a strong Caesarea cost money," Harari told Amit. He demanded bigger and bigger budgets, which he spent on training personnel and on the formation of more and more operational frameworks and networks. Harari's people opened hundreds of commercial firms in innumerable spheres and countries, which would serve the Mossad for many years after his departure. Most of them did not have an immediate use, but Harari had the foresight to see, for example, that it would one day be advantageous for Caesarea to control a shipping company in a Middle Eastern country. Sure enough, there came a time when the unit needed a civilian shipping vessel to provide cover for a Mossad team in the waters off Yemen. The Mossad unit loaded packages of meat onto a vessel, shipping it from place to place while secretly carrying out their espionage mission.

In 1967, Harari's changes began producing noticeable results, and Caesarea operatives in target countries were transmitting valuable information back to Israel on a daily basis, mostly related to Israel's main adversaries at the time: Syria, Egypt, Jordan, and Iraq.

The Mossad, AMAN, and the government justifiably allotted many resources to preparations for the next military confrontation with the Arab states, which indeed ended up coming that June.

However, Israeli intelligence failed to spot the next major challenge: the millions of Palestinians ready to fight for the return of their motherland. A wave of Palestinian terrorism against Israelis and other Jews would soon sweep through the Middle East and Europe.

"We were not ready for this new menace," said Harari.

# "ARMED STRUGGLE IS THE ONLY WAY TO LIBERATE PALESTINE"

BETWEEN 600,000 AND 750,000 Palestinians either fled or were driven out of the territory upon which the State of Israel was established and which it conquered during the war of 1948–49. The Arabs vowed to destroy the newborn state, and the Israeli leadership believed that if their precarious, vulnerable country was to have any chance of surviving, there had to be as few Arabs as possible within its borders. This was the rationale, however morally questionable, behind both the expulsions and the blanket refusal to allow any refugees to return—ever.

Refugees were settled into Gaza (a 141-square-mile strip formed along the southwest coast of Mandatory Palestine as a result of the 1948–49 war, controlled by Egypt until 1967 and by Israel since), the West Bank (the name given by Jordan to the 2,270-square-mile territory it controlled after the 1948 war in formerly Mandatory Palestine; Israel captured this territory in 1967), and other ramshackle camps in neighboring Arab countries, where the ruling regimes blustered that they eventually would wipe the Zionists from the map and return the Palestinians to their homeland. But that was mostly lip service. In reality, those regimes imposed harsh conditions of their own on the unfortunate refugees, who often had no rights, no significant control of their lives, no prospects for higher education or worthy employment. Living conditions were poor, and so were public health and even food security. The refugees who poured into the Gaza Strip during the 1948–49 war more than tripled the area's population.

From about 70,000 inhabitants in 1945, the number rose to about 245,000 in 1950. By 1967, there were 356,000 inhabitants, and by 2015, there were 1,710,000. The refugees had become stateless people, cast out of their own country and unwanted by any other. But they and the permanent Palestinian residents of the villages and cities in the West Bank and Gaza still considered themselves *a people*. In the squalid camps, young militants organized themselves into nationalist movements, driven by pride of self and hatred of Israel.

Among them was a boy named Khalil al-Wazir, who had been born in Ramla, a town southeast of Tel Aviv, in 1935. During the 1948 war, he and his family, along with many other residents of Ramla, were deported to Gaza, where they lived in a refugee camp.

By the time he was sixteen, al-Wazir already was the leader of one of the militant groups. Eager to avenge his family's deportation from Ramla, al-Wazir said, he "sought out mujahideen who had taken part in the [1948] Palestinian War so that we could learn from their personal experience in battle."

Those veterans of the '48 war trained al-Wazir and his friends, and they, in turn, trained other young Palestinians. In 1953, when he was just eighteen years old, al-Wazir commanded two hundred young men, all passionately motivated to fight the Zionist enemy. At the end of 1954 and the beginning of 1955, al-Wazir's men began a series of sabotage and murder operations inside Israel. The Egyptians, using the young militants as cheap proxies, sent reinforcements of Palestinian students from Cairo to Gaza. Among them was a young electrical engineering student at the University of Cairo, Mohammed Yasser Abdel Rahman Abdel Raouf Arafat al-Qudwa al-Husseini—Yasser Arafat.

Arafat's place of birth is disputed. According to the official Palestinian version, he was born in 1929 in Jerusalem, as might be expected from a Palestinian leader. However, it has also been argued that Arafat was born in Gaza or even in Cairo. Regardless, he came from an important Palestinian family with ties to the grand mufti, Hajj Amin al-Husseini, and to Abd al-Qadir al-Husseini, the commander of Palestinian forces in 1948, both of whom were primary targets for assassination at that time.

Arafat, who took the nom de guerre Abu Ammar, and al-Wazir,

who took the name Abu Jihad, became associates and confidants. They worked together to strengthen the Palestinian cells in the Gaza Strip.

Nevertheless, Israeli intelligence was not overly concerned with the festering militancy in the refugee camps. "In general, one could say that the Palestinian diaspora really didn't interest us," said Aharon Levran, who served as an AMAN officer at the time. "They did not constitute a significant force then." Rather than a long-term strategic issue, the militants were considered an immediate tactical problem, a concern only to the extent that they slipped over the border to harass and terrorize Jews. And that problem ostensibly had been solved by the 1956 Sinai Campaign: Egypt, fearful of Israeli reprisals and more concerned with preserving peace on the border than with the plight of Palestinians, stopped sponsoring those raids.

The militants, however, did not see matters the same way. Abu Jihad and Arafat, blindsided and betrayed when the Egyptians prohibited further infiltrations, decided the Palestinians could end their plight only by engaging in independent operations. Israel's military victory in the Sinai Campaign, which stopped the terrorist infiltration by Palestinians from Egyptian territory, thus also inadvertently led to the creation of a separate guerrilla movement.

After years of roaming from country to country, in late 1959 Arafat and Abu Jihad relocated to Kuwait. They had come to realize that in the eyes of Nasser, who was trying to unify the Arab world under his leadership, their activities would only be seen as obstructions. They knew that as long as they stayed in one of the major Arab states, they would never manage to create an effective all-Palestinian organization under their own authority.

Abu Jihad accepted the supremacy of Arafat, who was six years his senior and who already possessed a wide network of ties across the Palestinian diaspora. Arafat regarded himself as the leader, but he immediately identified Abu Jihad's operational capabilities, something he himself lacked. For two years, Arafat, Abu Jihad, and three comrades worked on developing a series of principles and operational frameworks for their organization. They did so in secret, to avoid arousing the opposition of the Arab states. Finally, on October 10, 1959, the Palestine Liberation Movement was officially established.

They soon discovered, however, that the Arabic acronym of their name, Hataf, spelled a word that ingloriously translates as "quick death." So Abu Jihad, who had a special sensitivity for symbolic matters, proposed that the letters be reversed to form the acronym Fatah—that word means "glorious victory."

The basic principles, disseminated at the time in the form of leaflets, would later be concentrated and expressed in the Palestinian National Covenant. Article 9 states, "Armed struggle is the only way to liberate Palestine," and Article 6 in effect calls for the deportation of all Jews who had arrived in Palestine after 1917. Article 20 notes, "Claims of historical or religious ties of Jews with Palestine are incompatible with the facts of history. . . . Nor do Jews constitute a single nation with an identity of its own; they are citizens of the states to which they belong." Article 22 mentions that "Zionism is . . . racist and fanatic in its nature, aggressive, expansionist, and colonial in its aims, and fascist in its methods." Most of the covenant's strictures against Zionism allege that it is a tool of international imperialism.

ISRAELI INTELLIGENCE, PREOCCUPIED WITH Nasser and convinced that Egypt posed the most credible and formidable threat, completely missed the founding of Fatah. It wasn't until early 1964, more than four years after the fact, that two Israeli spies filed the first field reports on the organization. Uri Yisrael (known in the Mossad as "Ladiyyah") and Yitzhak Sagiv ("Yisrael"), working under the cover of Palestinian businessmen, warned that the cells of students functioning with Fatah's support and inspiration were gaining more and more momentum in Europe and should not be belittled. On April 6, 1964, with the entire Mossad tied up with the affair of the German scientists, Ladiyyah wrote to his Mossad handlers, warning, "I am coming to the conclusion that the danger we face from the scholars, students, and educated [Palestinians] is of no lesser significance than the arming of the Arab states with weapons of mass destruction."

At first, their Mossad case officers were unimpressed, dismissing Arafat, Abu Jihad, and their friends as "students and intellectuals stronger with words than in actions." But Ladiyyah and Yisrael persisted, warning that their Palestinian acquaintances were speaking with increasing frequency about "the armed struggle against the Zionist entity."

Fatah was "something entirely different from anything that had existed before," they insisted in a May 1964 report. "These two"—Arafat and Abu Jihad—"are capable of inspiring the Palestinians to act against us."

FATAH CARRIED OUT ITS first terror attack on January 1, 1965, an attempt to bomb Israel's National Water Carrier, the huge pipe-and-canal system that brings water from the Sea of Galilee to the country's arid south. It was a highly symbolic act—threatening to cut out the source of life, water, in the desert of the Middle East—one that touched the raw nerves of all the residents of the region. The construction of the canal system had been a contentious issue, causing considerable agitation in Arab public opinion at the time. Although Prime Minister Salah Bitar of Syria declared in September 1963 that the Arab states had decided to wage "an unyielding campaign to prevent [Israel] from realizing its dream" of bringing water to the desert, those were empty words. It was only Fatah, still small and with few resources, that took the initiative and acted.

Planned by Abu Jihad, the operation was fairly amateurish, and an utter failure. The group that was supposed to carry out the first military act by Fatah was arrested in Gaza a whole week before the launch date. Another group was also arrested in Lebanon a few days before the launch date. Eventually, a third group coming from Jordan did manage to lay explosives at the National Water Carrier site, but they failed to go off and were discovered by a security patrol. The members of the unit were caught. Despite this evident failure, the news of the operation reverberated throughout the Arab world. At last there was a force ready to take on the Israelis. AMAN, for its part, took notice but did little more.

At the same time, Ladiyyah's connections, established over years of living a double life, paid off. Arafat and Abu Jihad maintained close contact with Palestinian students throughout Europe, particularly in East and West Germany. Ladiyyah had a Palestinian friend,

Hani al-Hassan, who headed West Germany's Palestinian Student Association and whose brother, Khaled, was one of Fatah's five founding members. Hani was in financial difficulties, and Ladiyyah came to the rescue. He offered to pay the rent on Hani's apartment, at Beethovenstrasse 42, Frankfurt, which also served as headquarters for the student organization. The leaders of Fatah periodically gathered there as well.

In January 1965, the Mossad's surveillance unit, Colossus, planted microphones in the apartment. For the next eight months, Israeli operatives eavesdropped on the Palestinians' strategy sessions from a post across the hall, listening as they vowed to "wipe Israel off the map," as Abu Jihad declared at one of the secretly recorded sessions.

Rafi Eitan, who years earlier had commanded the IDF force that expelled Abu Jihad's family from Ramla, was chief of the Mossad's European operations at the time. Listening to the plotting, he understood straightaway that this was a movement with potential, and that it had a particularly charismatic, dangerous leader. "Arafat's true nature was apparent even back then in the meetings in Frankfurt," Eitan said. "The students told Arafat and Abu Jihad that there were fifteen Palestinian organizations and that it was important to ensure that all of them operate under a single command. Arafat said that that wasn't necessary, and that it was actually a good thing for each organization to have its own militia and budget. Doing so would guarantee, he said, 'the continuation of the struggle against Zionism until we throw all the Jews in the sea.'"

Throughout the first half of 1965, Fatah carried out more and more guerrilla attacks, mining roads, sabotaging pipelines, and firing at Israelis with small arms. Most of these attacks failed, but their echoes reached Rafi Eitan in Paris. In May 1965, Eitan asked Mossad director Amit to order a Caesarea unit to break into the apartment on Beethovenstrasse and assassinate everyone there. "We can do it easily," he wrote to Amit. "We have access to the target and this is an opportunity that we may not get again."

But Amit, still reeling from the capture of Caesarea operatives Cohen and Lotz, refused to sign off. He didn't see the group as much more than a gang of young thugs with no real capability.

"Too bad they didn't listen to me," Eitan said decades later. "We could have saved ourselves a lot of effort, heartache, and sorrow."

In the months that followed, there were more attacks, and their frequency steadily increased, reaching a total of thirty-nine in 1965. It was clear that Arafat and Abu Jihad were a problem that wasn't going to go away. "At first their terror attacks were ridiculous," said Aharon Levran, who was then deputy chief of AMAN's intelligence collection division. "But as time went on, they became more serious. . . . Faced with those situations, the intelligence community reacted in two typical ways," Levran said. "First, they set up a special department to handle the matter. Second, they struck at the top of the pyramid.

The "special department," a secret committee to examine how to counter Palestinian terrorism, was established in August 1965 and had three members: Levran; Mike Harari, deputy chief of Caesarea; and Shmuel Goren, commander of AMAN's Unit 504.

The committee of three issued orders for the elimination of Arafat and Abu Jihad. Knowing that the unit's recent catastrophes made it extremely unlikely they would get authorization for a targeted killing operation using Caesarea, the committee instead recommended a return to letter bombs. Using information gathered by Ladiyyah and Yisrael, these bombs would be sent to a number of Fatah officials in Lebanon and Syria.

On October 8, Mossad director Amit met with Prime Minister and Defense Minister Levi Eshkol to submit the plan for his approval. "We have three targets," Amit said. "Our guy [Ladiyyah] has come back from the capitals [Beirut and Damascus], and we want to execute."

After identifying the targets, Amit noted that Ladiyyah "has brought all of the necessary information, and the proposal is to send each one of them a 'gift.'" The letters would appear to be from people known to the targets. To make them seem as authentic as possible, they would be mailed directly from inside Lebanon.

"It will be a woman doing it this time. She'll go to Beirut and slip the letters into a mailbox there. . . . [She is] South African, with a British passport, and she's ready to do it." Amit was speaking about Sylvia Rafael, daughter of a Jewish father and a gentile mother, who had developed a strong allegiance with the Jewish people, immigrated to Israel, and was recruited by the Mossad. She was trained by Moti Kfir and became the most famous female operative in the history of Caesarea.

Amit told Eshkol that there would be a whole wave of letter bombs. While the Mossad focused on its three targets, AMAN would simultaneously send twelve to fifteen of the lethal envelopes to Fatah operatives in Jordan.

Eshkol was skeptical. "Have we ever had an attempt that worked out all the way? . . . In Egypt it didn't work out all the way," he said, reminding Amit that the letter bombs sent to the German scientists in Egypt didn't kill them, but only caused injuries.

Amit reassured him, saying, "We're putting in more [explosive] material this time. Now we're putting in twenty grams."

Nevertheless, the booby-trapped envelopes didn't work this time, either. A few recipients of the letters were slightly wounded, but most of the letters were discovered and defused before they could do any harm at all.

At that time, Arafat and Abu Jihad were in Damascus, which had agreed to extend its patronage to Fatah's activities and to allow its military units to use some of Syria's training facilities. The possibilities for any sort of Israeli action in Damascus were very limited, especially after the capture of Eli Cohen and the panicky evacuation of the other operatives there. Furthermore, from Syria, Fatah could better coordinate its struggle against Israel, making frequent entries into the West Bank, which was then under Jordanian rule. Fatah established bases there, from which they launched terror attacks inside Israel. Most of the attacks were sabotage attempts of civilian targets, including private houses, institutions, and infrastructure, like water pipes, railways, and dirt roads.

In 1966, there were forty Fatah attacks in Israel. Though the frequency of the attacks remained the same as in 1965, there was a dramatic difference in the audacity and quality. Starting in the middle of 1966, Fatah began trying to hit Israeli military targets. In one such operation, on November 11, 1966, three Israeli soldiers were killed when their vehicle hit a land mine. Retaliation followed two days later when Israeli forces raided a Palestinian village, Samua, south of Hebron in Jordanian territory. The original goal was to de-molish houses in the village, in the hope of sending a signal that would deter the Arab states and motivate them to act against Fatah. However, the Jordanian army intervened. The result was sixteen dead Jordanian soldiers, one dead Israeli, and a sharp increase in ten-sion on the border.

Still, the urge to sweep the Palestinian problem under the carpet was so strong that the Israeli establishment did all it could not to even utter the name Fatah. "We didn't want to give Fatah credit, to say that this or that terror attack was its work," said Shlomo Gazit, head of the Research Division of AMAN from 1964 to 1967. "On the other hand, we had to refer to them somehow, so we decided on a neutral term." That word was *paha,* the Hebrew acronym for *hostile terrorist activity*. For decades, this was the term used by Israeli offi-cials when they told the public who was behind acts of terror.

In early 1967, the situation worsened rapidly. By the start of May, Fatah had launched more than a hundred attacks on Israel, across the Jordanian, Syrian, Lebanese, and Egyptian borders. Thirteen Is-raelis were killed: nine civilians and four soldiers. The back-and-forth of small-scale attacks—Palestinians raiding across the border, Israel retaliating—deteriorated Israel's already fragile relationships with neighboring Arab countries.

On May 11, Israel declared that it was warning Syria for the last time that if it did not restrain Fatah, Israel would take large-scale military action. That warning led to the establishment of a joint mili-tary command by Egypt, Syria, and Jordan and the concentration of enormous forces by all sides. Many Arabs believed that at last the time had come for the liquidation of the State of Israel.

In Israel, many people feared that another Holocaust was immi-nent. An atmosphere of gloom prevailed. Some expected tens of thousands to die. Mass burial sites were hastily prepared in public parks like Gan Meir, in the heart of Tel Aviv.

Prime Minister Eshkol gave a speech on Israeli radio on May 28, 1967, that only made things worse. Because the text had been changed at the last moment, Eshkol stuttered over key phrases. The Israeli public understood it as lack of resolve on his part, aggravating existing fears.

However, the heads of the Israeli Army and intelligence community were sure of their own capabilities and pressured Eshkol to let them strike first. Mossad chief Amit flew to Washington, where he met with Defense Secretary Robert McNamara. Amit understood from McNamara's response that he had obtained what he later described as a "flashing green light" for Israel to launch a preemptive attack.

The Six-Day War broke out at 7:45 on the morning of June 5, 1967, with the entire Israeli Air Force bombing and strafing dozens of enemy airfields. Thanks to detailed and precise intelligence gathered by the Mossad and AMAN over long years of preparing for war, Israel's Air Force was able to destroy, within hours, nearly every combat plane that Egypt, Syria, and Jordan owned. By the time the war ended, on June 10, Israel was occupying territories that increased its size by more than 300 percent. Its conquests included the Sinai Peninsula, as well as the Golan Heights, the West Bank, and the Gaza Strip.

It now oversaw more than a million Palestinian inhabitants in those territories as well, many of them 1948 refugees who now were occupied by the same forces that had dispossessed them of their land twenty years before. In less than a week, the face of the Middle East had been completely transformed.

The war proved that the Israeli intelligence community and its military enjoyed unchallenged superiority over its rivals in the Arab states. Yet some Israelis realized that the mighty victory was not just a reason to rejoice—it was also an opportunity to forge a lasting truce. AMAN research chief Gazit composed a special top-secret paper, distributed to the leaders of the government and the military, that included a warning that "we should not look like braggarts, mocking a defeated enemy, debasing him and his leaders." The memo called for immediate negotiations with the Arab states and the use of the conquered territories in a barter deal—an Israeli withdrawal and the establishment of an "independent Palestinian state" in exchange for an overall, absolute, and final peace treaty. In the Shin Bet, too, there were many who believed that this was a historic opportunity to end the national conflict between Jews and Arabs. Even Israel's number-one spy, Meir Amit, grasped the potential for peace. But his advice fell on deaf ears.

The sharp transition undergone by the Israeli public and its parliamentarians and cabinet ministers—from citizens and leaders of a country on the brink of destruction to those of a seemingly invincible empire—made everyone blind to the truth that even victory and the occupation of enemy territory could entail grave dangers.

Amit was one of the few who comprehended the profound and dangerous new trend in the national psychology. "What's happening now is a disappointment, a painful disappointment," he wrote in his diary two weeks after the war. "I am apprehensive and worried and fearful at this waste of a victory. . . . When I see how matters are being conducted, my hands go limp and I get a terrible feeling."

WHILE AMIT SAW ISRAEL'S victory as an opportunity for peace, Yasser Arafat and Abu Jihad saw the Arab nations' overwhelming defeat as a catastrophe to be exploited. They realized that the disgraceful failure of the Arab states' leaders would make room in public opinion for new leaders, who would be perceived as young, brave, and uncorrupted. Abu Jihad also grasped that it would now be easier to wage guerrilla warfare against Israel.

On June 20, just ten days after the war ended, Arafat and Abu Jihad announced from Beirut that Fatah would continue its struggle, only now from within territories Israel had just conquered. True to his word, Abu Jihad initiated a damaging wave of terror attacks in Gaza and the West Bank—thirteen attacks took place during September 1967, ten in October, eighteen in November, and twenty in December. The targets were mostly civilian: factories, houses, cinemas, and the like. In the wake of those attacks, no one in Israeli intelligence dared advocate negotiations with Fatah.

Although Abu Jihad was waging the war, it was clear to the Israelis that Fatah's leader was Yasser Arafat. He was the one who laid down the diplomatic and ideological lines, and who gradually managed to unite all of the various Palestinian factions under his authority. He had also begun to mediate relationships with the leaders of the Arab states, who had originally seen Fatah as a dangerous threat. In 1964, the Arab states founded the Palestine Liberation Organization and placed a puppet of theirs, Ahmad Shukeiri, at its head. But in the wake of the organization's dismal performance in the Six-Day War and with Arafat's rising prominence, Fatah gradually began taking control of the PLO, until Arafat was finally elected its chairman. Abu Jihad became the coordinator of its military activities, in effect the second in command.

Arafat, who took to wearing a kaffiyeh headdress draped to look like a map of Palestine, had become the symbol of the Palestinian struggle.

"Israel must strike at the heart of the terror organizations, their HQs," Yehuda Arbel, the Shin Bet commander in Jerusalem and the West Bank, wrote in his diary. "The elimination of Abu Ammar"—Arafat—"is a precondition to finding a solution to the Palestinian problem." Arbel pressed the committee of three to take steps to achieve this goal. For his part, he drew up and distributed a wanted poster, the first of many, which included the following description: "Short, 155–160 cm; dark-skinned. Build: chubby; bald spot in the middle of his head. Hair on temples—gray. Mustache shaven. Demeanor: restive. Eyes: constantly darting back and forth."

ISRAELI FORCES TRIED TO kill Arafat a few times during and immediately after the Six-Day War. In the days following Israel's victory, a Shin Bet informer identified his hideout in the Old City of Jerusalem, not far from Jaffa Gate. A contingent of soldiers was sent to get Arafat, dead or alive, but he managed to flee just a few minutes before they arrived. Two days later, soldiers acting on another tip from a 504 agent raided an apartment in Beit Hanina, a village just east of Jerusalem, but found only a pita full of salad and tahini, with a few bites gone. A day later, Arafat managed to cross over one of the Jordan River bridges, dressed as a woman, in a cab belonging to one of his supporters.

In the meantime, PLO terror attacks against Israel became more frequent and more deadly. Between the end of the war and March 1968, 65 soldiers and 50 civilians were killed, and 249 soldiers and 295 civilians were wounded. The attacks launched by Fatah from its headquarters in Karameh, in the southern Jordan Valley, led to frequent clashes between the IDF and the Jordanian army, and the long border between the two countries seethed with tension, making normal life on the Israeli side impossible. The IDF brass urged Eshkol to approve a massive military operation, but he was hesitant.

The Mossad was frustrated. "The humiliation caused by the terror attacks produced a feeling of helplessness," recalled Caesarea chief Zvi Aharoni. "I told the guys, 'Think outside the box. Think of an idea how to kill Arafat.'"

The plan they came up with in January 1968 called for shipping a large car from Europe to Beirut, where it would be packed with explosives and then driven to Damascus by a Caesarea man operating under the cover of a businessman. It would be parked outside Arafat's residence and detonated remotely at the right time. Amit went to Eshkol to seek approval but was met with a blunt refusal, on the grounds that the attack would invite and justify retaliatory attempts on the lives of Israeli political leaders. Eshkol saw Arafat as a terrorist, but one who had attained the status of a political leader, and this was perhaps the best proof of all of the PLO chairman's success.

But the Palestinian terror continued unabated. On March 18, a school bus hit a land mine. Two adult escorts were killed and ten children wounded. Now the reluctant Eshkol gave in to the pressure. He agreed that killing Arafat would be the primary aim of the operation against the Palestinian forces in and around Karameh.

On March 21, 1968, a unit from Sayeret Matkal, the elite IDF commando force, was flown by helicopter to a staging point in the desert near the Fatah base in Karameh. The commandos' orders were simple and clear: "Attack in daylight, seize control, isolate and kill the terrorists." At a cabinet meeting the night before, the chief of the general staff, Lieutenant General Haim Bar-Lev, had promised "a clean operation," by which he meant no or almost no Israeli casualties.

But things went very wrong, and the battle dragged on much longer than planned. The Jordan River is high at that time of year, the vegetation along its banks is thick and the terrain difficult to negotiate, which held up the mechanized forces that were supposed to support the commandos. Furthermore, due to faulty coordination, the air force dropped leaflets warning the civilian population to evacuate at a preset time. The element of surprise was lost and the Fatah forces had ample time to prepare for the assault. They fought back fiercely.

Arafat—again dressed as a woman—got away in a mad dash on a motorcycle.

Although the casualties—thirty-three Israelis dead, as well as sixty-one Jordanians and more than one hundred Palestinians— favored the IDF, for the first time in a face-to-face battle the Palestinians had succeeded in holding out against the strongest army in the Middle East. This showed who the real victors were.

Arafat, immediately grasping the public relations potential of Israel's bungled operation, turned it into a legend of Palestinian grit in the face of enemy attack. He even went so far as to (falsely) boast that his forces had wounded the Israeli defense minister, Moshe Dayan. Thousands of Palestinians were inspired to enlist in the PLO. After Karameh, no one doubted that there was a Palestinian nation, even if Israel continued to deny it officially for many years thereafter. And no one could be mistaken: Yasser Arafat was that nation's unchallenged leader.

The failure of the Karameh operation led Israel to adopt a more restrained policy in its raids into Jordan, and consequently engendered great frustration in the IDF. Transcripts of general staff meetings from that period reveal the extent to which the top brass was preoccupied with the PLO and with Yasser Arafat, who was regarded with great admiration by Palestinian youth.

The military and the intelligence community continued to look for ways to pinpoint and eliminate Arafat, but with no success. Eventually, out of desperation, they were even willing to adopt a particularly bizarre plan. In May 1968, a charismatic Swedish-born navy psychologist named Binyamin Shalit somehow heard about the secret three-man committee and proposed an idea based on the 1962 film *The Manchurian Candidate,* in which a Chinese intelligence hypnotist brainwashes an American prisoner of war and sends him to assassinate a United States presidential candidate.

Shalit claimed that he could do the same, with Arafat as the target. Shalit told the committee at a meeting attended by AMAN chief Major General Aharon Yariv that if he was given a Palestinian prisoner—one of the thousands in Israeli jails—with the right characteristics, he could brainwash and hypnotize him into becoming a programmed killer. He would then be sent across the Jordan, join the Fatah forces there, and, when the opportunity arose, do away with Arafat.

Incredibly, the committee approved the plan. The Shin Bet found several suitable candidates, and they were interviewed at length by Shalit, who picked the man he thought most suitable. Born in Bethlehem, he was twenty-eight, solidly built and swarthy, not particularly bright, easily influenced, and seemingly not entirely committed to Yasser Arafat's leadership. At the time of his arrest, he had been living in a small village near Hebron. A low-level Fatah operative, he was given the official code name Fatkhi.

AMAN's Unit 504 was assigned to provide the necessary infrastructure, but the unit's operatives vehemently opposed the plan. As Rafi Sutton, then commander of the unit's base in Jerusalem, said, "It was a foolish, crazy idea. The whole business reminded me of science fiction. Wild imagination and delusions."

Sutton's objections, however, were dismissed. A small structure containing about ten rooms was put at the Shalit team's disposal. Here, Shalit spent three months working on Fatkhi, using a variety of hypnosis techniques. The message drummed into the impressionable young man's head was: "Fatah good. PLO good. Arafat bad. He must be removed." After two months, Fatkhi seemed to be taking in the message. In the second stage of his training, he was placed in a specially prepared room and given a pistol. Pictures of Arafat jumped up in different corners and he was told to shoot at them instantly, without thinking first, right between the eyes—shoot to kill.

AMAN Chief Yariv and Aharon Levran, part of the three-man targeted killing committee and a senior AMAN officer, went several times to observe Shalit's work. "Fatkhi stood there in the middle of the room and Shalit spoke with him, as if they were just carrying out a normal conversation," Levran told me. "Suddenly Shalit banged his hand on the table and Fatkhi began to run around the table. He reacted automatically to all sorts of gestures by Shalit. Then he put him in a room and showed us how Fatkhi raised his pistol to firing position every time Arafat's picture popped up from one of the pieces of furniture. It was impressive."

In mid-December, Shalit announced that the operation could go forward. Zero hour was set for the night of December 19, when Fatkhi was scheduled to swim across the Jordan River into the Kingdom of Jordan. A fierce storm rolled in, and the rain was unrelenting. The usually calm and narrow Jordan overflowed its banks. AMAN wanted to postpone, but Shalit insisted that Fatkhi was in an "optimal hypnotic" state and that the opportunity had to be exploited.

A sizable entourage accompanied Fatkhi from Jerusalem. Shalit dropped him off and said a few hypnotic words. Fatkhi walked into the raging water, wearing a backpack that contained his gear. As he waded into the river, he was soon thrown off his feet by the current. He grabbed onto a boulder, unable to cross to the far side and unable to return. Ovad Natan, a driver from Unit 504 who had a large and muscular physique, jumped into the water and, at great risk, used a rope to tie himself to Fatkhi and pull him to his side. He then crossed the river with Fatkhi and deposited him on Jordanian territory.

Rafi Sutton was standing on the Israeli bank of the Jordan and watching as, soaked and shivering, Fatkhi waved goodbye to his operators. "He made a pistol out of his fingers and pretended to shoot an imaginary target between the eyes. I noticed Shalit was pleased with his patient. It was a bit after 1 A.M."

About five hours later, Unit 504 received a communication from one of its agents in Jordan: A young Palestinian man, a Fatah operative from Bethlehem, had turned himself in at the Karameh police station. He told the policemen that Israeli intelligence had tried to brainwash him into killing Arafat and handed over his pistol. A source inside Fatah reported three days later that Fatkhi had been handed over to the organization, where he had made a passionate speech in support of Yasser Arafat.

# MEIR DAGAN AND HIS EXPERTISE

FOLLOWING THE ISRAELI OCCUPATION, Palestinians in Gaza and
the West Bank—both the refugees and those who had always lived
there—found themselves governed by the enemy, the Jewish state
that the PLO had vowed to destroy. Palestinians who had been neither involved nor interested in nationalist politics were now caught
up in a maelstrom of conflicting currents—the Israelis' determination to control the occupied territories and the PLO's determination
to drive the Israelis out.

All of them had lived under cruel and dictatorial Arab regimes,
but a Palestinian could have chosen to be almost entirely isolated
from the armed conflict that was being waged on the borders between the Arab states and Israel. Now the camps, which had grown
into crowded slums, and the large Palestinian cities—Gaza, Nablus,
Ramallah, Jenin, and Hebron—were the main battlefield as Israel
aggressively tried to assert its authority in the face of PLO terror activity.

The mission of the IDF and its soldiers, particularly the eighteen-
to-twenty-one-year-olds doing their compulsory military service,
which had been in force since 1949, underwent a fundamental
change as well. Whereas, before, combat troops patrolled the country's borders, protecting it from external enemies, they were now reassigned to policing Palestinian cities and towns. The war also led to
profound changes in the intelligence community. The Mossad,
charged with collecting intelligence outside of Israel's borders, relin-

quished responsibility for the newly occupied territories. That task fell to the Shin Bet, a small agency of around seven hundred employees that had previously been responsible mainly for countering espionage and political subversion.

From 1968 through 1970, while PLO attacks on Israeli soldiers and civilians were growing more frequent, effective, and deadly, the Shin Bet was expanding rapidly. They obtained budgets, facilities, and personnel allocations and took on many Arabic speakers from AMAN, especially Unit 504, who'd been responsible for recruiting Arab sources. Soon, countering Palestinian terrorism became the principal objective of the organization.

The toughest theater of operations was the Gaza Strip, one of the most densely populated regions in the world. After the Six-Day War, Israelis drove through the Strip to reach Sinai, sought out bargains in its marketplaces, and ferried out Palestinian farm and construction workers. In 1970, Israel began establishing Jewish settlements in the Strip and northern Sinai. More and more often, the Israelis were attacked. The peak came in 1970, when five hundred terrorist attacks were perpetrated in the Gaza Strip. Eighteen Israeli civilians were murdered in these incidents, and hundreds wounded. By then, the IDF was able to control only the main transportation arteries; the PLO ruled everywhere else.

To suppress terror in the Strip, the Shin Bet drew up a list of Gazans suspected of being involved in attacks on Israelis. A great deal of information was gathered, and the list grew longer and longer. It quickly became clear that the Shin Bet—an intelligence-gathering organization—could not operate on its own. In order to arrest or eliminate wanted persons, it needed the manpower—and the firepower—of the military. It found an attentive ear in Major General Ariel "Arik" Sharon, who was appointed head of the IDF's Southern Command in 1969. Sharon began introducing more and more military units into the Strip to assist the Shin Bet in hunting down and arresting or killing terrorists. The intelligence for these activities was supplied mainly by Palestinian informers or extracted from detainees under harsh interrogation.

Not everyone agreed with Sharon's aggressive approach. Brigadier General Yitzhak Pundak, military governor of the Gaza Strip, responsible for civilian affairs, maintained that the way to curb Palestinian terror was to improve the quality of life for the territory's inhabitants and allow them to manage civilian and municipal affairs on their own, with a minimal military presence in inhabited areas. "Saber-rattling and killing for the sake of killing couldn't take us anywhere but to an intifada," or popular uprising, Pundak said. "[Minister of Defense] Dayan and Sharon did not see eye to eye about what had to be done in the Strip. Dayan wanted contacts and connections with the population, whereas Sharon was hunting the terrorists and could see them only through the sights of his rifle, and the population did not interest him at all."

Pundak was appalled by Sharon's tactics and complained bitterly. "I heard Sharon declare in front of all the officers, 'Whoever kills a terrorist will get a bottle of champagne, and anyone who takes a prisoner will get a bottle of soda.' I said, 'Good Lord, what kind of policy is this? Who speaks like this? After all, if we do not give them a little assistance, a little prosperity, they'll all turn to the path of terror.'"

Sharon insisted that there was no hope for accommodation with the Palestinians. Terrorist attacks should be answered with force, and there was no one on the other side to talk peace with, he maintained. If the goal of Arafat and the rest of the PLO leadership was to destroy Israel, what was left to negotiate?

THE REGULAR ARMY UNITS in Sharon's Southern Command had other duties, like patrolling the long border with Egypt and fighting the battles that broke out during the three-year War of Attrition along the Suez Canal, so Sharon needed a unit whose sole task would be to combat terrorism. No less important, Sharon wanted to create a small, closed body of men who would report directly to him and operate under the same mindset and codes.

When the time came to decide who could lead the new unit, Sharon's mind immediately turned to Meir Dagan, recalling an incident in northern Sinai in mid-1969. Fatah had placed Katyusha rockets, connected to timed fuses, in the middle of a minefield and aimed them at an IDF base. Not one soldier or officer dared to approach the rockets to disarm them. But Dagan, then a young recon officer, stepped forward. He simply walked up to the Katyushas, fearlessly, and defused them. He reminded Sharon of himself when he was a young officer.

Dagan was born in 1945. His parents had fled the Polish town of Łuków six years earlier, after a Russian officer warned them that the Germans were about to conquer the area and things would not be good for the Jews. They found refuge on the harsh plains of Siberia. At the end of the war, together with tens of thousands of other refugees, they made their way back to Poland, unaware that nothing was left of their homes or of the Jews who hadn't managed to flee. It was on one of the freight train's stops, somewhere in Ukraine, that Meir was born. His prospects for survival were slim in a cramped, cold freight car, but the dedicated care of his parents, plus his apparently innate physical robustness, saved him.

"My parents never spoke of that period," Dagan said. "It was as if someone had erased those years from 1939 to 1945 from the calendar. True, they survived and they saved us, but the war left them with broken spirits. They never really recovered." Only once was his father prepared to tell him about the return to their destroyed hometown. He found the valley of death where the Jews had been massacred and buried in a mass grave, and he wanted to erect a monument in their memory. He paid a Polish gentile from the village to help him. This man told him that during one of the last roundups of Jews by the Gestapo, the Germans asked him to take photographs. They had forgotten to take the film when they left the area, and the man gave it to Meir's father. When he developed it, he found that one of the pictures was of his own father, Meir's grandfather, moments before he was shot and tossed into the mass grave.

The grandfather, Dov Ehrlich, with his long beard and earlocks, and terror in his eyes, is seen kneeling in front of grinning German troops brandishing bayoneted rifles. "It suits us to think that it was the extreme fascists, the fanatics, who were the killers," he said. "The truth is otherwise: The battalion that carried out this massacre was a rear-echelon Wehrmacht unit. The fighting units were at the front. These men were lawyers and merchants, ordinary, normal people. The conclusion is terrible: You can take anyone and turn him into a murderer." Dagan's second lesson was even more essential: "Let's admit the truth: Most of the Jews in the Holocaust died without fighting. We must never reach that situation again, kneeling, without the ability to fight for our lives."

After five years in Poland, during which Meir learned the language, which he used decades later as director of the Mossad to break the ice in meetings with Polish counterparts, the family made its way to Italy, where they boarded a cattle ship that had been adapted to carry immigrants to Israel. A friend who was with Dagan on the boat says that even then, in miserable, overcrowded conditions, Dagan "behaved as if he was born to be a soldier." On the way, the ship was almost sunk by a storm, and Meir faced death once again, waiting on the deck, wearing a life belt and clutching an orange. That was what he remembered: the fruit in his hand. "There, on board the ship, was the first time I tasted oranges," he said, "and I remember the tremendous pride with which my father gave me the fruit, saying it was from the Land of Israel."

After a month at sea they reached Haifa. There, Jewish Agency officials sent the passengers to a transit camp, where they slept in rickety tents, and then on to temporary housing in an evacuated British Army camp near Lod. Six families lived in each room, with only a curtain separating them. There was one shower per barrack. Beyond the difficult living arrangements, the immigrants had to contend with the humiliating attitude of the veterans. The sabras, as the native-born Israelis were called, treated the Jewish refugees with contempt. Instead of fighting back against the Nazis, the sabras charged, the Jews of Europe had filed quietly into the gas chambers, like lambs to the slaughter.

Dagan dropped out of high school at the age of seventeen and enlisted in Sayeret Matkal, the elite force that carried out secret missions over enemy lines (and was also the forge from which many of Israel's later military and civilian leaders emerged). Of the thirty IDF recruits who volunteered for Sayeret Matkal in August 1963, only fourteen completed the grueling seventy-five-week training program. One of those who began the course with Dagan was Danny Yatom, who would later serve in a number of senior IDF positions and as Mossad chief—one of Dagan's predecessors. Yatom remembered being alarmed when he first encountered Dagan. "He'd whip out his commando knife and chuck it at every tree trunk or telephone pole," he said. "I thought to myself that I'd gotten to a unit of real killers— and that maybe I had no chance of surviving in such a place." Yatom made the cut, but Dagan didn't. "In retrospect," Dagan said, "and this is just my guess, I think I really did not fit in there. Not a sabra. Not a kibbutznik. Not from the Valley"—the Jezreel Valley, east of Haifa, site of many kibbutzim, whence hailed a high proportion of Sayeret recruits. "They thought to themselves, 'Who's this odd stranger trying to push in among us?'"

Dagan was assigned to the paratroopers and served in the brigade recon unit. He underwent an infantry officer's course and was discharged with the rank of lieutenant in 1966. In the Six-Day War, he was called up for reserve duty and served as the commander of a paratroop company. He fought first in Sinai and then on the Golan Heights.

"Suddenly we found ourselves in an unbroken string of wars," he says. "Where did I get the feeling that Israel's existence is not ensured? Only via my feet; only through all these battles." After the Six-Day War, he signed up again for the regular army and was posted to Sinai as an operations officer, where Sharon first encountered him and his bravery, defusing the Katyushas.

In 1969, he became commander of Sharon's new special-ops unit. It was a small force, 150 soldiers at its height, and highly secret, acknowledged in internal IDF documents only as Number 5176. Unofficially, it was known as Sayeret Rimon—the Grenade Rangers—because its insignia featured a hand grenade, a knife, and paratrooper wings. For a base, Dagan took over an abandoned villa on the beach, just south of Gaza City, that had once been used by Egypt's President Nasser.

Dagan "had a serious malfunction in his fear mechanism," one of his soldiers said. He was, by all accounts, exceptionally bold, focused, and aggressive. Suitably enough, then, his new force had few of the attributes usually associated with a military unit. It was free, wild, interested in only one thing: carrying out as many operations as possible. Every morning, Dagan would emerge, bare-chested, from his bedroom and head out to the yard, accompanied by his Doberman, Paco. He'd draw his pistol and take potshots at the soda cans his men had left scattered around the grounds. A team of aides would then make him breakfast and polish his boots. Dagan chose his soldiers personally, culling them from other units, looking for men who were willing to follow wherever he led.

Still in his mid-twenties, Dagan began to develop his battle doctrine, which is strikingly similar to the one the IDF and Israel's espionage agencies still follow today. The guiding principle of the doctrine was that Israel should avoid large wars, because "the great, speedy victory of the Six-Day War will never happen again." Going forward, he argued, Israel should not enter a full-scale military confrontation "unless the sword is at our throats." Instead, he believed, the Arabs could be beaten in a series of limited pinpoint engagements. Accordingly, enemy leaders and important field operatives should be pursued mercilessly, hunted down, and eliminated.

TOWARD THE END OF 1969, after about half a year of recruiting, training, and building his unit, Dagan decided it was time to go into the field. The Shin Bet handed over to him a file of wanted men in the Gaza Strip. "But the leaflet was only getting bigger," said Avigdor Eldan, one of the first recruits of the new unit. The Shin Bet might have known who it was looking for, but with the agency's shortage of firepower, it couldn't get its hands on them. The file contained more than four hundred names.

The Shin Bet divided the wanted list into two categories. "Black" targets were mostly minor operatives who did not know they were wanted for interrogation. Dagan's men tried to sweep these targets up with what he called "identification recon" missions. A captured PLO "black" operative would be interrogated by the Shin Bet and, if he refused to cooperate, tortured. He'd then be put into a taxi, squeezed between two of Dagan's men, who were armed with pistols, and told to point out hiding places, families that aided the PLO, routes that militants took, and more. Grenade Rangers following in jeeps acted immediately on the information divulged, arresting anyone the informer pointed out.

"Red" targets, on the other hand, knew they were wanted, which meant they were much more wary, already on the run, and usually heavily armed. Eliminating reds generally required getting close enough to draw quickly and kill. Accordingly, Dagan sent his best men deep into Gaza's neighborhoods, dressed as Arabs and accompanied by Palestinian collaborators, who gave them convincing cover.

This group, set up together with the Shin Bet, was code-named Zikit (Chameleon). Eight elite combat soldiers were selected to begin with. Project Chameleon was so secret that at first, "we didn't know what they were training us for," said Eldan. "All we knew was they tore our asses, and don't forget we were already fighting fit when we got there."

The Chameleons carried forged local papers supplied by the Shin Bet. They were able to sneak into the heart of heavily populated areas without being spotted until they drew their guns.

"We exploited the main weak point of these terror cells," Dagan said. "Because of their Marxist background, they practiced a very high level of 'need to know' compartmentalization. Each man knew only the members of his own cell and not those of other cells. If you appear as an armed local, and you can speak the target's language, he has no way of knowing that it is in fact a trick until it is too late."

For example, said Moshe Rubin, a veteran member of the unit, "We realized the terrorist organizations were getting their weapons and money via ships from Lebanon. They would sail in a mother ship from Beirut and, far out to sea, off the Gaza coast, get into small fishing boats and make for the shore. We said to ourselves, 'Why shouldn't we also arrive in a ship from Lebanon?'"

So, in November 1970, six Chameleon men boarded a fishing boat, which the Israeli Navy towed to a point off the Gaza coast.

The team included three Jewish IDF soldiers, headed by Dagan. They were joined by two Palestinian collaborators, one of whom had escaped from the massacre of PLO men that King Hussein of Jordan had carried out two months prior and was grateful to the Israelis for saving him. The other, code-named Submarine, had murdered a relative by thrusting a dagger into his skull and had been released by the Shin Bet in exchange for his cooperation. The final member was an Israeli Bedouin IDF officer whose job was to monitor the transmissions of the microphones carried by the Palestinians, who were meant to go ahead of the others and establish contact with the wanted men and then let the others know what was happening. The Bedouin had another task as well: to inform Dagan if the two Palestinians intended to betray him.

The Chameleon squad reached the beach and hid in the abandoned packing shed of an orchard for a number of days, with the collaborators making occasional ventures out to surrounding refugee camps. They claimed that they were members of the Popular Front for the Liberation of Palestine who had come from Lebanon.

At first, no one came. "They were scared of us—not because they thought we were Israelis, but because they were convinced we were PLO men," a member of the unit recalled. "The wanted terrorists were not always very nice to the local population. They would often extort them, demanding more and more food and raping the women. In the citrus groves, we often found bodies of Arabs who weren't killed by us, but by the wanted men, who settled personal accounts under the pretext of executing collaborators with Israel."

In a staged operation to establish credibility, the group was "discovered" by an IDF patrol that opened fire and pretended to give chase. Dagan and his men fled to an area of sand dunes south of the Beit Lahia refugee camp.

The engagement aroused the interest of the locals. "Submarine" managed to set up a meeting between the Chameleons and a woman who was known to be linked to senior wanted Popular Front members. The Chameleons killed a chicken and smeared its blood onto bandages that they wrapped around their throats, to explain why they couldn't talk, and left the speaking up to the collaborator. "We have come to help you," he told the woman. "Bring the top commanders to the dunes."

After a day, the terrorists showed up. "There were three of them—two men and a woman, armed, top commanders," Dagan recalled. After exchanging salutations, Dagan whispered the code word. The three soldiers opened fire at point-blank range with the 9-millimeter Beretta pistols they were carrying, killing the two men. They were each hit fifteen to twenty times.

"The woman wasn't hit," said Dagan with satisfaction.

Eldan recalled that "then Meir slid rapidly down the high dune we were on towards them, and took the Star pistol one of them had managed to draw and had used to fire at us, and carried out 'dead-checking'—another two bullets in the head of each of the men." Dagan took the Star for himself and gave the holster to Eldan.

Then they took the woman with them and handed her over to the Shin Bet for interrogation.

ON A WARM SATURDAY morning in early January 1971, a thirty-year-old advertising executive named Bob Aroyo took his family for a hike in the hills overlooking the Bardawil Lagoon, on the Mediterranean coast of the Sinai Peninsula. Born in Malta and raised in England, Aroyo had moved to Israel in 1969 with his wife, Preeti, and their two children, Mark and Abigail, and settled into a small suburb east of Tel Aviv. The kids were still young—Mark was seven, Abigail five—so Aroyo planned a short, gentle hike; they'd drive south for a day in the sun and fresh air, then head home for an early dinner. Both children were strikingly beautiful, and their faces were familiar sights in Israel, because their father used them in some of the advertisements he designed.

By 3 P.M. the Aroyos had finished their hike and climbed back into their Ford Cortina, bound for home. They drove north through Al-Arish before entering the Gaza Strip, where they passed Palestinian villages and refugee camps along the main highway. At that time, Israelis heading for Sinai would still often drive through the Strip, as it was the shortest and easiest route, and until then had been quite safe.

Just north of the city of Gaza, near a 7Up factory, they were stopped at a makeshift roadblock. A young teenager ran up to the car and tossed a hand grenade into the backseat. The explosion blew out most of the interior of the car, which erupted in a fireball. Aroyo, wounded, crawled out and begged two young men standing nearby to call for help. But they just laughed and jeered. Abigail died in the car. Mark died in the hospital. Preeti's wounds left her severely handicapped for the rest of her life. Two days later, the Aroyo children were buried in a single grave in Jerusalem's ancient cemetery on the Mount of Olives, in a ceremony attended by tens of thousands of

Israelis. The chief chaplain of the IDF, Major General Rabbi Shlomo Goren, offered a eulogy. All of Israel mourned.

Two weeks later, the Shin Bet captured the perpetrators. The kid who had lobbed the grenade was a fifteen-year-old named Mohammad Suleiman al-Zaki, from Gaza's Shuja'iyya neighborhood; his two accomplices were sixteen and seventeen. All three were students at the city's Falastin High School who had been recruited for the operation by a senior Fatah operative. The attack on the Aroyo family had not been their first mission.

The murder of Mark and Abigail Aroyo marked a turning point in the response to the flood of terrorist attacks that followed the Six-Day War. "We decided that things could not go on this way," Meir Dagan said. "After those kids were murdered, Arik [Sharon] took the matter of terror in the Gaza Strip personally." Sharon was no longer content to receive reports from Dagan, though he still had full confidence in him. From that point forward, Sharon "would turn up at our villa often and get involved in the planning of our missions and patrols, down to the tiniest detail."

The Aroyo killings also effectively ended the debate inside the Israeli defense establishment about how to handle the Palestinian population in the conquered territories. Sharon's approach triumphed. Massive forces poured into the Gaza Strip and, acting under Sharon's orders, demolished houses in order to create wide access roads through the crowded refugee camps. One night in January 1972, Sharon ordered the expulsion of thousands of Bedouin from a 2,500-acre area south of Rafah. General Shlomo Gazit, who was in charge of government activities in the occupied areas, was shocked. He boiled with anger when he heard about the action the following morning, and threatened to resign. "There is no other way to describe this act than ethnic cleansing and a war crime," he later said.

Sharon was given free rein to use special forces and secret units to unearth and kill terrorists before they could strike in Israel.

Meanwhile, Dagan and his men continually devised new methods for finding and disposing of these wanted Palestinians. One tactic was to ambush them in brothels. Another was to hide in trees in the citrus groves when they knew that terrorists were planning to meet there, communicating by pulling on fishing cord stretched out between them in order to maintain absolute silence. When the terrorists turned up, they were all shot dead.

They also frequently used a Palestinian collaborator to sell booby-trapped grenades to the Palestine Liberation Army. The fuses would be clipped from the usual three-second delay to a half-second, ensuring that whoever used them would blow himself up. And on one occasion, borrowing from Operation Mincemeat, a British World War II ploy, Dagan pretended to be a corpse and was carried by his comrades—two of them Palestinian collaborators and the others disguised as Arabs—into a terrorist hideout. Once inside, they killed everyone.

A month after the Aroyo killings, on January 29, 1971, two jeeps under Dagan's command were moving down a road that ran between the Jabalia refugee camp and Gaza City. Along the way, they encountered a local cab loaded with passengers driving in the opposite direction. Dagan identified two "reds" among the passengers: Fawzi al-Ruheidi and Mohammad al-Aswad, who was also known as Abu Nimr. Dagan ordered the jeeps to turn around and chase down the cab. The jeeps caught up and blocked the road, and Dagan's soldiers jumped out and surrounded the cab. Dagan approached the vehicle with his pistol drawn. Abu Nimr jumped out, holding a hand grenade, the pin drawn. "If you get any closer," he yelled, "we'll all die!" Dagan paused for a second or two. Then he yelled "Grenade!" and charged Abu Nimr, grabbing the hand holding the grenade and butting him in the head with his helmet. Bleeding profusely, Abu Nimr lost consciousness, and Dagan calmly and carefully removed the grenade from his grip, found the pin on the ground, and reinserted it. This act of bravery won Dagan a medal from the chief of staff. It also gave Sharon occasion to coin his black-humor description of Dagan: "His greatest expertise is separating an Arab and his head."

Indeed, there is little room for argument over the effectiveness of Dagan's chosen methods. The Shin Bet and IDF special forces, led by the Grenade Rangers and inspired and backed by Sharon, essentially wiped out terrorism in the Gaza Strip between 1968 and 1972. The Palestinian organizations had no response to Dagan's tactics.

They could not figure out how the Shin Bet learned their secrets, or how Israeli soldiers in Arab guise could suddenly appear, undetected, to capture and kill their fighters. The Shin Bet's list of four hundred wanted men (to which new names were continually added) had been reduced to ten in 1972. That year, only thirty-seven terror attacks originated in the Gaza Strip, down from hundreds in each of the preceding years. That number would continue to go down in each successive year, for four years.

But there was a price to be paid for those methods, too.

Yitzhak Pundak later recalled reading a report filed by the unit that read, "Our detail was chasing a wanted terrorist in Al-Shati [a refugee camp in Gaza]. He ran into one of the houses. The unit broke in after him, disarmed him, and killed him in the house." Pundak says he drew the attention of an intelligence officer to the possibility that if such a report reached the UN or the Red Cross, it would cause an international scandal. "So what's the problem?" said the officer, according to Pundak. "Destroy the report."

Pundak took this story to Southern Command chief Sharon, and when he refused to investigate further, Pundak recalled, he told Sharon, "You are a liar, a crook, and a knave." Sharon rose and raised his hand as if to slap Pundak, but Pundak wasn't scared. "If you do that, I'll break your bones right here in your office," he said. Sharon sat down. Pundak says he saluted, declared, "Now I know you're also a coward," and left the room.

Several journalists have collected accounts from Dagan's unnamed men saying they shot people after they surrendered, their hands in the air. One was quoted as saying that he and other soldiers had apprehended a Palestinian who was wanted for murdering an IDF officer. A Shin Bet agent who was with them purportedly said the man could never be brought to trial, because the secret service would be forced in court to name the collaborator who had provided the information that led to his capture. The soldiers let their captive "escape"—and then shot him as he ran.

Another unit veteran said, "The captive would be led from the house he was captured in to a dark alley off to the side, where the soldiers would leave a pistol or grenade in a certain way that made it very tempting for him to reach out for it. When he did, they'd shoot him. Sometimes they'd tell him, 'You have two minutes to run,' and then they'd shoot him on the grounds that he'd run away."

Other former Grenade Rangers said that when it came to the list of red targets, Dagan had unilaterally annulled the IDF's rule that suspects be given a chance to surrender before being killed. Under Dagan's command, a red was a target for assassination on sight. Dagan confirms this but says it was justified: "All the allegations about us being a death squad or a gang of killers are nonsense. We were acting under combat conditions, with us and the wanted men both in civilian clothes and armed with the same weapons. There is not, and there cannot be, from my point of view, an arrest procedure for an armed man. Almost all wanted persons at that time were armed. Any man carrying a weapon—whether he is turning, running, or fleeing but still holding a weapon—you shoot him. Our goal was not to kill them, but neither was it to commit suicide. It was clear that if we did not shoot first, they'd shoot at us."

After one arrest operation, on November 29, 1972, ended with the wanted man dead, Pundak demanded that Dagan's deputy, Shmuel Paz, be court-martialed. In the trial, it was reported that Paz had fired from a distance at the man, who was carrying a rifle, and he fell. Paz advanced toward him, firing the whole time to make sure he was dead. "And what exactly would you want me to do?" Paz asked. "The fact that the man fell does not mean that he is not putting on an act or that he's only wounded and still able to fire at us. There's no other way to act in such a situation," Dagan said.

Paz was given the benefit of the doubt and was acquitted. All the other complaints, rumors, testimonies—to say nothing of the many dead bodies—were swept into a closet, locked tightly to prevent any outside inquiry.

Without doubt, Dagan's unit was ruthless, and it operated under its own rules. One can reasonably argue that this was the beginning of an extrajudicial legal system parallel to criminal law in Israel, a system that developed quietly and in total secrecy. Dagan's unit was, for the first time, eliminating people in territory controlled by Israel, instead of arresting and prosecuting them, as required by international law. "In order to protect its citizens," Dagan said, "the state must sometimes perform actions that run counter to democracy."

All of this was embraced by the Israeli civil authorities, even as they ostensibly turned a blind eye. What the state's leaders wanted most of all was quiet in the conquered territories. That quiet allowed Israeli governments to enjoy cheap Palestinian labor and cheap imports from the territories, as well as a market for exports—an important matter for a country surrounded by hostile states with which it had no trade relations.

Moreover, it enabled the construction of Jewish settlements in the occupied territories. Right-wing Israelis believe that Israel must hold on to the areas that it conquered in 1967, in order to maintain the strategic advantage. In addition, many religious Jews believe that the conquest of biblical Judea and Samaria was an act of divine intervention, restoring the nation to its historical homeland and hastening the coming of the Messiah. Both of these groups hoped that establishing as many settlements as possible would forestall the establishment of a Palestinian state in the future.

In the absence of terror attacks, the political echelon interpreted the quiet achieved by the Shin Bet and the IDF as a complete victory and a vindication, as if history had come to a halt and there was no need to come to grips with the Palestinian question.

# THE PLO GOES INTERNATIONAL

AT 10:31 P.M. GMT on July 23, 1968, El Al Flight 426 took off from Rome's Leonardo da Vinci–Fiumicino Airport. A Boeing 707 with thirty-eight passengers, twelve of them Israelis, and ten Israeli crew members, the aircraft was scheduled to land in Tel Aviv at 1:18.

About twenty minutes after takeoff, one of three Palestinian terrorists on board barged into the cockpit. Initially, the pilots thought the man was drunk and asked a stewardess to remove him, but he pulled out a pistol. The copilot, Maoz Porat, hit the man's hand, hoping he would drop the pistol. He did not. The terrorist hit Porat on the head with his gun and wounded him, then fired a shot at him but missed. He pulled out a hand grenade, but the plane's captain reacted quickly and told him he would land the plane wherever he chose. At 11:07, the control tower in Rome received a message saying that the plane, then at an altitude of 33,000 feet, was changing its course and heading for Algiers, where it landed at thirty-five minutes after midnight, with the consent of the Algerian authorities. On the way, the hijackers broadcast to whoever was listening that they were changing the aircraft's call sign to Palestine Liberation 707.

Upon arrival, all non-Israelis, as well as all the women and children, were released. The remaining seven crew members and five passengers were held hostage at a facility of the Algerian security police close to the airport, where they were imprisoned for three weeks, until they were released in exchange for twenty-four of their counterparts in Israeli jails.

The seizure of Flight 426 was a stunningly audacious assault by a new faction, the Popular Front for the Liberation of Palestine. The PFLP had been founded the previous December in Damascus by two refugees, George Habash, from Lydda, and Wadie Haddad, from Safed—both pediatricians, Marxists, and Orthodox Christians. In one swift blow, the PFLP had won a short-term tactical and strategic victory, demonstrating that it had the terrifying capability to seize an Israeli civilian airliner and publicizing the Palestinian cause through-out the world. It also forced Jerusalem to negotiate with an organiza-tion it refused to recognize, a humiliating concession. Worse still, Israel was forced, in the end, to agree to a prisoner swap, an indignity it had declared would never happen.

But Flight 426 was merely a prelude. Though relentless efforts by the IDF and Shin Bet were making militant attacks inside and along Israel's borders increasingly difficult, Arafat and his followers—an endless array of splinter groups and sub-factions he could acknowl-edge or disown, depending on his momentary needs—realized the world offered a much bigger stage than the Gaza Strip or the West Bank.

Terror could erupt anywhere. And Western Europe was thoroughly unprepared to stop it: Borders were porous, barriers at airports and seaports were easily dodged, police forces were flaccid and impotent. Leftist student movements nurtured an empathy with Marxist-leaning Palestinians, and Europe's own radicals—the Baader-Meinhof Gang in Germany, for instance, or the Red Brigades in Italy—offered logis-tical as well as operational cooperation.

All of this posed an enormous challenge for Israel's intelligence community. As long as the Palestinian problem had been confined to the territories Israel occupied following the Six-Day War, things were relatively simple. But now the whole wide world was the front line, with Jews—and especially Israelis—the targets.

A LITTLE MORE THAN a year after the Flight 426 debacle, TWA Flight 840 took off from Los Angeles for Tel Aviv with 120 passengers—only six of them Israelis—and seven crew members. It stopped in New York, then landed in Rome to refuel. Half an hour after taking off for its last layover, in Athens, four Palestinians who'd boarded the plane in Rome went into action. One of them forced a stewardess at gunpoint to open the door to the cockpit. The copilot, Harry Oakley, was amazed to see that behind the man there was a woman, a grenade in her hand.

"She was very fashionably dressed, all in white," recalled Margareta Johnson, an air hostess on the flight. "A white floppy hat, white tunic, and white trousers." The "not unattractive lady," as one of the male stewards described her, ordered the captain to redirect the plane to fly over Haifa, saying it was her birthplace, which the Zionists would not allow her to return to.

Leila Khaled was indeed born in Haifa in 1944. After the Jewish victory in the bitter battle for that port city, her family fled to Lebanon, intending to return when the dust of war settled. But the newly established State of Israel barred the return of refugees, and Khaled grew up in an overcrowded refugee camp in Tyre, in southern Lebanon. She developed an acute political awareness, and by the age of fifteen she already was a member of the Jordanian branch of a pan-Arabic secular socialist movement headed by the later co-founder of the PFLP George Habash.

TWA 840 was not Khaled's first assault on civil aviation. On February 18, 1969, she had helped plan an attack against an El Al Boeing 707 as it was about to take off from Zurich airport. Four Popular Front members, tossing hand grenades and firing AK-47s, charged the plane from the tarmac, spraying the cockpit with bullets and fatally wounding the copilot. She also was involved, either directly or behind the scenes, in several other attacks. But the hijacking of TWA 840 made her famous.

After the demonstrative flight over Israel, escorted by Israeli Air Force fighters that could do nothing, for fear of harming the passengers, the plane landed safely in Damascus, where all the passengers and crew were released, with the exception of two Israelis who were held hostage for three months and then released in exchange for Syrian soldiers. The hijackers blew the nose off the empty plane and were spirited away to safety by Syrian intelligence.

Khaled, meanwhile, became a symbol of the era, the best-known female terrorist in the world. She was profiled in hundreds of articles and heralded in songs of praise for freedom fighters. Her picture appeared on posters, the most iconic of which featured her clutching an AK-47, black mane flowing from beneath her kaffiyeh, a striking ring on her finger. "I made it from a bullet and the pin of a hand grenade," she said.

On September 6, 1970, Khaled and her colleagues attempted to hijack an El Al flight out of Europe, but they failed. The captain, Uri Bar-Lev, a former Israeli Air Force fighter pilot, put the plane into a sudden dive, creating a negative g-force and flinging the hijackers to the floor. An undercover Shin Bet man shot and killed Khaled's partner, while another one came from inside the cockpit and overpowered her. She was handed over to the police in London when the plane landed.

But four other Popular Front squads were more successful, hijacking Pan Am, Swissair, and TWA planes that day (and, three days later, a BOAC plane), landing them in Jordan, and demanding the release of Khaled and many of her comrades.

The passengers were released, except for the fifty-five Jews and a male crew member, who were taken to a Palestinian neighborhood in Amman. The hijackers blew up the empty planes as television cameras broadcast the images to the world. The media called it "the blackest day in aviation history."

It also was a black day for Jordan's King Hussein, who was depicted in the international media as an inept monarch who had lost control of his kingdom. The Palestinians constituted a majority of the Jordanian population, and Hussein feared, justifiably, that the appetites of Arafat and his henchmen, who were behaving as if the country belonged to them, were growing and that they were planning to rob him of his kingdom. After the global embarrassment of the hijacked planes and an attempt on the king's life by a Palestinian cell, his retaliation was swift and severe. In mid-September, he ordered the Jordanian army, police, and intelligence services to launch a brutal attack against Arafat's people, massacring them indiscriminately. In a series of operations during a month that the Palestinians dubbed "Black September," thousands of Palestinians were killed, and the PLO was forced to relocate to Lebanon, where what remained of its decimated leadership began rebuilding.

Fatah and its factions soon regrouped and let loose a savage wave of international terror. The point, explained Bassam Abu Sharif, of the PFLP, was "to show that the expulsion from Jordan had not weakened us at all."

On November 28, 1971, just over a year after Jordanian prime minister Wasfi al-Tal ordered the assault on the Palestinians, he was shot dead in Cairo. Two weeks later, a group of gunmen tried to kill the Jordanian ambassador to Great Britain, Zaid al-Rifai. Two months after that, Palestinians executed five Jordanian citizens in Germany, supposedly for collaborating with Israel, and then bombed the offices of a Dutch gas company and a German electronics firm, accusing them of trading with Israel.

All of those attacks were carried out by a hitherto unknown organization called Ailool al-Aswad—Arabic for "Black September," so named to memorialize the massacre in Jordan. The name may have been new, but this was not a new organization. The Mossad quickly discovered that Black September was another of the ever-evolving Fatah factions, led by Salah Khalaf (nom de guerre: Abu Iyad), the former commander of Rassed, the PLO's intelligence branch, who was trying to maintain his terrorist standing amid recurring infighting. In order to act against a wider range of targets, Khalaf redefined the enemies of the Palestinian people, beginning with "U.S. imperialism, passing through the Arab regimes tied to it, and ending with Israel."

On May 8, 1972, four terrorists—three from Black September and one from PFLP—hijacked a Sabena airliner carrying ninety-four passengers and seven crew members from Brussels to Tel Aviv. More than half of the passengers were Israelis or Jews. When the plane landed at Lod (now Ben-Gurion) Airport, the hijackers demanded that 315 of their terrorist comrades imprisoned in Israel be released.

Two different response plans were presented to Defense Minister Moshe Dayan. Meir Dagan and members of the Chameleon unit suggested that they shave their heads and pose as Arab prisoners, mingle with the other newly freed prisoners, and board the plane with them, then, once the hostages were safe, draw their concealed weapons and wipe out the terrorists—and, as Dagan proposed to the high command, "also the freed prisoners, if necessary."

Dayan preferred the plan put forward by Ehud Barak, the commander of the Sayeret Matkal commando unit. Barak and his team approached the hijacked airplane in the guise of an airport ground crew, dressed in white overalls and carrying concealed Beretta .22 pistols. They then stormed the plane and killed or wounded all of the terrorists. A female passenger was killed in the firefight, and two others were injured. A young soldier by the name of Benjamin Netanyahu was also slightly wounded by a bullet fired by one of the other raiders.

The Sabena operation assumed mythic proportions in Israel. But despite its success, the Palestinians' main strategic aim was achieved as well. "For an entire day," a Black September commander said, "revolutionaries all over the world held their breath to see what would happen at the airport in occupied Palestine. The whole world was watching."

Many of those revolutionaries soon rallied to the Palestinian cause. The new wave of terrorist activity elicited a huge surge in applications to join the underground organizations. According to one member of Black September, nearly all of these applications contained some variation of the phrase "At last you have found a way of making our voice heard in the world."

These new recruits were used to devastating effect. On May 30, 1972, three members of the Japanese Red Army, underground leftists who'd been trained by the PFLP in North Korea and Lebanon, flew aboard an Air France flight from Rome to Lod Airport. Inside the Popular Front, there was some doubt whether their Maoist ideology was compatible with the Front's Marxism, but the Palestinians were impressed by the readiness of the Japanese—or, more correctly, their ardent desire—to die for the cause.

They attracted no attention at the airport. The screeners that the Shin Bet had posted around El Al counters were on the lookout for nervous Middle Easterners, not Asian tourists.

The three Japanese men pulled AK-47s and hand grenades from their baggage and began firing indiscriminately into the crowded terminal. "I saw twenty-five people piled up in a pool of blood near conveyor belt number three," one witness recalled. "One [man] stood near the belt with a submachine gun and fired across the entire length of the room. Another lobbed hand grenades whenever he saw people in large groups."

The sounds of ambulances filled the streets of Tel Aviv for hours. Twenty-six people, seventeen of whom were Puerto Rican Christian pilgrims to the Holy Land, were dead, and seventy-eight were wounded.

In a press conference in Beirut, Bassam Zayed, the PFLP spokesman (and the husband of Leila Khaled), defended the massacre of the pilgrims, declaring that it was the Front's contention that there were no innocents—that all were guilty, if only because they had not "raised a finger for the Palestinians." A feeling of bitter remorse permeated the Israeli defense establishment over the failure to prevent the massacre.

THROUGHOUT THIS NEW WAVE of terror, Israel struggled to come up with an adequate response. Initially, in the absence of any definitive intelligence, Prime Minister Levi Eshkol ordered a punitive operation against a relatively easy target: Arab civil aviation. This was based on the argument that the Arab regimes that controlled these airlines were responsible for what was happening and were backing the PLO.

In December 1968, a task force raided the international airport in Beirut and blew up fourteen empty planes belonging to Middle East Airlines, Lebanese International Airways, and Trans Mediterranean Airways. The operation succeeded in that it destroyed the planes without Israeli casualties, but it had no real impact on deterring future terrorist attacks on Israeli civil aviation. And the international reaction to the Israeli raid against civilian targets was fierce. On top of a UN Security Council condemnation, French president de Gaulle tightened his country's weapons embargo on Israel, canceling the sale of fifty fighter jets.

Further failures would follow. Intelligence information obtained by Junction identified a certain office in Beirut as the PLO headquarters in the city. On February 2, 1970, Caesarea operatives fired four RPG rockets from launchers fitted with timers into the windows of the offices. It turned out that the premises filled mainly an administrative function. "Some secretaries were wounded and some papers burned," a Caesarea operative said, but that was about it. This was one of the first counterterror operations approved by Israel's new prime minister, the redoubtable, hawkish Golda Meir, who had taken over the premiership after Levi Eshkol died, in February 1969.

Attempts to kill the founders of the PFLP were no more successful. Two Caesarea operatives were able to obtain the address of the apartment at 8 Muhi al-Din Street, in Beirut, that Wadie Haddad had used as both an office and a residence. "Haddad behaved like the lord of the manor in Beirut. There was no problem finding him—he wasn't scared and he took no precautions," said Zvi Aharoni, head of Caesarea. On July 10, Israeli naval commandos (Unit 707) debarked from a missile boat and landed on the beach near the Beirut Casino in a rubber dinghy and delivered two grenade launchers to the Caesarea assassins, who had rented an apartment opposite Haddad's. At 9 A.M., one of them aimed the rockets at the window of a room where he'd seen Haddad sitting, pressed the button on the timer, which was set at thirty seconds, and fled the scene.

"But what can you do," said Mike Harari. "Just then Haddad stepped into the other room, where his wife and kids were sitting, and he survived. Golda had ordered that not a hair on any innocent head should be harmed, otherwise we would have 'shaved' the whole floor."

Meanwhile, an Israeli agent in Lebanon located George Habash's villa at Bsaba, a mountainous area southeast of Beirut. He even photographed Habash sitting on his porch with some of his men. On July 15, an Israeli Air Force offensive was dispatched to bomb the house, but it struck and demolished a neighboring home instead. Habash escaped unharmed.

Shortly afterward, Aharoni resigned as head of Caesarea, partly due to the criticism leveled at him for not eliminating the terrorist chiefs. He was succeeded by Mike Harari.

Harari went straight for the top target: Yasser Arafat. Operation White Desert was Harari's plan to assassinate the PLO leader at a celebration for Colonel Muammar Qaddafi in Libya on September 1, 1970. A VIP platform was constructed adjoining the wall of the old city of Tripoli, the capital. Several ideas were put forward in Caesarea: placing a mortar connected to a timer on the other side of the wall and then shelling the platform, where Arafat and other leaders would be seated, or placing explosives underneath the platform and detonating them after obtaining confirmation that Arafat was there. "Eventually we reached the conclusion that this was a problematic operation, because, along with Arafat, another 120 souls would be dispatched skyward. So we decided to go with a sniper." Harari and his crew traveled to Libya a number of times to scout out the scene, rent safe houses, and plan escape routes.

Everything was ready to go when Mossad director Zvi Zamir brought the plan to Prime Minister Golda Meir for her final approval. But she feared that the operation would be pinned on Israel and would lead to severe international criticism and attempts to assassinate Israeli leaders. The plan was scrapped.

Disappointed, Harari sent two operatives to Europe, with orders to reactivate the letter-bomb setup. These bombs "had two clear advantages," Moti Kfir said. "They were easy to deliver to the target countries, because they looked harmless, and they provided a long getaway time—unlike gunfire, which attracts immediate attention." The Israelis did manage to maim a couple of militants with these bombs, but it wasn't long before PLO personnel learned to be more careful with their mail.

Fatah and its offshoots remained undeterred. And the Mossad's primary targets—Arafat, Abu Jihad, Habash, Haddad—remained alive, healthy, and a perpetual menace.

In closed meetings of the Israeli leadership, fingers were pointed at the intelligence community for having failed to stop terrorist attacks or to deter future attacks. "When a bus blew up in Jerusalem, they looked at me," said Harari. "Why don't I blow up four buses in Beirut or Cairo? After all, whatever they did here in Israel we could have done to them in Cairo, Damascus, Amman, or wherever anyone wanted. I could have done it simultaneously. But I was not prepared to do that sort of operation, to sink to their level. We weren't all that desperate. We looked for the selective strike, ones that the terrorists would know was Israeli but wouldn't leave any fingerprints."

In order to do that, Harari would have to overcome two significant obstacles. First, all the terrorist organizations' headquarters were located in the capitals of Arab states, which gave them asylum in places where it was very difficult for Caesarea to operate. Second, Caesarea's men at that time were simply not suited to the task. James Bond films and their ilk tend to portray spies as a homogenous lot—the same person can be a mole, an assassin, a break-in artist, and a surveillance expert, both gathering intelligence and analyzing it for the decision-makers. Reality, especially in the Mossad, is very different. Caesarea's operatives had been trained to carry out long-term assignments under deep cover. They were supposed to attract as little attention as possible, to have as little friction as possible with local actors, and to gather as much information as they could, so that Israel would have advance notice of any forthcoming war. "My people were not commandos," Harari said. "I would look for someone who could spend time in Cairo as an archaeologist and invite Nasser on a tour of his digs, or a woman who could serve as a nurse in a military hospital in Damascus. These people didn't have the training to take out a sentry, to draw a pistol or to throw a knife. In order to fight terror, I needed different people and other kinds of weaponry."

The PLO's transition into global activity also created a political challenge for the Israelis. European countries did not combat terror themselves during those years, and they didn't allow the Israelis to do so within their borders, either. The Europeans viewed the Middle East conflict as remote and inconsequential, and had no incentive to act. The Mossad gathered hundreds of tips about planned terror operations against Israeli and Jewish targets in Europe, but to deal with them, it needed the assistance of friendly European intelligence services. "We inform them of it once, twice, three times, or five times," Golda Meir explained at a secret meeting of the Knesset's Foreign Affairs and Defense Committee, "and nothing happens."

Frustration was building within the Mossad. "I don't get why we sit here quietly while, every day, terrorists are plotting how to kill Jews," Avraham "Romi" Porat, the intelligence officer of Caesarea, complained during a meeting in Mossad HQ. "We know where they are. Their offices in Germany and France and Italy and Cyprus are public knowledge. They don't even try to hide. Let's blow up one of their offices for every plane hijacking, and 'the land shall have rest for forty years,'" he said, quoting the Bible's book of Judges.

Harari's solution was to set up a special team within Caesarea that wasn't tasked with gathering intelligence prior to hostilities but rather was focused on "operating covertly and carrying out identification, surveillance, and execution of human targets and sabotage operations." The unit would be code-named Kidon (Bayonet), and it would function mainly in Western Europe and in democratic countries elsewhere.

The nucleus of Bayonet actually first began to take shape in mid-1969, under the command of an operative named Danny, but for many years Harari could not employ it in the field and had to limit its activities just to training and to working out a combat doctrine. Golda Meir, though wary of Western countries, nevertheless respected their sovereignty. She understood that otherwise friendly nations would never cooperate with Israel if it carried out targeted killings in their territory without their permission. In her words, European intelligence services "can decide what is permissible and what is forbidden on their territory. . . . There are friendly countries that say, 'You won't do it here; here we are the masters.' All of this is not simple. It's not our country."

Harari, who was convinced that Meir would eventually change her mind, quietly ordered Bayonet to continue its training. "In the end," Harari told Zamir, "we'll have no alternative but to kill them in Europe." Zamir agreed that training should be continued. "We respected the prime minister's policy, and therefore we only made information-gathering efforts, and prepared the personnel and the weaponry that would be required in the future."

This regimen of training and preparation was arduous. Recruits had to be adept at rapid movement, driving cars or motorbikes, tailing and getting rid of tails, breaking into buildings, and hand-to-hand combat. They also had to be able to function calmly under a variety of combat conditions. They were drilled in pistol marksmanship, with an emphasis on a method known as instinct shooting. Developed in part by a U.S. Army veteran named Dave Beckerman, who had helped liberate Dachau, it is based on speedy movement from rest to a firing position or attaining maximum accuracy while firing on the move.

Then recruits needed training in one more skill: makeup. Because most Bayonet missions would be short-term, various disguises could be used in order to change identities. According to Yarin Shahaf, who currently trains Mossad operatives in the craft of makeup, this is a complicated task: "You have to make sure that the mustache won't fall off even in a fight and that the wig fits and won't fly off even in a chase over rooftops. The warrior has to know how to put it on so that it looks believable, and also to clean himself up quickly if he has to escape."

Finally, a recruit would undergo one last test. The agency would send him home, to his own neighborhood and his own social circle, in disguise and with his alias. If he could circulate there, among those who knew him best, without being identified, he was deemed capable of operating in a hostile nation of strangers.

IN EARLY JULY 1972, eight members of Black September arrived at a training camp in the Libyan desert commanded by Muhammad Youssef al-Najjar, chief of the security-and-information apparatus of Fatah. The eight had all been Fatah activists and were chosen for a variety of reasons. Some had extensive combat experience. Others were familiar with Europe in general and Germany more specifically. Among these men was Mohammed Massalha, born in 1945, the son of the first head of the council of the Galilee village of Daburiyya. Fluent in both German and English and older than the others, he wasn't a fighter but rather served as the ideologue and spokesman for the group. The voice and figure of Massalha, who was given the code name Issa, would soon become famous all over the world.

In the Libyan camp, the eight men were met by Salah Khalaf (Abu Iyad), the founder of Black September, and Mohammed Oudeh (Abu Daoud), a longtime Fatah operative who was a trustworthy and capable confidant of Abu Iyad's. The latter informed them that they were about to take part in a highly important operation, without revealing precisely what that operation was. For the next few weeks the group underwent training in firearms, including pistols, submachine guns, and grenades, as well as hand-to-hand combat and fitness.

Special stress was placed on disguise. They were given code names and forged Libyan passports and were instructed to hide their faces throughout the operation and to change their clothing frequently, in order to give those watching them the impression that there were many more members of the group.

Israeli intelligence completely missed these preparations in Libya. On July 7, a Palestinain agent code-named Lucifer warned the Mossad that "Black September is planning an attack in Europe," and he reported on August 5 that "Black September is preparing an operation of an international nature." But he had no details. And so many terror alerts and tips were flooding the Mossad's research department that, inevitably, more than a few were overlooked. Lucifer's was among those that fell through the cracks.

On September 3 and 4, the eight Black September militants took separate flights into West Germany. They rendezvoused in Munich, where the 1972 Olympic Games were under way, watched by hundreds of millions of people around the world. The PLO, on behalf of the stateless Palestinians, had asked to participate but had been turned down by the International Olympic Committee. "Apparently, from the point of view of this reputable body, which pretends to be apolitical, we didn't exist," Khalaf said later. "The leadership of Black September decided to take things into its own hands."

On the eve of the operation, at a restaurant near the Munich railroad station, Oudeh finally told them the plan. The eight men drew up a joint last will and testament and joined Oudeh to collect weapons and explosives that had been smuggled in from Spain and Sweden and hidden in a locker at the railroad station. Oudeh collected their passports and sent them to gate number A25 of the Olympic Village. They easily climbed over the fence and walked to Connollystrasse 31, where the Israeli delegation to the Games was housed. At the time, there were thirty-two policemen in the village—two with handguns but the rest unarmed, because the German hosts wanted to create as peaceful and pacifistic an atmosphere as possible. None of them noticed what was happening.

At about 4 A.M. on September 5, Black September stormed the Israeli team's quarters. One of the athletes managed to escape. A wrestling coach, Moshe Weinberg, and a weight lifter, Yossef Romano, tried to resist the terrorists but were shot and killed. Their bodies were left lying on the floor for the next nine hours, in full view of the nine other members of the team, who were held hostage. Signs of severe mutilation were later found on Romano's corpse.

Massalha (Issa) conducted negotiations with representatives of the Bavarian state police and government as hundreds of millions of viewers across the globe looked on. That morning in Jerusalem, Golda Meir somberly informed the Knesset, "The murderers are demanding the release of two hundred terrorists from Israeli prisons in exchange for the release of the hostages."

As she had done in every case during her term as prime minister, Meir relied upon the judgment of the defense and intelligence establishments, with only one unequivocal stipulation: There would be no negotiations with terrorists, not under any circumstances.

The Germans firmly refused to halt the Games, contending that West German TV has no alternative programming. "Incredibly, they're going on with it," Jim Murray of the *Los Angeles Times* wrote. "It's almost like having a dance at Dachau."


A SAYERET MATKAL TEAM immediately began preparing a rescue operation. To Israel's astonishment, though, the Germans—far less experienced in such matters—refused to allow the Israelis into the country. Two senior officials—Mossad chief Zvi Zamir and the chief of the Shin Bet interrogation department, Victor Cohen—were permitted to observe the negotiation only from a distance.

Cohen, a native of Syria and a fluent Arabic speaker with a great deal of experience interrogating terrorists, was the man who had negotiated with the Black September hijackers of the Sabena jet. "In the Sabena affair, they let me work properly," Cohen recalled. "From the conversations with the hijackers I was able to learn a lot: from their dialects, where they were from; from their choice of words, precisely what mood they were in; from the energy I felt, how alert they were. When I sensed they were getting tired, I told Sayeret Matkal that it was time to break in."

In Munich, however, Cohen and Zamir's offers to counsel the Germans on how to handle the terrorists were repeatedly turned down. Instead, they watched as the surviving team members were led out of the dormitory building at gunpoint to two military Bell UH-1 helicopters parked nearby. The entire event left a deep impression in Zamir's mind: "The sight of the athletes being led to the helicopters, I will never forget until the day I die. On both sides of the pathway, which was a kind of lawn, stood tens of thousands of people from innumerable countries. Deathly silence. I stood alongside [German interior minister Hans-Dietrich] Genscher and [Franz Josef] Strauss, Victor at my side, and we watched the Israeli athletes, with their hands tied, flanked by the terrorists, and all in step they marched toward the helicopters. It was an appalling sight, especially to a Jew on German soil, in Munich."

The helicopters took the hostages to a nearby military airport, where a plane was supposed to fly them out of Germany as soon as the deal for the release of the Palestinian prisoners had concluded. The terrorists and the hostages were followed by additional helicopters with Zamir and Cohen and the German officials aboard.

Germany devised a rescue operation at the military airport, but the forces they deployed were untrained and disorganized, and they lacked the required intelligence on the terrorists, sniper equipment, and support for such a mission. They opened fire in an uncoordinated manner and did not hit or kill enough terrorists to neutralize the squad.

"The terrorists fired at the building where we were," Zamir said. "Victor and I ran down the stairs, groping in the dark, looking for the commanders of the operation, with firing going on all the time. We saw that the terrorists had shot the helicopter pilots, and they fell on their faces. When we located the [German] commanders [of the operation], I demanded to go up onto the roof to speak to the terrorists and warn them that if the firing continued, they would not get out alive. The officers refused, and we insisted, until they agreed on condition that we speak Arabic and not German."

Cohen took the megaphone and began trying to persuade the terrorists to surrender. "But it was too little and too late, and all I got was a burst of fire that nearly killed us both."

Zamir asked the Germans why there wasn't a force storming the terrorists. He was told that the police were waiting for armored vehicles that were stuck on the way to the airport in a traffic jam created by all the curious onlookers.

Zamir watched the terrorists lob grenades into the helicopters where the Israelis were being held; he saw them go up in flames after the grenades exploded. When he ran to the smoldering aircraft, he found only the nine Israelis' bodies, handcuffed to one another, charred, and some still burning.

To Zamir, the Germans' conduct in the hostage situation was telling: "They did not make even a minimal effort to save lives, or take minimal risks to rescue people—neither our people nor their own." He said he had seen one of the German pilots crying out for help. "I told [the German police], 'For God's sake, there are people bleeding in the helicopter. A wounded crewman has crawled two hundred meters. Get him out of there!' He crawled on all fours, wounded, and no one made a move to rescue him."

According to Cohen, "Later on, we learned that some of the policemen who were supposed to take part in the rescue operation made a decision before it started that they were not ready to risk their lives for the sake of the Israelis."

Just after 3 A.M., barely twenty-three hours after the initial terrorist assault, Zamir phoned Meir, who congratulated him on his success. She had been misinformed by a German source that all the Israelis were safe. "I'm sorry to tell you this, Golda," he told her, "but the athletes were not rescued. I have seen them all. Not one of them survived."

Almost immediately, historical parallels were drawn. Once again, Jews were slaughtered on German soil as the rest of the world continued with business as usual, as if nothing had happened. Worse, the State of Israel was rendered impotent by German authorities and forced to watch passively as terrorists slaughtered its citizens. In Israel, life came to a virtual standstill for days afterward. Rosh Hashanah celebrations all across the country were canceled, and a mood of gloom spread through the populace.

The Palestinians saw the operation as a success, as their cause had taken center stage in world public attention. One PLO organ wrote, "A bomb in the White House, a land mine in the Vatican, the death of Mao Zedong, an earthquake in Paris could not have had greater resonance with every person in the world than that caused by the Black September operation in Munich. . . . It was like painting the name 'Palestine' on a mountaintop visible from all corners of the globe."

In the immediate aftermath, there was little Meir's government could do. It issued a pro forma declaration that, "in anger and revulsion, the Government of Israel deplores the murder of eleven Israelis by Arab terrorists." Meir also ordered air strikes on a dozen "bases, camps, and headquarters of the terrorists in Syria and Lebanon. The intention is to harm terrorists and not civilians."

But that was only the beginning.

On the evening of September 6, Zamir returned from Munich. In two briefings that were to have a dramatic impact on Israel's future policy on terrorism, he described with emotion the attack and the German response—Germany's refusal to accept assistance or advice, and the chaos, lack of professionalism, and apathy that the German forces displayed.

"The German disgrace is immeasurable," he said. All the Germans wanted was to get the affair out of the way so the Games could continue, he told a shocked cabinet.

As Zamir's account circulated, the fury toward the terror organizations spilling Jewish blood—as well as toward the German authorities who had failed so miserably and refused to take responsibility—rose sharply. At a secret meeting of the Knesset panel, one of the participants seethed, "We must not only defend ourselves, but also go on the offensive. We have to seek out the terrorists and kill them. We have to turn them from the hunters to the prey." Menachem Begin proposed bombing Libya.

Meir, heavily criticized for the failure of the intelligence organizations under her command to detect and prevent the Munich massacre, and fearing for her chances of reelection, now came around. If the Europeans wouldn't even try to stop the terrorists on their own soil, Meir and her cabinet decided, the Mossad would be given a green light to do so. On September 11, the cabinet authorized the prime minister to approve targets even in friendly countries, without notifying local authorities. "Retaliation or no retaliation," Meir told the Knesset on September 12, "at any place where a plot is being laid, where they are preparing people to murder Jews, Israelis—Jews anywhere—it is there that we are committed to striking them."

Harari had been right: Meir changed her mind. Bayonet would be thrust into service immediately.

# "I HAVE NO PROBLEM WITH ANYONE THAT I'VE KILLED"

"THE BEAUTIFUL SARAH HAS left the building and is making her way to her house."

This was the message transmitted over the Bayonet team's radio network in Rome one night in October 1972. "Okay, get moving. Prepare to engage," ordered Mike Harari from his command post.

"The Beautiful Sarah" was not a woman, but the code name for a tall, thin, bespectacled man with a shock of shiny black hair and a very expressive face. His real name was Wael Zwaiter, and he was a Palestinian who worked part-time at the Libyan embassy in Rome as a translator. Zwaiter had nearly finished translating *One Thousand and One Nights* from Arabic to Italian, and he had spent the evening at the home of his friend Janet Venn-Brown, an Australian artist, discussing some of the finer points of his rendition of the colorful descriptions in the book. At the door, his hostess had given Zwaiter a loaf of bread she had baked for him. He put it into the envelope in which he kept his manuscript.

After he left, he headed for his apartment at 4 Piazza Annibaliano. He took two buses, and when he got off the second one he went into a bar, all the time holding a white envelope containing the last chapters of his translation.

A Bayonet surveillance team was watching Zwaiter the whole time. The Mossad believed he was not merely a translator—that this was only a cover and that he was, in fact, the commander of Black September operations in Rome. Italy was a particularly weak country when it came to counterterror enforcement, and Rome had become the European center of Palestinian terrorist activity at the time. The Mossad thought Zwaiter was responsible for smuggling in personnel and weaponry and selecting targets.

The Mossad also suspected Zwaiter of having masterminded an attempt in September to plant a bomb on board an El Al flight from Rome. Italian authorities had their suspicions as well: In August, police briefly detained him in connection with Black September attacks against oil companies trading with Israel.

Zwaiter left the café and headed home. The surveillance team radioed two of their comrades, confirming that the target was approaching. Zwaiter stepped into the dimly lit lobby of his apartment building and pressed the button for the elevator. He never saw the two assassins hiding in the shadows beneath the stairwell until it was too late. They pulled out Beretta pistols with silencers screwed to the barrels and shot Zwaiter eleven times. He was hurled backward by the impact of the bullets into a row of potted plants and fell to the ground, clasping his *Arabian Nights* manuscript. He died there on the floor.

Within hours, all seventeen Bayonet operatives were out of Italy and on their way back to Israel. None of them had been caught. The operation had gone exactly as planned.

Zwaiter was only the first on a very long list of militants and PLO staffers who were going to die.


THE CHANGE IN GOLDA Meir's attitude toward friendly European countries was immediate and severe. Born in Kiev and raised in Milwaukee, she saw the world in straightforward and sometimes rigid terms: Things were either black or white, good or bad. In Meir's mind, there was a direct link between the actions of the Palestinian terrorists and the atrocities of World War II: "Those who harm the Jews first harm other peoples later; that's how it was with Hitler, and that's the way it is with the Arab terrorists," she said to the publisher of *The New York Times,* Arthur Sulzberger, Sr.

She would blithely proclaim that she understood little about military affairs and intelligence—relying on Defense Minister Moshe

Dayan, cabinet minister Yisrael Galili, and Mossad chief Zvi Zamir—but after the Munich slaughter she understood clearly enough that Israel could not depend on other countries to protect its citizens. Rather than defer to any nation's sovereignty, Israel would now kill people wherever and whenever they reached the conclusion that it was necessary.

This policy change had a significant effect on Caesarea's operations. Prior to Munich, Meir had limited killings to "target" countries, those that were officially hostile to Israel, such as Syria and Lebanon. But it was difficult for Caesarea operatives to kill anyone in those countries because of the hazardous environment. Using a gun or a sniper rifle—methods that required close contact with the target—invariably drew quick attention from the local authorities, and even if the killers escaped cleanly from the scene, stringent border controls triggered by a high-profile murder would likely be put in place before they could leave the country. An Israeli assassin captured in a target country was likely going to die, and only after being brutally tortured. Distance killings might have been safer, but they also were less effective, vulnerable to many variables, and all too likely to kill or maim innocents.

Operating in so-called base countries—those with friendly relations, which included all of Western Europe—was much more convenient. At most, an assassin who got caught would serve a prison term. Moreover, the Mossad's Universe (Tevel) division, responsible for liaison with foreign intelligence bodies, had developed a network of close ties with many of Europe's services, known in Mossad jargon as "soft cushions" because they could provide local contacts to help smooth things over in the event of complications—sometimes in return for a favor. The bottom line was that in Europe it was a lot easier to kill a man and get away with it.

And there were a lot of men to kill. The first hit list consisted of eleven names: terrorists involved in the Munich massacre. It soon became clear that they were all holed up in Arab states or Eastern Europe, and it would be difficult to reach them. However, a lot of information had begun to accumulate in the meantime about other targets who were less important but who resided in Europe. After Munich, anyone the Mossad suspected of being involved with Black

September—in effect, anyone suspected of belonging to the PLO in general—became a legitimate target. That made for a lengthy list of targets.

"We wanted to create a noisy effect," one Caesarea operative said. "A genuine assassination, from close range, that would evoke fear and trembling, a deed that, even if Israel denied having anything to do with, it would be clear that an Israeli finger squeezed the trigger."

That finger would belong to Bayonet. In mid-September 1972, Zvi Zamir showed up at Bayonet's training center. "Israel is not going to sit idly by," he told the operatives. "We are going to get the people who did this. You will be the long arm of the Office."

"Those words," a Caesarea operative code-named Kurtz said, "roused a sense of pride in us." Within a year of Munich, fourteen Palestinian militants would be dead.


THE LEADER OF THE hit teams and commander of some of its operations was Nehemia Meiri, a Holocaust survivor born to a traditional Jewish family in the village of Demblin, in southern Poland. He was twelve years old when the Gestapo rounded up the Jews of his village and marched them into a nearby forest. The Jews were ordered to dig a pit and forced to line up along its edge. Then they were machine-gunned. Nehemia, already a resourceful and strong boy, dived into the pit a split second before the order to open fire was given. The Germans did not notice, and he lay quietly among the corpses of his family and neighbors until the killing was over. When the Germans were gone, he crawled out of the mass grave, soaked in blood.

Later in the war, after Meiri was captured and forced into hard labor at an airstrip, he saved the life of a senior Luftwaffe officer who crashed his Messerschmitt on the runway. Meiri climbed into the burning aircraft and rescued the unconscious pilot, thereby buying himself years of protection. After the war, he immigrated to Palestine on the famous illegal immigrant ship *Exodus*. He fought in the 1948 War of Independence, was taken prisoner, and once again miraculously survived after a Jordanian soldier began mowing the POWs down.

Afterward, he joined the Shin Bet, serving on Ben-Gurion's body-guard detail. His colleagues and superiors noted that he was cool-headed and had no moral qualms about killing anyone who harmed Jews.

"Nehemia used to get up in the morning with a knife between his teeth," one of his team members recalled.

Meiri was a member of the Birds, the joint Mossad–Shin Bet operational team. He took part in the abduction of Alexander Yisraeli, the con man who tried to sell Israel's secrets, and he participated in the campaign to assassinate and intimidate the Nazi scientists build-ing Nasser's missiles. Later on, he was transferred to Caesarea and assigned to the team that set up Bayonet. Eitan Haber, one of Israel's best-known journalists, who also served as Yitzhak Rabin's bureau chief, said he once chided Zamir for putting Meiri in Bayonet. It was immoral, Haber said, "an exploitation of Holocaust horrors in order to create a killing machine."

But Meiri had no problem being in Bayonet, and no compunction about what he did while he served in the unit. Over the years, people who knew of his covert life asked if he was ever haunted by images of the people he had killed, or if he had nightmares about them. "I dream at night about my family," Meiri would reply. "I dream about the valley of slaughter there, next to Demblin in Poland; I dream about the *Muselmänner* [starving, sick inmates] in the death camps. Those are the things that bother me. I have no problem with anyone that I've killed. They deserved a bullet in the chest and two in the head, each one of them."

Meiri was one of the men who shot Zwaiter to death in Rome. Two weeks later, the next target was marked: Mahmoud Hamshari, allegedly the number-two man in Black September.

The Mossad blamed him for a conspiracy to use international airmail to plant barometrically triggered bombs on planes flying from Europe to Israel. One such bomb exploded in February 1970, shortly after taking off from Frankfurt on a flight to Vienna, but the pilot managed to make an emergency landing. The pilot of Swissair Flight 330, from Zurich to Hong Kong, with a stopover in Tel Aviv, also tried to land after a bomb went off in his cargo compartment but crashed into a forest. All forty-seven passengers and crew members were killed. The Mossad also believed that Hamshari was connected to a failed attempt on Ben-Gurion's life during his visit to Denmark in May 1969, and that his apartment in Paris served as the arsenal for Black September.

Bayonet operatives watching Hamshari in Paris found that he spent a large part of his time with his wife and baby daughter at home, and the rest meeting various people, mostly in busy public places.

Being surrounded by so many innocents presented a problem, to which Meir was acutely sensitive. She invited Harari to her home and made him a cup of tea. "Mike," she said, "be sure that not a hair falls from the head of a French citizen. Not even a single hair. Do you understand me?"

Despite her newfound willingness to kill people in Europe, Meir still understood that certain protocols had to be followed. She also remained uncomfortable shouldering sole responsibility for condemning men to death. Whenever Zamir asked her to sign a "Red Page," as the kill order was called because of the color of the paper it was typed on, she would convene a select group of her cabinet ministers to deliberate with her—including her minister for religious affairs, Zerach Warhaftig, who would anoint each mission with a religious stamp of approval.

Killing Hamshari, then, would have to be done when he was alone inside his apartment. Meiri and Romi made the operational plan, which called for the participation of an additional unit—a departure from the usual protocols of Caesarea, which generally functioned as an independent unit within the Mossad.

On December 3, a team from Rainbow (Keshet in Hebrew, the new name of Colossus, the unit responsible for clandestine penetration) broke into Hamshari's apartment and took dozens of photographs, focusing especially on his work area. Those pictures were then flown to Israel and studied by Yaakov Rehavi, in the Mossad's technical department. He noticed that the telephone sat on a marble base. He and his staff crafted an identical base, stuffed with explosives.

On December 7, a man who introduced himself as an Italian journalist named Carl, but was actually Nehemia Meiri, phoned Hamshari and set up an interview at a café near his home the next day. As the interview was taking place, the Rainbow team broke in again and swapped out the phone base. A short time after Hamshari returned home, his phone rang. "Is this Monsieur Dr. Hamshari?" a voice asked. When the affirmative came, a button on a remote detonator was pushed and the marble base blew up. Hamshari was "almost cut in half" by the fragments of marble, according to Kurtz, who took part in the operation. He died several weeks later in a Paris hospital.

THE MOSSAD AND AMAN personnel coordinating the targeted killings devoted considerable time and thought to the ethics of each one. It was important that such acts be perceived as moral, at least in the assassins' own eyes. Even forty years later, Harari and his operatives described the deep conviction they held in both the end and the means. "In Caesarea there were no born killers. They were normal people, like you and me," Harari told me. "If they hadn't come to Caesarea, you wouldn't have found them working as contract killers in the underworld. My warriors in Caesarea were on a mission for the state. They knew that someone had to die because he had killed Jews and if he went on living he'd kill more Jews, and therefore they did it out of conviction. Not one of them had any doubts over whether it had to be done or not; there was not even the slightest hesitation."

Mossad chief Zamir also knew that having Meir's backing was important to his warriors. He knew how the prime minister's mind worked, too, so he always brought one or two Bayonet operatives with him when he met with her. One of them told her how important it was to know that their commander, Meir, was "a person with a world of moral values, with good judgment." Because of that, he continued, the assassins "feel much more comfortable with everything they've done, even if sometimes, once, there were question marks."

Meir beamed with happiness. "I sit facing them," she said after another meeting with Caesarea warriors, "full of wonder at their courage, composure, ability to execute, knowledge. They sit right in the jaws of the enemy. . . . I cannot explain to myself how we were blessed with a group like this."

Despite such mutual admiration, and the shared conviction in the morality of their actions, there were in fact a number of questions about the motives behind many of the post-Munich targeted killings, and whether the appropriate targets were chosen.

"Some of the Arabs we killed in that period, we didn't know why we were killing them, and they also don't know to this day why they died," a Caesarea officer said. "Zwaiter had nothing to do with the killing of the athletes, except, perhaps, that their plane flew over Rome on the way to Munich."

A top Mossad official who looked at the Zwaiter file years too late admitted that "it was a terrible mistake." Indeed, Palestinians have long insisted that Zwaiter was a peaceable intellectual who abhorred violence. (Granted, similar claims have been made about nearly every other Bayonet target from that period.)

But for some, that didn't matter. "Let's say that he [Zwaiter] was just the PLO representative in Rome, about which there's no disagreement," said an AMAN officer who dealt with identifying targets for Mossad hits. "We looked at the organization as one entity, and we never accepted the distinction between the people who dealt with politics and those who dealt with terror. Fatah was a terrorist organization that was murdering Jews. Anyone who was a member of such an organization had to know that he was a legitimate target."

Indeed, it is difficult to determine retrospectively whether the Zwaiter slaying was an error or part of an approach that had, and still today has, many disciples in Israeli intelligence: Every member of a terrorist organization, even if his function is not directly connected to acts of terrorism, is a legitimate target.

The problem inherent in this approach was that it allowed the Mossad to kill the people it *could,* not necessarily those the agency believed it *should.* Though the Mossad considered the targeted killing campaign a success, by early 1973 it was clear that it had not damaged the top echelons of the PLO. Those targets were sheltered in Beirut. That was where Israel would have to strike. And that would be a much more difficult mission.

.   .   .

ON OCTOBER 9, 1972, a coded message arrived at the AMAN base responsible for communications with Israel's agents in the Middle East. The base, which is situated on a ridge facing the sea and is surrounded by sand dunes, lies in one of Israel's prettiest landscapes. Hundreds of soldiers were employed there to receive, decipher, encode, and transmit top-secret material.

The message that night read, "Model requests urgent meeting."

Model was the code name for Clovis Francis, one of the most valuable agents AMAN and the Mossad had ever run in Lebanon. He was a well-groomed Lebanese man from a rich, connected Christian family, and he served Israel faithfully for decades. He'd been sending encrypted messages since the 1940s, when he relied on homing pigeons. Using a camera installed in the door of his car, he supplied Israeli intelligence with some 100,000 photographs over the years, documenting every corner of the country. He visited Israel periodically, traveling by submarine or naval vessel, to brief top intelligence officials. But he never asked for payment. He spied, he said, because "I believed in an alliance between Lebanon and Israel and, later, because I saw the Palestinians' activities in Lebanon as a great danger to my country."

Three days after his message requesting a meeting, a rubber dinghy slid up in the dark of night to a beach near Tyre, in southern Lebanon. Model climbed in and was ferried to a missile boat, which steamed to Haifa. The top officers of Unit 504 were waiting there to hear what he had to say. Model did not disappoint. He brought with him the home addresses of four top PLO officials in Beirut: Muhammad Youssef al-Najjar, the head of the PLO's intelligence apparatus, who had been involved in the planning and approval processes for the Munich operation; Kamal Adwan, responsible for Fatah's clandestine operations inside Israel, the West Bank, and the Gaza Strip; Kamal Nasser, the PLO spokesman; and Abu Jihad, Arafat's second in command. The first three lived near one another in a pair of high-rise buildings on Verdun Street.

The information was passed to Romi, Caesarea's intelligence officer, and he convened a series of meetings at the Caesarea HQ at Tel Aviv's 2 Kaplan Street. In addition to the information about the residences of the PLO men, large amounts of high-grade intel had been amassed on additional PLO targets in Lebanon—weapons workshops, command posts, offices. Harari said that he believed "there's a [targeted killing] operation here," but there were still too many gaps in the info for him to move forward. "It was a rule with me," Harari said, "that if there was no intelligence there would be no operation. Period."

In order to fill in those gaps in information, Caesarea decided to send a female operative into Beirut.

Yael (only her first name can be made public) was born in Canada in 1936 and grew up in New Jersey in a Jewish family without any link to Israel. Later on, she developed an emotional relationship toward the young country, and decided that "true Zionism entails making aliyah (immigrating) to Israel and forgoing the comforts of life in America." At that time, before the Six-Day War, "Israel aroused in me a sympathy for the underdog. Since childhood, I was attracted to people who were vulnerable, discriminated against." After immigrating and first finding work as a computer programmer, she was eventually recruited by the Mossad personnel division into the long and demanding Caesarea training course. In time, she became known as an exceptionally talented and coolheaded operative, who used her quiet charisma and her attractive appearance as a powerful weapon. When Harari sent Yael to Beirut, he told her, "With your femininity, delicateness, and beauty, who would suspect you?"

Yael—code-named Nielsen in the Mossad—and her handlers crafted a cover story of someone who'd come to Lebanon to write a TV series on the life of Lady Hester Stanhope, an aristocratic British woman who defied the conservative restrictions of the nineteenth century and became a groundbreaking political and social activist. Stanhope traveled extensively and spent her last years in Lebanon and Syria.

Yael arrived in Lebanon on January 14, 1973. She checked in at Le Bristol Hotel and, after a few days, rented an apartment in a luxury building exactly opposite the two buildings where the three targets lived. She quickly made friends with both locals and foreigners in Beirut, who agreed to help her in her research for the TV series about Lady Stanhope. Her cover story enabled her to move around freely and provided a legitimate pretext for traveling almost anywhere in the country.

She began walking around the potential landing areas and the target buildings, carrying a handbag with a camera inside it, which she operated by pushing a button on the outside. "Every detail was important," Yael later wrote in a journal. "Describing the day and nighttime routines in the three apartments, when the lights went on and off, who could be seen through the windows at what times, details about their cars, who came to call on them, whether the place was guarded."

With Yael's extensive reconnaissance work in hand, the Mossad now knew whom to hit and where to hit them, but enormous obstacles still remained. The homes of the top PLO men were in densely populated blocks in Beirut, so explosives couldn't be used—the likelihood of killing innocent civilians was unacceptably high. These would have to be close-contact hits. The problem, though, was that Lebanon was a target country, hostile to Israel, where a captured assassin would surely face torture and death. That meant that the Caesarea warriors already planted in Beirut were trained not in combat but rather in long-term, deep-cover surveillance. And the Bayonet warriors, who could execute a clean kill, lacked convincing cover stories for getting into a target country and remaining there long enough to do the job. Even if they did, getting out of the country quickly after hitting as many as seven PLO targets—three men and four installations—would be well-nigh impossible.

Romi and Harari came to an unavoidable conclusion: Caesarea couldn't carry out such a mission on its own. Only the IDF had the necessary forces and resources for a successful raiding party. This was a new proposition—until that point, the Mossad and the IDF had never cooperated in assault operations on the ground. It carried a special risk as well. Israel routinely denied responsibility for Mossad hits, but the moment a large military force started killing people, even if soldiers weren't in uniform, it would be impossible for Israel to claim it wasn't involved.

The IDF's initial plan was an unwieldy and time-consuming mess, requiring a contingent of a hundred men to storm both high-rise buildings and drive the residents into the street. A sort of police lineup would be held in order to identify the targets, who would then be killed.

Lieutenant General David Elazar, the IDF's chief of staff, had serious doubts about the plan. He asked Ehud Barak, the commander of Sayeret Matkal, the General Staff Reconnaissance Unit of the IDF, for some fresh ideas.

Sayeret Matkal was set up in the late 1950s with the aim of creating an elite force capable of clandestine penetration of enemy territory, which "would be trained to carry out combat operations, sabotage, and [intelligence] gathering," in the words of its establishment order. Until the 1970s, the unit specialized mainly in deep penetrations behind enemy lines in order to install highly sophisticated listening and observation devices. It was and still is considered the best unit in the IDF, always receiving the cream of the new recruits, who then undergo a twenty-month training course, said by some to be the hardest in the world.

Ehud Barak, who was the first officer to grow up in the Sayeret, became its commander in 1971. Kibbutz-born, short of stature, but athletic and determined, Barak embodied all the special qualities the unit required. He was also a skilled politician who knew how to handle his superiors, and he was boundlessly ambitious while always maintaining his composure. From the moment he took over command, Barak pushed for Sayeret Matkal to be a bigger part of IDF operations, beyond gathering intelligence behind enemy lines.

So when Elazar requested his assistance in planning the Beirut hits, "a look of satisfaction spread across Barak's face, like the look on the face of a chef starting to cook an extraordinary dish," one of his officers said. Barak examined the raw intelligence, the plot points on a map of Beirut, the previous hundred-man plan. "Chief, this is no good," Barak told Elazar. "A force of this size that enters Beirut and that may have to spend a long time there, until the 'police lineup' is done, will get involved in exchanges of fire. There could be many fatal casualties, on our side and on theirs. Civilians, too."

Elazar asked him, "How would you do it?'"

Barak replied, "Once we are sure the three targets are at home, we'll enter the city with a very small force, no more than fifteen men, get to the apartments, break in, shoot them, and pull out. All in a few minutes. With the right planning and means, and appropriate training, we can get in and out before additional enemy forces arrive on the scene. By the time they grasp what's happened, we'll be gone. Most important: to maintain the element of surprise."

Elazar smiled and gave Barak the green light to begin planning.


THE PLAN FOR OPERATION Spring of Youth—the Beirut raid—was outlined a few days later. The naval commando unit, Flotilla 13, would land the raiding party on the beach, where Caesarea operatives would be waiting with rented vehicles.

The Mossad team would then drive the troops to Verdun Street, where they would take the Fatah leaders by surprise in their apartments, kill them, then slip back to the beach and escape to Israel. At the same time, other commando squads would attack four different targets in Lebanon.

It was clear that after the operation it would be very difficult to carry out another one, and therefore the Israelis wanted to hit as many targets as possible. Barak has said that his sense was that Elazar was not confident that the Sayeret would succeed in hitting the three senior PLO men, and that he wanted to "spread the risk [of failing] out with additional objectives."

This was a complex exercise, involving the coordination and integration of different units, so Elazar oversaw some of the training sessions himself. He raised the concern that a group of men moving in the middle of the night through downtown Beirut might arouse suspicion. He suggested that some of the men wear women's clothing. "This way you'll also be able to conceal more weapons," Elazar said with a smile.

Some members of the Sayeret did not like their commander involving the unit in an operation that went beyond intelligence gathering. Before the raid, an internal argument broke out. Two of Barak's officers, Amitai Nahmani and Amit Ben Horin, both kibbutz members of the left-wing Hashomer Hatzair movement, argued that the unit had not been established as a death squad and that they had no intention of becoming assassins. Barak tried to persuade them, but they asked to see a higher authority. Barak set up a meeting with chief of staff Elazar, who spoke to them about the importance of the war on terror and the fact that Jewish blood had been spilled by Fatah in Israel and abroad. He said it was their duty to respond "with force and elegance." The two accepted the explanation and were assigned to the lead squad.

Barak said he saw the argument as "evidence of the unit's strength. Not only superior professional soldiers, but also men with opinions, men who ask questions, who are not satisfied with the mere command to execute but also demand to know the logic behind it."

While the Sayeret and the Flotilla 13 marine commandos were practicing the landing, Yael and Model continued gathering intelligence. Yael picked a suitable site for the landing—the private beach of the Sands Hotel, chosen because access was restricted to hotel guests and was close to the hotel's parking lot. Then she wandered through nearby streets, a small woman in a long skirt and sunglasses, carrying a handbag. Yael photographed the raiding party's entire route—the beach, the streets they'd drive, the telephone junction box they'd probably have to blow up so reinforcements couldn't be called, the buildings on Verdun Street, the concierge at the entrance.

Yael also gathered details about the nearby police station, which was only about six hundred feet from the apartment houses, and the patrols the police conducted and how long it would take them to reach the scene if they were called.

Before reporting to the chief of staff that the force was ready to set out, Brigadier General Emmanuel Shaked, chief infantry and paratroop officer and overall commander of the operation, insisted on meeting the Caesarea personnel who were to drive his men from the beach to the objectives and back again. Zamir, Harari, and Romi came with the Caesarea team to meet Elazar, Shaked, and Barak at a Sayeret training facility.

Shaked described the meeting as "no less than a catastrophe." He asked the Caesarea people to introduce themselves and describe their past combat experience. "When's the last time you had a gun in your hand and used it?" he asked. To his horror, most of them had never held a weapon. Only some of them had even served in the IDF. Those who did have some kind of military training had done only the absolute minimum and lacked any kind of combat skills.

Shaked exploded in anger and turned to Zamir, saying, "Get your sparrows out of the room." Shaked told Harari that he "wasn't prepared to let the operation go ahead with these people, who aren't combat troops."

"If they had been combat troops, we wouldn't have needed the IDF at all," Harari responded in anger. Elazar intervened and accepted Zamir's promise that "they are warriors of the highest order in the arena in which they are required to act, to enable the IDF soldiers to do their job."

On April 6, the six Caesarea operatives flew into Beirut from various European airports, carrying counterfeit German, Belgian, and British passports. They checked in separately at the Sands, rented large American-made cars, and parked them in the hotel parking lot.

On the afternoon of April 9, the IDF troops were bused to the Israeli Navy base in Haifa. At the final briefing, Shaked told them, "You don't shoot at your target and leave. You leave the apartment only after you make sure that he won't get up again."

At 4 P.M., on a calm Mediterranean Sea, eight Israeli missile boats set sail northward. Twelve miles off Beirut, they cut their engines and dropped anchor. At 5 P.M., one of the Caesarea operatives rendezvoused with Yael at the Phoenician Hotel. She confirmed that the three targets were at home. They parted, and the operative radioed the waiting force: "The birds are in their nests."

From the gunwales, nineteen rubber dinghies descended, each loaded with troops: twenty-one from Sayeret Matkal, thirty-four naval commandos, twenty soldiers from the Paratroop Reconnaissance unit. These elite combat units were supported by three thousand additional personnel. It was one of the biggest targeted killing operations of the twentieth century, if not the biggest. Harari, Zamir, Romi, Elazar, and Defense Minister Dayan were in a bunker beneath the Kirya-Sarona, the old Tel Aviv Templer neighborhood that housed the IDF command, monitoring the operation. Also in the Bor— Hebrew for the "Pit," as the bunker is informally known—was AMAN chief Eli Zeira. He knew that although almost the entire Israeli Navy was mobilized, Spring of Youth was "an operation for which there was no rescue option."

The dinghies glided toward the lights of Beirut. When they reached the beach, the men of Flotilla 13 carried the members of the raiding party onto dry land so that they wouldn't get wet and their disguises wouldn't be spoiled—taking extra care with the heavily made-up female impersonators on the team. The Mossad operatives were waiting in the parking lot of the hotel with the vehicles.

Barak, who was dressed as one of the women in the team, was in the front seat of one of the three cars. "Go!" he ordered, but nothing happened. The Mossad driver was sweating, his whole body shivering. Barak thought he was either sick or injured. But he was just scared. "I've never been anywhere where there's shooting," he admitted. "I did a last recon of the area. Two gendarmes armed with submachine guns are patrolling the street near the buildings." Barak and Muki Betser, a longtime Sayeret fighter, calmed the driver down, lying to him that there'd be no shooting.

"Go!" Barak repeated, having decided not to report about the gendarmes to Shaked, who'd stayed on the command missile boat, fearing that he'd call the operation off.

The three cars entered the upscale Ramlet al-Bayda neighborhood of Beirut. Two blocks from the target, the team got out and started walking—one man and one man in drag, paired together. It was late, around 11 P.M., but there were still a few people on the street. There were two armed cops standing there, bored, smoking. They ignored the couples who walked past them.

Muki Betser had his arm around Barak, the two of them just another couple on a romantic walk. "It reminds me of Rome," Betser whispered to Barak.

In one of the buildings, al-Najjar was asleep. In the other building, in separate apartments, the other two, Adwan and Nasser, were sleeping. At the entrances to the two buildings, the couples separated and the force split up—three details to each of the three targets, and another, under Barak's command, including a doctor, to cover the street.

The PLO guards they were expecting in the lobbies of the apartment blocks had fallen asleep in their cars and, unhindered, the soldiers began climbing the stairs, counting the flights to themselves as they ascended so that they wouldn't break into the wrong apartments. When each detail reached its objective, the men took up positions and placed small explosive charges next to the door, and each commander clicked three times on his radio mic. When Barak heard the three clicks from each of the three details, he replied with five clicks, which meant "Execute." At the same time, he signaled to Shaked that the other attacks in various places in Lebanon could begin. Maintaining the element of surprise required that the apartments be breached before they started.

The small explosive charges blew the three doors open. A woman who was woken by the pounding feet on the stairs and peeped through the eyehole of her door was killed when the blast blew her door open, too. Al-Najjar came out of his bedroom, grasped what was happening, and tried to shut himself in another room. Betser sprayed the door with automatic fire, killing him and his wife. The second target, Kamal Nasser, hid under his bed and fired his pistol, hitting one of the Israelis in the leg. The raiders turned the bed over, saw Nasser, and killed him with two long bursts of fire.

Inside the third apartment, Kamal Adwan stepped out of his door with a loaded AK-47 in his hands but was apparently confused to see what looked like a man and a woman facing him and hesitated for a second. This cost him his life as the Israelis opened fire with Uzi submachine guns hidden under their clothing.

At the same time, a PLO guard, who was supposed to be protecting the targets but had fallen asleep in his Renault Dauphine car, woke up and emerged from the car with his pistol drawn. Barak and Amiram Levin, one of his top officers, shot him with their silenced handguns. One bullet hit the car and set off its horn. This woke up the neighbors, who called the police. "More proof that there's always some new surprise," Betser says. "The unexpected is the thing that is most expected."

Police from the nearby station were soon speeding toward Verdun Street, where the Israelis were still rifling the apartments for documents. Finally, the raiding parties raced downstairs, almost leaving a man, Yonatan Netanyahu, the brother of Benjamin, behind. Now they had to engage the Beirut police. Levin stood in the middle of the street, his blond wig still on his head, swinging his Uzi left and right, spraying bullets. Barak stood in the road, firing at cops. Betser shot up a police Land Rover and covered Levin. A jeep with four Lebanese soldiers rolled up and screeched into the cross fire. The Israelis shot it, and Betser tossed a grenade at it, killing three of its occupants. The driver was slightly wounded. Yael saw him from her window, sitting on the sidewalk, sobbing for hours before he was taken to the hospital.

The assassins held off the police, and the soldiers piled into their rented cars and rushed back to the beach. They scattered sharp little steel tripods behind them, puncturing the tires of police cars that gave chase. Barak got on the radio, calling naval commandos to pick them up. Despite the chaos, he remained composed and was able to separate himself from the moment. "I remember looking in amazement at the streets," he said. "I had never been in such magnificent streets, I had never seen such beautiful apartment houses. It was a standard of building that we weren't familiar with in Israel." The wig made him hot, so he opened the window and felt a cool breeze caress his face. He relaxed. A man ran to the curb, yelling for the car to slow down. "Shoot him, Muki," he told Betser.

"He's a gas station worker, not a cop." Betser did not shoot.

The second raiding force, the Paratroop Reconnaissance troops who were hitting a building in a different Beirut neighborhood, was less fortunate. They killed the guards at the entrance of the PFLP building they were targeting, but they didn't know about a second guard post. A Palestinian opened fire, badly wounding three Israeli soldiers. Two of them were evacuated to a waiting car. The third, Yigal Pressler, was hit by fourteen bullets. A naval commando lifted him up and ran toward the car, but a PLFP man, apparently believing Pressler was a Palestinian, tried to rescue him, grappling with the commando. The three fell to the ground in a heap. One of Pressler's arms was paralyzed, but he managed to cock his pistol with his teeth. The Palestinian ran away. The commando chased after him, and Pressler thought he'd been left alone. He was thinking of blowing himself up with a grenade when the commando came back and picked him up again. The air was exploding with gunfire and explosions and yelling. Lights went on in the neighboring buildings.

Rather than withdraw immediately, the squad's commander, Amnon Lipkin-Shahak, with composure that earned him a citation from the chief of staff, ordered his men to remain and carry out their mission, attaching explosives to the building.

"My hardest moment," said Lipkin-Shahak, "was not during the actual combat, but when we got back to the vehicles. I was surprised to discover that the car with the wounded men wasn't there." He and his men, including the badly wounded Pressler, were stuck in the heart of Beirut with only two cars. The third, driven by a Caesarea operative and carrying two of the severely wounded men, had vanished. The radios weren't working. Hurried searches found nothing.

"It was very worrying," Lipkin-Shahak said. He did not want to withdraw without knowing where his wounded men were, but he had no option. He gave the order to pile into the two cars and head for the beach. Just after they set out, they heard a mighty blast and saw their target building collapse. Later, they learned that some thirty-five PFLP activists were buried in the ruins.

When they reached the beach, they found the Caesarea man sitting in his car, two of their comrades in the backseat, one already dead from blood loss. The driver was covered in sweat, smoking a cigarette with trembling fingers. "I asked him what happened," Lipkin-Shahak said, "why he didn't wait for us, why he didn't wait for the unit's doctor to treat the wounded. He was a little confused, but if I understood him correctly, he heard the gunfire at the beginning of the raid and thought we wouldn't get out alive, so he decided to get out and go to the beach."

Lipkin-Shahak's men were enraged. "It was a mistake to let people with no combat experience be involved in this," one of them said. "That guy from Caesarea saw that we were in trouble and got shell shock. He ran away."

The entire team boarded the dinghies and returned to the missile boat. Another one of the wounded men died during surgery on the boat. Two of the paratroopers couldn't restrain themselves and began yelling at the Caesarea operative that he was responsible for the deaths of their two comrades. He yelled back. One of the soldiers slapped him, he responded with a punch, and a fight broke out on the deck until the others separated them.

But by daybreak, all of the raiders were back in Israel. When Barak got home, his wife, Nava, was still asleep. He put his pack down and lay down next to her, exhausted, with his boots on. When she woke up, she was surprised to find her husband fast asleep at her side, with makeup on his face and traces of bright red lipstick on his lips.

The next morning in Beirut, surrounded by the wreckage of the previous night, no one paid attention to the skinny woman who came to the post office on Madame Curie Street. Yael had written a letter to her case officer that showed her trauma over what she had seen from her apartment window.

> Dear Emile,
> I'm still shaking from last night. Suddenly in the middle of the night I was woken up by the sound of many very loud explosions. . . . I was panic stricken—the Israelis are attacking! . . . It was horrible. . . . This morning it all just seemed like a bad dream. But it wasn't. Those terrible Israelis were really here. . . . For the first time I can see why there's so much hatred for that country and for the Jews. . . . Really this is such a nice, peaceful, residential area with gentle, very kind people.

Yael told "Emile" that she wanted to come see him for a vacation to calm down and that "I do miss you (more than I expected)." In invisible ink, she added, "It was a great show last night. Hats off!"

In order to avoid attracting suspicion, Yael remained in Beirut another week, despite the mounting fear that she was liable to be exposed due to the stringent security measures put in place after the raid. "When the plane took off and the wheels left the ground, I relaxed in my seat. I felt the stress of holding my cover character close to every one of my body's organs and my soul gradually weakening, torn off me piece by piece. When I landed at Heathrow, my arms were flaccid and it was hard to get out of my seat. I needed a few more seconds before I could leave the plane."

Back in Israel, Spring of Youth was considered a dazzling success. All of its objectives had been achieved. Three top PLO officials were killed, along with some fifty others, almost all of them PLO members. Salah Khalaf (Abu Iyad), the supreme commander of Black September, was saved by chance because shortly before the raid he left one of the targeted apartments where he often spent time. Four buildings and workshops for manufacturing weapons were destroyed. The seizure of a large number of documents from Adwan's apartment was deemed a catastrophe by the Palestinians. They supplied the Shin Bet with details about PLO cells in the occupied territories and led to a number of arrests, effectively wrecking the Fatah network there.

Because of this success, no attention was paid in Israel to the unprofessional conduct of the two Mossad drivers, both members of Harari's elite Caesarea unit, and the fact that they had prevented medical treatment from being given to two men who died of their wounds, and could have caused an even greater disaster.

The operation left Lebanon in shock. The Lebanese government resigned because of its impotence in the face of the "Israeli aggression." The Arab world was in an uproar, and in Egypt, the leading daily, *Al-Ahram,* commented that the goal of the operation had been "to drive into the Arabs' hearts the sense that Israel was in control of the region." Thanks to Spring of Youth, the myth that the Mossad could strike anywhere and at any time began to gain credence in the Arab world.

# "WRONG IDENTIFICATION OF A TARGET IS NOT A FAILURE. IT'S A MISTAKE."

THE RESOUNDING SUCCESS OF Operation Spring of Youth did not mean a letup in the string of Mossad targeted killings in Europe.

In the final days of preparation for the Beirut raid, Meiri and another operative were in Paris, waiting for Basil al-Kubaisi, a law professor at Beirut University and a low-level activist in the PFLP, to finish with a prostitute before they shot him dead. ("I decided that, just as they give a condemned man a last request, this guy also deserved some sex before he died," Meiri related.)

Then, only hours after the Spring of Youth forces returned to Israel, Harari, Meiri, and five additional operatives traveled to Athens, where they killed Zaid Muchassi with a bomb planted in the mattress of his hotel bed. Muchassi had just been appointed the Fatah representative in Cyprus, where he replaced Hussein Abd al-Chir—whom the Mossad also had killed, on January 24, with a bomb in a Nicosia hotel mattress.

On June 10, information came in indicating that Wadie Haddad had sent two of his men to Rome, to carry out an attack on the El Al airline office. The information came from a Junction agent deep inside Haddad's organization. This new and promising recruit, who would be described in AMAN's annual report as "an outstanding source with excellent and exclusive access to the Haddad organization," and who agreed to spy in exchange for money, was given the code name Itzavon, Hebrew for "Sadness." A team commanded by "Carlos," a Bayonet operative, began following the two men, who were driving around Rome in a Mercedes with German registration plates.

On the night of June 16–17, the Bayonet team planted a bomb under the car. In the morning, when one of the Palestinian men got into the car and started to drive away, he was followed by a Mossad car, with Harari driving and Carlos in the passenger seat, holding a remote control the size of a shoebox. In order for the bomb to be detonated, a minimal distance between the vehicles had to be maintained. After a few minutes, the Palestinian man in the car stopped to pick up his partner, who was staying at another address, and then drove off again. Carlos was about to push the button exactly when the car entered the Piazza Barberini, site of the Triton Fountain, an important work by the famous sculptor Gian Lorenzo Bernini.

Harari knew Rome well from the days after World War II when he was working to help refugees immigrate to Israel, and he was someone who appreciated art. "No! Stop! The statue . . . It's Bernini! Do not detonate!" he yelled at a confused Carlos, then proceeded to explain the importance of the work to him.

A few seconds later, when the car carrying the two Palestinians had moved away from the fountain, the button was pressed. The front part of the car exploded and the two men were very badly injured. One later died in the hospital. Police found weapons in the car and interpreted the explosion as a "work accident," assuming the two were terrorists who had a bomb in the car and had handled it incorrectly.

"Sadness" also reported on the activities of Mohammed Boudia, the head of PFLP operations in Europe. Boudia was a colorful combination of Algerian revolutionary, bisexual bohemian playboy, adventurer, and arch-terrorist who worked for both Haddad and Black September. The small theater he ran in Paris, Théâtre de l'Ouest, was used as a cover for his plans to attack Israelis and Jews.

Thanks to Sadness's reports, the Shin Bet managed to thwart some of his plans before they were executed. One was for simultaneous explosions of powerful TNT bombs in Tel Aviv's seven biggest hotels on the Seder night of Passover 1971.

During June 1973, Sadness reported that Boudia was plotting another big attack. A team of thirty Bayonet and Rainbow operatives followed him the length of Paris before an opportunity arose, when he parked his car in Rue des Fossés-Saint-Bernard, in the Latin Quarter. When he came back and started it again, a pressure-sensitive bomb placed under the seat of his car exploded and killed him.

Bayonet's string of triumphs instilled a sense of euphoria throughout the whole organization. "It seemed as if there was nothing the Mossad couldn't do," said a Caesarea veteran, "and that there was no one we couldn't reach."

That said, the reckoning with Black September remained open. Nine months after the horrific slaughter in Munich—the attack that had triggered the uptick in targeted killings—senior members of Black September were still at large. The Mossad had killed a lot of people, but not the eleven men it wanted most. These included the three surviving participants of the operation, who had been imprisoned but then sprung after Black September hijacked a Lufthansa plane and forced the Germans to release them. The other eight had been marked by the Mossad as tied to the conception, command, or execution of the attack.

At the top of that list was Ali Hassan Salameh, Black September's operations officer.

Ali Salameh's father, Hassan Salameh, had been one of the two commanders of the Palestinian forces in 1947 when war broke out after the UN decision on the establishment of Israel. The Haganah had repeatedly tried and failed to assassinate him, until he was finally killed in combat.

His son carried a heavy burden. "I wanted to be myself, [but] . . . I was constantly conscious of the fact that I was the son of Hassan Salameh and had to live up to that, even without being told how the son of Hassan Salameh should live," Ali Salameh said in one of the only two interviews he ever gave. "My upbringing was politicized. I lived the Palestinian cause, at a time when the cause was turning in a vicious circle. They were a people without a leadership. The people were dispersed, and I was part of the dispersion. My mother wanted me to be another Hassan."

But by the mid-1960s, the pressure from Ali's family, together with Yasser Arafat, was enough. Ali gave in and presented himself at the Fatah recruitment office. "I became very attached to Fatah," he recalled. "I had found what I was looking for."

"He very quickly became Arafat's favorite," said Harari.

In 1968, he was sent to Egypt by Arafat, for training in intelligence and the operation of explosives. He became an assistant to Abu Iyad, who assigned him to oversee the identification and liquidation of Arabs who collaborated with Israelis.

Salameh was young, charismatic, wealthy, and handsome, and enjoyed the high life that went hand in hand with membership in Rasd, the secret intelligence arm of Fatah. He combined his love of women and parties with his terrorist activities in a manner that "raised eyebrows in Fatah," according to an Israeli military intelligence report on him.

The Mossad believed that Salameh had been involved in a long list of terror attacks, some against Jordan and some against Israel, including the hijacking of the Sabena airliner. Documents seized in al-Najjar's apartment in Beirut indicated that Salameh's responsibilities included liaising with European terrorist organizations, and that he had invited Andreas Baader, co-founder of the German Baader-Meinhof Gang, to a Palestinian training camp in Lebanon. "We showed the documents to the Germans," said Shimshon Yitzhaki, head of the Mossad's counterterror unit, "to make it clear to them that the danger of Palestinian terror was their concern as well."

There is no disagreement about these charges, but the Mossad was also convinced that Salameh was implicated in the planning and execution of the Munich massacre, and that he had even been present not far from the scene when the terror squad was dispatched to Connollystrasse 31 in the Olympic Village. However, Mohammed Oudeh (Abu Daoud) maintained that Salameh wasn't involved at all and that he, Oudeh, planned and commanded the operation. Doubts about Salameh's role were also raised in two books on the subject, Kai Bird's *The Good Spy* and Aaron Klein's *Striking Back*.

But to this day, Yitzhaki remains confident: "The fact that Abu Daoud, years after the event, when Salameh was no longer alive, wanted to take all the credit for himself makes no difference. Ali

Salameh was not present when the attack went down in Munich, but he was involved in the deepest manner possible in the planning, recruitment of personnel, and perpetration of that shocking murder."

In any case, Salameh was a marked man. "Ali Hassan Salameh was the number-one target," Harari said. "We hunted him for a long time." The Mossad had only one recent photograph of him, though, which they used, without success, to try to locate him. Information about him took Bayonet operatives to Hamburg, Berlin, Rome, Paris, Stockholm, and other European cities. Each time, they seemed to have missed him by moments.

The breakthrough came in mid-July 1973, after an Algerian named Kemal Benamene, who was working for Fatah and had links with Black September, left his apartment in Geneva for a flight to Copenhagen and waited for him there. The Mossad had reason to believe he was planning an attack with Salameh, and he was followed. If they could stick close to Benamene, the Israelis reasoned, they would reach Salameh and be able to kill him.

The Caesarea men trailing Benamene saw that he didn't leave Copenhagen airport, but instead went to the area for passengers in transit and then immediately boarded a flight to Oslo. From there he took a train to Lillehammer. The whole time, he was followed by Mossad operatives. Harari and Romi concluded that he was going to meet their target in the sleepy Norwegian town.

Commandeering personnel from two Bayonet teams engaged in missions elsewhere in Europe, Harari rapidly formed a task force. The team of twelve was headed by Nehemia Meiri and comprised a mixture of trained assassins and other operatives and Caesarea staffers who knew Norwegian and were available for the job. One of these team members was Sylvia Rafael, the operative who traveled the Arab world posing as an anti-Israeli Canadian photojournalist named Patricia Roxburgh and gathered much valuable information on the armies in the region.

Other members of the squad included Avraham Gehmer, who had been Rafael's training officer; Dan Arbel, a Danish-Israeli businessman who occasionally took part in Mossad operations in Arab countries, helping with logistics and renting cars and apartments;

and Marianne Gladnikoff, an immigrant from Sweden and former
Shin Bet employee who had just recently joined the Mossad but who
spoke Scandinavian languages fluently.


WHAT HAPPENED NEXT IS a matter of some dispute. In one version, likely the most accurate, the Caesarea surveillance team lost
Benamene's trail in Lillehammer. They then began using the "combing method," a technique Meiri helped devise in the 1950s when he
was looking for KGB agents in Israel, which enabled the search team
to cover large urban areas and quickly locate their target's position.
After a day's search, they zeroed in on a man sitting with a group of
Arabs in a café in the center of the town. He looked, they thought,
exactly like the man in the photograph of Salameh they were carrying, "like two brothers look like each other," General Aharon Yariv, the
former head of AMAN who was now Prime Minister Meir's adviser
on counterterrorism, later said.

In another version, the man identified as Salameh was not just
sitting with some unknown Arabs in a café, but was actually spotted
in a meeting with known Fatah activists. In this version, then, the
Israelis saw that the suspect was associating with other known terrorists, and thus they had an additional indication, apart from the photograph, that this was most likely the man they were looking for.

Either way, a report that Salameh had been positively identified
was transmitted to the Mossad HQ, on Shaul Hamelech Street in Tel
Aviv. But Harari was told that it was not possible for him to speak to
the director, Zvi Zamir, because he had decided to travel to Lillehammer himself in order to be there when the hit was carried out. Harari
instructed his team to continue with the surveillance.

They soon discovered that the man they thought was Salameh
lived a quiet life in Lillehammer. He had a blond Norwegian girlfriend
who was heavily pregnant. He went to the movies and to an indoor
pool in town. He didn't betray any of the skittishness or caution of a
man concerned that the Mossad might be looking for him. Marianne
Gladnikoff purchased a swimsuit and went to the pool to watch and
observe him. What she saw only made her question whether this man
really was the most wanted Palestinian terrorist after all.

She was not the only one. But when Gladnikoff and others expressed their doubts to Harari—who in turn discussed them with Zamir, already in Oslo, en route to Lillehammer—they were dismissed. "We told them that we thought this wasn't our man," an operative nicknamed Shaul said. "But Mike and Zvika [Zamir] said it made no difference. They said, 'Even if it isn't Salameh, it's clear that he's some other Arab with connections to terrorists. So even if we don't hit Salameh, the worst we'd do is kill a less important terrorist, but still a terrorist."

Harari had his own opinion: "Seven operatives make a positive identification between the photograph and the man we'd seen in the street, and only a minority think it wasn't him. You have to decide, and you go with the majority. The easiest thing is to say 'Don't pull the trigger,' but that way you'll end up doing nothing."

The target was kept under observation. In a phone call on Saturday, July 21, Zamir, who had not managed to get the train to Lillehammer, ordered Harari to proceed with the hit. That night, the man and his girlfriend left their apartment and took a bus to a movie theater. The Bayonet team, in vehicles and on foot, did not let them out of their sight. At about 10:30, the couple left the theater and took the bus home. When they got off the bus, a gray Volvo stopped nearby, and Shaul and Y., another operative, got out. The two drew silenced Beretta pistols and shot the man eight times before running back to the car and making off. They left the woman, who was not hit, kneeling over their victim, screaming as she cradled his bloody head.

The hit men drove to a prearranged meeting place, where some of the other team members and Mike Harari were waiting. Shaul reported that the job was a success, but added that they had seen a woman who had witnessed the killing write down the Volvo's license number as they drove away.

Harari told the logistics man, Arbel, to park the car on a side street and toss the keys into a storm drain. Then Arbel and Gladnikoff were to take a train to Oslo and fly to London and then Israel. The other operatives were to wait in rented apartments for a few hours and then fly out as well. Meanwhile, Harari and the two assassins would drive south to Oslo, where they would take a ferry to Copenhagen.

Shaul and Y. took separate flights out of Denmark. Harari boarded a plane for Amsterdam, confident, flush with success. Salameh's elimination was the final rung on the ladder of Harari's climb to the directorship of the Mossad once Zamir's term ended. Only in Amsterdam, while watching the news on TV, did he finally understand that a catastrophe had just occurred.

THE MAN THE ISRAELIS killed in Lillehammer was not Ali Hassan Salameh, but Ahmed Bouchiki, a Moroccan working as a waiter and cleaning man at the swimming pool. He was married to a woman named Torill, who was seven months pregnant. She described what happened:

> All of a sudden, my husband fell. I did not understand what had happened, and then I saw those two men. They were three, four meters away from us. One of them was the driver of the car, and the second was his passenger. They stood outside the car, on both sides, firing pistols. I fell flat on the ground, sure they wanted to kill me, too, and that I would die in a moment. But then I heard the car doors slam and it drove away. My husband didn't shout. . . . I got up and ran as fast as I could to the nearest house and told them to call the police and an ambulance. When I got back, there were already people around my husband trying to help him. An ambulance came and I drove with my husband to the hospital, and there they told me he was dead.

Mossad chief Zamir tried to dismiss the disaster: "Not one of us has the means of making only correct decisions. Wrong identification of a target is not a failure. It's a mistake." Zamir placed some of the blame on the victim's conduct: "He behaved in a manner that seemed suspicious to our people who were following him. He made a lot of journeys, the aim of which it is difficult to know. He may have been dealing in drugs."

Meiri was not at the scene because he'd torn a ligament the day before and had been sent back to Israel by Harari. In his version of events, Bouchiki was seen meeting with known Fatah operative

Kemal Benamene. He insisted the operation was therefore still a success. "It angers me that it is seen as a failure," he said. "What difference does it make if I kill the arch-murderer or his deputy?"

But there's no substantive evidence that Bouchiki was anyone's deputy. In truth, he had no connection at all to terrorism, and the Lillehammer affair was nothing but the cold-blooded murder of an innocent pool attendant.

And Bayonet's problems were just beginning. According to Shaul, while waiting for the hit to go down, Dan Arbel had bought a faucet and a few other items for a house he was building in Israel. He put them in the trunk of the gray Volvo—the car Harari later told him to dump because a witness had gotten the plate number. But Arbel didn't want to carry his rather heavy purchases, so instead of getting rid of the Volvo, he drove it to the airport in Oslo with Gladnikoff.

The police were waiting at the rental car return at the airport. Arbel broke down fairly quickly under interrogation because of his claustrophobia. "Only after the operation," Shaul said, "did we read in Arbel's file [about] his fear of closed places and how apprehensive he was about getting caught and interrogated. It was very unprofessional behavior on Caesarea's part. A man writes an honest report and no one reads it. If they had read it, he would have been suspended immediately from operational duties."

Arbel told the police where to find Avraham Gehmer and Sylvia Rafael, and a search of their hideout led to the capture of two more operatives. It was already clear to the Norwegians that this was a targeted killing and the Mossad was behind it. Documents found on the detainees (which the operatives were supposed to have destroyed after reading them) led to the discovery all across Europe of safe houses, collaborators, communications channels, and operational methods. The information also helped the Italian and French security authorities with their investigations into targeted killings that had been carried out in their countries.

The six detainees were put on trial, making headlines all across the globe and causing extreme discomfort in Israel. Particularly embarrassing was that Arbel had given up everything, even the phone number of Mossad HQ in Tel Aviv. Israel did not admit that it was responsible for killing Bouchiki, but the state provided legal defense and other assistance for the prisoners. The court found that the Mossad was behind the murder. Five of the six were found guilty and sentenced to prison terms ranging from one to five and a half years, but they were all released after serving only short periods because a secret agreement was reached between the governments of Israel and Norway. Upon their release from prison, they were greeted as returning heroes in Israel.

Harari and Zamir kept their jobs, although the snafu probably cost Harari his dream of becoming head of the Mossad. "Lillehammer was a real failure all down the line, from those who tailed the target to the shooters, from the Mossad to the State of Israel," said Caesarea veteran Moti Kfir. "By a miracle, precisely those who were truly responsible for what happened came out of it without any harm."

That miracle was Golda Meir, the Mossad's greatest fan. Harari claimed that he and Zamir acknowledged their responsibility for the debacle and that "we offered our immediate resignations to Golda. She wouldn't hear of it. She said there were important things to be done, that we were needed, and that we must stay." During the weeks afterward, while Harari was trying to get his people out of jail, the prime minister invited him to her modest apartment in north Tel Aviv and, Harari said, she "made me tea in her kitchen and tried really hard to cheer me up."

Still, the failure in Lillehammer led to a much more cautious Caesarea policy. On September 4, Harari was in charge of a wide-ranging operation by Caesarea and Rainbow in Rome, tracking a Black September squad headed by Amin al-Hindi, another of the figures on the list of eleven Israel wanted to kill because of their roles in the Munich massacre. This squad was acting on behalf of the Libyan ruler, Muammar Qaddafi, who had equipped them with six SA-7 Strela shoulder-launched antiaircraft missiles, with which they were planning to shoot down an El Al airliner just after it took off from Fiumicino Airport. Harari and his team followed them as they transported the missiles to an apartment in Ostia, a suburb of Rome that was "a catapult shot from the runway," in Harari's words. They intended to fire the missiles from the roof of the building.

In a nearby playground, sitting on a lawn with kids playing around their mothers, Harari and Zamir sat and argued with Meiri, who pleaded, "Let me go in. I'll knock them all off in a minute and take the missiles."

But after the Lillehammer fiasco, Zamir was wary. Over Meiri's vociferous objections, Zamir said, "Nehemia, not this time. We'll inform Italian intelligence and let them take care of it."

"And what'll we get out of that?" Meiri asked. "The Arabs will hijack an Italian plane or threaten them some other way, and they'll let these guys go."

"If an El Al plane was in immediate danger, then we'd blow up not only the apartment but the whole building, but there are still many hours before they're planning to fire the missiles," Harari responded. "Besides, when we blasted Hamshari, we knew the bomb would hit only the lamp and the desk and his head, but here? How can I let you start a gunfight in a six-story building when I don't know who their neighbors are and who else is likely to get hurt? Perhaps the prime minister of Italy lives in the apartment across the hall? Perhaps the prime minister's grandmother?"

Meiri wasn't persuaded. His fury soared when Zamir ordered him to be the Mossad representative to go with the Italian police and point out the apartment, because he was the one who knew how to speak Italian best. "If they see me, I'll be burned, and I'll never be able to take part in another op," Meiri complained.

Harari tried to calm him. "Don't worry, Nehemia. There are some excellent plastic surgeons in Israel. We'll give you a new face, even better than the one you've got now. Go show them where the apartment is."

The Italians arrested all the members of al-Hindi's squad, but, exactly as Meiri had predicted, they were freed after three months because of pressure from Qaddafi.

Bayonet was in effect disbanded because of the Lillehammer affair. The fake Italian passport Meiri had used for the operation was exposed during the investigation by the Norwegian police, and his travels abroad were severely curtailed. He left the Mossad shortly afterward.

# HUBRIS

THE LILLEHAMMER MESS NOTWITHSTANDING, the general mood in the defense establishment remained euphoric following Operation Spring of Youth. There was a newfound sense of confidence, and it was not limited to the Mossad, but spread through all of the Israeli leadership.

Two days after the operation, Defense Minister Moshe Dayan climbed to the top of the mountain fortress of Masada. It was here that Jewish zealots rebelling against the Roman Empire killed themselves and their families rather than be taken captive, thus creating the nation's major heroic myth. Dayan declared, "We shall establish a new Israel with wide borders, not like those of 1948. . . . These days are blessed with conditions the likes of which it is doubtful that our nation has ever seen in the past." Chief of staff Elazar, in a letter to Zamir, boasted that after Spring of Youth, "the prestige of the IDF has soared to new heights and its glory has increased." And Golda Meir, on April 15, 1973, wrote, "Perhaps the day will come when the stories of heroism and resourcefulness, sacrifice and devotion, of these warriors will be told in Israel, and generations will recount them to those who follow them with admiration and pride, as yet another chapter in the heritage of heroism of our nation."

Yet confidence can too easily slip into overconfidence, the pitfalls of which weren't limited to Caesarea and the Lillehammer fiasco. Forty years after the raid, Ehud Barak, the leader of the Beirut hit team and later chief of staff, prime minister, and minister of defense, suggested that this hubris had disastrous consequences for the entire nation. "In retrospect," he said, "it seems to me that we came back from Beirut that night and the country's leaders drew the wrong conclusions from the success of the operation. It created a self-confidence that lacked foundation. It is impossible to project from a surgical, pinpoint commando raid onto the abilities of the entire army, as if the IDF can do anything, that we are omnipotent.

"They—the prime minister, the defense minister, and all the rest—saw us, the Sayeret and the Mossad, get the order and, within a few weeks, act on it. And we acted on it well. This gave them the sense that such a capability was common to the entire military. But our successes, both in the Six-Day War and in the operations that followed it, sprang from accurate planning and optimal use of the element of surprise. We were the ones who initiated. We set the timetables as well as the outcomes.

"And with our new sense of security came complacency as well. We did not think that they could take us by surprise, too, that they could damage us just as badly."

Unwavering faith in the armed forces and the belief that the three branches of the defense establishment—the IDF, the Shin Bet, and the Mossad—could save Israel from any danger whatsoever led the country's leadership to also feel that there was no pressing need to reach a diplomatic compromise with the Arabs. Others outside Israel disagreed.

In 1972, U.S. National Security Adviser Henry Kissinger launched a secret diplomatic initiative aimed at achieving a peace agreement, or at least a non-belligerency pact, between Israel and Egypt. He realized that as long as Israel held on to the Egyptian territories it had conquered in 1967, Egypt would do whatever it could to reconquer them, and the next conflagration in the Middle East would be only a matter of time.

The high point of the initiative came during dramatic meetings at a CIA safe house in Armonk, New York, on February 25 and 26, 1973, between Kissinger and an Egyptian emissary. The emissary declared that Egypt was prepared to sign a peace treaty with Israel, the terms of which—Israeli recognition of Egypt's sovereignty over the Sinai Peninsula, but retention of Israeli forces there, with a full retreat later on in exchange for the establishment of diplomatic relations between the two countries—were unprecedentedly favorable to Israel. Yet Egypt's president, Anwar Sadat, also warned that if his offer was not taken up by September, he would go to war.

Meir refused. "We'll pass on this," Meir told Kissinger.

Dayan concurred. "I prefer Sharm el-Sheikh without peace," he said, "to peace without Sharm el-Sheikh."

By this time, Egypt and Syria were already feverishly engaged in preparing their armed forces for war: massive troop movement toward and then away from the front lines; air force exercises in conjunction with the advanced surface-to-air missile systems the Soviets had supplied them; training commando forces in the use of Sagger antitank missiles; and vast maneuvers to prepare for crossing the Suez Canal in great force. These were all obvious preparations for war, but without any intelligence explicitly confirming that fact, the Israeli defense establishment dismissed them as mere war games.

Elazar had been convinced that the Mossad and AMAN would be able to give Israel at least forty-eight hours' warning before the outbreak of war, enough time to mobilize the reserves. He and his cohorts weren't much worried, in any case, confident as they were that the Arabs were frightened of Israel and wouldn't dare start a war. If they did, the Israelis were sure that "we would break their bones" in short order.

They were wrong.

On October 6, at 2 P.M., the Egyptian and Syrian armies launched massive, concerted surprise attacks against Israel. It was Yom Kippur, the Jewish Day of Atonement, when Israelis, even nonreligious ones, fast and go to synagogue or stay at home, so the forces on the front lines were thinly spread. The Egyptians threw 2,200 tanks, 2,900 armored personnel carriers, 2,400 artillery pieces, large amounts of antiaircraft and antitank weaponry, and hundreds of thousands of infantry and commando troops into the battle, much of it across the Suez Canal. On the Golan Heights, the Syrians invaded Israeli territory with 60,000 troops, 1,400 tanks, and 800 guns. Both also activated the bulk of their air and naval forces. The Israeli units facing them were made up of a few hundred men, mostly reservists who'd been kept there to allow the regular forces to go home for the holy day.

Within the first few days, the Arab armies scored notable victories against the Israelis, who, in addition to being taken by surprise, also read the other side's tactics incorrectly. The Egyptians established a formidable beachhead on the Sinai side of the canal, and the Syrians penetrated deep into the Golan Heights and were threatening to sweep down into the Jordan Valley and the Galilee.

However, by dint of massive effort and sacrifice, the Israelis managed to stem the invasions and, after nineteen days of counterattack, turned the tables on the enemy. The Egyptians were expelled from almost the entire beachhead. Israeli units crossed the canal and, after surrounding the enemy forces on the western side of the waterway, advanced toward Cairo, reaching a point only sixty miles from the Egyptian capital. The Syrians were driven out of the Golan, and Israeli forces advanced until they were within artillery range of Damascus.

But the victory came at a heavy cost. More than 2,300 Israeli soldiers died in the Yom Kippur War, a war that could have been prevented through negotiation, or at least prepared for with adequate prior intelligence.

A wave of protest swept through Israeli society, which led to the establishment of a commission of inquiry and the forced resignation of chief of staff Elazar and AMAN chief Zeira, along with other top officers. The war dispelled, at least temporarily, Israelis' sense of military and espionage supremacy and, thus, their sense of security. Although the panel did not explicitly blame Meir or Dayan, due to heavy public pressure, the prime minister tendered her resignation on April 11.


A MONTH LATER, AT around 4:30 A.M. on the morning of May 13, 1974, three members of the Democratic Front for the Liberation of Palestine (DFLP), a PLO splinter group not connected with the PFLP, sneaked across the Lebanese border into Israel. They hid in a cave until nightfall. An Israeli Border Police patrol found their footprints but did not manage to track them down. Under cover of darkness, the three began making their way toward Maalot, a town about six miles from the frontier populated mostly by new immigrants. On the way, they ambushed a vehicle carrying women on their way home from work, killing one and wounding another. IDF troops called to the scene failed to apprehend the terrorists.

At 3:30 A.M., the three came to a house on the outskirts of the town. Two of them were natives of Haifa and could speak Hebrew, and they told the people inside the house that they were police looking for terrorists. When the door opened, they burst inside and murdered Yosef and Fortuna Cohen and their four-year-old son, Moshe, and wounded their daughter, Bibi. They did not notice sixteen-month-old Yitzhak, a deaf-mute who didn't make a sound. As they left the house, the Palestinians ran into Yaakov Kadosh, an employee of the local government, and demanded that he tell them the way to the school. He did so, and then they shot and injured him.

The three arrived at the Netiv Meir school, intending to lie in wait for the children arriving the next day. They did not expect to find eighty-five teenagers, aged fifteen to seventeen, and ten adults already sleeping there. The children were from a religious school in Safed, and they were on an overnight field trip in the Maalot region. When security forces arrived on the scene, the terrorists shouted that if twenty of their comrades in Israeli prisons were not released by 6 A.M., they would kill all their hostages.

The normally aggressive Golda Meir, who had not yet been replaced as prime minister, was prepared to concede to the terrorists' demands. After the shock of the Yom Kippur War, the conclusions of the inquiry, and the angry protest demonstrations against her, Meir did not want her last act as prime minister to be one that endangered the lives of children. The cabinet endorsed her recommendation. However, Minister of Defense Dayan, also about to be replaced, disagreed. The fallout from the Yom Kippur War had had the opposite effect on him: After thousands of protesters in Tel Aviv had demanded his resignation, Dayan saw his political career on the brink of a humiliating conclusion, and he wanted to project determination and authority. "The only way to handle terrorists is to not give them what they want and not let them get out of here alive. We have to kill them," he urged the prime minister. Eventually, Meir gave her consent. At 5:15 A.M., the order was given for Sayeret Matkal to break into the school.

This time, the Sayeret proved inadequate to the task. The sniper who fired the first shot only slightly wounded his target, and a force commanded by Amiram Levin entered the wrong room on the wrong floor. The terrorists responded by firing and tossing grenades into the classroom where the hostages were being held. Because the hostages were devoutly religious, they were sitting separately—the boys along the walls and the girls in the middle—and the girls took most of the fire. In the thirty seconds before the Sayeret managed to reach the terrorists and kill them, twenty-two children—eighteen of them girls—four adult hostages, and one soldier were killed. Sixty-eight people were wounded, including every surviving hostage.

It was a dismal end to Meir's political career. On June 3, 1974, she was replaced by Yitzhak Rabin, the Six-Day War chief of staff and former ambassador to the United States. Rabin was fifty-two, the youngest person to serve as prime minister at that point, and the first Israeli-born sabra in that position. He was also utterly different from Meir in that, while she refrained almost entirely from interfering with the recommendations of her military and intelligence advisers, Rabin involved himself in the minutest details of all military and counterterror operations.

And there were many such operations to come.

THE MAALOT ATTACK WAS the beginning of a new round of terror, yet another reverberation from Operation Spring of Youth.

The PLO had undergone a number of organizational and structural changes following the deaths of their three leaders in Beirut. The Mossad believed that the operation had had a chilling effect. "It instilled in them great fear," said Shimshon Yitzhaki.

"It obliged them to hide and run," added Harari. "We managed to disrupt them. It was not for nothing that Arafat didn't sleep in the same bed for two nights running."

On the other hand, Spring of Youth had also strengthened the hand of Abu Jihad. Most of his internal rivals were now out of the way, thanks to the efforts of Israel. After Spring of Youth, Arafat and Abu Jihad decided to terminate the activities of Black September and put a stop to attacks on targets outside Israel and the occupied lands. Some journalists and historians, including prominent Palestinians, believe that they did so because they realized that acts of terror against Israelis or Jews in Western countries ended up harming the Palestinian cause more than helping it. They also undoubtedly realized that the moment they committed acts of terror in Europe, they bestowed legitimacy upon Israel's targeted killing operations against their own people on that continent, making the price of each terrorist attack very high.

Others credit the fact that the PLO obtained international standing in 1974, when Arafat was invited to address the UN General Assembly. The truth is probably somewhere in between.

Either way, as the head of the PLO's Supreme Military Council, Abu Jihad ordered all terrorist attacks to be targeted inside "the occupied motherland." Militants slipped into the country through airports and seaports from Europe, came over the Jordan border or, like the three terrorists who attacked Maalot, launched raids from Lebanon.

The Maalot attack, orchestrated by the DFLP, reflected Abu Jihad's strategy. It was the most lethal attack by the Palestinians since Munich and the worst that had ever been launched across the border into Israeli territory. But it was not the last, merely an indication of what was yet to come.

At around 11 P.M. on March 5, 1975, eight of Abu Jihad's men sailed into Israeli waters on a ship disguised as an Egyptian merchant vessel. Under the dark of a moonless night, the terrorists climbed into a rubber dinghy and landed on a beach in Tel Aviv. They walked through the sand toward the street, then sprayed the Herbert Samuel Esplanade with automatic fire.

Their ship was made to look Egyptian because the terrorists wanted to sabotage an upcoming visit to the region by Secretary of State Henry Kissinger, who had not given up on his attempts to bring peace between Israel and Egypt.

The terrorists seized the Savoy Hotel, a down-market establishment a block away from the beach. The men burst into the lobby, killed the reception clerk, and herded all the guests they found into one room.

This was "the first time terrorists had succeeded in getting a squad into the heart of the country," said a secret military report on the incident shortly after it ended. The terrorists were so close to the Kirya compound, the former Templer neighborhood where Israel's military and intelligence outfits were headquartered, that a stray bullet from an AK-47 flew through a window and landed in a meeting room where the IDF's top commanders were gathered.

Inside the Savoy, the eight terrorists, armed with AK-47 assault rifles and grenade launchers, placed a series of explosive devices around the room where they were holding the eleven hostages. (Another eight civilians were hiding elsewhere in the hotel.) They threatened to kill them all unless twenty Palestinian prisoners were released within four hours.

In addition, although almost two years had passed, the Palestinians announced that their raid was retaliation for Operation Spring of Youth.

Negotiations continued through the night, conducted through one of the hostages, a resourceful young Arabic-speaking woman named Kochava Levy, who gave the Israelis much valuable information on what was happening inside the hotel. She also persuaded the terrorists to allow her to take a badly wounded German tourist, who'd lost a leg in the exchanges of fire and was lying in the hotel lobby, out of the building, and although she could have stayed outside, she bravely went back in to help with the negotiations.

But Israel never had any intention of releasing the Palestinian prisoners. Instead, while the Israeli negotiator stalled for time, a Sayeret Matkal force plotted a rescue operation. At 5:16 A.M., forty-four commandos stormed the hotel. They killed seven of the terrorists and later captured one. But only eleven of the hostages were rescued. Eight civilians were killed when the terrorists realized they were under attack and detonated the charges. Three soldiers were also killed, including a staff officer who was a former commander of the unit and had followed the raiding party into the hotel.

This was seen as yet another significant failure in a seemingly endless cycle. "It was a terrible time," said Omer Bar-Lev, a Sayeret Matkal soldier who took part in the raid on the hotel and rose to become the unit's commander. "Every few weeks we scrambled in the middle of the night and were put on a chopper to go to the scene of another terror attack. You knew that in the few hours you had before dawn, you had to eliminate the problem. Although it was all happening inside Israel, the nature of the operations was different from what the unit was used to—all the initiative, all of the element of surprise, all the planning was the other side's. Terribly scary."

WITH THE ATTACKS CONTINUING unabated, it was clear that Israel needed to redouble its efforts to eliminate the PLO leadership. But even when Bayonet was functioning at full strength, the Mossad had found it difficult to operate in target countries such as Lebanon, where the heads of the Palestinian terror organization lived. Moreover, security precautions had tightened up considerably after Operation Spring of Youth. Using Mossad operatives to eliminate the PLO leadership was now seen as impractical, if not impossible.

Instead, Israel turned to its air force. In mid-August 1975, a Mossad mole inside Fatah reported that the PLO was planning a rally in a stadium, Al-Madina al-Riyadiyyah, in south Beirut, on October 1, and that one hour before that rally the entire Fatah leadership would be meeting in a nearby office. This was seen as an ideal opportunity to get rid of Yasser Arafat, Khalil al-Wazir (Abu Jihad), Farouk Kaddoumi, Hani al-Hassan, Wadie Haddad, and many other senior officials all at once. Prime Minister Yitzhak Rabin ordered that a plan be drawn up immediately.

While the chief of staff and the air force were in favor of an attack, the head of AMAN, General Shlomo Gazit, vigorously opposed it. "I told Defense Minister Shimon Peres that we must not get involved in something open like this. I was prepared to combat terrorism with full force, but only in clandestine operations that did not leave a calling card. There were some Israelis who were not ashamed of the targeted killings. My attitude was the opposite: I was ashamed. I sat quietly and didn't brag about them."

His objections were overruled, and planning began. Major Aviem Sella, then a rising star in the air force, was appointed to coordinate the operation. Eight A-4 Skyhawk attack aircraft and one F-4 Phantom fighter-bomber were scheduled to take part. Helicopters were readied in case any pilot was shot down or crashed and needed rescue. Everything was going according to plan.

Then, on the morning of the operation, the weather report came in. The forecast was for heavy clouds over Beirut. Because the Israelis' bombs at that time lacked precise, all-weather guidance mechanisms, there would be no certainty of hitting the target. "But it was so inviting, so once-in-a-lifetime," Major Sella said. "And all those vast preparations—a large part of the air force was on operational footing. We decided to give it a go. I told Benny [Peled, commander of the air force], 'Come on, let's take a chance—send the planes up and maybe a miracle will happen.'"

The pilots took off, hoping that the skies would clear. The skies didn't oblige, and clouds were still covering Beirut when they reached the city.

But Sella "had not taken into account the motivation of the pilots," as he later acknowledged. The pilots had been ordered not to drop their bombs if they couldn't see the target, but that still gave them a significant amount of discretion. They knew the nature of the target and grasped how important it was to Israel that the PLO's leaders be eliminated.

The pilots dived under the cloud cover to a lower altitude than their orders permitted. When they saw they were over the target, they released their bombs, which contained an arming device operated by a cable connected to the aircraft. But since they were flying lower than they were supposed to, the fuses remained unarmed, and the bombs fell onto the ground and the roofs of buildings without going off, "like a batch of abandoned eggs," in Sella's words.

Only Abu Jihad's driver was killed in the air raid, crushed by one of the undetonated bombs. The next day, a Beirut newspaper ran a cartoon showing a Palestinian boy peeing on an Israeli bomb. Abu Jihad ordered an investigation to find out who had leaked the intel about the meeting. Three months later, another Mossad asset was exposed and executed.

WHILE FATAH WAS NOW concentrating its terror activities inside Israel, the Popular Front for the Liberation of Palestine kept up its murderous attacks against Jewish and Israeli targets abroad, particularly in Europe. The PFLP bombed synagogues, Israeli legations, and

El Al offices. Its militants hijacked planes flying to Israel, a technique in which they had grown quite skillful.

George Habash was still the leader of the PFLP, but the organization's most brilliant operational mind belonged to Habash's deputy,
Wadie Haddad.

"He had a virtuoso talent for clandestine transportation of explosives to the site of an attack and their concealment there," said Ilan
Mizrahi, who ran agents inside Haddad's organization. "He preferred
quality operations, sometimes far away, after careful planning," said
Shimshon Yitzhaki, the Mossad's counterterror chief. "The training
he gave his men at a base in South Yemen was of a different league
from what we were used to."

Others admired Haddad's professionalism as well. The KGB,
which gave him the code name Nationalist, granted him generous
assistance in order "to reach some of our own objectives through the
activities of the PLFP while maintaining the necessary secrecy," as
the head of that agency, Yuri Andropov, wrote to the Soviet leader,
Leonid Brezhnev, in 1969. Haddad eliminated Soviet defectors and
attacked targets connected to the CIA, and in return he received
funding, training, advanced weaponry, and intelligence from the
KGB and the Stasi.

Haddad was independent and resolute. When Habash announced
internally that he was weighing compliance, even "only temporarily,"
with Arafat's request that terrorist acts outside the Middle East be
put on hold, Haddad declared that Habash could do as he pleased
but that he and his men would carry on in their own way.

For many long years, Haddad planned a major attack, one that
would shock the world. He invested much time in the planning and
intelligence gathering but kept on postponing it because of various
operational snags. One of the most difficult challenges was that he
needed to find operatives who looked European. In mid-1975, the
solution cropped up.

The PLO had excellent ties with a number of militant extreme
left-wing organizations in Europe and had even set up training camps
for them in Lebanon and South Yemen, which had close ties with the
Soviet Union and took an extreme anti-Israeli line.

Haddad was on especially good terms with West Germany's Red

Army Faction (RAF), also known as the Baader-Meinhof Gang. Its members espoused an anarchist-Marxist ideology and practiced urban guerrilla tactics against Germany's law enforcement and big businesses. They saw Israel, with its oppression of the Palestinians, as another front in the war against the evils of imperialism.

Two RAF members, Thomas Reuter and Brigitte Schulz, who had just been released from prison, slipped out of Germany and turned up at a PFLP training camp near Aden, where they joined up with other RAF comrades. These were the Westerners Haddad needed.

Three of the PFLP's own men were ordered to wait outside the airport in Nairobi, Kenya, for an incoming El Al airplane while the two Germans watched the airline's counter in the terminal to ascertain the final arrival time of the flight and to alert the squad waiting outside.

Immediately after the plane flew over them, the PFLP men were supposed to shoot it down with Strela SAM 7 shoulder-borne missiles.

In the two months before the operation, the men had practiced firing Strelas and studied sketches of the Nairobi airport made by PFLP operatives who had conducted a preliminary reconnaissance. Together, they identified an area outside and slightly west of the airport, studded with clumps of tall trees and cactuses, between the main Mombasa Road and the fence of Nairobi National Park. From this spot, there was a clear line of sight to the airport's runway.

A week before the operation, two Strelas supplied to Haddad by the KGB were smuggled into Kenya. The eight members of the squad had entered Kenya separately, with forged passports, nine days before, and they checked into a hotel downtown.

Everything was ready for the attack, but the Mossad had gotten wind of the plot through the Junction agent Sadness.

An argument broke out inside the agency, with the head of Junction, Shmuel Goren, wanting more than anything else to protect Sadness and fearing that if the Mossad revealed the details of the planned attack to the Kenyan authorities and assisted them in thwarting it, Haddad's group would realize that the Mossad was running an agent with access to its secrets. That could have spelled the end of Sadness. Goren proposed foiling the plot using "Hebrew labor"—i.e., targeted killings of the perpetrators by Bayonet—"without sharing it with the locals."

On the other side, the head of the Mossad's foreign relations division, Nahum Admoni, who had been in charge of the agency's Africa operations for a long time and knew President Jomo Kenyatta and his intelligence chiefs well, vigorously opposed carrying out such an action under the noses of "the locals."

There were also operational considerations: Bayonet had only just begun to reorganize after the disastrous Lillehammer affair, and "we felt that to handle several people simultaneously, while they were holding missiles in their hands, could be too complicated," said former Mossad official Eliezer Tsafrir.

Yitzhak Hofi, an ex-general who had taken over as Mossad director from Zamir in 1974, was visiting his CIA counterparts at Langley and was informed there about the developments. He sent an encoded message to Rabin with his recommendation: to collaborate with the Kenyan authorities and not to use Bayonet.

"The principle had not changed—if someone kills a Jew, his blood be on his own head," said Yitzhaki. "But it's impossible to bump people off every day. Targeted killings entail a severe risk to your own people and the danger of fouling up relations with the country where you carry them out—in this case, Kenya. In operations, the rule is not to do unnecessary things. You have a target, execute a clean op. Forget everything else. Our supreme goal was to make sure nothing would happen to the El Al plane, and at the same time to protect the security of our source as fully as possible."

So instead of attempting to kill the terror squad, the Israelis enlisted the help of Kenya's security forces. On Friday, January 23, 1976, late at night, a team of seventeen Israelis flew out of Israeli Air Force Base 27, headed for Nairobi. The operation was code-named Heartburn. "There was great anxiety," recalled Tsafrir, who was a member of the team on the plane. "So many lives at stake, depending on us and the success of the operation."

As soon as the Israeli team landed, Admoni met with Kenyan intelligence agency officers to inform them of the impending attack. The Kenyans were shocked. President Kenyatta was particularly incensed when he grasped that Somalia was involved. The Kenyans willingly agreed to cooperate—they were pleased that the Mossad wasn't acting on its own under their noses. They did insist on knowing the identity of the Mossad's sources, in order to be sure that they were about to act on the basis of reliable information, but Admoni politely declined.

A combined Mossad-Kenyan team soon located the Germans and the Palestinians and placed them under close surveillance. They also located the white minibus, with license plate KPR338, in which the missiles had been deposited. Later, the team followed the three Palestinians when they drove out to scout the launch site.

On January 25, El Al Flight LY512 was due to take off from Johannesburg en route to Tel Aviv. The plane, a Boeing 707 with some 150 people on board, was scheduled to stop off in Nairobi at 5 P.M. Shortly before, the three Palestinians and the two Germans set out in their white minibus and another rental vehicle. Their first stop was to drop off the Germans at the terminal. Then they left the airport and got onto the main road, before turning right onto the dirt track in the direction of the planned launch site. But before they could reach it, Kenyan secret service operatives charged the group; immediately after that, they picked up the two Germans near the El Al counter in the terminal. All five surrendered without a struggle.

Thus far, the Kenyans had been completely cooperative with the Israelis, but they didn't want anything to become public, fearing the heavy Arab pressure they'd have to face in Third World and African forums if the affair came to light. They suggested two solutions: "Either we take them to the desert and feed them to the hyenas for lunch," or the Israelis could have them, with the understanding that they would never disclose that the prisoners were in their hands.

The Israelis hoped they'd be able to extract from the prisoners more information on Haddad and his activities, so they chose the second option: to effectively "disappear" the terrorists by whisking them off to Israel, where they would be held in isolation under extreme conditions and then face a secret trial. This was perhaps the first case of the West being involved in an activity that, after 9/11, the CIA would call "rendition"—the clandestine, undocumented, extrajudicial transfer of suspects from one country to another.

Interrogators from AMAN's Unit 504 and the unit's medical officer flew to Nairobi. The five prisoners were tied to stretchers and sedated before the six-hour flight to Israel.

Meanwhile, in Tel Aviv, some were reconsidering the wisdom of bringing the prisoners to Israeli land. General Rehavam Zeevi, the prime minister's counterterror and intelligence adviser, proposed an alternative to Yitzhak Rabin: "Let's drop the five righteous souls into the Red Sea and get rid of the problem," he said. "The Kenyans have kept quiet about the whole story. Nobody knows they've been caught. We have information that Wadie Haddad promised them that if they were captured, he'd hijack a plane to get them released. If we bring them to Israel and it gets out, it will only spark another wave of terror against us. Let's finish it off now."

Rabin looked at Zeevi and remained silent for a long while. Then he told an aide to convene an urgent meeting of the cabinet forum on targeted killings.

"What do you say?" Rabin asked the assembled ministers after they'd listened to Zeevi's proposal. They all agreed that bringing the five prisoners to Israel would endanger Israeli travelers everywhere in the world. Haddad was a seasoned hijacker who would do what he could to free his people. Rabin also agreed with this assessment but nevertheless refused to sign off on the execution of the sedated prisoners "unless the attorney general also agrees," he said. "Call Aharon in now."

Aharon Barak, who would later become chief justice of Israel's Supreme Court and the country's most renowned jurist, listened in silence to a description of the secret operation and the proposal to dump the perpetrators into the sea. "Have you finished?" he asked Zeevi when his exposition was over. "That's good," he said angrily, "because I think you must be insane. These are two German citizens you want to kill while they are tied up and sedated on an Israeli military plane. I cannot by any means approve of this."

The three Palestinians and two Germans landed safely in Israel and were taken to Unit 504's secret interrogation facility in a base code-named Stalk, southeast of Tel Aviv. They were placed in dark cells with bare walls, receiving doses of sedatives all the while. As they began to wake up, "we decided to play ghost games with them," says the head of the Shin Bet interrogation division, Arieh Hadar.

"We put on masks and wailed while they were coming to, as if they had died and were in the world hereafter."

The Israelis were very eager to learn as much as they could about the structure and methods of the PFLP, and perhaps even something about where Wadie Haddad could be found.

The senior 504 interrogator, Y., an officer with the rank of lieutenant colonel who sported the skullcap of an Orthodox Jew and was known for being a political right-winger, was put in charge of the three Palestinians. Y. was the man who ran the POW drills for the IDF's special-ops forces, with their simulation of harsh captivity conditions and torture. Shortly before the arrival of the Nairobi five, he had caused a permanent spinal injury to a Sayeret Matkal man by striking him with a baton. A few months after that, one of the Palestinians who'd been under Y.'s interrogation collapsed and was rushed to a hospital, where he died.

"Y. didn't kill him. He did not kill him. He died," said Yigal Simon, the commander of 504 at the time. "It was a long interrogation. Very long. He was beaten, but it was established that his death was not connected to this. The autopsy proved it."

When the three Arab operatives were brought from Kenya, Y. "worked them very hard," according to a Shin Bet operative. One of them was badly injured and also hospitalized, but he recovered.

The German prisoners enjoyed completely different treatment and were questioned politely by Shin Bet personnel. AMAN chief General Shlomo Gazit visited the interrogation facility. "The lady [Schulz] made a remarkable impression," he said. "A very strong woman, in control of herself and her surroundings with an iron hand. The guy was a drip." In the end, Hadar, who conducted the interrogation in his quiet, cunning way, won Schulz over with his soft speech and innocuous appearance.

The two Germans confessed, pleaded guilty, and provided information about Haddad. "They told us a lot, including plans for future terror attacks," said Hadar. "All of this time the woman from the Mossad [the German-Hebrew interpreter] is sitting there and telling me in Hebrew, 'I'd like to slaughter her.'

"Before we parted, I took Schulz's hand and asked, 'Brigitte, let's say that one day you go back to Germany and friends tell you that you have to kill Harry'—that's how she knew me. 'What will you do?' And she answers, without blinking, 'I couldn't kill you, Harry, after everything you've done for me.'

"I was pleased. I thought that perhaps at least something in her had changed for the better. But then she added, 'I'd ask someone else to shoot you.'"

ON JUNE 27, 1976, six months after the Kenyan attack was thwarted, Rabin and his cabinet convened for a meeting in the prime minister's office, in the Kirya-Sarona in Tel Aviv.

The ministers were discussing a proposal by Defense Minister Shimon Peres to increase the pay of IDF soldiers when, at 1:45 P.M., the military secretary entered the room and handed Rabin a note. Suddenly his face became grave. He cleared his throat to get everyone's attention. "Before we go on, I have an announcement to make," he said. "An Air France plane that took off from Lod at 9:50 has lost contact. Apparently hijacked. Apparently flying the other way. On the plane there are about eighty-three Israelis."

The military aide, Efraim Poran, told Rabin that intelligence agencies did not know yet who had perpetrated the hijacking and that he'd update him when more information came in.

There was a moment, Rabin confided to an associate later, when he regretted not giving the okay to throw the Nairobi five into the sea.

"Forget it," Rabin told Poran. "I know. It's Wadie Haddad."

There were four hijackers—two from the PFLP and two German leftist extremists. They had boarded the Paris-bound plane during a stopover in Athens, and after takeoff, they got up, drew guns, and burst into the cockpit, ordering the pilot to fly first to Benghazi, for refueling and to pick up three more terrorists, and then to Entebbe, Uganda.

Wadie Haddad had proved once again that he was the best strategist in the terrorist world. He had learned from his own and others' mistakes and had produced a large-scale operation based on accurate intelligence, meticulous preparations, and coordination with at least two despots, Libya's Muammar Qaddafi and Uganda's Idi Amin, both of whom extended logistical assistance and asylum to the hijackers, far from Israel's reach.

Amin, an ex-boxer and a sergeant in the British Army, had seized control of Uganda with the assistance of the Mossad and the Israeli Defense Ministry, which maintained secret ties with the country. In exchange for bribes Amin received in suitcases with double bottoms, he awarded Israel large military and civilian contracts and gave the Mossad a free hand in Uganda.

But Amin's bloodlust and cruelty were matched only by his lust for money, and in 1972, when Qaddafi began offering him bigger bribes than Israel had, he expelled its representatives and became its avowed enemy. He agreed to host the hijackers and their hostages at Entebbe, 2,200 miles from Israel.

Haddad believed that Israel would have no alternative but to negotiate with him. In Entebbe, his operatives released the 209 non-Israeli and non-Jewish passengers and the twelve Air France crew, though the crew, in a courageous act of solidarity, insisted on staying with the remaining eighty-three Israeli and eight non-Israeli Jewish passengers. The hijackers then demanded the release of fifty-three "freedom fighters" in exchange for the Israeli and Jewish hostages. This demand came via Idi Amin, who made telephone contact with Israel himself. The list of "freedom fighters" included Archbishop Hilarion Capucci, a man of the cloth who had used his diplomatic status to smuggle a large shipment of weaponry in his Mercedes sedan to Fatah cells in Jerusalem; Kozo Okamoto, one of the perpetrators of the 1972 Lod airport massacre; and the five terrorists who had been on the Nairobi mission, who Haddad was sure were in Kenyan or Israeli hands.

The Mossad was in turmoil. There were now many who regretted that the Nairobi five had not been dumped into the sea. At a command meeting, Tsafrir said, "They want the five? With pleasure. Let's fly them to Uganda and drop them from the plane onto the roof of the terminal so Haddad will realize that that's all he is going to get from us."

Meanwhile, the IDF planned a rescue operation involving a huge force that would land in the area of Lake Victoria, then secure the whole airport and a wide swath of land around it. Rabin listened to the plan, growing angrier by the minute.

"In the time that it takes to secure the whole area, the hijackers will slaughter all the hostages, and Idi Amin will have time to bring in reinforcements," he fumed.

"Rabin told the IDF that he wanted to see a plan in which no more than three minutes would elapse from the moment forces land until the rescue operation begins," said the director general of the prime minister's office, Amos Eiran. But from such a distance, without any intelligence, this seemed an impossible request.

Lacking any viable alternatives, Rabin was inclined to comply with the hijackers' demands. Though he loathed the idea, he saw no other way to save the hundred-plus innocent lives. But this action would entail a breach of the ironclad law laid down by Golda Meir and accepted thereafter as Israeli policy: no negotiations with terrorists. Shin Bet director Avraham Ahituv demanded that, if there truly was no other way, then, at the very least, no prisoners "with blood on their hands"—a phrase that has since been invoked repeatedly in similar situations—should be exchanged for hostages. In other words, only junior PLO functionaries, who had not been directly involved in spilling Israeli blood, could be considered for release. "Anyone who has killed a Jew," said Ahituv, "must either be eliminated or die in an Israeli prison after being sentenced to life."

For four days, the debate continued. Demonstrations by relatives of the hostages raged outside the gates to the Kirya, within earshot of Rabin's office. The daughter of the director of Israel's main nuclear reactor was one of the hostages. He had access to Rabin and exerted heavy pressure on him to reach a compromise with the terrorists.

If all that wasn't enough, Rabin then received a secret report from the Military Censorship Bureau that it had barred the publication, in an Israeli daily newspaper, of a story that included all the details of Operation Heartburn. Ahituv informed Rabin that he had ordered the reporter's phone to be tapped but had still not managed to determine the source of the leak. Rabin was furious: "I am really shocked . . . [that] it is impossible in this country to take a military correspondent and lock him up and grill him about where he got it from. . . . This [leakage of information] is going to be a disaster for us."

Rabin understood that breaking Israel's promise to Kenyatta of total secrecy about the Nairobi five would lead to a crisis in their relationship with Kenya. More important, disclosure of the affair could paint Israel, which was now asking for the world's support against the hijackers, as a pirate state employing terrorist-like methods. On the other hand, how could Israel negotiate with the terrorists when both they and Kenya denied having any knowledge of their whereabouts?

In the end, Caesarea came up with a solution that didn't require a hostage-for-prisoner swap. Five years earlier, Harari had decided that he needed an operative who could pose as a pilot. Why, exactly? "Because perhaps we'll need it one day" was his customary answer to any questions about preparations he'd made without any immediate cause. He persuaded Zamir to make the financial investment, and an operative code-named David underwent the lengthy training in Israel and Europe.

Now the investment paid off, big-time.

David rented a plane in Kenya and circled the Entebbe terminals and tarmac, taking photographs from the air. When he landed, he posed as a wealthy, pampered English hunter living in a Central African country who needed the assistance of the control tower on a number of matters. The Ugandan air controllers cooperated willingly and even had a drink with him, sharing their impressions of "the big mess of the last few days," their term for the hostage situation in the nearby terminal.

Twelve hours later, when Harari brought David's detailed report and the hundreds of photos he had taken to Rabin, the prime minister's face lit up. "This is just what I needed," he said. "This is the intelligence for an operation." Especially important to Rabin were the shots of Ugandan soldiers all around the terminal, which he took as proof that Wadie Haddad's men hadn't booby-trapped the building. "Idi Amin wouldn't have allowed his men to be there," he said. It was also clear from the pictures that the Ugandan force guarding the terminal was very small.

Sayeret Matkal came up with an original and daring plan: A small Sayeret contingent would land, under cover of darkness, in an unmarked C-130 Hercules military transport aircraft, using the runway lights that were lit for a civilian cargo plane scheduled to land before it. The force would disembark and travel toward the terminal in a number of vehicles behind a black Mercedes similar to the one used by Idi Amin, in order to confuse the Ugandan guards. Close to the terminal, the force would dismount and storm the building from several different entryways, taking advantage of the surprise and confusion to eliminate the terrorists. All of this was supposed to be accomplished in less than two minutes. More IDF forces would land immediately afterward and would deal with the control tower, the Ugandan soldiers, and the Ugandan air force jets, so that they would not be able to pursue the Israeli planes once they took off with the hostages and troops aboard. Kenyatta agreed to allow the Israeli aircraft to land in Nairobi to refuel on the way back.

Defense Minister Shimon Peres believed that the plan could succeed, and he pressed Rabin. On July 3, the prime minister gave the green light for the raid.

The commanders of the operation asked Rabin what to do if they ran into Amin himself. "If he interferes, the orders are to kill him," Rabin said. To which the foreign minister, Yigal Allon, added, "Even if he doesn't interfere."

The Israeli task force set out for the mission on four planes. Each soldier was given a map of Uganda and a sum of money in American dollars, in case they were stranded and had to escape on their own. "But it was clear to us that this was mere talk, and that in fact this was an operation without a getaway plan. If something were to go wrong, we'd be stuck there and would have to fight to the death," said Yiftach Reicher, the deputy to Yonatan Netanyahu, brother of Benjamin and now commander of Sayeret Matkal.

The first Hercules landed as planned. Reicher, who was in one of the Land Rovers following the black Mercedes, recalled the scene: "There was total silence and total darkness, blacker than black, in the huge, deserted airfield. Wide runways with nobody moving on them. All I thought to myself was 'Mommy, this is scary.'"

The element of surprise was almost lost when the force encountered two Ugandan guards and Netanyahu decided that they constituted a danger and opened fire at them with a pistol fitted with a silencer. The soldiers were not killed by the shots, and the man sitting behind Netanyahu, believing they were still dangerous, shot them with his unsilenced rifle.

The sound of the rifle brought other Ugandan troops to the area, and a firefight began. The Israelis' vehicles reached the terminal and the charge began, but Netanyahu was hit, and he later died of his wounds. However, the terrorists were taken by surprise when the raiding party, headed by Muki Betser, broke into the terminal, and he killed all of them before they could get organized. Reicher's force broke into an adjoining building manned by Ugandan troops and killed them, too. Another detail seized the control tower. Another destroyed eight Ugandan air force MiG fighters parked on the runway.

All eight hijackers had been killed. Three of the hostages, caught in the cross fire, also died. Another hostage, an elderly Israeli woman who had been taken to the hospital the previous night, was murdered, on Amin's instructions, in retaliation for the raid.

But a hundred people had been rescued, and Israel had made no concessions. The operation became a model for how to handle hostage situations: no negotiation and no compromise with terrorists, but a steadfast willingness to go to extraordinary lengths and even to risk lives in order to free hostages.

But though the raid on Entebbe was a significant tactical victory, the man who'd ordered the hijacking—the man Golda Meir had signed a kill order on more than six years earlier, the terrorist who'd been only slightly wounded by a barrage of RPGs fired through his Beirut office window, the zealot who'd survived a bomb dropped on a Beirut stadium in 1974, who topped Israel's hit list, and who was the target of a number of assassination plans still on the drawing boards— was still alive and still at large.

Rabin told the Mossad to spare no expense. Wadie Haddad must die.

# DEATH IN THE TOOTHPASTE

IN MAY 1977, ISRAEL'S Labor Party, which had ruled the country since its establishment in 1948, lost a national election for the first time. It was defeated by the Likud, a nationalist right-wing party led by Menachem Begin, the former commander of the Irgun, the anti-British underground. A combination of various factors—the discrimination and humiliation suffered by Jewish immigrants from Arab countries, revelations of corruption in the Labor Party, the shortcomings of the Yom Kippur War, and the ability of the charismatic Begin to take advantage of these factors and ride a wave of populism—led to an upset that shocked both Israelis and observers abroad.

Begin was viewed by many foreign leaders and local top officials as an extremist and a warmonger. Some of the chiefs of Israel's military and intelligence agencies were convinced that they would soon be replaced by partisans of the new government.

But Begin's initial moves as prime minister surprised everyone, foreign and domestic. At a dramatic summit meeting with Presidents Jimmy Carter and Anwar Sadat at Camp David in 1978, he agreed to a breakthrough peace treaty with Egypt that provided for Israel's eventual total pullout from the Sinai Peninsula, conquered from Egypt in 1967. The withdrawal of the army, the dismantling of settlements, and the relinquishment of oil fields and tourism facilities were bitterly opposed by Israel's right wing. But Begin, risking his own political standing, forced his party to comply. He also greatly strengthened the security alliance with the United States and bolstered the overarching authority of the Israeli Supreme Court.

Internally, there was no purge. Indeed, Begin even asked two men with strong ties to Labor—Shin Bet chief Avraham Ahituv and Mossad head Yitzhak Hofi—to remain in their jobs. "It was very strange for us," Hofi said. The Labor Party was hard-boiled and pragmatic when it came to matters of the military and intelligence. "But for Begin," Hofi said, "the army was something sacred."

As a practical matter, that meant Begin gave the military and intelligence agencies carte blanche. He had been given very limited access to the intelligence community when he was leading the parliament opposition, and he had to be taught a great deal. But even after he'd been exposed to the nuts and bolts, his oversight was superficial at best. "It was as if he was hovering above us at eighty thousand feet," said Mossad deputy chief Nahum Admoni.

Begin signed off without question on all of the Red Page targeted killing orders that the Mossad submitted to him. The prime minister did not even insist on the standard operating procedure of having an aide transcribe meetings with the Mossad chief to approve sabotage and targeted killing operations. This surprised Hofi. "Rabin," he said, "would bring the issue to be approved before a kind of inner cabinet." But Begin signed off on operations "face-to-face, without a stenographer and without his military aide. . . . I advised him that it was important to put things in writing."

The only point of disagreement between Begin and his intelligence chiefs was one of shading and priorities. At his first meeting with Hofi, he said he wanted the Mossad to launch a large-scale targeted killing campaign against at-large Nazi war criminals. "I told him," Hofi said, "'Prime Minister, today the Mossad has other missions that concern the security of Israel now and in the future, and I give priority to today and tomorrow over yesterday.' He understood that, but he didn't like it. . . . In the end, we decided that we'd concentrate on one target, [Josef] Mengele, but Begin was a very emotional person and he was disappointed."

At the same time, though, Begin understood Hofi's point. "Unlike other Israelis who saw the Holocaust as a one-time historical catastrophe," said Shlomo Nakdimon, a prominent Israeli journalist who was close to Begin and served as his media adviser when he was prime minister, "Begin believed with all his heart that the lesson of the Holocaust is that the Jewish people must protect themselves in their own country in order to prevent a renewed threat to their existence."

Begin equated Yasser Arafat with Adolf Hitler and believed that the Palestinian Covenant, which called for the destruction of the Jewish state, was nothing less than *Mein Kampf II*. "We Jews and we Zionists, guided by experience, will not take the path taken by leaders in Europe and across the globe in the thirties," Begin said in a fulminating speech in the Knesset on July 9, 1979, attacking the West German and Austrian chancellors, Willy Brandt and Bruno Kreisky, for their ties to Yasser Arafat.

"We take *Mein Kampf II* seriously, and we shall do all we can—and with God's help we will be able—to prevent the realization of the horror . . . uttered by that son of Satan [Arafat] . . . the leader of a despicable organization of murderers, the likes of which has not existed since the Nazis."

SINCE 1974, AS TERROR attacks in Europe tapered off, Arafat had been putting special emphasis on political efforts in the international arena to obtain diplomatic recognition for the PLO and to present himself as someone who was ready to negotiate with Israel. Over Israel's vociferous objections, official and overt PLO diplomatic missions were opened all over the world, including in Europe. At the height of this campaign, in November 1974, Arafat appeared before the UN General Assembly and delivered a speech that generally was accepted as being relatively moderate.

Moreover, Arafat's efforts to appear an advocate for a political solution to the Israeli-Palestinian conflict began a thaw in relations between the PLO and the United States. Israeli intelligence was deeply concerned about a potential rapprochement between its main ally and its chief enemy. A December 1974 paper prepared by AMAN for then–Prime Minister Rabin warned that "the United States has an interest in acquiring maximal influence inside the PLO so that it will not remain an exclusively Soviet stronghold." The paper also said, about Secretary of State Henry Kissinger, who was considered pro-Israel, "We do not find in his words an absolute negation of PLO with regard to the future."

Israel's intelligence community wasn't persuaded by the PLO's diplomacy. To AMAN, it was nothing more than "a draft strategy for the liquidation of Israel." While Arafat wooed American diplomats and was toasted at the United Nations, his people were continuing to attack Israeli citizens. "Arafat was the complete opposite of his ludicrous appearance. He was a kind of genius," said Major General Amos Gilad, long a prominent figure in military intelligence. "He had two deputies for running terror operations, Abu Jihad and Abu Iyad, but, except in one attack, you won't find any direct connection to Arafat. It's like a zookeeper letting a hungry lion loose in the streets and it eats someone. Who's responsible? The lion? Clearly it's the zookeeper. Abu Jihad got directives in principle, and he did the rest on his own. Arafat didn't want reports, didn't take part in planning meetings, didn't okay operations."

Arafat's increased prominence on the world stage led to a sharp debate between the Mossad and AMAN about whether he was still a suitable target for assassination. Brigadier General Yigal Pressler, then head of the AMAN department that dealt with assassination targets, argued passionately that Arafat should be left at the top of the list: "He is a terrorist. He has Jewish blood on his hands. He orders his people to keep on carrying out terror attacks. Everything must be done to get rid of him."

The head of counterterror at the Mossad, Shimshon Yitzhaki, disagreed: "After Arafat's speech at the UN, he has become a political figure. He's the head of the snake, but the world has given him legitimacy, and killing him will put Israel into an unnecessary political imbroglio."

Ultimately, the latter opinion won the day. That meant that Arafat's name was removed from the kill list and Wadie Haddad's name was pushed to the top.

FOR EIGHTEEN MONTHS AFTER the Entebbe raid, Wadie Haddad lived securely and very affluently in Baghdad and Beirut.

The Mossad was apprehensive about using firearms in Arab capitals such as Baghdad, Damascus, and Beirut, however, because the risk of capture was simply too great. And so more silent methods of assassination were sought, ones that had a less visible signature and made the death appear natural or accidental, the product of, say, a disease or a car crash. In such cases, even if there were to be a suspicion of foul play, by the time anything could be done, the killers would be long gone, whereas, in a hit using firearms, it is immediately clear that the killers are still in the vicinity.

The Mossad decided to exploit its deep intelligence penetration of Haddad's organization and to allocate the job of eliminating him to Junction. The assassination, using poison, was assigned to the agent Sadness, who had a high degree of access to his home and office.

On January 10, 1978, Sadness switched Haddad's toothpaste for an identical tube containing a lethal toxin, which had been developed after intense effort at the Israel Institute for Biological Research, in Ness Ziona, southeast of Tel Aviv, one of the most closely guarded locations in Israel. It was founded in 1952 and still serves as the facility where Israel develops its top-secret defensive and offensive biological warfare agents. Each time Haddad brushed his teeth, a minute quantity of the deadly toxin penetrated the mucous membranes in his mouth and entered his bloodstream. The gradual accretion in his body, when it reached a critical mass, would be fatal.

Haddad began feeling sick and was admitted to an Iraqi government hospital. He told the doctors there that in the middle of January he had begun suffering from severe abdominal spasms after a meal. His appetite faded, and he lost more than twenty-five pounds.

He was first diagnosed as suffering from hepatitis and, later, a very bad cold. Doctors treated him with aggressive antibiotics, but his condition didn't improve. His hair began to fall out and his fever spiked. The doctors in Baghdad were at a loss. They suspected that Haddad had been poisoned. Arafat instructed an aide to approach the Stasi, East Germany's secret service, to ask them for help. In the 1970s, the Stasi had provided Palestinian terror organizations with passports, intelligence, shelter, and weapons. The East German leader, Erich Honecker, and others in that country regarded Arafat as a true revolutionary, like Fidel Castro, and were ready to help him.

On March 19, 1978, Haddad was flown to the Regierungskrankenhaus, in East Berlin, a prestigious hospital that catered to members of the intelligence and security communities. His aides packed a bag for him with his toiletries, including a tube of the deadly toothpaste.

Intelligence material reaching the Mossad after he boarded the plane from Baghdad to Berlin gave cause for satisfaction. "Haddad was absolutely finished when he reached Germany," read a report at a Junction command meeting. "Biological Institute experts say he is a dead man walking."

He was admitted under the pseudonym Ahmed Doukli, forty-one years old, five feet six inches tall. He was indeed in bad condition: hemorrhaging in many places, including subcutaneously, from the pericardium around his heart, at the root of his tongue, his tonsils, his pleural membranes, and inside his cranium, with large quantities of blood in his urine. Bone marrow functioning was suppressed, with a resulting drop in the red platelet count in his blood. Despite his being treated as a privileged patient, Haddad's condition continued to deteriorate. The military physicians, the best doctors in East Germany, put their patient through every conceivable test: blood, urine, bone marrow, X-rays. They believed he had been poisoned, either with rat poison or some heavy metal, perhaps thallium, but they could find no physical evidence. According to information reaching Israel from an agent in East Germany, Haddad's screams of pain reverberated throughout the hospital, and the doctors gave him increasing doses of tranquilizers and sedatives.

Wadie Haddad died in great agony in the East Berlin hospital on March 29, ten days after he had arrived. Shortly afterward, Stasi chief Erich Mielke received a full report, including results of an autopsy conducted by Professor Otto Prokop, of East Berlin's Humboldt University, one of the world's leading authorities on forensic medicine. He wrote that the immediate cause of death was "brain bleeding and pneumonia by panmyelopathy" and that, in view of the symptoms and the person under discussion, there was room for suspicion that someone had assassinated him. But in hairsplitting forensic medicalese, he was actually admitting that he had no idea what had killed Haddad.

At the time of his death, Haddad was effectively in command of an entirely separate organization from that led by George Habash. But Habash grieved his comrade's demise, and he had no doubt that Israel was behind it.

The Mossad and the leaders of the Israeli defense establishment were overjoyed at the operation's outcome. One of Israel's most potent and effective enemies had been neutralized. No less important, five years after the Lillehammer fiasco, the Mossad had returned to targeted killings, and had done so in an eminently sophisticated manner. This may have been the first time that the phrase "low-signature," to describe an assassination in which the death appears to be natural or by chance, entered the Mossad's vocabulary.

"I was very happy when I heard Haddad was dead," said Shimshon Yitzhaki. Because Israel never admitted that it had killed Haddad, he stressed, "Don't take my words as confirmation of involvement in the case," but he declared that "anyone who has Jewish blood on their hands is doomed to die. Without Haddad, incidentally, his organization couldn't exist. It was already functioning separately from George Habash, and it split between Haddad's deputies and then kept on splitting until it melted away."

WITH HADDAD ELIMINATED, THE Mossad moved on to its next target: Ali Hassan Salameh.

The reasons Salameh had to die are a matter of some dispute. Israeli intelligence believed he had planned and implemented the slaughter of the Israeli Olympic team in Munich, though people who worked with Salameh strongly deny this accusation. In any case, the desire to eliminate him was likely intensified by the fact that the attempt to assassinate him in Lillehammer had turned into the most embarrassing and damaging fiasco in the Mossad's history. Salameh himself poured oil on the flames by mocking the agency for botching the Norwegian operation. "When they killed Bouchiki, I was in Europe," Salameh said in an interview with the Lebanese *Al-Sayad*. "Bouchiki was a swimming pool employee. His face and figure did not match my description." Salameh said he was saved "not so much because of my skills, but rather because of the weakness of Israeli intelligence."

This interview was distributed to the heads of the intelligence community by the AMAN department that deals with open-sources intelligence—Harari had asked the unit to collect every detail it could about Salameh. "Do not fear," he told his people when the interview was read out at a Caesarea meeting. "His day will come."

Salameh was undoubtedly connected to a number of acts of terrorism against both Israeli and Arab targets. He himself admitted involvement in Black September operations in the two interviews he gave. But Black September was not in existence anymore in 1978, and Salameh had taken on a number of internal roles in Fatah, leaving the terror activities to others. Was revenge for what he had done in the past a sufficient reason to take him out?

"Killing Salameh was first and foremost a matter of closing the Munich account," said Yair Ravid, who was the commander of Unit 504's northern region and one of the top experts on PLO attacks originating in Lebanon. "In our view, he was not an initiator of terrorist attacks" in the late 1970s. Other Caesarea operatives of the time, however, insisted that Salameh remained a threat as a commander of the PLO's Force 17, Arafat's bodyguard unit. "We've got to remember that Force 17 not only was guarding Arafat, but also carried out various terrorist operations," said one Caesarea veteran.

But there was also a deeper motive.

On July 10, 1978, during a high-level meeting at the Mossad, Caesarea chief Mike Harari reported that there had been "significant progress" made toward the goal of eliminating Salameh. But David Kimche, the head of Universe (Tevel), the Mossad branch in charge of relations with the intelligence agencies of other countries, said that his CIA counterparts had hinted that Salameh was an asset of theirs. "They didn't say explicitly that they wanted to protect him, but this has to be on the table, and we have to ask ourselves whether our relations with 'Helga'"—the Mossad's nickname for the CIA—"should alter our attitude toward him."

Shimshon Yitzhaki responded sharply, "So what? Suppose he's connected to the Americans. This man has Jewish blood on his hands. He was involved in Munich. He's still operating against us. I don't give a damn if he's an American agent."

In fact, Salameh was not just any source for the CIA. MJTRUST/2, as he was labeled by his controllers at Langley, was one of the CIA's most important contacts in the Middle East. Moreover, he was acting with the full knowledge and approval of Yasser Arafat, serving as the channel for exchanges between the Americans and the PLO.

"Dominick," a senior Mossad official involved in the hunt for Salameh, said that throughout the 1970s, the Mossad learned of the depth of the ties between the CIA and Salameh. The Mossad, and Prime Ministers Rabin and Begin, saw these ties as "no less than base treachery on the part of an ally, a stab in the back."

According to Kai Bird's *The Good Spy,* an authoritative biography of Robert C. Ames, one of the CIA's savviest field operatives in the Middle East, Salameh and Ames met for the first time in 1969, at the Strand café, in Beirut, and continued to meet later on in CIA safe houses in the same city. Ames reported to the CIA that Arafat valued Salameh highly.

The PLO was officially considered a terrorist organization by the United States, but the CIA wanted to preserve a back channel. In 1973, with Kissinger's approval, this channel became a secret but formal link between the United States and Arafat. Over the years, the two met in Europe and Beirut many times. The connection continued even after Salameh took a leading role in Black September. The Americans persisted not because they disagreed with the Mossad's evaluation of Salameh's role and responsibility in terrorist activities, but in spite of that.

Salameh even admitted to Ames that he had recruited Mohammed Boudia, the Paris theater owner who had sent agents to blow up a hotel in Israel, to Black September. Ames considered this to be "interesting intelligence," and he even expressed sympathy for the Palestinian cause: "I am fully aware of the activities of our friend," he wrote in a letter to the intermediary who passed messages between him and Salameh, "and although I do not agree with all of them, I can sympathize with his organization's feeling that they must carry them out."

Ames did all he could to persuade Salameh that "we are not out to 'get' his organization. Contrary to his beliefs, we are not an action group like his group is." He also kept on reassuring him in order to keep the connection with him alive: "Our friend should know that he still has friends in high places, and so does his cause."

The only point over which Ames saw fit to admonish Salameh was the possibility that Black September would act in the United States: "His activities in Europe, which are fully documented, and his plans in our territory, which we know of completely and will hit hard and expose to his organization's embarrassment, are the only points on which we disagree."

In other words, as long as Salameh would be careful not to harm Americans or act on American soil, he could continue attacking other targets without fear of reprisal from the United States. Ames even went so far as to offer, "I could arrange safe travel to . . . [a] European point, if he so desires."

Through the Ames-Salameh middleman, a meeting between CIA deputy director Vernon Walters and top Fatah officials was arranged and held in Rabat, Morocco, on November 3, 1973. The understanding that existed between Ames and Salameh became an official position—Fatah would not harm Americans, and the secret channel of communication would remain open.

Ames wasn't present when Salameh traveled with Arafat to the General Assembly in New York in 1974, but he organized the visit and arranged meetings at the Waldorf Astoria. "We watched him escorting Arafat around New York," said Dominick. This was insulting, wounding, "as if they had poked a finger in our eye."

Salameh, as Arafat's emissary, tried to obtain official American recognition of the PLO as the sole representative of the Palestinians. It didn't happen, but the very existence of the channel was a significant achievement from Arafat's point of view. In exchange, Salameh helped Ames with various kinds of information about developments in Lebanon and in the PLO, and on attempts by the PLO's rivals to harm the United States.

A deep friendship had formed between Ames and Salameh, which, due to Ames's rising standing in the agency, was gradually affecting the U.S. administration's attitude toward the PLO as well. After the Lebanese Civil War broke out, in 1975, turning Beirut into a war zone, Salameh posted his own men to guard the American embassy. The Israelis looked on and ground their teeth.

The link with Salameh was not Ames's private initiative or a rogue operation, although the American did have sharply critical positions toward Israel. It in fact was a high-priority project of the entire CIA. In late 1976, the agency's director, George H. W. Bush, sent an official invitation to Salameh, via Ames, to come to Langley. The visit, which took place in January 1977, combined business and pleasure. Salameh told Ames that he "really needed a vacation"—he had just married a former Miss Universe, the Lebanese beauty queen Georgina Rizk, and wanted to make her dream come true of having their honeymoon in Hawaii and Disneyland. Ames promised to take care of it.

The CIA organized the trip, and a senior official escorted the couple wherever they went, including on all the rides in the California theme park. Rizk greatly enjoyed herself. Salameh hated Disneyland but was very happy with the gift he received from CIA operations officer Alan Wolfe—a splendid leather shoulder holster for his handgun.

The CIA escort, Charles Waverly, recalled the visit: "All he [Salameh] really wanted to do was eat oysters. He thought they were an aphrodisiac. I was in the adjoining hotel room—so in the evenings I heard the results."

Because of the relationship between the Israeli and American intelligence communities and Israel's overall dependence on the United States, the Mossad refrained from operating on American soil. Salameh knew he wasn't threatened there. This meant that the couple could have a real holiday, without bodyguards getting in the way.

Normally, however, Salameh hardly ever left Beirut, and he surrounded himself with very heavy security. He would move around in a convoy of vehicles loaded with armed bodyguards, with a Dushka 22-millimeter heavy machine gun mounted on a Toyota pickup truck bringing up the rear.

Ames and his CIA colleague were not impressed. In his book, Bird mentions that Sam Wyman, one of the CIA liaison officers with Salameh in Beirut, once asked Salameh, "How is that damn cannon going to protect you? It just announces to everyone where you are." Salameh just laughed and said, "Oh, it is good."

Bird notes that Salameh was given dozens of CIA alerts, some in a very firm tone, that the Mossad was out to get him.

"I warned him," said Wyman. "I told him, 'You idiot, they're going to get you, the way you drive around Beirut. It is only a matter of time. . . . You are violating every principle of good intelligence practice. The Israelis know who you are, and they know what you did, and so you should be careful.'"

The CIA even supplied Salameh with encrypted communications equipment to enhance his security, and it considered sending Salameh an armor-plated car to protect him from the Israelis as well.

To Dominick, there was only one way this relationship could be interpreted: "Imagine that we, the Mossad, set up a secret relationship with Osama bin Laden, not because we recruited him as a spy working for cash but a friendly relationship, almost like allies, swapping info and mutual favors. Imagine that we invited him on a visit to our Tel Aviv HQ, kowtowed to him, expressed understanding and sympathy for the Twin Towers attack, told him that it was okay for him to go on blasting American embassies as long as he didn't blast ours, gave him and his wife royal hospitality, and did everything to protect him from the Navy SEALs coming to kill him. How would that be seen by America?"

The Mossad eventually reached the conclusion that "cutting this channel was very important, to show that no one was immune—and also to give the Americans a hint that this was no way to behave toward friends." Prime Minister Begin was informed by Mossad director Hofi about the relationship between Salameh and the Americans, but even with this knowledge, he accepted the Mossad's recommendation to assassinate him.


IN JUNE 1978, THREE months after Wadie Haddad was killed, Operation Maveer (Burner), the hunt for Salameh, went into high gear. For the first time since Operation Spring of Youth, Caesarea would kill someone in a target country: "a blue-and-white job to ensure that the job will be done," in Harari's words. A top agent for AMAN's Unit 504, code-named Rummenigge, after a German soccer star of the time, was asked to supply information about the quarry's habits.

Rummenigge was Amin al-Hajj, a member of one of Lebanon's prominent Shiite families and a well-connected merchant. His recruitment was facilitated by his hatred of the Palestinians and his desire to obtain permission to move his goods (which some say included a lot of illicit drugs) freely around the Middle East, sometimes via Israel, without hindrance by the Israeli Navy. Meetings between Rummenigge and his controller were usually held on an Israeli missile boat off the coast of Lebanon.

Al-Hajj used his network of sources to come up with a plethora of details on Salameh's daily routines, discovering that he spent a lot of time at the gym and spa of the Continental Hotel in Beirut and that he shared an apartment with Rizk in the upscale Snoubra neighborhood of the city.

Harari was pleased. "Salameh was by nature a playboy, a prominent figure in Beirut's glitzy social class," he said. "It's easy to get close up in such circles. I sent my warriors in to rub shoulders with him."

A Caesarea operative went to Beirut, booked a room in the Continental Hotel under a false European identity, and signed up at the gym. He went there every day, and now and again he ran into Salameh. He knew Salameh took a keen interest in luxury watches and fashionable clothes, and he dressed himself accordingly in the locker room, always standing as close as he could get to the Palestinian.

One day, some of the other gym members were congratulating Salameh on an award Rizk had received at a ball the previous night. The Caesarea operative joined in and struck up a conversation with Salameh. "There was some male bonding there," said Harari.

The two became friendly and chatted every now and again. "The idea in encounters like these is to let the target initiate contact," said a source involved in the operation. "Otherwise it would seem suspicious, especially for a hunted person like Salameh."

When the Caesarea operative returned to Israel, a "low-signature" hit on Salameh was discussed, including the possibility of "slipping some 'medicine' into his toothpaste or soap or aftershave lotion," Harari said. But the risk for the operative, were he to be discovered, looked too great.

Another alternative, placing an explosive device in Salameh's locker at the gym, was rejected out of fear that an innocent bystander might also be hurt. Eventually, Harari decided to drop altogether the idea of taking him out at the gym or his office or home, because of the heavy security at those sites.

The solution Harari adopted was new to the Mossad: a bomb on a public street, hitting a moving target. Salameh would be dispatched while driving through Beirut, escorted by the Toyota truck with the heavy machine gun and a third vehicle occupied by bodyguards. Somewhere along the route, as the three cars passed by, a large explosive device would be triggered by a Mossad operative positioned unobtrusively a safe distance away.

Yaakov Rehavi, a former NASA scientist recruited by the Mossad to head the technology department, created a special device for the agents to practice executing the operation. In the drill, the operator had to push a button at the exact moment a car chassis on metal wheels, towed at speed by another vehicle, passed a certain point. There was no explosion, just an electronic signal showing whether the button had been precisely synchronized with the passing of the vehicle.

Agents who took part in the drills recalled that Rehavi and two other male operatives couldn't get the timing right. "Maybe you'll let me try," asked a female desk hand in the counterterror department, who was present at the drills. Rehavi smiled patronizingly and handed her the remote. She timed it perfectly, several drills in a row. Finally they tried it with explosives, with store-window mannequins in the car, and once again the woman's timing was perfect.

"As long as men were pushing the button, there was an atmosphere of despair," said Harari, "but after she aced it again and again, in differing light conditions, I realized that women apparently were better at it than men, and I made a decision accordingly." A female operative, code-named Rinah, would push the button in Beirut. "This wasn't an easy decision," said Harari. "We had to change all the cover stories and to construct something that would suit a woman who would possibly have to remain for long hours at a site with a view of the street. It wasn't enough for her just to know how to push the button. Salameh didn't leave his home at the same times every day. Sometimes it was necessary to be on the alert for as much as eighteen hours, and sometimes she'd have to close her eyes or go and do pee-pee. It's no simple matter."

RINAH'S REAL NAME WAS Erika Chambers, and she was born in England in 1948, the daughter of Marcus Chambers, an engineer who designed race cars and spent most of his life at the tracks, and his wife, Lona, a singer and actress from a wealthy Czechoslovakian Jewish family, most of whom were killed in the Holocaust. Erika studied at the University of Southampton in the 1960s, where she was remembered most vividly for her wild driving. She traveled to Australia and then to Israel, where she enrolled in a master's program in hydrology at the Hebrew University. In early 1973, she was contacted by a recruiter for the Mossad. She liked the idea of combining adventure with what she described as "making a significant contribution to the security of the state." She passed all of the screening tests, was inducted into Caesarea, and then underwent the grueling training program. In mid-1975, she left Israel, assumed a false British identity, and began carrying out missions abroad.

Rinah and two men were selected for the assassination of Salameh.

The complex plan once again called for close cooperation with the IDF's special-ops units, who were to execute those aspects of the operation that the Mossad couldn't carry out itself.

Rinah arrived in Beirut in October 1978, presenting herself as an NGO staffer interested in assisting Palestinian orphans at a shelter in the Tel al-Zaatar refugee camp. She lived in the city for some two months and, together with another operative, clandestinely gathered information about Salameh's movements. Early in the new year, she rented a flat on the eighth floor of a high-rise building on Beka Street, overlooking Salameh's apartment. On January 16, the other two operatives arrived in Beirut separately, one with a British passport and the other with a Canadian one.

On January 18, a team from Sayeret Matkal crossed the border into Jordan, in the Arabah region, south of the Dead Sea, carrying a hundred kilograms of plastic explosive and a detonation device. On the other side of the border, a 504 agent was waiting. He put the explosives in his car and drove to Beirut. On January 19, in an underground parking garage, he met the two male operatives. He said the password—two words in English—and they gave the prearranged two-word reply. The agent then handed over the explosives and the detonation device, said goodbye, and left. His part in the operation was done.

The operatives loaded the bomb into the trunk of a Volkswagen they had rented two days before, set the detonation device, and parked the car down the street from Salameh's apartment block.

Harari himself traveled to Beirut to oversee the culmination of Operation Maveer. He could not allow himself another failure like Lillehammer. Leaving the Volkswagen containing the bomb parked on a busy street for what might be a long time was a problem. A parking inspector's suspicion could be aroused. The solution: "To switch cars, at a time when we were sure that Salameh would not be passing. Just making sure we kept the right parking spot was an operation in itself." On January 21, 1979, Harari took leave of Rinah and the two men and flew out, to ensure that there would be as few operatives as possible in the field.

The next day, shortly after 3 P.M., Salameh finished eating lunch with his wife, kissed her goodbye, and left. He got into his Chevrolet and drove off at 3:23 toward the Force 17 offices, his bodyguards traveling in the Land Rover in front of him and the Toyota behind him. He had gone only about sixty feet when his Chevy drew level with the Volkswagen. Rinah pressed the button. A huge explosion shook Beirut, and the Chevrolet became a ball of fire. One of the two male operatives, who was watching from a distance, would later recount to his friends that Salameh had managed to get out of the car, his clothes in flames, and fall to the ground. The operative muttered through his teeth, "Die, motherfucker! Die!"

Abu Daoud (Mohammed Oudeh), the commander of Black September's Munich operation, who by chance was passing by, ran up and tried to help. He saw a huge metal fragment lodged in Salameh's skull. Salameh was rushed to the American University Hospital, where he died on the operating table.

Eight others were also killed in the blast: Salameh's driver and two bodyguards, three Lebanese citizens, a German, and a Briton. Harari acknowledged that an operation such as this, with the explosion of a large device in an area teeming with passersby, would never have been approved in a non-Arab country.

Rinah and the two other operatives waited on a beach near Jounieh, north of Beirut, for a rubber dinghy manned by Flotilla 13 men to pick them up at around midnight. A young naval commando lifted Rinah into the boat. The man, on one of his first missions, was Holiday, who would one day become head of Caesarea. The dinghy met up with a navy missile boat waiting out at sea, and within hours the hit team was in Haifa.

The killing of Salameh was a terrible blow to the PLO. "I warned them!" Arafat exclaimed, with heavy pathos, in a television interview shortly afterward. "I warned my brothers, 'Be careful! The Mossad will hunt us, one by one, commander by commander.'" At Salameh's huge funeral, Arafat took Hassan, the dead man's son, who was named after his grandfather, the Palestinian commander in the 1948 war, on his knee, holding an AK-47—just as he had held Ali himself at a memorial for his father twenty-five years before.

Frank Anderson, head of the CIA station in Beirut, wrote Hassan an emotional condolence letter: "At your age, I lost my father. Today, I lost a friend whom I respected more than other men. I promise to honor your father's memory—and to stand ready to be your friend."

Israel had closed its account with Ali Salameh, but it had not managed to cut the ties between the United States and the PLO. Robert Ames was very saddened by the death of his friend, and he tried hard to forge ties with the man the PLO appointed to replace him, Hani al-Hassan. After the slaying, Ames espoused positions that were considered pro-Palestinian, and he was a key figure in the formulation of the Reagan Plan, which was in effect the first official American recognition of the right of the Palestinians to establish a state of their own.

# A PACK OF WILD DOGS

ABOUT A WEEK BEFORE Wadie Haddad, writhing in agony from Mossad poison, was admitted to an East German hospital, the Shin Bet learned from one of its sources, code-named Housemaid, about a PLO squad training for a raid into Israel. Amos Gilad, from the AMAN unit that dealt with Palestinian terrorism, met Housemaid in a Shin Bet safe house in Jerusalem and left the meeting feeling very worried: "I understood they were planning something terrible, and they wanted to cause as many casualties as possible."

The information, confirmed by wiretaps at the PLO offices in Cyprus, was very specific. The Shin Bet knew the names of the terrorists and the exact location of their base on the beach of Damour, in Lebanon. They knew that the terrorists were planning an attack from the sea, and that the assault was intended to disrupt peace talks Begin had initiated with Egypt. Arafat and Abu Jihad had ordered it because they feared, correctly, that a truce between Egypt and Israel would leave the Palestinians in the lurch, as Egypt had thus far been their chief advocate. The raid was so important to the PLO that Abu Jihad himself had briefed the guerrillas, together with his operations commander in Lebanon, Azmi Zrair.

Gilad wanted to strike first, to eliminate the threat with a preemptive attack on the terrorist base. On March 5, 1978, the naval commandos, Flotilla 13, carried out Operation Lucky Man (Bar-Mazal). The aim was to eliminate all the terrorists at the Damour base, but they actually killed only those who were in one building, while those who were in a nearby structure and didn't come out or open fire were unharmed. Housemaid was able to report this as well.

Gilad demanded that the commandos go in again to finish the job, but Defense Minister Ezer Weizman said, "Forget about all these commando raids. I'm going to Washington tomorrow and it'll only ruin my visit."

Gilad protested vehemently: "By now Abu Jihad knows that we know that he's preparing something. That will only spur him on to get them on the move as soon as possible. There is going to be a murderous attack."

Weizman may have been correct that headlines about an Israeli military action in the sovereign territory of another country would cast a dark shadow over his first visit to the Pentagon as defense minister, but it turned out to be a costly decision.

On March 11, 1978, at 2:30 P.M., eleven Fatah men landed on the beach near Kibbutz Maagan Michael, south of Haifa, in a nature preserve bounded by fish-breeding ponds where flocks of migrant birds stop on their way to and from Africa. An American nature photographer named Gail Rubin was taking pictures of the birds when the raiding party stumbled upon her. The Palestinians were close to despair after three exhausting and hazardous days at sea, during which two of their number had drowned. Because the waters were so stormy and they had been washed miles out to sea, they had lost their bearings and thought they'd landed in Cyprus. They were relieved when Rubin told them they were in Israel, halfway between Haifa and Tel Aviv. They thanked her and shot her dead.

Then the attackers made for the Coastal Highway, the road between Haifa and Tel Aviv. At gunpoint, they hijacked a taxi and then a bus, and took the drivers and passengers hostage. They ordered the driver of the bus to head south, toward Tel Aviv. Abu Jihad had instructed them to seize a hotel, but the raiders, now in bold high spirits because of the dozens of hostages in their hands, decided to change the nature of the operation. The IDF's classified report on what followed noted, "The terrorists' improvisation led to a new method of assault—an attack on the move (along a route of over 50 kilometers), which was a surprise and against which there was no deployment at all on the part of the security forces."

The terrorists fired from the bus windows at vehicles on the road and stopped another bus, taking its passengers hostage as well. Because of the novel nature of the attack, "security forces found it difficult to read the situation, to maintain an updated evaluation and to take the initiative, which affected the course of the incident and its results."

Although the police managed to stop the bus at the northern outskirts of Tel Aviv, the confusion led to utter chaos: "The predominant factor was the lack of central control, both among the terrorists, who were trying to defend themselves by firing in all possible directions, and among the security forces."

One of the terrorists rested the hand holding his pistol upon the head of the daughter of one of the hostages, Avraham Shamir. Shamir saw the man was wounded and he charged at him, grabbed his gun, and shot a terrorist standing at the front of the bus. Then he fired three shots at another terrorist. "Behind you!" warned a female hostage, and Shamir turned to see one of the Arabs aiming his weapon at him. They both fired at the same time and wounded each other. The courageous Shamir, still functioning, saw that the man whose gun he had grabbed was lying on the floor, muttering, his face covered in blood. He had a grenade in his hand, the safety pin removed. Shamir tried to stop him from dropping it, but he failed, and the grenade rolled onto the floor. He tried to use the terrorist's body to block the blast, but that didn't work, either. The grenade exploded, seriously wounding Shamir's eyes and killing the terrorist and five hostages. The blast set the bus on fire. Some of the terrorists and hostages managed to escape, but most were burned alive.

In all, thirty-five Israelis, thirteen of them children, were killed, and seventy-one were wounded. Nine of the terrorists died. One was captured at the scene, and another was found in a hospital where the casualties had been taken. "I see him lying there," said Arieh Hadar, the top Shin Bet interrogator, "lightly wounded but with a feeding tube and an IV infusion, mocking us, right in our face. The doctor understood what was up, and he turned his back to us and said, 'You'll do what you do, and I'll do what I do.' We pulled out the tubes. He screamed a little from pain and began talking right away. 'Abu Jihad sent us,' he said."

The Coastal Road massacre, as it became known in Israel, is one of a handful of terrorist attacks, out of the thousands Israel has suffered, that have been branded into the collective consciousness. Defense Minister Weizman, full of remorse at having forbidden a preemptive attack, rushed home and ordered the IDF to launch a large-scale invasion of southern Lebanon, Operation Litani. Three days after the massacre, Israeli armor and paratroops crossed into Lebanon with the goal of killing as many PLO fighters as they could, destroying their bases in southern Lebanon, and pushing them north of the Litani River, some fifteen miles north of the Israeli border.

The incursion achieved only a few of its objectives. Some three hundred PLO operatives were killed, their bases wrecked and arms depots seized. In addition, a United Nations Interim Force in Lebanon (UNIFIL) was set up and posted in the area, and a pro-Israel, mainly Christian militia, the Free Lebanese Army, was established. But with time, even all of these new forces could not prevent the firing of Katyusha rockets at Israel, or cross-border penetrations by PLO squads.

Due to the fury engendered by the slaughter of civilians, Israeli soldiers also committed a few acts of killing prisoners and of looting during the weeklong Operation Litani. Once again, Israel sustained sharp international condemnation.

Weizman understood that large-scale operations in Lebanon were out of the question. Mossad operations, meanwhile, required months of preparation: figuring out how to get into a target state under a cover identity, execute a hit, and get out without being discovered. So Weizman opted instead for precision raids and targeted killings by special-forces units—less complicated, faster, and requiring no cover story—undertaken by commandos in full combat gear. The division selected to carry out most of these missions was the naval commando unit, Flotilla 13.

THE MAN WEIZMAN PUT in charge of the operations in Lebanon was General Rafael "Raful" Eitan, who became chief of staff in April 1978. Eitan, a farmer and a carpenter, was a tough paratrooper who knew no fear during battle and a political hawk who "believed in taking the war against the PLO to the enemy's rear, to harass them at their staging bases."

Eitan never saw himself bound by the rules of political correctness. Responding to rock throwing by Palestinians on the West Bank, he suggested to the Knesset that new Jewish settlements should be established there until the Arabs could only "run around like drugged bugs in a bottle." One of his first moves as chief of staff was to pardon two convicted IDF criminals—Y., the POW interrogator under whose grilling a Palestinian terrorist suspect had died and another, who was involved in the Nairobi plot, was hospitalized, as well as Lieutenant Daniel Pinto, who had tortured and murdered two prisoners during Operation Litani, throwing their bodies into a well.

A bearlike man of very few words, Eitan addressed the naval commandos at their base at Atlit shortly after taking over as chief of staff. "You, Flotilla 13, are like a priest's balls," he said. "Not used—but it's nice that they're there." He paused for a moment and looked around to make sure everyone was smiling at his crude wisecrack. Then he became serious, cleared his throat, and delivered the main message: "All that is going to change."

Flotilla 13 was founded in late 1949 as a secret commando unit responsible for clandestine penetration and sabotage and targeted killing operations via the sea. The motto selected by the founders fit this spirit: "Like a bat out of the dark, like a blade slicing in silence, like a grenade shattering with a roar." The unit's insignia is a bat's wings with the Israeli Navy emblem at the center. Its eighteen-month training program is as arduous as that of Sayeret Matkal, if not more so. Toward the end of it, recruits also undergo a hellish POW simulation.

Between 1978 and 1980, Flotilla 13 carried out twenty-three raids against the PLO on Lebanese territory or at sea. In these operations, some 130 enemies were killed, hundreds were wounded, and stores of arms and ammunition were destroyed. Some of the attacks were aimed at wiping out entire terror squads preparing to attack inside Israel. Others targeted specific individuals, particularly Abu Jihad's men.

Under Eitan's supervision, old rules of engagement began to bend. During the preliminary stages of the targeted killing of Abu

Jihad's senior operational commander, Azmi Zrair, who was responsible for many attacks against Israelis, including those at the Savoy
Hotel and the Coastal Road, Rummenigge and his network of sources
discovered that he operated out of the refugee camp at the port city
of Tyre and regularly met an aide in a seaside café there.

On August 5, 1980, commandos were to ride rubber dinghies to a
point a kilometer from the beach, then swim underwater to the seawall, and from there use sniper rifles to take out Zrair and his aide.
In a final briefing, Eitan ordered his men to booby-trap the seawall
with a trip wire and an explosive device, in order to stop any attempt
to chase the snipers and fire at them.

Ami Ayalon, the commander of Flotilla 13, objected. "I said to
him, 'Chief, we will not leave booby traps,'" Ayalon recalled. "'Kids
might come along, or maybe a romantic couple.' But Raful insisted.
He didn't even try to justify his order."

Then Eitan went further. "After you've killed Zrair," he ordered,
"spray the entire pier with your light machine guns, to make sure no
one will return fire."

"I said to him, 'Listen, where's the logic here?'"Ayalon continued.
"Who do we spray? All the civilians there? Why send us at all to pick
off someone? Send in the air force. They'll drop a one-ton bomb on
the pier and it'll all be over.'"

Eitan's orders didn't matter in the end: On the day of the raid,
IDF units on the border responded to rocket fire from Lebanon by
shelling the Tyre refugee camp. Because of the panic there, no one
went to the port for coffee.

But the argument between Ayalon and Eitan was born of a new
and problematic reality that Israel's activity in Lebanon had created.
When the Mossad targeted PLO personnel in Europe, it followed a
strict policy of avoiding harm to innocent civilians. More than a few
plans were dropped because civilians might have been endangered.
But as long as the targets were located in enemy countries, and as
long as the innocent civilians were Arabs, the finger on the trigger
became quicker. Moreover, Mossad operations had to be approved
by the prime minister, a civilian answerable to politics, who usually
was involved to some extent in the planning. On the other hand, only
some of the IDF operations required approval at the political level,

and only after they had already been hammered out inside the army. Even then, the approving authority was usually the defense minister, not the prime minister. Incursions into Lebanon were considered acts of war—and much more is permitted in war, particularly on Arab soil. The issue of collateral casualties became less important.

The standards of conduct prevalent in corrupt and civil-war-torn Lebanon began to infect the Israelis, who went there to kill in order to protect their own citizens. Eitan presided over, and even encouraged, that trend. "Raful's attitude was that it made no difference which Palestinians we killed in Lebanon—they either were terrorists or would become terrorists or they gave birth to terrorists," said David Shiek, deputy commander of Flotilla 13 at the time. "Once, Raful joined us on the missile boat on the way to a raid and an officer asked him how we were supposed to identify the terrorists. Raful answered, 'If they haven't got [birthday party] balloons, they're terrorists.'" Another former naval commando recalled an operation after which the IDF spokesman reported that "thirty terrorists were killed," but in fact the raiders had hit a truck by mistake and many of its passengers were women and children.

IN ADDITION TO THE increasingly bloody commando operations, Weizman authorized Eitan to significantly step up the activities of intelligence units in Lebanon, particularly those of AMAN's 504. But in the wildness that was Lebanon in the late 1970s, seemingly everything was permitted. On several occasions, 504 allowed its agents to kill people without the authorization—or even the knowledge—of the unit's superiors. For example, in December 1978, an agent by the name of Muhammad Abdallah suspected that a certain man had seen him broadcasting to Israel. "The same night, that man died of natural causes by swallowing a pillow," said Yair Ravid, who commanded the unit's northern region. In yet another case, in July 1979, a Syrian operative named Qasim Harash threatened to expose Israeli agents. "We called a session of the special tribunal," Ravid boasted, "with me as the judge, prosecutor, and defense counsel, and unanimously sentenced him to death, without the right of appeal." A 504 agent code-named the Brazilian shot Harash dead. Agents from 504 brought his body to Israel and buried him in the cemetery for enemy dead, facedown, in a final jab of debasement.

Israeli intelligence was establishing a permanent presence in Lebanon, both to gather information on Arafat and to destabilize the PLO. With Begin's vigorous support, they forged a secret alliance with the Phalange, the militia of the Lebanese Maronite Christians, the Palestinians' most bitter enemies. The Christians had their own sources, and they shared the information they gathered with Israel. Under the protection of the Phalange, the Mossad was also able to set up its own base close to Beirut, and IDF officers were able to conduct scouting parties throughout Lebanon, gathering important intelligence about the PLO and Syrian forces.

However, this partnership came at a moral price. The Phalangists were exceptionally brutal, "a fundamentally corrupt gang of murderers that reminded me of a pack of wild dogs," said Uzi Dayan, Moshe Dayan's nephew and a commander of Sayeret Matkal at the time.

They adorned their belts with ears severed from the people they killed, gruesome trophies of war. They boasted of the massacre they had carried out in the Palestinian refugee camp Tel al-Zaatar—the Hill of Thyme—in August 1976. "One thousand Palestinians in the ocean is pollution," the Phalangists said, almost as a war slogan, "but five million Palestinians in the ocean is the solution."

The Phalangists didn't limit their brutality to Palestinians. Their chief executioner, an Israeli-trained Maronite militant named Robert Hatem, said he personally killed or oversaw the killing of some three thousand people. The Phalangists had commandeered an old cow slaughterhouse in Beirut's Karantina quarter, where prisoners were taken. "Almost no one who came there to be questioned left alive," Hatem said. "We used to shoot them in the head and dump their bodies into lime pits—Syrians and Shiites and Palestinians and son-of-a-bitch officers of the Lebanese army. Everyone who wanted to kill us, we killed them first."

Hatem said that Mossad officers approved the killing of only a few prisoners, including four Iranian diplomats who were tortured before being shot and dumped in the pits. But the Phalangists' wider rampage was clearly carried out with the strong backing of the Israelis.

"At the outset of our relationship with them, I took a pill against nausea and carried on," said Reuven Merhav, the Mossad official heading the unit that liaised with the Phalange. "Because the enemy of my enemy is my friend, and they really helped us against the PLO. But the more the days went by, I reached the conclusion that linking up with people like these could only lead to disaster." Merhav left the Mossad as a protest against the continued relationship, but the agency's strategic alliance with the Maronites only deepened.

The leaders of the Phalange accurately gauged Begin's sentimental nature and realized how to enlist his support. "Begin saw himself as the savior of the oppressed, a helper of people in distress," said Mordechai Zippori, who had served under Begin in the Irgun and was a close friend of his since those days, becoming a senior IDF officer and deputy defense minister in Begin's government. "He wasn't really well versed in the history or the conduct of affairs in the Middle East, and he was convinced that the Phalangists were a Western Christian minority that the PLO wanted to annihilate. Just like he saw us, the Jews in Israel."

Zippori was the only politician in the administration to stand up to the Mossad and the IDF, and he tried to persuade them and Begin that "we must not be the Phalangists' patrons and get embroiled in their conflicts." But it was in vain. "The delights of the lavish banquets at Jounieh (where the Phalange HQ was situated) totally addled the judgment of the army brass."

Still, despite all the bodies eaten away in Hatem's lime pits, the PLO's various militias managed to consolidate their positions in southern Lebanon. They fired shells and rockets into Israeli communities along the border, and the IDF responded by bombarding Palestinian strongholds with artillery and from the air. During 1979, the two sides had settled into a rote and seemingly endless pattern of exchanging blow for blow.

ON APRIL 22, 1979, at close to midnight, a terror squad from the PLO-affiliated group headed by Abu Abbas landed in a rubber dinghy on the beach at Nahariya, an Israeli city seven miles south of the Lebanese border. One of its four members was Samir Kuntar, then sixteen and a half years old. After trying to break into a house and being frightened away by gunfire, and after killing a policeman who tried to arrest them, the four broke into the apartment of the Haran family and took the father, Danny, and his daughter Einat, four, as hostages. They dragged them to the beach, where soldiers and police had already deployed, and a firefight ensued. Kuntar shot Danny and then grabbed Einat by the hair and dashed her head, with all his might, against a rock, again and again, until she was dead.

Danny's wife, Smadar, hid in a crawl space in their apartment with their two-year-old daughter, Yael. Smadar covered the toddler's mouth with her hand, to keep her from crying out and allowing the attackers to find them. "I knew that if Yael cried out, the terrorists would toss a grenade into the crawl space and we would be killed," she wrote in an article in *The Washington Post,* aimed at rousing the world's awareness of the horrors of terrorism. "So I kept my hand over her mouth, hoping she could breathe. As I lay there, I remembered my mother telling me how she had hidden from the Nazis during the Holocaust. 'This is just like what happened to my mother,' I thought."

In her panic, Smadar pressed too hard. She smothered her little girl.

The head of the IDF's Northern Command, Major General Avigdor "Yanosh" Ben-Gal, arrived at the scene shortly after the incident. He saw Einat's shattered head, Yael's lifeless body, and Smadar screaming with anguish after realizing she had lost everything dear to her. "You cannot imagine the dimensions of the atrocity," Ben-Gal said. At the funeral for Danny and his two children, Prime Minister Begin quoted a line from Israel's national poet, Hayim Nahman Bialik: "Satan has not yet created vengeance for the blood of a little child."

The horrendous murder in Nahariya was to become yet another milestone in the degeneration of the conflict between Israel and the PLO into total warfare. Chief of staff Eitan gave Ben-Gal a simple order: "Kill them all," meaning all members of the PLO and anyone connected to the organization in Lebanon.

Such a policy had never been approved by the government of Israel. There is no way of knowing to what extent Defense Minister Weizman, who had once been a hawk but by this time was much more moderate, was aware of it. "We had a lot of disagreements about many current matters" was how Eitan described their relationship. "I was in favor of carrying out retaliatory actions against the terrorists in Lebanon. [Weizman] used to change his positions . . . in order to find favor and placate public opinion. Ezer simply didn't understand the Arabs. . . . Concessions to the Arabs are taken by them as a sign of weakness and weariness of the struggle. . . . Ezer did not accept my opinion, and I didn't accept his opinion."

With Eitan's blessing, Ben-Gal appointed the man he called "the IDF's top specialist in special ops," the man who'd suppressed terrorism in Gaza ten years before, Meir Dagan, to head a new unit known as the South Lebanon Region (SLR). Dagan was promoted to colonel, and Ben-Gal took him to the summit of one of the hills overlooking the south of Lebanon. "From now on," he told him, "you are emperor here. Do whatever you want to."

Ben-Gal and Eitan defined the goal for Dagan: to intimidate, to deter, to make it clear that Israel would be aggressive on offense, not merely reactive on defense. More specifically, the object of the covert activities during the first stage was to hit PLO bases throughout southern Lebanon, as well as the homes of residents who assisted the terrorists and gave them lodging before they set out on operations against Israel.

Based on that directive, Dagan did as he pleased. At the SLR headquarters in Marjayoun, he and a number of intelligence and operational personnel set up a secret organization that reported directly to him. "I gave his secret operations complete freedom," Ben-Gal said. "Meir loved to be involved in secret, small-scale warfare, in shadows and dark places, in espionage activities and in weaving conspiracies, small or big. That's his forte. He's a very brave guy, very creative, very opinionated, who's ready to take huge risks. I knew what he was doing but ignored it. Sometimes you have to turn a blind eye."

David Agmon was head of the Northern Command staff, one of the few who were in on Dagan's secret ops. "The aim," he said, "was to cause chaos amongst the Palestinians and Syrians in Lebanon, without leaving an Israeli fingerprint, to give them the feeling that they were constantly under attack and to instill them with a sense of insecurity." In order to leave no Israeli fingerprints, Dagan and his crew recruited Lebanese locals, Christians, and Shiite Muslims, who detested Arafat and were infuriated by the way the Palestinians treated Lebanon and its people, as if it were their own land. Using those "operational squads," as they were called, Dagan's SLR began a series of targeted killings and sabotage operations in southern Lebanon.

"Raful and I used to okay missions with a wink," Ben-Gal said. "I used to tell him, 'Raful, we've got an op to do.' He'd say, 'Okay, but nothing in writing. It's between me and you, personal. . . . I don't want it to become known.' We didn't act through the military bureaucracy, because we both did and did not carry out these actions. We used them [the locals] as proxies, mercenaries. We put motivation into them—Christians and Shiites and Sunnis—and we played them against one another."

The primary method used for those attacks was explosives concealed in cans of oil or preserves. Since the activity was not officially sanctioned by the IDF and had to be hidden from the rest of the army, Ben-Gal asked the secretariat of Kibbutz Mahanayim, where he was living at the time, for permission to use its Diyuk metalworks. ("Of course, we gave him the keys and total backing," one of the secretaries said. "This was the head of the command. He was like a king to us.")

The explosives were provided by the IDF's bomb disposal unit, whose commander had been ordered by Eitan to cooperate without knowing what the purpose was. The unit specialized in neutralizing old, unexploded ordnance—rockets, mines, and grenades, including spoils taken by the Israelis. By using such explosive material, the IDF was able to greatly minimize the chance that any connection with Israel might be revealed if the explosive devices fell into enemy hands.

"We'd come there at night," Ben-Gal said, "Meir and I and the rest of the guys, with the Northern Command's chief engineer, who brought the explosives, and we'd fill those little drums and connect the fuses." Those little drums were then dispatched to couriers in large backpacks, or, if they were too big, on motorcycles, bicycles, or donkeys. Soon the bombs began exploding at the homes of the PLO's collaborators in southern Lebanon, killing everyone there, as well as in PLO positions and offices, mostly in Tyre, Sidon, and the Palestinian refugee camps around them, causing massive damages and casualties.

For Ben-Gal and Dagan, the stealth measures—manufacturing bombs in a kibbutz in the dark of night, deploying Lebanese irregulars—were necessary to keep their operations secret not just from the PLO but also from their own government, and even their own colleagues in the IDF. They had launched a covert and unsanctioned campaign on foreign soil. The Northern Command reported to AMAN, which was supposed to be involved in such matters, as well as the Operations Directorate of the General Staff, which was supposed to approve them. "But we kept them absolutely out of the loop," Ben-Gal said. According to Dagan, AMAN "interfered with us all the time. They didn't understand what a clandestine operation was and how important this activity was."

To be more precise, the military intelligence branch disagreed about the importance of these unsanctioned killings. The head of AMAN at the time, Major General Yehoshua Saguy, was a cautious man who doubted the effectiveness of the kind of operation Dagan was conducting. He didn't see the situation in Lebanon in black-and-white, as Eitan did, and he repeatedly warned that Israel could become embroiled in something too big for it to handle there. "Ben-Gal even tried to bar me from entering the Northern Command headquarters or to visit the region," Saguy recalled.

"There was a constant struggle with the Northern Command," said AMAN's Amos Gilboa. "They bypassed us, worked behind our back; Yanosh [Ben-Gal] lied to us all the time. We did not believe any of their reports. What made it even more grave was that it was being done with the approval of the chief of staff, who kept the activity a secret from the General Staff. This was one of the ugliest periods in the history of the country."

According to Ben-Gal, Saguy "realized that something irregular was going on," and he tried to ferret out the facts. Saguy ordered his field security unit, Vulture—normally responsible for ensuring that soldiers didn't give away military secrets on insecure lines—to tap into the Northern Command's phones. "But my command communications officer caught them connecting to my switchboard, and I tossed them into the lockup," Ben-Gal said, proud of having discovered "AMAN's plot."

Ben-Gal had an encrypted connection set up between his office in Nazareth and Dagan's command posts on the northern border and inside Lebanon. "This was the first thing he showed me," recalled Efraim Sneh, who was a senior officer in the Northern Command at the time, describing the first time Ben-Gal informed him of the covert activity. "He pointed at that certain handset and said, 'That's so that Yehoshua [Saguy] won't be able to listen in, and AMAN can go jump in the lake.'" Sneh said that Ben-Gal and Eitan "were right in their attitude to Saguy, who was a stool pigeon and tried to squelch any original initiative."

Not long after, Saguy went to Prime Minister Begin to complain that Ben-Gal had told Dagan to booby-trap the corpses of terrorists who'd been killed in firefights, in order to take out their comrades when they retrieved the bodies. Ben-Gal concluded from this that AMAN had apparently managed to tap his encrypted phone.

"Then we had no option," he said. "To keep our secrets, we had to hold all of our discussions in person." From time to time, usually once a week, Eitan would drive from Tel Adashim, the agricultural village where he lived, to the nearby Northern Command headquarters near Nazareth, to meet Ben-Gal and plot the next moves in their shadow war.

Even still, not everything could be kept secret. Early in 1980, various elements in the IDF, headed by Saguy, began informing Deputy Defense Minister Zippori that Ben-Gal was conducting rogue ops inside Lebanon. They turned to him because they knew that he was the only politician who dared to speak out about what was going on there. "They tell me about the explosions in Lebanon and even that Yanosh was mining roads taken by IDF troops, to make it look as if the PLO was behind it."

In June, Zippori heard that women and children had been killed in an operation two months earlier, when a car bomb was exploded on a main road in the Western Sector of southern Lebanon, with the aim of hitting PLO personnel. "Raful had not submitted it upstairs for approval, because we feared that we wouldn't get authorization for a thing like that," said Ben-Gal. Both in internal army reports and publicly, the Northern Command claimed that the operation had been carried out by one of the local South Lebanese militias, something that was feasible but was in fact totally untrue.

"One of the cars managed to get away. Two cars caught fire and blew up. Can I tell you there were any big stars there? No, there weren't. But we zapped a few operatives," said Ben-Gal.

"I thought it was a terrible thing," said Zippori. He demanded that Begin, who was serving as defense minister (Weizman having resigned in May), throw Ben-Gal and Dagan out of the army. "Menachem, we are a sovereign state. Everything the army does, it can do only with the authorization of the cabinet. And in the cabinet, if such a thing came up for discussion, I would express my opinion. But it has not come up, and no one authorized it."

Ben-Gal was summoned to the defense minister's bureau in Tel Aviv, where Begin, Zippori, Eitan, and Saguy were waiting for him. "You are carrying out unauthorized actions in Lebanon. In these activities, women and children have been killed," Zippori charged.

"Not correct," Ben-Gal replied. "Four or five terrorists were killed. Who drives around in Lebanon in a Mercedes at 2 A.M.? Only terrorists."

Zippori immediately protested. "The head of the Northern Command, who is doing things without the approval of the general staff, must be dismissed," he said. "I am deputy minister of defense, and I knew nothing. You, Mr. Begin, are prime minister and minister of defense, and you knew nothing. The chief of staff didn't know."

Ben-Gal made small movements with his hand, signaling to Eitan that he should stand up and say everything was done with his approval. But Eitan, realizing that he couldn't implicate himself, ignored him, playing with his wristwatch, which he had taken off and was turning over and over.

Finally, Begin spoke. "General Ben-Gal," he said, "I want to ask you, as an officer and on your word of honor: Did you obtain approval for the operation from anyone above you?"

"Yes, Prime Minister. I obtained approval."

"I believe the head of Northern Command. A general in the army would not lie," Begin said. "The matter is closed. I hereby end this meeting."

Was Begin aware of what was going on around him? Zippori, who still saw Begin as a venerable commander and an esteemed leader, believed that the military men deceived the prime minister time and again, exploiting his romantic attitude toward generals. Others believe that Begin, a seasoned politician, fully grasped the situation but preferred to retain plausible deniability of the egregious activities. Either way, the top brass realized there was no point in asking the prime minister to rectify the situation.

Though the infighting between AMAN and the Northern Command continued, and AMAN later learned from its sources in Lebanon about the Northern Command's car and donkey bombings, eventually they decided to let go of the issue. "There were a lot of ops that were seen as small, kind of tactical, so we decided to drop it," said Gilboa. "We said, 'Perhaps it is better we don't know, as long as it isn't causing political damage.' Something like 'Let the young men arise and play before us.'"

Gilboa's quote is from the Bible, 2 Samuel 2:14, and it means, basically, "Let the kids have their fun." Ben-Gal's targets were low-level PLO operatives, and his missions little more than tactical skirmishes. None of the PLO leadership was touched in his secret war. The operations, he said, were a kind a game for Dagan. "Just as he has a hobby of painting—and he paints very nicely—that's the way it was with these ops," Ben-Gal said. "They were Meir's hobby."

"It was convenient for me that the activities took place in a gray area," Ben-Gal continued. "Sometimes one does not have to know. There are subjects about which you don't have to be a worm like Zippori, and investigate the truth all the way to the end. Just let things flow, and know how to back Dagan up if things go wrong. True, Dagan was a wild man, but a wild young horse that jumps the fences and sometimes breaks a leg is better than some mule that you have to beat with a whip to make him take two paces forward."

ON AUGUST 5, 1981, Prime Minister Menachem Begin appointed Ariel "Arik" Sharon as defense minister of Israel. Begin had a deep admiration for the former general—"a glorious commander of armies," he called him, "an international strategist"—though he was somewhat apprehensive about Sharon's aggressiveness and his un-willingness to accept the authority of his superiors. "Sharon is liable to attack the Knesset with tanks," Begin had half-joked two years before.

Still, Begin believed he was the right man to oversee the with-drawal from the Sinai in the wake of the peace treaty with Egypt, a task that, despite some violent demonstrations by settlers and the far right, Sharon accomplished without bloodshed.

At the same time, though, Sharon exploited the powers of his position to build more Jewish settlements in the West Bank and the Gaza Strip, which, as occupied territories, fell under the jurisdiction of the Defense Ministry. He also instilled a pugnacious, enterprising spirit throughout the defense establishment. Sharon and Eitan, who in the 1950s had served as an officer under Sharon's command in the IDF's Paratroopers Brigade, both saw supreme importance in com-bating the PLO and its bases in Lebanon, and they ordered the mili-tary to start planning a major military campaign there.

"Sharon's plans were revealed to us very, very slowly," said Efraim Sneh. "At first, he ordered us to prepare a limited military penetra-tion [to Lebanon], and only later on to draw the maps for a massive invasion, up to the Beirut-Damascus road." David Agmon, Northern Command chief of staff, said that at a later stage, Sharon ordered him to plan the occupation of the whole of Lebanon and even parts of Syria. "It was clear to us that we didn't know everything," said Sneh, "and that the government knew even less than we did."

But even Sharon realized that Israel could not simply invade Leb-anon and occupy parts of it. In July 1981, President Reagan's special envoy to the Middle East, Philip Habib, mediated a ceasefire be-tween Israel and the PLO in the Lebanese arena. Sharon and Eitan fiercely opposed the agreement, which did not include an undertak-ing by the PLO to refrain from attacks against Israelis in other places, like the occupied territories or Europe. To Sharon, a grenade thrown at a synagogue in Paris should have been considered a breach of the ceasefire. Furthermore, Begin and Sharon saw Arafat as responsible for any act by any Palestinian anywhere in the world, even if they belonged to organizations that were not affiliated with the PLO. But the outside world saw things differently, and Habib made it clear to the Israelis that the United States would back a land incursion into Lebanon only in response to a gross provocation by the PLO.

Sharon thought, correctly, that every day that went by peacefully gave Arafat and his people a gift of time to consolidate their position in Lebanon and improve their military deployment there. He decided to speed things up a little so he could execute his plan, and to activate Dagan's secret apparatus in the Northern Command. "The aim of the second phase of this activity," according to Sneh, "was to sow such chaos in the Palestinian areas of Tyre, Sidon, and Beirut that there would be a genuine and cast-iron reason for an Israeli invasion."

Sharon also dispatched Rafi Eitan as a personal emissary to keep an eye on the clandestine activities in the north. Eitan—the slayer of the Tel Aviv Templers, the captor of Eichmann, and commander of the operations against the German scientists in Egypt—had left the organization in a huff when he was passed over for the directorship. In 1981, he was serving as the prime minister's counterterrorism adviser and as the head of Lakam, an espionage arm of the Defense Ministry that dealt mainly with military technology.

By mid-September 1981, car bombs were exploding regularly in Palestinian neighborhoods of Beirut and other Lebanese cities. One went off in the Fakhani quarter of Beirut on October 1, killing eighty-three people and wounding three hundred, including many women who were trapped in a fire in a clothing factory owned by the PLO. Another one exploded next to the PLO headquarters in Sidon, killing twenty-three. In December 1981 alone, eighteen bombs in cars or on motorcycles, bicycles, or donkeys blew up near PLO offices or Palestinian concentrations, causing many scores of deaths.

A new and unknown organization calling itself the Front for the Liberation of Lebanon from Foreigners took responsibility for all of these incidents. The explosives were now packed in Ariel laundry powder bags so that if the cars were stopped at roadblocks, the cargo would look like innocent goods. The Israelis in some cases enlisted women to drive, to reduce the likelihood of the cars being caught on the way to the target zone.

The car bombs were developed in the IDF's Special Operations Executive (Maarach Ha-Mivtsaim Ha-Meyuchadim), and they involved the use of one of the earliest generations of drones. These drones would relay the beam that would set off the detonation mechanism of the device. One of Dagan's local agents would drive the car to the target, under aerial or land observation, park it there, and then leave. When the observers identified the moment they were waiting for, they'd push a button and the car would explode.

Sharon hoped that these operations would provoke Arafat into attacking Israel, which could then respond by invading Lebanon, or at least make the PLO retaliate against the Phalange, whereupon Israel would be able to leap in great force to the defense of the Christians.

The Front for the Liberation of Lebanon from Foreigners also began attacking Syrian installations in Lebanon, and it even claimed responsibility for operations against IDF units. "We were never connected to activities against our own forces," said Dagan, "but the front took responsibility in order to create credibility, as if it was operating against all of the foreign forces in Lebanon."

Yasser Arafat was not hoodwinked by this ploy. He accused the Mossad of being behind the blasts and the "front." That was not quite right, either, however. The Mossad was in fact vehemently opposed to what Ben-Gal and Dagan were doing.

"With Sharon's backing," one Mossad officer of the time said, "terrible things were done. I am no vegetarian, and I supported and even participated in some of the assassination operations Israel carried out. But we are speaking here about mass killing for killing's sake, to sow chaos and alarm, among civilians, too. Since when do we send donkeys carrying bombs to blow up in marketplaces?"

Another Mossad man who was in Lebanon at the time said, "I saw from a distance one of the cars blowing up and demolishing an entire street. We were teaching the Lebanese how effective a car bomb could be. Everything that we saw later with Hezbollah sprang from what they saw had happened after these operations."

Dagan and Ben-Gal strongly denied that the front ever intended to harm civilians. "The targets were always military targets," said Ben-Gal. Dagan said there was no alternative to using proxies. "I am ready to shed countless tears on the grave of a Lebanese who was killed on a mission for us, as long as no Jew's life is endangered." But he added that using mercenaries had its disadvantages. "You can give

him explosives and tell him to go blow up a PLO headquarters somewhere, but he has his own accounts, and now he's also got a bomb to
settle them. So sometimes it happened that it went off somewhere
else."

Arafat realized that Sharon was trying to goad the Palestinians
into breaching the ceasefire so that he could launch his invasion, and
Arafat made a genuine effort not to oblige him, including a partly
successful attempt to stop violence in the occupied territories. In the
face of this Palestinian restraint, the leaders of the front decided to
move up a level.

Sharon had Arafat returned to the wanted list—he'd been removed in 1974, when the Mossad reached the conclusion that he'd
become a political figure and that therefore Israel must not harm
him—and in late 1981, Ben-Gal and Dagan began planning an operation that they expected would change the course of Middle East
history. Operation Olympia, code-named for a popular Tel Aviv restaurant, was a plan to bring in truck bombs loaded with something
like two tons of explosives and surround a theater in east Beirut
where the PLO was scheduled to hold a festive dinner in December.
One massive explosion would eliminate the entire PLO leadership.
But the idea was abandoned, and Olympia 1 was scrapped in favor of
Olympia 2. This one called for Israeli agents to plant a massive set of
bombs under a VIP dais under construction in a Beirut stadium
where, on January 1, 1982, the PLO was going to celebrate the anniversary of its founding. With the push of one button would come
wholesale destruction.

Ben-Gal was no longer head of the Northern Command by the
time this plan went into its operational stage. Sharon had little use
for him. The general who was plotting to blow up dozens of Palestinians and who'd waged a secret war in Lebanon was, in Sharon's view,
softhearted and lacking in resolve. In December 1981, he dismissed
Ben-Gal from the Northern Command and appointed someone more
to his liking—a move that foreshadowed Sharon's plans for Lebanon.

It was at this time that Olympia 2 moved into high gear. On December 20, 1981, three agents recruited by Dagan managed to get to
the VIP dais and plant large amounts of explosives underneath the
place where the PLO leadership would be seated, all linked to a re-

motely controlled detonation device. In addition, at one of the unit's bases, three miles from the border, three vehicles—a truck loaded with a ton and a half of explosives and two Mercedes sedans with 550 pounds each—had been prepared. These vehicles were to be driven to Beirut by three Shiite members of the Front for the Liberation of Lebanon from Foreigners and parked close to a wall of the stadium behind the VIP dais. They would be detonated by remote control about a minute after the explosives under the dais, when the panic was at its height and the people who had survived were trying to get away. The death and destruction were expected to be "of unprecedented proportions, even in terms of Lebanon," in the words of a very senior officer of the Northern Command.

In a note Rafi Eitan passed to Efraim Sneh at a meeting about the planned operation, he wrote, "If this works, we [Israel] will immediately be blamed." This was written not in fear, but rather in hope, because, as Sneh later said, "those PLO leaders who weren't killed by the blast in the stadium would know right away what they had to do: to attack Israel, to breach the ceasefire, and to give Sharon, who was desperate to invade Lebanon, the pretext to do that."

Everything was in place, but then someone leaked the plan to Saguy, who informed Deputy Defense Minister Zippori what was afoot. "Foreign diplomats are likely to be on the dais with Arafat, and in particular Alexander Soldatov, the Soviet ambassador to Lebanon," Saguy told Zippori.

Zippori detested Sharon and was always suspicious of his intentions, so he contacted his old commander in the pre-state underground, the Irgun: Begin. "The ambassador matter was grave enough in itself," Zippori said. "But far more grave, much more, was that once again they were carrying out such acts without the approval of the cabinet."

Early on the morning of December 31, a day before Olympia 2 was scheduled to take place, chief of staff Eitan called Dagan. "All of a sudden, I hear that Sharon is ordering us to go to the prime minister in order to present the plan and get his final approval to act," Dagan recalled. "It was a very rainy day. Raful informs us that in order to maintain secrecy, he would come to Northern Command headquarters to pick me up and fly us together to Begin."

In Begin's office, the prime minister stared at them inquiringly. "They say that it's possible that the Soviet ambassador will be there on the platform," Begin said.

"That's simply incorrect," Dagan said. "There's a very low probability that he or any other foreign diplomat will be there."

Begin asked Saguy what he thought. Saguy said it was likely that a Soviet diplomat would attend. "If something happens to him," he said, "we are liable to get into a very grave crisis with the USSR."

Years later, Saguy said, "My duty as head of AMAN was to take care of not only the operational-military aspects, but also the diplomatic aspect. I told Begin that it was impossible to kill a whole stadium just like that. And what would happen the next day after such a massacre? The whole world would pile on top of us. It would make no difference if we never admitted responsibility. Everyone would know who was behind it."

Dagan, Eitan, and Sharon tried to persuade Begin, saying this was an opportunity that would not come again. But the prime minister took the danger of a Russian threat seriously and ordered them to abort.

"In the end, of course, it turned out that I was right and there was no Soviet ambassador or any other foreign diplomat there," Dagan said. "But what could we do? The PM said abort, so we abort. There was a very complicated business afterward, getting the explosives out."

Begin quickly green-lit another operation, one that carried little risk of harming either diplomats or civilians. Surveillance of the top PLO leaders had revealed that once a month, on a Friday, they left Beirut in a convoy of seven or eight luxury Mercedes sedans and sped toward Syria, and from there to Jordan, where they held leadership meetings. It was both business and pleasure, and Arafat often joined the delegation.

One night in early February 1982, a squad of Caesarea operatives came to one of the main junctions the convoys passed through each month. They dismantled the top of one of the traffic lights and replaced it with one manufactured in the Mossad's technological department. It contained a camera to transmit images to Mossad HQ. On Friday, March 5, at 3 A.M., a few hours before the PLO convoy was due to pass by, another, larger Caesarea squad arrived at the junction, with a large amount of explosives that they began planting in ditches along the sides of the road, connected by a detonating cord and linked wirelessly to headquarters. According to the plan, the Mossad personnel would leave the scene after setting up the bombs and return to Israel. The convoy would be watched by local agents after it departed Beirut. When it passed a certain point, marked on one of the trees and clearly visible in the transmitted images, the bombs would be detonated and the PLO leadership would be liquidated.

Everything went well until dawn, when a local policeman saw the two vehicles the Israeli team had arrived in, and the men kneeling near them. "What are you doing there?" the cop asked in Arabic. "We've been to a wedding and they served bad food," one of the Mossad agents told him. "We've all got the runs. We stopped to empty our stomachs." Two of the team had already surreptitiously drawn their pistols and cocked them. But the cop decided to go on his way.

The operatives wondered whether he had believed them or if he'd gone for reinforcements. HQ decided not to take any risks. The prime minister and the defense minister agreed that the mission should be aborted, and the team returned to Israel. Once again, the iron law that any mission must be sacrificed if it could allow operatives to fall into captivity was strictly observed.

What would have happened if Begin had allowed Dagan to go ahead with Olympia, or if the Arab policeman hadn't driven by? History, Dagan argued, would have run a completely different course. "If they had permitted us to act and the PLO leadership been put out of play," he said, "we all would have been spared the Lebanon War six months later, and any number of other troubles."

It's impossible to know for sure. Others feel that Sharon and Eitan would not have been satisfied even then, and that they had a grand strategy to create a new order not only in Lebanon, but in the whole of the Middle East.

For now, they kept silent, waiting for the inevitable pretext for war.

# "ABU NIDAL, ABU *SHMIDAL*"

EVERY SPRING IN LONDON, the De La Rue company, a British-based currency-printing and security-system firm, hosts a black-tie dinner for diplomats and business executives in the city. In 1982, it was held on the night of June 3 at the posh Dorchester Hotel. Eighty-four ambassadors and CEOs from all over the world feasted, networked, and swapped gossip.

When it was over, shortly after 10 P.M., and the guests began to wander out, Israel's ambassador to the Court of St. James's, Shlomo Argov, stopped in the hotel lobby to chat with another diplomat. They discussed the gifts their respective countries would give to the first child of Prince Charles and Princess Diana, who was due to be born in two weeks. Then, right at the exit, Argov shook hands with the press mogul Robert Maxwell and thanked him for his papers' friendly attitude toward Israel.

The Shin Bet's VIP protection unit wasn't allowed to operate in the United Kingdom, so Argov was protected by a British bodyguard, Detective Colin Simpson. The two men stepped out of the hotel and quickly walked the thirty feet to an armor-plated ambassadorial Volvo sedan. Simpson opened the back door for Argov.

Neither one of them saw the assassin on the sidewalk until it was too late.

Hussein Ghassan Said was part of a secret cell of the Abu Nidal terror group. He and two comrades had been waiting, watching the front door of the Dorchester for an hour and a half. "The day before the operation," Said said, "Russan, our commander, came to me and told me that tomorrow would be a great day for the Palestinian nation, that we were going to kill an important Zionist."

Carrying a Polish-made WZ-63 miniature submachine gun, he approached Argov from behind. "I came close to him," he said, "and he began getting into the car. I took my weapon out of my bag and held it with both hands, as I had been taught. The other man opened the door for him. I came closer, until I was only a few meters away, and then I fired at him, one shot in the head."

Simpson pushed Argov into the car and told the chauffeur to drive to the hospital. The ambassador was gravely injured. Then Simpson chased Said, who was fleeing up Park Lane toward a car in which two friends were waiting for him. The detective testified later that at the corner of South Street, several blocks from the Dorchester, Said turned and fired at him. He missed, and the bullet hit a car belonging to a member of the royal family, whose clothes were covered by shattered glass. At almost the same moment, Simpson fired his .38 pistol and hit Said in the neck just below the right ear, bringing him down. "I began running toward the car," Said said. "My weapon jammed. Suddenly I felt a terrible blow to my neck and I fell down to the ground."

Said's companions were caught forty minutes after the incident. British intelligence had a double agent inside the Abu Nidal cell, but they missed his tip-off about the planned assassination bid and realized too late what was happening.

Argov survived but was paralyzed and suffered from grave ailments that led to his death in 2003. Shortly after the assassination attempt, Israeli intelligence learned that Abu Nidal, Arafat's sworn enemy, whose real name was Sabri al-Banna, "had ordered the attack on behalf of Barzan al-Tikriti, the head of the Iraqi intelligence services," said Yigal Simon, a former commander of Unit 504, who at the time was serving in the Mossad's London station.

Barzan's half brother and boss, the Iraqi despot Saddam Hussein, hoped that the assassination would bring about a large-scale military clash between Syria and the PLO and Israel, his three bitter Middle Eastern rivals, and perhaps even embroil the biggest rival of all: Iran.

As it happened, Saddam and Sharon's cadre of hawks had similar interests. At the Israeli cabinet's meeting on the morning of June 4, 1982, Prime Minister Begin declared that "an attack on an ambassador is tantamount to an attack on the State of Israel, and we will respond." He wouldn't listen to his own intelligence personnel, who tried to tell him that the PLO had been behaving for a year, since the American-initiated ceasefire of the previous summer, and that Argov had been shot by a member of a dissident fringe Palestinian group, which itself wanted to eliminate Arafat. "They're all PLO," Begin proclaimed. Chief of staff Eitan was less refined: "Abu Nidal, Abu *Shmidal*. We've got to whack the PLO."

The cabinet approved a massive aerial bombardment of Beirut and PLO bases. Clearly, Arafat could not let this pass without reacting. Soon after, twenty-nine northern Israeli communities had come under heavy PLO artillery fire.

In London, Said was sentenced to thirty years in prison. In telephone interviews and letters, he said he didn't believe his shot had started the Israeli war in Lebanon. "It would have happened anyway," he said. "It may have affected the timing of the invasion, but Raful and Sharon wanted to conquer Lebanon in any event. They used what I did as an excuse."

He was probably correct. In any case, the war in Lebanon was on.


ARIEL SHARON PRESENTED THE Israeli cabinet with a plan to avenge the shooting of Argov and silence the PLO forces on June 5. He called it Operation Peace for Galilee, a name designed to give the impression this was an almost reluctant mission of self-protection. It would be a limited incursion, Sharon told the cabinet, aimed only at removing the threat PLO artillery posed to Israeli communities. The IDF would advance into Lebanon no more than forty kilometers, the range of the PLO's biggest guns at the time.

The only minister who opposed the plan was Mordechai Zippori, now serving as minister of communications. He suspected that Sharon had much greater goals. With his military background, Zippori also grasped that a thrust of such depth, along the flank of the Syrian forces in Lebanon, would by necessity lead to a clash between the

Israeli and Syrian forces. But Begin rebuffed Zippori's objections and declared, "I have said that we will not attack the Syrians."

Zippori's suspicions, however, were once again entirely justified. This was indeed only the beginning of Sharon's actual plan. Along with his chief of staff, Eitan, he had a secret agenda that was far more grandiose: He intended to use the IDF's tanks to remake the whole of the Middle East. In his vision, Israeli forces and their Phalange allies would conquer Lebanon from the border to Beirut, destroying all PLO forces and inflicting serious damage on Syrian units deployed there. With the capital secure, the Israelis would install the Phalange's leader, Bashir Gemayel, as president, thus transforming Lebanon into a reliable ally. Next, Gemayel would expel the Palestinians to Jordan, where they would be a majority able to establish a Palestinian state in place of the Hashemite Kingdom. This, Sharon reckoned, would eliminate the Palestinian demand for a state in Judea and Samaria—the West Bank—which thus would become part of Israel.

In that fantastical plan, there was one more critical element: killing Yasser Arafat. Sharon believed that in a war against a terrorist organization, emblems and symbols were as important as body counts. To send a signal, to crush the Palestinians' spirit, he and Eitan were determined to get to Beirut, find Arafat's lair, and kill him.

To this end, a special task force was set up, code-named Salt Fish. Sharon appointed his two experts on special ops—Meir Dagan and Rafi Eitan—to run it. "I thought that hitting him would change everything," Dagan said. "Arafat was not only a Palestinian leader, but a kind of founding father of the Palestinian nation. Killing him would unleash a large part of the internal conflicts inside the PLO and significantly hinder their capability to make any strategic decisions from then on."

The AMAN chief, Major General Yehoshua Saguy, and the head of the Mossad, Yitzhak Hofi, formerly an IDF general, both firmly opposed invading Lebanon, because they knew that behind Sharon's and Eitan's promises of "an incursion of no more than forty kilometers" there was another, hidden plan that would place Israel in a damaging situation. "I knew them both," said Hofi, "and I knew that they had not given up their ambition and that somehow they would try to achieve what they always wanted"—to reach Beirut and kill Arafat. Hofi warned Begin that an invasion of Lebanon "would be the Yom Kippur War of the Likud," Begin's party—a disaster for the state and for his own career, just as the 1973 conflict had ended the hegemony of the Labor Party.

But Begin dismissed the intelligence organizations' objections, and on June 6 the IDF stormed into Lebanon.

An army of 76,000 troops, 800 tanks, and 1,500 armored personnel carriers advanced northward on three axes, with a fourth force landing from the sea.

The beginning was promising, from Sharon's point of view. The Israeli forces achieved most of their objectives, thanks to their vastly superior firepower but also to the top-grade intelligence that AMAN and the Mossad had supplied them after penetrating deep into the deeply corrupted PLO. The militiamen performed even worse than AMAN had predicted. Most of the senior commanders fled, leaving their men to perish.

Just as Zippori had predicted, the Syrians responded to the blatant Israeli provocation. Eitan, whose forces had almost been overrun by the Syrians on the Golan Heights in 1973, took advantage of the opportunity to settle the score and ordered a counterattack in force. The Syrians also withered under the Israelis' fire.

But along with the military victories, it very quickly became clear to Israeli cabinet ministers that the "forty-kilometer incursion" against the PLO that they were promised was becoming something completely different. Sharon ordered the IDF to keep advancing, claiming that this was necessary for various operational reasons. In the face of his charismatic and overbearing personality, the ministers raised almost no objections.

"I very quickly saw that the forty-kilometer plan was melting away, and the IDF was penetrating deeper into Lebanon," said Begin's military secretary, Brigadier General Azriel Nevo. "Sharon lied and misled Begin and the cabinet. Sharon's greatness was that he knew how to describe, in the most vivid way, why it was necessary to advance another few kilometers, because otherwise tomorrow morning the Syrian Army would be sitting on some hill and endanger our troops.

That's how he managed to extract authorization from the cabinet for the creeping invasion."

On June 25, the IDF completed its encirclement of Beirut, far beyond the range that had been agreed upon, and commenced a harrowing siege and bombardment of the city's western neighborhoods.

Sharon had hoped that the Maronite Christian Phalangists would help fight the PLO, serving as Israel's cannon fodder, especially in the densely populated areas. The Phalange had similar ideas, but the other way around: that the Israelis would do the fighting to establish their hegemony in Lebanon. "The Mossad, which was managing the connection with the Phalange, was absolutely wrong in the way it read the situation in Lebanon and the capability and intentions of the Christians. They led us up the garden path," said Nevo.

The Phalange's leaders urged the Israelis to conquer more and more territory, promising military assistance that never materialized. In a meeting with chief of staff Eitan on June 16, the Phalange leader Bashir Gemayel pleaded for the IDF to conquer Beirut. "Your declarations that you won't enter Beirut," Gemayel said, "don't help, because they strengthen the fighting spirit of the Palestinians and the Muslims and obstruct the political process." At the same time, Gemayel had advice about how to treat his hometown: "You must continue with the aerial bombardment, because artillery shelling has no effect, because they are already used to them."

Together, Sharon, Eitan, and the Phalange were clandestinely plotting how to take Beirut in a combined operation code-named the Spark. During a meeting at Sharon's home on August 1, attended by the heads of the IDF and the Mossad, Sharon asked Gemayel, "Can you cut off the water again?" reflecting his desire to apply as much pressure as possible to get the PLO and the Syrians to pull out.

Gemayel said, "We can, with your cover."

"Okay," Sharon said. "But we have to leave the water open on Monday, when [U.S. Secretary of State George] Shultz meets [Foreign Minister Yitzhak] Shamir."

Israel's cabinet ministers heard only afterward about Sharon's orders to conquer, for the first time in Israel's history, the capital of another sovereign state. Indeed, all throughout the war, Sharon never stopped assuring the cabinet, the Knesset, and the nation that "there is no intention to enter Beirut," repeating this promise many times. But the command Sharon gave the IDF was perfectly clear: "We have to finish off the southern part" of Beirut, where the refugee camps and PLO bases were located, he said at a meeting in his office on July 11, "to destroy whatever can be destroyed . . . to raze it to the ground."

THE FULL-SCALE INVASION OF Lebanon and the siege of Beirut would become a quagmire for Israel, an occupation that would last—at least in the south—for another eighteen years.

The whole world, even President Ronald Reagan, who had a good relationship with Begin, came out against Israel. "You are causing a holocaust in Beirut," said Reagan in an angry phone call to Begin. "Please, Mr. President," Begin responded, no less angry, "don't teach me about holocausts. I and my people know very well what 'holocaust' means."

The Mossad tried to balance the picture by leaking to the London *Observer* documents purporting to show that the PLO had stockpiles of weapons for 100,000 men, which were in fact the Soviet Union's emergency stores in the Middle East. They also claimed that the USSR intended to send Cuban soldiers in to fight alongside the Palestinians, to conquer the Galilee, destroy the Jewish settlements, and set up an independent state there. It is doubtful that these tales contained even a grain of truth, and they certainly didn't swing world opinion in Israel's favor. The Middle East conflict once again was perceived as a David and Goliath story—but with Israel as the powerful and brutal giant, and the Palestinians as the pitiable underdog.

The full extent of the deception that Sharon perpetrated against the government and the public of Israel emerged only gradually. But the steadily increasing Israeli casualty count, the indistinct and fluctuating goals, and the stories of destruction and suffering in Lebanon brought home by soldiers began to arouse protests and opposition.

Sharon's chief of staff, Eitan, realized that most of the IDF's moves in Lebanon were being made without the approval of the cabinet, so he deliberately absented himself from the meetings of that body, claiming that he was with the fighting forces. He left the job of compartmentalization and concealment to Sharon, who simply ignored all the opposition and pressed ahead. ("He Doesn't Stop on Red" was a song written about him by Israel's leading rock musician, Shalom Hanoch.)

It is unclear exactly how much Begin knew about Sharon's complicated plan. In time, Sharon would sue a journalist who wrote that he had lied to Begin and concealed information from him. Sharon lost the case.

As for the plan to do away with Yasser Arafat, there are no complete transcripts of cabinet sessions or of Sharon's meetings with Begin, so it is impossible to say precisely what Begin and his other minister knew, if anything, about Operation Salt Fish.

Still, whatever Begin may have known about the specifics, he made no secret of his opinion about the larger need to dispose of Arafat. In a letter to Reagan on August 2, Begin wrote that he felt as if "I have sent an army to Berlin to wipe out Hitler in the bunker." In a speech in the Knesset the same week, he again called Arafat "that despicable man with the hair on his face, the killer of our children."

The Salt Fish task force, set up by Meir Dagan and Rafi Eitan, continued operating outside of the broader war command, and was staffed mostly by Sayeret Matkal soldiers commanded by the outgoing chief of that unit, Lieutenant Colonel Uzi Dayan. Its mission, though, was complicated by the realities of urban warfare. The team couldn't simply send a platoon of soldiers to storm through Beirut to kill one man, a tactic that would have wreaked unimaginable havoc. "So the main task was to locate Salt Fish and put him in the air force's bombsights," Dayan said. "But without causing too much collateral damage."

Colonel Yossi Langotsky, one of the founding fathers of AMAN's technological unit, was summoned to Beirut in June to tap into all of the PLO's communications systems. Thanks to the intercepted calls, which were cross-checked against covert deep observation carried out by Sayeret troops and information from Mossad agents, the Salt Fish teams had an abundance of information on the hideouts used by Arafat.

Still, "it was a very complicated mission," said Dayan. "We had to collate the information from the various sources, to understand which building or cave was the right one, to pinpoint it on the map, to narrow it down to ten-figure coordinates, to transmit them to the air force, giving them enough time to put a plane in the air and bomb it."

The long days and nights at the Salt Fish command post were mostly frustrating times as Arafat escaped time and again. Langotsky and Dayan would hear the bodyguards arranging Arafat's arrival at a certain place and time and quickly give the air force the coordinates. Once they even heard Arafat himself on the phone and sent in a pair of fighter-bombers that razed the building, but Arafat had left "not more than thirty seconds earlier," according to Dayan.

The Palestinian leader understood that it was not a coincidence that bombs were repeatedly falling at places he had just entered or just left. He told his people that Sharon, in Beirut, was acting like a "wounded wolf" and wanted to kill him in revenge for the way the war was dragging on. He began taking more precautionary measures, arranging several meetings at the same time in different places. He scattered disinformation around among his aides, suspicious that one of them might be a Mossad agent, and he moved around all the time.

"Arafat kept on breaking his routine," said Moshe Yaalon, a Salt Fish officer. "There was no regular pattern in his behavior, nothing that could enable the preparation of a raid by land against a bunker or a house."

The team, growing increasingly desperate, came up with innumerable ideas. On July 3, the left-wing Israeli magazine editor Uri Avnery crossed the front line in Beirut to interview Arafat (together with reporter Sarit Yishai and photographer Anat Saragusti) in the heart of the city. The meeting was highly controversial in Israel. Arafat was seen as the country's worst enemy, and this was his first time meeting an Israeli. "My goal was to begin paving a path to Israeli-Palestinian peace by changing the Israelis' way of thinking," Avnery said. The Salt Fish team didn't particularly admire this initiative ("I won't even begin to say what I think about Avnery and his outrageous act," said Yaalon) but decided to take advantage of the opportunity to track the three Israelis and to let them lead a group of assassins straight to Arafat.

Among the Salt Fish team members, a discussion took place over whether it was permissible to endanger the lives of the Israelis, or perhaps even kill them, while carrying out their mission. Avner Azoulai, the Mossad representative in the Salt Fish forum, summed up the outcome of this debate: "If the conditions were right from the operational aspect, it is reasonable to assume that both Arafat and these three dear Jews would not have remained alive."

But the ever cautious Arafat suspected that the Mossad might be keeping tabs on Avnery and the two journalists with him. Arafat's security guards took strict deceptive countermeasures, and the Salt Fish team lost their trail in the alleys of south Beirut.

As more days went by, and the reality of a messy, fomented civil war refused to conform to Sharon and Eitan's wildly overambitious plan to restructure an entire region of the planet, the two hawks put increasing pressure on the air force and the Salt Fish teams to get Arafat. "From the start of the siege of Beirut, the matter of killing Arafat assumed huge importance. The feeling was that it was something personal for Sharon," said Major General David Ivri, then an air force commander. "Every now and again, people from the Mossad or AMAN would show up at Canary"—the air force command post, in a subterranean bunker deep beneath Tel Aviv—"and tell us that Arafat was here or there. Sharon or Raful would order us to bomb those places immediately."

"I thought that it was messy, with the danger of harming civilians," Ivri continued. "I was not ready to okay a bombing party like that without getting an order in writing from the general staff's operations branch. I hoped that placing the matter into an organized framework of information-sharing and decision-making would lead to better judgment. In fact, many of the orders never came in writing. They just disappeared somewhere on the way."

Uzi Dayan had the same misgivings. "Arafat was saved by two things," he said. "His interminable good luck and me. I thought Arafat was a legitimate target, but I did not think that hitting the target justified any means. If I saw that it entailed large-scale killing of civilians, even if we knew Arafat was there, I did not agree to have a place bombed."

"Raful used to blow up with anger," Dayan continued. "He'd call me up and say, 'I understand you have information on such and such a place. Why aren't the planes in the air?' I replied that it was impossible because there were a lot of people around. Raful said, 'Forget about it. I'll take responsibility for it.' I wasn't prepared to allow it. Raful would not teach me the ethics of war."

Rafael Eitan would remind Dayan that he was not authorized to decide whether to drop a bomb. But as Dayan explained, "All I had to do was to report when the target was ripe from the intelligence point of view. So from that point on, each time we knew that bombing would lead to massive civilian casualties, we reported that the target wasn't ripe from the intelligence angle."

On the evening of August 4, Eitan asked the head of the air force operations department, Aviem Sella, to come and see him. The two had a close relationship, and Eitan had a soft spot for Sella, a highly promising officer considered a potential commander of the air force.

Eitan greeted Sella and told him that the next day he wouldn't be working in Canary as usual, but would be "going on a trip."

"Anything like our last trip together?" asked Sella, alluding to a visit to Beirut in May, in preparation for the invasion and the operation to assassinate Arafat.

"Something like it," Eitan replied. "But from above. Meet me tomorrow morning at Hatzor [an air force base in the south]. You'll fly the plane, and I'll navigate and operate the combat systems. We're going to bomb Beirut." The target was a building where Arafat was supposed to be the next morning, according to information obtained by Operation Salt Fish.

Sella knew that Eitan had a pilot's license for light aircraft, but he still was convinced he wasn't hearing right. "It was totally insane," he said. "I was in shock. If someone had told me that the chief of staff, who isn't really an airman, was taking the head of the air force operations department for a break in the running of the war while they bombed Beirut for fun, I would never have believed it."

But chief of staff Eitan was obsessive about killing Arafat. The next day, the two met at Hatzor. They were part of a quartet of Phantoms on an expedition to bomb the al-Sana'i office block, in west Beirut, where Arafat was supposed to be attending a meeting. "Raful's functioning was so-so; I think he was feeling a little bit sick. I did my own navigation. He operated the munitions systems, which by today's terms were rather primitive. We made two bombing runs over the target, and then another one to see if we'd hit it. Raful was happy, and we flew home to Israel."

Arafat was once again saved by a miracle: The bombs wrecked part of the building just before he arrived. Sella returned from Hatzor to Tel Aviv to manage the operations of the air force, and Eitan took a helicopter ride to Beirut. "In the evening," Sella recalls, "I saw him on TV, being interviewed on the outskirts of Beirut. He declared that Israel was refraining from bombing targets in civilian surroundings—which was exactly what he had been doing himself that morning."

THE PROBLEM WITH OPERATION Salt Fish, for Sharon and for Israel, was that the entire world was watching. With each failed assassination attempt, Israel looked more and more like a military power overrunning a sovereign nation in a monomaniacal quest to kill a single man. Arafat, rather than being seen as a bloodthirsty terrorist, was now the hunted leader of a nation of refugees trampled by the Israeli war machine. Sharon had achieved precisely the opposite of what he wanted.

Its main target now an object of global sympathy, the invasion sank deeper into a swamp of military misadventure. The stalemate had to be broken, a quasi-victory salvaged. On August 1, the IDF began exerting heavy pressure on the PLO forces in Beirut (Operation King Kong), with an unbroken seventy-two-hour artillery bombardment aimed at persuading Arafat to withdraw from Lebanon. The Israeli Air Force carried out more than a hundred expeditions in a ten-hour period. The barrage from the air, land, and sea continued after that as well and reached a climax on August 12, which became known as Black Thursday because of the vast devastation wrought.

The pressure worked. On August 13, with the Americans mediating, Arafat agreed to evacuate Beirut with his forces. Uzi Dayan departed the city and left the Salt Fish team under Yaalon's command, with mixed feelings. "I didn't spend the rest of my life mourning, but I thought then and I still believe today that it's a pity the mission was not executed," he said. "On the other hand, the war was a very distressing affair from a humanitarian point of view. We watched the Lebanese population around us, the poverty, the destruction caused by the fighting. Among us, among the fighting forces, there was a great argument. I knew friends, comrades in arms, who really believed that someone should go and kill Sharon, who actually contemplated assassinating him, to save the State of Israel. I had supported the war from the outset, but I also understood that there was deadlock, that the war wasn't going anywhere. Sharon and Raful were deceiving everyone. I left Beirut with a feeling of great relief."

On August 21, the PLO forces evacuated Beirut by sea. Israel's relationship with the United States was very tense, considering the invasion of Lebanon and the siege of Beirut. Prime Minister Begin was eager to calm things down. When the evacuation agreement was signed, he promised the American mediator, Philip Habib, that no harm would be inflicted on the evacuees. Keeping this promise was important to Begin, and he firmly instructed Sharon to drop any plans that had been made to exploit the withdrawal as a way to settle scores with Arafat.

The Salt Fish team remained in Beirut and on August 30 took up positions, together with Shin Bet and Mossad officers, on the adjacent roofs of the Lebanese national oil and power companies, overlooking the port. "From a distance we saw a large convoy of vehicles," one of the Shin Bet operatives remembers. "All of a sudden, we saw the famous kaffiyeh on the famous head of the number-one wanted man coming out of one of the cars. He stood among a crowd of people, as if surrounded by a swarm of bees."

It would have been so easy to kill him. "We were 180 meters away," Yaalon said. "At that range, with the sniper rifle that our team was holding, it's hard to miss." Others who were there remember that Arafat was in the sights of at least five snipers at the same time.

One of the commanders was in radio contact with chief of staff Eitan in the command bunker in Tel Aviv, updating him on when Arafat would be out of range. "We can do it. We have him in our sights. Do we have authorization?" Eitan delayed, and the officer continued: "He's about to go inside, in ten, nine seconds—please give us authorization—eight, seven . . ."

Finally, Eitan replied in his nasal voice, audibly disappointed: "Negative," he said. "I repeat: negative. There is no authorization."

Twenty-four hours later, Begin gave Habib a picture of Arafat in the crosshairs of a sniper's rifle to prove that, despite the opportunity, Israel had stood by its word. By then Arafat was already in Athens, en route to the PLO's next stop in Tunis. Begin's goal to "wipe out Hitler in his bunker," as he had declared to Reagan, had become watching Hitler get airlifted out of Berlin.

# BLACK FLAG

SHARON HAD PROMISED TO withdraw the IDF from Lebanon as soon as the PLO departed, but he instead remained fixated on his grand plan of remaking the Middle East. With Israeli forces firmly entrenched and the Mossad exerting heavy pressure, the Lebanese parliament voted on August 23, 1982, to install the Phalange leader, Bashir Gemayel, as president. In Sharon's fantasy, Gemayel would expel the Palestinians from Lebanon.

More immediately, Sharon wanted to knock out what he called "the terror nucleus [PLO militiamen] and the left-wing forces [Communist and other leftist groups allied with the PLO], which are armed with heavy weaponry and remain in west Beirut."

Sharon knew that the United Nations would soon deploy a multinational peacekeeping force (MNF) in Beirut, and once that happened, he would no longer be able to do what he wished. At a meeting with the heads of the Mossad and the Shin Bet, he wondered aloud, "How will we be able to take care of the terrorists when the MNF is active? These would be entirely different methods. . . . We'll have to be certain that the problem has been solved, with every step we take today making things easier then."

Sharon didn't want to put the IDF into the heart of the Palestinian refugee camps, so he suggested that the Phalangists go into west Beirut "to ensure that whoever [from the PLO] was there would be killed or arrested." Begin liked this idea and approved of giving the job to the Phalange, because "our boys won't spill their blood on this matter."

The Mossad embellished this proposition. "We had a long list of names of European leftist activists who were with the Palestinians," said Avner Azoulai, the Mossad's liaison with the Maronite militia. "The idea was to hand it to the Phalangists so they could find them and kill them. After that, the Mossad would be able to secretly report to the European countries from which these bandits came, such as Germany, France, and Italy, that their problem was solved, and this way they would owe us a favor."

As it happened, Gemayel was instead murdered three weeks later, together with a large number of his associates, blown up by a bomb planted by a Syrian agent, that demolished the Phalange HQ in Beirut. In response, the Lebanese Christian militias secured permission from the Israelis to search for PLO fighters in the Palestinian refugee camps of Sabra and Shatila.

On the morning of September 16, Yair Ravid, the head of the Junction team in Beirut, was at the Phalange HQ, where the Mossad had placed its Beirut station. "All of a sudden," Ravid said, "I saw the boys of Elie [Hobeika, the Phalange military chief] sharpening their knives, and they tell me, 'Today it is the turn of *silah al abyad*,' the white weapons, which is what the Lebanese call slaughtering with knives. They didn't say against whom exactly, but it was clear to me they were going to cut throats. I didn't inquire any deeper. I was just a guest of theirs." Ravid didn't report to his superiors what he'd seen.

Robert Hatem, Hobeika's executioner, recalled that when the 350 Phalangists set out on their mission, "Hobeika told us, 'Fuck everybody there. Erase the camp.' We even took a D9 [bulldozer] to demolish everything."

The camp, Hatem said, "was made up of shacks, tin shanties. When we fired, everything came tumbling down. We shot in all directions. We didn't check to see who was behind those walls."

The lion's share of the damage was inflicted by a group commanded by Marom Mashalani. "Its members," Hatem said, "including the commander, took a lot of drugs, as much as it is possible to take. They didn't distinguish between fighters and noncombatants or between men and women. They shot them all."

The result was a horrific massacre. The number of the dead is disputed—the Israelis say 700, and the Palestinians say 2,750. Sharon would later claim that "Lebanese forces [i.e., the Phalangists] would conform to the conventions of war when the IDF was controlling them, overseeing or coordinating their actions. . . . The terrible outcome is in the nature of an unanticipated and unexplained breakdown." In other words, Sharon argued that he could not have foreseen what had happened.

Classified IDF and Mossad documents, however, prove that the barbaric behavior pattern of the Phalange had long been known by the heads of the Israeli defense establishment. The prevalent assumption was that, straight after the evacuation of the PLO from Beirut, "the Phalange would find a way to move in, to settle scores— that murder would begin in Beirut from the first day."

Sharon himself had spoken with contempt about any possible military contribution the Phalange could make, asserting, "Forget about them. They won't do a thing. Maybe later, when . . . it'll be possible to loot, to kill, to rape. Yes, then they will rape and loot and kill."

The IDF and the Mossad didn't contribute directly to the massacre, but the patronage they extended to the Christian forces and their failure to protect the occupied Palestinians tarred Israel's name. As soon as the Israelis discovered what the Phalangists had done, they ordered them to cease and expressed their outrage. At the same time, however, they also began counseling the Maronite militia on what to tell the legions of journalists now covering the atrocity.


FIERCE INTERNATIONAL AND DOMESTIC censure followed. The leaders of the opposition, Yitzhak Rabin and Shimon Peres, withdrew their support for the war when they became aware of the scale of the killing.

Sharon's response was typical. Testifying behind closed doors before a 1982 Knesset oversight panel on the secret services, he read from a sheaf of classified documents about the massacre of Palestinians perpetrated by the Maronites at the Tel al-Zaatar refugee camp in 1976, when Rabin and Peres were running the country. Sharon dwelled at length on the horrendous slaughter of children, the blades that slashed open pregnant women's bellies.

# THE PALESTINE POLICCE FORCE

# REWARD

A REWARD OF L.P. 2000 WILL BE PAID BY THE P.PALESTINE GOVERNMENT TO ANY PERSON GIVING INFORMATION WHICH LEADS DIRRECTLY TO THE APPREHEN-SION OF THE PERSON WHOSE NAME AND PHOTOGRAPHH APPEAR HEREUNDER.

قـــــوة بوليـــــس فلسطــين

مـــكافـــأة

تعطي حكومة فلسطين مكافأة قدرها ٢٠٠٠٠ جنيه فلسطيني لأي شخص يعطي اخبارية تؤدي مباشرة لالقاء القبض على الشخص الذين اسمه وصورته ادناه :—

משטרת פלשתינה (א"י).

# גמול

פרס בסך 2000 לא"י ישווילם ע"י הממשלה הא"י לכל אדם שימסור ידיעה שתוביל באופן ישר לידי מאסרו של האדם ששמו ותמונתו נקובים להלן.

| מנחם ביגין | MENACHEM BEIGIN | مناحم بيجين |
|---|---|---|
| גיל : 36 שנים. | Age: 36 years | عمره : ٣٦ سنة |
| גובה : 175 ס"מ. | Height: 175 cms. | طوله : ١٧٥ سنتمترا |
| מבנה הגוף : צנום | Build: thin | البنية : ضعيف |
| אף : גדול וכפוף. | Nose: long, hooked | أنفه : طويل معقوف |
| שניים : במצב רע. | Teeth: bad | أسنانه : رديئة |
| מדבר : פולנית, אנגלית ועברית. | Speaks: Polish, English, Hebrew. | يتكلم : البولونية الانكليزية والعبرية |
| תכונתו : נראה בלתי מגולח טוב. הליכתו אופיינית ופוסע בצעדה כרגל שטוחות. | Peculiarities: Appears to be badly shaved. Walks with a peculiar flat-footed stride. | الخصائص المميزة : يظهر ان لذقه ليست محلوقة جيدا وبمشي مشية عربية بارجل مبطلعة |

INFORMATION MAY BE GIVEN AT ANY TIME TO ANY POLICE OFFICEER OR TO ANY POLICE STATION

Jerusalem,
July, 1945

**J. M. RYMER JONES**
Inspector-General.

يمكن اعطاءاله الاخبارية في اي وقت لاي ضابط بوليس او اي مركز بوليس

ج. م. رايمر جونز
مفتش البوليس العام.

القدس.
تموز سنة ١٩٤٥

את הידיעה אפשפשר למסור בכל זמן לכל שוטר או לכל תחנת משטרה.

ג. מ. רימר־ג׳ונס
המפקח הכללי

GPP. 33295—300—22.8.45

ירושלים,
יולי 1945.

A most-wanted advertisement published by the British Criminal Investigation Department for Menachem Begin, the commander of the Irgun.

Ariel Sharon (center), Paratroopers Brigade commander, August 1955.

Alexander Yisraeli.

Moshe Tsipper (right), the son of Alexander Yisraeli, hears for the first time what really happened to his father from Raphi Medan (left). (RONEN BERGMAN)

The Mossad team: Rafi Eitan (second from right) and Zvi Aharoni (second from left) in São Paulo, shortly before they saw Josef Mengele, "the Angel of Death" from Auschwitz. [ZVI AHARONI COLLECTION]

Egyptian president Gamal Abdel Nasser (right) during a missile test with German and Egyptian scientists.

The Mossad warrior Oded, who captured Dr. Hans Krug and brought him to Israel for interrogation.

A Mossad surveillance photo of Dr. Hans Krug.

President Nasser (right) and King Hussein of Jordan at the 1965 summit in Casablanca, where their conversations were recorded by the Mossad.

Prime Minister Levi Eshkol (fourth from left, in a black hat and tie), Mossad chief Meir Amit (center, smiling), chief of staff Yitzhak Rabin (in uniform), and former Mossad director Isser Harel (third from right), 1965.   (MOSHE MILNER, GOVERNMENT PRESS OFFICE)

Eli Cohen, hanged in Damascus.

Meir Dagan's "Chameleons" on their way to an operation in Gaza, dressed as guerrillas returning in a boat from Lebanon. From left to right: Dagan (commander of the operation), Meir Botnick, and Avigdor Eldan, a Bedouin IDF officer. The other men are Palestinian agents.

David Ben-Gurion (sitting, with glasses and a map), with Yitzhak Pundak (left) and General Rehavam Zeevi (standing with sunglasses).

Leila Khaled, the Palestinian terrorist and plane hijacker, depicted in a 2001 graffiti illustration on the wall dividing Israel and the Palestinian Authority.

Mike Harari, the man who ran Caesarea for fifteen years and had the most influence over the Mossad's targeted killing and sabotage operations, during preparations for Operation Spring of Youth.

Mike Harari in Italy in 1977, commanding a covert Mossad operation.

Nehemia Meiri, commander of Bayonet, dressed as a beggar.

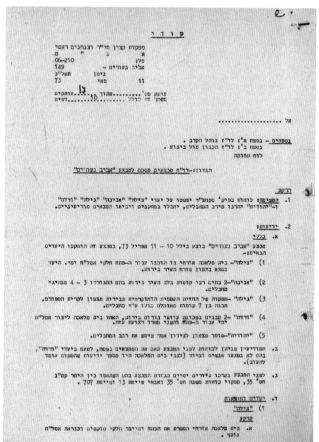

The operation order for
Spring of Youth, 1973.

Surveillance photographs of the apartment building where Kamal Adwan, one of the top leaders of the PLO, lived, taken by Mossad warrior Yael.

Adwan's apartment and body after the targeted killing operation.

Adwan's funeral.

Photo from the air patrol over the Entebbe terminal, taken by Mossad operative David.

Ali Hassan Salameh, who the Mossad was convinced was behind the murder of the athletes in Munich.

The critically wounded Ali Salameh is carried out of a car a few seconds after an explosion. He died shortly afterward at the hospital.

Robert Hatem (right), one of the Phalangist assassins, confesses to killing hundreds of people in an interview with the author in 2005.

Prime Minister Menachem Begin (third from left), Minister of Defense Ariel Sharon (second from left), and the prime minister's military secretary, Brigadier General Azriel Nevo (left) examining a PLO post in southern Lebanon after its capture by Israel, June 1982. (MINISTRY OF DEFENSE ARCHIVE)

Yasser Arafat (right) and the journalist Uri Avnery in an interview during the siege in Beirut. (ANAT SARAGUSTI)

Peres responded angrily, "Who knew [what was going on]?"

Sharon replied, "The Red Cross reported that during those days of the massacre, our ships prevented the entry of vessels carrying medical aid. . . . You built the relationship and we continued it. . . . You also helped them after the massacre. We didn't complain to you then. And I would not have raised the matter if you did not behave the way you behaved. . . . You, Mr. Peres, after Tel al-Zaatar, have no monopoly on morality."

Sharon's menacing tone was clear. One of his aides hinted to the heads of the Labor Party that if they pushed for an official inquiry into the Sabra and Shatila massacre, these classified documents about their actions during the Tel al-Zaatar massacre would be leaked to international media as well. The criticism from the Labor Party duly died down.

Public protests, however, were still ramping up as the official count of Israeli troops killed in Lebanon rose every day. Demonstrations were held outside the prime minister's residence, with protesters shouting slogans and carrying placards condemning Begin and Sharon. Every day, the protesters updated a giant sign facing Begin's residence that counted the number of dead soldiers from Sharon's misbegotten war.

Sharon seems to have been indifferent to the protests, but Begin was ailing. He sank deeper and deeper into what became a clinical depression, gradually losing the ability and desire to communicate with those around him, cutting himself off almost entirely from the apparatus of governance.

"I watched Begin withering away, shrinking into himself," said Nevo. "He realized that Sharon had hoodwinked him, that he had entered a swamp that he had not wanted to enter. The victims and the protests were killing him. The man was a very sensitive person, perhaps too sensitive."

His condition deteriorated so much that his aides refrained from reporting bad news to him, out of fear that he would slip over the edge.

"I also saw him during his period of decline," said Nahum Admoni, who became Mossad chief in September 1982. "I begin a briefing, and after a few minutes I see his eyes are shut and I don't know whether he's listening to what I'm saying, whether he's asleep or awake. A very embarrassing situation, very embarrassing. I ask Azriel [Nevo], his military aide, 'Do you think I should go on talking or stop?' . . . We didn't refer the problem to anyone else, but everyone knew. Everyone knew this was the situation."

And yet, though nearly everyone around Begin knew he was hardly functioning, let alone fit to run a country at war, instead of moving to replace him, they decided to cover for him, and his aides worked to conceal his true condition from the Israeli public. The secretaries in his bureau went on typing out the prime minister's schedule every day, but it was empty. "And so, to conceal it, I told them to classify the schedule 'Top Secret' so that no one could see it," said Nevo, adding that he believed that he and the other bureau staff "were criminals, and we perpetrated a grave offense. You can't hide the fact that the prime minister is actually not functioning, and acting as if he is. It calls to mind benighted regimes."

With Begin all but absent, Sharon was now free to do what he wished with the military. During this whole period, in fact, Sharon was effectively running the country, unconstitutionally and without any restraints. He even took charge of the Mossad, although it formally came under the prime minister's jurisdiction. "He was practically commander in chief of the military, giving orders over chief of staff Eitan's head," recalled Aviem Sella, head of air force operations. "No one could stand up to him."

"Sharon dominated the meetings [of the cabinet]," Admoni said. "He never gave an accurate or full picture either at cabinet plenums or at sessions of the inner cabinet [which was supposed to decide defense issues]. There were also times when Sharon would introduce a subject, the cabinet would discuss it, make a decision, and Sharon would call us out after the meeting—the chief of staff [Eitan], me, the other officers—and say, 'They decided what they decided. Now I'm telling you to do this or that,' which was not exactly what they had decided."

With his well-deserved but also carefully cultivated image of a George Patton–like war hero, and his freedom from doubts or misgivings about getting what he wanted on a personal or national level, Sharon was known in Israel as "the bulldozer." Cynical and ruthless, sometimes menacing, but more often charming and congenial, he had no qualms about twisting the truth when he deemed it necessary. "Arik, King of Israel," his supporters used to sing about him, and during this time he did obtain almost monarchical rule.

YET DESPITE HIS NEWLY amassed power, Sharon was also a realist, and he quickly grasped after the death of Bashir Gemayel that his aspirations for Lebanon were not to be.

Amin Gemayel, who was elected president instead of his brother, Bashir, was far less connected and committed to Israel, and after a short time he annulled the peace pact that Israel had forced him into. He was not a particularly strong leader: He lacked the charisma and aggression of his brother, as well as the ability or desire to drive all the Palestinians out of Lebanon.

Sharon's plans to kill Yasser Arafat, however, never faltered for a second. After the battles in Beirut were over and the PLO leaders and forces had been evacuated from Beirut, "Arik and Raful [Eitan] were dying, simply dying, to kill him," said then–Brigadier General Amos Gilboa, head of AMAN's Research Division.

Sharon realized that by this point, Arafat was such a popular figure that an open assassination would only make him a martyr to his cause. So he instructed the intelligence organizations to intensify their surveillance of Arafat and to see if they could find a more subtle way to dispose of him.

Operation Salt Fish morphed into Operation Goldfish. But the mission remained the same, and Sharon ordered that it be given top priority. Every day, and sometimes twice a day, the Goldfish team gathered in Eitan's office. "We had a thousand matters that were a hundred times more important," said Gilboa. But Sharon insisted.

At that time, any intelligence about the PLO leader's movements was partial at best. Wartime isn't an ideal place to gather information, and because the PLO had not yet found a permanent base to replace the one in Beirut, its officials and militiamen were moving constantly, living out of suitcases all over the Middle East and Europe. Arafat was traveling frenetically, meeting leaders, mobilizing support, giving interviews, and shifting funds around. "When someone's on that kind of routine, and yet under heavy protection, it's hard for us to plan a hit operation against him," one of Caesarea's intelligence officers told the Goldfish forum.

The Mossad told Sharon that under these circumstances, it was impossible for them to get to Arafat. At best, they could report on his whereabouts in whatever country he was visiting that day or whatever flight he was on the next. AMAN told the defense minister that Arafat often used an executive jet provided by Saudi Arabia and that the two pilots were carrying American passports. There was no question of shooting it down. "Nobody," said AMAN's Amos Gilad, "touches Americans." The bottom line was that AMAN saw no possibility of assassinating him at that time. "We have to wait until he settles down in a permanent place," said an AMAN representative at the Goldfish forum, "and then to begin planning an operation there."

But Sharon was in a hurry. And Arafat sometimes used other, private aircraft, too. Occasionally he even flew commercial. To Sharon's thinking, blowing an aircraft out of the sky, especially over deep water, where the wreckage would be hard to find, was a perfectly acceptable way to deal with the issue.

The next problem was how to be sure Arafat was on a certain flight. General Gilboa demanded that a number of operational steps be taken in order to ascertain whether he was: "From my point of view, it would be positive identification only if we could prepare in advance, before his arrival at an airport, and have someone there standing at the door to the plane to tell us, 'That's him; I saw him with my own eyes.' Then I could say, 'The bells are ringing,'" an intelligence phrase meaning near total certainty.

Once the basics of the plan were settled, Sharon pushed hard to get the mission rolling. He instructed air force commander General Ivri to keep fighter planes ready to intercept Arafat's aircraft. Ivri grasped the potential for disaster in such an operation and once again informed chief of staff Eitan that he was not prepared to take orders directly from Sharon, and that IDF regulations required that all orders come via the Operations Directorate of the General Staff. This was not much of an obstacle for Sharon, and the orders that soon came down through the proper channels were largely the same, although words such as "shoot down," "destroy," and "eliminate" had been omitted.

Finally, they found their opening in Greece. Arafat occasionally flew through Athens, with the consent of the locals. "The Greek authorities did not take rigorous measures against terrorism," says Admoni, "and the PLO did more or less whatever it wanted to there."

On October 22, 1982, two Junction agents reported that Arafat would take off the next day in a private plane from Athens to Cairo. The Mossad immediately dispatched two Caesarea operatives to find out more details. The two operatives took advantage of lax security at the Athens airport and reached the area where private planes were parked, looking for Arafat.

Back in Tel Aviv, Sharon kept up constant pressure for the operation to move ahead. The air force put two F-15 fighters on alert for immediate takeoff from the Tel Nof air force base, southeast of Tel Aviv. But Ivri, ever cautious, briefed the airmen himself. He understood the stakes. It was clear to him how disastrous it would be if Israel shot down the wrong aircraft. "You don't fire without my okay," he told the fighter crews. "Clear? Even if there's a communications problem, if you don't hear my order"—he emphasized that part: *hear my order*—"you don't open fire."

At 2 P.M., one of the Caesarea operatives in Athens called Mossad HQ and said, "He's here. Positive ID." His excitement was audible. He reported that he had watched the PLO leader and his men making final preparations to board a DHC-5 Buffalo (a Canadian-made twin-engine cargo plane) with a tail painted blue with brown marks, and the registration number 1169.

To Ivri, something seemed off. "I didn't get this whole story," he said. "It wasn't clear to me why Arafat would be flying to Cairo. According to intelligence, he had nothing to look for there at the time. And if he was going there, why in that kind of a cargo plane? Not at all dignified enough for a man of his status. I asked the Mossad to verify that he was the man."

The two operatives insisted that they were certain. "The objective has grown a longer beard to mislead," they reported, but they reconfirmed their positive identification.

At 4:30 P.M., they reported that the plane had taken off. Ivri was informed, as was Eitan, who ordered it shot down. Ivri told his pilots to take off. The Buffalo is a very slow aircraft, especially when compared with the F-15, but the flight path was some distance away over the Mediterranean, out of the range of Israeli radar. The jets took off and headed for the anticipated interception point, but at a certain distance from the Israeli coastline they had to rely only on their on-board radar, with its limited range.

Ivri still felt a pang of doubt. He told his aide to contact the Mossad and demand that they activate more means of making sure that Arafat was on the plane. He wasn't showing any emotion, as was usual with him. "But we could see he was very worried," said one of his subordinates who was there.

Ivri needed to buy time. He knew that pilots could be overeager, that sometimes they'll look for a reason to fire upon a target, interpreting a burst of radio static as an affirmative to shoot, for instance. He needed to calm twitchy trigger fingers. "Hold your fire," he reminded his pilots over the radio. "If there's no radio contact, do not open fire."

Sharon and Eitan weren't in the bunker, but Eitan kept on calling Ivri to find out what was happening and to see whether the order to shoot down the plane had been given. Ivri gave the same reply each time: "Raful, we do not yet have positive confirmation that it is him." This despite the fact that the Mossad had in fact already confirmed and then reconfirmed a positive identification.

Separately, Ivri told AMAN and the Mossad that the visual identification was insufficient and he demanded yet another cross-checked confirmation that Arafat was on the plane.

The F-15s' radar screens picked up the blip of the Buffalo 370 miles into Mediterranean airspace. The fighters closed rapidly and flew tight circles around the lumbering target. They read the tail number, saw the blue and brown markings. They were positive they'd found the right plane.

The lead pilot keyed his radio. "Do we have permission to engage?"

Ivri, in the Canary bunker, knew that, by all accounts, the answer should be yes. His fighters had a positive visual ID and a clear shot in open skies over empty ocean. Their job—*his* job—was to eliminate targets, not select them.

But Ivri's doubts overcame him. "Negative," he answered the fighter pilot on the radio. "I repeat: negative on opening fire."

He was still stalling for time, but he knew he couldn't do so for much longer. His justification for delaying the attack—that he was waiting for additional information from the Mossad and AMAN—was weakening in the face of a chief of staff directly demanding over the phone that he give the attack order. Ivri understood that if he didn't do so very soon, he would have to explain why to Eitan and, more troublingly, to Sharon.

Tension was heightening in Canary. The minutes dragged on.

And then, five minutes before five o'clock, only twenty-five minutes after the fighters took off, a phone jangled in Canary. It was the encrypted line connected directly to the Mossad. "Doubts have arisen," the voice on the line said with embarrassment. It was the same intelligence officer who'd previously confirmed that Arafat had been identified as he boarded the aircraft.

The Mossad had other sources who insisted that Arafat had been nowhere near Greece, and that the man on the plane couldn't possibly be him.

In the absence of another order, the pair of F-15s continued to circle the Buffalo. Ivri picked up the handset again and repeated his orders. "We're waiting for more information. Keep eyes on the target and wait."

At 5:23, another report came in to Canary. Sources from the Mossad and AMAN said the man on the Buffalo was Fathi Arafat, Yasser Arafat's younger brother. He was a physician and the founder of the Palestinian Red Crescent. On the plane with him were thirty wounded Palestinian children, some of them victims of the Sabra and Shatila massacre. Fathi Arafat was escorting them to Cairo for medical treatment.

Ivri breathed a sigh of relief. He keyed the radio. "Turn around. You're coming home," he ordered.

EVEN THIS NEAR DISASTER—COMING within one jittery pilot's finger of murdering a doctor and thirty wounded children—did not weaken Sharon's hand or dissuade him from the idea of targeting

Arafat in the air. In fact, he became even more reckless. When the Mossad reported that Arafat was flying more commercial flights, with the PLO often buying up the entire first-class or business-class cabin for him and his aides, Sharon decided that one of those would make a legitimate target.

He ordered Eitan, the air force, and the operations branch to come up with a plan to shoot down a civilian jetliner.

Sharon sketched out the broad parameters. The flight would have to be shot down over the open sea, far from the coast, so that it would take investigators a long time to find the wreckage and establish whether it had been hit by a missile or had crashed due to engine failure. Deep water would be preferable, to make recovery even more difficult.

Aviem Sella couldn't believe his ears. "It was a direct and clear order from him: Shoot the plane down," he said. "I had no problem with killing Arafat, who deserved to die, in my opinion. The problem was with shooting down a civilian airliner with innocent passengers aboard. That is a war crime."

In contrast to his brutal image, Eitan was a very cautious man politically, and it was evident that he did not want to be involved in such an adventure, Sella said. "But Sharon was so domineering that no one could stand up to him."

The air force drew up a detailed plan to shoot down an airliner. Its representatives at the Goldfish forum explained that they had chosen a precise spot on the commercial air route across the Mediterranean, one where there was no continuous radar coverage by any nation and where the sea below was a daunting three miles deep. A salvage operation there would be extremely difficult, perhaps impossible, with the technology of the time. This complex plan set strict parameters for where the Israeli aircraft could shoot down Arafat's plane undetected, which meant there would be a fairly narrow window of opportunity for executing the attack.

Because the operation would take place far from Israeli airspace, beyond Israel's radar and radio range, the air force had to set up an airborne command post, in the form of a Boeing 707 fitted with radar and communications equipment. Sella would command the operation from this aircraft.

Under Sharon's direct orders, then, surveillance of Arafat was maintained continuously, and four F-16 and F-15 fighters at the Ramat David air force base were placed on interception alert. Over the course of nine weeks, from November 1982 to early January 1983, these planes scrambled at least five times to intercept and destroy airliners believed to be carrying Arafat, only to be called back soon after takeoff.

General Gilboa expressed his sharp opposition to these operations time and again. "It was clear to me that the air force would execute it as well as could be, and the plane would vanish forever. They do what they are told, and if you give them an order to build a pipeline to move blood from Haifa to the Negev, they'll do it excellently and won't for a moment ask whose blood it is, but I had additional responsibility."

As head of AMAN research, it was Gilboa's job to evaluate the political impact of each operation. "I told chief of staff Eitan that it could ruin the state internationally if it were known that we downed a civilian airliner."

On one occasion, with a commercial plane believed to be carrying Arafat from Amman to Tunisia over the Mediterranean, and the Israeli jets closing in, Eitan asked Gilboa if he thought their target was definitely on the plane. The two were standing in the central space inside Canary.

"Chief of staff, do you really want to hear what I think?" said Gilboa. Eitan nodded.

Gilboa could feel his heart thumping in his chest. He stalled, elaborating all the many reasons for believing Arafat might be on the plane, then enumerating all the many reasons to doubt he was on the plane.

Eitan grew impatient. "Gilboa," he barked. "Yes or no?"

"My gut feeling," Gilboa said, "is that he isn't on the plane."

Eitan turned around and went to the red encrypted phone at the side of the room. "Arik," he said to the defense minister, waiting impatiently in his office, "the answer's negative. We'll have to wait for another day."

. . .

THERE IS A LESSON taught in IDF training—a lesson so important that the basics are mandatory for every recruit, and the details are a critical part of the officer training program as well. The lesson dates back to October 29, 1956, when an Israeli Border Police unit, ostensibly enforcing a curfew in the village of Kafr Qasim, rounded up a large group of residents as they were returning from work. Then they shot them. They killed forty-three people, including nine women and seventeen children. The policemen claimed they were obeying an order to shoot curfew breakers, but Judge Benjamin Halevy, in one of Israel's most important judicial rulings, said that soldiers must not obey an order that is clearly illegal. "The distinguishing mark of a manifestly illegal order," Halevy wrote, "is that above such an order should fly, like a black flag, a warning saying: 'Prohibited!' Not merely formally illegal, not covered up or partly covered . . . but an illegality that stabs the eye and infuriates the heart, if the eye is not blind and the heart is not obtuse or corrupt."

This lesson, ingrained in every soldier, was undoubtedly one of the only reasons that a war crime was not committed, despite the fact that on five different occasions, F-16 and F-15 fighters were called upon to intercept and destroy commercial airliners carrying Arafat. Indeed, the air force command intentionally obstructed these operations, refusing to obey orders that they believed to be manifestly illegal. "When we received the order," Sella said, "I went with Ivri to see Eitan. I told him, 'Chief of staff, we do not intend to carry this out. It simply will not happen. I understand that the minister of defense is dominant here. No one dares to stand up to him, and therefore we will make it technically impossible.' Raful looked at me and never said anything. I took his silence as consent."

On each of the five occasions, Israeli planes identified their target over the sea, Sella said, but the mission was sabotaged. Once, the radios on the flying command post, the air force Boeing 707, were silenced by being set to the wrong frequencies, blacking out communications long enough to make the whole operation impossible. A second time, Gilboa determined at the last minute that there wasn't enough evidence that Arafat was on the target plane. A third time, Sella informed Eitan, falsely, that the target plane had been identified too late and there was a danger that the interception would be detected by a nearby maritime nation. On the other occasions, "we simply drew the time out until the plane had left the zones in which it would have been possible to hit them without discerning what had happened."

In the end, though, Sharon's plans for an intentional war crime were finally derailed by his past unscrupulousness. Under intense pressure from the Israeli public and after heavy international criticism, Begin was compelled to establish a judicial inquiry into the massacre at the Beirut refugee camps. It was headed by the president of the Supreme Court, Justice Yitzhak Kahan, but the real force behind it was Aharon Barak, the opinionated and conscience-driven attorney general who had blocked the killing of the Nairobi terrorists and had since been appointed as a justice of the Supreme Court. For three months, the panel heard evidence from all the Israelis involved and pored over thousands of documents.

This inquiry and its hearings made the first cracks in Sharon's monolithic power. After listening to Barak's penetrating questions, it didn't take long for the chiefs of the defense and intelligence communities to understand that their careers were also on the line. They quickly hired attorneys, who then instructed their clients to lay the blame at someone else's door. The commission soon became a spectacle of mutual recrimination.

The Kahan Commission published its findings and recommendations on February 7, 1983. The Phalange was found to be directly responsible for the massacre, but the commission ruled that some Israelis had to be held accountable as well: "It is our opinion that a fear of a massacre in the camps if the Phalange's armed forces were introduced there . . . should have been aroused in anyone who had anything to do with what was happening in Beirut." The commission found that Prime Minister Begin had "a certain degree of responsibility," but it placed most of the blame on Defense Minister Sharon, chief of staff Eitan, and AMAN chief Saguy, along with some other senior officers and Mossad director Admoni. The commission recommended that Sharon be dismissed immediately.

Sharon refused to resign, so Begin and his ministers fired him.

Then, on September 15, 1983, Begin himself, stricken by anguish and sorrow, resigned the premiership and was replaced by Yitzhak Shamir.

For the time being, the hunt for Arafat was called off. The fallout from Sharon's relentless hunt for him, and the enormous collateral damage that hunt created, had raised Arafat's stature even further. Arafat was now a man of international prominence and prestige. Much of the world now considered him a statesman rather than a simple terrorist. "Gradually," Gilboa said, "the awareness grew that Arafat was a political matter, and he must not be seen as a target for assassination."

"Of course," Gilboa continued, "everyone under him in his organization was an entirely different matter."

# THE SHIN BET COUP

TRAVELING SOUTH FROM TEL Aviv to Ashkelon on Route 4, a driver moves along a thirty-two-mile two-lane major highway, the green Mediterranean scenery gradually giving way to sparser vegetation as the Negev Desert approaches. Route 4 runs parallel to the Mediterranean coastline, past the site of the ancient Philistine city of Ashdod, where the Israelis have built a new port city. Much of the sand-dune scenery that once dominated the terrain is now developed, all the way down to the Gaza Strip.

On April 12, 1984, at 6:20 P.M., a bus set out to Ashkelon from Tel Aviv's central terminus. There were forty-four passengers, among them four Palestinians, sitting apart from one another and pretending not to know each other, concealing their nervousness as they prepared to hijack the bus to Gaza and take the passengers hostage.

These were difficult days for Israel. The country was still licking its wounds from the war in Lebanon, and still occupying part of that country. More and more soldiers were coming back in body bags, victims of the frequent clashes with guerrillas there. Inside Israel as well, violence reigned. On April 2, three terrorists from the Democratic Front for the Liberation of Palestine, who had entered Israel as tourists, opened fire with submachine guns and grenades in a busy street in central Jerusalem, wounding forty-eight people, one of whom died later. They were stopped only thanks to action taken by armed civilians. There were also acts of Jewish terrorism against Arabs. Right-wing extremists attacked Palestinian mayors, burned houses, and plotted to blow up five crowded buses. The Shin Bet caught them just before they carried out the latter attack.

The four young Arab terrorists on Bus 300 had been caught up in this maelstrom of violence. They were from the Khan Yunis area in Gaza. Their leader, twenty-year-old Jamal Mahmoud Qabalan, was the oldest son in a family of sixteen. He had borne the burden of their livelihood since their father died, working as a dishwasher in various Tel Aviv restaurants. He had also served a year in an Israeli prison for minor terrorism infractions. His three companions were Muhammad Baraka, nineteen, and two cousins, Majdi and Subhi Abu Jumaa, both high school students less than eighteen years old. Qabalan had persuaded them to join him in the hijacking, which he hoped would stir wide international resonance. But beyond their nationalistic zeal, they had no links with any organization, nor any firearms apart from a lone hand grenade. Instead they carried knives, a bottle of yellowish liquid that looked as if it might be acid or some flammable substance, and an attaché case with some wires protruding, which was in fact nothing more than that, although they told their hostages it contained a bomb made up of two RPG rockets.

Forty minutes out of Tel Aviv, when the bus reached the Ashdod junction, a passenger spotted the knife that one of the Arabs was carrying. He asked the driver to stop, pretending he was sick and wanted to throw up. As he got off the bus, he shouted "Terrorists!" and jumped out. The four realized they had been made, and Qabalan ran to the driver, pressed his knife to his throat, and ordered him in Hebrew to "Go—fast."

The passenger who had gotten away called the police, who placed roadblocks along the bus's route, but the bus sped through all of them. It reached a spot near Deir al-Balah, in the center of the Gaza Strip, where security forces managed to puncture its tires and bring it to a stop against a stone wall. Some of the passengers were wounded by the gunfire. Their shouts mingled with those of the other hostages and the hijackers. The driver jumped out and yelled to the passengers to do the same. Some succeeded, but then Qabalan closed the doors, and most were trapped inside.

Soon the bus was surrounded by soldiers and special forces, as well as senior IDF officers and top Shin Bet personnel. The media also arrived in force at the scene, as did a swarm of curious onlook-ers. Qabalan shouted out that he would free the hostages only when five hundred Palestinian prisoners were released from Israeli jails.

Conducting the negotiation was the Shin Bet's senior expert on Arab affairs, Nahman Tal. He soon realized who he was dealing with. As he declared in a later testimony, "Right away I understood that they were not serious people and they did not constitute a danger." Ehud Barak, then chief of military intelligence, got the impression that if the Shin Bet managed to draw out the negotiations for another few hours, "the hijackers would agree to let the hostages go in ex-change for some sandwiches."

Nevertheless, the Israelis still felt that if it was possible to free all the hostages immediately using force, there should be no negotia-tions. At 4:43 A.M., the chief of staff, Lieutenant General Moshe Levy, who was on the scene, ordered Sayeret Matkal to storm the bus. A sniper immediately took out Qabalan, who was standing at the front of the bus, and he fell, dead, onto the steering wheel, sounding the vehicle's horn. The Sayeret fire also killed a young woman pas-senger. The soldiers also shot Baraka dead and found the Abu Jumaa cousins hiding among the passengers. At first, the commander of the Sayeret, Shai Avital, ordered that they be killed, but when he realized they were not dangerous, he rescinded the order immediately, "be-cause, fuck it, I saw that from the moment the fighting was over, they were prisoners of war and it was forbidden to kill them."

The two were taken off the bus, and after a brief interrogation by Brigadier General Yitzhak Mordechai, the chief paratroop and infan-try officer, to ascertain whether there were explosives or other terror-ists on the bus, they were handed over to the Shin Bet, whose personnel were gathered together in a nearby wheat field.

Micha Kubi, one of the Shin Bet's senior investigators, was ques-tioning both of them, but the conditions weren't ideal. "I was trying to do things quietly," Kubi said, "but everyone there was in a frenzy."

And then Avraham (Avrum) Shalom showed up.

Shalom was the head of the Shin Bet, and had been for four years. The son of Austrian Jews who fled the Nazis, he'd joined the Pal-mach underground militia when he was eighteen. After the establish-ment of the state, he joined Shin Bet's operations unit. In the early

1960s, he collaborated with Yitzhak Shamir, then head of the Mossad's targeted killing unit, in Israel's efforts to stop the German scientists working on Egypt's missile program. The two became fast friends. When Menachem Begin resigned and Shamir became prime minister in 1983, "Shalom became the most important person in the security establishment," said Carmi Gillon, who headed the Shin Bet in the 1990s. "And I think that what happened to Avrum was that he felt as if he could do whatever he wanted to do."

Shalom ran the organization without constraints, and many of his subordinates considered him a manipulative and ruthless dictator. "Toward Avrum there was no awe," said Yuval Diskin, an operative under Shalom who, twenty years later, would be head of the agency. "There was fear. We feared him. He was a strong man, brutal, clever, very stubborn, uncompromising, and an ass kicker."

As soon as the storming of the bus was over, Shalom had consulted with chief of staff Levy before joining his men in the wheat field.

"Avrum [Shalom] was holding a pistol," Kubi said. "And he brought its butt down with all his strength on the head of one of the terrorists. I saw the butt actually entering the skull."

"He was in a frenzy," said another Shin Bet man.

Kubi announced that he wasn't prepared to carry on in the commotion going on at the scene and demanded that the prisoners be moved to the Shin Bet's interrogation facility in Gaza. Members of the agency's operations unit, the Birds, who were guarding the two prisoners, took them out of the field. Shalom signaled to the unit's commander, Ehud Yatom, to come aside with him, and he quietly told him, "Finish them off."

Shalom didn't want terrorists tried in a court of law. Allowing men who hijacked a bus to receive a proper trial, he believed, would only encourage more terrorism.

Still, two criminals couldn't be summarily executed on a public highway, in full view of soldiers, reporters, and civilians. So Yatom and his team drove the two to an empty and isolated field a few miles away. Subhi and Majdi, battered and dazed by the night's events, were taken off the vehicle and made to lie on the ground. Yatom explained to three others what had to be done, picked up a large rock, and brought it forcefully down on Majdi's head. The others joined in.

They beat them to death with rocks and iron bars, a brutal method chosen so that it would appear the two were murdered by enraged, renegade (and unidentifiable) soldiers and civilians immediately after the raid on the bus.

Kubi was waiting at the Gaza interrogation facility when he was informed that the terrorists had died on the way, from the beating they had supposedly received from civilians and soldiers. "I realized exactly what had happened," Kubi said. "Avrum's policy was that terrorists carrying out an attack should not end up alive. I wasn't surprised when they told me that they wouldn't be coming in for questioning. I went home to bed. I thought that the whole thing was over and done with."

KUBI THOUGHT THAT BECAUSE such incidents typically *were* over and done with as soon as the bodies were cold. Over the years, as terror attacks multiplied, public pressure increased on the government and armed forces to adopt stricter counterterror measures. As Israel's responses intensified, however, the checks and controls over those responses gradually weakened. Targeted killing—which had once been practiced sparingly, far from the country's borders, and been subject to high-level authorization—had begun to be used much more frequently, much closer to home, and with far less supervision. The isolated "irregularities" perpetrated by a few unscrupulous units during and after the Six-Day War, for instance, had become an accepted practice by the mid-1970s, albeit one of dubious legality.

The Shin Bet, which was responsible for thwarting PLO attacks in the occupied territories, had used illegal tactics since the 1960s. Shin Bet interrogators feared, not without cause, that if they did not squeeze information out of their captured prisoners, more Israelis would be killed. What began as intimidation and humiliation during interrogations evolved into outright physical and psychological torture: mock executions, sleep deprivation, forcing prisoners to endure painful stress positions and extremes of heat and cold. Prisoners were sometimes administered supposed "truth serums" that, the subjects were told, caused impotency.

The dark and filthy basement rooms where the Shin Bet carried out its interrogations took on such a sinister character that even "a normal person who crossed that threshold would be prepared to confess to killing Jesus," said Gillon.

Even Avraham Shalom said he was shocked by what he saw when he visited the Hebron detention facility as head of the Birds and witnessed the grilling of "an Arab who in my eyes was elderly. He was fifty-five then, the Arab, but looked much older. And our guy, who knew Arabic, was shouting at him, 'Why are you lying?' The Arab was dilapidated, old, wretched, and I began to feel sorry for him. I asked, 'Why is he shouting at him?' And finally the interrogator took a chair, and he broke the chair on the floor, took one of the legs of the chair, and smashed his hand. He said, 'Put your hand on the table,' and he smashed all of his fingers." On another occasion, said Shalom, "I saw an interrogator kill an Arab. Not with blows. He flung him from one wall to another, from wall to wall, wall to wall . . . then he took his head and almost broke the wall with that Arab's head. A week later, the Arab died from a cerebral hemorrhage. It was blurred over."

Some prisoners died while being tortured, and some were driven to suicide. In other cases, PLO activists who were detained for questioning were found dead without even reaching a detention facility.

Every now and again, a PLO activist would simply disappear. Their families would suspect they were in Israeli custody, and they would ask the police for assistance. The police would then publish a photograph of the missing person in a newspaper—standard procedure in such cases—and they would ask the Shin Bet if they had any information. "We used to have a fixed formula then," said Yossi Ginossar, a senior Shin Bet official. "It went: 'There is no information in the security establishment as to the whereabouts of this person.' This is what we told the police every time they asked us, although we knew very well what hole he was buried in."

Some of those disappeared people were killed as part of the secret program code-named Weights. In one Weights operation, Abu Jihad had his men smuggle large amounts of weaponry into the occupied territories, which were stored in caches until other Palestinian operatives could deliver them to attack squads. Sometimes the Shin Bet discovered the location of the cache, placed it under surveillance, waited for the pickup team to arrive, and captured them. On multiple occasions, however, the Shin Bet rigged the caches with powerful explosives, which would be remotely detonated when the pickup squads showed up.

"The basic idea behind Weights," said a Shin Bet source, "was taken from the concept imported from [the Israeli military activity in] Lebanon, which said that there are times when it's not worthwhile to take prisoners. Doing that is both a greater risk for our forces and also makes the other side want to take hostages for bartering exchanges. And in any case, they deserve to die. The way we saw things then, whoever came to a weapons cache to take the arms and use them to kill Jews, it's better if they have a work accident."

Weights operations—summary executions of suspects who posed no immediate threat, a violation of the laws of Israel and the rules of war—were not renegade acts by rogue operatives. They were officially sanctioned extrajudicial killings, proposed to the head of the Shin Bet by his senior commanders, approved by him and then by the prime minister, first Rabin and then Begin and Shamir.

Some of the detonations in Weights operations were carried out from afar by means of a ray or a beam code-named Plate, considered to be a cutting-edge technological innovation at the time. "That's all very well in theory," said a senior Shin Bet operative who took part in these operations, "but these caches were sometimes concealed only very superficially, under a heap of construction debris or under a big rock. Sometimes it was a PLO man who came to collect the stuff, but sometimes a shepherd would lift the rock, or a couple on a romantic stroll in the countryside who got curious. More than a few innocent people were killed in incidents like that." The IDF Chaplains Corps would remove the bodies at night and take them to be buried in the graveyard for enemy fallen.

The Shin Bet implemented a strict policy of telling the truth inside the organization and institutionalized lying to the outside world. Prisoners complained in court that they'd confessed only after being tortured, but it didn't matter. When the interrogators were called to testify, they would execute what was called, inside the Shin Bet, the

"Let him look me in the eye" maneuver. Asked if they had struck the prisoner or tortured him in any way, they would look at the judge, and then at the prisoner, and then back at the judge, and say, "I did not touch him. Let him look me in the eye now and say we did anything to him."

"We denied everything," said Arieh Hadar, the head of the interrogation department then. "The judges believed us, of course. Because some of the Arabs tended to exaggerate in their descriptions of what we did, refuting it all was no problem at all."

Hadar and every other member of Shin Bet interviewed for this book insisted that the material produced by the interrogations saved the lives of many Israelis by averting terror attacks. They also repeatedly claimed that only the guilty were abused. "We never fabricated evidence," he said. "We never invented facts we did not believe to be true. We never came to court if we were not one thousand percent convinced that the person was really guilty."

The Weights program was canceled on April 8, 1979, after a flawed bomb killed a Shin Bet operative. Avraham Shalom was appointed to head Shin Bet in 1980, and he immediately reinstated the campaign, at an increased clip.


SHALOM'S SHIN BET EMPLOYED aggressive tactics against the Palestinians in the occupied territories and Lebanon, but he was well aware that, ultimately, the occupation was a problem that could not be solved by force. "All we did was control the war," he said. "We could keep the flame at a certain level so the state could do what it wanted, and that was important. But it didn't solve the occupation problem."

He was not alone in this opinion. Almost all the heads of the intelligence community held liberal leftist views on the Palestinian issue and backed a political solution entailing a compromise that would produce an independent Palestinian state. But if they ever spoke out about this, it was in a very soft voice. Despite his own personal opinions about the occupation, Shalom did not push back against his superiors, but merely continued to implement, very efficiently, the policy of preventing terrorism.

At that time, Shin Bet was finding it difficult to handle an outbreak of terrorist acts against IDF troops in Lebanon, a land where the agency was not subject to any laws, and accordingly employed particularly brutal methods. "Lebanonization affected the Shin Bet," said Shimon Romah, who headed the agency's operations in that country. "With no civilians or journalists moving around, the sense of work freedom without it all getting into the media was great, and that had an effect."

That freedom of action affected Avraham Shalom. "There was a process of corruption at all levels because of Lebanon," said Yossi Ginossar. "So it could be that Avrum, who was involved in what was going on in Lebanon in the most intimate way, gave instructions that he could get away with in Lebanon but did not work in the Israeli reality."

By the time of the Ashkelon attack, Shalom had already been overseeing operations at the Shin Bet with impunity for four years. There was no reason to suspect that another couple of dead Palestinians would cause a problem.

But one of the people who had rushed toward the bus when the rescue operation began and who was standing right next to it when it ended was an Israeli press photographer named Alex Levac.

In the commotion that ensued, Levac photographed everyone around him. He saw two burly men leading a shorter, black-haired young man away. At first, he didn't see that he was handcuffed. "When I snapped that shot, I didn't know who he was. At first I thought he was one of the rescued passengers," Levac told an investigative panel. "But when one of the escorts stormed at me in a fury, I thought he objected to their being photographed because the man was a secret operative." In fact, it was Majdi Abu Jumaa, along with two Birds operatives.

"We dragged him," one of them testified. "After a few meters, there was a flash. One of the escorts shouted, 'Get the film!'"

Levac had not yet grasped exactly what was happening, but he realized that there was something important in his last picture, so in the time before the Birds operative reached him and demanded the film, he quickly switched the rolls in his camera and shoved the exposed roll into one of his socks.

The IDF announced that the "terrorists had died when troops attacked the bus at dawn today, ten hours after it was taken over on the coastal highway." Editors at the newspaper Levac worked for, *Hadashot*, realized they had a scoop and wanted to print the picture, but the military censor stopped them. Someone leaked it to foreign papers, however, including the German weekly *Stern*, which printed it. Subsequently, *Hadashot* defied the censor and ran the story anyway, quoting *The New York Times* and then showing the photograph as well.

Majdi Abu Jumaa was identified by relatives and neighbors in the Gaza Strip as the man in the photograph. No wounds are visible, his eyes are open, he is handcuffed, and the agents do not appear to be supporting him, indicating that he is standing on his own.

The publication of the photographs after the official announcement that all the terrorists had been killed during the raid caused a public uproar that coincided with a lack of confidence in the authorities created by the Lebanon War, and led to a general assault on the government by several liberal media outlets.

Prime Minister Shamir and Shalom were opposed to an inquiry into the affair, but their appeals fell on deaf ears. Defense Minister Moshe Arens ordered the establishment of an inquiry panel and, later, another one was instituted by the Justice Ministry.


ON APRIL 28, TWO days after the first inquiry was announced, Avraham Shalom ordered ten of his associates—the Birds personnel who took part in the killings, the agency's legal advisers, and other top officials, including Yossi Ginossar—to gather in an orange grove near Netanya, north of Tel Aviv. He chose an isolated spot where no one would see them, far from the Shin Bet installations, which were covered with listening devices. Those devices usually served the purposes of the organization. Now, though, Shalom feared they might disrupt his plans.

That night, underneath the stars, Shalom and his men took an oath never to reveal the truth, and to do whatever it took to paper over the affair, because if they didn't, Shalom told them, "grave damage would be caused to state security and the Shin Bet's secrets would be bared."

They knew that if they told the truth, or if the truth were to be uncovered by these inquiries, they could be tried for torture, even for murder. "They simply swore to one another that they would never let this thing out," said Reuven Hazak, Shalom's deputy. "Not the matter of the Krenk ['Sickness' in Yiddish, the code name for the killing], nor the matter of the cover-up."

In the orange grove and at subsequent meetings at their homes, they crafted a plan that Hazak, who attended some of the meetings, described in retrospect as "a preplanned campaign against the institutions of law and government of the state."

The plan had two interdependent parts. First, Shalom suggested to Arens and Shamir that a representative of his be made a member of the inquiry committee, so that "the Shin Bet's position would be represented and to make sure that the organization's secrets would not be harmed." This apparently innocent proposal was accepted, and Yossi Ginossar was named a member of the Defense Ministry inquiry.

Ginossar would serve as Shalom's Trojan horse. He was one of the men who took the secret oath in the orange grove, and he himself was personally offended by the very existence of the commissions. "What happened? Two terrorists who hijack a bus and kill its passengers died," he would protest later. "For this you bring down a whole world? Hypocrisy! For years we were cleaning out Israel's sewage, and everyone knew more or less how the sewage was cleaned."

Ginossar said, "I neither had nor have any moral problem with the slaying of the terrorists." His problem was "with the facts on the ground. That so many actors outside of the Shin Bet were there." His solution: "The supreme rule after a failed op is the erasure of the fingerprints of the State of Israel. Not telling the truth is an integral part of removing the problem."

During the day, the commission sat in a Defense Ministry meeting room and heard witnesses—soldiers, Shin Bet operatives, civilians, hostages, and the photographer Alex Levac. Then, at night, Ginossar sneaked off to meet Shalom and his inner circle at the home of the legal adviser, to fill them in on details of that day's session and help prepare the witnesses for the next day.

This led to the second part of Shalom's plot: framing innocent Israeli soldiers for the two murders he'd ordered. Along with Ginossar, the Shin Bet's legal counsels, and members of the Birds squad, Shalom concocted a sophisticated plan to shift the allegations of murder from themselves to the men who had laid their hands on the Palestinians first: IDF soldiers under the command of Brigadier General Yitzhak Mordechai.

This plan was breathtaking in its treachery. It required perjury, conspiracy, and a deep, dizzying betrayal of an honorable man and friend. Ginossar and Mordechai had been close since they collaborated during the 1982 invasion of Lebanon. Ginossar had even awarded Mordechai a special Shin Bet decoration on June 27, 1982, as a token of recognition for helping the Shin Bet kill Azmi Zrair, the Fatah operations officer in southern Lebanon.

Ginossar spun an intricate web of lies. He well understood what the panel required. "Guys, don't delude yourselves," he said at one of the clandestine gatherings. "Someone has to be found guilty here. Otherwise this committee hasn't done its job. . . . The only person who can be made to be guilty is Mr. Yitzhak Mordechai."

The key testimony was that of Birds commander Ehud Yatom. Shalom, Ginossar, and the others rehearsed it with Yatom over and over the night before. He told the panel, "I and the head of the Shin Bet arrived at the scene. I saw two clumps of people, about ten meters from each other. There were twenty to thirty people in each clump. . . . [W]hen I pushed my way in, I saw a clump of people that today reminds me of descriptions of the Syrian fellahin who attacked our pilots [who were downed over Syria]. They were doing whatever they felt like with their hands and feet. When I saw the terrorist, I also gave him a slap. I was carried away by the atmosphere of mob anger." He said that he saw no Shin Bet men in the mob, but he did see General Mordechai striking one of the terrorists with his pistol.

Yatom told the panel that when the terrorists were given to him, they were in very bad condition, and he took them to the hospital, where they were pronounced dead. The head of the inquiry, retired

Major General Meir Zorea, was deeply impressed by Yatom's honesty. He was the only witness who confessed, and he even expressed regret for slapping a terrorist. This "confession" was of course intended to cover up a much greater secret.

"Who did you see doing the hitting?" another Shin Bet official was asked during his testimony, after he described the scene he'd witnessed as a lynching. "It's very complicated, hard to recall," he replied. "The only person that I can single out is Itzik [Yitzhak] Mordechai. His blows cried out to the heavens." Yet another Shin Bet witness said, "I saw Itzik hitting them on the head, serious blows," but he could not identify anyone else. A parade of witnesses from the agency all followed suit.

The conspirators tried to get Kubi to perjure himself, too. Ginossar "came to me to make sure I'd testify that I saw Mordechai beat them to death," Kubi said. "I told him that I didn't see that. He went on and asked if, from my point of view, Avrum was not present while the terrorists were being beaten. I said that, actually, he had been there—and had even been the first to strike them. 'If so,' he said, 'then from my point of view, you weren't there at all.' Afterward they sent me on a permanent mission in Italy. I realized they wanted me as far as possible from the inquiry commissions."

The Justice Ministry's inquiry panel, however, insisted on questioning Kubi. He was secretly flown to Israel, and, in an acrimonious meeting with Avraham Shalom, he told his boss that he would not back up his version of events. Shalom yelled, "This is treachery!"

Kubi, who had faced severe danger many times during his thirty years in the Shin Bet, said he'd never been more frightened for his life than at that moment. "I feared I wouldn't get out of there alive," he said. He did, but his feelings were indicative of the depths to which the Shin Bet had sunk.

In the end, a compromise was reached between Kubi and Shalom, Ginossar, and the legal counsel. Kubi testified—falsely—that he had been busy with the interrogation and he hadn't seen who hit the terrorists.

The testimonies of the other witnesses—spun by master craftsmen of subterfuge and obfuscation, practiced over many hours—all cross-checked perfectly with one another. The cumulative effect of thirteen identical narratives from ostensibly honorable men made a strong impression on the inquiry panels.

ON MAY 20. THE inquiry commission issued its findings: "It emerges clearly from the investigation material that the IDF forces and the Shin Bet personnel were not given any order from which it was liable to be understood that the two terrorists who remained alive should be killed or harmed."

The inquiry gave complete credence to Avraham Shalom's testimony, and noted that Mordechai's testimony and claim that he was not the person who killed the terrorists "does not conform in part with a number of testimonies that we have heard and is supported in certain details by other testimonies."

The commission did not determine who had killed the prisoners but recommended that the military police conduct an investigation against Mordechai. This led to his indictment on a charge of manslaughter. In July 1985, the Justice Ministry's inquiry came to similar conclusions.

Shalom's plot had worked. An innocent man would be tried for his crimes.

Mordechai vigorously denied the allegations against him, but almost no one believed him. "Any other man in Mordechai's place would have killed himself," said Ehud Barak.

"For two years, I and my family went through hell," Mordechai would say.

Fortunately for him, though, a young and energetic military advocate by the name of Menachem Finkelstein, who was the military's representative on the Justice Ministry inquiry panel, was later involved in the process of judging whether Mordechai should be indicted.

Finkelstein, an Orthodox Jew with a bent for Talmudic hairsplitting and skepticism, who would later become a prominent district court judge, examined the evidence and felt that something was wrong. "On the one hand, the testimony of the Shin Bet personnel was unequivocal," he said. "It was inconceivable that any of them would lie. But this attempt to lay the blame on Mordechai looked odd to me."

Mordechai had admitted that when the two terrorists were led off the bus, he struck them once each while questioning them, but a careful perusal of all the evidence clearly indicated that the Abu Jumaa cousins had been handed over to the Shin Bet in far better condition than its operatives claimed. Finkelstein fought against the Shin Bet and the Justice Ministry, both of which were pressing to have Mordechai put on trial for murder, and obtained a forensic affidavit that noted that there was no possibility that Mordechai's blows could have killed the two terrorists, who appeared to be in good condition in Levac's photographs.

Finkelstein's efforts could not prevent Mordechai's indictment on two counts of manslaughter, and Mordechai had to go to trial in a special court-martial. But his meticulous legal work was instrumental in the trial itself, and after a single session and a brief hearing of the evidence, the court acquitted Mordechai.

This appeared to be the end of the Ashkelon affair. A good man was dragged through the mud and his name was tarnished, though he was cleared in the end. No Shin Bet secrets were revealed, and nobody was held accountable for their crimes.


THE WHOLE AFFAIR WOULD have been forgotten entirely but for three senior Shin Bet officials whose consciences gave them qualms. One of them was Reuven Hazak, the deputy director, who was scheduled to replace Shalom as head of Shin Bet soon. At first, the three men tried to warn Shalom to stop lying. Peleg Raday told Shalom that "Nixon fell not because of the stupid break-in, but because of the cover-up." Shalom did not respond. Although Hazak had been involved when the perjury conspiracy began, he later came to the conclusion that closure could be obtained only if all the conspirators, including him, resigned. Shalom refused, point-blank.

On October 29, 1985, Hazak managed to get an audience with Prime Minister Shimon Peres, who had replaced Shamir in September 1984, under a rotation agreement, because their parties had tied in the Knesset election. Peres listened attentively to Hazak, who came with a page of notes that spared no detail in their description of the killings or the cover-up. "The moral basis upon which the Shin Bet relied for performing its duties has collapsed," Hazak told Peres.

Peres responded, "I usually think before I make a decision."

Hazak left with a sense of relief, feeling that his indictments had been taken seriously and that an appropriate response would be forthcoming. But he was wrong. Shalom was a much more sophisticated tactician. He'd already met with Peres earlier and laid out a totally different scenario for the prime minister: This was an attempted rebellion by three lawbreakers, whose aim was to oust him and take over the Shin Bet.

With Peres's full backing, Shalom dismissed the three whistleblowers. They departed in disgrace from the service they had given their lives to, estranged from all their colleagues, who were given to believe that they were traitors.

But the whistleblowers fought back. Late at night on March 9, 1986, the three came to the Ministry of Justice's almost deserted main bureau, in East Jerusalem, and entered the office of Attorney General Yitzhak Zamir.

The meeting lasted three and a half hours, and the three whistleblowers laid out the entire story—not only the killing of the Palestinians and the attempt to frame Mordechai, but also the extrajudicial executions, the torture, and the perjury that had been practiced by the Shin Bet for decades.

The deputy state attorney, Dorit Beinish, found it difficult to believe that Peres had heard the story and failed to act: "At your meeting with the prime minister, did you speak about the cover-up?"

"Everything came up," Hazak said.

"I felt as if the sky had fallen down," said Yehudit Karp, the deputy attorney general for special duties. "It is not possible to exaggerate what happened there. It was a gross undermining of the rule of law, and corruption of all the systems. I do not remember an event of similar gravity in the history of the State of Israel."

Two new inquiries were then launched: a police investigation into the Ashkelon affair and a broader probe of the Shin Bet's practices by a committee headed by Karp.

For Shalom, this was a disaster. He'd survived two inquiries

through perjury and sheer mendacity, and he'd gotten the three whistleblowers dismissed. But the two dead Palestinian hijackers kept
coming back to haunt him, and now that the full conspiracy had
been opened up, it would be much harder for him to persuade the
investigators with another concocted scenario.

Still, Shalom and his allies did not retreat. Instead they launched
"a broad campaign of lies, gossip, and mud-slinging against the three
whistleblowers and against the Justice Ministry," Karp said. Ministry
officials were placed under surveillance and their phones were
tapped, in a bid to collect information for blackmail and try to outma-
neuver their opponents. Anonymous threats were leveled at the ministry officials in the dark of night, and Zamir was given round-the-clock
bodyguards. One night, an intensive-care ambulance was dispatched
to his home, even though he was perfectly healthy, and a funeral
wreath was sent there as well. Journalists were told by Shin Bet
sources that one of the whistleblowers was having a romantic affair
with Deputy State Prosecutor Beinish.

"The astonishing thing that came out during that time was the
untrammeled powers of the Shin Bet," said Beinish. "Only when we
were dealing with it did we grasp that this power could be aimed at
anyone, even the legal system, and if necessary also at the political
echelon. We found ourselves besmirched, exposed, menaced."

But Beinish, Karp, and the police investigators did not back down.
The inquiries continued into April and May of 1986, despite the
smears and attempts at intimidation.

Eventually, Shalom resorted to simply lying under oath. Questioned by the police, he first claimed that Defense Minister Moshe
Arens had ordered him to kill the Ashkelon hijackers. When Arens
met with him on April 16, 1986, and emphatically denied this, Shalom apologized and said, "I had the impression that you'd given such
an order, but now that I am speaking with you I see that I was wrong
and it was not so."

Next he blamed Shamir, who had been the prime minister at the
time. Shalom claimed that Shamir had in fact given the order to beat
the Palestinians to death, and then ordered, or at least approved of,
the cover-up that followed. Shamir, too, denied any such thing.
Caught again, Shalom dissembled further. Shamir, he claimed, had

told him in a November 1983 meeting that captured terrorists should be killed. Shamir denied that, too. In the end, Shalom was reduced to insisting that he'd been given blanket authority to decide what to do with terrorists—even before an attack—if he could not reach the prime minister for guidance.

By May 1986, Attorney General Yitzhak Zamir was insisting on prosecuting all those involved in the affair on charges of murder, perverting the course of justice, perjury, and any number of additional counts.

Shalom was backed into a corner. He had only one card left to play.

IN LATE MAY, SHALOM had met with Yossi Ginossar and their legal counsels in Ginossar's room at the Grand Beach Hotel, in Tel Aviv. Together they began compiling a list of the dead. They worked from their files and from memory, writing down the names, places, and dates of people killed by the Mossad, AMAN, and the Shin Bet in the years before the Ashkelon hijacking.

"We sat there for a long time. Everything went into the document, with Avrum's approval," said Ginossar.

On the list, there were the four Iranian diplomats the Mossad had allowed to be tortured and executed in Beirut by the Phalangist butcher Robert "the Cobra" Hatem. There were the targets of AMAN's Unit 504, who "died naturally by swallowing a pillow" and were buried facedown. There was the operation by the Shin Bet in June 1984 in the village of Bidya, where fifteen operatives arrived in three Mercedes sedans at the garage owned by the local Shiite commander, Murshid Nahas, who was pulled into one of the cars and was told, according to an eyewitness, "You can choose how to die." His bullet-riddled body was later found on the outskirts of the village. The names of people who'd simply disappeared from the occupied territories were written down, as were those of all the men killed in the Weights program.

It was by no means a complete list—just three pages and sixty-seven names long—and it covered only deaths in Lebanon, the West Bank, and Gaza. But it was a devastating compilation.

Ginossar called it the Skulls Dossier. Ostensibly, it was a legal document, meant to demonstrate that Shalom's order to kill the two Ashkelon hijackers was both routine and acceptable, part of a sanctioned program of extrajudicial killing. In reality, it was pure blackmail, an implicit threat that if Shalom and his allies were indicted, they would take others with them, including prime ministers.

"We understood very well the significance of the Skulls Dossier that they laid on the table," a former cabinet minister said. "It was clear to us that we had to stop the general hysteria and make sure that the Shin Bet personnel involved did not have to go to court."

It was a shocking maneuver, but an effective one. "I offered my resignation to Shamir" (the foreign minister and part of the trio running the state), Shalom said. "He told me, 'Don't you dare.' He feared that if I did, he would have to also. So he [Shamir] went to see [Prime Minister] Shimon Peres and Rabin, who was defense minister, and said, 'You also gave such approvals. So if you abandon us, the Likud, we'll drag you down with us.'"

Ultimately, a dubious agreement, first proposed by a very influential attorney who was advising both the prime minister and the heads of the Shin Bet, was made. The state president, Chaim Herzog, would hand down all-encompassing pardons to the implicated Shin Bet personnel, covering all of the proceedings against them. Eleven men were thus exonerated before they'd even been indicted. No one would be called to account for the Ashkelon killings, or any of the others. In return, the only requirement was that Shalom resign from the Shin Bet.

Even after walking away scot-free, Shalom clung to his fabrications. He wrote that he had acted "with permission and with authority," sticking to his claim that it was Shamir who gave the order to kill the Palestinian hijackers. In the wake of the affair, it was decided that all meetings between the heads of the intelligence services and the prime minister would be attended by his military secretary and by a stenographer who would record the proceedings.

The day after Herzog signed the pardons, the daily *Hadashot* provided an account of what had happened: "So this bunch of folks sat down and, in an act similar to the meeting of a junta in some remote Latin American state, removed the noose from around their necks."

President Herzog, a former head of AMAN, defended the action in a statement to the media, but only a few grasped what he was hinting at: "The process of investigating the affair would have necessitated uncovering the modus operandi of the Shin Bet over the years. That way, perhaps sixty to eighty affairs from the past would have emerged. Would that have been good for the country?"

# THEN CAME A SPARK

AT A CAMP NOT far from the PLO headquarters in Hammam Chott, a Tunisian resort town, twenty-eight of Abu Jihad's best guerrillas trained for almost a year for a spectacular attack. The plan was to sail in a mother vessel from Algiers to the sea off Tel Aviv, then travel in rubber dinghies to the beach at Bat Yam, a suburb south of Tel Aviv. They would come ashore at first light, hijack a bus or two, and force the drivers to take them to the IDF General Staff headquarters, in Tel Aviv's Kirya government compound. They would gun down the sentries at the gate and storm the compound, rushing toward the offices of the chief of staff and the minister of defense, killing as many people as they could along the way. Then they would capture one of the buildings or block the entrance and exit to one of the streets of the compound and hold as many hostages as possible, threatening to kill them if their demands—the release of PLO terrorists from Israeli jails—were not met.

The attack would come on April 20, 1985, two days after Holocaust Remembrance Day and four days before Memorial Day, one of the most significant days in the Israeli calendar, when all of Israel's citizens stand at attention for two minutes as sirens are sounded all across the country to honor the nation's fallen soldiers and victims of terror. Abu Jihad wanted to give the Israelis something new to mourn: "We want to turn the light of day to a dark night in Tel Aviv," Abu Jihad told his fighters during a final briefing before they set out.

"With the help of Allah, this Sabbath day will be a black day in the history of Tel Aviv, and so will Sunday. On this day, the whole of Tel Aviv will close down, witnessing rivers of blood, ruin, and destruction."

Abu Jihad spread out a map of the Israeli shoreline south of Tel Aviv, marked with three arrows showing the landing sites of the three dinghies: "We will attack their headquarters, with the help of Allah, and then we will close the streets. In one street, for instance, we will imprison five hundred people—five hundred people at one time—and then we will be able to use them as bargaining chips."

The supreme military commander of the Palestinian people marked out a clear goal for his fighters: "With the help of Allah, he will also send Sharon there. We know what he looks like."

One of the fighters chuckled, "He has a potbelly."

"He has a potbelly," Abu Jihad said. "Whoever aims well will be able to hit him. May a bomb fall on his head, with the help of Allah. He [Allah] can do it, boys. There is nothing Allah cannot do."

Abu Jihad must have known that this was a futile wish. Sharon had been ousted as defense minister two years earlier, and the chances that on that day he'd happen to be at the ministry he'd been shamefacedly driven out of were minimal. But Sharon was the embodiment of evil in Palestinian eyes, and Abu Jihad must have thought this was the best way to encourage his men.

MORE THAN TWENTY YEARS had passed since the first Mossad kill order had been issued against Abu Jihad. He'd settled in Tunis, the capital of Tunisia, after the PLO's evacuation of Beirut in the summer of 1982. He lived in a rented villa not far from the beach, some twenty-five miles from the ruins of the ancient city of Carthage. Israeli intelligence kept tabs on him as he traveled to Syria and Jordan and other countries in the Middle East, issuing orders, organizing, encouraging his troops, and planning operations against Israel.

As the military commander of the PLO, second only to Yasser Arafat, Abu Jihad was responsible for multiple acts of terrorism against Israelis, more than any other Palestinian actor by a wide margin. He remained imbued with nationalistic-revolutionary fervor, now bolstered by a desire to prove to Israel that the PLO was down but not out, and that it could still strike back and inflict heavy damage. To that end, he made the decision to once again begin planning attacks in Western countries, particularly in Europe, where he and Arafat had not operated since the first half of the 1970s. He put an emphasis on maritime operations—those carried out on ships, by means of ships, or in the vicinity of ports.

To achieve this, he deployed Force 17, the well-trained special unit of Arafat's bodyguards, alongside his own special-operations squad, the Western Sector, and Fatah's naval division.

An Israeli plan to kill Abu Jihad in Amman had been developed in 1983, but it was put off a few times, usually for operational reasons. The Mossad did plan operations targeting Abu Jihad's subordinates, however. Following the restart of Fatah's operational activities in Europe, the Mossad also resumed aggressive action against the PLO on the subcontinent.

Since the Lillehammer disaster, Caesarea had been busy rebuilding Bayonet, its targeted killing unit. "I used to call it 'sharpening the sword,'" said Mike Harari, who made a number of changes to the unit before his retirement in 1980. In the new Bayonet, the old-time Holocaust survivors and the former liquidators from the anti-British underground no longer played leading roles. The stars were now graduates of IDF combat units with rich battle experience, endowed with large stores of courage and readiness, if not eagerness, to squeeze the trigger.

Heading the new Bayonet was "Carlos," a Caesarea operative who had reached the Mossad via combat duty in Ariel Sharon's Paratroopers Brigade. His colleagues said that Carlos carried out killings coldly and methodically, that his heart didn't miss a beat.

In August 1983, Abu Jihad sent the deputy commander of his naval unit, Mamoun Meraish, to Greece to acquire a ship and weapons to be used in a terror attack on Haifa. As he was on his way to close the deal in Athens, a motorcycle drew up alongside Meraish's car at a traffic light. Carlos, the man on the passenger's seat of the motorcycle, drew a silenced pistol and pumped bullets into Meraish until he was certain he was dead. All of this happened in full view of his three children, aged four, nine, and thirteen, who began shrieking with terror.

On August 16, 1984, Zaki Hillo, a member of George Habash's PFLP, arrived in Madrid on a flight from Beirut. The Mossad believed that he, too, was on a mission for Abu Jihad, who had enlisted him for one of his planned operations in Europe. A day later, while Hillo was walking on the street in the center of Madrid, a motorcycle passed by him, and the man on the passenger's seat shot him several times. Hillo survived the hit but lost the use of his legs.

Munzer Abu Ghazala, the commander of Fatah's naval arm, had been the object of a number of Bayonet targeted killing attempts before October 21, 1986, when he parked his car in an Athens suburb, giving "Eli" enough time to do his job. Eli, an assassin with a predilection for explosive devices, slid his burly body underneath the car and attached one of his "Eli-Ears," a lethal bomb of his own design. Abu Ghazala entered the car, and Eli, now a safe distance away, pushed a button, blowing up the car and its driver.

In the wake of these hits, as well as other PLO operations in Europe that were thwarted after the Mossad tipped off the local police, Abu Jihad came to the conclusion that the Israelis had agents inside his European networks. He decided then on a naval operation that would be run entirely from inside his headquarters in Tunis and a training base in Algeria, under strict secrecy. This operation became the plan to seize the General Staff building and take as many hostages as possible.

In the spring of 1985, Abu Jihad's troops embarked on a leased 498-ton diesel-powered Panamanian-flag cargo ship called the *Attaviros*. Abu Jihad had plotted an extended voyage for his commandos, from the port of Oran, in Algeria, westward into the Atlantic, around the Cape of Good Hope, up the east coast of Africa, through Bab al-Mandeb Strait, and into the Red Sea. From there they hoped to slip unnoticed through the Suez Canal in a merchant convoy until they were in Israeli waters.

But unbeknownst to Abu Jihad, AMAN's Unit 504 had a network of agents within the Western Sector apparatus, Abu Jihad's military wing. For almost a year, Israel had known that an attack of some kind was planned for around Memorial Day; on April 24, a task force of four missile boats and Flotilla 13 commandos sailed 1,800 miles and blew up a second ship leased for the operation, *Moonlight,* when it was empty and docked in Algeria. And when the *Attaviros* reached the Mediterranean on April 20, two Israeli missile cruisers and Flotilla 13 naval commando units were waiting, thirty miles off Port Said.

The PLO operatives on the ship refused the Israeli call to surrender and opened fire on one of the Israeli vessels. In response, the Israeli forces sank the Palestinian ship, killing twenty people on board.

Eight others were captured and taken to Unit 504's subterranean interrogation facility, known as "Camp 1391," north of Tel Aviv. The site is not marked on maps, and Israeli law bars the publication of its location.

The prisoners were stripped naked and hooded, then tied to the wall. Loud music blared in their cells, making it impossible for them to sleep, and they were subject to occasional beatings.

After four days, the prisoners confessed the details of Abu Jihad's plan. They described how they were planning to seize the General Staff building and take the defense minister and chief of staff hostage. Were it not for AMAN's precise intelligence, it would have been "a disaster on a scale we had not yet known," said Oded Raz, a senior AMAN officer.

Relying on intelligence to merely prevent attacks already in motion was no longer an acceptable option.

IMMEDIATELY AFTER THE CONFESSIONS extracted by Unit 504's interrogators, Defense Minister Yitzhak Rabin ordered the IDF to plan two operations against Abu Jihad's base in Tunis. Rabin, who was one of the main targets of Abu Jihad's foiled attack, wanted two options to choose from, both of which would be big and noisy. One was a large-scale land incursion that would involve forces from Flotilla 13, Sayeret Matkal, and Shaldag (the air force's elite commando unit). Altogether, there would be about a hundred warriors under the command of Brigadier General Yitzhak Mordechai, the man whose life was almost ruined by the Shin Bet's attempt to frame him. These men would all land on the Tunisian shore in dinghies launched from navy vessels, raid the PLO compound, and kill Abu Jihad and his men.

The other possibility was a bombing run by Israeli aircraft. Both Mordechai and the air force began training, pending the cabinet's approval.

There were tactical and strategic problems with both alternatives. Tunisia is a long way from Israel—1,280 miles, farther than almost all IDF operations had reached before. For a complex, combined-ops land assault far from Israel, that meant there would be very limited possibilities for extracting the forces if things went south. Slogging through a major city also meant that the risk of casualties for the Israeli fighters would be precariously high.

Sending in bombers, on the other hand, was also risky. Israel suffered from a dearth of intelligence on the air defenses in both Tunisia and neighboring Libya.

Since the PLO headquarters had moved to North Africa two years earlier, Israel had asked the United States for the requisite information on the radar facilities and military and naval deployments of the two countries, but it was turned down. The Americans were justifiably worried about the repercussions of an Israeli attack outside of its immediate neighborhood.

Since it couldn't get the intelligence legitimately, Israel simply stole it. Jonathan Pollard, an American Jew with delusional dreams of becoming a spy and influencing the course of history, had tried to enlist in the CIA but was turned down because of "significant emotional instability." The agency didn't share its evaluation with other branches of U.S. intelligence, however, and Pollard was hired by the U.S. Navy, where he was considered a brilliant analyst and an outstanding employee.

Pollard later claimed that he had witnessed "anti-Israeli attitudes among his colleagues" and "inadequate U.S. intelligence support for Israel," so he tried to get both the American Israel Public Affairs Committee and the Mossad to recruit him as a spy. He was firmly rejected by both organizations but then managed to get recruited by Lakam, the Defense Ministry's espionage arm. From the Hebrew acronym for "Bureau for Scientific Relations," this secret body, known to only a very small group of people, was headed by Rafi Eitan, who was still bitter that he had not been made head of the Mossad. "The information Pollard gave was so good that I could not resist the temptation," said Eitan. He said that his superiors, the prime ministers and the ministers of defense, knew about the situation but turned a blind eye in the face of the ocean of information Pollard gave them.

From the moment he was recruited, Pollard started sneaking huge quantities of documents out of his workplace and taking them to be photocopied at a safe house in Washington, then returning them. These documents, coded "Green Material," were then sent to Israel and stored in large safes at the Research Division of AMAN and at air force intelligence.

In June 1985, Yossi Yagur, Pollard's handler at Lakam, asked his spy for all available information on the PLO headquarters outside Tunis, and on Libyan and Tunisian air defense. Pollard went to the Navy Intelligence archives and borrowed all the required information, which found its way to Israel in a matter of days. Yagur passed Pollard thanks from "the highest levels of the Israeli Government" for his outstanding intelligence support for the upcoming raid.

Although they now had the necessary intelligence, Shimon Peres and Yitzhak Shamir, who were alternating as prime minister, were still hesitant to green-light the operation, as was Defense Minister Rabin. Mordechai tried to persuade Rabin to back the sea-land proposal because "there's a difference between an air raid and the effect that you have when you come up on someone with a gun at his head." But Rabin was afraid that something unexpected would go wrong, "and I couldn't promise him that such a thing wouldn't happen," said Mordechai.

By contrast, an air bombardment would pose relatively little danger to the airmen, especially with the high-quality information Pollard had supplied, but Israel shared the Americans' strategic concerns. Tunisia had no border with Israel and no present conflicts. Invading an ostensibly neutral country, by air or land, could have serious international repercussions.

There was another, external factor for the delay as well. Targeted killings, especially those involving high-profile targets such as Abu Jihad, are not merely military or intelligence operations. They are also political tools, and as such they are often driven by political concerns, a useful method to either assuage or rally public opinion. In 1981, for example, polls were predicting a handsome majority for the leftist Labor Party in an upcoming election until Prime Minister Begin, from the right-wing Likud, ordered the bombing of the nuclear reactor near Baghdad where Saddam Hussein was trying to develop nuclear weapons. This was enough to tip the balance in Likud's favor.

At the moment, however, domestic politics were stable. There was no election campaign that required rousing the public with flashy militarism, nor was there any demand from the public for immediate vengeance. A delay of indefinite length, then, seemed to be the obvious choice, since the tactical and diplomatic risks of the operation were too high, and the opportunities too uncertain.

But all that would change just a few months later.

ALL THROUGHOUT THIS PERIOD, both the PLO and Israel were especially active in Cyprus, and in the sea between that island and Lebanon. Abu Jihad used Cyprus as the main route for the transfer of his fighters back to Lebanon and as a logistics base for the whole Mediterranean zone. The small island became a hive of terrorist activity, smuggling, espionage, and then, of course, targeted killings.

The Mossad took advantage of the mutiny declared by some Fatah elements, who received backing from Syria in their fight against Arafat and his leadership, and began executing a clever sting hit operation, in which one of its operatives would pose as a Palestinian who wanted to take revenge against Arafat and offered his services to Syrian intelligence. The Mossad man gave the Syrian intelligence station in Larnaca, Cyprus, information about Palestinian fighters returning to Lebanon. "The Syrians, who were then in control of the sea and airports of the country, waited for the Palestinians to arrive, picked them up, and then they were never seen again," said Yoni Koren, an AMAN officer at the time. "It was a remarkably successful operation. The Syrians were so pleased that they began to pay us by the head. We managed to get rid of about 150 PLO people."

Some of the ships sailing from Cyprus to Lebanon were stopped by the Israelis themselves. On September 9, 1985, intelligence came in that a group of high-ranking Palestinians would set sail from Limassol for Lebanon the next day, on a ship named *Opportunity*.

Aboard this vessel was a man whom Israel had long wanted to eliminate: the deputy head of Force 17, Faisal Abu Sharah. He had been involved in a number of terrorist attacks, the most serious of which, had it materialized, would have taken place in November 1979. Force 17 was planning to use a shipping container departing from the port of Piraeus, Greece, for Haifa, carrying several tons of raisins, to deliver a huge quantity of explosives that would go off when the container was unloaded. Abu Sharah sent one of his top aides, Samir al-Asmar, to take charge of the operation. But the Mossad's Junction division got wind of it and located the container and the Palestinian team. A Bayonet squad went to Piraeus and killed al-Asmar. A month later, on December 15, Bayonet disposed of another member of the team, Ibrahim Abdul Aziz, after he arrived in Cyprus, and a member of the PLO diplomatic mission there who was hosting him, Samir Toukan. Abu Sharah was supposed to have been with them, but his life was saved thanks to a change in his schedule of meetings that day, and he continued operating for five more years, until the Israelis found him on the *Opportunity*.

Flotilla 13 commandos boarded the ship off the coast of Lebanon and captured Abu Sharah and three other senior Force 17 men. They then took the prisoners to Unit 504's Installation 1391. "They made me stand with my hands on my head, pulled my hair, bashed my head against a wall," Abu Sharah said later. "They told me to crawl on the floor, stripped almost completely naked, and to lick the floor. I remained naked and they poured cold water over me, hit me on my testicles, and whipped them with rubber cords." According to medical documents submitted to the court, the beatings and kicks that he sustained were so hard that his scrotum burst.

Arafat wanted to avenge the capture of Abu Sharah and his men, so he responded in kind. Two weeks later, on September 25, 1985, a Force 17 squad raided an Israeli yacht berthed in the marina at Larnaca, snatched three civilians, and demanded that their Palestinian comrades be released. But then, rather than wait for their demands to be answered, for no discernible reason, they instead murdered the three hostages and surrendered to the Cypriot authorities.

"The bastards killed three Israelis in cold blood, shot them in the back of their necks," a former cabinet minister said. "Of course, Israeli public opinion wouldn't have tolerated it if we sat back with our arms folded."

An urgent meeting of the Israeli cabinet was called. At the urging of Defense Minister Rabin, Operation Wooden Leg—the assassination of Abu Jihad and Force 17 commander Abu Tayeb, and the bombardment of the Western Sector and Force 17 buildings in Tunis—was approved.

The goal, as Rabin put it, was to make clear that "there is no immunity for any PLO element anywhere in the world. The long arm of the IDF will be able to reach and punish them. Israel will determine the manner of combat and the place of the attack, solely in accordance with its own considerations."

Only Ezer Weizman, a minister without portfolio in the cabinet and former commander of the Israeli Air Force, who would later be president of the state, was opposed. At the time, he was conducting secret unauthorized talks with the PLO. "[Jordan's] King Hussein and [Egypt's] President Hosni Mubarak are in the United States now," he said at the cabinet meeting. "There is an effort under way to advance the peace process. The timing is wrong."

Peres responded with sarcasm: "And in a week or two weeks' time, will the time be right?"

Preparations for the attack began immediately, and on October 1, ten F-15 fighters flew to Tunis, armed with GBU-15 guided bombs. Also in the air were two Boeing 707 tankers, which would refuel the fighters twice. Another Boeing served as an airborne command, control, and communications post. Two Hawkeye spy planes were tasked with jamming radar installations in Tunisia, Libya, and Algeria.

The F-15s dropped their bombs, then turned back toward Israel. All the targets were hit, including the principal objectives: the offices of the Western Sector Apparatus and Force 17. More than sixty PLO personnel and local Tunisian workers were killed, and seventy were wounded.

"When we turned around to head back, there was a great feeling of release," said one of the pilots. "I let out a huge roar in the cabin, to relieve my stress. Flying home was much more significant than usual. I saw the shores of Israel with different eyes. I was filled with elation that I'd never felt before."

Prime Minister Peres, speaking at a high school in southern Israel after the initial reports of the raid came out, said, "Terrorist headquarters are not immune. We have a right to attack them. Cold-blooded murderers cannot be allowed to get away with it. Every act of theirs has a guiding and organizing hand."

Yasser Arafat, who toured the wrecked buildings later that afternoon, used the opportunity to inflate the legend that his life was always saved by miracles. "I have been saved by a miracle from certain death," he declared, in his theatrical manner. "I was on my way to my office in the headquarters at Hammam Chott, a quarter of an hour's ride away. I told the driver to turn off the road and to head for another headquarters, and it was there that I heard about the raid. I picked up the phone and called Cairo and Amman. I said I had not been hit and was continuing to direct the struggle."

In fact, information in Israel's possession had shown that he was not supposed to be at the site during the time of the raid. "We knew where Arafat's residence was located, but we decided he wasn't a target and we didn't propose it to the government," said Yoni Koren, of AMAN.

Still, the general feeling of elation in Israel was mixed with some sour disappointment. None of the PLO's commanders had been in their offices when the missiles struck. Abu Iyad, commander of Black September and initiator of the operation against the Israeli Olympic team in Munich, whose name was very high up on Israel's hit list, even accompanied Arafat on his visit to the site, as if to spite the Israelis even more.

Only one senior official, Nur Ali, was killed, and he was considered very moderate. Indeed, he'd actually been in touch with Israeli officials in secret negotiations over prisoner exchanges and was one of the PLO officials who had held secret contacts with Defense Minister Weizman. As for Abu Jihad, he had been at a meeting in his home, not very far away, and had heard the bombs exploding.

The failure to eliminate more of the PLO leadership led the Mossad to initiate its own pinpoint operation. It began planning a "negative treatment"—a euphemism for targeted killings commonly used by the Mossad at the time—to be meted out in Tunis to Abu Jihad. For more than a year and a half, Caesarea explored a variety of

plans and ideas, including targeting his home with remotely controlled missiles, selling a booby-trapped limousine to him through a
double agent, and placing a sniper in the center of Tunis to shoot him
on his way to work.

All of these ideas were discarded, either because of the high risk
of innocent civilians being killed in the attack or because of the risk
to the operatives themselves. Tunisia was considered a "target country," which demanded the most stringent safety precautions while
Caesarea personnel operated there and meant that after the targeted
killings, extricating the operatives involved would not be easy.

Caesarea command eventually concluded that it would need the
IDF's firepower and transportation capabilities. The Mossad requested assistance from Sayeret Matkal and the naval commandos,
just as it had done in Operation Spring of Youth, in Beirut in 1973.
The Mossad turned to the head of AMAN, Major General Amnon
Lipkin-Shahak, who was in charge of the Sayeret. He himself had
commanded one of the Spring of Youth forces and afterward became
a senior officer, known for his restraint and caution. He firmly opposed Sayeret's involvement in the mission. He believed that the
Mossad could and should execute the mission itself and that "there
was no need to endanger so many soldiers." In an interview a few
months before he died, in 2013, Lipkin-Shahak said, "It was clear to
me that we could do it, but I thought that a small Mossad force
wouldn't leave the footprint that a commando raid would, making it
clear that Israel was behind it."

The plans for the assassination of Abu Jihad and the lingering
question of whether the army would be involved caused a significant
amount of tension between the IDF and the Mossad. The final decision could be made only by the politicians, but for the time being,
Prime Minister Shamir and Defense Minister Rabin refrained from
intervening.

And then the whole paradigm shifted.


APPROXIMATELY 2.5 MILLION PALESTINIANS (no general census
was conducted during that period) lived in the West Bank and the
Gaza Strip, having been under Israeli rule since 1967. Their frustra-

tion and bitterness had been growing steadily year after year. Israel
had opened its gates to Palestinian workers, and some 40 percent of
the workforce crossed the border every day to work in Israel, but only
menial jobs were available, at exploitation wages and in difficult conditions. Palestinian construction laborers and dishwashers watched
resentfully as Israelis thrived and reached an almost Western European level of economic prosperity.

Inside the occupied territories themselves, unemployment grew,
and there were few jobs available for those with higher education.
The cities were intolerably overcrowded, and Israeli authorities did
nothing to improve municipal services, nor did they provide land for
building and agriculture to meet the needs of a burgeoning Palestinian population.

Israel did, however, confiscate Palestinian lands and settle increasing numbers of its own citizens there, a blatant violation of international law. Many of these settlers were ideologically driven,
believing in the idea that "Greater Israel" belonged to the Jews. Others were simply seeking a better standard of living and taking advantage of the heavily subsidized housing.

After enduring these aggravations, wretched conditions, and visible injustices for years, the West Bank and the Gaza Strip were on
the verge of exploding. But this was something that Israeli intelligence either could not see or did not want to see. A longtime focus
on pinpoint warfare against the PLO and its leaders had concealed
the swelling rage of the Palestinian people from Israel's intelligence
community and its politicians. The Israelis' tactical achievements
and ability to locate and eliminate PLO leaders and militants nearly
anywhere in the world had given them the sense that Israel could
forever impose its rule over the millions of Palestinians in the occupied territories without consequence.

Israeli intelligence had also overlooked another dramatic development: A young, vibrant, and charismatic leadership stratum had
evolved in "occupied Palestine" and was functioning independently
and separately from Arafat, Abu Jihad, and the PLO command. A
large majority in the West Bank and Gaza supported the PLO's spectacular acts of terrorism, but many were also finding those theatrical
displays of violence to be less and less relevant to their everyday

problems. Arafat was still seen as the father of the nation, but his actions, especially those now undertaken from distant Tunis, did not appear likely to bring about the independence that he had promised anytime soon.

Then came a spark.

On October 4, 1987, five dangerous terrorists belonging to the Palestinian Islamic Jihad (PIJ) escaped from the IDF's Gaza prison. Two days later, the Shin Bet, with the help of local agents it was running in Gaza, located the terrorists in a hideout apartment in the Sejayieh neighborhood. A team from the agency's Birds unit, disguised as Arabs, kept the apartment under observation. Nearby, special forces of the YAMAM, the police counterterror unit, prepared to act, under the command of David Tzur. "The Shin Bet guys saw them getting into two Peugeot 404 cars, one white, the other light blue, heavily armed, and driving off. We tailed them, and the moment they spotted us, they opened fire. Next to the soccer field, we caught up." Four of the terrorists were killed by the first volley fired by the YAMAM. A fifth man, who escaped from the vehicles, was shot later. A Birds operative, Victor Arzuan, was also killed in the exchange of fire.

The funerals for the five Palestinians turned into a stormy demonstration. Protesters shouted in the streets that the five had been murdered. The rioting was more violent than anything the IDF had witnessed in the occupied territories thus far.

"From an operational point of view," said Tzur, who was later to become a deputy commissioner in the Israeli police and chief of the Tel Aviv region, the location and liquidation of the five terrorists "was a clear-cut success for the YAMAM." But Tzur also admitted that this tactical accomplishment, and others like it over the years, had blinded Israeli intelligence from seeing the big picture and made them "miss the dramatic development that was about to take place." Even the violent funerals were not perceived as being more than localized outbursts of anger.

Then, on December 8, the driver of an IDF tank carrier lost control and crashed into a line of cars carrying Palestinians on their way back into the Gaza Strip from work in Israel. Four were killed, and seven injured. The fallacious rumor soon spread that the accident was actually an intentional Israeli act of revenge for the fatal stabbing of an Israeli two days before. The funerals of the dead workers once again became mass protests.

A wave of demonstrations swept across the West Bank and Gaza in December 1987, marking the start of the Palestinian uprising against Israeli rule, the Intifada. The Shin Bet, the IDF, and the government were stunned and "for weeks failed to grasp the significance of the protests, so much so that it did not even occur to Defense Minister Rabin, when they began, that he should curtail a trip abroad and come back to Israel," says the PM's military secretary, General Nevo.

The IDF had believed for years that it could control the Palestinians with minimal forces. But when rioting mobs hurled rocks at small detachments of soldiers, who had no crowd dispersal equipment or protective gear, the soldiers responded with gunfire. More than a thousand Palestinians were killed, many more were wounded, and Israel's international standing took a nosedive. Each evening, the world saw on TV how the Israeli troops aggressively suppressed masses of Palestinians demanding political independence and an end to occupation. The underdog equation had reversed completely: Israel was now Goliath, and the Palestinian Arabs, in the eyes of the international community, were now David, with his slingshot and stones. "The Intifada," said then–Mossad director Nahum Admoni, "caused us a lot more political harm, damage to our image, than everything that the PLO had succeeded in doing throughout its existence."

Lacking an adequate response to the uprising, and without a real understanding of its causes, Israel once again turned to the weapon it was so familiar with, and which many believed could change the course of history: targeted killings. Abu Jihad, who'd already survived repeated Israeli attempts on his life, was once again the primary target. Partly that was because of his own boasting. In an interview on Radio Monte Carlo in January 1988, he claimed to have given the order to start the Intifada. The PLO reiterated this in some of its publications. The Arab world applauded. Israel's political leadership accepted his declarations as the absolute truth. The heads of the intelligence community acknowledged, or at least did not contradict, their authenticity.

But Abu Jihad was lying. Neither he nor Arafat had given any order for the commencement of the Intifada. It had surprised them just as it surprised Israeli intelligence. In truth, it was a popular uprising, and it was young men in their late teens and early twenties, acting independently from the leaders in Tunis, who ignited the flame. But the facts of the matter did not interest the heads of the PLO, the Arabic media, or Israeli intelligence.

Moreover, that overeagerly accepted "truth," however misconceived, was an attractive one for the Israelis. If the uprising was caused by discontent built up among the Palestinian population in the occupied territories over long years of arbitrary military rule and Israeli encroachment on their land, its root causes would have to be addressed. If it was all a PLO plot, it could be brought to an end simply by killing the man behind it.

After the Intifada broke out, Defense Minister Rabin ordered the IDF to give the Mossad all the assistance it required to plan Abu Jihad's assassination. AMAN chief Lipkin-Shahak was "still not convinced that such a large and complex operation was necessary," but he grasped that the political circumstances had changed and he withdrew his objections, at least during the planning and training stages.

Meanwhile, Abu Jihad and Arafat tried to ride the wave of international sympathy that the uprising generated. While covert preparations for the raid on Abu Jihad's home in Tunis were under way, he and Arafat initiated their own clandestine operation, a clever public relations exercise. They called it the "Ship of Return" operation. The idea was to sail a vessel into Haifa carrying 135 Palestinian deportees from Israeli-controlled areas, and also as many journalists and camera crews as would accept the invitation to cover the voyage and its dramatic ending. The PLO leaders wanted the voyage of the "Ship of Return" to look like that of the *Exodus,* the well-known steamer that illegally carried Jewish immigrants to British Mandatory Palestine back in 1947. Fatah tried to keep the plans a secret until the last minute but failed, and the Mossad received real-time notification. The Palestinians had chartered a ship in Piraeus, but the ship's owners canceled after Israel warned them that if they let the project go ahead, their ships would never be allowed to berth in Israel again.

Instead the PLO purchased a Japanese-built ferry ship named the *Sol Phryne* in Cyprus for $600,000.

An urgent meeting of the Israeli cabinet was called to discuss the subject, and they approved a joint IDF-Mossad clandestine operation to block the *Sol Phryne*, "even before it could sail from Limassol port." The hope was that thwarting the plan and killing its participants "would produce a sense of despair in the Palestinian leadership, a reduction in the media coverage in the occupied territories, and deal a blow to the motivation for continuing the Intifada," said one of the ministers who took part in the meeting.

On the morning of February 15, 1988, three of the PLO activists who had been sent by Abu Jihad to Cyprus to organize the voyage of the Ship of Return got into their car, not far from the hotel where they were staying. "Rover," chief of Bayonet, and Eli were sitting in another car, watching them, after many tense hours of surveillance, during which the local police almost caught the Israelis. When the three Palestinians got into their vehicle and started it, Eli pushed a button, detonating another of his bombs. The three Palestinians were killed.

Eighteen hours later, naval commandos dived under the *Sol Phryne* and attached a small limpet mine to its hull. It blew a hole in the side of the vessel, which began to sink. The voyage of the Ship of Return—the Palestinian *Exodus*—was over before it could begin. "Listen, history plays strange games," said Yoav Galant, commander of the naval commandos, as he climbed, dripping, from the Black Sea at 3 A.M. onto the Israeli missile boat waiting for him. He was referring to the voyage by his own mother, Fruma, in the original *Exodus* many years before.

ON MARCH 14, THE Israeli security cabinet under Prime Minister Shamir met again to discuss the killing of Abu Jihad. The prior approval of his elimination by various prime ministers over the years, including Levi Eshkol, Golda Meir, and Yitzhak Rabin, was not valid under a different premier. And even if the same man was heading the government, the security forces would still have to seek renewed approval if much time had gone by, because it was possible that the political circumstances had changed or the prime minister had changed his mind. Approval had to be given immediately before a targeted killing was carried out, the moment that operational readiness was reached, even if it had been green-lighted some time before.

On the face of things, "Shamir could have made do with his own order to do away with Abu Jihad," says Nevo. However, Shamir was aware that Abu Jihad was no ordinary target, and the reactions to hitting him could be out of the ordinary. He decided not to take sole responsibility and instead to bring the matter to the security cabinet for its approval. The Likud and Labor each had five ministers on the panel. Shimon Peres, head of the Labor Party and then serving as foreign minister, declared that he was firmly opposed to the assassination. "My information was that Abu Jihad was a moderate," he said. "I thought it would be unwise to kill him." The four other Labor members—including Rabin, who had already approved killing Abu Jihad earlier—expressed apprehension about the international condemnation that would be leveled at Israel, as well as the danger to Israeli soldiers and Mossad operatives, and they joined Peres in opposing the operation. Shamir and the four Likud representatives voted for it. A tie meant there would be no operation.

Finance Minister Moshe Nissim, of Likud, decided to try persuasion. He asked Rabin to join him outside the meeting room. "Look at what the Intifada's doing to us," he said. "The public's mood is very despondent. The IDF has in the past executed actions with great resourcefulness and creative thinking, but it hasn't happened for a long time. We have to renew the sense in the world, in the international community—but first and foremost, among the citizens of Israel—that the IDF is the same IDF that has done marvelous things over the years. We have to carry out this mission for the sake of the national morale." Politics, the withering of the national morale, demanded a blood sacrifice. Killing Abu Jihad, at least the way Moshe Nissim saw it, was an act more symbolic than practical.

Rabin was persuaded. He returned to the cabinet room with Nissim and announced that he was changing his vote. By a vote of 6 to 4, Operation Introductory Lesson was given the green light.

Nissim, who was the son of a chief rabbi of Israel, would never regret that he'd persuaded Rabin. "In the whole world," he said, "there isn't another army that is as meticulous as the IDF about values and norms of conduct and assuring that innocent people aren't hurt. But there is a Talmudic precept: 'If a man comes to kill you, rise early and kill him first.'"

ABU JIHAD'S HOME IN Tunisia, Israeli intelligence operatives believed, was the perfect place to kill him. It was located on one of the prettiest corners of a well-tended and exclusive development of private homes and broad, clean streets, just a few thousand yards from the beach, which gave a team of assassins relatively easy access. Tunisian police patrols would need to be avoided or distracted, but otherwise Abu Jihad was protected by only two men. "It was a relatively isolated location, only lightly guarded," said Nahum Lev, the deputy commander of Sayeret Matkal. "Furthermore, Abu Jihad returned there each night when he was in the country. It was a superb place to lay an ambush. Abu Jihad simply never believed that someone would reach him there. The Mossad had operated in Beirut or Syria or Europe, but never in Tunisia. So Abu Jihad felt relatively safe."

Killing Abu Jihad in his home, Israeli intelligence believed, would also be suitably menacing, suggesting to the Palestinians that no one is safe anywhere, even in his own bedroom.

The plan to assassinate Abu Jihad in Tunisia had been developed by Caesarea over the previous year. Three Caesarea operatives disguised as Arab businessmen had scouted routes from the beach and mapped the neighborhood in detail. The Mossad and AMAN's Units 504 and 8200 tracked Abu Jihad's movements, charted his travels, noted his habit of buying tickets on multiple flights to make it difficult to know when he would be traveling and where. His home and office phone lines were monitored. Oded Raz, then an officer in the section of AMAN's Research Division that dealt with terror, said that, "in following Abu Jihad, I came to know and respect the man we were facing off against. True, he was a terrorist, but also a model family man and an authentic leader who had the good of his nation in mind."

Still, the Israeli political and intelligence leadership wanted to kill him. The good of the Palestinian nation, to their minds, was a direct threat to the good of their own country. As they saw it, Abu Jihad was—and about this there can be no argument—the man behind the deaths of hundreds of Jews.

Defense Minister Rabin, the punctilious military man, was concerned about many details of the getaway route and the safety of the troops. No less important, he wanted to know what would happen if, "once we get to Tunis with this whole armada, and we break into the house, and then our 'patient' isn't in at all?" The Mossad people explained their plan to make sure that Abu Jihad would be home before the signal was given to commence the raid. Rabin was satisfied, and with the occupied territories in chaos and Abu Jihad, rightly or wrongly, claiming credit, Operation Introductory Lesson finally was authorized.

IDF deputy chief of staff Ehud Barak was the overall commander of the operation, and a short time before it was scheduled to begin, he led a planning meeting at General Staff headquarters, in Tel Aviv. AMAN officers showed him their scale model of Abu Jihad's neighborhood. Barak abruptly pointed to the house across the street from Abu Jihad's.

"Who lives there?" Barak asked.

"Abu al-Hol," one of the AMAN officers replied. "The PLO's internal security chief."

"And who lives here?" Barak asked, pointing at a house nearby but not next door to Abu Jihad's house.

"Mahmoud Abbas—Abu Mazen," a Mossad operative answered, using the real name and nom de guerre of another top PLO official.

"It's pretty close," Barak mused. "Why shouldn't we visit him as well? What with this entire huge armada going to Tunisia, it's two birds with one stone."

"Ehud," a senior Mossad official interjected, "drop it. It will only complicate an operation that is really complicated as it is." A short discussion—an argument, really—followed. Barak insisted on using the opportunity to take out two targets. Such a strike, he maintained, would send PLO morale plunging and could have a desirable effect on the wave of unrest in the territories. The representatives of the Mossad and AMAN were categorically opposed. "We can't guarantee that both targets will be home at the same time," they argued. "You are the commander, but we recommend sticking with Abu Jihad alone. It's quite enough if we give him what he deserves."

In the end, Barak gave in. Thus, the life of Mahmoud Abbas, the man who would succeed Arafat as head of the Palestinian Authority and whom Barak, among others, in time would come to regard as a bold partner in peace efforts, was saved.

"It's difficult to judge such matters in retrospect," Barak said. "In real time, from the operational point of view, it was very enticing. On the other hand, it was clear that a strike at that level against their leaders would actually have legitimated attacks on our leaders by them."

SIX CAESAREA OPERATIVES ARRIVED in Tunis on April 14, on four different flights from Europe. Three of them—two men and a woman, traveling on bogus Lebanese passports and speaking perfect French—paid cash to rent two Volkswagen Transporters and a Peugeot 305 sedan, all of them white and each from a separate company. Those vehicles would be used to drive the Sayeret Matkal men from the beach to Abu Jihad's home and then back again. The other three operatives were shadows: They found a clump of trees from which they could monitor the house and make sure Abu Jihad was inside. The drivers would evacuate by sea with the kill team, while the shadows would leave Tunis on commercial airlines once the operation was over.

Meanwhile, five Israeli missile boats were steaming toward Tunisia, carrying the raiding party, a mobile hospital, and powerful communications equipment. A larger vessel, fitted out as a helicopter carrier but disguised to look like a regular cargo ship, had a reserve Sayeret unit ready to be flown in, should something go wrong.

The convoy halted twenty-five miles from the Tunisian coast, well beyond the country's territorial waters, on April 15. Below, in the water, the Israeli submarine *Gal* provided a quiet, invisible escort. Far above, an air force Boeing 707 served as a communications relay station, while also monitoring Tunisian frequencies for any trouble. It was capable of jamming Tunisian radar and air control if needed.

Israeli F-15s were patrolling just off the coast as well, ready to intervene if necessary.

The sun was sinking into the waters to the west when rubber dinghies went over the sides of the missile boats. Each held two naval commandos and six Sayeret Matkal soldiers. They motored quietly toward shore, dusk turning to dark on a moonless night. A third of a mile from the beach, seven Flotilla 13 commandos dived off the dinghies and swam underwater toward the beach. The first to set foot on Tunisian soil was the commander of Flotilla 13's raiding force, Yoav Galant. The beach was deserted. The commandos set up a broad semicircular perimeter to secure it, while establishing radio contact with the boats and with the Mossad operatives waiting in their cars. The commandos told the Mossad operatives to approach the waterline, then told the twenty-six men in the dinghies that it was safe to come ashore. The Sayeret men hustled to the waiting Caesarea vehicles, where they changed into dry clothes that they'd brought in waterproof duffel bags. They were going to slip into Abu Jihad's neighborhood posing as civilians—some male and some female—then break into his house and kill him. Still, they all carried POW cards to prove that they were soldiers in case they were captured.

The naval commandos spread out to keep the beach secure until the Sayeret squad returned. The three Caesarea operatives who'd been monitoring the house watched through powerful binoculars as Abu Jihad's car pulled up just after midnight. Two bodyguards, one of whom was also the driver, went inside with him. The driver stayed only briefly, then went back to the car and dozed. The other sat in the living room for a few moments, then went down to the basement and fell asleep. In another bedroom, Abu Jihad's baby boy, Nidal, slept in his crib. His wife, Intisar, and his sixteen-year-old daughter, Hanan, were waiting for him in the bedroom. Intisar recalled their conversation:

> I was very tired. I asked him if he was tired, and he said no. I asked him to come in to sleep, and he said that he had a lot of work to complete. He sat at the table in our bedroom and wrote a letter to the Intifada leadership. Hanan was with us in the room. He

asked her what she had done during the day. She said that she had gone horseback riding. Then she remembered that she wanted to tell him about a dream she'd had the previous night. She dreamed that she was in Jerusalem with a few friends. They prayed at a mosque, and then suddenly Israeli soldiers expelled them and chased after them. She ran and ran until she went outside the city walls, and then she saw her father. She asked him where he was going, and Abu Jihad said that he was going to Jerusalem. She asked him how he could get into Jerusalem, because it was full of Israeli soldiers. He said that he would ride a white horse.

After she finished telling him the dream, Abu Jihad took off his glasses and said, "Oh, Hanan, yes, yes, I am on my way to Jerusalem."

The phone in the villa rang. Abu Jihad picked it up. Israeli agents tapping into the line listened as the aide who handled his travel arrangements told him that he had a seat on a flight to Baghdad leaving Tunis a little after 3 A.M. This was a problem for the Israelis. They'd planned to enter Abu Jihad's house at about 1:30 A.M. to be as sure as possible that everyone would be asleep. But if they waited until then, it was likely that their target would already be on his way to the airport.

They couldn't wait that long. The operation had to happen immediately. Yiftach Reicher, head of the Special Operations Executive, who was also at the seaborne command post, called Sayeret commander Moshe Yaalon on the radio. They spoke in code and in English, in case the conversation was picked up.

Reicher: "Bogart, this is Richard. You can leave the station. You can leave the station. Do it fast. I say again: Do it fast."

Then Reicher realized that, because Abu Jihad was getting ready for a flight, both he and his staff would likely be awake. "Bogart," he said, "this is Richard. Because the boss is leaving I want to tell you there are people who are not sleeping at the office."

Yaalon: "Okay, Richard, I understand."

Reicher called one of the Caesarea operatives watching the house from the trees: "Willy, is there anything new near the office, including the red car?"

Willy: "Negative."

Reicher: "Bogart is on his way. Before entering the office, he will call you. If there is any change in the situation, let him know, because he needs the okay. Your okay."

The two Transporters hauled twenty-six Sayeret Matkal men, armed with Micro Uzi and Ruger .22 pistols fitted with silencers and laser pointers, into the neighborhood. Two Caesarea operatives, a man and a woman, drove the Peugeot a quarter-mile ahead to scout the road and make sure that the main force would not run into anything unexpected.

All three vehicles stopped about five hundred yards from the house. The commandos began creeping forward. But final, positive identification still had to be made. Lookouts had seen Abu Jihad's car arrive and watched him and his bodyguards go into the house. But according to the protocol Rabin had signed, that was not sufficient. Three fluent Arabic speakers from Unit 8200 who'd been co-opted to the Mossad for the mission had put in hundreds of hours studying Abu Jihad's voice and quirks of speech. Wearing earphones, they sat in the command bunker in Tel Aviv while technicians set up a phone call to the al-Wazir residence via an exchange in Italy, the way he generally communicated with the occupied territories.

The technicians played crowd noises in the background. "*Ya, Abu Jihad,*" one of the voice experts shouted into the receiver. "They've arrested Abu Rahma! And now the sons of bitches want to take the whole family to prison!" He added an Arabic curse: "*Inshallah yishrbu waridat al-nisa!*" ("May they drink menstrual blood!") Abu Jihad tried to calm the speaker down so he could get more details. In the meantime, the technicians in Tel Aviv kept the conversation going until all three experts raised their hands to indicate that they had identified the voice for certain.

"Introductory Lesson, you have a green light," the command bunker in Tel Aviv radioed to the forward command post at sea. That message was immediately relayed to the force on the ground. Nahum Lev and another soldier dressed as a woman went first. Lev was holding a large box, apparently of candies, but inside was a pistol with a silencer. He walked up to the guard sitting in a car next to the house, showed him a hotel brochure, and asked him how to get there. The sentry studied the brochure. Lev pulled the trigger and shot the man in the head.

Lev signaled the rest of the squad. A small detail moved forward with a hydraulic jack to force open the door. In training sessions, the door had opened silently. Now, though, it creaked. The fighters tensed. But there was no reaction from within the sleepy house. One of the team signaled to the men in the other cars that the coast was clear. The rest of the fighters took up positions around the house. One detail circled into the backyard.

The Sayeret Matkal men burst through the door and down the front hall. A few rushed to the basement, where the second bodyguard had just awakened. They shot him before he had time to cock his rifle. Then they saw another sleeping man—the family's Tunisian gardener, who had decided to spend the night. They shot him, too. "He really hadn't done anything," Lev said. "But on a mission like this, there's no choice. You have to make sure that any potential opposition is neutralized."

Upstairs, Abu Jihad's wife, Intisar, woke up to the sound of men shouting below. Abu Jihad was sitting by his desk. He pushed it back, got up quickly, and took his pistol from the closet.

"What happened?" Intisar asked him. "What happened?"

A Sayeret Matkal man, clad in black, his face masked, bounded to the top of the stairs. Lev, the commander, followed close behind. Abu Jihad pushed his wife farther into their bedroom.

The first Israeli shot him. Abu Jihad fell. Then Lev fired a long burst. Abu Jihad was dead.

Intisar crawled to her husband, wrapped her arms around him. A commando put a pistol in her back, shoved her hard to the wall. She was sure she'd been shot. Instead, she'd been moved out of the way so she wouldn't be.

A third commando came in and shot Abu Jihad again. He stood aside, and a fourth Israeli shot him once more.

Nidal, the baby boy, was awake and screaming. Intisar was sure he'd been hit, too. A voice downstairs was yelling, *"Aleh! Aleh!"*— Faster! Faster!

Finally, Lieutenant Colonel Yaalon stood over the body and fired, the fifth man to do so.

"*Bas!*" Intisar cried. Enough!

Abu Jihad had been shot fifty-two times. Twenty-three years after Golda Meir signed the first red sheet on his life, he was dead.

Recalling the assassination many years later, in 2013, Yaalon, at that time minister of defense, said, "Listen, it certainly wasn't a pleasant scene. The woman was standing there, wanting to rush forward, and only because one of the men was pointing a gun at her she didn't move, and we are firing into her husband, over and over. It is impossible to say that it didn't bother me or make me feel very uncomfortable. On the other hand, it was clear to me that it had to be done, although it was in front of the wife and the daughter."

Yaalon had no regrets, however. He called the operation "the perfect hit" and added, with characteristic cynicism, "I don't understand why they say why we, Israel, are losing the war for minds. If I put a bullet between Abu Jihad's eyes, right in the middle of his mind, doesn't that mean I've won?"

ALL OF THE ISRAELIS escaped Tunisia unharmed. The local police were busy responding to multiple, bogus reports made by the Caesarea operatives of a fleet of cars racing from Abu Jihad's neighborhood toward downtown Tunis—exactly the opposite direction from the one taken by the assassins. The police set up roadblocks and searched dozens of cars. Three hours later, they found the rented Volkswagens and Peugeot abandoned on the beach.

The next afternoon, Shamir was asked by a reporter about Israel's involvement in the targeted killing. "I heard about it," he said drily, "on the radio."

Abu Jihad was buried a few days later, with military honors. He had been made a martyr. Yasser Arafat walked behind the coffin with the widow, Intisar, and her eldest son, Jihad.

At the time, the Israelis considered the killing of Abu Jihad to be a tremendous success. "Rabin thanked me later for persuading him," Moshe Nissim said. "'You cannot guess how right you were,' he told me. 'People are cheering me, shaking my hand, giving me the thumbs-up. What joy it has brought to the nation! What a feeling of high morale, how right it was for our deterrent force.'"

Indeed, Abu Jihad's death was a severe blow to the PLO. Abu Jihad was a seasoned and shrewd commander, and without him Fatah was able to launch far fewer successful attacks against Israel.

But the immediate, professed reason for killing him was to dampen the Intifada—and by that measure, the assassination failed to achieve its goal. In fact, the targeted killing had precisely the opposite effect: The elimination of Abu Jihad greatly weakened the PLO leadership but bolstered the Popular Committees in the occupied territories, which were the true leaders of the uprising. And Israel still had no reply to the waves of protesters or the growing tide of international condemnation.

With the benefit of hindsight, many Israelis who took part in the operation now regret it. Some believe that Abu Jihad's powerful presence had a restraining and sobering effect on Arafat and that his voice would have been highly beneficial after the establishment of the Palestinian National Authority, in 1994. If the adored and charismatic Abu Jihad had been alive, Hamas might not have been able to consolidate its position and to dominate large parts of the Palestinian public.

Amnon Lipkin-Shahak, who was head of AMAN at the time of the assassination, and later chief of the General Staff, said that in an ideal world, "if we had known that a short time after Abu Jihad's elimination, the PLO would take the diplomatic course, then perhaps we would have raided his house and first of all talked with him about his attitudes toward a compromise with Israel, and only then decided whether to kill him or not. In retrospect, his absence is indeed evident to a certain extent. He could have made a significant contribution to the peace process."

# INTIFADA

ON JUNE 23, 1988, an ABC News crew came to the Palestinian village of Salfit, on the slopes of the Samarian Hills in the West Bank.

At that point, the occupied territories were still in the turbulent throes of the Intifada. Violent protests, terrorist attacks, rocks, and Molotov cocktails were all daily occurrences. There were many dead on both sides.

The international media was attracted by the action.

In the small village of Salfit resided the Dakdouk family. One of their sons, Nizar, figured prominently on the Shin Bet's wanted list, though he was only eighteen years old. Intelligence information indicated that he was the leader of a gang of teenagers who hurled gasoline bombs at Israeli buses. Responding to the provocation with a form of collective punishment often used at the time, the IDF had demolished the Dakdouk family home on June 16. The next day, Israeli TV broadcast an interview with Nizar and his mother, standing next to the ruins of their home. With a smile, Nizar denied all the accusations against him, but he didn't object strongly when the interviewer suggested that he was considered a local hero. It was evident that he was not averse to media attention.

When a separate crew from ABC News arrived a week later and asked the family if it could interview Nizar, he appeared within minutes. The reporter explained that he had been impressed by the Israel TV interview with him and that he wanted to produce a major story about him. The crew suggested that the interview with Nizar take place on a hilltop overlooking the village. Nizar agreed but asked them to wait for a few minutes so he could change his shirt.

"No need," said the interviewer, friendly as could be. "I've got a stock of clean shirts in the van. What size do you wear?"

Pleased as any young man would be with the attention, Nizar jumped into one of the crew's two vans, both carrying press signs and the ABC logo. The party headed up the hill for the interview.

When Nizar failed to return home after a few hours, the family began to worry. The next morning, they called the ABC bureau in Tel Aviv. The people at the news bureau were surprised to hear that Nizar had disappeared. In fact, they were surprised to hear that anyone from the network had been in Salfit at all. A brief investigation revealed that it was not, in fact, anyone from ABC who had taken Nizar away. ABC suspected Israeli intelligence.

Roone Arledge, president of ABC's news division, contacted Prime Minister Yitzhak Shamir. The friendship between the two gave him access, but Arledge was furious. The action of the Shin Bet, he said, "presents grave peril to the safety of legitimate journalists." He demanded that "an investigation be conducted immediately to ascertain who authorized such an action" and to "affirm that it is not the policy of the Israeli Government to pose as journalists for whatever reason."

Shamir was not aware of the Salfit incident, but he realized that this was a matter that could very quickly become a scandal of major proportions, and he summoned a meeting for that evening with the heads of the military and the intelligence community.

THE INTIFADA WAS CHARACTERIZED by two types of Palestinian activity against the Israeli occupation: huge popular protests, and acts of terror against Israeli soldiers and settlers.

Back in 1986, Major General Ehud Barak, then the head of the IDF Central Command, together with the head of the operations department of the General Staff, Major General Meir Dagan, set up a highly secretive unit, Duvdevan (Hebrew for "Cherry"), to combat terrorists in the West Bank. The unit was now put into action.

Its fighters were Mistaravim who would work undercover, generally posing as Arabs, deep inside Palestinian territory, and hit the people on the wanted list. The nucleus of Duvdevan comprised graduates of elite IDF units, particularly the naval commandos.

The Cherry troops exhibited exceptional operational capabilities, thanks to the long and grueling training they underwent, which included special instruction to become familiar with the Arab territories, dress, and disguise techniques. They were uniquely capable of blending in when they were in crowded and hostile Palestinian environments, even in small villages where strangers attracted immediate attention.

It was Cherry that had posed as an ABC crew and abducted Nizar Dakdouk in Salfit.

Prior to that operation, the men chosen for the mission—one of them born and raised in Canada and another from the United States—had undergone a few days of intensive training at Israel's state-run television studios in Jerusalem. They learned how a television crew works, how an interview is conducted, how the camera is used, and how the sound man holds the boom mic. Israel's television stations also loaned them the equipment. The Shin Bet was responsible for forging the ABC signs and logos and press credentials.

After the fake TV crew picked up Dakdouk and left Salfit, ostensibly headed toward the hilltop interview site, their van was stopped by what looked like a routine IDF roadblock but was in fact another Cherry detail. These men then handcuffed the wanted youth, blindfolded him, and handed him to the Shin Bet for interrogation.

Shamir was furious that he had not been asked to approve the Salfit operation, and he immediately forbade the use of fake media cover from that point forward—and "definitely, definitely not American" media. Major Uri Bar-Lev, the officer in charge, who in 1986 was the one who had set Cherry up, tried to calm Shamir down and explain why it had been important to use the ABC News ruse.

"Mr. Prime Minister," said Bar-Lev, "we understood that he was just looking for a chance to talk. We knew this was the easiest way to get him out of the village without causing a commotion."

Bar-Lev says he brought the videotape shot by the "crew" to prove how efficient the job had been, "and gradually you could see Shamir's

crumpled turtle face becoming softer, and even that he was beginning to like it."

Shamir smiled. "In the underground, we also had to use disguises
sometimes," he said. But he soon snapped out of the nostalgia and
repeated his order: "What's done is done. But from now on, no more
use of media cover."

"Prime Minister, we are in the middle of another operation with
the same cover," Bar-Lev said. "I am asking you not to categorically
forbid the use of this modus operandi."

After a moment's reflection, Shamir said, "Well, okay, but I forbid
the use of the cover of American journalists."

Dakdouk was interrogated and eventually given a long jail term,
but in the end he came out alive. In many other cases, however—the
IDF refuses to this day, more than thirty years afterward, to release
precise figures—the targets of Cherry operations ended up dead.
"The essence of Cherry was to carry out low-signature killings of terror operatives," said Yoni Koren, an officer in AMAN and a close associate of Barak's.

"The orders of engagement are very straightforward," observed
Bar-Lev. "If the wanted person is seen with a weapon in his hands,
i.e., is a danger to our troops, he is to be shot right away."

Conversations with former members of the unit revealed that in a
large number of its operations, it was clear that the suspect would be
armed, and that they were therefore de facto targeted killing missions. Often, it was even obligatory to perform "dead checking"—
pumping more bullets into the man after he was down. All this
without giving him the chance to surrender.

The IDF denied that Cherry performed the dead-checking procedure, but proof came after a soldier in the unit, Sergeant Eliahu Azi-
sha, was killed by friendly fire when he was mistaken for a wanted
Palestinian. An IDF Criminal Investigation Division probe revealed
that he had been shot multiple times to make sure he was dead.

Cherry and other units like it carried out hundreds of missions
during the Intifada. Peddlers, shepherds, taxi drivers, female pedestrians on the street—just about any type of person one might have
encountered in an Arab city or village at that time could have turned

out to be a Cherry soldier and suddenly drawn a concealed weapon. "A terrorist trying to survive doesn't execute attacks. Our activity put the members of the terror cells into absolute uncertainty," said Bar-Lev. "They didn't know where it was coming from, didn't know who could be trusted or where they could feel safe."

Sometimes Cherry soldiers even posed as Israeli Jews. In February 1990, the Shin Bet learned that an armed squad with ties to Fatah intended to attack IDF reservists in Manara Square, in the center of the West Bank city of Ramallah. Cherry men dressed like reservists: in sloppy uniforms, potbellies peeking out of their shirts and their rifles out of reach as they sat eating hummus in a restaurant on the square. After two weeks of waiting, the anticipated attack took place. The "reservists" sprang into action. They ripped off their latex potbellies and drew out the Micro Uzi machine pistols secreted inside them. They opened fire and killed some of the assailants. Snipers posted nearby took care of the rest.

Cherry and similar units set up by the police and the Shin Bet achieved their goal: severe damage, sometimes fatal, to Palestinian terrorist groups, thus reducing their level of activity to a significant extent.

But this success, as important as it may have been, only highlighted the larger strategic failures in the war against the popular uprising. Against the mass protests, Israel had responded with all the grace of a clumsy giant trying to repel a swarm of nimble dwarves. Soldiers rounded up thousands of protesters, and they were sent to special detention camps set up in the south of the country. Large parts of the population of the Palestinian areas were placed under lengthy curfews, the family homes of activists were demolished or boarded up, and they themselves were deported. Many schools remained shut for most of the year.

Television footage of the violence led to greater decline in Israel's international standing and an increase in pressure, now from President George H. W. Bush and Secretary of State James Baker, to sit down and negotiate with the Palestinians.

But despite the mounting international criticism, domestic discontent, and the need to send more and more troops to quell the protests, Prime Minister Yitzhak Shamir and his Likud-led government refused to hold talks with the PLO over the occupied territories. Shamir and his right-wing ministers continued to view the organization as the force behind the Intifada, and continued to believe the Intifada could be quelled by targeting the mob leaders in the occupied territories as well as Arafat's men in Tunis. The fact that the assassination of Abu Jihad had done nothing to quiet down the popular uprising did not sway them from this view.

The prime minister ordered the Mossad to remain focused on gathering intelligence on the PLO and figuring out how to kill its operatives. Mossad director Shabtai Shavit, whose politics were very similar to Shamir's, happily complied. In fact, he wanted to go even further: With the Intifada whirling, Shavit requested permission to settle old scores and eliminate former members of Black September.

The PLO, however, had dramatically tightened its internal security. The Israeli Air Force's strike on Tunis in 1985 and the subsequent commando raid on Abu Jihad led to the establishment of a number of Fatah inquiry panels to locate the leak that provided intelligence to the Israelis. Those investigations came up empty, but nevertheless, stringent precautions were instituted at PLO facilities—background checks for candidates trying to join the organization, strict compartmentalization, polygraph tests administered by Tunisian intelligence—making it very difficult for the Mossad to spy on them.

There was no way for the Mossad to recruit agents in Tunis. The local authorities were enraged by the Israeli actions in their territory, and they provided open assistance to the PLO, helping it to tighten its security.

So instead, as it had done in many of its recruitment operations, the Mossad looked for likely agents among Palestinians traveling in so-called base countries, those states in which operatives and case officers could function in relative freedom and where Israel had diplomatic representation.

The most convenient country for these activities was France, through which most PLO officials passed after leaving Tunis. Many of them stayed at Le Méridien Montparnasse, in Paris, an established, respectable hotel popular among Middle Eastern business travelers. To the surprise of the Mossad personnel, as soon as they began investigating the hotel, they discovered that El Al, the Israeli national airline, enjoyed a corporate discount at the same hotel, and pilots and cabin crews spent their layovers there. Each morning, Mossad surveillance crews watched as senior members of the PLO munched croissants and sipped café au lait in the same cafeteria as El Al pilots, many of whom were officers in the Israeli Air Force reserves, all purely by coincidence.

Among the PLO men who frequented the hotel was Adnan Yassin, a midlevel activist who was responsible for logistics and security at the Tunis HQ. Yassin also assisted his bosses with their personal comforts, coordinating their vacations, arranging their medical care, and procuring luxury goods: sports cars shipped in containers from Marseille, expensive perfumes, Cuban cigars, and alcoholic drinks. Life in exile, far from the hardships of their people in the occupied territories, had made some of the PLO officials exceedingly corrupt.

Yassin took care of his own comforts, too. During the late eighties, many of the senior officials in the organization dipped their hands into the coffers, enjoying the good life at the expense of the Palestinian revolution. In the Mossad, these men were referred to mockingly as *midawar*—Arabic for "loafers"—or as the "Champs-Élysées Revolutionaries."

Besides his PLO duties, Yassin also frequented Paris because his cancer-stricken wife received chemotherapy there. The couple always stayed at Le Méridien Montparnasse. Yassin had a reliable address, a basic routine, and a wealth of PLO intelligence. In late 1989, Avi Dagan, the head of the Mossad's Junction division, green-lit Operation Golden Fleece to recruit Adnan Yassin.

ONE MORNING IN MARCH 1990, Adnan Yassin sat down to breakfast with some of his PLO colleagues at the hotel. At a nearby table, a well-dressed man of Middle Eastern appearance, his room key on the table, read a newspaper printed on pale green pages. These items—the key, the paper—were not there by chance. Rather, they were props of a Junction recruiter trying to establish initial contact with a potential agent. This is a delicate stage, requiring discipline and patience. "Most important at this moment," a Junction case officer who was involved in Operation Golden Fleece explained, "is to try to cause the other side to make the first move and initiate contact. Or, at least, not to look as if you are trying too hard, not to act with suspicion-arousing aggression. For example, you might well be suspicious of a person who comes to the bus stop after you, but much less so of someone who was already there when you came. If I enter an elevator and someone hurries in after me and then gets off at the same floor as I do, that looks suspicious. If he was there already, much less so. We are talking about innumerable delicate nuances, the aim of which is to allow a situation to flow naturally along. Only rarely will you meet someone sufficiently corrupt for you to wrap things up by handing him a suitcase full of cash. For everyone else, you need real craft, great patience."

The room key on the table was there to create a feeling of familiarity, to indicate that the man sitting there was also a guest at Le Méridien. The newspaper with the green pages was well known to any Arabic reader who traveled abroad: *Al-Shark al-Awsat,* published in London by a member of the Saudi royal family and considered relatively moderate.

The Mossad was lucky that morning in Paris. One of the people in the PLO breakfast group, though not Yassin himself, asked the Mossad man about something in the paper. The Mossad recruiter congenially handed the man the paper. A conversation then developed between the Palestinians and the Mossad man, who was at pains not to pay any particular attention to Yassin. One member of the group invited the Mossad man to join them, but he refused politely and left the room, so as not to arouse suspicion by appearing too eager.

The next morning, the Palestinian group again ran into the Mossad operative, who introduced himself as an Egyptian businessman by the name of Hilmi, and they struck up a lively conversation. Two days later, Yassin came to the dining room on his own and looked around for some company. He spoke only Arabic, and he was pleased to see Hilmi reading his green newspaper again. He asked if he could join him. Hilmi was happy to say yes.

It was the perfect contact method. Yassin was convinced that he had initiated the relationship, and there was no reason for him to be suspicious. Hilmi said that he was in the import-export business between France and the Arab world, hinting that he made quite a bit of money from it. The rapacious Yassin asked to meet later for lunch at a nearby restaurant, and Hilmi agreed. Later, they met twice more.

From Hilmi's conversations and information already in the Mossad's possession, Junction developed an understanding of Yassin's character. It was not especially flattering. In his Junction dossier, Yassin is depicted as vulgar, uneducated, aggressive, and coarse, his chief concern being his social status and lining his own pockets. Hilmi reported that Yassin tried to get him involved in petty illegal currency deals and in smuggling contraband into Tunis. Later on, Mossad men witnessed his degrading behavior toward his wife, including one time when he slapped her in public.

In short, he was an ideal Mossad recruit.

Hilmi and Yassin's friendship progressed. Eventually, Hilmi told Yassin about a friend, a businessman who was connected to the Iranian embassy in Paris. Hilmi had made a lot of money, he said, because of that friendship. But he never offered to introduce Yassin. He just dangled his connection like bait, waiting patiently for Yassin to take it. And when Yassin finally asked if he could accompany Hilmi the next time he met his contact, Hilmi demurred, like a fisherman playing out a line, not ready to set the hook. Yassin badgered, and Hilmi refused. Finally, after a month of repeated entreaties, Hilmi agreed to introduce him to his Iranian contact.

The businessman with the Iranian connections was, of course, just another Junction operative. Playing his part perfectly, he described to Yassin a number of future business initiatives he had planned and told him that he could have a stake in some of them. In the meantime, he said, the Islamic Republic of Iran was very concerned about the plight of the Palestinians. It was important for the Iranians to know that the PLO was functioning well and "doing the correct things," by which he meant keeping up terror activities against Israel outside its borders and stepping up the Intifada in the West Bank and Gaza. "The Islamic Republic," he said, "will do all it can to destroy the Zionist entity and to return to the Palestinians what is theirs."

Any information Yassin could provide from PLO headquarters would be welcome, and handsomely rewarded.

Junction was betting that it would be easier for Yassin to betray the PLO if he believed he was selling its secrets to Iran, rather than the enemy.

The bet paid off. Yassin turned out to be an exceptional investment for the Mossad. In exchange for a few tens of thousands of dollars, he supplied an enormous amount of high-quality intelligence during regular debriefings in Paris. Primarily, he provided information about Hammam Chott, the PLO headquarters in Tunis, giving details about the day-to-day activities there and about the plans hatched there. Yassin outlined everything, including shifting organizational structures, who sat in which office, who met with whom, how Abu Jihad's powers had been dispersed and reassigned, weapons transfers, how the Intifada was stoked, preparations for terror attacks, and personnel recruitment. He interspersed his detailed operational reports with quality gossip. He was the first to tell of the close relationship developing between Suha, the daughter of the Palestinian national poet, Raymonda Tawil, and Chairman Arafat, who had made Suha an adviser in his bureau. The two were married a short time later.

Adnan Yassin also brought a plan by Arafat and one of his operatives, Jibril Rajoub, to the attention of Israeli intelligence. The plan was to kill Yitzhak Shamir and Ariel Sharon as revenge for the assassination of Abu Jihad. The designated assassin, a frustrated and debt-burdened Israeli Jew by the name of Rafael Avraham, landed in Israel in October 1992, carrying a large amount of cash and the assassination plan with him. Adnan Yassin knew about the plan because he had booked Avraham's travel arrangements.

Birds operatives were waiting for Avraham when he got off the plane. Rajoub was stunned: "I really did not understand how the Shin Bet got on to him so quickly. He didn't manage to do anything. Just got off the plane and hop! He was captured."

Yassin was an endless fountain of information, an asset of almost unimaginable value. Through him, the Mossad was able to instantly track many of its top assassination targets, primarily because, once again, he was the man who made all their flight and hotel reservations. One such instance occurred in late January 1992, after the French authorities, via the Red Cross in France, permitted George

Habash, the head of the Popular Front for the Liberation of Palestine, to visit the country for medical treatment, despite the fact that he was on their most-wanted list and those of several other countries. Acting on Yassin's intelligence, the Israelis examined the possibility of eliminating him, but the French were taking precautions to protect him. Instead of the hit, then, the Mossad leaked the scandalous news of his visit to the media, causing considerable embarrassment for the government of François Mitterrand.

Yassin also kept tabs on men the Mossad believed had been involved in the 1972 Munich massacre. Despite the fact that the Red Pages for these men had been signed by Golda Meir almost twenty years earlier, some of them remained at large. "From our point of view, the Red Pages were open-ended," an aide to Mossad director Shavit said.

One of the names high up on that list was Atef Bseiso, who had been a member of Black September at the time of the terror attack and, by 1992, had become a top PLO official. It was never clear exactly what role he played in the Munich attack. The PLO claimed he was not involved at all. But the Mossad insisted he was, and in any case, it made no difference—Shavit was determined to avenge Munich, and anyone connected to Black September was, in his mind, a legitimate target. Still, it was an odd distraction. At this point, the entirety of the Middle East was consumed by the Intifada. The occupied territories were in flaming turmoil. Israel had far more pressing intelligence needs than killing people for atrocities they may or may not have been involved in two decades earlier. Nonetheless, Shamir re-endorsed the Red Page for Bseiso. The reason, a Caesarea operative said, was "simply because we had access." That access was Yassin.

In early June 1992, Bseiso left Tunis for a series of meetings with the German and French intelligence services, as well as with the CIA's Robert Baer. "In 1979, the Mossad assassinated Ali Salameh, who was the liaison with the CIA," Baer said. "We were certain they did it to cut off the link with us. Hani al-Hassan and then Atef Bseiso replaced him. I arrived in Paris on that day to hold the periodic meeting with him."

According to a number of sources, these meetings were another primary reason the Mossad wanted to kill Bseiso. The Mossad realized he was one of the main links between the PLO and intelligence agencies in the West, including those of Germany, France, and America, and top Israeli intelligence officials believed that these ties were one more step toward the West's bestowment of full international diplomatic legitimization upon Arafat and the PLO, and the isolation of Israel. The fact that the Palestinian liaisons were former members of Black September only stoked the Israelis' rage further. Their protests to the Western states fell on deaf ears, so Israel decided to convey its displeasure in a more direct manner.

Because he had once again made the travel arrangements, Yassin knew that at the last minute Bseiso had decided to drive from Bonn to Paris, rather than fly, and that he had changed his hotel from Le Méridien Etoile to Le Méridien Montparnasse. Ironically, Bseiso made these changes because he was concerned about his safety.

A Bayonet team was waiting for Bseiso in the hotel lobby. They tailed him up to his room and waited while he unpacked, showered, and dressed for the evening. They kept close to him as he went out for dinner with friends at the nearby Hippopotamus restaurant and then returned to the hotel. As he left the car at the entrance of the hotel and headed for the lobby, two Bayonet men shot him five times. The pistol they used was equipped with a silencer, and immediately after the killing they collected their empty cartridges in a bag, in order to make things more difficult for investigators.

A man purporting to be a spokesman for the Abu Nidal Organization claimed responsibility for the slaying, but this claim was immediately denied by one of the organization's real spokesmen. Arafat was quick to accuse Israel. AMAN's chief at that time, Major General Uri Sagie, declared soon afterward that he did not know who had carried out the killing—but he added that Bseiso had been involved in the Munich massacre, the abortive attack on an El Al plane in Rome in 1978, and the attempted murder of the Jordanian ambassador in London.

The backlash to the targeted killing of Bseiso was swift. The CIA was infuriated that the Mossad had again interfered with its ties to the PLO. The French were even more angry. To them, the hit—in front of an elegant Paris hotel—was a grave violation of national sovereignty. French agents began to rein in Mossad operatives in Paris, placing them under surveillance, breaking into their meetings, identifying and burning their sources. A judicial inquiry into the murder remains open in France.

Killing Bseiso, in fact, served as little more than a distraction at a critical time. Israel, already pilloried internationally, needed all the allies it could get.

On the other hand, there's no doubt that eliminating a senior figure in the PLO who was in charge of Arafat's contacts with Western intelligence agencies did have an effect. The targeted killing, along with other operations based on intelligence supplied by Yassin, badly weakened the PLO during this period. In mid-1990, the Mossad and AMAN's Special Operations Executive hacked into the computer network of Al-Sammed al-Iktisadi, Fatah's financial arm, and transferred money from one account to another inside it, in a manner that made members think their colleagues were stealing the organization's funds, thereby sowing mistrust and confusion. Headquarters was in disarray, preoccupied with finding traitors and moles. The result was a significant reduction in the organization's attacks against Israel.

The biggest blow, however, was a strategic blunder made by Arafat himself, without the help of the Mossad. In August 1990, Saddam Hussein sent 90,000 Iraqi soldiers and seven hundred tanks rolling over the border into tiny, oil-rich Kuwait. The invasion was almost universally condemned, by both the West and most of the Middle East, and eventually was repelled by a massive, multinational, American-led force. Arafat and Libya's Muammar Qaddafi were the only Arab leaders who backed Saddam, and they refused to join an Arab League resolution calling on him to pull his forces out of Kuwait. Arafat likened the American-led coalition, which included many Arab states, to a "new crusade" and declared that Saddam was "the defender of the Arab nation, of Muslims and of free men everywhere."

This infuriated the surrounding Gulf states, upon whose cash the PLO, with its now insatiable pit of corruption, relied. By mid-1992 the organization was broke. The PLO, for years Israel's nemesis, finally had been pushed to the wall.

At the same time, the Intifada was still fully aflame, a struggle that was increasingly wearying the Israeli public. The IDF deployed tens of thousands of troops in the occupied territories; in total, throughout the uprising, hundreds of thousands of soldiers, most of them eighteen- to twenty-two-year-old conscripts, were charged with policing the Palestinian population. Instead of fighting to defend the country's borders, the putative central mission of the Israeli Army, they were assigned to duties like suppressing demonstrations, searching men and women at roadblocks, and chasing down kids who'd thrown rocks at them, all part of the Sisyphean task of suppressing the Palestinian uprising against the occupation.

When these young soldiers came home on short furloughs, they brought with them a sense of the hopelessness of the job, and the political debate in family living rooms and workplaces between worried parents and siblings revolved around the question "Why are we there at all?"

Over four years, the Intifada morphed from an isolated disturbance on the nightly news into a seemingly endless crisis that affected hundreds of thousands of Israeli families. Adding to the growing unease about the situation in the occupied territories was the anxiety and anger injected by a series of stabbing attacks by Palestinians inside the "Green Line" borders of Israel proper. The most significant of these was the murder of a young girl by the name of Helena Rapp, in the Tel Aviv suburb of Bat Yam, in May 1992. It led to stormy protests against the government and to a feeling that Shamir was incapable of ensuring the safety of the citizenry. At the same time, Shamir became embroiled in an angry confrontation with the American administration over the continued construction in the occupied territories, and President George H. W. Bush refused to approve financial benefits sorely needed by Israel for the absorption of a million Jewish immigrants pouring in from the disintegrating Soviet Union.

The Intifada and the severe financial crisis eventually brought down the Shamir government. On June 23, 1992, Yitzhak Rabin, who was perceived by the electorate as a pillar of security but also someone who would make genuine efforts to achieve peace with the Palestinians, was elected prime minister by a significant majority—a win by the center-left more decisive than any Israel has seen since.

Rabin, who had served as defense minister during the Intifada, was himself deeply affected by the conflict with the Palestinians, and had reached the conclusion that a compromise must be reached.

HOBBLED BY ISRAELI INTELLIGENCE operations and reeling from his Iraqi debacle, Yasser Arafat once again resorted to his tried and tested survival technique. Palestinian historian Yezid Sayigh described it as *"hurub ila al-amam"*—running away by running forward.

Backing an illegal invasion had made him a pariah, even among his wealthy Arab sponsors. On the other hand, even if he hadn't initiated and couldn't control the Intifada, he was still *perceived* as the Palestinian leader, the one man who might be able to negotiate a peace. It was Arafat's gift to exploit the latter crisis to cover up—run away from—the former crisis.

Arafat permitted his people to open a secret back channel with a group of Israeli academics, first in London and later in Oslo. Initially, the Israeli professors acted on their own, but later they brought in Deputy Foreign Minister Yossi Beilin, who reported directly to Foreign Minister Shimon Peres.

When Peres informed Rabin about the contact with the Palestinians, the premier instructed him to drop it immediately, but shortly afterward he changed his mind and decided to give the initiative a chance.

The negotiations, however, were kept secret, even from the heads of Israel's military and intelligence organizations. Rabin instructed Unit 8200, which eavesdropped on Palestinian communications, to report anything they heard about the discussion directly and solely to him. Officially, this was for operational security—any leak that got out to the various Palestinian factions could derail the talks. Unofficially, Rabin wasn't entirely certain that men who'd spent years trying to kill Arafat and his minions, who ran agencies that had invested enormous effort in the war on Palestinian terrorism, could make the mental adjustment necessary to see a former enemy as a partner in peace.

Rabin knew that any diplomatic process with the PLO could end in agreement only if it included territorial concessions. A large segment of the Israeli population, however, was bitterly opposed to any such compromise, for ideological and religious reasons. Any leak disclosing that secret negotiations were under way—emanating, say, from sources inside the defense or intelligence communities who thought that it was a strategic error—would have revealed the possibility of territorial concessions and thereby killed the negotiation instantly.

This exclusion of the military and intelligence from the negotiation process created an odd situation, however. While the highest levels of the Israeli government were trying to negotiate peace, the country's intelligence agencies continued fighting a covert war, unaware that anything had changed.

The Mossad had invested heavily in Adnan Yassin and Operation Golden Fleece, and it was still paying dividends. In the spring of 1993, more than four years after Yassin had first been targeted as an asset, he told his case officer of a conversation he'd had with Amina, the wife of Mahmoud Abbas (Abu Mazen), the PLO's second in command, who was also in charge of the organization's diplomatic activities. Her husband was badly overweight, she'd told him, and suffering from severe back pains. She knew Yassin could get hold of almost anything, and she thought an orthopedic chair from Europe might help Abbas.

"Of course," Yassin told her, asking if she needed anything else for the office. She requested an especially bright lamp, as Abu Mazen's eyesight was weakening. Yassin promised to do what he could.

The Mossad jumped at the opportunity and supplied Yassin with a luxurious leather office chair and a decorative table lamp, both fitted with microphones and transmitters.

Yassin brought the new items to Abbas's office, even taking the trouble to move the old chair himself, cursing whoever gave "such miserable furniture to such important people." He put the new chair in place, then put the lamp on the desk, plugged it in, and switched it on.

The lamp was the more important of the two pieces of furniture, because, while the bugs planted in the chair required batteries that would have to be replaced, the lamp could serve as a transmitter for years, powered by a constant supply of electricity direct from the grid. The chair contained two separate energy-saving devices: spring switches that turned the microphones on only when someone was putting weight on them, and a voice activation system, which meant that if someone was sitting on the chair but not talking to anyone, the batteries still would not get used up.

Transmissions from the chair were picked up and relayed to Tel Aviv from the very first day it was placed in Abbas's office. Mossad director Shavit realized what an achievement this was: Abu Mazen was at the hub of the PLO's activities, and innumerable people passed through his office, sharing the organization's most important secrets with him.

Yet, very quickly, another matter emerged, one much more unexpected. The director of the Mossad learned from "the singing chair," as it was known, that the Israeli government was conducting advanced negotiations with the PLO behind his back.

Rabin had ordered AMAN's SIGINT Unit 8200 to bring anything they heard about the negotiations directly to him, but he had not done the same with the Mossad.

Shavit angrily confronted Rabin, complaining about the Mossad being left out of the loop. Rabin placated Shavit by saying that it was "a marginal initiative" by Peres, to which he, Rabin, did not ascribe any significance.

Then, as abruptly as they'd begun, the transmissions stopped. Three and a half weeks after the concealed microphones had been planted, the giant antennas at Mossad headquarters quit picking up signals. At first, the Israelis thought there might be a technical problem, but an inspection showed that all the links between the Mossad and Abbas's office were in good working order, and anyway, it was highly unlikely that both would malfunction at the exact same time. This almost certainly meant that both microphones had been discovered, that Operation Golden Fleece had been blown, and that their prize asset, Adnan Yassin, was in mortal peril. "We couldn't understand," a source in the Mossad's counterterrorism division said, "how it was possible, how it could *be,* that so short a time after we managed to put the equipment in place, it was discovered, together with the agent who did it."

It was Jibril Rajoub who detected the presence of the equipment, with the assistance of the local intelligence agency. Rajoub said, "Our people in Oslo sensed that the Israelis were seeing through them, that they knew exactly what they were going to say next, and what positions to take. This aroused the suspicion of eavesdropping, and that's why we went to scan Abu Mazen's office."

However, most Mossad operatives involved in Golden Fleece had a very different explanation: Their own people had betrayed them. According to this theory, which is unprovable but is supported by some serious circumstantial evidence, one of the Israeli negotiators in Oslo saw the reports on the intelligence gathered during the operation and distributed to the prime minister and the heads of the intelligence community. He grasped that the source of the intelligence was some kind of eavesdropping device in Abu Mazen's office or a tap on one of his communication lines. He then tipped the Palestinians off, knowing that they would immediately locate the devices and dismantle them. Once that happened, Israeli intelligence would have no way of knowing what was happening at the talks, which would mean none of the hardliners could leak the details to the media and ruin the negotiations. In other words, an Israeli diplomat betrayed Israeli intelligence to prevent Israeli intelligence from sabotaging Israeli diplomacy. The fact that a valuable asset would likely be killed was beside the point.

Yassin was arrested and tortured until he confessed everything: how he'd been recruited, the information he'd provided, how his greed had turned him against his own people. Arafat, stunned that such a trusted aide had been arrested, went to see Yassin in his cell at the Fatah interrogation facility to hear the story for himself. It was a foregone conclusion that Yassin would be executed. He was undeniably a traitor, and he'd been deeply involved in the killing of Bseiso.

Soon after, in Oslo, a Palestinian delegate fumed about the Yassin arrest and the Bseiso killing. He asked one of the Israelis what he knew. "I know nothing about this story," said the Israeli, who truly was not party to any intelligence secrets but understood what had happened from the little he had heard from Peres and Beilin. "But let's all drink to that being the last assassination." He added one last word in Arabic. *Inshallah.* God willing.

The delegates around the table—four Palestinians, three Israeli

Jews, and two Norwegians—all lifted their glasses. The atmosphere was optimistic. The negotiations had lasted six months so far and had generated historic letters of mutual recognition between the two nations—from Rabin to Arafat, and from Arafat to Rabin. These letters would evolve into a series of agreements that became known as the Oslo Accords. At the first stage, the accords begat the autonomous Palestinian Authority (PA), which was to rule over most of the territory populated by Palestinians. The Palestinians undertook to stop the Intifada and to renounce terrorism.

The bloody conflict in the Middle East seemed as if it might finally come to a peaceful end. Yasser Arafat and most of the PLO and Fatah leaders left Tunis and took up residence in the autonomous occupied PA territories.

Even Adnan Yassin appeared to benefit from the newfound cooperation. The Oslo Accords engendered security coordination committees, with delegates from the military and intelligence apparatuses of both sides. For the first time, top Mossad and Shin Bet officials were meeting with men who, a few short months earlier, had been their targets for either espionage or assassination. The meetings were held in the Palestinian territories or in hotels in Tel Aviv or Jerusalem. The two sides overcame their initial suspicions through lighthearted mutual teasing about the past—who had succeeded in tricking whom, whether the Palestinians had conducted operations the Israelis didn't know about, where and when the Israelis had foiled Palestinian plans.

The Israelis took advantage of this genial atmosphere to request clemency for Yassin. "We raised it as a plea for a goodwill gesture in return for the thousands of Palestinian prisoners that Israel had undertaken to release as part of the deal," said one of the Mossad participants in the committee meetings.

The pressure, and the atmosphere, worked.

In the end, Yassin was not executed, but only sentenced to fifteen years in prison. It was a lenient sentence, all things considered. In the summer of 1993, it seemed Yassin would live to see a lasting peace in the Middle East. *Inshallah.*

# NEBUCHADNEZZAR

ON THE NIGHT OF April 6, 1979, outside a shipping hangar on the waterfront, a pair of headlights poked through the darkness, casting two cones of yellow-white on the pavement, widening as the car came closer. It was a Fiat 127 sedan, the engine sputtering and clanking, then stalling two hundred yards from the front gate.

The two French guards outside the hangar—at La Seyne-sur-Mer, just west of Toulon on France's Mediterranean coast—eyed the car warily. The hangar belonged to the CNIM Group, which specialized in manufacturing large-scale, complex components for ships and nuclear reactors. There were always two guards on duty—three shifts a day, eight hours each, all of them boring.

The guards took a few steps toward the fence as the doors opened. Two women got out. Pretty girls, the guards thought. But the women seemed confused, almost angry, as they tottered toward the gate.

*"Pouvez-vous nous aider?"* one of them asked from the other side of the fence. Can you help us? They were British tourists, she said, out for a night on the Riviera, but their lousy car kept breaking down. She smiled. A flirt. Maybe later, she said, the guards could join them at one of the bars.

The guards gathered some tools, opened the gate, walked toward the car. They were smiling.

Behind them, five Bayonet operatives hustled over the fence, quickly and noiselessly, a maneuver they'd practiced endlessly at a military base on Israel's southern coast. Just as quietly, they forced their way into the hangar. Inside, they attached five powerful explosives to two enormous cylinders. They set timers on the detonators, then slipped back out, over the fence, and into the night.

They'd needed less than five minutes to get in and out.

On the street in front of the hangar, the guards managed to get the car started. It had been surprisingly easy. Then the women—both Israeli operatives—promised to meet them later and drove off.

At the same time, some distance away, a man and a woman holding hands walked along slowly. They seemed preoccupied with their romance. The man, his hair slicked back, looked a little like Humphrey Bogart. He peered over the woman's shoulder and saw the car starting up and driving off. The couple turned around, and a few streets away, they got into a car and also drove off. They were Mike Harari, Caesarea's boss, and Tamara, a female Mossad operative.

Thirty minutes later, the hangar exploded. Flames ripped into the night sky and lit up the waterfront in orange and red. Firefighters extinguished the blaze before the building was completely destroyed, but everything inside was badly damaged, including some carefully crafted machines that it had taken more than two years to manufacture. Fully assembled with the rest of the components, they would make a seventy-megawatt nuclear reactor, large enough that it was known as an Osiris-class reactor.

Osiris is the ancient Egyptian god of the afterlife, the underworld, and the dead. The French were selling it to Saddam Hussein, the Iraqi dictator, who saw himself as the modern embodiment of Nebuchadnezzar, the Babylonian king who destroyed the Kingdom of Israel.

A few hours after the bombing, a spokesman for Groupe des Écologistes Français telephoned a newspaper to claim responsibility. But no one, certainly not French intelligence, believed him. Everyone assumed that it was the Israelis, because they had the most pressing motive.

WHILE MANY OF ISRAEL'S defense and intelligence assets were bogged down in the bloody muck of Lebanon, existential threats to the tiny nation continued to haunt the Mossad. Chief among them was Iraq, a country ruled by an unhinged butcher with a long-standing ambition to become the next Saladin. One of the IDF's nightmare scenarios was a massive Iraqi army joining up with the Jordanians to create a menacing eastern front.

Israeli forces had been covertly involved in Iraq since the 1960s, when the oppressed Kurdish minority rebelled against the Baghdad regime. The country supplied arms to the Kurds, and IDF soldiers and Mossad personnel trained fighters in commando warfare. The idea, according to Meir Amit, who ran the Mossad then, was "to create a Middle East in which we would be able to act against our enemies on several fronts simultaneously." To put it more simply, Iraq was a declared enemy of Israel, and the Kurds were an enemy of Baghdad—the enemy of my enemy is my friend. At the same time, such alliances—for example, with the shah of Iran and Emperor Haile Selassie of Ethiopia, two states that bordered Israel's hostile Arab neighbors—allowed the Mossad to establish listening posts and other intelligence assets inside otherwise unfriendly countries.

Starting in 1969, Israeli advisers, among them explosives expert Natan Rotberg, began hearing about the man the Kurds called "the Butcher of Baghdad." Saddam Hussein al-Tikriti had been part of the Baathist coup that had taken power the year before, and he was appointed vice chairman of Iraq's Revolutionary Council—second in command of the new regime and in charge of the armed forces and intelligence services. He ordered bombs dropped on civilians, choked off food supplies to starve dissident populations, and set up a network of torture chambers in which he often did the torturing himself.

The Kurds asked the Israelis to help them kill Saddam—Rotberg even prepared a booby-trapped Koran for the task, the same tactic he had used to assassinate the chief of Egyptian intelligence in 1956. But PM Golda Meir refused to sign the Red Page. She feared that the Kurds would not keep Israel's involvement a secret and that her government would get embroiled in an international scandal with the Russians and the Americans, both of whom were wooing Saddam assiduously at that time. Earlier, Meir had also dismissed the notion of assassinating Egypt's Nasser, for fear that killing him would legitimize attempts on her life and those of her ministers.

Left alive, Saddam, as ruthless as he was ambitious, took over the

Baath Party and, thus, Iraq. By 1971, when he was thirty-four years old, Saddam had removed all of his serious rivals in the regime and had assumed power in all but name, leaving the president, Ahmed Hasan al-Bakr, as nothing more than a figurehead. (He would finally push out al-Bakr completely in 1979.) He saw himself as a historic figure, a pan-Arab leader who would make Iraq a regional power, the leading force in the Arab world and the equal of Iran.

Saddam thought that Jews were "a mixture of the garbage and leftovers of various nations," and he wanted to redraw the whole of the Middle East, erasing Israel entirely. The Iraqis made no secret of this. "The existence of an artificial Zionist entity symbolizes the negation of the Arabs' historical right to existence and is a slight to their honor," the Baath Party newspaper *Al-Jumhuriya* wrote in March 1974. "This bellicose entity is nothing but a terrible cancer that dangerously spreads beyond its borders. We must fight Zionism . . . in every possible way. Arab Jerusalem awaits the Arab Salah al-Din [Saladin] who will redeem it from the pollution with which Zionism has stained our holy places."

The clear implication was that Saddam Hussein would be the modern version of Saladin and drive the infidels out of Palestine.

But Saddam realized that Iraq would never be a credible power without a formidable arsenal. The only way to conquer the Middle East was to have the ability to destroy it. Saddam wanted nuclear weapons.

In 1973, the dictator brought Iraq's nuclear program—ostensibly a peaceful civilian enterprise—under his direct control and began investing "budgets of billions, practically unlimited," in the words of Amatzia Baram, a prominent biographer of Saddam, into developing reactors that eventually could produce an atomic arsenal. Ideally, a dictator already known for bombing his own people and hell-bent on becoming a nuclear menace would be shunned by civilized nations. But geopolitics is a complicated business: Several Western powers, including the United States but most notably France, wanted to exert their own influence in the Middle East. And what's not complicated is merely crass: Saddam was throwing around a lot of money.

.   .   .

FRANCE AND ISRAEL HAD a long and complicated history that was reaching its low point in the 1970s. The relationship had been rife with hostility and distrust ever since de Gaulle had turned on the Jewish nation in the sixties. To the French, the possibility that Iraq represented a mortal threat to the nation of Israel seemed, at most, a manageable concern.

President Valéry Giscard d'Estaing and his prime minister, Jacques Chirac, orchestrated a number of deals with Iraq in the first half of the seventies. The most significant was the sale of two nuclear reactors: one very small one-hundred-kilowatt reactor, designated Isis-class, and a larger forty-megawatt Osiris reactor, which was expandable to seventy megawatts. The Iraqis combined the name of the reactor with the name of their country, calling it Osirak.

Although Iraq's stated intention was to use the reactor for research purposes, the French knew that a reactor of that size would almost certainly end up being used to process fuel for nuclear weapons. The reactor's core held twelve kilograms of 93 percent enriched uranium—enough to make an atom bomb—so if the French kept their promise to replace spent fuel rods, the Iraqis would be able to simply convert some of them into material for use in nuclear arms.

The Iraqis admitted as much: "The search for technology with military potential is a response to Israel's nuclear armament," Saddam declared in an interview on September 8, 1975, just before he visited Paris to sign more deals. "The Franco-Iraqi agreement is the first Arab step toward gaining nuclear arms, even if our declared goal in building the reactor is not the manufacture of atom bombs." But it takes years and very specific expertise to build atomic bombs. Any legitimate threat, the French seemed to assume, could be dealt with when and if it arose.

The Iraqis paid very generously. Some seven billion francs ($2 billion at the time) were transferred directly to France. The French also received favorable terms and a price reduction on their import of Iraqi oil.

A number of French companies were connected to the vast project, and joint management was set up to run things in Paris and Baghdad. Not far from the construction site, luxurious living quarters were constructed for two thousand French engineers and technicians.

Israel could not stand idly by. A joint Mossad/AMAN/Foreign Ministry team, dubbed "New Era," was set up "to make a special, concentrated effort to zero in on Iraq's intention to obtain nuclear weapons," in the words of Nahum Admoni, then the deputy director of the Mossad, who headed the team.

Under the guise of European businessmen or NATO European military officers, Junction case officers approached Iraqis working in France who they believed might potentially become informants. One scientist, whose son had cancer and was receiving inferior treatment in Iraq, traded secrets for better medical care. He believed that Yehuda Gil, Israel's top recruiter, was the deputy CEO of a European firm concerned with nuclear safety.

But that was a one-time success. Saddam had frightened all those involved in the project into silence with a video of Iraqi cabinet ministers executing other officials. "It was a terrifying tape," said Khidir Hamza, one of the directors of Iraq's nuclear program. "He was sending a message that if he's unhappy with you for any reason, you are dead."

Still, the Israelis had other sources: French scientists, technicians, secretaries, and midlevel managers. Some were paid handsomely. Others, Jews, did so for ideological reasons. Through one of these sources, the Mossad obtained the "project book," a document detailing all the deals signed with Iraq. Several hundred pages long, it had been written in English by the French scientists. "From that book," says Lieutenant Colonel Dr. Raphael Ofek, a nuclear physicist at Ben-Gurion University recruited by AMAN, "we learned a lot, including the layout of the project site where the reactor and adjoining laboratories were situated at Tuwaitha Nuclear Research Center."

Unit 8200, AMAN's SIGINT arm, established a top-secret task force, nicknamed "Apocalypse," that tapped into telephone and telex lines, and Rainbow agents planted bugs in the Iraqis' Paris offices.

With reams of damning intelligence, Israel called on the international community to halt the program. But exasperated foreign leaders, critics of Israel, and even some domestic opponents of Begin charged Israel with alarmism. The Iraqi project could not possibly harm Israel, they insisted. The French continued to maintain that the project was an entirely legitimate research program and that they were using enough security mechanisms to ensure that Iraq would not be able to develop nuclear bombs.

Foreign Minister Moshe Dayan, who returned from a visit to Paris appalled at the French indifference to his requests, tried the Americans next, asking Washington to pressure the French, also to no avail.

Israel concluded that the diplomatic path had failed. In November 1978, the security cabinet authorized the prime minister to take "necessary actions" to halt the Iraqi nuclear project. The Mossad was given the green light to act. "Osiris," the cabinet concluded, "must be killed."

Not long after came the explosion at the shipping hangar on the French Riviera. The components the operative blew up that night were badly damaged, and the Israelis believed they'd set back Saddam's nuclear ambitions by at least two years, the amount of time it would take the French to manufacture new components.

But the Iraqi dictator would not allow such a delay. He ordered the project to proceed on schedule. Iraq's minister of defense demanded that the French repair the parts and deliver them on time. The French countered that a repaired casing would not be as strong. It would be risky to use and would almost certainly have to be replaced in just a few years. But no one dared cross Saddam Hussein.

Iraq could still have nuclear weapons within a few years. Frustrated Mossad officials decided that they needed to begin using more aggressive tactics.

They would start killing scientists.


THE MOST OBVIOUS TARGETS for elimination were the heads of the Iraqi program, Khidir Hamza and Jafar Dhia Jafar. The latter was "the brains of the project, the most important scientist," according to Dr. Ofek. He was a graduate of Birmingham University, held a Ph.D. in physics from Manchester University, and had worked as a researcher at the Centre for Nuclear Engineering of Imperial College, in London.

But both men rarely left Iraq, where successfully killing either one would be extremely difficult, if not impossible. Yet just as Nasser had hired Germans to build his missiles, Iraq had recruited Egyptians to help develop its nuclear program. The most important among them was Yehia al-Mashad, a nuclear physics prodigy at Alexandria University who became a senior scientist at the Nuclear Research Center at al-Tuwaitha, in Iraq. Mashad traveled frequently between Egypt, Iraq, and France. The Mossad began to track his moves in February 1980 and shadowed him constantly whenever he was in Paris or at the French Institute for Radiological Protection and Nuclear Safety at Fontenay-aux-Roses, near the capital.

In early June, the French prepared a shipment of uranium for the Iraqis to use in their Isis small reactor. Mashad came to France to check the quality. He traveled with two aides who never left his side, making him difficult to reach. The Mossad's plan, then, was to poison Mashad via some common and innocuous item, similar to the way Wadie Haddad had been killed with tainted toothpaste in 1978.

But at the last minute, Mashad decided to cut short his stay in France. He wanted to visit his family in Egypt. That meant the Mossad operatives didn't have enough time to implement their original plan. But Mashad also decided to spend his last night in Paris alone. "He let his two Iraqi assistants go, because the hotel he was in was very expensive," Hamza said. "He was a kind man. He told them, 'Okay, you might want to stay in a more convenient shopping neighborhood and a cheaper hotel that would be more accessible to you. So you can go ahead.'"

With no aides to protect him, Mashad suddenly became a much more vulnerable target.

He returned to his hotel at about six o'clock on the evening of June 13. He showered and changed, had a drink and a sandwich in the lobby, then went back to his room on the ninth floor. Carlos, the commander of Bayonet, and another operative hid in a recess in the corridor, watching the door. The plan had changed so rapidly, they weren't sure what to do. Carlos had a pistol, but the standing orders were that guns could not be used in hotels under any circumstances, since bullets can go through walls and hit innocents. Carlos was adapting on the fly.

The elevator opened at about 9:30. A young woman got out, a

prostitute. She walked by the two Bayonet men but ignored them. She knocked on the door of 9041. Mashad let her in.

Carlos and his partner waited for four hours, until the prostitute finally left at 1:30 A.M. By then Carlos had found an ashtray with a stand near the elevator, a yard tall, with a heavy base, a narrow leg, and a plunger mechanism at its top end for disposing of accumulating cigarette butts. He examined it carefully, weighed it in his hands, felt its heft. He decided it was solid enough to use.

"Take out your blade," Carlos told the other operative, who was armed with a large Leatherman pocketknife. The two men approached Mashad's door and the companion knocked.

"Qui est là?" Mashad said. "Who's there?" He sounded sleepy, relaxed.

"Hotel security," Carlos told him. "It's about your recent guest."

Mashad shuffled across his room and opened the door. Carlos brought the ashtray down hard on his head. Mashad lurched backward and crumpled to the floor. Carlos lunged after him, hit him again, and then once more. Blood formed a spreading stain on the carpet. There was no need for the knife.

The two operatives washed the blood off their arms and rinsed off the ashtray. Carlos removed his bloodstained shirt, crumpled it up, and shoved it into his pocket. As they left, they made sure the DO NOT DISTURB sign dangled on the doorknob. They put the ashtray back where it belonged, took the elevator down to the lobby, and sauntered out of the hotel.

Hotel security found Mashad's body fifteen hours later. Police at first thought he'd been battered in a sex game gone wrong, but they found the prostitute and quickly cleared her. Mashad hadn't been robbed, and he'd had no other visitors. But the prostitute remembered seeing two men in the hallway.

The French figured out pretty quickly that the Mossad had killed Mashad. So did the Iraqis. "I thought we were all targeted," Hamza said. "After that, I would travel only with an Iraqi intelligence officer with me."

Saddam Hussein understood that the targeted killings could devastate morale among the scientists working on his nuclear project.

He handed out luxury cars and cash bonuses to all the senior scientists and paid Mashad's wife compensation of $300,000, an enormous sum at the time in Egypt, and promised her and Mashad's children a lifelong monthly pension.

It did nothing, however, to stop the killings. Three weeks after Mashad was killed, a British-educated Iraqi engineer named Salman Rashid was sent to Geneva for two months of training in the enrichment of uranium by means of electromagnetic isotope separation.

He had a bodyguard who never left his side. A week before he was to return to Iraq, Rashid became violently ill. Doctors in Geneva suspected a virus. Six days later, on September 14, Rashid died in agony. An autopsy showed that there had been no virus: The Mossad had poisoned him, though how, and with what toxin, no one could say for certain.

Two weeks later, another senior Iraqi engineer, Abd al-Rahman Rasoul, a civil engineer who handled the construction of the various buildings for the nuclear project, took part in a conference sponsored by the French Atomic Energy Commission. Immediately after the cocktail party and official reception that opened the conference, he came down with what seemed to be food poisoning. He died five days later in a Paris hospital.

In early August, many of the French participants in the Iraqi project received a letter containing a blunt warning that they would be in danger if they did not leave immediately. Saddam Hussein was furious, and a few days later he delivered a particularly angry speech against Israel, not mentioning the attacks against the scientists but threatening to "reduce Tel Aviv to rubble with bombs."

Saddam's scientists began to panic. "Nobody would want to travel," Hamza said, "so we were given bonuses if we traveled." They also received training in personal security and self-defense. "A Mukhabarat [intelligence] man would tell us how to eat, not to accept an invitation after dark, always be accompanied. We were trained to carry with us our toothpaste, our toothbrushes, our shaving equipment, either in a small bag or in our pocket."

A few French contractors resigned in fear, and the Iraqi nuclear project was slowed down slightly. But Saddam had put the resources of an autocratic nation into building a bomb, and he could spare a technician or three in the process. All of the scientists, both the dead and the frightened, were quickly replaced. France sent twelve kilograms of enriched uranium and filled a second order shortly afterward.

At best, Israel had bought some time before Saddam could complete the construction of the reactors and begin to activate them: perhaps eighteen months, perhaps two years. But Iraq still expected—and Israel still feared—that Saddam would have fully operational nuclear weapons and the means to deliver them by the end of the decade.

Yitzhak Hofi, the Mossad director, knew that intelligence, targeted killings, and sabotage operations could do only so much. "I give up," he told Begin in October 1980. "We will not be able to stop it. The only way still open is bombing from the air."

The only way left, in other words, was an outright act of war.


THERE WAS DISAGREEMENT AT the top in Israel. Some of the country's leading intelligence officials warned that bombing the Iraqi reactor would have dire international consequences, that it would take years before the reactor would produce enough fuel for a bomb, and that destroying it would push Saddam to take an alternate, more secretive approach, about which it would be far more difficult to gather information. There was so much tension that at one stage Begin stopped inviting the head of his own Atomic Energy Commission, Uzi Eilam, because he opposed the attack. One of Eilam's staffers, Professor Uzi Even, who feared that destroying the reactor would only lead to the transfer of the Iraqi nuclear project to secret installations, which Israel would not be able to keep under surveillance, leaked the plan for the anticipated attack to the head of the opposition, Shimon Peres. He, in turn, wrote a memo in his own handwriting to Begin, warning that if Israel went through with the attack, it would be isolated internationally, "like a bramble in the wilderness," using the prophet Jeremiah's metaphor for how alone Israel would be if God abandoned it.

But Prime Minister Begin, Ariel Sharon, who had recently been promoted to minister of defense, and IDF chief of staff Rafael Eitan rejected every argument against the mission. They subscribed to the opinion of Admoni and other top intelligence officials that the reactor should be attacked as soon as possible, before it became "hot," in order to avoid the horrific humanitarian disaster that would take place in the event of a nuclear radiation leak. At the New Era forum, the physicist and officer Dr. Ofek repeatedly insisted that in order to ensure the total destruction of the reactor, one objective had to be achieved: "Enough explosives to wreck the internal pool in which the uranium rods were to be immersed."

On June 7, at four o'clock in the afternoon, eight F-16 planes took off from the Etzion base, in Israeli-occupied Sinai, to attack the Osirak reactor. They were escorted by six F-15s to provide cover, and another sixty aircraft were deployed to support the operation—some of which circled in the air while others remained at the ready on the ground. They included Boeings adapted for midair refueling and for airborne command and control, Hawkeye planes to provide intelligence, and helicopters in case a plane went down and a rescue operation was necessary. The F-15s could handle any Iraqi MiG that might challenge the Israeli planes, and they also carried advanced electronic warfare systems to jam the radar of antiaircraft missile batteries on the ground.

The route was six hundred miles long, crossing northern Saudi Arabia and the south of Jordan. The pilots flew very low, less than three hundred feet above the ground, in order to avoid Jordanian, Saudi, and Iraqi radar.

The planes reached the target toward sundown, at about 5:30 P.M. The eight F-16s climbed to an altitude of one thousand feet, executed a roll maneuver, and released their bombs at an angle of thirty-five degrees. One after the other, they dropped two one-ton bombs each on the concrete dome of the reactor. Half of the bombs were set to explode on contact, and the other half would go off only after they had burrowed deep into the structure. Seven of the eight pilots hit the target, and twelve of the sixteen bombs penetrated the dome. Ten Iraqi soldiers and one French technician were killed as well.

The Iraqis were taken completely by surprise. Not one missile was fired at the attacking planes, and only sporadic, harmless antiaircraft fire was aimed at them on their way back. All the planes made it safely home to base. To this day, they bear an image of the reactor on their nose, along with the circles that represent planes downed in combat.

By midnight, the video footage taken by the airborne cameras had been analyzed, documenting the huge damage done to the reactor. At 3 A.M., Unit 8200's Apocalypse Team intercepted a phone call made by one of the engineers describing an inspection of the bombed-out site in darkness. The engineer had looked for the pool, the critical part at the heart of the structure, but, with the help of his flashlight, he found only "chunks of blasted concrete covered by the water"— the sections of the dome that had collapsed inward. In the "immediate intelligence survey" that was distributed to the top government officials and heads of the intelligence community, AMAN confirmed that the reactor pool had been irreparably damaged and that "the reactor has been totally destroyed."

Before the attack, the intelligence community had recommended that Israel not claim responsibility. They believed that without an embarrassing public humiliation, Saddam would not feel pressure to stage a counterattack on Israel. He would have room to maneuver.

In the end, however, Begin decided otherwise. The bombing raid had been perfectly executed, Iraq's reactor left in smoldering ruins, and Saddam's nuclear ambitions perhaps permanently stalled. Begin wanted to acknowledge those facts, even to boast of them. He had a keen sense of the mood of the Israeli public. In a speech in the Knesset, he equated Saddam with Hitler, and the perils of a nuclear Iraq with the Nazis' Final Solution. "What could we have done against such a terrible danger?" he asked.

"This country and its people would have been annihilated. Another Holocaust would have happened in the history of the Jewish people."

Saddam delivered a speech of his own in private to the leadership of the Baath Party. "It is painful," he admitted with a sigh, referring to the bombing, "because this is a dear fruit that we labored very hard to harvest, one of the fruits of the revolution and one for which we have exerted tremendous efforts politically, scientifically, economically for a long period of time."

But he quickly moved into his customary pugnacious tone, cursing the "Zionist entity" and Menachem Begin.

Saddam then continued: "Begin and others have to realize that what they call preemptive strikes, which aim to prevent the advancement and rise of the Arab nation, and prevent it from using science and technology, will not prevent the Arab nation from moving toward its goals, and this method of preemptive strikes will not provide the Jews with the security of which he is speaking."

Three weeks later, Begin celebrated again, this time with a victory in the general election.

The Mossad and the IDF were also triumphant over the success of the operation and what they saw as the destruction of the Iraqi nuclear project. They relegated Iraq to the bottom of the list of intelligence priorities.

BUT SADDAM'S REACTION TO the bombing of the reactor in Baghdad was precisely the opposite of what Israeli intelligence had expected.

"Saddam under pressure . . . becomes more aggressive and becomes more determined," said Dr. Hamza. "So the $400 million project became a $10 billion project and the four hundred scientists became seven thousand."

Saddam issued orders for a major effort to be invested in any and all scientific paths that could lead him in the shortest possible time to the acquisition of an atomic bomb, and the means for delivering it to a target. Very quickly, he found Western companies that were ready to supply him—in exchange for vast sums of money—equipment and raw materials that, while ostensibly for civilian purposes, could also be applied to military ends for the development of nuclear, biological, or chemical weapons of mass destruction.

Israel uncovered only small traces of these efforts. One plan it did uncover was the Condor project, a joint Iraqi, Egyptian, and Argentinean effort to develop missiles of various types. A large amount of information about the project was obtained and conveyed to Israel by Mossad agents in the German companies involved in the project and in Argentina's scientific world, as well as by Jonathan Pollard, the spy working for Israel deep inside an American intelligence agency. The Mossad began torching the offices of the European companies involved, and systematically terrorizing the scientists, in a manner similar to the way the German rocket scientists in Egypt had been intimidated in the 1960s. They received anonymous phone calls telling them, "If you don't desist immediately, we'll kill you and your family."

The Mossad drew up plans to eliminate some of the scientists as well, but it turned out that the pressure, the arson, and the break-ins, as well as the Mossad's lethal reputation, obviated the need for targeted killings. The scientists departed, and Argentina and Egypt thinned out their financial participation.

In his distress, Saddam turned to a Canadian rocket scientist, formerly employed by NASA, the United States Army, and Israel, named Gerald Bull, asking him to develop missiles and a super-cannon, inspired by Jules Verne's science fiction novel *From the Earth to the Moon,* that could send huge payloads enormous distances—as far as Tehran (430 miles from Baghdad) and Tel Aviv (570 miles from Baghdad). Bull assured his clients that his super-cannon would not only have an immensely long range but would also be a more accurate and effective way to fire biological and chemical agents, because the warheads would heat up less than the Scud missiles Iraq possessed.

In 1989, Bull and the Iraqis erected the cannon at Jabal Hamrayn, 125 miles north of Baghdad. Three test firings were conducted.

To his great misfortune, Bull never took seriously the threatening anonymous phone calls and letters he had received, which warned him that if he did not immediately terminate his relationship with Saddam, "we will have to take harsh action against you, your companies, and the people involved with you."

On March 22, 1990, a Bayonet squad lay in wait for him at his home, a short drive away from his office in Brussels. Two men were hiding just behind the stairwell door. From their vantage point, they could see Bull walking toward his apartment, fumbling in his pockets for his keys. As soon as he passed and his back was to them, they leapt out from behind the door with their silenced Makarov pistols drawn. One of them fired two bullets into Bull's head and three into his back, while the other remained behind him, securing the area. Bull was dead before he hit the floor. The assassin whipped out a camera and took several pictures of the scientist's shattered head. One was a close-up, and another showed Bull lying on his belly in a huge pool of blood.

The pictures were sent that day to the staff at Space Research Corporation, Bull's company. "If you go to work tomorrow," they wrote in an accompanying note, "you'll end up like this." No one turned up at the office the next day, and the company was soon terminated. The Mossad made sure that all of Bull's straw companies got the message as well.

The project was dead in the water. On April 2, after Saddam learned from his intelligence services that Gerald Bull had been killed, he addressed his nation and vowed to "make the fire eat up half of Israel."

Indeed, the death of Bull only slowed down Saddam's effort to obtain long-range delivery tools and did not impede his nuclear project in any way. It turned out that the intelligence agencies of Israel and other Western nations were utterly ignorant of the major part of Saddam's military R&D efforts.

"This huge and very sophisticated network operated right under everyone's noses," said Brigadier General Shimon Shapira, of AMAN's research division. "This was without a doubt one of the biggest failures in the history of Israeli intelligence."

Israel, said Shapira, "had more luck than sense." Saddam Hussein made a mistake by invading Kuwait in August 1990, assuming that the United States and the rest of the world would sit by, arms folded, in the face of his aggression. He was wrong. He brought upon himself a broad international coalition, one that included some Arab states, that kicked him out of Kuwait and forced him to accept stringent international inspection.

UN inspectors then found what the Mossad had missed completely: By the time Operation Desert Storm to liberate Kuwait was launched, in January 1991, Saddam was only a few years away from full nuclear, chemical, and biological weapons capability, as well as the ability to manufacture missiles and warheads that could deliver those weapons to Israel.

Even after the end of the war, when President Bush decided not to invade Iraq and to leave Saddam in place, IDF chief of staff Barak still believed that Saddam remained a clear and present danger to Israel. Saddam would certainly try again to develop weapons of mass destruction, and there was no possibility of entering into any sort of negotiation with him.

On January 20, 1992, Barak ordered "the formation of a team to examine the possibility of striking at the target [Saddam]." Two months later, on March 12, the team, headed by Amiram Levin, reported to the chief of staff on the plan's progress. Barak told the team, "The target is among the most important that has ever faced us in any pinpoint operation," and he ordered that preparations be made for execution of the plan in July of that year.

Barak spoke to both Prime Minister Shamir and to Rabin, who replaced him in 1992, and tried to persuade them that the assassination weapon should be used for the first time against the leader of a sovereign state.

"In retrospect," Barak said years later, "just imagine how we could have saved the world an entire decade with this terrible man. History would have looked different."

The two premiers both gave him the go-ahead to plan the hit. Many ideas were put forward: crashing an Israeli aircraft or even a satellite somewhere in Iraq, preferably in Baghdad, waiting for Saddam to come and inspect the wreckage, and then blowing it up with him and his entourage; setting up a straw company in Europe that would sell Saddam a new and modern television studio from which to broadcast his speeches to the nation, fitting it with equipment that would broadcast to Israel, and blowing it up while his face was on the screen; switching a monument to one of his revolutionary comrades with a booby-trapped substitute and detonating it as Saddam stood with his head bowed before it at a memorial ceremony—and many other schemes for disposing of the Iraqi dictator.

In the end, it was decided to strike at Saddam at the only place outside of prohibitively well-guarded Baghdad where everyone could be sure that he himself, and not one of his doubles, would be: his family's plot in the cemetery at Tikrit, for the funeral of someone very close to him. That someone would be his uncle, Khairallah Tulfah, the man who had raised him, who was very ill.

The Israelis closely followed the treatment Tulfah was receiving in Jordan and waited for news of his death. But he kept clinging to life, so an alternative plan was decided upon. Instead of Tulfah, the Mossad would eliminate Barzan al-Tikriti, the Iraqi ambassador to the United Nations.

Sayeret Matkal commandos would be flown to Tikrit in helicopters that would land some distance away and then proceed to the cemetery in jeeps that looked exactly like the ones the Iraqi army used but were in fact equipped with a special system that turned the roof of the car upside down and pulled out guided missiles. When Saddam came to attend the funeral, they would launch the missiles and kill him.

If this plan succeeded, many of those involved believed, chief of staff Ehud Barak would go into politics and become a candidate with a good chance of becoming prime minister. This would be only natural for a man who was marked for greatness from the time he was a young lieutenant.

At the huge Tze'elim training camp, in Israel's Negev Desert, Sayeret Matkal built a model of the Hussein family's cemetery and practiced the operation. When they were ready, on November 5, 1992, the IDF's top brass came to watch a dress rehearsal. The hit team with the missiles took up positions, with members of the unit's intelligence and administrative staffs playing Saddam and his entourage.

But because of serious planning flaws and weariness from the long training schedule, the men with the missiles mistook what was supposed to be a dry run, with the soldier posing as Saddam waving at the invisible crowds, for the wet run, in which the live soldier would be replaced by a mannequin. Things were so disorganized that the same code words, "Send a cab," were used for both the dry and wet runs.

The commander of the force, believing that this was the dry run, gave the order: "Send a cab." But the commander of the firing jeeps thought that the wet run had begun. "Launch missile one," he ordered, and one of his men pushed the button and began guiding the missile toward the target. When approaching it, he noticed that something was wrong, and according to some witnesses he yelled, "What's this? I don't understand why the dolls are moving."

But it was too late. The missile landed right in the middle of the entourage. Seconds later, the second missile hit the ground a few yards away, but it did almost no damage, because all of the men in the target area were already lying on the ground, dead or wounded. The commander realized that something had gone terribly wrong. "Cease fire!" he yelled. "Cease fire! I repeat: Cease fire!"

Five soldiers were killed, and all the others in the target area were wounded.

Embarrassingly, the man playing Saddam was among the men who were only wounded. The incident became the cause of a fierce political storm and an ugly quarrel between Barak and some other generals over who was responsible.

The accident at Tze'elim put an end to the plan to assassinate Saddam Hussein. Later, it turned out that, contrary to Barak's expectations, Saddam had not, in fact, resumed his attempts to obtain nuclear weapons after Operation Desert Storm.

In any case, Israel by now was facing new enemies, much more dangerous ones.

# GREEN STORM RISING

ON MARCH 13, 1978, a luxury executive jet took off on a secret flight from Tehran, carrying two worried passengers: Uri Lubrani, Israel's ambassador to Iran, and Reuven Merhav, the Mossad station chief in Iran. They were on their way to meet His Imperial Majesty Mohammad Reza Cyrus Pahlavi Shah, who was at his vacation residence on the island of Kish, ten miles off the Iranian shore in the Persian Gulf.

The shah was Iran's omnipotent ruler, a ruthless, megalomaniacal despot who wanted to transform his country rapidly into a land "more developed than France." He invested Iran's huge oil revenues in the establishment of a powerful army, the construction of up-to-date infrastructure, and a modern economy. He imposed an accelerated process of Westernization on his subjects, something that many of them, from the merchants in the Great Bazaar of Tehran to the Muslim clerics, found offensive and detrimental. But their objections didn't faze the shah, and he ordered the army and his brutal secret service, SAVAK, to suppress any opposition with an iron fist.

The shah's foreign policy was based on close political, military, and civil links with the United States. He also formed an intimate intelligence alliance with Israel. This led to Iran acquiring a great deal of military weaponry and equipment from the Jewish state, in exchange for both cash and oil. He also allowed the Israelis to stage a number of important operations against Arab states from Iranian soil.

But Lubrani and Merhav had good reason to be perturbed. While Iran's links with the United States and Israel were as strong as they'd ever been, the shah's rule over his country was beginning to crumble. The demonstrations against him were getting more intense by the day, and protest movements from all sides—merchants, Communists, right-wingers, Islamists—were gaining power. The White House, which had hitherto turned a blind eye to the shah's human rights violations, was now run by liberal president Jimmy Carter and began to display increasing discomfort at the use of force against protesters, which led to the shah's being reluctant to deploy his army against them.

Iran's royal family and leadership did not put any checks on their lavish lifestyle, however. Soon after landing on the island of Kish, Lubrani and Merhav were witness to this. The island was the shah's favorite residence, the location of his headquarters during parts of the year. "It was the playground for all the top people," says Merhav. "Evidence of the astonishing corruption was everywhere. We were shocked by the hedonistic atmosphere, the extravagance."

The two Israelis had come to Kish to meet the shah and his close advisers, in order to evaluate the strength of the regime in the face of the mounting opposition. Fueling their concern was the fact that extremist Shiite elements, the most important component of the opposition, had linked up with their brethren in Lebanon and had begun training in camps set up for them by Yasser Arafat. "That combination," said Merhav, "between what was then perceived as the main terrorist force operating against us—Arafat's PLO in Lebanon—and the extremist Shiites, seemed to us to have significant potential dangers."

The most prominent leader of the religious opposition was Ruhollah Khomeini, who bore the hereditary title *sayyid,* meaning "lord," used only by descendants of the Prophet Muhammad, and had earned the highest Shiite clerical rank, Grand Ayatollah. As a young man in his family's hometown of Khomein, the future revolutionary was a well-known preacher, acutely expert in the intricacies of the faith, but lacking in charismatic oratory. In 1962, however, at age sixty, Khomeini underwent a dramatic change: After a period of seclusion, he emerged from his bedchamber convinced that he had been visited by the Archangel Gabriel, God's special messenger, who had told him that Allah had destined him for great things.

To accomplish his mission, Khomeini transformed. He abandoned his hitherto complex style and began to speak simply, never using more than two thousand words, and repeating certain phrases over and over again until they took on the sound of magical incantations. "Islam is the solution" was one of his favorites. He began to portray the world as a clash between good and evil. The evil must be uprooted and destroyed, a duty that had to be performed by the good, who were both judges and executioners. His followers among the poor found this persuasive.

Later on, Khomeini reshaped Shiite Islam to conform with the leadership role he had designed for himself. He shook off the basic separation of civil and religious authority that had always prevailed in the Muslim empires, and declared that there was no longer a need for a king advised by religious sages. The government should be in the hands of the sages themselves. All of the monarchies and the other regimes in the Muslim world that were not manifestly religious—the presidents of Egypt and Syria, the king of Saudi Arabia, and the shah of Iran—were illegitimate and had to be replaced. "Islam is the only solution," he decreed.

Khomeini's attitude on the issue of martyrdom was also meant to prepare the ground for his assumption of power. He explained to his supporters that the highest sanction in the hands of the state was the power to execute its citizens. Take this sanction away, by changing death to a desired reward, and the state becomes powerless. "Please kill us," Khomeini proclaimed and wrote. "For we, too, are going to kill you!" He would later instruct the bereaved families of martyrs and their neighbors to hold joyous celebrations to mark the deaths of their sons in Iran's holy war.

Khomeini's next step was to shatter the most important traditional custom of Shiite theology. He allowed the believers—even encouraged them—to call him "imam," a term in the Shiite tradition that is largely similar in meaning to the Judeo-Christian concept of the Messiah, whose advent heralded the End of Days.

In 1963, a short time after formulating his new doctrine, Khomeini launched an open campaign against the shah from Qom, Iran's holiest city. The shah couldn't risk killing the ayatollah, so instead he was exiled. Khomeini found refuge in Turkey, Iraq, and finally France.

The lessons he taught there attracted more and more students. During the 1970s, he became, from afar, the most powerful of the shah's opponents. By the time Lubrani and Merhav came to Kish, Khomeini had already flooded Iran with an estimated 600,000 cassette tapes of his sermons. In the mosques and the markets, in rural regions and on the mountains surrounding Tehran, in the bazaars and even, very quietly, in government offices, many millions were listening to the incendiary preaching of the fanatical, stern-faced cleric.

They heard him say things like "the despised shah, that Jewish spy, the American snake, whose head must be crushed with a stone," or "The shah says that he is giving the people freedom. Listen to me, you puffed-up toad! Who are you, to grant liberty? It is Allah who grants liberty. It is the law that grants liberty, it is Islam that grants liberty, it is the constitution that grants liberty. What do you mean when you say you have granted us liberty? What gives you the ability to grant anything at all? Who do you think you are?"

The distribution of the Khomeini cassettes was observed, of course, by the watchful eyes of the SAVAK, the shah's secret service. The organization's leaders asked the shah for permission to raid the ayatollah's distribution centers. But the request was refused, because of President Carter's pressure to refrain from violating civil rights and the weakness and confusion that the shah was suffering from due to the cancer treatment he was undergoing. Lubrani and Merhav were not aware of the shah's illness, which was a well-kept secret.


ONLY LUBRANI WAS GRANTED an audience. The shah welcomed him warmly, but the ambassador soon realized that the conversation would go nowhere. Lubrani left the magnificent, gilt-decorated chamber in a somber mood. "The shah is detached from reality, living in a world of his own, almost delusional," he told Merhav. "He is surrounded by sycophants who don't tell him the truth about the situation in the country." Merhav's meetings with the heads of Iranian intelligence led him to the same conclusions.

Soon after the visit, the two transmitted a warning to the Israeli security establishment: The rule of the shah was crumbling. The rare coalition established between secular and religious opponents of his regime, along with the flagrant corruption and the monarch's obliviousness to the outside world, were leading to the imminent demise of the Pahlavi dynasty.

But the warnings fell on deaf ears. In the Foreign Ministry and the Mossad—and in the CIA, too—officials were convinced that Merhav and Lubrani were wrong, that the shah's rule was firm, and that Iran would remain an ally of Israel and the United States forever.

It was a grave mistake. From his latest headquarters in Paris, Khomeini directed the mass protests of thousands, which soon became tens and then hundreds of thousands, in cities throughout Iran.

On January 16, the shah, ailing and debilitated, decided that without American backing, he had best pack up and leave. He took a box with a few clods of Iranian soil and, along with his wife and a handful of aides, he flew to Egypt.

The following day, the secular prime minister the shah had appointed to rule the country, Shapour Bakhtiar, turned to the new head of the Mossad station in Tehran, Eliezer Tsafrir, with a straightforward request: Would the Mossad please kill Khomeini in the Parisian suburb where he was living? The head of the agency, Yitzhak Hofi, called an urgent meeting of his senior staff at headquarters, on Tel Aviv's King Saul Boulevard.

The benefits for Israel were obvious: The SAVAK would owe a deep debt of gratitude to the Israelis. Furthermore, it was possible that a hit would divert the course of history and prevent Khomeini, who had made his views on Israel and the Jews quite clear, from seizing power in Iran. The attendees of the meeting discussed several points: Was the plan operationally feasible? Did the ayatollah actually represent such a grave danger? If so, would Israel be prepared to take upon itself the risks of eliminating a top clerical figure, and to do so on French soil?

A representative of Caesarea chief Mike Harari said that from an operational point of view it was not a complicated matter, but obviously, as in all such operations, especially ones that had to be executed with such limited lead time, things could go wrong.

One divisional head who had served in Iran said, "Let Khomeini go back to Iran. He won't last. The military and SAVAK will handle him and his people protesting in the streets of the cities. He represents Iran's past, not its future."

Director Hofi made it clear that he was inclined "to turn the request down for reasons of principle," because he was "opposed to the use of assassinations against political leaders."

Yossi Alpher, the senior research analyst dealing with Iran, told the meeting, "We do not have sufficient information about Khomeini's positions or about his chances of realizing them, and therefore I cannot accurately evaluate whether the risk is justified." Hofi accepted Alpher's opinion and ruled that Tsafrir should give Bakhtiar a negative reply.

This episode was another demonstration of how the State of Israel—though often willing to use targeted killings as a tool—remains very hesitant when it comes to killing political leaders, even if they have not officially been designated as such.

Looking back, Alpher would say that "as early as a couple of months after that meeting, I realized what he [Khomeini] was all about," and that he was "very sorry" about the decision. If the Mossad had killed Khomeini, according to Alpher, history might have taken a better course.


ON FEBRUARY 1, KHOMEINI landed in Tehran's Mehrabad International Airport, greeted by triumphant rejoicing such as Iran had never before witnessed. By the strength of his taped voice alone, Khomeini crumbled the shah's monarchy. The dream of an Islamic republic became reality. With almost no use of force, Khomeini and his supporters seized control of Iran, a vast country rich in natural resources, with the sixth-largest military force in the world and the largest arsenal in Asia.

"Islam has been dying or dead for 1,400 years," Khomeini said in his first speech as supreme leader. "We have resurrected it with the blood of our youth . . . very soon we will liberate Jerusalem and pray there." As for the government of Shapour Bakhtiar, who had been appointed prime minister by the shah before he left, Khomeini dismissed it with one short, sharp statement: "I will break their teeth."

The United States, the "Great Satan," as Khomeini thundered, and Israel, "the Little Satan," saw the ayatollah's rise as a passing episode. After all, American and British intelligence services had restored the shah to power once before, after left-wing rebels deposed him in 1953. But Khomeini's rise was the culmination of years of foment, girded by enormous popular support and protected by seasoned, sophisticated lieutenants who identified and crushed all attempts at counterrevolution.

In November, a mob of angry student supporters of Khomeini broke into the U.S. embassy in Tehran, occupied it, and took the diplomats and other workers there hostage. They also seized a vast trove of American intelligence material. The ensuing crisis and the abject failure of a rescue attempt (Operation Eagle Claw) humiliated the United States and contributed to Carter's failure to win reelection. "We felt helpless in the face of this new threat," said Robert Gates, at the time a senior official at the Office of Strategic Research of the CIA (and later CIA chief and secretary of defense).

It was clear to both Washington and Jerusalem that what was once their closest ally in the Middle East was now their bitterest enemy.

It also soon became clear that Khomeini's vision was not restricted to the Islamic republic that he declared in Iran. Rather than clinging tenuously to power, the ayatollah was determined to spread his Islamic revolution throughout the Middle East.

He intended to begin with Lebanon.


ONE OF KHOMEINI'S CLOSEST allies during his years in exile, a Shiite cleric named Ali Akbar Mohtashamipur, was given the mission of spreading the revolution. He first met Khomeini when studying in Najaf, a city holy to Shiites in Iraq, where the ayatollah had found refuge after being expelled by the shah. He accompanied him throughout his years of exile both there and in France. In 1973, Khomeini had sent him, together with a group of other loyal associates, to the Middle East to establish links with Muslim liberation movements in the region. It was Mohtashamipur who wove the alliance with the PLO that led to the acceptance of Khomeini's men into the training bases of Force 17.

At the training bases, PLO experts taught young men the arts of sabotage, intelligence operations, and terror tactics. For Arafat, having Khomeini's men train at his bases was a way to acquire support for the Palestinian cause and to make himself into an international figure. But for Khomeini and Mohtashamipur, it was part of a long, focused strategy: to eventually extend the Islamic revolution they were fomenting in Iran to Lebanon, a small country in the heart of the Middle East, with a large population of impoverished Shiites ripe for incitement. Khomeini wanted to stake out "a forward strategic position that brought us close to Jerusalem"—Lebanon's border with Israel. By 1979, hundreds of Shiites were being trained as a guerrilla army.

When Khomeini returned to Iran and seized power, Mohtashamipur took a central role in the formation of the Islamic Revolutionary Guard Corps, the force that preserved Khomeini's rule inside the country.

Before the Iranian Revolution, the ideal of an Islamic state was an abstract desire, remote from reality. But now, men who had spent their lives in the extremist Muslim colleges of Iran and training camps in Lebanon had become the lords of the land.

Almost three years after the fall of the shah, with the revolution firmly established in Tehran, Khomeini named Mohtashamipur Iran's ambassador to Syria. That post came with two roles. Overtly, he was an emissary of his country's foreign ministry, like all other ambassadors. Covertly, he was also a senior member of the Revolutionary Guards, receiving direct orders from Khomeini and commanding a huge number of personnel and a budget of millions of dollars per month. That second, secret role was by far the more important of the two.

At the time, though, much of Lebanon was controlled by the Syrian military. In order for his revolutionary forces to operate effectively, then, Khomeini needed to broker a deal with Syrian president Hafez al-Assad. That was Mohtashamipur's job: finessing the diplomacy that would allow a military alliance.

Despite their common enemy—Israel—Assad initially was wary of Mohtashamipur's overtures. The Iranian ambassador was imbued with an unbridled revolutionary zeal. Assad, a secular Arab, feared that the Islamist rage Mohtashamipur was inciting would ultimately prove uncontrollable and be turned against his own regime. The potential repercussions seemed to outweigh any immediate benefit.

But after Israel invaded Lebanon in June 1982, Assad recalculated.

The war was a catastrophe not only for Israel but also for Assad. In the confrontation with Israel, the Syrian forces were dealt a knockout blow. The most devastating damage was sustained by the Syrian air force, a source of pride for Assad, who had commanded it in the past and had continued nurturing it. A total of eighty-two Syrian warplanes were destroyed in forty-six hours, while Israel lost just one plane.

Assad concluded from the Israeli invasion that Syria would have no chance against Israel on the traditional battlefield and that it would have to try to inflict damage indirectly. Israel played right into his hands by leaving its forces inside Lebanon. Israel's intent was to ensure quiet for its communities in the north, but in so doing it merely created another front for itself, exposed and vulnerable to guerrilla attacks.

"Assad, Sr."—that is, Hafez, the father of Bashar, who would succeed him—"was, to my great regret, a clever man," says Meir Dagan, who commanded the Israeli forces in Lebanon at the time. "He built up an apparatus for squeezing blood out of Israel without paying a penny."

That apparatus was the Iranian-backed Shiite militia that Mohtashamipur was so eager to establish. In July 1982, Iran and Syria signed a military alliance that allowed the Revolutionary Guards under Mohtashamipur's command to operate in Lebanon. In the open, they gave civilian assistance to the Shiite population, building social and religious institutions, such as schools and mosques. They provided welfare aid to the poor and other needy folks, like drug and alcohol addicts, and a relatively high-level health system. Iran was supplying the Lebanese Shiite public with everything that the government of Lebanon, dominated by a combined Sunni and Christian majority, had never given them.

In secret, they began to train and arm a guerrilla force that filled the vacuum left by the PLO and, within two decades, would become one of the dominant political and military forces in the Middle East. Sensing the historic importance of the nascent movement, Mohtashamipur gave it a grandiose name.

He called it Hezbollah—the Party of God.

AHMAD JAAFAR QASSIR WAS a sixteen-year-old boy born to a poor Shiite family in the tiny Lebanese village of Deir Qanoun al-Nahr. His parents said that as a child "he was alert and perceptive, characteristics which led him to develop into a self-starting and independent youth." As early as four years old, he would run past his father to a patch of farmland in order to pick some vegetables and return home before his father had barely set out on the chore. The local mosque soon became his home away from home as Ahmad frequently went there to pray and read the Koran.

He was one of the Shiites swept up in the fervor of Hezbollah, and in the autumn of 1982 he was recruited into a covert military division known as Islamic Jihad. Ahmad secretly carried out several military operations against the Israeli enemy. He also used his resourcefulness to move armaments from Beirut to "wherever they were necessary to confront the enemy [Israeli] troops."

On the morning of November 11, just before seven o'clock, he drove a white Peugeot packed with explosives toward a seven-story building the IDF used as a regional military and government headquarters in the southern city of Tyre. When he got closer, Qassir stepped hard on the accelerator and aimed for the base of the building.

Then he blew himself up.

The blast destroyed the building and killed seventy-six Israeli soldiers, border police, and Shin Bet operatives, as well as twenty-seven Lebanese: workers, civilians requiring various permits from the army, and prisoners. It was the first Islamist suicide terrorist attack outside of Iran, and it killed more Israelis than any other such attack before or since.

For years, Hezbollah kept its involvement and the identities of those involved a secret. Only later did the militia build a memorial monument to Qassir in his village, publish a letter of appreciation that Supreme Leader Khomeini had written to the family, and declare the date of his death the annual Martyrs' Day.

This secrecy was convenient for Israel's defense establishment, which quickly tried to cover up its own enormous negligence in allowing the suicide attack to happen. The head of the Shin Bet on the northern front then was Yossi Ginossar, whose unit was responsible for collecting information and preventing attacks like Qassir's suicide bombing. Ginossar, together with some of his subordinates and senior officers of the IDF, misled the inquiry into the disaster, steering it away from the truth until it came up with the conclusion that the blast had been caused by "a technical fault in the gas canisters in the kitchen" and not a daring operation by the new militant Shiite organization.

But while Ginossar might have been grossly self-serving in this instance, on a larger scale, Israeli intelligence was indeed unaware of the new militant force rising from the smoking ruins of Lebanon. The first terrorist attacks carried out by Hezbollah—gunfire attacks and roadside bombs aimed at military vehicles—were dismissed by AMAN and Shin Bet as "no more than a tactical nuisance to IDF troops."

"We began to grasp everything only after a time," said Yekutiel (Kuti) Mor, a senior AMAN officer and later the military secretary to Defense Minister Rabin. "We missed the process. Instead of hooking up with the Shiites, we kept up the link with the Christians, and we made the majority of Lebanese our enemies." Even worse, no one at the time recognized the connection between the Iranians and Lebanon's Shiites—that the balance of power was being tipped by Khomeini's revolutionaries, allied with Assad. "For a long time," said David Barkai, of Unit 504, "we never realized that the significant activity was coming out of the office of Mohtashamipur in Damascus."

Likewise, Israel's formidable intelligence apparatus was unaware of the shadow army forming around it, made up of both new recruits and seasoned guerrillas such as Imad Mughniyeh. Born in 1962 to devout Shiites, Mughniyeh grew up in the poor and crowded neighborhoods south of Beirut. "His father was a worker at a candy factory in Beirut," recounted Israel's spy Amin al-Hajj (Rummenigge), himself a Shiite. "We were in touch when we were kids. He was very naughty. Later on, I heard he'd dropped out of school and joined a training camp of Force 17, and the connection between us was broken."

In mid-1978, Mughniyeh became a member of Force 17, Yasser Arafat's guards and the Fatah's elite force. Ali Salameh took Mughniyeh under his wing until he was killed by the Mossad in 1979. Mughniyeh wanted to belong to something larger than a local gang in south Beirut, and he wanted action. Salameh and his successors saw in him an able and intelligent person, charismatic and uninhibited. Although they were Palestinian Sunnis and Mughniyeh was a Lebanese Shiite, the interests of both sides intersected. At the time, Khomeini's followers—poor, exiled Iranians and their Lebanese allies—were grateful to the PLO for their hospitality and support.

Mughniyeh was acting under the auspices of Force 17, but he also acquired a reputation as the boss of a gang of thugs enforcing Islamic laws and modest conduct in the streets of Beirut, which was then perceived as a bastion of liberal European customs in the heart of the Middle East. Around this time, Israeli intelligence began receiving reports of "an extremist, uninhibited psychopath" who was kneecapping hookers and drug dealers in Beirut.

Three years later, when the PLO evacuated Beirut, Mughniyeh and his brothers, Fouad and Jihad, decided to remain in Lebanon and join up with what they rightly saw as the next rising force, Hezbollah. Mughniyeh immediately became one of the organization's most important operatives. For half a year, he headed the detail that guarded Sheikh Mohammad Hussein Fadlallah, the supreme Shiite authority in Lebanon, and "Hezbollah's spiritual compass." He also represented the sheikh at meetings in Mohtashamipur's office in Damascus, where senior Iranian officials and Syrian intelligence personnel plotted a strategy for Lebanon. The south was occupied by Israel, and some of the rest by the Multinational Force—American, French, and Italian soldiers who had been deployed there to try to bring an end to the horrendous civil war ravaging the country.

Both the Syrians and the Iranians wanted the occupiers driven

out, but neither could afford—or win—a direct military confrontation. In those meetings, they agreed on a stealth campaign of sabotage and terror.

Mughniyeh was put in charge of organizing it. He, along with
Mohtashamipur, created Islamic Jihad, which recruited Qassir, the
boy who blew up the IDF headquarters in Tyre. It was a devastating
inaugural strike, and it was only the beginning. Sheikh Fadlallah
hinted at what was coming in an article published in a collection of
religious essays in February 1983. "We believe that the future has
surprises in store," he wrote. "Jihad is bitter and harsh; it will well up
from inside, by virtue of effort, patience, and sacrifice, and the spirit
of willingness to sacrifice oneself."

By "sacrifice oneself," Fadlallah was referring to the religious
sanction given by Khomeini to his young soldiers, some no more than
children, who'd been brainwashed into marching forward into certain death through minefields laid by invading Iraqis. Fadlallah took
it a step further, granting approval for *intentional* suicide in the service of jihad. Hezbollah began carrying out suicide operations in
Lebanon, and before long Mughniyeh and Hezbollah had perfected
the method, turning it into something of an art.

On April 18, 1983, one of Mughniyeh's men drove a van through
the front door of the American embassy in Beirut, detonating the ton
of explosives stuffed inside. The entire front of the building was demolished, and sixty-three people were killed, including almost all of
the members of the CIA station in Lebanon, as well as the agency's
senior Middle East expert, Robert Ames.

Then, on October 23, suicide bombers drove trucks packed with
huge quantities of explosives into two facilities of the Multinational
Force in Beirut and detonated them. At the U.S. Marine barracks,
241 peacekeepers were killed, and at the French paratroopers' base
there were 58 fatalities. Mughniyeh sat atop a high-rise building
nearby and watched the proceedings through a telescope. Concrete
fragments and body parts fell on the Shin Bet HQ in Beirut, about a
mile away from the burning Marines facility.

On November 4, 1983, Nakad Sarbukh, an Israeli border policeman who was guarding an army base in Tyre, saw a suspicious pickup
truck speeding in the direction of the base. He opened fire at the ve-

hicle, spraying it with 130 bullets, but failed to stop it. The suicide driver smashed into the base and detonated the five-hundred-kilogram bomb he was carrying. The building housing the Shin Bet's operation on the base crumpled, and surrounding buildings and tents were also hit. Sixty people were killed, and another twenty-nine were wounded.

If Israel had been able to write off the first Tyre attack, almost exactly a year earlier, as a technical mishap, by the time of the second bombing in Tyre this was no longer possible. Thanks to these suicide attacks, which were planned and directed by Mughniyeh, Mohtashamipur got almost exactly what he had wanted: The Multinational Force was disbanded, and Israel withdrew by stages from most of Lebanese territory, until its forces were concentrated in a shallow "Security Zone" in the south of the country.

After the second attack in Tyre, the Israeli intelligence community also began to grasp that it was facing a new type of enemy, one that posed a significant challenge. Top members of the Mossad, Shin Bet, and various branches of the IDF began contemplating the possibility of once more employing targeted killings, this time against a new adversary.

To the Mossad, it was clear that Imad Mughniyeh was the first priority. But they had little intelligence—only a faded photograph—and no idea where to find him. Nevertheless, the Mossad realized that the coordination between Iran and Hezbollah took place in Mohtashamipur's Iranian embassy in Damascus, and not in Beirut.

At the end of 1983, Mossad director Nahum Admoni gave Prime Minister Yitzhak Shamir a Red Page to sign. The attached dossier included a litany of suicide bombings and other terrorist attacks, including the attacks against the American embassy and the U.S. Marines barracks in Beirut.

The name on the Red Page was Ali Akbar Mohtashamipur, the Iranian emissary to Syria. A diplomat, officially. This was not a recommendation made casually, and Shamir signed it only after much hesitation and debate. As a rule, Israel abstained from targeting officials of sovereign states, no matter how hostile they were to the Jewish nation. But something had to be done to stop Hezbollah. Someone—someone important—had to die.

Shamir signed the Red Page.

.   .   .

THE FIRST PROBLEM WAS getting to Mohtashamipur. He spent his
time in either Tehran or Damascus, both capitals of target countries,
where Bayonet did not operate and where Caesarea was not supposed to carry out targeted killings, except in extraordinary cases.
Both capitals were considered particularly difficult arenas, crawling
with suspicious police and members of the countries' secret services.
Moreover, the ambassador was always accompanied by an armed
bodyguard and a driver. Every proposal that involved getting close to
Mohtashamipur or into the areas he frequented—shooting him,
planting a bomb, poisoning—was ruled out, for fear that the operatives would be caught.

One option remained: a booby-trapped package, delivered by
mail. But when the idea was suggested, objections were raised immediately. Israeli intelligence already had extensive experience in
the use of such packages. Twice, the method had worked—in the
liquidation of the head of Egyptian military intelligence in Gaza
and in that of his colleague the Egyptian military attaché in Amman,
Jordan, in 1956. But in all other cases—German scientists in
Egypt, a Nazi war criminal in Damascus, and PLO functionaries
all over the world—the parcels either were discovered in time,
blew up in the wrong person's hands, or caused only injuries and
not death.

"I told them that it was foolish, and even a little infantile," one
Caesarea veteran said, "that they chose a modus operandi that did
not assure the total neutralization of the objective." But the opposition was shut down. A postal explosive was the only option that
wouldn't put an agent in unnecessary danger.

On February 14, 1984, a large parcel arrived at the Iranian embassy in Damascus, ostensibly mailed by a well-known London publishing house owned by Iranians. The embassy receptionist saw that
it was clearly marked PERSONAL FOR HIS EXCELLENCY THE AMBASSA-
DOR and passed it on to Mohtashamipur's second-floor office. The
emissary's secretary unwrapped it and saw a cardboard box containing a magnificent volume in English about Shiite holy places in Iran

and Iraq. She made do with a peek at the binding, then took it into the ambassador's room.

Mohtashamipur opened the book, and there was an explosion. The blast tore off one of his ears, his hand, and most of the fingers on his other hand. Shrapnel destroyed one of his eyes. "If I had opened the book like this," he later told an Iranian TV journalist, holding his hands open near his face and neck, "my head would have been blown off. But I put the book on a table and opened it like this"—here he kept his face and body away from the imaginary book—"and the blast made a hole in the wall, and my hand was there, inside the wall. And if the book had opened like this"—near his face—"my face would have been torn off, from my neck. The marks on the rest of my body are from the fragments of the explosion."

Another mail bomb had gone wrong. "The aim of a negative treatment operation is to kill the object," the Caesarea veteran who had objected to the plot said. "There's no such thing as half dead. If he remains alive, it means we have failed." Israel did not claim responsibility, but the Iranians had no doubt the Mossad was behind the operation.

Even worse, Mohtashamipur was now a symbol for the revolutionary cause, a maimed survivor of Khomeini's holy war. "I was sorry about the regrettable occurrence that world imperialism has caused to happen to you," his friend the ayatollah wrote to him. "I hope that your health will soon return and that you will continue your persistent struggle at the front of Islam and the revolution on behalf of the wretched of the world."

Moreover, disabling the ambassador had absolutely no effect on Hezbollah's operations, and killing him probably wouldn't have done much more. The attempt on his life had come too late: The ragtag army of impoverished Shiites that Mohtashamipur had begun organizing a decade earlier was by then a huge organization. Hezbollah wasn't one man's guerrilla force—it was a movement. The enormous enterprise that Mohtashamipur had launched in Lebanon was already up and running, having enlisted thousands of young Shiites as well as most of the important Shiite clergy in the land.

Israel now had a powerful adversary that was both an Iranian proxy and a legitimate grassroots social movement.

Hezbollah clerics, most of them operating and residing in the Shiite villages in southern Lebanon, knew how to combine fanatical, messianic religious fervor with a new type of Lebanese patriotism, which centered on the consolidation of the Shiites and hatred for the Zionist occupier.

The most prominent of these local religious leaders during the founding of the movement was Sheikh Ragheb Harb, the imam of Jibchit, a town in southern Lebanon. A brilliant, fiery-eyed cleric, he had received his training in the holy city of Najaf, in Iraq, where Khomeini spent much of his exile from Iran, and upon his return he took charge of Hezbollah's propaganda and preaching in the south of the country.

Harb was a man of the cloth, not a fighter, but stories about him were reaching Meir Dagan, who argued that "Harb was becoming an important religious authority in the south and he was constantly advocating attacks against Israel and Israelis."

Dagan requested authorization to eliminate Harb. Though Harb never took part in terrorist actions against Israel himself, he incited them constantly, and in those years Israel, mired in its battle with Hezbollah and feeling impotent, welcomed every idea for action. Dagan dispatched two Lebanese agents he'd used in past operations of the Front for the Liberation of Lebanon from Foreigners, the proxy guerrilla movement Dagan created. On the night of Friday, February 16, two days after the blast in the Iranian embassy meant to kill Mohtashamipur, Harb was on his way home in Jibchit. The two Lebanese agents were waiting at a bend in the road, and as Harb slowed down for the curve, they sprayed his car with bullets, making sure that the young leader was dead.

Harb was immediately proclaimed a martyr. At the religious colleges in Qom, prayers were held in his memory, and the Grand Ayatollah Hossein Ali Montazeri, one of Iran's top clerics, sent a cable of condolences to his Shiite colleagues in Lebanon, praising Harb's feats. To mark the hundredth day after his death, a postage stamp in his memory was issued. His portrait appeared above all the pictures of all the martyrs, whose number was gradually increasing as the years went by. His statement advocating absolute rejection of any contact whatsoever with the Israelis, "A stance is a weapon and a handshake is an acknowledgment," has since that point been Hezbollah's primary motto.

Meanwhile, Dagan also targeted Mohammed Saad, one of Harb's close associates and another prominent Shiite figure in the south. Saad was a frequent participant in guerrilla activities against Israel and had amassed a huge quantity of weaponry and explosives in the *hussainia*, a place of prayer separate from the mosque, that he managed in the village of Marakah. On March 4, 1985, Dagan's agents blew up Saad's weapons cache. He and one of his men were killed in the blast along with thirteen others.

The attempt on Mohtashamipur's life and the elimination of Harb and Saad reveal much about the operational difficulties Israel faced when confronting Hezbollah. The Mossad generally took pains for its targeted killings to be "blue and white" (the colors of the Israeli flag) or carried out by Israeli operatives, but local agents were used in the killings of Harb and Saad, and the Mossad had to resort to the postal bomb method, long considered inefficient and liable to harm innocent bystanders, in order to try to dispose of Mohtashamipur. These three victims were not senior Hezbollah commanders, either. There was almost no information about the top target, Imad Mughniyeh.

An attempt to do away with the "spiritual compass" of the organization three days later was no more successful. On March 8, 1985, a car bomb exploded near the home of Sheikh Fadlallah in Beirut.

Fadlallah was unhurt, but eighty people were killed and two hundred injured, most of them worshippers at the mosque where Fadlallah preached. Some of the sheikh's bodyguards were killed as well, including Imad Mughniyeh's brother Jihad.

Still, Israel continued to try to solve its Lebanon problem through targeted killings. In 1986, Israeli intelligence discovered that Ahmed Jibril, the commander of the Popular Front–General Command Palestinian terror organization, was working with and assisting Hezbollah. On the strength of this information, coupled with Israel's long-standing desire to eliminate Jibril, Shamir signed a Red Page for him. Gathering the intelligence took a long time. Eventually it was established that Jibril often visited his organization's headquarters, in a warren of caves at Naameh, on the Mediterranean coast north of Lebanon's border with Israel. On the night of December 8, 1988, the IDF launched a large-scale land operation aimed at killing Jibril and destroying the network of caves.

Operation Blue and Brown (Kachol Ve'hum) was an embarrassing flop. The intelligence about the target area was dangerously incomplete. The soldiers ran into unexpected natural obstacles, and a lookout post they did not know about spotted them, depriving them of the element of surprise.

One of the commanders of the assassination force, a lieutenant colonel, was killed. Four soldiers went astray and had to be extricated later in a complicated air force operation. In addition, a trained dog, which was loaded with explosives and was supposed to run into one of the caves, where the device on its back would be exploded by remote control, was frightened by the shooting and ran away. Hezbollah later found the animal, which exposed the IDF's secret Sting (Oketz) canine unit. Most embarrassingly, Ahmed Jibril wasn't even there that night at all.

By the late 1980s, then, Hezbollah had far better intelligence, critical in waging a guerrilla war. One of the reasons for the absence of sufficient intelligence on the Israeli side was that Hezbollah gave Lebanon's downtrodden and beleaguered Shiites a community and a cause. Every attack against it drew its followers closer to the organization, strengthening the distinction between the good guys and the bad in their eyes. This, in turn, made it especially difficult for Israel to recruit live agents. Shiites willing to work for money grew fewer and farther between. Nobody wanted to betray Hezbollah.

Imad Mughniyeh used this superior intelligence to devastating effect. Backed by Iran's Revolutionary Guards and Intelligence Ministry, Mughniyeh honed and perfected Hezbollah's battlefield tactics. Suicide bombs and roadside explosions and carefully staged ambushes wreaked havoc on the large and unwieldy IDF forces. The price of having almost zero information about the Shiite militia was paid with the blood of Israeli soldiers. Between 1984 and 1991, there were 3,425 operations against the IDF and the South Lebanon Army, the pro-Israel Lebanese militia set up by the Israelis. Most of these attacks were carried out by the Shiite organization. In these attacks,

98 Israeli soldiers and 134 Lebanese allies were killed, and 447 Israelis and 341 Lebanese were wounded. Two Israeli MIAs were later
discovered to have been killed as well.

Frustrated by their weak position, in 1991 Israel's intelligence operatives began looking for what they termed "the tiebreaker," the
symbolic attack that would rock Hezbollah to its foundation and give
Israel back its edge.

# THE AGE OF THE DRONE

THE IMAMS IN THE village of Jibchit began calling people to the *hussainia* at ten o'clock in the morning. The *hussainia* is a Shiite meeting hall, named for the Imam Hussein, the son of Ali, cousin of the Prophet Muhammad, and founder of Shi'a Islam. Shiites believe that Ali was the true heir to Muhammad and that his inheritance was brutally usurped by the Sunnis. The Shi'a became a sect that was oppressed and discriminated against. In the *hussainia,* they would hold their religious rites in secret, for fear of the Sunnis.

But on that day in Jibchit, there was no longer any need for secrecy. Iran had become the first country in the world ruled by Shiite clergy. In Lebanon, the extremist Shiite Hezbollah, founded by Iran, was the predominant political and military force. The *hussainia* in Jibchit, abutting the imposing village mosque on the main street, had been renovated and expanded, its walls lined with shining white marble.

For seven years, the call had come from the loudspeakers on the mosque's minarets every February 16, the anniversary of the death of Sheikh Ragheb Harb, the first spiritual leader of Hezbollah in southern Lebanon. By assassinating him in 1984, Israel had unintentionally created a martyr, and the leaders and commanders of Hezbollah made annual pilgrimages to his memorial, before attending a political rally.

By 10:30, the main street was crowded with men and women, all of whom had set aside whatever they were doing, locked up their homes or stores or offices, and made their way to the *hussainia*. They moved slowly, following two SUVs, one gray and the other black, apparently a Hezbollah security escort.

At about 9,500 feet above the streets of Jibchit, a camera in the nose of a small, quiet aircraft panned the length of the procession. There was no pilot, but rather an operator controlling the plane from a trailer on the northern border in Israel. The images from the camera, in high resolution and real time, were beamed to a screen in the small AMAN war room overlooking a rose garden outside the Defense Ministry, in Tel Aviv. It was, in 1992, a marvel of intelligence technology: a drone that put Israeli eyes on a surveillance target without risking any Israeli personnel.

The drone's camera continued the length of the procession. At the end, four vehicles were clearly visible—two Range Rovers and two Mercedes sedans. In Tel Aviv, intelligence officials watched as those four slipped away from the crowd, passed the *hussainia,* and stopped in a parking lot behind the building.

"We've got him," one of the analysts watching the video feed said. Two hundred miles away, intelligence operatives had a clear view of a target. "Suddenly," an internal review of that morning later reported, "the scent of a hunt was in the air."

EVER SINCE THE OPENING offensive of the Yom Kippur War, which had taken the Israelis completely by surprise, Major General Benjamin "Benny" Peled, the commander of the Israeli Air Force, had been haunted by failure. At the beginning of the war, in 1973, the air force had received more than half of the defense budget, and yet it completely collapsed during the initial Egyptian and Syrian attack. Peled believed that one of the main reasons for the failure was that important intelligence had reached him too late. If he'd known Egyptian forces were launching—if he could have seen, in real time, the preparations—his own forces would have been better able to respond.

In the aftermath of that assault, Peled decided to develop a network of secret communications and real-time intelligence-gathering systems. It would be designed to serve the air force independent of the "Greens" (as the "Blues" of the IAF somewhat condescendingly called the ground forces, because of their olive drab uniforms). Using aircraft for that end would have been the obvious plan, but that was complicated by another trauma of the Yom Kippur War: The IAF had lost more than a quarter of its warplanes, and many of the rest were damaged and unfit for action. Furthermore, many of the IAF's airmen, who until then had enjoyed an aura of invincibility, had been shot down and taken prisoner or killed.

But what if airplanes didn't need pilots? Or the multi-million-dollar munitions systems? What if, Peled wondered, the IAF could remotely pilot smaller, cheaper aircraft equipped with only cameras and communications links?

A decade earlier, when he ran the weapons department, Peled was the first to introduce drones into the air force, although at the time it seemed a fantastical idea. He was worried about the Arab forces' acquisition of Soviet-made surface-to-air antiaircraft missiles, and, as a result, he "wanted to fill the air with decoys that would be very cheap, and with similar profiles as fighter planes on their radar screens." These UAVs, an Israeli improvement on an American invention, were launched by rockets, and in order to return to the ground they would eject a parachute, which a helicopter with long poles fixed to its fuselage would then sweep up. Later, the drones were also equipped with cameras.

But after the 1973 war, Peled reached the conclusion that this was not enough. The launch and recovery systems were costly, clumsy, and very dangerous. Processing the photographed material took a long time, too. Hours elapsed between taking the pictures, developing the film, and finally transferring the photos to the intelligence analysts.

And so, in the wake of the 1973 defeat, a new type of drone was developed. This drone could take off and land independently, it was controlled from a command caravan, and it had cameras that transmitted video footage in real time. By 1982, drones were a key element in providing real-time intelligence for the top air force brass sitting in Canary, the command post deep underground in central Tel Aviv. They also played a key role in knocking out Syrian antiaircraft missile batteries in Lebanon.

The drone that targeted Syrian defenses was the first model of the Scout (known in Israel as the Zahavan), made by Israel Aerospace Industries. The Israeli Air Force, hoping to convince the United States to cooperate in drone development, wanted to demonstrate to the Americans how effective its miniature, pilotless planes could be. When U.S. Defense Secretary Caspar Weinberger visited the Middle East—first Beirut and then Tel Aviv—he met with the top IDF and Defense Ministry officials. He was then shown a video taken by an Israeli drone of his arrival in Beirut, and the movements of his motorcade in the Lebanese capital. Weinberger didn't much appreciate the surveillance, but the members of his entourage were very impressed with the technology.

Weinberger's visit to Israel paved the way for a huge deal between Israel Aerospace Industries and the Pentagon for the sale of 175 upgraded Scout UAVs, which were given the name Pioneer in the United States. They were used by the U.S. Navy, Marines, and Army until 2007.

Improvements to the drones were made over the years to allow them to carry more fuel, and to update the cameras. In 1990, Israel equipped its drone fleet with lasers so that they could emit a beam and designate a static target for warplanes.

The upgrades to the drones were part of a larger technological push in the IDF, which in the late 1980s invested significant resources to acquire and develop precision ordnance—"smart bombs" that could hit their targets more accurately, making them more effective and less likely to inflict collateral damage. This process was accelerated when technology buff Ehud Barak, who wanted to build "a small, smart army," became chief of staff in 1991, in effect shaping the Israeli war machine for the coming decades. Under his direction, the IAF's Apache attack helicopters were equipped with laser-guided Hellfire missiles.

At the same time, a meeting between the heads of the IAF operations department and Arieh Weisbrot, commander of the first IAF drone unit, Squadron 200, came up with the revolutionary idea of combining all of these technological advances into a single five-step process, to create a new and particularly deadly method of targeted killing.

First, a drone would track a moving target, either a person or a vehicle. Second, the drone would transmit an image of the target directly to the operational command, providing a real-time connection with the decision-makers, right up until the order to fire. Third, the drone would designate the target with a laser beam that could be picked up by an Apache helicopter's laser detector—a stage known as "passing the baton," from the intelligence-gathering cycle to the operational cycle. Fourth, the Apache's own laser would mark the target, which a Hellfire missile could then lock on to. Fifth, the Apache pilot would fire the missile and destroy the target.

Combining and synchronizing both systems—intelligence and operations—was a major breakthrough. Drones already had proven themselves invaluable in gathering information. But now they'd evolved from a support role into a direct combat tool.

Squadron 200 began training with the Apache pilots of Squadron 113, the "Wasp" squadron, in late 1991. There were skeptics in the IAF, especially among pilots who'd been trained in, and had long practiced, specific combat tactics. The idea that flying robots could be effective in war seemed, to some, preposterous.

But in December 1991, they tried a number of "dry runs," using vehicles on Israel's roads as targets. Three or four drones were launched, and a vehicle selected at random for them to track with their cameras, transmitting everything to the control caravan. Then the vehicle was "lit up" with a laser beam, and after a few miles the chase was joined by two Apaches, and the whole team would practice "passing the baton" as the Apaches' sensors would lock on to the drone's laser beam. At the moment the Apache indicated that the target was locked, the exercise ended.

But simulating missile fire onto cars on a friendly road was one thing. Killing a live target in hostile territory was something else altogether.

ON A ROUTINE BOMBING run in southern Lebanon in October 1986, a bomb dropped by an F-4 Phantom exploded too early and ripped off one of the plane's wings. The two airmen ejected and landed in enemy territory. The pilot was rescued by an IAF Cobra helicopter, but not before hanging from the undercarriage, under fire from Hezbollah militiamen. The navigator, Ron Arad, could not be located.

Israelis attach great importance to the Jewish religious injunction of redemption of captives, and it is an Israeli fixation to do everything and more to get MIAs and POWs home. Losing an airman to Hezbollah in hostile territory was a tremendous blow.

Not surprisingly, then, the search for Arad was massive, the largest rescue operation in Israeli history. A Mossad official who was involved in Operation Body Heat (Hom Haguf), the code name for the effort to find Arad, said it was "the biggest search operation ever conducted in modern history for a single person. There was no stone that we left unturned, no source that we didn't enlist, no bribe that we didn't pay, and no scrap of information that we didn't scrutinize."

It all came to nothing. Arad was passed from one militia to another, year after year. In 1989—three years after Arad had disappeared—Israel abducted two relatively minor Hezbollah officials in an attempt to locate the airman. One of them, Abdal-Karim Obeid, was the man who had been named to succeed Sheikh Ragheb Harb as Hezbollah's chief cleric in southern Lebanon after Harb was killed. Their interrogation revealed nothing, and Hezbollah responded with indifference to an offer to begin negotiations for an exchange.

The search for Arad was partially hobbled by errors and oversights, as well as simple bad luck. Mostly, though, the continuous search highlighted Israel's inability to penetrate Hezbollah or the Iranian intelligence agencies that supported the organization.

More broadly, the militia was now carrying out increasingly sophisticated guerrilla actions, orchestrated by its military chief, Imad Mughniyeh, inflicting casualties and severe damage to the morale of the IDF. Finally, in the summer of 1991, AMAN top brass worked out a plan to shift the balance in Israel's favor: Israel would abduct Hezbollah secretary general Hussein Abbas al-Mussawi, or one of his two deputies, and hold him hostage until Ron Arad was returned. A concomitant goal was to stage "an emblematic operation that would reverberate and clarify who was really in charge of the situation," in the words of one of the Israeli officers involved.

.  .  .

MUSSAWI WAS ONE OF the poor Shiites the Iranians began organizing in the 1970s. He also underwent guerrilla training in a PLO Force 17 camp before becoming more devout and devoting years to studying Shi'a theology, first in Lebanon and then in Muslim colleges in Najaf, in Iraq, which were run by disciples of Khomeini, in accordance with his religious precepts. His astute mind, excellent memory, and loyalty to Khomeini, which matched his fanaticism, soon made him a well-known religious authority in Iraq and Lebanon and led him to become one of the core founders of Hezbollah. Mussawi, according to information gathered by the Israelis, was involved in the decisions that allowed Imad Mughniyeh to begin his campaign of suicide terrorism against the United States and Israel. He believed that one of Hezbollah's main aims, although not the primary one, should be the expulsion of the IDF by means of guerrilla warfare. "The future will be for the Resistance [against the Israeli occupation]," he repeatedly declared in his speeches, "while arrogance [of the Israelis] will be defeated. It is only a matter of time." In May 1991, he became secretary general of Hezbollah, by now already the most powerful political and military position in Lebanon.

From the outset, it was clear that any abduction operation in Beirut would be exceedingly difficult, if not impossible. So efforts instead focused on obtaining information about a future visit by Mussawi to southern Lebanon, closer to the Israeli border, where he would be easier to grab.

The head of operations for the AMAN research division's counterterrorism section, Lieutenant Colonel Moshe Zarka, had the idea to concentrate on the village of Jibchit, where seven years earlier, on February 16, 1984, Israeli agents had eliminated Ragheb Harb. The village is located in southern Lebanon, making it a far easier place to act in than Beirut, where the Hezbollah headquarters were located.

On February 12, 1991, AMAN received the information it was waiting for: As had become tradition, Hezbollah would hold a large political rally on the anniversary of Sheikh Harb's death. The rally would be attended by top Hezbollah officials, including Secretary

General Mussawi and the commander of the Iranian Revolutionary Guards in Lebanon.

The initial plan was merely to gather intelligence, study the rally, and plan an abduction the following year. This was crucial because of the wretched state of Israel's intelligence on Hezbollah at the time. Indeed, at one planning meeting, it became clear that no one in the room knew even the basics of Shiite memorial rites—when the widow is visited, for instance, or when the men gather at the *hussainia*. (A lieutenant colonel who'd written his doctoral thesis on Hezbollah was summoned to explain.) Brigadier General Dani Arditi, head of the Special Ops Executive (SOE), was emphatic: With such tenuous intelligence, there was no way he could recommend an immediate abduction mission. Still, he was in full support of preparing for the next year's rally at Jibchit.

Major General Uri Sagie, the chief of AMAN, was more ambitious. "SOE does not want to do it," he said at an AMAN command meeting on February 13. "I accept the proposal for building an intelligence model, but let's not stop ourselves from operational thinking. We'll carry out an intelligence model, with an 'operational tail.' Get some choppers ready for attack alert."

At this point, a critical misunderstanding crept in. Chief intelligence officer Brigadier General Doron Tamir, under Sagie in the command hierarchy, said he considered the reference to an "operational tail" to be merely part of an intelligence model. "Choppers would take off and practice the acquisition of the target, but in no circumstances would they open fire," he said. "Just a dry training run." The people who were supposed to assess the risks and repercussions of an operation thought so, too—which was why they didn't prepare those assessments.

But Sagie and his immediate associates, as well as chief of staff Barak, were thinking of something entirely different. To them, the "operational tail"—airborne helicopters armed with laser-guided Hellfire missiles—would leave the option of killing Mussawi open.

This was not part of the original plan, but now that the opportunity had arisen, the temptation was simply too great: Eliminate a tenacious enemy while employing a brand-new targeted killing protocol, using drones and Hellfires. This was precisely what Barak, who had just been fawned over by the media during his fiftieth birthday, wanted—to see a small, smart, and lethal IDF in action.

Unwittingly, however, two parallel plans had thus been created, without anyone's even realizing it.

ON FRIDAY, FEBRUARY 14, the AMAN counterterrorism section issued its summary, which made it clear that Operation Night Time was intended only to gather intelligence for a later abduction. The summary contained the following details: "Mussawi's convoy of cars usually includes three to five vehicles. Of these, two or three are escort vehicles at the head and the end of the convoy. The vehicle Mussawi rides in is a Mercedes 280 or 500. His place in the convoy isn't fixed. Sometimes he is in the first car behind the lead escort vehicle, and sometimes in the second or third. The other vehicles are Range Rovers."

That same day, the air force's intelligence wing issued its own orders, indicating an entirely different plan: "Units of the intelligence wing and AMAN will carry out a collection model in the execution zone. Later, in accordance with the intelligence collected, the operation will move into the attack stage."

This was a dangerous contradiction, with one unit beginning to prepare for an attack the other hadn't properly planned for. Yet because the operation was still officially a dry run, it wasn't put on the agenda of the weekly "operations-and-sorties" forum, attended by the minister of defense and the chief of staff. Defense Minister Moshe Arens was totally unaware of even the existence of Operation Night Time.

That night, a Friday, only hours after conflicting orders had been issued by Israeli officials, a squad of Islamic Jihad guerrillas slipped into an IDF field camp. Fresh recruits on a training exercise were asleep in their tents. The jihadists killed three of them with knives, axes, and pitchforks. Reporting on the attack at the end of the Sabbath, Haim Yavin, the chief anchor on Israel's only television channel, called it "the Night of the Pitchforks."

The national mood sank to a new low.

.  .  .

ON SUNDAY, THE DAY of the operation, the small AMAN war room opened at 7 A.M. Everyone was crammed in: SOE chief Arditi and representatives of the collection department, Unit 8200, the AMAN counterterrorism section, the drone unit, and the air force intelligence wing. The actual drone operators were in a trailer near the Lebanese border.

The Unit 504 agent who had provided the tip-off about Mussawi going to the rally reported that the target had left Beirut. Other intelligence coming into the war room indicated that "a convoy of activists left Beirut this morning, and that a 'VIP' had arrived in the south." None of that was confirmation that Mussawi was in Jibchit, but it appeared likely.

At about 10 A.M., the loudspeakers in Jibchit began calling citizens to come to the meeting place for the memorial rally, the village *hussainia*. At 10:30, the screen in the war room showed images, relayed from the drone, of a massive procession making its way to the site. Abutting the *hussainia* was a mosque, and its high minaret was clearly visible on the screen. The procession moved slowly behind a number of vehicles, apparently a Hezbollah security escort. The drone scanned the procession. At the end were two Range Rovers and two Mercedeses. "We've got him!" Zarka yelled.

At around noon, chief of staff Barak returned to his office, sullen and furious. He'd been summoned to Jerusalem that morning to testify to the security cabinet about the Night of the Pitchforks.

"Three terrorists have disgraced us," he blurted out angrily. Barak received a brief update on Operation Night Time, and then he went to the AMAN war room. He watched the drone's images intently.

It was a special occasion. For the first time, a commander in his headquarters could have his own eyes on the leader of a hostile terrorist organization in real time, with the possibility of acting on that image.

Sagie stood next to Barak, the two of them grim-faced, tense. From their demeanor, it was clear that the original objective of Operation Night Time—simply gathering intelligence—had fallen completely by the wayside. Others in the war room got the impression that the two senior commanders were eager to make the kill. They were waiting only for confirmation that Mussawi was in Jibchit, information they could take to the defense minister for his approval.

Barak told an aide to update the defense minister's military secretary on the situation. "Prepare Moshe Arens," he said, "for the possibility that he might be asked to green-light an operation." That was the first time that anyone had taken the trouble to fill the minister in on Operation Night Time.

Sagie took Zarka aside. "What do you think? Should we attack?" he asked. "We have a golden opportunity to take him out here."

"Yes," Zarka replied. "But know that we'll be moving up a level in fighting Hezbollah."

The ceremony at the *hussainia* ended a little after one o'clock. A massive crowd poured out and walked toward the cemetery where Sheikh Harb was buried, a short distance away. At 1:10, research division head Kuti Mor called an urgent meeting of his senior staff to formulate the division's position.

They were unanimous in their opposition to killing Mussawi. At the very least, they felt that a comprehensive discussion of the subject should be held before acting. Mussawi was a religious figure, the head of a political organization that happened to have a military arm, a lieutenant colonel argued. Israel had refrained from attacking such persons in the past. Besides, Hezbollah was not a one-man show, and Mussawi was not the most extreme man in its leadership. He would be replaced, perhaps by someone more radical.

During the meeting, a note was handed to Mor. He read it, then said to the attendees, "This is a Radio Lebanon report saying that Abbas Mussawi addressed the rally in Jibchit today." A murmur ran through the room. Now there was certainty that Mussawi was in Jibchit, and high probability that he was in the convoy. But there was still some room for doubt, and Mor stressed it. The questions now were: Which car was Mussawi riding in? And were any senior Lebanese or Iranian government officials in the car with him?

Nobody questioned whether his wife and child were with him.

One of Mor's officers called the Shin Bet's VIP bodyguard division. "Let's say that you have to guard the prime minister," he asked, "and there are four cars in the convoy. Which one would you put him in?" There was a brief discussion at the Shin Bet, and they came back with the reply: Most likely, he would go in the third car.

But that was only a supposition, and even if Mussawi was in the third car, it was still completely unclear who might be with him. Mor couldn't recommend firing missiles at a target with that kind of unknown. "It is impossible to attack," he said, ending the meeting.

Sagie came into the room immediately after. The relationship between the two men was already tense because of other issues, and Mor didn't mince words. "The intelligence circle is not complete," he told Sagie. "There are too many unknowns. The majority opinion here is that there's no room for implementation. I cannot recommend an attack."

Sagie rose, smiled, and said, "We'll see." He left abruptly and, with chief of staff Barak, went directly to the Defense Ministry to brief Arens.

Sagie told Arens he had no doubt that Mussawi was in the convoy. It was possible that there was some other person with him, perhaps a Lebanese cabinet minister. If Israel were to kill a Lebanese minister, the damage would be very great, "but both by analysis of the circumstances and intuitively, that is not the most reasonable conclusion." Killing Mussawi, he said, carried very little risk.

Arens was of two minds. On the one hand, he was being offered an opportunity to eliminate an enemy leader who was, in his view, a notorious terrorist. On the other, he was being asked to make an immediate decision—Mussawi could leave the village at any minute, and there were not many hours of daylight left—without time to give it full consideration. It could be disastrous if there was some error, if the intelligence wasn't solid, or if some extraneous detail or improbable scenario had been overlooked. He looked at Barak.

"We're talking about the leader of a terrorist organization and an enemy emblem. A lot of time could go by until another chance like this turns up," Barak said. "And even if it does, there could be so many circumstances that will stop us from executing for political reasons. What we have now is a one-time opportunity, one and only."

Arens paused for a moment. "To kill a person whom you didn't have to kill," he said, "is a disaster."

"Minister," said Sagie, "I have a commander's intuition that we must act."

Barak, who always had a keen sense of what makes people tick, decided to try inviting Arens, an aeronautical engineer by profession, to come to the war room to see the drone's images himself. The minister accepted and said he'd be along shortly. In the meantime, he told his military secretary, Brigadier General Yeremi Olmert, to call Prime Minister Yitzhak Shamir. It was 2:35 in the afternoon, and Arens was told that Shamir was at home napping after eating a lunch prepared by his wife, as he did every day.

He couldn't make a decision without the prime minister's approval. But time was running out.

Forty-five minutes passed. At 3:20, a group of people whose faces could not be identified left the home of Sheikh Harb's widow and climbed into a convoy of four vehicles. The convoy drove a short distance, then stopped at the home of a Hezbollah activist in Jibchit. This dovetailed with another item of information: that a meeting of top officials of the Shiite organization was due to be held at that home on that Sunday. This meant there were no Lebanese ministers present, because they could not be a party to such a meeting, and they would not be left waiting in the car until it was over. The likelihood that a high-ranking figure from outside Hezbollah was traveling in the convoy and might be hit was greatly diminished, then, and the likelihood that Mussawi was there increased even more.

Sagie told Barak that, although there could never be absolute certainty, he recommended attacking. Mor gave a more ambiguous opinion: "The intelligence circle is not complete, although all circumstances indicate that it is Mussawi. Therefore, it is now up to the commander to decide whether to attack or not to attack."

Barak decided. He ordered the air force to send the helicopters in, and, on another phone, he persuaded Arens that circumstances had changed. Arens gave his approval for the attack.

Next, just after 3:30, Barak phoned the prime minister's office. Still, no one had spoken to Shamir. He was asleep, and all attempts to reach him had failed. His wife was also napping, and no one answered the phone.

Everyone was waiting for him to get back to the office, as he did every day, at around four o'clock. The problem was that every elapsed minute could make the operation impossible because of the approaching darkness. At 3:50, the convoy began leaving the village. The voice of the drone operator came over the loudspeaker: "Start of movement."

Tension mounted in the war room. Barak, seeing the unfolding scenario as a historic opportunity, moved one of the crew and sat in his seat, taking over radio contact with the drone command and the control caravan, directing them where to point the airborne cameras while simultaneously analyzing the possible routes the convoy might take from Jibchit to Beirut. Barak kept an open line with the air force commander, who was in Canary, several dozen feet under the war room. "Take off, all take off," came the order to the Apaches from Canary.

At about 3:55, Shamir reached his office. He heard a rundown of no more than one minute's duration on a targeted killing operation about which he'd had no advance knowledge. Still, he gave it his unhesitating approval. "Let them kill him," he said. Arens's military secretary informed Barak, who told the air force commander, "They are all yours."

The convoy began moving again at 3:57. The drone watched as it traveled slowly north through Jibchit and across the bridge over the Zahrani River. Then the vehicles picked up speed, a Range Rover in the lead, the two Mercedeses following, spaced about a hundred yards apart, while the second Range Rover brought up the rear.

At 4:05, the operator reported, "Another twenty seconds and the road curves west," to pinpoint the precise location for the Apache pilots.

"Approaching zone; activate [laser] designator," the pilot in the lead attack helicopter said.

"Designator activated," said one of the operators in the drone command trailer.

"I can't see it," one of the pilots radioed, but moments later he reported, "Designation acquired," indicating that he could now see the drone's laser stain on the target.

"Positive identification of target," came the confirmation from the Canary duty commander. At 4:09, he told the Apache pilot, "*Rashai,*

*rashai.* I repeat: *Rashai*"—Hebrew for "You have authorization," similar to "permission to engage" in American military dialect.

The Apache pilot fired a single Hellfire missile.

It struck the third vehicle in the convoy. The Mercedes exploded in a ball of flame. No one had scanned the road ahead, though, to make sure civilian cars weren't traveling toward the target from the other direction. In fact, there was one, and it was very close to the Mercedes when it was struck by the missile. It, too, was engulfed in fire.

A second missile was fired at the second Mercedes in the convoy: another direct hit on the target.

Doors opened in one of the two Range Rovers, which had stopped at the roadside, and people got out and began to run away. "We were there, watching every movement and passing it on to the air force's air control unit," recalled one of the drone operators.

The second Range Rover picked up the casualties from the two Mercedeses and sped off in the direction of Nabatieh. "Take him," Canary ordered the drone operators tracking the car. At 4:32, they designated it, with their laser, as a target for the second pair of Apaches, which then destroyed it. Smoke billowed from the vehicle. The Apaches then sprayed the area with machine-gun fire.

Absolute silence fell over the war room. Barak made his way out, slapping his colleagues on the shoulders and congratulating them with the English words "Well done."

But was Mussawi dead? The AMAN officers waited in their respective offices for final confirmation of the kill. At around 6:00, it came. Mussawi had indeed been in the third car. So had his wife and son.

The 504 agent who had provided the tip-off to the AMAN war room at the start of the operation later claimed that he had mentioned that Mussawi's wife, Siham, and his son, Hussein, age six, were traveling with him in his car. Others involved in the operation denied knowing this, but Meir Dagan believed the agent. "The claim that AMAN didn't know that at least Mussawi's wife was in the car was concocted after the fact. They must have known, or else they are a bunch of fools. Mussawi's wife had first-degree relatives in Jibchit, and there was no chance in the world that she would have missed the chance to go and visit them."

Two hours after the hit, Barak held a meeting in his office to try to anticipate Hezbollah's possible reactions and retaliations. Security alert and public relations steps were discussed. Shortly afterward, Israel TV opened its newscast with an item about the attack, which it called "a daring operation." Defense Minister Arens took the trouble to go to the studio to appear on the news. "This is a message to all terrorist organizations," he said, "that whoever opens an account with us, that account will be closed by us."

That is, until another one is opened and it, too, needs to be closed.

# MUGHNIYEH'S REVENGE

ABBAS MUSSAWI'S CHARRED CORPSE was extricated from the burned-out Mercedes. Because of its condition, it was impossible to observe Hezbollah's usual rites and hold an open-casket funeral. Instead, the remains were cleaned, wrapped in a shroud, and placed in a magnificent coffin that was specially constructed out of carefully carved wood, then painted blue-gray and given silvered metal fittings.

The heads of Hezbollah did not hasten to carry out the burial within the first twenty-four hours, as is customary. For one thing, there were security problems. The shock over the aerial attack on the secretary general's motorcade was so great that Imad Mughniyeh feared that the funeral could also become a killing field. Moreover, the funeral had to be delayed to allow high-level Iranians to attend. Hezbollah had been founded by Iran, and its leaders were under the influence of the Islamic Revolutionary Guard Corps (IRGC) in their day-to-day conduct, and followed the religious authority of the ayatollahs' regime in Tehran. Iran, for its part, saw Hezbollah as its main ally in the Middle East.

The Supreme Leader of the Islamic Revolution, Grand Ayatollah Sayyid Ali Khamenei, who had replaced Khomeini when he died, in June 1989, declared, "The martyrdom of Sayyid Abbas is a turning point in the course of resistance," and dispatched a delegation to help stabilize and calm the organization, to display public support during its difficult hour, and to select a new secretary general immediately.

In Israel, there had been no serious discussion before the hit took place about what would happen in the aftermath of Mussawi's death. From their perspective, there were no significant differences between the various members of Hezbollah, and no one had bothered to ask who was likely to replace Mussawi, and whether the replacement might be better or worse for Israel. "From our point of view," said an officer serving in AMAN at the time, "they were all painted in black." After the killing, AMAN's best guess was that the Iranians would appoint Mussawi's well-known and popular deputy, Subhi al-Tufayli.

They were wrong.

Immediately after Mussawi was interred, the Iranian delegation took part in a meeting of the Shura Council, Hezbollah's twelve-member supreme religious leadership council, where they delivered a message from Iranian president Hashemi Rafsanjani, recommending a successor. Soon afterward, the council announced its decision to appoint a pious thirty-two-year-old cleric, Sayyid Hassan Nasrallah.

If the Israelis had any illusion that Hezbollah would be tempered by the killing of Mussawi, Nasrallah's promotion quickly disabused them of it. Compared with Mussawi, Nasrallah was a wild-eyed radical. It turned out that even black has its shades. Nasrallah was blacker than black.

Nasrallah was born in 1960, the eldest of nine siblings, in the Shiite Bourj Hammoud neighborhood northeast of Beirut. Although the family was not very religious, as a child, when the other boys in his Beirut neighborhood were playing in the streets or at the beach, Hassan displayed an affinity for the faith and spent most of his time in the mosque, studying.

With the outbreak of the civil war, in 1975, the family relocated to southern Lebanon, where, in a mosque near Tyre, Nasrallah caught the exacting eyes of several Shiite clerics with ties to Khomeini. They sent him to Najaf, Iraq, for higher religious studies, and there he got to know Abbas Mussawi and became his star disciple. When the two returned to Lebanon in 1978, after Saddam Hussein expelled the Lebanese Shiite students, Mussawi set up a study center, and Nasrallah became one of its head teachers, attracting large numbers of admirers. In 1982, with the founding of Hezbollah, Nasrallah and his disciples joined en masse and began taking an active role in the guerrilla warfare. Nasrallah spent the ensuing years alternating between commanding a Hezbollah unit and furthering his higher religious studies in Iran.

Israel was a "cancerous growth, this contaminating germ," he said in a television interview, "a forward imperialist garrison in the heart of the Arab and Islamic world. It is a society of war, a warlike society of warriors, men and women alike. There is no civil society in this entity." The meaning was clear: All Israelis, whatever age or gender, were a legitimate target for jihad.

Gradually, a sharp ideological rift grew between Nasrallah and his former teacher. Mussawi advocated further cooperation with the Syrians, the most important political and military force in Lebanon, who welcomed Hezbollah's actions against Israel and even agreed to allow the Iranians to send large consignments of weaponry through Syria to the organization's militia. But Nasrallah was opposed to any form of cooperation with the regime of the Assad family, who were Alawites, an Islamic sect that he regarded as pagan heretics.

The two men also differed in their attitude toward Israel. Mussawi regarded it as a secondary issue and believed that most resources should be devoted to attempts to take control of the governmental machinery in Lebanon. Nasrallah argued that the guerrilla war against Israel should be prioritized.

Nasrallah lost the argument—Mussawi was made secretary general, and Nasrallah was exiled to serve as Hezbollah's envoy in Iran. He returned to Lebanon only after declaring that he was giving up his opposition to ties with Syria and that he accepted Mussawi's authority in the matter of the struggle against Israel.

All this changed in February 1992.


IRONICALLY, BEFORE MUSSAWI WAS killed, Hezbollah and its Iranian sponsors had been more concerned with consolidating their position as a social and political force in Lebanon than with attacking Israel. Though there were guerrilla attacks against the Israelis during the 1980s, largely at the urging of the extremist faction in

Hezbollah led by Nasrallah, they were not a high priority and were in no way indicative of the full damage the organization could have inflicted.

But after the targeted killing, priorities shifted. The Iranian Revolutionary Guards began to prefer Nasrallah's approach, and they came to believe that dealing with their enemy to the south had to be their top priority. They now felt that Hezbollah would not succeed in transplanting the Khomeini revolution to Lebanon without first getting rid of the Israeli occupation.

The man Nasrallah ordered to implement the new policy was Hezbollah's military chief, Imad Mughniyeh, "the extremist, uninhibited psychopath" who'd been kneecapping Beirut hookers and drug dealers thirteen years earlier, the guerrilla ideologue who'd created Islamic Jihad and sent suicide bombers to destroy barracks and apartment houses occupied by American, French, and Israeli troops and diplomats, the ghost on the grainy photograph the Israelis hadn't been able to kill or even locate in the early eighties. "He was responsible for building Hezbollah's military strength, and not Nasrallah, with all due respect to Nasrallah's excellent television appearances," said Meir Dagan. "Because of him, and a group of operatives close to him, the organization became a strategic threat to the State of Israel."

Mughniyeh had already been a tactical annoyance for years. To defend its northern border, Israel in 1985 had created a Security Zone, a strip of territory inside southern Lebanon controlled by the IDF. The aim was to keep hostile forces as far as possible from Israel's civilian settlements and to confine the confrontation with them exclusively to Lebanese territory. In addition, to spare the lives of its own soldiers, Israel established a proxy militia, the South Lebanon Army (SLA), made up mostly of Christians and Shiites from the villages in the region, who were sworn enemies of the Palestinians in Lebanon and Hezbollah. The use of the SLA allowed the Israelis to see Hezbollah as merely an occasional threat to its border, rather than as a guerrilla army waging an asymmetrical war. A few soldiers, mostly SLA men, were killed from time to time, but the status quo, from the IDF's perspective, was preferable to a full-scale confrontation with the Hezbollah forces.

But now Mughniyeh was unleashed by Nasrallah, and retaliation for the assassination of Mussawi was swift. As soon as the funeral for the murdered leader was over, Hezbollah fighters launched a barrage of rockets into western Galilee. For five days, they bombarded the communities of northern Israel, which was brought to a standstill, most of its residents confined to bomb shelters. It was more firepower than Hezbollah had used against Israeli civilian communities in its entire history up to that point.

Only one person was killed—a six-year-old girl, Avia Alizada, in the communal farming village of Gornot HaGalil—but the message that Nasrallah and Mughniyeh had delivered to Israel was clear: From now on, any action against Hezbollah would bring about a direct attack not only on the IDF but also against civilians in northern Israel.

Israel responded by shelling Shiite villages and bolstering its forces in southern Lebanon. The Israelis hoped that would be the end of this particular round of fighting, and that Hezbollah would feel at least temporarily satisfied in its own show of force as a response to the slaying of Mussawi.

Mughniyeh, however, was planning something far more grandiose than a few days of rocket barrages: He intended to target the thousands of Israelis serving abroad as diplomats and in other official capacities, as well as the world's Jewish communities, for whose security Israel considered itself responsible. To him, the battlefield was global. Mughniyeh wanted to rewrite the rules of the game: Any attack on any important Hezbollah asset would draw a response not only in what he and Nasrallah called "the region" (Israel and Lebanon), but also beyond that region: Israeli and Jewish targets all across the globe.

He struck first in Turkey. On March 3, 1992, an explosive device went off near a synagogue in Istanbul, but, miraculously, no one was killed. Four days later, Ehud Sadan, the chief security officer at the Israeli embassy, was killed when a large bomb exploded under his car, planted by members of a group calling itself Hezbollah Turkey. From there, Mughniyeh targeted Argentina: On March 17, a terrorist exploded a car bomb outside the Israeli embassy in Buenos Aires, killing twenty-nine people, including four Israelis, five Argentinean Jews, and twenty children at a nearby school. Two hundred forty-two people were injured. In its claim of responsibility, delivered to a Western news agency in Beirut, the Islamic Jihad Organization declared that the action was dedicated to the memory of Hussein, Mussawi's son, who burned to death with him in the vehicle, and that it was "one of our continuing strikes against the criminal Israeli enemy in an open-ended war, which will not cease until Israel is wiped out of existence."

The Israelis were surprised by how quickly Mughniyeh had been able to pull off the attacks in Turkey and Argentina. Only later did it dawn on them that he had planned those operations, and surely many others, years in advance, to be executed only when the occasion arose. An in-depth investigation by the Mossad and the CIA's Counterterrorism Center (CTC) revealed that the squad that carried out the Buenos Aires bombing was one of forty-five sleeper cells deployed all over the world, including Europe and the United States, by Hezbollah's "special research apparatus—Unit 910." This is the code name for the militia's elite secret force, consisting of between two hundred and four hundred of its best and toughest fighters, most of them trained in Iran by the Revolutionary Guard's Al-Quds Brigades.

"The aim of the cells is to provide an immediate response outside of the Middle East in the event of an Israeli attempt to strike at Hizballah in Lebanon," said Stanley Bedlington of the CTC. The Buenos Aires bombers, for instance, were from a cell that had been cultivated in Ciudad del Este, a city in Paraguay, near the border with Brazil and Argentina and the great Iguazú Falls, where a large number of Shiite Lebanese émigrés had settled. Long before the hit on Mussawi, the cell had collected a great deal of information on possible Israeli targets, for use when the need arose. After the assassination, Mughniyeh ordered a team to leave Lebanon for Ciudad del Este, where the locals provided them with intelligence, vehicles, explosives, and a suicide bomber.

In the immediate aftermath of the attack, though, the Israelis decided not to retaliate. Some Mossad operatives argued for an aggressive response in South America. A Mossad team visited Ciudad del Este. "A town called Hell," they reported. "We're speaking of a clear and present danger. The next attack is on its way."

But the heads of the Mossad responded with apathy, largely because any other response would have entailed significant bureau-cratic changes for the Mossad. If Israel started to consider Hezbollah a global threat, the matter would then fall under the Mossad's re-sponsibility and require vast institutional realignment, including an extensive deployment in South America, where its presence had hitherto been extremely thin. The top Mossad command instead pre-ferred to regard the attack in Buenos Aires as an isolated, one-off event, a chance success for Hezbollah, and to continue seeing the Shiite organization as a localized phenomenon that the IDF and the Shin Bet had to handle in southern Lebanon. Nevertheless, Mughni-yeh's message was clearly understood, and Israel abstained for many years from any attempts on the lives of the heads of Hezbollah.

Mughniyeh felt he had achieved his goals in Buenos Aires, and for the time being he halted plans for more attacks outside the Mid-dle East arena. But while he refrained from activating any sleeper cells, Mughniyeh continued his provocations in the Security Zone. From month to month and year to year, Hezbollah's performance improved and its daring increased. With generous aid from Iran, it employed increasingly sophisticated electronic systems, monitored IDF radio communications, improved its roadside explosive devices so they would not respond to Israel's remote detonation equipment, planted spies inside the SLA, sent suicide bombers against IDF troops, and carried out blitz raids aimed at conquering Israeli fortifi-cations in southern Lebanon.

Nasrallah had a fine understanding of the Israeli public's mood and its sensitivity to casualties. His militia shot video footage of its operations and broadcast it on Hezbollah's Al-Manar TV station. Those clips were then picked up in Israel and often rebroadcast on Israeli channels. They had the intended effect, which was more stra-tegic than tactical: Over time, watching the numerous videos of Hez-bollah's successes began to gnaw away at the national consensus to maintain an IDF presence in Lebanon. Israel responded with re-peated bombardments against Hezbollah positions and settlements where it was active, killing both militia and civilians.

At some point, Mughniyeh apparently felt that Israel had crossed a red line. No one in Israel could point to a single, specific action that set him off, but two years after the Buenos Aires bombing,

Mughniyeh staged another attack outside of the Middle East. On March 11, 1994, a suicide bomber drove a truck packed with tons of explosives from the outskirts of Bangkok toward the Israeli embassy. If the attack had been successful, it would have caused hundreds of casualties. Fortunately, the man had second thoughts about becoming a *shahid,* stopped the truck in the middle of the road, short of the embassy, and ran away.

This time, the Israelis decided a response was necessary. The question was what form the retaliation should take. At consultations in the prime minister's office, AMAN officers said that it wasn't enough to strike Hezbollah; rather, its sponsors, the Iranians, should be targeted. General Ali Reza Asgari, the commander of the IRGC's Al-Quds Brigades, was a suitable candidate for assassination, they argued. This proposal would also have transferred responsibility for the operation to the Mossad.

But Prime Minister Rabin wasn't keen to get the Iranians involved, and in any case, no one in Israeli intelligence knew where Asgari was or how to get close enough to kill him.

Rabin did endorse another target, however. That spring, two Unit 504 agents learned of a Hezbollah camp near Ein Dardara, close to the Lebanese-Syrian border, where an officers' training course was under way. Aerial photographs from a Scout drone and radio communication monitoring by Unit 8200 confirmed it. Then, on June 2, after weeks of careful planning, Israeli Air Force Defender helicopters attacked. Cadets scattered in all directions, desperate for cover from the helicopters' machine guns. Fifty of them were killed and another fifty wounded. Among the trainees were the sons of some senior Hezbollah officials and two others from the Iranian Revolutionary Guards who were related to officials in Tehran. "It was more or less the same as someone bombing Eton College in England," said one Israeli official.

Hezbollah radio stations called the raid "barbaric" and promised "a comprehensive response at all levels." Forty-six days later, Mughniyeh struck in Buenos Aires once again. On July 18, 1994, a suicide terrorist blew up a van packed with explosives in front of the Argentinean Jewish AMIA community center. The seven-story building collapsed, killing eighty-five and injuring hundreds. It took weeks to extricate all of the bodies from the wreckage.

This second bombing finally woke Israeli intelligence to the full reality of the international threat posed by Hezbollah. What two years before had seemed like a localized incident had turned out to be the work of a worldwide network, supported by Shiite communities and under the protection of Iranian embassies.

The Israelis grasped that these remarkable capabilities—"better than most of what we had ever seen from any Palestinian organization," an AMAN operative said—sprang first and foremost from the mind of Imad Mughniyeh.

Retaliation, for the Israelis, would come in two stages. First, the Mossad would kill Mughniyeh's other brother, Fouad. Then operatives would wait at Fouad's funeral for Mughniyeh and either kill him there or, at the very least, start a surveillance operation against him, which would ultimately lead to an assassination. Fouad had to die because the Israelis didn't have the slightest idea how else to find Mughniyeh, who remained no more than a grainy photograph in their files.

Caesarea, however, couldn't pull off the job on its own in Beirut. So local agents had to be employed, and they eventually settled on a young Palestinian named Ahmad al-Halak, who had been taken prisoner by Israel in the Lebanon War in 1982 and recruited by the Mossad's Junction division. Halak was something of a roughneck, with no discernible ideology other than money. He dealt in smuggled goods and protection rackets, which gave him access to the dodgier areas of Beirut that interested the Mossad. By 1994, he was one of Junction's key agents in the city. Acting on orders from his case officer, whom he met from time to time in Cyprus, Halak found pretext for an ostensibly coincidental visit to Fouad Mughniyeh's hardware store, in the Shiite neighborhood of al-Safir, and, over the next few months, made friends with him.

On December 21, 1994, a few minutes before 5 P.M., Halak and his wife, Hanan, parked their car outside Fouad's store. Halak went inside to make sure Fouad was there, chatted with him briefly about a debt he had undertaken to collect for the store owner, and left. His wife quickly got out of the car, and the couple walked away. When they were about a hundred yards from the store, Halak turned around, looked at the store and the car parked outside, and put his hand into his pocket. Fifty kilograms of high explosives in the trunk of the car detonated, destroying Fouad's store, killing him and three passersby, and seriously wounding fifteen others.

A statement issued by Hezbollah after the bombing read: "There is no doubt as to the identity of the criminal hand that committed this crime against civilians in a shopping area in the al-Safir neighborhood in Beirut. Today, after repeated threats, the Zionist enemy and his destructive agencies carried out a despicable crime against a number of people while they were doing their shopping."

The funeral was held the next day. The Mossad had four lookouts posted at different points along the route and at the cemetery. But Mughniyeh saw through the ploy: He stayed away from the funeral, fearing the Mossad would be waiting for him.

Hezbollah, meanwhile, was quickly on Halak's trail. He managed to escape by reaching the beach and rendezvousing with a submarine waiting to take him to Israel. (Hanan, who had planned to fly out of the country, was caught on her way to the airport, brutally interrogated, and sentenced to fifteen years of hard labor.) The Mossad sent Halak to a Southeast Asian country with a new identity, but he never fit in. "I don't get these people; they're small and strange," he complained at a meeting with a Junction operative who was keeping in contact with him. After six months, the Mossad offered to place him in an Arab town in Galilee, but Halak insisted on returning to Lebanon. In March 1996, an Israeli double agent working for Hezbollah managed to lure him into accepting an invitation to lunch. Halak was drugged and taken by truck to Beirut, where he was tortured by Mughniyeh and his cohorts. Then he was handed over to the Lebanese authorities and indicted, sentenced to death, and executed by a firing squad.

MORE THAN THREE YEARS had passed since the hasty assassination of Abbas Mussawi. Many dozens of people had died in a bloody cycle of revenge, and yet Hezbollah had only grown stronger, with a new leader, Nasrallah, who was several times more powerful and effective than Mussawi had been.

"I did not accurately foresee Hezbollah's reaction," Major General

Uri Sagie said. "I did not accurately evaluate Imad Mughniyeh." And Defense Minister Arens admitted, "It was too hasty a decision-making process."

As for then–chief of staff Ehud Barak, he admitted the facts, but not the error. "The question," he said, "is how did things look at the time of the act? We had identified Mussawi as a threat, and we thought it was right to strike at him. This was correct thinking for that moment. It was very difficult to foresee then that he would be replaced by Nasrallah, who seemed less significant then and less influential, and that he would become a leader with such great power. It was also difficult to know that Mughniyeh would come to be his number two, who turned out to be super-talented at operations."

By 1995, he remained alive, and he was now only one of Israel's antagonists.

# "JUST ONE SWITCH, OFF AND ON"

TWO BUSES, ONE FULL of Israeli soldiers, were parked in the lot of a roadside kiosk near Mehola, a settlement in the Jordan Valley, on April 16, 1993. After a little while, a car pulled off the road and slipped up close to the buses.

Then it exploded.

Set against the damage the terrorist intended to inflict, the actual number of casualties was fortunately relatively low. A Palestinian from the nearby village, who worked in a snack bar, was killed, and eight people were lightly wounded. But Shin Bet investigators noted that inside the car were the charred remains of its driver, along with cooking-gas cylinders used as explosive material. A suicide bomber.

By now, suicide attacks were common enough, but up until this point, they had all occurred in other places, not Israel. The Mehola attack began a wave of such bombings inside Israel. Within a year, suicide bombers were blowing themselves up all over the country. In eleven months, they killed more than one hundred Israelis and wounded more than a thousand.

Shin Bet's top officials tried to understand where they had erred, and how the situation had become so horrific. They started tracing most of the attacks back to just three men. But two of them, Ahmed Yassin and Salah Shehade, were in Israeli prisons. And the third, Yahya Ayyash, was in Poland, or so they believed.

The Israelis had no idea how these three managed to communicate with each other, let alone how they had explosive devices prepared and how they successfully recruited and dispatched so many suicide bombers.

YASSIN WAS BORN IN the Palestinian village of Al-Jura, and became a refugee in the 1948 war, ending up in the Egyptian-ruled Gaza Strip with his family. Like many young Palestinians, he joined the Muslim Brotherhood, where he met another refugee, two years older, by the name of Khalil al-Wazir, the charismatic leader who became known as Abu Jihad. Al-Wazir feared that being identified with the Brotherhood, then in conflict with the Egyptian government, could be an obstacle in his path, and he abandoned it to go his own way. But Yassin, quiet and introverted, felt that he had found his life's true vocation, and he turned out to be a prodigy of Islamic studies.

After the Arab defeat in the Six-Day War of 1967, while al-Wazir launched a huge campaign of guerrilla warfare against Israel, believing that only force would finally destroy Israel, Yassin came to a different conclusion. He believed that the Arab defeat was the result of their own moral failings, and that secular and decadent regimes had strayed too far from Allah. Redemption, therefore, was to be found in devotion to Islam. *"Al-Islam hua al-Khal,"* he said repeatedly—"Islam is the solution"—echoing in Arabic the same slogan Ruhollah Khomeini had used to rouse his followers in Farsi.

In the late 1960s and early '70s, in an effort to build a movement based on Islamic values, with himself as its leader, Yassin set up mosques and Islamic educational institutes, as well as a network of welfare and social assistance bodies. A frail and slender man who spoke in a high-pitched voice and used a wheelchair—the result of a boyhood accident—Yassin appeared to be a sensitive social reformer, doing godly works in Gaza. Certainly, the Shin Bet assumed, he was no threat to Israel.

In fact, many Shin Bet operatives liked Yassin. In contrast to the PLO, he didn't try to conceal his activities, and he even held long conversations with Israeli officials whenever they requested a meeting with him. "He was an excellent conversationalist, knowledgeable about Zionist history and Israeli politics, sharp-minded and very pleasant," recalls a senior Shin Bet officer posted in Gaza at the time, code-named Aristo. "He was so different from the PLO terrorists whom we used to interrogate."

With Arafat gathering support in the territories and recognition around the world, it seemed best to leave Yassin be. "In a certain sense, the Shin Bet grew the jihadist," said Amnon Lipkin-Shahak, head of AMAN in the late 1980s.

"The agency was one of the factors which supported the Islamist elements," said Ami Ayalon, head of the Shin Bet in the 1990s. "Our thinking was that in order to create a counterweight to the PLO's Palestinian national movement, we'd encourage Islam, which does not have a nationalist element—at least that's what we believed then." The hope was that the Muslim clergy, increasingly popular thanks to their social activities in preschools, clinics, youth centers, and mosques, would drain support from Fatah and weaken Arafat.

At the time, the Muslim Brotherhood in Gaza was seen mainly as a social movement, devoid of political ambitions. Throughout the 1960s and '70s, that was largely accurate. But then Ayatollah Khomeini overthrew the shah in Iran. A religious scholar, pious and holy, had led a revolution, raised an army, and instituted a functioning government. He demonstrated to Muslims everywhere, not only to Shiites like him, that Islam was not only a religion, constrained to sermons in mosques and charity in the streets, but also an instrument of political and military power—that Islam could be a governing ideology, that Islam was the solution for everything.

In the Palestinian territories, preachers' tones began to change. "The apologetics that had characterized Islam began to disappear," said Yuval Diskin, who became head of the Shin Bet in 2005 and who'd spent most of his career as an intelligence operative acting deep inside the Palestinian population. "The passivity and the waiting for the long process of preparing people's hearts for 'salvation' gave way to activism and preaching for struggle, for jihad. From humble doormats, they turned into very energetic activists. It happened here in Gaza as well as across the entire Middle East and Africa. They were on a higher personal level and were more ideologically dedicated than the PLO folks, and their need-to-know compartmentalization capability was infinitely better than anything we'd seen. Neither we nor the rest of the Western world saw these processes in real time."

Yassin was one of the early adapters, which the Shin Bet discovered quite by accident in April 1984. One day, a young Palestinian activist was detained in Gaza on suspicion of involvement in acts of terrorism sponsored by Fatah. He was taken to a spare interrogation room, where he was questioned by the Shin Bet interrogator Micha Kubi (the same man who had questioned the two terrorists who hijacked the Ashkelon bus just before they were murdered by the Shin Bet, and who refused to lie about the incident later on).

The suspect was talking, giving up snippets of information, but Kubi sensed he was holding something back, a secret too important to tell. Kubi leaned forward, as if to whisper something in the Palestinian's ear. Then he swung his huge arm, his hand rising swiftly from his hip, and gave an open palm slap to the man's face, knocking him off his chair and into the wall. "I don't want to hear all the garbage that you're telling me!" Kubi yelled in Arabic. "Now, start giving me the really serious stuff, or else you don't leave here alive today."

That was all the prompting the man needed. The interrogation soon revealed that Sheikh Yassin was operating under the orders of the extreme wing of the Muslim Brotherhood in Jordan, whose leader was a Palestinian, Abdallah Azam. At the time, Azam was also active in Peshawar, a large city in northwestern Pakistan, where he had met a member of a wealthy family of Saudi Arabian building contractors and persuaded him to adopt the same militant jihadist ideology. The rich Saudi began using his family's money to finance the organization and support networks of fanatical Islamists, some of them graduates of the training camps the CIA was running in Afghanistan as a proxy force against the occupying Soviets. The man's name was Osama bin Laden.

Azam's men in Jordan had been sending money that they obtained from wealthy individuals in Jordan and Saudi Arabia to Yassin, who used it to set up armed cells, preparing to launch a jihad against Israel. Thanks to the information supplied by the interrogated Palestinian, the Israeli authorities arrested Yassin and began rounding up his closest associates. The most important of those men was Salah She-hade, a social worker by profession, educated and astute. Thanks to Yassin, he had become a devout Muslim and eventually his mentor's chief aide, in charge of the organization's clandestine activities.

Shin Bet personnel, angry at having been deceived by the sheikh and his men, subjected their prisoners to very harsh treatment. The first to break was Shehade, who was badly beaten, deprived of sleep, and starved. Shehade suffered from claustrophobia, and the Shin Bet took advantage of this, locking him up—blindfolded, and with his hands and feet bound—in a cellar and then playing tapes of the sounds made by rats and roaches. He begged to be taken out, and when he was, Kubi was waiting for him.

Kubi told Shehade he could eat in exchange for information. She-hade, exhausted and hungry, agreed, on the condition that Kubi wouldn't reveal that he'd been the first to talk.

The next to break was Yassin himself, though no physical means were used against him. The Shin Bet interrogator Aristo handled the questioning. Aristo said:

> We knew, from the weeks of surveillance of his home, that a female admirer of Sheikh Yassin, a respectable married woman, came to visit him now and again, and that out of her admiration for him and her desire to make his difficult life more pleasant, she'd get into bed with him. During one questioning session, I leaned over him and whispered in his ear, "I know all about you. I know what you speak about with the people who are closest to you. I know who comes to visit you and when. I know when you get a hard-on and when you don't."
>
> I did not mention the woman, but he knew exactly what I was getting at, and right away he rethought his situation. He saw that he had no choice, that if he didn't speak up and give us the correct details, we'd spread the story about the woman and place him in a very embarrassing situation.

Fear of public humiliation proved to be a reliable tactic. Another senior prisoner was made to undress and stand naked, facing the interrogators, for hours. They saw that he had an abnormally small penis, and out of fear that they would spread word around, he began to talk as well.

From the interrogations, it became clear that Yassin had been preparing for violent jihad for a long time. Since 1981, he'd ordered his men to break into IDF bases and steal arms and ammunition, and they had accumulated a large amount of weaponry. Altogether, forty-four firearms were located, the organization's first arsenal.

Yassin, the investigation revealed, had secretly set up a small military unit under the command of Salah Shehade. This unit consisted of two separate parts—one that would operate against wayward Palestinians, and another that would wage jihad against Israel. Yassin and his men selected personnel for the two units by observing a training program conducted by the sports and culture committees of his welfare organization, which showed them who was physically fit and who had organizational ability and ideological commitment to the movement.

In a summary he wrote after questioning all the detainees, Kubi observed that Shehade's men were "very smart, a little better educated than the average, fanatically religious, hovering around in their own space, almost impossible to penetrate" for intelligence. His report came up for discussion by the Shin Bet's top echelon. "But," says Aristo, "Avrum [Avraham Shalom, director of the agency] said there was no need at all to deal with it, and nothing harmful would come of it. *Tzileigerim* [Yiddish slang for 'losers' or 'cripples'] was what he called Yassin and his gang. I got the impression that it was very important for Avrum to please the political echelon above him—that is, the Likud government and Shamir, who detested the PLO—and to tell them with that smile of his that he was clandestinely working on a sophisticated conspiracy that would bring about significant damage to Arafat. In the historical perspective, it may be that he was right—there was indeed a sophisticated conspiracy, so sophisticated that he himself and the whole Shin Bet missed it completely."

YASSIN WAS SENTENCED TO thirteen years for his involvement in a series of weapons thefts but released a year later as part of a prisoner exchange with Ahmed Jibril's PFLP. He immediately returned to where he'd left off—building the infrastructure for the organization. Yassin had a phenomenal memory, and he knew by heart the 1,500 code names he had devised for the various operatives, operations, and letterboxes. He could recite the résumé of every member, and he displayed astonishing awareness of technological innovations and Middle Eastern current affairs.

In the years afterward, Yassin also developed and disseminated his doctrine advocating the use of suicide attacks. He noted, for the benefit of his disciples, the differences between suicide, which is absolutely forbidden, and self-sacrifice on the battlefield, which is a religious commandment and ensures the martyr, and even his family members, a place in Paradise. Whenever the suicide has received the blessing of a qualified Islamic sheikh, Yassin ruled, the dying person is not acting out of personal motives, but is considered a *shahid*, a martyr, who has fallen in the jihad for the sake of Allah.

The Shin Bet, meanwhile, was in a difficult period of transition. The agency was trying to cope with a series of shocks caused by the Ashkelon bus affair and its aftermath. Within a brief period, most of the organization's leadership had been replaced by younger men, and it took time for them to reach professional maturity. Several case officers and investigators have said that during this time they warned their superiors about the danger of extremist Islam, but the agency was too helpless to tackle it. When the First Intifada broke out, in late 1987, Yassin was already the most important religious-political figure in Gaza and the West Bank, standing at the head of a movement that had hundreds of members and tens of thousands of supporters. That December, Yassin declared that the jihad had begun. He named his organization the Islamic Resistance Movement, and its Arabic acronym was "Hamas," which also means "enthusiasm."

During the ensuing months, disjointed reports about the movement started coming in to the Shin Bet, and in August 1988 a large-scale operation was planned against it. The Shin Bet rounded up 180 people and put them through intensive questioning, but they were all well prepared and didn't reveal the most important bit of information: that Salah Shehade, the most senior member detained in the roundup, had set up a secret military wing and was now commanding it. At first, he and Yassin, wry and clever men, called it Unit 101, after Ariel Sharon's legendary command unit. Later, the name was changed to the Special Unit, Izz al-Din al-Qassam Brigades, after a Palestinian leader who had carried out attacks on British and Jewish targets in the 1930s.

Shehade continued to command the military wing from prison, smuggling out encoded messages. In 1989, he and Yassin sent two members of the unit, Mahmoud al-Mabhouh and Muhammad Nasr, to abduct and kill two Israeli soldiers. They lay in wait, in a car with Israeli plates, at an intersection where they knew soldiers hitched rides, a very widespread practice in Israel, where many motorists are only too happy to help soldiers on brief furloughs to get home or back to their bases.

Two decades later, al-Mabhouh told Al Jazeera TV network how they had grabbed one of the soldiers, Ilan Saadon:

> We disguised ourselves as religious Jews, with skullcaps on our heads, like rabbis. Another car came to the junction and dropped off passengers. Our car had boxes in it [to take up space, so only one hitchhiker could get in]. I was the driver. The boxes were behind me, and the door behind me was out of order. I told him [Saadon] to go around to the other side.
>
> He did that and sat on the backseat. I and Abu Sahib [his partner, Nasr] had a prearranged signal that at the right moment I would make a sign with my hand, because I could see what was happening on the road ahead and behind. And about three kilometers after the junction, I gave the signal to Abu Sahib and he fired his Beretta pistol. I heard him [Saadon] breathing heavily. . . . He took two bullets in the face and one in the chest, gasped, and that was it—finished. Afterward, we laid him on the seat and took him to the prearranged place.

Mabhouh added that he had wanted to shoot Saadon himself, but to his great regret it was his partner who enjoyed this privilege. In both abductions, al-Mabhouh and Nasr took photographs of themselves treading on the corpses of the soldiers to celebrate their victory.

Al-Mabhouh and Nasr fled to Egypt before the Shin Bet could arrest them. Al-Mabhouh became a key operational figure in Hamas abroad. The other members of the Izz al-Din al-Qassam Brigades who had provided logistical support to the two killers were arrested and subjected to torture, including mock executions and injections of sodium pentothal. All of them confessed, and one of them was dressed in an IDF uniform and driven around the Strip and made to point out where they had hidden Saadon's rifle and dog tags, along with the weapons they had used.

Yassin was given a life sentence for his part in the slayings.

ON THE MORNING OF December 13, 1992, two masked men entered the office of the Red Cross in Al-Bireh, a town in the West Bank, and handed the receptionist a letter. They warned her not to open it until half an hour after they had left, and ran away.

It read, "Today, 13.12.92, the fifth anniversary of the founding of Hamas, an officer of the occupation army has been abducted. He is being held in a safe place. . . . We notify the occupation authorities that we are demanding that they and the Israeli leadership release Sheikh Ahmed Yassin in exchange for the release of this officer."

The letter was signed, "The Special Unit, Izz al-Din al-Qassam Brigades, the Military Arm, Hamas." Attached to the letter was a photograph of the police ID card of First Senior Sergeant Nissim Toledano of the border police.

The prime minister and minister of defense, Yitzhak Rabin, decided not to comply with the kidnappers' demand and instead launched a wide campaign of raids and arrests. Meanwhile, the Shin Bet tried to buy some time. A top official, Barak Ben-Zur, was sent to see Yassin in prison, to ask him to agree to be interviewed by the media and to instruct his followers not to harm the kidnapped police officer.

The sheikh received Ben-Zur sitting in his wheelchair, wrapped in a blanket, with "a smile that was almost cordial." He gave a number of interviews and, in each, repeated the requested statement.

Only afterward did the Shin Bet realize why Yassin had been so obliging. He had foreseen the situation and had instructed his men in advance that whatever they heard him say in any interview, they should pay no attention and should not obey him, because the message would most likely have been extracted from him against his will.

Prison had not lessened Yassin's influence, nor broken his will. "There will never be peace," he told Ben-Zur, after the interviews were over and the cameras were switched off. "We'll take what you give, but we will never give up our armed struggle. As long as I, Sheikh Yassin, am alive, I shall make sure that there will be no peace talks with Israel. I do not have a time problem: Ten more years, a hundred more years—in the end you will be wiped off the face of the earth."

The Hamas men, as previously ordered, ignored Yassin's public instructions not to harm Toledano. That night, the four abductors, dressed in ninja costumes and armed with knives, came to the cave where Toledano was being held. "We asked Israel to free Sheikh Ahmed Yassin for you," they told him. "But your government refused, and this is proof that the lives of their soldiers do not interest them. We are sorry that we have to kill you."

Toledano began to cry. He begged to be released.

"What is your last wish?" one of the Hamas men said.

"If you have decided to kill me, kill me when I'm wearing my uniform."

The Hamas men strangled him, then stabbed him when it turned out he was still alive.

For Rabin, the murder of Toledano was the final straw. The week before, five other Israelis had been killed in terror attacks, most of them orchestrated by Hamas. The Rabin government, which now grasped the danger presented by Hamas, decided it was time to strike a decisive blow against the movement. Some in the Shin Bet proposed poisoning Yassin in prison, which would be relatively easy to do. Rabin rejected the idea out of hand, for fear of the riots that would inevitably ensue when it became known that Yassin had died while in Israeli custody.

IDF chief of staff Ehud Barak suggested a different alternative: the mass expulsion of Hamas activists to Lebanon. "We had tried a lot of methods against Hamas," said Major General Danny Yatom, head of the IDF Central Command. "And it seemed to us, for some reason, that this expulsion to Lebanon would very severely damage the motivation of the terrorists whom we expelled—and of those who think about it in future."

This was a problematic decision, ethically, legally, and pragmatically. The IDF and the Shin Bet hoped to execute the expulsion covertly, before the world could get wind of it, which put them under immense time pressure. Starting on December 16, they rounded up four hundred persons suspected of having links with Hamas—not one of them directly connected to the latest acts of terror—blindfolded them and handcuffed them, then loaded them onto buses and took them to the Lebanese border.

But news about the operation had leaked out anyway, and in Israel a number of NGOs, as well as the families of some of the deportees, petitioned the Supreme Court to halt it, which delayed the bus convoy for hours. The attorney general's office refused to represent the government, believing that the expulsion was in fact a war crime, and chief of staff Barak himself had to go to the court to try to persuade the justices.

He succeeded, but in the meantime an international scandal had broken out. It turned out that about a quarter of the deportees had been loaded onto the buses by mistake, and were not the people the Shin Bet had meant to expel. Meanwhile, Lebanon blocked its borders, and the buses were stuck in a no-man's-land between the Israeli-controlled Security Zone to the south and territory controlled by the Lebanese Armed Forces and Hezbollah to the north.

The IDF military police escort gave each deportee $50 in cash, a coat, and two blankets, then forced them off the buses, removing their blindfolds and plastic handcuffs. Then they turned the buses around and headed back into Israel. The deportees eventually pitched a tent camp at Marj al-Zuhour, near the Druze town of Hasbaya. At first, the government of Lebanon blocked attempts by the Red Cross to extend assistance, out of a desire to intensify the deportees' distress and to embarrass the Israeli government even more.

As it happened, the expulsion was in fact a serious blow to Hamas. At this point, its two top leaders, Yassin and Shehade, were in an Israeli prison, and the rest of its leaders were now in a remote tent camp on a freezing, windy hillside in Lebanon, without electricity, without means of communication, wet and miserable.

But the situation changed dramatically a week after the expulsion, when a group of Lebanese came to visit. Their leader introduced himself as Wafik Safa of Hezbollah, greeted them in the name of Secretary General Hassan Nasrallah, and asked if the deportees needed any help.

This visit had come after a series of meetings held between Nasrallah, the IRGC, Mughniyeh, and Safa, who had become a kind of foreign minister for the organization. Mughniyeh had seen the expulsion and the sufferings of the Hamas group as a godsend. In his mind, Hezbollah could and should use the opportunity to expand its influence beyond the borders of Lebanon, with partners who were not necessarily Iranian or Shiite. In the end, he managed to persuade the others, too.

Militant Shiites did not, as a general rule, make alliances with Sunni Muslim Palestinians. This was a surprising gesture toward Sunni Muslim Hamas, then, and Hamas, too, was initially hesitant. The link didn't seem natural to them, either, but their predicament was decisive, and they shared a hatred of a common enemy. They responded affirmatively, and within a short time, convoys of donkeys and mules began bringing in more weatherproof tents, warm clothes, heating stoves, and fuel, as well as large quantities of food and cleaning and laundry materials to see them through the harsh winter.

Next came the Lebanese media—some under the control or influence of Hezbollah, but others simply covering a good story—to tell the world about the sufferings of the deportees. Then came military and terrorism instructors. Until that point, Hamas had had almost no training in combat operations or intelligence. In this respect, the expulsion turned out to be a godsend for them, too.

Mughniyeh's men, commanded by his brother-in-law, Mustafa Badreddine, along with instructors from the Al-Quds force of the IRGC, set up a guarded area near the tent camp, but far enough away to avoid the prying eyes of the media that were now constantly covering the camp. Within this area, courses were held in communications, encryption, and field security, light arms, rocket launchers, espionage and counterespionage, urban warfare, hand-to-hand combat, and more.

Mughniyeh's instructors were particularly impressed by a twenty-eight-year-old electrical engineer from the northern West Bank, a graduate of Bir Zeit University named Yahya Ayyash, who would, appropriately, come to be known as "the Engineer." The Iranian and Hezbollah experts taught him how to clandestinely make explosives from domestic items that were easy to buy, how to make small but deadly explosive devices using nails and screws as shrapnel, and how to make car bombs. Mughniyeh himself came to the camp to talk with Ayyash and some of his comrades about the ways in which potential candidates for suicide bombings could be located and recruited—how to approach them and how to handle the sensitive and difficult process of persuading them to do the deed.

While his men were being trained on a desolate mountain, Yassin's organization was being rebuilt in the West Bank and Gaza. Over the years, Hamas had established a vast network of activists and fundraisers in the Persian Gulf, Jordan, and the United States, under the overall command of Mousa Abu Marzook, a U.S. citizen. Wealthy sheikhs from Saudi Arabia, along with counterparts from the Gulf emirates and wealthy Muslims in the West, had contributed funds to the organization. After the mass expulsion, Marzook dispatched one of his aides, Muhammad Salah, from the United States to the occupied territories with hundreds of thousands of dollars in cash.

International pressure on Israel mounted daily. There was continuous media coverage of the camp, a sharp condemnation by the UN Security Council and the threat of sanctions, and an increasingly acrimonious confrontation with the administration of newly sworn-in president Bill Clinton and his secretary of state, Warren Christopher. By February 1992, Rabin realized that the whole thing had been a big mistake, and he agreed to Christopher's proposal to repatriate some of the deportees immediately and the rest by the end of the year, in exchange for a U.S. veto on Israel's behalf in the Security Council.

The deportees returned to the Gaza Strip and the West Bank as victors. Ayyash was made a commander of the Izz al-Din al-Qassam Brigades in the West Bank, and a short time later he organized the suicide bombing at Mehola in April 1993, in which the terrorist and a civilian were killed. For his next attack, though, Ayyash waited for a defining moment, something that would forever justify and legitimize suicide bombing in the eyes of the Palestinians.

That moment came on February 25, 1994, when Dr. Baruch Goldstein, a Brooklyn-born follower of Rabbi Meir Kahane and the Jewish Defense League, who had immigrated to Kiryat Arba, a settlement near Hebron, opened fire on Muslims worshipping in that city's Ibrahimi Mosque, located at Cave of the Patriarchs, the site revered by both faiths as the burial place of Abraham.

During a minute and a half of shooting, using his IDF-issued Galil rifle and wearing an IDF uniform, Goldstein managed to replace four magazines. Then one of the Muslims threw a fire extinguisher at him and knocked him down. The worshippers pounced on him and beat him to death. Before he was incapacitated, he managed to murder twenty-nine worshippers and injure more than a hundred.

Throughout the Muslim world, there were many who saw this act as not only a despicable crime against innocent people, but also a declaration of war by the Jews against Islam itself.

This was the moment Yahya Ayyash had been waiting for. He counted the ritual forty days of mourning before striking, and then, on April 6, a suicide bomber recruited by Ayyash blew himself up close to two buses in the Israeli town of Afula, just north of the West Bank, taking eight civilians with him. A week later, another suicide bomber killed five Israelis in the bus station in Hadera. On October 19, Ayyash struck in the heart of Tel Aviv, where a Palestinian detonated his suicide belt on a No. 5 bus on the city's Dizengoff Street, killing twenty-two. The bombings went on and on.

"Until then, the Palestinian terrorists we were acquainted with had a lust for life," the Shin Bet's Avi Dichter said. "Even Leila Khaled, in her last hijacking with two grenades in her hands, when faced by an Israeli security guard with a pistol, didn't have the guts to blow herself up. The change in 1993 was dramatic, and it surprised us.

"The power of the terrorists had grown exponentially. A suicide bomber doesn't need operational skill; it's just one switch, off and on. When there are four hundred on the waiting list to be suicide terrorists, everyone can see the gravity of the problem."

Hamas's competitors took notice of Ayyash's successes and the support his activities received in the Palestinian streets. On November 11, 1994, a member of the Palestinian Islamic Jihad (PIJ) blew himself up at an IDF post at Netzarim Junction, in the Gaza Strip, killing three reserve officers. On January 22, 1995, an Islamic Jihad (IJO) terrorist wearing an IDF uniform pushed his way into the center of a crowd of soldiers waiting at a bus stop at Beit Lid, twenty-five miles northeast of Tel Aviv. He pushed a switch that detonated twenty-two pounds of explosives on his person. Dozens of soldiers were cut down by the huge blast. When others ran toward the wounded, who were screaming for help, a second suicide bomber blew himself up in their midst. A third terrorist was supposed to follow that up minutes later but got cold feet and ran away.

Twenty-one soldiers and one civilian were killed in that attack, and sixty-six were wounded, some very badly. Prime Minister and Defense Minister Rabin came to the scene shortly after the blasts, the junction still littered with body parts and stained with blood. A spontaneous demonstration of angry citizens took place while he was there. However, the protesters were not chanting slogans against terror, but rather against Rabin. "Go to Gaza!" they yelled, a curse that, in Hebrew, sounds similar to "Go to Hell."

On his return to Tel Aviv, Rabin, "his blood boiling with fury," in the words of his bureau chief, Eitan Haber, called a meeting of all the heads of the defense establishment. "This madness must be stopped," he said. "Bring me Red Pages to sign."

# "BRING US THE HEAD OF AYYASH"

THIS WAS NOT THE way Yitzhak Rabin had imagined his second term as prime minister of Israel would turn out.

He had been elected on the promise to deliver both security—he was perceived as a tough military leader, uncompromising in the war on terror—and a diplomatic initiative that would extricate Israel from its isolation, bring economic prosperity, and put an end to the intifada.

Rabin had indeed reached the conclusion that the occupation of Palestinian lands needed to end. He agreed to the Oslo process, initiated by Shimon Peres and his associates, though he did so rather sourly, with much doubt and skepticism of the intentions of the Palestinians. All this was evident in his face and body language when President Clinton coaxed him into a handshake with Yasser Arafat at the signing ceremony on the White House lawn on September 13, 1993.

Rabin believed that the process should be conducted gradually, with Israel pulling out of only Gaza and Jericho at first, instead of signing a comprehensive agreement right away. That would allow Israel to hand over parts of the occupied territories to the Palestinian Authority while continually checking to make sure Arafat was fulfilling his end of the agreement. It would also mean that the main items still in contention—the right of return for Palestinian refugees, the status of Jerusalem, the future of the settlements in the West Bank and Gaza, and whether the Palestinian Authority would become a sovereign state—would be left to be decided on at a later date. Rabin hoped this would allow him to avert the divisive controversy that would almost certainly arise in Israel when these issues came to a head.

But controversy followed Rabin anyway. A large section of the Israeli public believed that the Oslo Accords had increased the likelihood of terror attacks, and that because of the peace process and the transfer of territory to Arafat's control, terrorism was on the rise. All the Israeli right wing had to do was quote, word for word, what Yassin was saying—that there would never be any compromise, that he would never accept the existence of a Jewish state. What began as minor demonstrations by small groups of extremist settlers grew into a protest campaign across the length and breadth of Israel, drawing increased strength after each terror attack and focusing more and more on vicious incitement against Rabin himself. These protests were spurred on by the leaders of the Likud, Ariel Sharon and Benjamin Netanyahu.

Meanwhile, the Palestinians saw with rising frustration how they were being dispossessed of their lands—Rabin did restrict the construction of new settlements, but he did not stop construction altogether, and he did not evacuate even a single existing settlement in the occupied areas—and they had no sense that the process would lead to the establishment of a state of their own. At the same time, because Arafat wanted to avoid a confrontation with the Islamist opposition, he refrained from any attempt to combat the guerrilla and suicide terror attacks of Hamas and Islamic Jihad.

"Neither of the sides grasped the meaning of the other side's demands," said Ami Ayalon, head of the Shin Bet in the second half of the 1990s, "so that ultimately it transpired that both sides felt cheated, with a great degree of justifiability. We didn't get security, and they didn't get a state."

Efforts to resolve the conflicts on Israel's northern borders were no more successful. Secretary of State Christopher mediated between Israel and Syria, with the goal of reaching a peace agreement under which Israel would withdraw from the Golan Heights and perhaps also from Lebanon, while Syria would work to put a stop to Hezbollah's actions against Israel. But no significant breakthroughs were made. Hezbollah, egged on by the Syrians, who were trying to exert pressure on Israel, continued inflicting casualties on the IDF forces in Lebanon.

The status quo in the Lebanese Security Zone was wearing thin for the Israelis. The IDF's field commanders were furious, demanding that they be given free rein to go into action. The most prominent of these commanders was Brigadier General Erez Gerstein, a burly man with enough charisma and self-confidence that many saw him as a future chief of staff. Gerstein saw parallels between southern Lebanon and Vietnam, mostly in terms of lessons to be learned from American mistakes. "We sit in the fortresses scratching our balls instead of going out, thinking like them [Hezbollah], hitting them where they don't expect it, and killing their commanders," he said.

The SLA troops were also dissatisfied, feeling like cannon fodder, restrained from fighting back. Aql al-Hashem, the deputy commander of the militia, had for years pleaded with Israel to at least target Hezbollah officers.

These calls didn't fall on deaf ears. On January 1, 1995, Amnon Lipkin-Shahak succeeded Ehud Barak as chief of staff. Determined to escape the shadow of his predecessor, he decided to change the policy in Lebanon. From now on, it would be a war, and Hezbollah would be treated as a full-fledged enemy. He needed resources: personnel who could gather intelligence and special-operations squads skilled in sabotage and assassination.

Lipkin-Shahak and the head of the Northern Command, Major General Amiram Levin, one of the IDF's leading experts in commando warfare, quickly organized a new commando unit, known as Egoz (Hebrew for "Nut"), to wage counterguerrilla warfare against Hezbollah. One of its first commanders, Moshe Tamir, explained that "a large part of the tactics that I developed in the Egoz unit . . . came from books compiled by the British Army about fighting in the Himalayas, in Indochina. Also, the experience of the Americans in Vietnam, especially at the lower levels, was instructive." Like the officers of the British and American forces, and the French in Algeria, Tamir, Gerstein, and their colleagues believed that if they were given adequate resources, time, and support from the rear, it would be possible to defeat Hezbollah.

Egoz began conducting ambushes and raids inside Lebanon, in the areas where Hezbollah felt safe, surprising the militiamen and killing large numbers of them. One of the men killed was Hadi Nasrallah, the son of the leader of the movement.

Levin had taken part in Operation Spring of Youth, and he saw great importance in targeted strikes against Hezbollah commanders. Ronen Cohen, who had just become head of the Lebanon desk in the Northern Command's intelligence section, had to apply the new policy. The two decided to focus on killing middle-ranking militia officers, regional commanders in southern Lebanon, and not the top-level officials. Levin believed that Hezbollah distinguished between operations targeting one of its leaders or the center of its activities in Beirut and tactical warfare of the kind being waged in southern Lebanon. The former would provoke an extreme reaction, perhaps even outside the Middle East, whereas the response to the latter would be limited in scope and confined to Lebanon and northern Israel.

Until this point, the Mossad had carried out all targeted killings outside of Israel, while the IDF only provided support, at most. But the Mossad didn't see Hezbollah as much more than a border problem that the IDF should cope with, and even if it had changed its order of priorities, the organization was almost incapable of operating offensively in Lebanon. "In brief," Cohen said, "it was clear to me that if we wanted to hit quality Hezbollah targets we, the IDF, would have to do it on our own."

The hit on Mussawi, strategically flawed as it was, seemed to Cohen to be a good tactical model: Identify a target with a drone, mark him with a laser, then fire a missile. It was an inexpensive, efficient method.

Northern Command intelligence picked a target, a man by the name of Rida Yassin, better known as Abu-Ali Rida, commander of Hezbollah in the Nabatieh area, who lived in the village of Zawtar al-Charkiyeh. As an intermediate-level commander in southern Lebanon, Rida fit the profile perfectly, and he was accessible in a way that other commanders of similar seniority were not.

After two weeks of surveillance, Cohen managed to gather enough information about Rida, who was given the code name Golden Beehive, to plan an operation. Once a week, Rida went to a meeting of

Hezbollah senior staff in Beirut, returning late at night, then driving to his office at about 8:30 the next morning. The original plan called for an agent to stand lookout at that time to be sure that Rida got into his car and that no one else was with him. Once that was confirmed, a drone would track him until he left the village, then identify the car with its laser for an Apache helicopter to fire its missile.

Operation Golden Beehive, which was managed from the Northern Command war room, was almost called off. On March 30, 1995, the agent posted near Rida's house was surprised to see Rida's parking space empty. He couldn't remain there for long without arousing suspicion, and had to leave. But the drone remained in the sky above, transmitting images from a distance until the monitors saw Rida's car returning home. Someone got out and went into the house, but Levin, Cohen, and their subordinates in the command bunker could not see his face. Nor could they identify the person who left the house an hour later, started the car, and drove out of the village, crossing the Litani River and moving south toward Nabatieh. The dilemma was clear: Who was driving the car now? Was it Rida or one of his children? Should the order be given to fire the missile?

Levin gambled. He told the Apache pilot to fire.

About three hours later, Hezbollah's radio networks exploded with transmissions about the killing. Rida, and only Rida, had been in the car. In the radio chatter, Israeli monitors could hear that Mughniyeh's men were rattled, their confidence undermined. One of their own had been assassinated from afar, marked by a silent and unseen flying robot. It was only the second time a drone had been used to kill a man.

Nasrallah vowed revenge, and Hezbollah once again responded with a barrage of rockets into northern Israel. A seventeen-year-old jogging on the beach didn't hear the alerts and was killed by a direct hit. Nevertheless, Hezbollah, just as Levin and Cohen had predicted, regarded the incident as a local matter and did not try to avenge the slaying of Rida beyond the Middle East.

Operation Golden Beehive was the model for additional attacks on other midlevel officers. But the Golden Beehive MO wasn't the only one employed. In others, Egoz or another unit moved in at night and placed a bomb in the target's car or along his expected route, which then would be remotely detonated by either an aircraft or a lookout on the ground.

Meanwhile, Levin and Cohen were restructuring the command-and-control networks of targeted killings—who decided on targets and who gave the final *rashai* (permission to engage) order. This was a critical matter. Until this point, all Red Pages for "negative treatment" had to be reported to VARASH, the committee of heads of intelligence agencies, chaired by the director of the Mossad. Then they had to be approved at the highest civilian level, signed by the prime minister himself, who often brought in other ministers as well before making a decision.

Because of the high risk of a diplomatic tangle in the event of failure, every Red Page required deliberation and a great deal of time, and it often ended in non-approval.

Levin and Cohen, however, avoided that process through a clever use of semantics. In Lebanon, a targeted killing was no longer an assassination—it was an "interception." Those, apparently, did not require such scrutiny, although of course the authorization of the chief of staff was still necessary.

At the time, this workaround of the system was not seen as troublesome. Rabin, who served as both prime minister and minister of defense, trusted chief of staff Lipkin-Shahak and was satisfied with being informed during the weekly operations-and-sorties meeting in the defense minister's office.

Nevertheless, "a precedent was created," one former Northern Command officer said, "by which an assassination operation was called something else so that it would fall under a different decision-making protocol, in order to enable a lower echelon to approve it." In other words, killing a man no longer required the prime minister's approval.

There was no doubt the new procedures were effective, though. After years of frustration in the Security Zone, the IDF had constructed a complete targeted killing system, rapidly gathering intelligence and turning it into operations. In two and a half years, IDF squads carried out twenty-seven targeted killing operations, mostly against Hezbollah personnel, twenty-one of which were successful.

·   ·   ·

WHILE LEVIN AND COHEN were rewriting the assassination protocols in the Security Zone, Israel's intelligence agencies were figuring
out how to execute two Red Pages Rabin had signed in early 1995.

The evening after the Beit Lid terror attack, when two suicide
bombers killed twenty-one soldiers and one civilian waiting at a bus
stop, Israeli intelligence already knew who was responsible and who,
therefore, was going to be assassinated: Fathi Shaqaqi, the leader of
the Palestinian Islamic Jihad. His organization had grown out of a
nucleus of Palestinian students studying medicine in the 1970s in
Egypt who were politically active at Zagazig University, a hotbed of
Islamist fanaticism. After a brief career as a pediatrician in the Gaza
Strip, Shaqaqi set up a small and secretive organization, in some
ways a competitor to Sheikh Yassin's Hamas. Shaqaqi differed ideologically from Hamas in his belief that jihad must take precedence
over social reform, while Hamas was equally devoted to both. The
group that coalesced around Shaqaqi had only one function: anti-
Israel terror.

Shaqaqi was in and out of Israeli jails for three years, until ultimately he was expelled from Gaza to Lebanon in 1988. The Iranian
Revolutionary Guards took him under their wing and arranged permission for him to make Damascus his base, providing him with
funds and weaponry. Within a short time, his organization was operating under the patronage of the Iranians, and PIJ soon launched a
series of terror attacks. The worst of these was a well-organized gunfire assault on a bus carrying Israeli tourists in Egypt, some thirty
miles east of Cairo, in February 1990. Nine Israeli passengers and
two Egyptians were killed and nineteen wounded. Following Hamas's
success with suicide terrorism, the Iranians gave Shaqaqi a green
light to begin carrying out those kinds of attacks as well. PIJ's Beit
Lid bombings were the climax of this campaign.

Four days after the suicide bombings, Shaqaqi gave an interview
to *Time* magazine correspondent Lara Marlowe in his Damascus office. Shaqaqi did not admit that he had been directly involved in the
attack, but he detailed how it had been planned, smiling and chuck-
ling throughout the interview, evidently quite pleased that twenty-
two Israelis were dead.

By then, Rabin's signature on Shaqaqi's death warrant was already three days old. But this order was a highly unusual one. In fact, it was the first Red Page that Rabin had signed since becoming prime minister. At the time, the pact with the PLO and Arafat's establishment of the Palestinian Authority had led many Israelis to conclude that the war with the Palestinians—the bombings, the terror attacks, the assassinations and abductions all over the world—was over. The Mossad saw the suicide terrorists as an internal problem, within the jurisdiction of the Shin Bet, and there were some who even proposed cutting the Mossad's counterterror division by half.

Moreover, Fathi Shaqaqi was a Palestinian leader with many admirers in the occupied territories. The decision to eliminate him, despite the accompanying risk of rebellious responses from the Palestinians, was indicative of Rabin's painful recognition that the war with the Palestinians was still far from over.

Indeed, the terror attack at Beit Lid led to a change in the way Prime Minister Rabin conceived of Israel's security. In its wake, Rabin began defining terror differently: from "bee stings" to "strategic threat." Until then, the phrase "strategic threat" had been reserved for full-scale enemy military moves that endangered large parts of the Israeli population and its territory or that could lead to the destruction of the state, such as the surprise by the Arab armies in October 1973, or the possibility of Saddam Hussein obtaining nuclear weapons. "The reason for Rabin's changing the definition—which I totally agreed with," said Carmi Gillon, deputy Shin Bet chief at the time, "sprang from the fact the terror had succeeded in making a sovereign government change its decisions or delay their implementation because of the effect of the terror attacks on the Israeli street."

Despite this change in approach and in perceived threat, executing the Red Page on Shaqaqi was still a careful operation, and it took months of surveillance. Mossad operatives were able to wiretap the phones in Shaqaqi's home and office, but killing him in Damascus was not ideal. It was physically treacherous to operate in Syria, and it was politically risky as well: Uri Sagie, head of AMAN at the time, told Rabin that such an operation would harm the peace negotiations then under way between Israel and Syria, under American patronage.

But killing Shaqaqi outside of Syria would not be a simple matter, either. Shaqaqi knew he was in jeopardy, and when he traveled, it

was only to other Arab states or Iran—equally difficult places for Israeli assassins to penetrate. For almost six months, the Mossad's
Caesarea tried to pinpoint a time and place where it would be possible to orchestrate an attack. Then, on April 9, the pressure on the
Mossad increased: A car bomb driven by a PIJ suicide terrorist exploded next to an Israeli bus in the Gaza Strip, killing seven soldiers
and Alisa Michelle Flatow, a twenty-year-old student from West Orange, New Jersey. More than thirty people were injured. A short time
afterward, another car bomb injured twelve people. "Find a solution,"
Rabin told Director Shabtai Shavit. "We've got to nail this man."

A month later, the Mossad came up with a proposal, though it,
too, aroused immediate opposition. Like Spring of Youth, in 1973,
and the hit on Abu Jihad in Tunis, in 1988, it called for the IDF to
extend its assistance to the Mossad, which could not execute it on its
own.

Chief of staff Lipkin-Shahak, whose relations with Shavit were
already shaky, had no objection, in principle, to killing Shaqaqi, but
he believed that the Mossad should be able to do so on its own, and
that there was no need to involve IDF personnel in an operation a
long way from Israel's borders. A loud argument between the two
men broke out in Rabin's presence, until he silenced them and decided in Shavit's favor.

Surveillance had shown that Shaqaqi was in regular contact with
Muammar Qaddafi—who had given the jihadist a Libyan passport
under the name Ibrahim Shawish—and that he visited the Libyan
dictator frequently, either alone or with other top terrorists. At the
time, Libya was under rigorous international sanctions because of its
involvement in terrorism, and most airlines did not fly there. So
Shaqaqi would fly from Beirut or Damascus to Malta and then to
Tunis, where he would rent a luxury car, usually a BMW or a Jaguar,
and drive the 480 miles to Tripoli on his own.

A bomb along the desolate highway seemed ideal, and in June a
squad of Flotilla 13 naval commandos landed on a Tunisian beach
and hiked toward the roadway, sinking in the soft sand under the
weight of four crates, each packed with 450 pounds of explosives.
They were placed on special tungsten pallets, strong but flexible, that
could be carried by four burly soldiers across the dunes to the Tunis-

Tripoli highway. The plan called for the raiders to dig a pit next to the road, on which traffic was minimal, and bury the huge bomb in it. Meanwhile, Caesarea operatives would be watching Shaqaqi as he rented a vehicle in Tunis and attach to it a transponder, or "pinger," in trade jargon, which transmitted a particularly strong signal. This device would activate the bomb's detonating device as the car passed by, blowing it and its driver to pieces.

"Almost no one ever uses this road," one of the Caesarea planners said at the final briefing, "so there's a very, very high probability that the target will go to the world hereafter when he is on his own, and it will take a very long time before anyone notices what has happened, and many more hours before some search party or crime scene investigators get to the scene."

On June 4, 1995, the signal came in: Shaqaqi had made a reservation for a flight to Malta a week later. The assassination operation began. Two Israeli Navy missile boats set sail from Haifa, loaded with equipment and naval commandos, under Yoav Galant, commander of Flotilla 13. It took two and a half days to sail the 1,200 miles, before anchoring a safe distance from the coast at the point where the border between Tunisia and Libya meets the Mediterranean. Ami Ayalon, now commander of the navy, directed the operation from a distance.

It had been seven years since Galant led the naval commando detachment that landed a Sayeret Matkal unit on the Tunisian beach on its way to eliminate Abu Jihad. Now the IDF was equipped with much more advanced technology. On a giant screen in the Pit, Ayalon saw accurate, real-time indications of the locations of all the forces involved.

Proceeding in extra-strong rubber dinghies, the commandos landed some six miles west of the Libyan seaside town of Sabratha.

"Moving across those dunes was very tough," said one of the commandos, "with each one of us gripping the end of a pole and trying not to sink into the sand and sweating ourselves to death. I still remember that yellow, perfectly clean sand. I thought that in a different situation, I'd be happy to stretch out on it near the sea and grab a tan. But not that day. It was already beginning to get light, and we had to get the burying done quickly. We kept moving until all of a sudden we heard on our headsets 'Cease advance now!' from the force's forward squad. Very soon we realized why."

It turned out that although the Israelis' intelligence on Shaqaqi's movements was accurate, they had not anticipated a Morocco-to-Egypt car rally under way right then. Some of the drivers reached the road at the same time as the commandos and decided to take a break. They broke out drinks and chatted loudly in English, German, and French, laughing and cursing the sand that was getting into their engines. Galant consulted with Ayalon. The danger of being discovered by the rally drivers was growing minute by minute. ("One of them may step aside to take a leak or worse, and do it right on our heads," Galant radioed.) Also, it was not clear how much longer they would stay at that spot or whether more cars would come along the road later. This meant that even if the bomb was placed and set off by Shaqaqi's car that evening, "innocent non-Arab people" might be harmed. Ayalon ordered the commandos to withdraw. The risk of killing a civilian, or many civilians, was too high, and the operation was aborted.

Four more frustrating months passed. Finally, in mid-October, the Mossad got a break that enabled them to do the hit themselves, without any complicated combined operations with the IDF.

The phone, which was still tapped, rang in Shaqaqi's office in Damascus. On the line was an aide to Qaddafi, inviting him to a conference, in Libya, of several heads of Arab guerrilla organizations. Shaqaqi said he would not be attending. But the Mossad then learned that Said Mussa al-Muragha—Abu Mussa—commander of an extremist Palestinian faction that had mutinied against Arafat and quit the PLO, and was now based in Damascus and operating under Syrian protection, would be there. Abu Mussa was also a rival of Shaqaqi's.

"If Abu Mussa goes, our client won't be able to stay away," Mishka Ben-David, Caesarea's intelligence officer, told a meeting called to discuss the subject at Mossad HQ. "Tell the guys to get ready."

It wasn't clear what Shaqaqi would decide in the end. But the Mossad reasoned that if he went, he could be vulnerable during his stopover in Malta, or farther along his overland route to Libya.

A few months earlier, "Jerry" had been appointed commander of the targeted killing unit. Not particularly liked by his Mossad colleagues, Jerry was a man of few words, who had done his military service in a special naval diving unit. He had already been part of the teams that eliminated Gerald Bull and Ataf Bseiso, and he believed that this new position would elevate him in the ranks of the Mossad toward what he really wanted: to be head of Caesarea. "I want to sit in Mike Harari's chair," he told a friend. Killing Shaqaqi, then, was a matter of both national interest and personal ambition.

On October 22, Jerry and his team traveled to Malta and waited at the airport, examining the incoming passengers. After a few flights had landed, Jerry radioed his partners and the Mossad in Tel Aviv. "There's someone sitting on the side here," he said. "I'm going to check him out." Tension mounted. A minute later, he came back on the air: "I think we've got an ID. He's got a wig on, but there's a high probability he's our man."

Shaqaqi never left the airport, but instead boarded the next flight to Tunis. The Mossad knew, however, that he would usually spend a day or two at the Diplomat Hotel, in the Maltese resort town of Sliema, either on the way to Libya or on his return trip. So the odds were good that if they waited a few days, Shaqaqi would be vulnerable.

Shaqaqi landed in Malta again on the morning of October 26 after attending the conference. He was spotted at the airport by a Bayonet lookout, and by 10 A.M. two operatives were posted in the lobby of the Diplomat. Shaqaqi arrived by taxi and checked in for one night. He took his own bags up to his room, not allowing a bellboy to do it for him. One of the Israelis followed him and saw him entering room 616.

The tranquil and tourist-packed Malta was considered a "base country" in which it was not particularly dangerous to operate, and it was therefore left up to Jerry himself to decide which way the hit would be made. Jerry summoned his team to the street corner outside the hotel and briefed them.

At 11:30 A.M., Shaqaqi left the hotel, turned left, and strolled down the street, enjoying the pleasant weather. He went into a Marks & Spencer store, and an operative trailed him, watching as he bought a shirt there and then three more at another store. Jerry was standing across the street. When he saw Shaqaqi coming out, he whispered two words into the microphone of the radio in his sleeve: "Honey Bun." The code for action.

Shaqaqi had not noticed anything unusual, and he continued his stroll. He didn't pay any attention to the Yamaha motorcycle that began closing in on him at 1:15, until it drew level with him very slowly. Then, when Shaqaqi was alone on the sidewalk, the passenger on the back of the bike drew a pistol fitted with a silencer. He shot Shaqaqi twice in the side of the head and, after he fell, once more in the back of his neck. The pistol was equipped with a small bag that collected the shell casings, leaving the crime scene investigators of the Malta police force very little to work with.

The motorcycle sped away, and two rental cars picked up the rest of the team. They gathered at a nearby beach, where a speedboat crewed by three commandos, dressed in civilian clothing and looking like three unremarkable tourists, picked them up and whisked them away to an Israeli Navy missile boat waiting far offshore. The next day, the Malta police found the motorcycle on the beach.

IN THE WAKE OF the change in approach to the terror threat after the attack at Beit Lid, Rabin also ordered an intel collection on leaders of Hamas, focusing first and foremost on Yahya Ayyash, "the Engineer," who'd been trained in exile and imported suicide bombings into Israel in the spring of 1993. During 1994 and '95, Ayyash was responsible for nine suicide attacks, in which fifty-six people were killed and 387 wounded. Israeli public opinion was brimming over with the sight of spilled blood and charred bodies in buses. Rabin knew he had to do something, and so he signed a Red Page against Ayyash.

This, too, was very unusual. Ayyash ran suicide terrorists from inside the West Bank and Gaza, territories under the control of the Palestinian Authority. It was the PA's jurisdiction, and they were supposed to arrest him and his men. Israel and the PA were negotiating the next stages of the Oslo Accords at the time, and operating inside its territory would be considered a breach of the peace agreement and could become a political crisis.

Rabin had repeatedly demanded that the PLO chairman act firmly and decisively to disrupt the suicide bombings. One of the intelligence officials who was present with Rabin during a phone conversation with Arafat remembered him rebuking Arafat harshly. When he put the phone down, Rabin "was red in the face," complaining that Arafat and his people were doing nothing at all to rein in Hamas and the PIJ.

For his part, Arafat denied that Palestinians were even behind the attacks. A noted conspiracy theorist, Arafat had his own, completely unfounded explanation. "A secret Israeli organization by the name of OAS," he said, "that functions inside the Shin Bet and in cooperation with Hamas and the Islamic Jihad, whose aim is to disrupt the peace process, is behind these attacks and many others."

By early 1995, the Israelis realized that any hopes they harbored of the Palestinian Authority stopping the terror attacks themselves were, at best, highly unrealistic. "Along with all the contacts, talks, requests, and demands that we raised with the Palestinians, we decided ultimately that we would rely solely on ourselves and to make every effort to combat terror," said Gillon.

By coincidence, at the same time the two suicide bombers attacked Beit Lid, on January 22, Shin Bet chief Yaakov Peri summoned Yisrael Hasson and asked him to become head of the agency central command, which covered the entire West Bank.

Hasson, one of the Shin Bet's most experienced operatives, said he would agree only if the agency radically altered the way it was handling Yahya Ayyash.

"If you think," Hasson told Peri, "that it's a local problem for the case officer in charge of Rafat [the village where Ayyash was born], you are making a big mistake. This man is derailing the political process. The only way to get to him is for the entire agency and every one of its members to get up in the morning and ask himself, 'What can I do today to catch Yahya Ayyash?'"

Peri asked him what he wanted.

"I want supreme responsibility, over all other factors in the agency, for handling him," Hasson said.

Peri, himself a skilled runner of agents who knew how to make people feel good, responded with a smile: "I hereby appoint you head of the agency for Yahya Ayyash affairs."

"So then I want a promise that you can't overrule me and that any decision of mine on the subject is final," Hasson said.

Peri was confident that he'd be able to persuade Rabin to sign a Red Page against Ayyash, but he was also sophisticated enough to steer clear of organizational mines, and he only replied, "Yisrael, the entire agency is behind you. Get going, and bring us the head of Ayyash."

Hasson took up his new post and reviewed all the intel they had on Ayyash. There was very little. It emerged that for more than a year, not one reliable Shin Bet source had been in touch with Ayyash or with any of his closest associates, and that there was no clear indication of his whereabouts, apart from one report that said Hamas had managed to help him flee to Poland, for fear the Shin Bet would lay its hands on him.

Hasson doubted the veracity of this report. "How can he be in Poland, when we are finding his fingerprints all over the suicide bombings here?" he asked at a meeting in early February. He announced then that he was changing his entire way of looking at the subject.

Until that point, the Shin Bet's chief foes were the various member organizations of the PLO. They generally functioned in small cells, from certain locations, usually where they lived. Consequently, Shin Bet operations had been built around geographical areas—villages, towns, districts, regions—in which intelligence operatives and agent handlers gathered material on everything that was happening. Each unit acted almost entirely independently, and coordination between them was limited and implemented only at the command level. Operatives working on the same subject never met in any kind of organized manner to swap information and discuss various actions to implement.

But Hamas functioned within a completely different framework. Activists did not carry out the tasks Hamas gave them in their own place of residence, but elsewhere. With each mission, they were in a different place, while remaining under a nationwide command. Thus, a Shin Bet operative's specialized awareness of what was happening in his specific geographical area did not yield any significant results.

Hasson was taking a new approach to Ayyash, who was given the code name Crystal. All intelligence on Crystal, he announced, was to be concentrated in his office, under his command. Operation Crystal was transformed from a localized matter handled separately by a number of operatives in the Shin Bet—each one under a different commander with his own order of priorities—into a nationwide matter, with Hasson making all the decisions. This was something of a small-scale organizational revolution: Hasson could now issue an order over the heads of the local commanders, and this aroused quite a bit of resentment.

Hasson ordered various Shin Bet units to try to recruit a number of Palestinians who could possibly help. He also ordered operatives to re-interrogate dozens of Hamas activists in Israeli prisons. Following those operations, another thirty-five Hamas activists were arrested and interrogated. They were put together in cells at night, in different groupings, and their conversations were taped. In addition, Palestinian prisoners recruited to act as Shin Bet agents—Muppets, they were called—were planted in their cells to get them to talk.

They quickly discovered that Ayyash was exceptionally clever. Long before it was widely known that law enforcement and intelligence agencies could secretly collect a large amount of information from private telephones, Ayyash took pains not to use the same cellphones or landlines regularly, and to constantly change his sleeping places. Most important, he seemed to never trust anyone.

Eventually, though, the efforts to locate Crystal bore fruit. It turned out he was not in Poland, and never had been. He was in the northern West Bank, operating in the vicinity of Qalqilya, in an area partly under the control of Israel and partly under the PA—right under the Shin Bet's nose. "It is impossible to lay the blame for his not being captured only on the shoulders of the PA," said Carmi Gillon, who had taken over from Peri as head of the Shin Bet. "It was our failure, and we've got to admit it."

In April, four months after the Red Page was signed, the Shin Bet got a tip that Ayyash was going to attend a Hamas meeting in Hebron. Hasson thought that acting then was too risky, and that the intelligence penetration of Hamas had to be improved, but the pressure from Prime Minister Rabin to hit Ayyash was too great to withstand. Disguised as Arabs, the Birds team lay in wait for him close to the meeting place, in the heart of a very hostile and crowded location. "To his good fortune and to our good fortune, he never turned up," said Hasson. "I doubt that we would have been able to get all of our people out of there alive. It was an absolutely insanely dangerous mission, but because of the danger that this terrible individual represented, we had decided to go ahead with it nevertheless."

Ayyash didn't turn up anywhere else that was strategically convenient, either. In May, it emerged that he had managed to slip away to Gaza, by identifying and exploiting loopholes in the Israeli security system around the Strip. "That, too, was a failure of ours," said Gillon.

For months, Shin Bet operatives tried to track him in the Gaza Strip, where they knew he was operating but where Israeli authorities were not authorized to make an arrest. They searched for patterns in his behavior, routines, lapses in field security—any weakness to exploit.

Finally, in late August, the Shin Bet learned that on rare occasions, Ayyash made some phone calls from the home of a follower and a childhood friend of his, Osama Hamad, who lived in the town of Beit Lahia, in the northern Gaza Strip. Using Hamad's phone, he would speak with Iran and Lebanon, and with a number of his subordinates in Hamas. Also, every time he visited Hamad, he would have a lengthy phone conversation with his father, in the West Bank.

This was valuable information.

But Hasson thought that the hit against Ayyash should be part of a larger, comprehensive operation in which the Shin Bet would implement a much deeper intelligence penetration of Hamas and gain control of the smuggling routes in and out of the Gaza Strip. "But the guys' pants were on fire," said Hasson, implicitly criticizing Avi Dichter, the head of the southern region (and the man who would triumph over him five years later, when they both ran for the director's post). "They wanted above all to have this achievement under their belts. They said, 'First of all, let's eliminate him, and then see what happens.' Pity."

A plan to assassinate Ayyash was presented to Dichter. Ayyash always made his calls from a room adjoining the living room of the Hamad family. When there was no one home, members of the Birds would enter the house and hide an explosive device, along with a camera that would transmit images. When Ayyash sat down there, and his voice was heard on the wiretapped phones, the device would be detonated.

"But here's the dilemma faced by a country that wants to thwart terror in a surgical manner and remain faithful to moral principles," said Dichter. "It was very easy to ensure that Ayyash would be blown sky-high. But we knew that he was in a house with children in it, and we had no way of ensuring that they would not be harmed by the explosion. The whole operation had to be changed because of this."

The Shin Bet needed a smaller bomb, one measured in grams, lethal enough to kill Ayyash but not so powerful as to put others at risk. One, perhaps, that Ayyash would hold to his head.

The solution came when the Shin Bet managed to find a link between Hamad and an Israeli collaborator. His uncle was a wealthy builder named Kamal Hamad, who had been in contact with Israeli officials in the past. Shin Bet approached Kamal, got his cooperation, and asked him to find a convincing pretext to give his nephew a gift of a new cellphone, a Motorola Alpha with a folding mouthpiece.

The assumption was that it would eventually be used by Ayyash.

"We concealed a small transmitter in the phone, so we can listen in to the calls," they told Kamal, who was given a package of benefits allowing him and his family to relocate to the United States after the operation.

The Shin Bet handlers were lying. Instead of a transmitter, the phone contained a fifty-gram explosive charge with a remotely triggered detonator. On October 28, two days after the slaying of Shaqaqi, Ayyash came to visit Hamad, who gave him the new cellphone and left the room, allowing the commander to make his calls alone. The Shin Bet's technological capabilities at the time were quite meager, and it took a special air force plane to pick up the phone's transmissions. The plane relayed the calls to the Shin Bet's southern region headquarters, where an experienced monitor familiar with Ayyash's voice was listening in. When he identified "the Engineer," he gave the signal to trigger the device.

The monitor began to remove his headphones in order to avoid exposure to the deafening blast that was about to come, but instead the conversation went on as if nothing had happened. The sign was given again, but still Ayyash continued talking. "You press once, you press twice," said Dichter, "but the coffee stays in the machine."

The tiny bomb had failed, but at least it had not been discovered. Kamal later told his nephew that there was a problem with the billing and he needed the phone for a couple of days. The Shin Bet lab fixed the problem, the phone was returned to Hamad, and everyone waited for Ayyash to return.

ON THURSDAY, NOVEMBER 2, a senior member of the VIP protection unit of the Shin Bet, responsible for the safety of the prime minister, made an encrypted phone call to a colleague, Yitzhak Ilan, who was in charge of intelligence collection for the agency's southern region. "The day after tomorrow in the evening," the caller told Ilan, "there's going to be a huge rally in Tel Aviv's Kings of Israel Square, in support of the government and the peace process. Rabin will be speaking. Since the hit on Fathi Shaqaqi, have you got any info on whether Islamic Jihad aims to avenge their leader by trying to kill the prime minister?"

Ilan replied that there was no specific information, but there was a lot of agitation in the area in the wake of the Shaqaqi assassination, and although Israel hadn't taken responsibility for it, the PIJ had no doubt who was behind it. Ilan's chief concern was that there might be a car bomb at the rally, and he recommended clearing the whole area around the square of vehicles. After their conversation, the VIP protection unit decided to put on extra precautions.

The peace rally was organized by left-wing groups as a counter to the angry protests the right had been staging, which had become spectacles of vicious incitement against Rabin. Pictures of him were set aflame, he was depicted in the uniform of the Nazi SS, and coffins bearing his name were carried along. At some of these protests, demonstrators had tried, and almost succeeded, to break through the security cordon and attack him. Shin Bet chief Gillon warned that Jewish terrorists might try to harm a government leader, and he even asked Rabin to travel in an armor-plated car and to wear a flak jacket. Rabin, who didn't take Gillon's warnings seriously, recoiled at the latter idea, and complied only on rare occasions.

The rally was a great success. Although Rabin had doubted that the supporters of the left would come out and demonstrate, at least a hundred thousand crammed into the square and cheered for him. They saw Rabin, generally a very introverted man, showing rare emotion. "I want to thank each one of you for standing up against violence and for peace," he began his speech. "This government . . . has decided to give peace a chance. I've been a military man all my life. I fought wars as long as there was no chance for peace. I believe there is now a chance for peace, a great chance, and it must be taken.

"Peace has enemies, who are trying to harm us in order to sabotage peace. I want to say, without any ifs or buts: We have found a partner for peace, even among the Palestinians: the PLO, which was an enemy and has ceased terror. Without partners for peace there can be no peace."

Afterward, Rabin shook hands with the people on the platform and headed for the armor-plated car waiting nearby, accompanied by his bodyguards. Shin Bet security personnel saw a young, dark-skinned man standing in the prime minister's path. But because of his Jewish appearance, they did not try to move him out of the way. The young man, Yigal Amir, a law student close to the extremist settlers in Hebron, slipped past Rabin's bodyguards with astonishing ease and fired three shots at the prime minister, killing him.

Lior Akerman, from the Shin Bet's investigation division, was the first to receive Yigal Amir at the Shin Bet's interrogation facility: "He arrived with a smirk that remained stuck on his face for many hours. He explained to me that Rabin had betrayed the homeland and that someone had to stop him. 'You'll see,' he said to me. 'My shots will stop the peace process and the handing over of territory to the Palestinians.'"

The murder hit Israel like a thunderclap. As in America after the assassination of John F. Kennedy, everyone would remember exactly where they were when the news was broadcast. Hundreds of thousands of Israelis went out into the streets, lit candles, and wept. The shock was all the greater because it had occurred to almost no one—including the people responsible for guarding the prime minister—that a Jew might kill the leader of the Jewish nation. The Shin Bet had failed horrifically, two different times: first by not knowing about the terror cell run by Amir, and then by allowing him to get close to Rabin with a gun in his hand. A mood of despondency spread through the organization.

But Ayyash was still alive, and Shimon Peres, who replaced Rabin as prime minister and minister of defense, signed the Red Page against Hamas's "Engineer." The head of the Shin Bet, Carmi Gillon, decided not to resign immediately after the assassination of Rabin but to continue on until Ayyash had been eliminated, so that his term would not be seen as an entirely embarrassing failure.

And there was still a bomb in a mobile phone. On the morning of Friday, January 5, 1996, Ayyash returned to Osama Hamad's house from where he'd been hiding the night before, a cellar in the Jabalia refugee camp. At 9 A.M., his father, Abd al-Latif Ayyash, called Hamad's cellphone, the one he'd gotten from his uncle Kamal. "I gave Ayyash the phone and heard him ask his father how he was," Hamad said. "I left the room to leave him alone."

Ayyash told his father how much he loved him and was missing him. It was enough for the voice recognition expert to give the sign. This time, the signal reached the phone, via the aircraft, and detonated the charge.

"Suddenly the line went dead," said Abd al-Latif Ayyash. "I thought there was no reception, and I tried dialing again, but it was dead. That afternoon, I was told he'd been killed."

Ayyash was buried in Gaza the next day, in a funeral attended by thousands. That night, Hamas operatives started recruiting suicide bombers in the West Bank. A Hamas spokesman said, "The gates of Hell have been opened."

# "SLY AS A SNAKE, NAÏVE AS A LITTLE CHILD"

BY THE TIME THE Shin Bet caught up with him, Yahya Ayyash was responsible for the death and maiming of hundreds of people and had done incalculable damage to the State of Israel and to the peace process.

At the time, there were several other senior commanders at the top of Hamas, in charge of regional forces in the West Bank and the Gaza Strip, and they, too, were responsible for bloody attacks against Israelis. But there was a substantial difference between Ayyash and the rest. Most of them operated inside the occupied territories, mainly in firearms ambushes against soldiers on the roads. Ayyash was primarily responsible for the suicide bombings that took place inside Israel itself, directed against civilians.

Ayyash's revolutionary work outlived even his untimely death. In the last months of his life, he trained a group of Hamas activists in the art of building small, lethal explosive devices for suicide bombers, and in the methods of recruiting and prepping them. One of those men was Mohammed Diab al-Masri. After he made the Shin Bet's wanted list, he became known in Hamas as Mohammed Deif, which means "Mohammed the Guest" in Arabic, because each night he would sleep in a different place. He was born in 1965 in the Khan Yunis refugee camp, in the Gaza Strip, to a family that had fled from a village near Ashkelon in the 1948 war. Deif joined Hamas soon after it was established in 1987. In May 1989, he was arrested for the first time and sentenced to sixteen months for being a member of the military wing of Hamas, but he returned to activity immediately after being released and participated in the workshops Ayyash was secretly teaching on the sand dunes outside Gaza. In November 1993, he was put in charge of Hamas terror operations inside the Strip.

The day Ayyash was buried, Deif became the head of the Izz al-Din al-Qassam Brigades, Hamas's military wing. That night, he began recruiting suicide bombers. The next month, he began retaliating.

Deif and his men carried out four terror attacks. On February 25, 1996, a suicide bomber blew himself up on a bus in Jerusalem, killing twenty-six people. That same day, another suicide terrorist killed a soldier and wounded thirty-six others at a hitchhiking station for soldiers outside Ashkelon. A week later, on the morning of March 3, another suicide attack took place on a bus in Jerusalem, killing nineteen and wounding eight. The next day, on March 4, a bomber detonated his device near the line for an ATM at Dizengoff Center, a busy shopping mall in the heart of Tel Aviv, killing thirteen and wounding more than a hundred.

Shimon Peres, who had succeeded Rabin as prime minister, grasped the impact of these terrorist attacks on Israeli public opinion, its support for the peace process, and his own prospects in the upcoming elections, scheduled for May. He signed a Red Page against Mohammed Deif and ordered the Shin Bet to do everything it needed to get rid of him, but Deif managed to stay alive. The Palestinian Authority, which was supposed to be helping the Shin Bet fight terrorism as part of the peace negotiations, did nothing. Jibril Rajoub, one of the heads of the Palestinian security apparatus who was close to Arafat, claimed, "I did not have the power. I wanted to [fight Hamas terror], but I didn't have the men, the instruments, the authority." Yuval Diskin, Shin Bet liaison with the Palestinians, disagreed. "Jibril's a liar," he said. "He had huge powers, but he got orders from Arafat not to try too hard."

Before the four attacks, Peres had tried to get Arafat to arrest Deif and thirty-four other terror suspects. He traveled to Gaza for an urgent meeting with Arafat on January 24. With them was AMAN chief Yaalon, who told Arafat, "You must arrest these people right away, or everything will sink into chaos."

"Arrest Mohammed Deif immediately!" Peres demanded.

Arafat looked at them with eyes wide open in perplexity. "Mohammed *shu?*" he asked in Arabic. Mohammed who?

Eventually, though, Arafat realized that the suicide bombers made him look, in the eyes of his own people, as if he couldn't control the Palestinian Authority and, in the eyes of the international community, like someone who was lending a hand, even if only by omission, to the murderous terror. He realized that the peace process would come to an end if Israelis continued to be blown up in buses and shopping malls. After the fourth attack, his security forces waged a vigorous campaign against Hamas, rounding up 120 of its leading members and grilling them using the harshest torture techniques. But by then it was too late.

"Arafat was a very complicated person," Peres said, "with a psychology that we weren't familiar with. On the one hand, he was as sly as a snake. On the other hand, as naïve as a little child. He wanted to be everything at the same time, both a man of peace and a man of war. On the one hand, he had a phenomenal memory—he remembered all the names, all the birthdays, all the historical events. On the other hand, facts and the truth did not always interest him.

"We sat together, and I ate from his hand—the one with the eczema, and that takes courage. I brought him information on the top Hamas terrorists in his territories. He knew very well that it was accurate, but he lied to my face without any problem. When he was persuaded, it was already too late. The terror ruined me, finished me off, removed me from power."

The wave of terror in February and March 1996 was a case study in how suicide attacks could alter the course of history. At the beginning of February, Peres was up twenty points in the polls over his opposition, the conservative hawk Benjamin "Bibi" Netanyahu. By the middle of March, Netanyahu had closed the gap significantly, and Peres led by only five percentage points. On May 29, Netanyahu won by 1 percent of the vote. This was all due to the terror attacks, which Peres simply couldn't stop. Yahya Ayyash's disciples had ensured the right wing's victory and "derailed the peace process," in the words of the deputy head of the Shin Bet, Yisrael Hasson.

Curiously enough, though, after the election, the attacks stopped for almost a year. Some said this was because of Arafat's campaign against Hamas, and the arrest of many members of its military wing. Others believed that Hamas no longer had any reason to carry out suicide attacks, because Netanyahu had already almost completely stopped the peace process, which was the short-term goal of the attacks anyway.

Netanyahu did not abrogate the Oslo Accords, but his government heaped innumerable difficulties on the process, and for the duration of his first term, the peace process was almost completely stalled. On the other hand, Netanyahu never hastened to use force or initiate aggressive action. His modus operandi was to do nothing: never taking the initiative, to war or to peace.

Arafat, for his part, was furious over the continual delays in Israel's withdrawal from Palestinian territories, and in retaliation he freed some of the Hamas activists he had detained. On March 21, 1997, the organization struck again in the heart of Tel Aviv, when a suicide bomber blew himself up at a sidewalk café, not far from the former home of David Ben-Gurion. Three women were killed and forty-eight people were wounded, some seriously. In the wake of this attack, Netanyahu again displayed restraint, and despite his associates' suggestions to take military action in the Palestinian areas, he refrained from ordering any use of force.

The Tel Aviv bombing highlighted a growing gap between the way Israel's two main counterterror intelligence arms viewed Arafat. The Shin Bet, under Ayalon, thought the Palestinian leader was passive and weak, allowing the attacks to continue and not making an effort to rein in Hamas because he wanted to avoid a confrontation with the fundamentalist Islamist movement.

AMAN, headed by the charismatic and opinionated Major General Moshe Yaalon, thought Arafat was central to the problem. Though both the Shin Bet and AMAN saw the same transcripts of secret conversations between Arafat and Hamas leaders, only Yaalon believed that the intelligence material implied that Arafat had given a green light for terror attacks in order to break the deadlock in the negotiations. Yaalon told the three prime ministers under whom he'd served as head of military intelligence—Rabin, Peres, and Netanyahu—that in his estimation, "Arafat is not preparing his people for peace with us, but for war." Yaalon said that in retrospect, Rabin's dictum that Israel should "pursue peace as if there is no terror, and fight terror as if there is no peace" was a "dumb statement," because the man they were trying to make peace with was the same figure who was creating the terror.

Yaalon was a member of a kibbutz in the Arabah Desert, and a prominent son of Israel's leftist labor movement. But, he said, what he saw in the intelligence material as head of AMAN, and later chief of the General Staff, made him change his mind and swing to the right. His meteoric rise in military and political rank amplified his hawkish opinions, and they ended up having a dramatic effect on the shape of Israeli policies in the decades to come. The right warmly welcomed him, since he was one of the few members of the intelligence community to espouse such opinions. He would become one of the closest associates of Netanyahu, who appointed him to his cabinet as minister for strategic affairs and then defense minister, though he forced him out in 2016 after Yaalon, a stickler for law and discipline, insisted that a soldier who shot and killed a helpless wounded terrorist should be prosecuted.

Yaalon is also considered one of Israel's most honest politicians, and there's no doubt that his disgust at Arafat was totally authentic. He remained steadfast in his belief that Arafat continued actively supporting terror. "The Shin Bet is used to collecting evidence that will stand up in court and lead to a conviction," he said. "But Arafat is clearly much more sophisticated. He doesn't tell the heads of Hamas, 'Go and carry out attacks,' but rather speaks to them about holy war, and releases all their top people he had arrested. There's no need for more than this. To this day, no order signed by Hitler has been found ordering the extermination of the Jews. Does this mean he didn't order it to be done?"

Brigadier General Yossi Kuperwasser, one of AMAN's senior analysts, backed up his boss's words: "When he wanted to, Arafat shut down nineteen Hamas institutions and arrested some of its activists. Then he began letting them go after he decided that it was time to resume terror attacks. Hamas demanded proof of his seriousness. 'Release Ibrahim al-Makadmeh,' they told him. 'That's the only way we'll know for sure that you're giving us a free hand.' Why Makadmeh? Because he headed a squad that was going to assassinate Arafat himself. Arafat complied, and a short time later they carried out the attack near the former Ben-Gurion residence." Kuperwasser argues that Arafat was sophisticated enough to release Hamas prisoners who lived in areas under Israeli control, so that the Israelis would be able to blame only themselves, and in any event to release men who had no links with Fatah, so as to keep as much distance as possible between himself and the terror attacks.

JERUSALEM'S MAHANEH YEHUDAH MARKET is almost always crowded with people shopping for cheap produce and clothing. Located between the city's main artery, Jaffa Road, and Agrippas Street, it has served the populace since the end of the nineteenth century. With vendors loudly hawking their meat, fish, flowers, and falafel, and all the colors and smells and sights of an authentic, busy market, it's also a popular tourist attraction.

At noon on Wednesday, July 30, 1997, nobody paid any attention when two men wearing black suits, white shirts, and neckties walked through the bustling crowd. The men were carrying heavy attaché cases, and they strode purposefully to the heart of the market, stopping at a distance of 150 feet from each other—just as Mohammed Deif had instructed them. They pulled their bags in close to their bodies, as if they were hugging them.

The bags were each filled with some thirty-three pounds of explosives, nails, and screws.

The men detonated them, and the enormous blasts and flying shrapnel killed sixteen people and wounded 178.

Hamas took responsibility for the attack in a statement sent to the Red Cross. But Deif had also realized that the Shin Bet, after earlier bombings, had identified the remains of the perpetrators and used the information to pinpoint who they'd been in contact with before the attack. So this time, the bombers went to great lengths to conceal their identities. They cut the labels from their clothing, for instance, so Shin Bet investigators wouldn't be able to trace them to a particular storekeeper who might recognize them. They held their bombs tightly, to destroy as much of their own bodies and faces as possible. Hamas militants had told their families not to set up tents for condolence calls, as is customary among the Palestinians, so the Shin Bet would not be able to identify them and construct a picture of their contacts.

Nevertheless, after considerable investigative work, the agency was able to report to the prime minister that it had identified who the dead terrorists were, and that Mohammed Deif was behind the planning of the attack and the recruitment of the suicide bombers.

Ten days after the bombing, Prime Minister Netanyahu convened a meeting of the security cabinet. At the beginning of the meeting, he made it clear that he was done showing restraint. After Mossad and Shin Bet officials explained to the ministers that many of the leaders of Hamas had found refuge in Jordan, Syria, the Gulf states, the United States, and Europe, Netanyahu declared that he was in favor of taking action against them. The cabinet authorized the prime minister and the defense minister to set the specific targets.

The next day, Netanyahu called in Mossad director General Danny Yatom and demanded a hit list. Yatom was accompanied by the head of Caesarea, HH, and Caesarea's chief intelligence officer, Moshe (Mishka) Ben-David.

Ben-David was something of an odd man out in the Mossad. Short and solid, he wore an unconventional long beard and had entered the Mossad, in 1987, at the relatively advanced age of thirty-five. His mother, a translator and editor, had spoken to him only in Russian, so he spoke that language before he learned Hebrew. When he turned eighteen, his knowledge of Russian made him a natural candidate for Unit 8200, where he listened in on the Russian advisers who were then assisting the Egyptian and Syrian armies. When he retired from the IDF, he represented an Israeli youth movement in the United States for a while, then returned to run a youth center in Israel. He raised horses in the Jerusalem mountains, wrote books, and earned a Ph.D. in literature and a black belt in karate. He also married and raised three children.

It was only after achieving all this that Ben-David decided to apply to the Mossad. "It really interested me," he explained, "and I also understood the Zionist and national importance of contributing to the country's security after a number of years doing things for myself. I saw that war was raging in Lebanon and that peace was still far off, and that it didn't really matter to anyone from Jerusalem to Tel Aviv."

It wasn't that no one cared, exactly, he said. It was simply easier to pretend the world was not such a dangerous place. "The Tel Aviv café crowd gets edgy when they encounter a clear view of a world in which the State of Israel still faces an existential danger, and the fact that there are not a few people and institutions that really are making every effort and sparing no expense on plotting how to hurt and destroy us," Ben-David said. "It's much more pleasant not to think about the bad people and just sit back. . . . I think that the great majority of the people in the Mossad are like me. The love of adventure, of intrigue, and the desire for a good career are good only up to the final call for Flight 337 to Tehran. That's when it all ends. Without conviction that your cause is just and strong patriotic motivation, you can't survive your second operation."

Yatom and his aides arrived at Netanyahu's office with dossiers on several potential Hamas targets in Europe and the Middle East who were responsible for weapons acquisition or fundraising. One of them was Mahmoud al-Mabhouh, who had abducted and killed two Israeli soldiers in 1988 and later escaped to Egypt. Netanyahu rejected the list. "Bring me some big fish, not these minnows," he said. "I want leaders, not merchants."

Netanyahu's order posed a difficult problem for Ben-David and his colleagues. The senior leadership of Hamas was in Jordan, a country with which Israel had signed a peace treaty three years before; Israeli intelligence, under an order from Rabin and out of basic diplomatic courtesy, couldn't operate there without the Jordanians' permission. And it was clear that King Hussein—whose subjects were mostly Palestinians—was not going to grant that permission.

Whether the Mossad made these logistical difficulties clear to Netanyahu is a matter of some dispute. "Netanyahu told us he wanted execution without footprints," Ben-David said. "The head of Caesarea [HH] told him, 'I know how to carry out such an operation with rifles, pistols, or bombs. I have no experience in directing a silent operation. When you have to act to hit a target, you have to reach actual contact with the target, and everyone is watching—it isn't clandestine, and if something goes wrong, you can't drop the gun and run away.' Netanyahu said, 'This is important enough for you to carry out a silent mission . . . because I don't want to jeopardize relations with Jordan.' He also said, 'I need the leaders of Hamas to be wiped out. I cannot allow more suicide bombings like these to happen.'"

On the other hand, Brigadier General Shimon Shapira, the prime minister's military secretary, who was present at all the meetings, maintained that the Caesarea representatives never suggested that executing a mission in Jordan would be a problem. "They gave us the impression it was a stroll in the park, the same as doing it in the center of Tel Aviv," Shapira said. "Everything was simple. No risks, nothing that could go wrong."

The Mossad came back with a list of potential targets—four Hamas leaders living in Jordan. Netanyahu's eyes lit up. He was familiar with one of the names: Musa Abu Marzook, head of Hamas's political bureau. Marzook had been working unimpeded in the United States up until Israel requested his extradition. The request was approved, but Prime Minister Rabin decided to give up on it, because the Shin Bet warned him that a trial would likely expose its sources of information. Instead, the Americans deported Marzook to Jordan.

Marzook also was an American citizen, which didn't bother Netanyahu—he was fine with killing him—but it made the Mossad wary. In order to avoid the damage to relations with the United States that might be incurred, the Mossad put Marzook last on its list of targets. This meant his name was behind Khaled Mashal, Marzook's deputy, behind Hamas spokesman Muhammad Nazal, and behind Ibrahim Ghosheh, a senior member of its political bureau.

The Mossad had only a little information on each of them, and a scarcity of resources or time with which to fill in the gaps. A targeted killing could be executed only if there was sufficient intelligence about the target, so it was reasonable that the person at the head of the order of priority should be selected, if only because there was more intelligence about him. This way, the life of the last person on the list should have been relatively safe.

Eight days later, six Bayonet members went to Jordan on a scouting mission, under the command of the unit's head, Jerry. They began collecting intelligence about Mashal, age forty-one, who ran Hamas's political bureau out of "the Palestinian Aid Center," in a glitzy shopping mall in downtown Amman. Within a few days, the Israelis knew where he lived, how he traveled, and the basics of his daily routine. They devoted little time to following Ghosheh or Nazal, and never got to Marzook at all. When the recon team came back from Jordan, the Mossad reported to Netanyahu that they had enough intel on Mashal to move forward with a plan to eliminate him, but far from sufficient information to act against the other three.

While Bayonet was gathering information in Jordan, operatives at Mossad HQ were figuring out how to pull off the "silent operation" Netanyahu had demanded. The killing could not cause a commotion, could not draw attention to the assassins, and, ideally, would make it look like Mashal had died of natural causes. Various options, such as a road accident, were considered and rejected, finally leaving only one: poison. Consultations over which toxic agent to use were held in the Mossad's technological unit, in cooperation with the Israel Institute for Biological Research, a top-secret government facility located in Ness Ziona, south of Tel Aviv. They eventually settled on levofentanyl, an analogue of the powerful opioid fentanyl, which itself is one hundred times stronger than morphine. (Pharmaceutical companies that have tried to develop levofentanyl for use as a surgical anesthetic found that it could not be controlled sufficiently to avoid killing the patient.)

The plan was to surreptitiously administer a fatal dose to Mashal. Levofentanyl is a relatively slow-acting drug—over a period of hours, Mashal would feel more and more drowsy, until eventually he'd fall asleep. Then the drug would slow his breathing, finally stopping it. His death would appear to be nothing more than a stroke or a heart attack, and levofentanyl leaves almost no signs. Unless someone tested for it specifically, an autopsy would reveal nothing. "Potion of the gods," some in Caesarea called it.

The next problem was how to get the substance into his system without being discovered. The Biological Institute suggested using an ultrasound device, similar to ones used to immunize children, that could inject substances without the use of a needle. This device would still require getting close to Mashal, who would likely feel a slight blast of damp air. Caesarea decided that the best place to carry out the killing would thus be in the open, on a crowded street where pedestrians occasionally jostle each other. Two operatives would approach him from behind, one would open a well-shaken can of soda, and at the same moment, the other would spray the toxin from the ultrasound instrument taped to the palm of his hand (imagine Spider-Man shooting his web). When Mashal turned to see what had wet him, there would only be two tourists with a can of fizzy soda. Because the substance was so dangerous, a Mossad doctor would be in Amman carrying the antidote, in case a drop touched one of the operatives by accident.

The assassins were still practicing their technique—a lot of pedestrians got sprayed with Coca-Cola on Ibn Gabirol Street—in early September when three suicide bombers, one of them dressed as a transvestite to avoid inspection, blew themselves up on Jerusalem's Ben Yehuda pedestrian mall. They killed five, including a fourteen-year-old from Los Angeles who was visiting family, and wounded 181. Netanyahu, visiting the wounded at Shaare Zedek Medical Center, said he'd had enough. "I want to make this very clear," he said. "From this moment, our path will be different."

The first step was to kill a Hamas leader. The prime minister ordered Mossad director Yatom to proceed immediately with Operation Cyrus, the hit on Mashal. Yatom once again tried to persuade Netanyahu to instead act first against the Hamas agents in Europe, but without success.

All the considerable problems that were to follow, however, rose not so much from Netanyahu's order but from the Mossad's agreement to execute it. Operatives have the right—which they had exercised more than once in the past—to tell their commanders, or even the prime minister himself, that they think a mission "isn't ripe" or that the risk is unreasonable. Of course, it's not easy or comfortable to say so to a prime minister exerting pressure.

But the moment the Mossad agreed to immediately carry out the hit on Mashal, its personnel were obliged to forgo a series of routine preparatory steps. For example, on their recon visit, they'd posed as European tourists, personas they'd used before in other operations, which had been tested and could withstand intense scrutiny. But because they were returning to Jordan so soon, they were given Canadian papers, identities with which they were much less familiar. In addition, the operatives never went through a thorough dress rehearsal in a mock-up of the operation zone. One of the members of an internal Mossad panel of inquiry into the event said, "It isn't that the way in which it was planned could not have ended up a dazzling success. It certainly could have. But an operation of this nature has to end in success, or at least not to fail. The idea of taking innumerable precautionary measures is not to allow unexpected events or bad luck to screw things up."

Furthermore, Defense Minister Yitzhak Mordechai, who should have been asked to check and approve the operation—prime ministers have the formal authority to order Mossad operations on their own, but they usually make the final decision with another minister or two—was not even aware that it was taking place. Earlier, he had approved the intelligence gathering, but he wasn't informed about the final go-ahead or the operation's location. Mordechai was a former combat general and a stickler for detail, and he might very well have improved Caesarea's preparations, as he had in other cases. But he simply didn't know about it.

Mossad director Danny Yatom said he was convinced that it was possible to pull the mission off "smoothly and quietly, or else I would have told Netanyahu otherwise. It may be, in retrospect, that the operations wing personnel didn't give me correct estimations of the risks."

Netanyahu did not feel that his judgment or agenda were to blame: "What's the prime minister's duty? To set policy. The Mossad has intelligence units and an operational unit, which in my opinion, since the killing of Shaqaqi, had been quite sleepy. I said, 'Give me targets.' They gave me, inter alia, Khaled Mashal, who in my opinion was a suitable target. It's not my job to be the Mossad's internal investigator. My job was to ask, 'Can you carry out the mission? Are you ready?' and from the moment they said yes, I have to rely on them."

THE FIRST TWO MEMBERS of the Bayonet team went to Jordan on September 19. A day later, Jerry and five other operatives, including one woman, checked into the InterContinental Hotel in Amman. Separately, Caesarea intelligence officer Ben-David and a female anesthesiologist, "Dr. Platinum," also checked in. The Mossad occasionally employed Platinum for special missions. For instance, she had sedated nuclear technologist and whistleblower Mordechai Vanunu in Rome, in 1986, so he could be brought back to Israel to face trial. This time, Platinum was carrying the antidote to levofentanyl.

The Mossad team decided to ambush Mashal at the entrance to the Hamas office, which was on the third floor of the Shamiya shopping center. To get to the office, Mashal would have to walk from his car, at the curb, through an open arcade, an arched corridor about thirty yards long. Jerry told two operatives to wait behind one of the arches and to start walking toward the entrance when Mashal was getting out of the car. They would come up behind and spray him with the poison and cola simultaneously.

For five mornings, conditions weren't right. Once, Mashal didn't show up. Another time, there were too many people in the designated attack zone.

Every morning, Ben-David and Platinum waited at the hotel until they were notified that the hit was off for that day. "Then we did what tourists do: sightseeing," Ben-David said. "Amman is a very interesting city."

On September 24, the two Bayonet men on lookout duty aroused the suspicion of a worker at Shamiya center. Jerry realized that it was too dangerous to loiter around the area much longer. The team would have to leave Jordan the next day, whether the mission was accomplished or not. They were going to have to rush.

But the team had not collected enough information about Mashal's movements, and they didn't know, for example, that sometimes he would accompany his children when his driver took them to school in the morning. That's exactly what he did on September 25, the last possible day to execute the operation. Worse, the small children were sitting low in the backseat of the car, and the surveillance team didn't see them at all.

At 10:35 A.M., the car arrived at the shopping center. Jerry got out of the surveillance vehicle and signaled the two operatives waiting with the soda and the poison to begin the operation. No one was carrying any communications equipment, a precaution taken so that if something went wrong, the operatives wouldn't have any incriminating gear on them. But that meant there was also no way to tell them to abort. Once put in motion, there was no way to abort the mission.

Mashal got out of the car and began walking toward his office, the two Bayonet men following. The driver was supposed to continue on and take Mashal's children to school, but his little daughter didn't want to leave her father. She jumped out of the car and ran after him, calling out, *"Ya baba, Ya baba,"* Arabic for "Hey, Dad!" The driver ran after her. Jerry saw what was happening, but the hit men did not. He tried to signal them to hold back, but at that precise moment they were behind one of the arcade's arches and couldn't see him.

They came close to Mashal, and one of them lifted the canister of poison taped to the palm of his hand and prepared to spray Mashal on the nape of his neck. The other one began to snap open the Coke can. Just then, the driver chasing the little girl caught sight of Mashal and thought that the man raising his arm behind him was about to stab him with a knife. He yelled out, "Khaled, Khaled!" Mashal heard him and his daughter calling and turned around. The jet of toxin hit him in the ear, instead of the back of his neck.

The poison would still be just as effective, but their cover was blown. Mashal, finding himself face-to-face with a man who had sprayed him with something from a strange cylinder, immediately understood that his life was in danger. He began running away from the two Bayonet men. The driver picked up the little girl and ran back to the car. The hit men also ran, jettisoning the poison canister and the soda can in a garbage bin on their way to the getaway car.

Danny Yatom said the operatives had not acted appropriately. "The basic presumption of the operation was that it would be silent, that the target would not know he had been affected. The operatives blatantly disobeyed my orders. I had made it unequivocally clear, both in writing and verbally, on the two occasions that I observed their practice runs, that if there was anyone at all next to Mashal, they must not go ahead. But they did nevertheless. That was the reason for the failure: execution out of overmotivation, in conditions that clearly indicated that there should not be execution."

Ideally, a second Caesarea team would have been posted nearby, waiting to create a diversion if needed. But there wasn't. Even worse, a man named Muhammad Abu Seif, a trained guerrilla fighter and a Hamas arms and currency courier, happened to walk by as the incident took place. Abu Seif did not immediately grasp what was happening, but seeing his boss run one way and two strangers run the other was an obvious clue. He chased after the two Israelis until they got in their car and jotted down the license plate number as they drove off.

The Israeli driver saw Abu Seif write the number down and told the two operatives. The car got caught up in heavy traffic and turned right into a side street and then right again twice. When they thought they were far enough from the scene, the operatives told the driver to stop. Since the car had been spotted, they figured it was best to get rid of it, even though, in hindsight, it was clear it would have taken the Jordanian police hours to organize a search. But the Israelis did not realize that the tenacious Abu Seif had commandeered a car and was still following them. He arrived just as the two operatives started walking away in separate directions, one of them already across the street.

Abu Seif was an expert in hand-to-hand combat, trained in mujahideen camps in Afghanistan. He tackled the Israeli closest to him, yelling that the man was from Israeli intelligence and that he had tried to kill the leader of Hamas. The second operative sprinted back and punched Abu Seif in the head. Abu Seif was dazed and bleeding, but instead of simply running away, the Israelis stayed to strangle him into unconsciousness.

Good fortune was on Hamas's side that day. As it happened, a former Palestine Liberation Army guerrilla and current Jordanian security operative named Saad al-Khatib was in a passing taxi. He saw the crowd watching two foreigners choking a local and told his driver to stop and wait while he went to separate them. "One of them had picked up a big rock and was about to bring it down on Abu Seif's head," al-Khatib said.

"I jumped on him, threw him down, and sat on his chest and tried to restrain him." Then he told the two Israelis that he was taking them to the police station. Afraid that they might be lynched by the mob they'd attracted, the two operatives agreed to go without a struggle. Bystanders, meanwhile, helped Abu Seif into the taxi—al-Khatib told him to sit in front—and someone loaned him a cellphone so he could call Mashal.

The Mossad operatives were confident that their cover identities would hold up under questioning. At the police station, they showed their Canadian passports and told the police that they were tourists who'd come to enjoy Jordan's attractions when all of a sudden, in the middle of the street, they had been pounced upon by "this nutcase," pointing at Abu Seif, who began beating up on them.

But then they were searched, and the authorities found, on the arm of one of the operatives, bandages that were not covering any wounds—the adhesive strips that had held the ultrasound device. They were arrested. They used their prison phone calls to contact "relatives abroad."

Two hours after their arrest, the Canadian consul in Amman came to the station. He entered their cell and asked where they had grown up, and some other questions about Canada. After ten minutes, he came out and told the Jordanians, "I don't know who they are. Canadians they are not."

Mashal, still at his office, called his two colleagues in Hamas, Musa Abu Marzook and Muhammad Nazal. They decided to put out a statement saying the Mossad had tried to kill Mashal, and that the Jordanian Royal Court was complicit in the plot. While they were talking, Mashal began to feel very weak and drowsy. The poison had seeped into his bloodstream. His colleagues and some bodyguards rushed him to a hospital.

In a few hours he would be dead.


THE CALLS THE ARRESTED Bayonet men made were, of course, to their Mossad teammates. One of them, a female operative, immediately proceeded to the InterContinental to report to Ben-David, who was sitting in a swimsuit next to a magnificent pool in the hotel's vast courtyard, reading Salinger's *Catcher in the Rye*. "From her face I could tell that something was very wrong," he said. "We exchanged a few words, and I realized that a grave incident had occurred." According to the original plan, the team was supposed to fly out of Amman to different destinations, but after what had happened, it was certain that the Jordanians would keep a close eye on the airport.

Ben-David called Mossad headquarters, in Tel Aviv, and was instructed to collect all the members of the team from their hiding places and bring them to the Israeli embassy.

By coincidence, news of the operatives' arrest reached Mossad headquarters while the prime minister was already there, wishing the organization's staff a happy Rosh Hashanah. Netanyahu was due to give a speech, and many hundreds were gathered together waiting for the ceremony to begin. Meanwhile, Yatom reported the bad news to the prime minister.

The two men decided to proceed as if nothing had happened. Almost all of the Mossad staff was unaware of the crisis, and Netanyahu wanted to convey a message of business as usual. He spoke briefly, thanked the staffers warmly for their contribution to the security of the country, then hurried with Yatom to the director's office.

He ordered Yatom to fly immediately to Amman and tell King Hussein what had happened. He was to do "everything necessary" to secure the release of the two operatives. "And if it is necessary to save Mashal's life," Netanyahu told Yatom, "then let them do so."

Yatom was received by the king. Hussein was stunned and stalked out of the room in anger. Yatom recalled that "it was [Jordanian intelligence chief General Samih] Batihi who got the king angry, because he was personally offended by me. Without him, we would have been able to finish the matter much more quietly with the king, and at a much lower price.

"During the discussions, Batihi started complaining to me for not telling him, saying that we could have planned the operation together, et cetera, et cetera. That's pure nonsense. We asked the Jordanians many times to curb Hamas and they did nothing. Rabin criticized them severely several times, but it didn't help. It is therefore obvious why we never shared our plans for Mashal with them."

By that time, Mashal was rapidly deteriorating, and doctors at the Islamic Hospital were at a loss. King Hussein's director of the Private Office, Ali Shukri, came to ask how he was, and Mashal's colleagues berated him, accusing him of being part of a murder conspiracy. Ordered by the king to make sure everything was done to save Mashal's life, Shukri had him transferred to the Royal Wing at Queen Alia Military Hospital. Mashal's comrades refused at first, fearing that Hussein was planning to finish killing Mashal, but eventually they assented to the transfer, as long as they could stay by his bedside, surrounded by Hamas security, and have every detail of his treatment explained to them.

Dr. Sami Rababa, the personal physician to the Royal Court, a colonel in the Jordanian army's medical corps, and one of the most prominent doctors in the country, was summoned. He had only a vague idea of who Mashal was, and he knew little about Hamas. "But from the bustle all around at the hospital," he said, "and the fact that Ali Shukri was there, I understood that this was a very important guest and it was very important to the king that he be cured."

Mashal, who was very dazed, told Rababa what had happened outside his office. As he spoke, he repeatedly nodded off, and the medical staff had to keep waking him. Then Rababa noticed that Mashal stopped breathing when he was asleep. "It was clear we had to keep him awake or he would fall asleep and suffocate," he said.

The doctors had Mashal get to his feet and walk around, but that helped for only a short while. They dosed him with naloxone, which is used to counter some kinds of opioids, but the effect wore off quickly and weakened with each new dose. Rababa hooked Mashal up to a ventilator—if they couldn't keep him awake, at least a machine could breathe for him.

No one wanted Mashal to die. King Hussein feared, justifiably, that the death of a Hamas leader would trigger riots in his kingdom, perhaps even a civil war. Netanyahu and Yatom knew that Hussein would then be forced to have the two prisoners tried and executed. Moreover, they knew that Jordanian intelligence suspected, correctly, that the other members of the Bayonet team were still sheltered in the Israeli embassy. A Jordanian commando battalion was standing by, prepared to attack, with Hussein's son, Prince Abdullah, the future king, in command. King Hussein wanted to make it clear that he took the incident very seriously.

Everyone knew that such an ugly series of events would undoubtedly destroy all ties between Jordan and Israel.

"All this time," Ben-David said, "I was walking around with the antidote, which wasn't needed, because none of our guys was affected. . . . Then I got a call from the commander of Caesarea. At first, because what he said was so fantastic, I thought that I had heard wrong. I asked him to say it again."

HH told Ben-David to go to the hotel lobby, where he would meet a captain from Jordanian intelligence and go with him to the hospital. Ben-David understood that a hastily arranged deal had been made: Mashal's life in exchange for the lives of the two Mossad operatives. In other words, Ben-David was going down to the lobby to save the life of a man whom he and his team had been trying to kill only hours before.

"We were in a tough spot," Ben-David said. "But in situations like that, you can't give your feelings too much room. You can't say, 'Oh, we screwed up and let them go to hell.' No. You do what you have to do—you execute in the best possible way that you can, and that's it. There's no room for feelings in this kind of situation."

Ben-David went to the lobby, where a captain was waiting for him. "I still remember his hostile look. But he also had his orders, and he carried them out." Yatom had told Dr. Platinum and Ben-David to accompany the officer to the hospital and to give Mashal the injection that would save his life. But the Jordanians refused.

Platinum was taken to Rababa's office. "She said she was part of the operation, but only if one of the operatives touched the poison," Rababa recalled, "and that she had no idea at all what the aim of the mission was. She placed two ampoules on my desk. I ordered them to be checked in the laboratory. We couldn't rely on what they said it was. Maybe they just wanted to finish the job."

Rababa maintained his professional decorum toward Platinum, befitting his medical and military rank. But inside, he was furious. "To my mind, medicine should not be recruited to kill people," he said. "And the Israelis do it again and again."

Afterward, Mashal made a rapid recovery. Yatom returned to Israel with the two would-be assassins and Ben-David. The two men reported that they had been severely beaten but had not given up any information.

But Hussein was not content to leave it at that. He told the Israelis that the deal they'd made included only the two prisoners, and that the Israelis would have to pay a higher price in order to get the rest of the team—the six Bayonet members holed up in the embassy. In the meantime, he suspended all ties with Israel.

Netanyahu consulted with Efraim Halevy, a Mossad veteran who had served as deputy director of the agency and was Israel's ambassador to the European Union at the time. The London-born Halevy, who had spent most of his time in the Mossad in the Universe foreign relations division, was a controversial man, but certainly a skilled and sharp-witted diplomat who knew how to behave with rulers and kings. He'd played a key role in hammering out the Israel-Jordan peace treaty of 1994, and he knew Hussein well. The king respected him, too.

After meeting with Hussein, Halevy told Netanyahu and Yatom that to free the six operatives, they would have to give the Jordanians a serious ransom, "enough to enable the king to be able to publicly defend the release of the hit team." His proposal was to let Hamas founder Sheikh Ahmed Yassin out of jail, where he was serving a life sentence for his role in terror attacks against Israel.

The suggestion was met with "wall-to-wall opposition, from Netanyahu down to the last of the organization's operatives," according to Halevy. Israelis had endured abductions and murders and terror attacks, all designed to scare them into freeing Yassin, the argument went. Now they were expected to just give in to King Hussein's request?

Netanyahu consulted with Shin Bet director Ami Ayalon, who called in his top expert on Hamas, Micha Kubi, and asked for his opinion. Kubi responded angrily. "Don't heed Hussein's threats. In the end, he'll have no choice but to let the operatives go, one way or another. If you free Yassin, who should rot in jail until his dying day, he'll go back to Gaza and build a Hamas that will be more awful than anything we've known so far."

Ayalon conveyed this message to Netanyahu. But Halevy was persuasive, and gradually, as he shuttled by helicopter between Jerusalem, Tel Aviv, and Amman, he convinced the prime minister that there were no other options. Netanyahu understood that he was caught in a huge crisis and, first and foremost, he had to set his priorities: He wanted to get the Caesarea men back home. The calm and confident way that Netanyahu managed the Mashal crisis, from the time he learned that the operatives had been captured, was one of his finest hours as the leader of the State of Israel.

In the end, an agreement was signed: Yassin and a large number of other Palestinian prisoners, including some who'd been involved in the murder of Israelis, were released, in exchange for allowing the six Mossad operatives to return to Israel.

The deal once again demonstrated the enormous commitment and sacrifices undertaken by Israel to bring home its men from behind enemy lines.

It came at a great cost. The botched operation in Jordan exposed a number of the Mossad's operating methods and blew the cover of the entire Bayonet squad, which now had to be rebuilt again. It took Israel years to repair the damage caused to the delicate and important relationship with the Hashemite Kingdom. An official reconciliation between Hussein and Netanyahu took place only in late 1998, during a mutual visit to the United States. The Mashal affair also embroiled Israel in awkward diplomatic situations with Canada and other countries whose passports had been misused by the hit team. Yet again, Israel had to apologize and promise, like a scolded child, not to repeat the mistake.

The internal and external inquiry panels set up in the wake of the affair uncovered multiple contradictory accounts of who had known about, and who had authorized, the operation. Netanyahu and the Mossad insisted that they had informed all relevant personnel, but Defense Minister Yitzhak Mordechai, AMAN head Moshe Yaalon, and Shin Bet director Ayalon all claimed they had not known about the operation in advance, apart from a general reference to the idea of killing Mashal made months earlier at a meeting of intelligence chiefs, where it was described as only one of many potential possibilities.

Ayalon was severely critical of the entire operation, even its motive: "Khaled Mashal was not part of the terrorist operational circle. He was, therefore, from the outset, not a legitimate target. Mashal was less involved in Hamas military activity than a defense minister in a democratic state."

An internal Mossad investigation, written up by Tamir Pardo, later to become Mossad director himself, issued one of the most severe reports in the history of the organization. In harsh terms, it blamed everyone who was involved in the planning and execution of the operation. The commanders of Caesarea and Bayonet, Ben-David, the operatives, and several others all came in for their share of criticism. There wasn't one area examined by the committee that was found to be faultless. However, the panel referred to Yatom's role in these failures only implicitly.

The head of Caesarea, HH, resigned. Jerry, whose ambition had once served him so well, was removed from his post as head of Bayonet. Ashamed and bitter, he left the organization.

On top of everything, Yassin was now a free man. The entire point of killing Mashal had been to weaken Hamas, but instead, its founder and spiritual leader had now been released. He left Israel for the Gulf states, supposedly for medical treatment. In reality, he used his travels to raise funds. "A great confrontation" with Israel was coming, he boasted.

There was no reason not to believe him.

# A LOW POINT

A FORCE OF FLOTILLA 13 naval commandos landed, undiscovered, on the beach near the Lebanese coastal town of Ansariyeh. Under cover of a moonless night, the sixteen men disembarked from their small, powerful Zaharon raiding boats and began a long march inland. It was the night of September 4, 1997, and the commandos were going to kill a man.

The mission was the twenty-seventh since Levin and Cohen had developed the IDF targeted killing protocols for midlevel Hezbollah leaders in Lebanon. Twenty of them had been successful. In this case, however, the two Northern Command officers believed the mission was unnecessary. They felt that the target, Haldoun Haidar, was minor and insignificant, and that there was no significant strategic gain to be had from killing him. But the Israelis had gathered enough actionable intelligence on him, and the system had proved itself so many times before, that in the minds of some, there was also no reason *not* to kill him. Still, enough Northern Command officers objected that the responsibility for the mission was transferred to the General Staff. Critics were left out of the decision-making loop.

The plan called for the commandos to march inland some two and a half miles and lay a number of roadside bombs along a route taken by Haidar every morning. They were then supposed to withdraw to their boats and sail back to Israel. When the operators of the drones circling above saw Haidar passing by, a radio signal transmitted through the drones would trigger the explosion. Metal fragments of the type used in devices made by Lebanese terrorists were packed into the bomb, to make the attack look like an internal Lebanese affair.

At first, everything went according to plan. In favorable weather conditions, the men landed, quickly crossed the Lebanese coastal road, and reached a wall on the eastern side that bordered a large area of groves and orchards. Two of the men hopped over it, broke the hinges of the gate, and opened it for the others. Most of the way was uphill, in an area difficult to navigate because of irrigation ditches and thick vegetation.

When the force reached the point marked on their coded map as G7, they hit another gate, with a road on the other side. They were supposed to cross that road and advance another quarter-mile before reaching the road that Haidar used. The commandos climbed over the gate, and the point detail crossed the road and began moving forward, combing the area for hostile elements. After the clear signal was given, the point man of the second group began crossing the road.

When he was halfway across, there was a huge blast, and then another.

In these blasts and an ensuing firefight while rescue operations were under way, twelve of the commandos were killed.

An IDF inquiry into the incident concluded that it had been a chance ambush by Hezbollah, impossible to foresee or prevent, and that the rounds the guerrillas fired had detonated the explosives the Israelis brought to kill Haidar.

That may have been the most convenient explanation to all concerned, but it turned out not to be true. In fact, Hezbollah apparently had been able to plan and coordinate the ambush because of a complete breakdown in Israeli intelligence in the weeks and even hours before the commandos set out. The video transmissions from drones that flew reconnaissance missions over the area were not encrypted, and Hezbollah was able to intercept them. Moreover, supposed Israeli intelligence assets in the South Lebanon Army were actually double agents, reporting to Hezbollah who and what their IDF handlers were interested in.

With a video of the area the IDF was reconnoitering and intel from the IDF handlers that they were targeting Haidar, it wasn't difficult for Hezbollah to figure out where the ambush would be laid. Indeed, according to sources who served in Flotilla 13 at the time, video from a drone flight hours before the raid showed three figures loitering suspiciously at G7. If that video, which has never been released, had been analyzed in real time, the mission would probably have been postponed or canceled.

The "Shayetet (Flotilla) Disaster," as it became known in Israel, had a deep impact on the public in Israel, mostly because the men who were killed belonged to one of the IDF's two best units. Nasrallah intensified this effect by uploading gruesome pictures of the body parts collected at the site to Hezbollah's website, including the head of one of the soldiers.


THE ANSARIYEH DEBACLE UNFOLDED just a day after a triple suicide bombing in the Ben Yehuda pedestrian mall in Jerusalem, an attack that Israeli intelligence had no advance knowledge of, and only weeks before the disastrous Mossad attempt on Khaled Mashal in Jordan.

In many ways, then, September 1997 marked one of the lowest ebbs in Israeli intelligence history. Each of three different intelligence arms had racked up a number of failures. The Shin Bet had failed to protect the prime minister or to stop a wave of suicide bombings. The Mossad had not managed to target the command centers of the jihadist terror organizations abroad. AMAN's efforts to penetrate and disrupt Hezbollah had been far from effective. And the latter two had altogether missed, as it would later transpire, the WMD projects of Iran, Syria, and Libya.

The Ansariyeh debacle, meanwhile, intensified the public controversy over the Israeli military presence in Lebanon, which some saw as comparable to the American embroilment in Vietnam. Protests demanding withdrawal were led by the Four Mothers, a movement named after the four matriarchs of the Bible, started by four women whose sons were serving in the IDF in Lebanon. The IDF and the political leadership treated them with contempt—one senior officer called them the "four dishrags"—but their protests were resonating.

Because of the Ansariyeh disaster, the targeted killings in Lebanon stopped. The IDF repeatedly put forward ideas for killing Hezbollah officers, but they were rejected by the chief of staff or by the weekly operations-and-sorties forum with the minister of defense. Hezbollah hadn't become less of a menace, but targeting its officers had become more of a potential political liability.

The Mossad, fresh off nearly destroying diplomatic relations with Jordan, botched another operation barely five months later, this time in Switzerland. The target was Abdallah Zein, a senior figure in Hezbollah's logistical and financial network. The Mossad's plan was to tap his telephone, keep him under surveillance, and eventually kill him. But they made enough noise trying to install a bug in the basement of Zein's apartment building that they woke up an old lady, who called the police. One operative was arrested. Mossad chief Danny Yatom, after one too many botched plans, resigned.

Yatom was replaced by Efraim Halevy, who had scored points with Netanyahu for the way he handled the Mashal case.

Afraid of any more fiascoes, Halevy effectively shut down Caesarea, refusing to approve almost every high-risk operation and allowing the unit to decay.

"It can honestly be stated," said Avi Dichter, who was deputy head of the Shin Bet at the time and would become head of that agency in 2000, "that the defense establishment was not giving the people of Israel the protective shield that they deserved."

That would be worrisome under any circumstances. But it was especially so in the late 1990s, because Israel's enemies were becoming more menacing. From Iran to Libya, from Hezbollah in Lebanon to Hamas in Gaza and Amman, a front of adversaries had been created who were much more innovative and determined than anything the Mossad, AMAN, or the Shin Bet had grappled with before.

THE SHIN BET WAS the first of the intelligence agencies to regain its footing. Its chief, Ami Ayalon, and the inquiry panels he set up to find out what had gone wrong reached the conclusion that the Shin Bet had become weak and ineffective in two of its main areas of activity.

The first was the acquisition of information. For decades, the Shin Bet had relied upon intelligence obtained from human sources, but this reservoir had almost dried up. No substitute had yet been found for the hundreds of Palestinian agents that it had lost when Israel withdrew from Palestinian territory after the Oslo Accords. The Shin Bet failed to develop alternative methods and was unable to recruit agents inside Hamas, an ideological-religious movement whose members were less likely to be tempted by bribes. One of the Shin Bet inquiry panels put it succinctly—and damningly: "The organization is not attuned to the environment it works in."

The second inadequacy was what the Shin Bet did with information once it was obtained. Ayalon visited the organization's archives and stared incredulously at the huge containers stuffed with hundreds of thousands of cardboard binders. "We are behaving like a medieval organization," he told the senior command forum of the Shin Bet. "An archive like this does not make it possible to construct a real-time intelligence picture. Even if all the information were to be found in the files, it wouldn't help us at all."

Ayalon declared that "the Shin Bet is not an intelligence body, but rather a preventive body." In other words, the agency's purpose was not merely to gather information for the sake of collection, but rather to thwart the enemy's intentions in real time. In order to do so, the Shin Bet had to collect intelligence and analyze it in the briefest of time spans.

Ayalon argued that the solution was to be found in advanced technologies. Tech-based sources would replace human sources, producing a multi-dimensional, real-time intelligence picture. In 1996, these were revolutionary thoughts that generated a crisis of confidence in the Shin Bet, drew harsh criticism of Ayalon, and even led many to quit the agency. But Ayalon stuck to his guns. He created a number of new teams and departments that developed cutting-edge techniques for collecting information: penetrating various data systems and intercepting emails, phone calls, and, later on, social media communications. They also developed new ways to use the information: state-of-the-art techniques for analyzing vast amounts of data and extracting the most important bits of intel.

Ayalon and his tech teams shifted the focus of the Shin Bet so that more emphasis was placed on the connections between people—more emphasis on the network, rather than on each separate individual. The Shin Bet was the first to grasp the huge potential of tracking mobile phones, first through the phone calls themselves and later through geolocation, texting, video transmissions, and online surfing.

Under Ayalon, the agency's entire operational structure changed. It no longer relied on regional case officers, deployed geographically, who ran agents and functioned more or less independently, but instead concentrated activities around a "desk," whose personnel sat at computer monitors, gathering information, piecing it together, and ordering operatives to gather missing pieces of the puzzle.

The makeup of Shin Bet's personnel was also changing rapidly. Many of the agency's old case officers left, while young men and women from the IDF's tech units were being recruited at a quick pace. Soon, 23 percent of the agency's personnel were operatives trained extensively in the development of innovative technologies. "We set up an entire division of Q's," said Diskin, referring to the tech wizard of James Bond movies. "In it, dozens of amazing startups are under way simultaneously."

THE FIRST PROBLEM THE newly revamped Shin Bet had to deal with was Mohi al-Dinh Sharif, a student of Yahya Ayyash's who became the Hamas military wing's top explosives expert after Ayyash's assassination and who was known as "Engineer Number 2." Ayyash and his deputy at the time, Hassan Salameh, had taught Sharif to make improvised bombs out of a very powerful explosive material, triacetone triperoxide, as they themselves had learned from the Islamic Revolutionary Guard Corps. Sharif was the one who had built the bombs that were used in the four suicide attacks Hamas launched to avenge Ayyash's death.

Like Ayyash before him, Sharif trained others in his craft, teaching a squad of men in Jerusalem how to configure remote-controlled bombs, build time-delayed fuses, and improvise explosives from readily available materials. He also taught them how to hide bombs in videocassettes. Eleven such cassettes were made in a plot to detonate them at bus stops, lottery stalls, and phone booths. One of them blew up in Netanya on February 11, 1998, wounding ten civilians. The Shin Bet identified the bomb makers before they planted the others and arrested them, thereby preventing a major disaster.

The Shin Bet compiled a thick dossier on Sharif, monitoring his movements and habits by tracking the calls and locations of mobile phones he and some of his men used. Most critically, the agency uncovered a plot to detonate a massive bomb stuffed inside a Fiat Uno on the eve of Passover, when Jerusalem's sidewalks would be crowded with people doing last-minute holiday shopping. The Shin Bet's operations wing, the Birds, managed to attach a detonator to the Fiat before Sharif delivered it to the suicide bomber. On March 29, 1998, when Sharif drove the car into a garage in Ramallah, away from innocent civilians, it exploded.

Even with Sharif's demise and the arrest of many of his associates, the Shin Bet sensed that a piece was missing from the puzzle. The agency concluded that there was a "multi-tentacled octopus" at work, with "one person who was operating all of the tentacles, each one separately, independently from the others."

The Shin Bet's new data-mining systems, which monitored thousands of Palestinians designated as targets, began to zoom in on one man. The Israelis singled out Adel Awadallah, who had taken over as head of Hamas's military arm in the West Bank, the counterpart to Mohammed Deif in the Gaza Strip.

Awadallah had been on the wanted list for some time, but thanks to a Hamas support network known as "the assistance and service apparatus," which served as a buffer between him and the cells that he ran, he wasn't caught, even when subordinates were captured and gave away information under interrogation.

This support system, which enabled Awadallah to avoid apprehension by the Shin Bet and at the same time launch many terror attacks, was run by Adel's younger brother, Imad, who had escaped from a Palestinian Authority prison. The two began planning the next series of terror attacks, the most ambitious of which involved five car bombs in the center of Israel's five largest cities. According to the plan, the first one would be detonated in Tel Aviv, presumably causing heavy casualties. Then an ultimatum would be presented to the

Israeli government: Free all the Palestinian prisoners or another car would explode, then another, and so on. At the same time, they laid plans for the abduction of soldiers and prominent Israeli political figures—large amounts of sedative drugs were acquired on the black market for this purpose—to use as bargaining chips. Among the men they intended to kidnap or assassinate were Ehud Olmert, then mayor of Jerusalem; Rafael Eitan, the former IDF chief who had become a Knesset member and cabinet minister; and two former Shin Bet directors, Yaakov Peri and Carmi Gillon.

Awadallah was a first-class operational leader, but he was not aware of the changes in the Shin Bet, including the stringent surveillance of phone calls—who called whom, when, and precisely where both sides were at the time—so that, even though he hardly ever used the phone himself, at least some of the members of his network did, making it possible to map his movements and keep tabs on him.

And he never grasped that his main adversary was, in Ami Ayalon's words, "the best operational chief the agency had ever had." That man was Yuval Diskin, whom Ayalon had appointed commander of the Jerusalem and West Bank region, the areas where the brothers lived and were most active.

Diskin, born in 1956, had done his military service in the Shaked recon unit, rising to the position of company commander. In 1978, he joined the Shin Bet and served as a case officer in the Palestinian territories and in Lebanon. His command of Arabic was outstanding, and he excelled at his work and rose rapidly in rank. Diskin was extremely tough and highly critical of both subordinates and superiors. It was clear that if he succeeded in smashing the Hamas terror networks in the West Bank, he'd be a good candidate for director of the Shin Bet.

"Adel was very suspicious," Diskin said. "He relied only on his HUMINT communications network, each of whose members had undergone loyalty testing by him. Thanks to them, he survived a few years. Until the last moment, we found it very difficult to get close to him."

Adel and Imad's caution came from seeing the fate of Mohi al-Dinh Sharif and the arrest of many of their comrades. They suspected that a Hamas activist, perhaps even a very senior one, had been collaborating with Israel or with the Palestinian Authority, divulging secrets and, eventually, setting up Sharif.

Since no collaborator had been flushed out, the brothers assumed that he might still be active among them. Because of this suspicion, the brothers decided to approach people outside of Hamas, though still known to be loyal to the Palestinian nationalist cause, when they looked for a place to sleep and eat.

They settled on a group of activists from the Popular Front for the Liberation of Palestine who, in the past, had served years in an Israeli prison for membership in a terrorist organization and illegal possession of firearms. These activists let the brothers stay in a two-story farmhouse with a large yard, surrounded by a wall, in the village of Khirbet al-Taiybeh, west of Hebron, which belonged to a member of one of their families. That house quickly became a trove of intelligence information that included the archives of the Hamas military wing, which Adel took with him from hideout to hideout, for fear they would fall into the hands of the Shin Bet. The brothers also brought with them the plans for their next major attack, which included poisoning Tel Aviv's water supply.

The Shin Bet managed to identify one of the brothers' contacts in this group of activists, and put heavy pressure on him to act as their agent, threatening that if he didn't, he'd be prosecuted for collaborating with Hamas and go to jail for many years. The stick was matched by a big carrot: a hefty payment and a new and easy life abroad for him and his family if he cooperated. The man agreed.

The first task was to get the house wired for video and audio surveillance. Capturing the Awadallahs could wait. More important, Diskin believed, was learning precisely what the brothers were planning. The Shin Bet waited for a tip-off from their agent that the brothers were leaving the house.

The next time one of the PFLP friends brought the brothers their provisions, they told him they were in a hurry to go somewhere. They all left together, the brothers in one car and the collaborator in another.

The Birds were waiting outside, watching. When the cars were out of sight, they went into action. Using a copy of the key, they went inside the house and installed cameras and microphones in every room.

The brothers returned later that night. For four solid days afterward, every word of the head of Hamas's military wing was recorded. Adel and Imad talked about various tactical improvements they wanted to make to their plan, and the possibility that Hamas would begin making rockets like the ones that Hezbollah was using.

The resulting documentation gave the Israelis not only details about specific plans, but also a sense of the brothers' broader worldview. In one conversation, for example, Imad, who had suffered harsh torture at the hands of Palestinian Authority jailers, spoke with bitter hatred about Yasser Arafat's men. "The next time they come for me," he said, "I'll open fire immediately."

His brother, who had been lounging on one of the sofas, leapt to his feet. "Never!" he thundered. "We do not shoot Muslims. Do you hear me? Even if they do the most terrible things to you, you do not kill a Muslim."

The Shin Bet informed the IDF of its impressive intelligence coup. Knowing full well that, at some unpredictable point in time, as a routine security precaution, the brothers would move to another hideout, they also requested an allocation of forces to kill them. The military, however, was not eager to assassinate another Hamas official—the aggressive response to Ayyash's death had made them anxious. So, instead, Ayalon and the Shin Bet went to the Israel Police's counterterror unit, the YAMAM. There was a long-standing rivalry between YAMAM and the IDF's special-operations units, and the army rightly interpreted Ayalon's decision to enlist the help of the police as an intentional disparagement.

Later on, a disagreement arose between Diskin and Ayalon. Diskin thought the YAMAM commando squad should break into the house and kill the two brothers on the spot. Ayalon was, in principle, willing to assassinate them, but he believed that an effort should be made to capture them alive so they could be interrogated, which he was sure would produce a valuable crop of information. In the end, a compromise was reached: If they could find a way to ensure that the two could be caught alive without endangering the YAMAM operatives, they would go for it. If not, the two would be killed.

Ayalon took the plan to Prime Minister Netanyahu, who was

much less decisive than he'd been when the Mossad brought him the assassination plan for Khaled Mashal. He now fully understood that every operation, even ones that seem easy and safe, can fall apart in the execution, with disastrous results for the personnel involved and for the entire nation. The hit on Mohi al-Dinh Sharif had left no Israeli fingerprints, but this time it was quite possible that the brothers would be killed in the YAMAM raid, and Israel would not be able to deny responsibility. Hamas would launch massive retaliatory attacks.

Shimon Peres had lost power because of the wave of Hamas terror in the wake of the Ayyash assassination. Netanyahu had no desire to risk his own office. He refused to sign the Red Page.

"If we are not willing to take care of the head of the military arm that is operating against us," Ayalon argued to Netanyahu, "what are we worth? If you don't sign the authorization, I will resign as head of the Shin Bet."

This was a formidable threat, with repercussions that went beyond the stated position itself. The prime minister was already seen as weak for releasing Sheikh Yassin. The public generally believed that he was not doing a good job in the war on terror. If Ayalon resigned, Netanyahu was sure someone would leak the reason. It would be framed as the prime minister's having refused to eliminate a major threat to the State of Israel and Jews everywhere. He would then be considered even weaker.

After a few hours, he signed off on the operation.

The plan was to incapacitate the Awadallah brothers before the assault. In one of his conversations picked up by Shin Bet, Imad Awadallah had mentioned his love of baklava. So on the night of September 11, 1998, Shin Bet specialists dosed a baklava with a sedative, then had it delivered to the house in Khirbet al-Taiybeh. They would wait until the brothers dozed off, then enter the house, load them into a vehicle, and take them to an interrogation facility.

It didn't quite work. Imad was overjoyed by the baklava and gorged himself on it. Soon he was overcome by sleep and began to snore. But the Shin Bet wasn't aware that Adel hated baklava and wouldn't touch it. When it became clear from the video surveillance that Adel was not under the influence of the drug and did not intend to go to bed soon, the YAMAM was given the order to storm the house. The squads surrounding the building moved in from several directions, accompanied by an attack dog. They climbed the wall and broke in.

Adel went for his rifle, fired, and hit the dog, but was immediately cut down. Imad, woken by the shooting, tried to reach his weapon and was killed by a long burst of automatic fire. After the YAMAM gave the all-clear, a Birds team entered the house and soon found the archive, hidden in one of the rooms.

Ayalon called Netanyahu to tell him that the operation had succeeded and the Awadallahs were dead. To forestall a violent Palestinian reaction, Netanyahu instructed Ayalon to drive to the Mukataa, the Palestinian Authority's governmental compound in Ramallah. When he arrived, Arafat was awake and waiting. Ayalon told Arafat that Israel had killed the brothers. "Before he could deny knowing who they were, I said, 'Please don't ask me, "Awadallah *shu?*" We know that you know who they are and what they have done,'" Ayalon said. "'In the name of the State of Israel, I demand that you do everything to ensure that Hamas doesn't begin to run wild.'"

Arafat asked to have the news of the slayings held up for four days so he could get organized. Ayalon informed him that there was nothing he could do to delay the news, and that he believed that the Palestinians had no more than four hours before the media got hold of the story.

"Please give Jibril [Rajoub] and [Muhammad] Dahlan"—the two heads of the Palestinian security apparatus, who were sitting on either side of Arafat—"the order to act now," Ayalon said. "They know what has to be done. If that doesn't happen and there's a terror attack, Israel will react in the harshest possible manner, including an absolute stop to the peace process."

Arafat told his two lieutenants to act decisively. That same night, the leading activists of Hamas were rounded up and held in detention, and the organization was put on notice that any activity against Israel would draw a severe response from the Palestinian Authority. Rajoub and Dahlan did everything they could to assure the Israelis that this time Arafat was serious about carrying out his threats.

Meanwhile, Shin Bet desk officers and analysts immediately began poring over the Hamas military archives, plugging names and dates into their computers—all part of "an intensive effort aimed at the rapid scrutiny of the archive documents in order to act before the members of the military wing could regroup and go into hiding." Units from the IDF, the YAMAM, and the Shin Bet itself began rounding up dozens of suspects—"senior commanders, explosives experts, procurers of weapons and materials for bomb manufacture, training and support staff, including liaison personnel and members of the Dawah," the social-civilian arm of Hamas.

The archives the Awadallah brothers had guarded so closely would now be used to bring Hamas's military infrastructure to the brink of collapse.


ONE OF THE NAMES gleaned from the Hamas archive was Iyad Batat, a senior military operative focused on attacks inside the West Bank. The records showed that he had been involved in ambushing IDF soldiers on a number of occasions.

After several months, the Israelis eventually tracked him down to a safe house in the village Beit Awwa. An operation—code-named Dungeons and Dragons—was drawn up to kill him.

Moshe Yaalon, who had ended his term as head of AMAN and was now serving as head of the IDF's Central Command, came to the operation's forward command post, a large and musty tent near the village Beit Jubrin, not far from Beit Awwa, on October 19, 1999. Though his operatives had already had three days to plan, he immediately realized that they had only a fraction of the intelligence they needed. No one from Unit 8200 (AMAN's SIGINT arm) was there, nor anyone from Unit 9900 to operate the drones. Even if they had been there, there were no monitors on which the information could be presented. The Shin Bet's relevant intelligence officer was in another area, and access to him depended on the fluctuating quality of his cellphone reception.

"I come from another place, another culture," Yaalon said, referring to Sayeret Matkal, which he had once commanded, "and there things are conducted differently. It was inconceivable that someone else should know something relevant to the operation and it would not be available to the commander of the force about to go into action."

Yaalon and Diskin decided that it was unacceptably risky to continue. They canceled the operation and put a temporary hold on all efforts to kill Batat. "In Beit Awwa, we realized that we had been totally dumb," Diskin said. "We asked ourselves what had to be done to ensure that next time we wouldn't be."

In theory, the solution was simple: Put all the necessary people in the command post so they could talk to one another and watch monitors displaying a single summary of the data. The Shin Bet, YAMAM, IDF commando units (Matkal, Flotilla 13, Cherry/Duvdevan), AMAN's 8200, 504, and 9900, and, eventually, the air force, would all be stationed in one room—"under fluorescent lights, not in some miserable tent," Diskin said—into which all of the available and necessary data would flow.

However, the implementation of this solution was difficult, because of a number of issues of accountability, command, and control. The various arms of the military and intelligence services had become accustomed over the years to functioning in parallel, and because the operatives came from different units, they spoke in different professional jargons. At times, some people were also just more concerned with turf than with national security.

Diskin, in the Shin Bet, and Yaalon, in the military, had to shatter quite a few entrenched bureaucratic procedures and navigate various interpersonal difficulties to get everyone into the second-floor space of the Jerusalem Shin Bet headquarters, which would now be called, appropriately, the Joint War Room (JWR). Especially tough was the resistance of 8200, the glamorous SIGINT unit of AMAN, who tried to insist that Shin Bet come to them instead.

On December 11, 1999, everything was ready for action. Information reaching the Shin Bet indicated that Batat was due to go to his safe house in Beit Awwa in the next few days. The house and its environs were placed under close surveillance. As a security precaution, Batat did not carry a phone, but his driver had one, and the Shin Bet tracked it. They saw it come to the house on December 13, stopping there for a while and then moving on, apparently after dropping someone off. A camera in a drone overhead also saw the car stop and saw someone get out of it and enter the house. Information coming in from an agent indicated that Batat had posted a camouflaged lookout on the roof of the house to warn him of any danger. This intel was fed into the JWR computers, and heat sensors in the drones were then activated, which showed that there was indeed a man sitting under a shelter on the roof.

Taking all this information into account, soldiers of the Cherry unit, disguised as Arabs, took up positions at a number of spots around the house. Four of them took cover under a little staircase along an outside wall, close enough to the entrance but hidden from the lookout on the roof.

"Eleven o'clock at night. The village is asleep. At first, there's adrenaline and you aren't scared, and later, when you're in position, the fear begins," Alon Kastiel, one of the raiders, recounted. "We received permission to open fire from the commander of the unit. . . . We killed Batat's man on the roof of the house. There were some exchanges of fire. . . . After the firing, we executed 'freeze' [cease fire], to get some intelligence. Then more noise from the house, and Iyad Batat comes out with a handgun. The whole force identified him and opened fire."

Afterward, the IDF put out a brief statement saying that one of its units had "encountered" Batat and another wanted Hamas man and killed them. The purpose of the statement was to cover up the vast intelligence activity that had taken place behind the scenes.

But to the Israelis themselves, it was clear that the Shin Bet's reforms and the JWR were proving effective. Over the next nine months, the JWR model was used in fifteen different arrest and targeted killing operations. This model was based on total transparency among agencies and a system of "baton passing" from one agency to the next as an operation unfolded.

The first principle of the JWR model calls for the presence of all the "sensors"—the intelligence-gathering agencies connected to the operation—in the form of both actual representatives and real-time feeds of the information they produce. The Shin Bet put a great deal of work into integrating all of the relevant computer systems—the innumerable hardware and software elements utilized by many different intelligence and operational bodies—so that they would interface with one another and communicate with the IT equipment in the war room. The goal was to have all the data displayed in a manner that would create a single, easily digestible picture of the situation. "This intelligence superiority, the concentration of all possible sources, lies at the foundation of our ability to hit our targets," said Yaalon.

To implement the second principle, passing the baton, the war room was in effect divided in two. One part, under the control of the Shin Bet, was called the Intelligence War Room. It was here that the target of the operation was identified. In other words, the Intelligence War Room's responsibility was to point out the specific location of the target and to guarantee that he was in fact the right person. This part was termed "framing."

Once there was a positive identification, the baton was passed on to the second part of the war room, the operational section. For the most part, this was the responsibility of the IDF, which supervised the execution of the hit. (At first, most of the targeted killings were carried out by ground forces. Later, execution passed into the hands of the air force, but the general principle remained the same.) In cases where the baton has been passed on to the operational war room, but something has happened on the ground that hinders the capability of hitting the target, such as a temporary loss of the surveillance picture, responsibility returns to the intelligence war room, and the framing procedure starts over from the beginning. And so on, until execution.

In September 2000, two months after Diskin had been appointed deputy director of the Shin Bet and Yaalon had been named deputy chief of the IDF General Staff, the two recommended that the model they had developed for the Central Command region be replicated for the entire country—that a permanent war room be set up for implementing major operations and targeted killings. The proposal was accepted, and space was set aside inside a building under construction at the Shin Bet HQ, in north Tel Aviv.

The timing was fortuitous. "If we had not implemented the technological revolution and hadn't set up the special war room," Diskin said, "it's doubtful whether and how we would have coped with the huge challenge that was posed for us by the Second Intifada."

# ALL-OUT WAR

BENJAMIN NETANYAHU DID NOT wait for the final results of the elections. On May 17, 1999, shortly after the TV exit polls began indicating a clear victory for the Labor Party and its leader, Ehud Barak, Netanyahu announced his retirement from political life.

Netanyahu had been elected because of Hamas suicide bombings, but his years as prime minister had been marked by a series of political scandals, coalition crises, security debacles like the Mashal affair, and a diplomatic dead end with the Palestinians. Barak was perceived by the electorate as Netanyahu's exact opposite—the IDF's most decorated soldier, a disciple of and successor to Yitzhak Rabin who had promised to get the army out of Lebanon and to bring peace. In his victory speech, Barak said that it was "the dawn of a new day" as he stood before hundreds of thousands of supporters in Tel Aviv's central plaza, now called Rabin Square, after the prime minister who'd been assassinated there four years earlier. "Peace is a common interest, and it bears within it enormous benefits for both peoples," Barak told the Knesset a few months later, declaring, "True peace with Syria and the Palestinians is the peak of the realization of the Zionist vision."

With his tremendous energy, decisiveness, and sense of purpose, Barak set about implementing his policies. Once the master of special ops, he was imbued with self-confidence, and sure that he could plan diplomatic maneuvers the same way he had planned targeted killing operations behind enemy lines—with strict attention to detail, careful planning to anticipate all possible contingencies, and aggressive action when necessary. But it turned out that although these methods worked well on a small scale, they did not always work with complex international processes. And Barak seldom listened to the advice of his aides.

Under America's aegis, Israel engaged in negotiations with Syria. Acting as Barak's emissary, President Clinton met with President Hafez al-Assad in Geneva on March 26, 2000. Clinton told Assad that Barak was willing to withdraw from the entire Golan Heights, except for some very minor border adjustments, in exchange for peace, though Clinton's language was somewhat less enthusiastic and alluring than might have been expected. Assad, who came to the meeting suffering from a variety of ailments, including incipient dementia and exhaustion, was more obdurate than ever about getting every inch back. The encounter blew up only a few minutes after the two presidents had finished initial formalities and begun discussing the substance of the dispute.

Barak had to keep his promise and pull out of Lebanon, but without any agreement with either Syria or Lebanon. In order to prevent Hezbollah from exploiting the retreat to kill a large number of IDF troops, however, it had to be carried out overnight and kept a complete surprise.

Shortly before the pullout, AMAN managed to locate Imad Mughniyeh, Hezbollah's military chief and number one on Israel's wanted list, as he conducted tours of inspection along the confrontation lines in southern Lebanon to see whether Barak was about to keep his promise and pull out, and to prepare his militia for the day after.

They planned to have him assassinated. But Barak, who came to the northern border and met with top military officials there on May 22 for an urgent consultation, ordered them only "to continue intelligence surveillance of the object M," and not to strike him, in effect liquidating the entire project. Barak's first priority was to make sure the retreat was carried out without any casualties, and he feared that assassinating Mughniyeh would provoke Hezbollah into bombarding Israeli communities or launching major attacks against Israeli targets abroad, which would require an Israeli response and make a quiet, surprise retreat all but impossible.

Barak was right, at least in the short term. The day after the meeting at the northern border, he ordered the immediate withdrawal of the IDF from Lebanon. The entire withdrawal was carried out without any casualties.

But Nasrallah celebrated the withdrawal as a complete victory for his side, depicting the Israelis as cowardly and fearful, running away from Mughniyeh's army. "Israel is feebler than a spider's web," he crowed. "A spirit of defeatism is prevalent in Israeli society . . . the Jews are a lot of financiers and not a people capable of sacrifice."

In retrospect, the end of the Israeli occupation in Lebanon came at the worst possible moment for Barak. He saw that he couldn't reach a deal with the Syrians, so he decided to speed up the handling of the Palestinian situation. But there were many Palestinians who saw the retreat from Lebanon as proof that guerrilla tactics and terrorism could defeat the strongest military and intelligence forces in the Middle East, and they began contemplating the possibility of applying these methods to their own arena.

Clinton invited Barak and Arafat to Camp David in July 2000, in order to hold marathon negotiations and, hopefully, reach a peace agreement. "I knew that such an agreement had to include a Palestinian state and a compromise in Jerusalem," Barak said, "and I was ready for that. I was sure I would be able to persuade the public in Israel that it was to our advantage, that there was no other option."

Arafat, for his part, did not want to come, and he agreed only after Clinton promised him that he would not be blamed if the talks failed.

During this time, Israeli intelligence indicated that ferment among the Palestinians had reached new heights. The Palestinian Authority was reported to be making preparations for an armed confrontation with Israel in order to pressure it into making far-reaching concessions.

"We were not preparing, and we did not intend to start, a confrontation with Israel, but 'hope is by nature an expensive commodity,'" said Jibril Rajoub, quoting Thucydides. Barak told his associates, "We're on a giant ship that's about to collide with an iceberg, and we will manage to divert it only if we succeed at Camp David."

The atmosphere at the meetings was festive. Barak was ready for concessions that left the American participants "open-mouthed and overjoyed," including a major compromise that would have given the Palestinians parts of East Jerusalem and international rule over the Temple Mount, the site of the Al-Aqsa Mosque. No Israeli leader had ever agreed to give away so much, or to make compromises on matters that until then had been considered taboo.

But Barak hadn't done enough in advance to prepare the ground for the meeting; he hadn't tried to get the broader Arab world to press Arafat to compromise on Palestinian principles like the right of return of refugees. He also behaved in a manner that was perceived as bossy and conducted the negotiations with Arafat via emissaries, even though his cabin was no more than a few hundred yards away.

Arafat refused to sign, perhaps because he thought he would get better terms from Israel if he held out, or perhaps because he simply didn't see any Arab leader ever backing a compromise with the great enemy. Clinton blew up in anger. He ended the summit and broke his promise to Arafat not to blame him for the failure. "If Clinton had adopted Carter's strategy and knocked their heads together until they agreed to a compromise, history would have been different," said Itamar Rabinovich, one of Israel's top Middle East scholars and diplomats.

In the ensuing two months, attempts were made to bridge the gaps. But by now the tension and suspicion between the two sides had passed the point of no return. "We were living with the feeling that we were breathing gunpowder," said one of Barak's close associates.

And wherever there is gunpowder, there'll be a pyromaniac to set it alight. This time the pyromaniac was Ariel Sharon.


WHAT THE JEWS CALL the Temple Mount and the Muslims call the Noble Sanctuary is perhaps the most sensitive place in the world today. Located inside Jerusalem's Old City, it is revered as the site of the rock from which God created the world, and where he called upon Abraham to sacrifice his son Isaac. It is also where the First and Second Jewish Temples stood, where Jesus walked and preached, and where Muslims believe the Prophet Muhammad took off on his flight to Heaven with the angel Gabriel. The Dome of the Rock and the Al-Aqsa Mosque stand there today.

Over the years, many confrontations have flared up there. In 1982, a group of Jewish terrorists plotted to blow up the Dome of the Rock, "to remove the abomination," as they put it, in the hope that the act would lead to a world war, thus hastening the coming of the Messiah. Though they failed in their mission, their strategy was not entirely off-base: Any incident on the Temple Mount would be a snowball that could quickly set off an avalanche.

Ariel Sharon was aware of all this. As the leader of the opposition to Barak's administration, he decided to defy, in the most flagrant manner possible, Barak's readiness to give up Israeli sovereignty over the Temple Mount. On September 28, he led a group of Likud politicians, surrounded by hundreds of police officers, to a demonstration at the holy site. He declared, "It is the right of every Jew in Israel to visit and pray on the Temple Mount. The Temple Mount is ours."

The Palestinians who were there at the time called out to him, "Butcher of Beirut . . . murderer of children and women," and very soon they clashed with the police who were guarding Sharon.

By the time of the next morning's prayers, Radio Palestine broadcasts and sermons in the mosques were already sharply condemning what they said was an Israeli attempt to harm Islam's holy places. A crowd of twenty thousand mostly young men angrily awaited the commencement of prayers at Al-Aqsa. Many of them were armed with rocks and other objects, and they began to hurl them at police and down onto the Jewish worshippers at the Western Wall. In those riots, seven Palestinians were killed, and more than a hundred were wounded. The next day, the violence had spread across the occupied Palestinian territories and the Arab-populated areas of Israel. Twelve Israeli Arab men and boys were killed (along with a Palestinian and an Israeli Jew). Within a short while, the local clashes had become a war.

Inside Israeli intelligence, the argument over what was going on in Yasser Arafat's mind flared up once again. The heads of AMAN and the IDF, especially Moshe Yaalon, believed that the intifada was part of a sophisticated and preplanned strategy of Arafat's and that he "controlled the height of the flames" from his office, at first with "spontaneous" demonstrations organized by his people, then with gunfire at Israeli troops from inside the crowds, then with planned shooting attacks against soldiers and settlers, and finally with suicide bombings inside Israel. Arafat was "trying to attain diplomatic achievements by means of spilling Israeli blood," said the chief of staff at the time, Lieutenant General Shaul Mofaz.

On the other side, the Shin Bet believed that Arafat had never had any such strategy and that the war had begun as a spontaneous outburst by students frustrated by a number of issues—some of them intra-Palestinian—who were then egged on by local leaders. The demonstrations led to a sharp response by the IDF, which was "over-prepared" for the outbreak of violence. That response left a large number of Palestinians dead or wounded and led to further deterioration. Arafat, the Shin Bet claimed, was being dragged along by the tide of events.

YOSSI AVRAHAMI WAS AN independent businessman from Petah Tikva, thirty-eight years old, married, with three children. In his spare time, he volunteered as an auxiliary traffic cop. Vadim Nurzhitz was three years younger, a native of Irkutsk, in Russia, and a truck driver by occupation. Neither was a professional soldier, but, like many Jewish Israelis, they were reservists, on permanent standby to reinforce the IDF.

The Second Intifada, as the latest war between Israel and the Palestinians became known, required reinforcements. Avrahami and Nurzhitz were called up on October 1, 2000, to guard settlers' school buses from attacks by Palestinians. On October 11, they were given a one-day furlough. The next day, on their way back to their base in Nurzhitz's car, they took a wrong turn and ended up in the West Bank city of Ramallah. There had been some rioting in Ramallah in the preceding weeks, and a number of Palestinians had been killed by IDF gunfire. Tension was running high. When the car entered the city, passersby saw the yellow Israeli license plates and began throwing stones at it. The two tried to flee but were blocked by traffic.

Palestinian policemen dragged them from their car at gunpoint,

Yasser Arafat leaving Beirut. This photograph was taken by a sniper of the Sayeret Matkal commando unit and transferred by Menachem Begin to American mediator Philip Habib in order to prove that Israel could have killed Arafat if it had wanted.

(FIRST PUBLISHED IN SCHIFF AND YAARI, *ISRAEL'S LEBANON WAR*)

The picture taken after the Bus 300 kidnapping, which exposed the Shin Bet's illegal liquidations.
(ALEX LEVAC)

Amin al-Hajj, aka "Rummenigge," a merchant with connections throughout the Middle East, who belonged to a prominent Shiite family in Lebanon, and who became one of the most important Mossad agents in Lebanon.
(ELAD GERSHGORN)

The eighteen-month training program of the naval commando unit Flotilla 13 is considered the most arduous in the IDF. Since the late 1970s, the unit has taken part in many targeted killing operations.
[ZIV KOREN]

In the command room for the targeted killing of Abu Jihad: Ehud Barak (sitting, left) and Yiftach Reicher (sitting, with telephone in hand).

Dr. Gerald Bull (left) with former Quebec premier Jean Lesage, inspecting one of the giant cannons Dr. Bull developed.

Project director Amiram Levin (left) and Doron Avital, commander of the Sayeret Matkal commando unit, in one of the rehearsals for the assassination of Saddam Hussein.

Ali Akbar Mohtashamipur, the man who founded Hezbollah, points with a two-fingered hand, the result of an attempted targeted killing by the Mossad.

AMAN chief Uri Sagie (left) and Prime Minister Yitzhak Shamir.

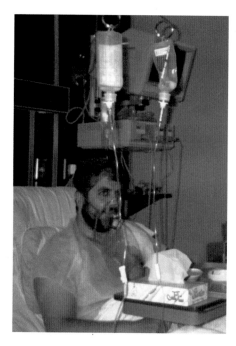

Khaled Mashal recovering from a poisoning at the Royal Hospital in Amman.

A "Cherry" drill to arrest or kill wanted men.

(COURTESY OF URI BAR-LEV)

A woman is carried away for medical treatment after a suicide bomber exploded himself in a restaurant in Tel Aviv. This is one of the photographs Sharon forced foreign diplomats to look at when he made his arguments for the use of targeted killings as a national security tool.
(ZIV KOREN)

The Israeli drone Heron TP can stay in the air for up to thirty-six hours, fly at a maximum speed of 230 miles per hour, and carry more than a ton of cameras and bombs.
(IAI)

The Grass Widow method was developed to draw armed Palestinians out into an open area and then shoot them from a hidden sniper position. [RONEN BERGMAN]

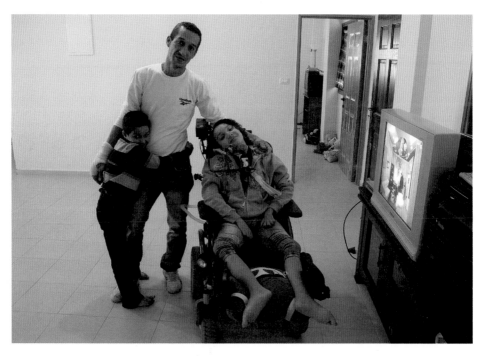

Maria Aman was with her family in a car in Gaza in May 2006 when the blast from a missile fired at an Islamic Jihad operative in a nearby vehicle also hit them. Her mother, six-year-old brother, and grandmother were killed. She was mortally wounded and remained paralyzed from the neck down. Her father, Hamdi (pictured here), has since devoted his life to treating her. [RONEN BERGMAN]

Hamas leader Sheikh Ahmed
Yassin at a press conference,
taking responsibility for sending
Reem Riyashi to kill herself.

Sharon (right) appointing Meir Dagan to be head of the Mossad.

One of the photographs of Imad Mughniyeh that the Mossad used to locate him and kill him in 2008.

Mossad surveillance photographs of Mughniyeh's deputy and brother-in-law, Mustafa Badreddine, whom Mughniyeh appointed to take care of affairs during his absence in Beirut.

Hezbollah secretary general Hassan Nasrallah at Mughniyeh's funeral.   (ULRIKE PUTZ)

A poster memorial in Jabalia for Mahmoud al-Mabhouh, along with one of his sisters.

Al-Mabhouh exiting an elevator, followed by two "tennis players."

Mostafa Ahmadi-Roshan, a chemical engineer at the Natanz uranium enrichment facility.

On January 12, 2012, the Mossad killed Ahmadi-Roshan in his car.

"Israel must be wiped off the map": a propaganda announcement on a Tehran street with targets on the heads of AMAN chief Amos Yadlin, Mossad director Dagan, and Defense Minister Barak.

Mossad chiefs Yossi Cohen (2016–present), left, and Tamir Pardo (2011–2016). Both of them have continued to use targeted killings as one of the primary tools of national security.

(GOVERNMENT PRESS OFFICE)

confiscated their weapons, and took them to a police station for questioning. Then they left them at the mercy of a raging lynch mob that had gathered outside.

The two reservists were beaten, their eyes were gouged out, and they were stabbed multiple times. Nurzhitz's head was bashed in before he was disemboweled with a stick shoved down his throat, and his body was set on fire. When Avrahami's wife, unaware what had happened, called his cellphone, one of the killers told her, "I slaughtered your husband a few minutes ago." One of the Palestinians was photographed at the second-floor window of the police station ecstatically exhibiting his bloody hands to the cheering crowd below. The mob then dumped the bodies through the window, onto the ground, and dragged them through the city.

The event left a profound impression on the public in Israel, which quite rightly blamed the Palestinian Authority, whose personnel had not provided protection for the Israelis in their territory but had instead arrested them without any reason and had allowed the mob to murder them inside the police station.

The Shin Bet designated the lynching an "emblematic attack," whose perpetrators had to be hunted down in perpetuity, "like those responsible for the massacre of the Israelis at the Munich Olympics." The hunt went on for months and years afterward.

Even more significantly, in the eyes of many in the Israeli leadership, the attack was seen as a fundamental betrayal, proof that the Palestinian Authority's goal—and, by extension, Arafat's goal—was not actually peace, but conflict. From that point forward, the PA and Arafat himself would be treated as part of the problem.

In the wake of the Ramallah lynch mob, the IDF greatly stepped up its use of force. Firearms were used more frequently against rioting protesters. The IDF hit back against Palestinian policemen, too, blowing up police stations at night, when they were empty. By the end of 2000, 276 Palestinians would be killed.

The bloodshed was a political disaster for Ehud Barak. Already hobbled by the failure at Camp David, the uprising left him unmoored and ineffectual. He openly and repeatedly blamed Arafat for what had happened, but that only made him look like more of a failure to the Israeli public, for having trusted the Palestinian leader in the first place. And his insistence on continuing the peace process with Arafat brought his popularity level down to unprecedented depths. Close associates described the last months of his term as manic, lacking in focus, and devoid of any clear sense of direction. His governing coalition began to unravel, and in December he was forced to call for elections in February 2001.

Barak was defeated by the very man whose provocation at the Temple Mount had kick-started the intifada: Ariel Sharon.

Sharon had been a political pariah for almost two decades, ever since he orchestrated the disastrous invasion of Lebanon. He'd been forced to abdicate the office of defense minister in 1983, but his misbegotten military adventure—his foolhardy plan to rearrange the whole of the Middle East—dragged on for eighteen years, costing Israel 1,216 lives and more than 5,000 wounded, as well as untold thousands of Lebanese casualties.

Large crowds of Israelis protesting in the streets had called him a murderer and a war criminal. The United States had imposed an unofficial boycott on him—only junior U.S. officials were allowed to meet with him when he was in America, and even then only at his hotel, outside of regular work hours. The man who never stopped on red, as the song went, was publicly scorned and widely loathed for years, despite serving in the Knesset and as a cabinet minister.

But Sharon saw politics as a Ferris wheel. "Sometimes you're up and sometimes you're down," he used to say. "Just stay on it." In early 2001, when Israelis were desperate for a strong leader who could stop the violence, he defeated Barak by 25 percent.

The contrast was immediately evident. Aides who remained in the prime minister's office after Barak left said the atmosphere immediately became calmer and steadier. Sharon was the complete opposite of Barak: warm, attentive to moods and personal quirks, careful to show respect toward everyone. He was naturally suspicious, but as soon as he came to feel that someone could be trusted, he gave them a great deal of freedom.

He also felt it deeply whenever Israelis or Jews anywhere were killed in a terror attack. "I would come in with news about this or that suicide attack," said military secretary Yoav Galant, "and see how his heart was crushed. It pained him in the most personal way. Any child or woman or man in Israel who was murdered on a bus or in a mall, he would take it as if they were his relatives, his family."

Sharon marked a seemingly clear path to end the violence. "He radiated to us all confidence that we were about to win this war, the war on terror," Galant said. "As Napoleon said, the Roman legions didn't cross the Rubicon; Julius Caesar crossed the Rubicon. Sharon was a leader, and he led the war on terror."

Immediately after assuming the premiership, Sharon declared that political negotiations would not take place while the terror attacks continued. Only when calm was achieved, he said, would Israel return to the negotiating table. At the same time, he pressed the IDF and the Shin Bet to step up their operations. "Think outside of the box," he told the commanders. "Come to me with creative ideas." He repeatedly reminded them of his own tumultuous times in Unit 101 in the 1950s, and of how Meir Dagan, under Sharon's command, had successfully hunted terrorists in the 1970s.

Since his stint as defense minister in the early 1980s, Sharon had had his doubts about the IDF's capabilities, harboring a suspicion that it had "lost its fortitude over the years." He was mistrustful of army officers as well, perhaps because he remembered how he himself had lied to the politicians when he was in uniform, deceiving his superiors so they would allow him to carry out operations. Now that he was prime minister, he felt that IDF officers were scared of failing, and he was therefore "convinced that senior commanders were lying to him so they would not have to take responsibility," said Galant.

On the other hand, Sharon felt much more comfortable with the Shin Bet, and he had great confidence in its chief, Avi Dichter. In the war against terror, the first and most important matter on his agenda, Sharon increasingly relied on the agency, giving it more missions and authority.

AT THE BEGINNING OF the Second Intifada, a significant number of people who'd been involved in terror attacks over the previous decade were sitting in prisons operated by the Palestinian Authority. After the suicide attacks of 1996 toppled Shimon Peres's government and disrupted the peace process, Arafat had realized that he needed to keep the top Hamas and Islamic Jihad leaders behind bars for at least as long as he was negotiating with the Israelis. But over six months, starting in October 2001, Arafat ordered their release.

Once again, the IDF believed that Arafat was trying to instigate more attacks on Israel, while the Shin Bet believed he was just frantically trying to avoid losing the support of the Palestinians to Hamas. By that point, hundreds of Palestinians had been killed in the intifada, while only a handful of IDF soldiers and settlers had lost their lives. Hamas's suicide attacks, however, were starting to even the scales. "The more the suicide attacks increased and succeeded, support for Hamas grew in direct proportion," said Yuval Diskin, the Shin Bet deputy chief.

The loss of the Awadallah brothers and of its archives had been a powerful blow, but Hamas had begun to rebuild under the leadership of Sheikh Yassin. And as it rebuilt, it began using suicide attacks against Israeli civilians more and more.

On May 18, 2001, a Hamas operative wearing a long, dark blue coat came to the security checkpoint outside the HaSharon Mall, near Netanya. He aroused the suspicion of the guards, who stopped him from entering, and then blew himself up, killing five bystanders. On June 1, another suicide bomber killed twenty-one young people, most of them new Jewish immigrants from Russia, in the line outside a discotheque on the beach in Tel Aviv. The owner of the dance hall, Shlomo Cohen, had served in the naval commandos, "but this was the worst thing I had seen in my life," he said, with despair in his eyes.

By early November, suicide bombers were striking in the streets of Israel almost every week, and sometimes every few days. On December 1, three bombers in succession killed eleven people in Jerusalem's Ben Yehuda pedestrian mall, the same place where a suicide attack in 1997 had led to the attempted assassination of Khaled Mashal. The next day, a man from Nablus blew himself up on a bus in Haifa, killing fifteen and wounding forty. "We are facing an all-out offensive," the Northern District police commander said when he reached the scene.

The offensive did not stop. In March 2002 alone, 138 men, women, and children were killed by suicide bombers, and 683 were wounded. The most atrocious of the attacks occurred on Passover, on the ground floor of the Park Hotel in Netanya, where a Seder banquet was being held for 250 of the city's disadvantaged people. A suicide bomber dressed as a religious Jewish woman entered the hall and blew himself up, killing thirty—the youngest aged twenty and the oldest ninety—and wounding 143 others. George Jacobovitz, a Hungarian-born Nazi death camp survivor, was there with his wife, Anna, also a Holocaust survivor from Hungary. They were celebrating Seder night with Andrei Fried, Anna's son from a previous marriage, and his wife, Edit. All four were killed.

The year 2002 was, according to Shin Bet chief Dichter, "the worst year for terror attacks against us since the establishment of the state."

Chief of staff Mofaz said, "This was a national trauma. It cast upon us loss of life, damage to our national security, damage to our economy. There was no tourism, people were scared to go to shopping malls, scared to sit in restaurants, and didn't ride in buses."

The Israeli intelligence community had come across suicide bombers before, "but we did not realize that it could be done in such huge numbers," said Major General Yitzhak Ben-Yisrael, head of the Administration for the Development of Weapons and Technological Infrastructure (Maf'at in Hebrew) at the Israeli Ministry of Defense. "Even when we grasped that this was the main threat, we had no solution for it, neither in combat doctrine nor in weaponry. What can you do against a suicide bomber when he's already walking around in your streets looking for somewhere to blow himself up?"

Terrorism in general, and suicide attacks in particular, created a strange and frustrating situation within the Shin Bet and IDF. "Unequivocally, there was a sense of impotence," said the head of the IDF Planning Directorate at the time, Major General Giora Eiland. "The frustration was huge. We were under great pressure to do something, both from above [the IDF command and the political echelon] and from below [officers and soldiers in the field]. And your neighbors and relatives and people in the street stopping you and asking,

'Where are you military commanders? A fifty-billion-shekel budget—
what do you do with the money? What do you do with yourselves all
day?'"

IN THE ABSENCE OF any larger strategy for how to respond to the
suicide-terrorism offensive, the Shin Bet just continued doing what
it had always done: assassinating the people instigating and organizing the terror.

During the first year of the intifada, the hits were carried out in a
diffuse manner, without any clear direction. The first one took place
shortly after the intifada began, when the Shin Bet discovered that a
Fatah operative by the name of Hussein Abayat was behind many of
the shooting attacks on the roads in the West Bank and in the Jerusalem neighborhood of Gilo.

Since the lynching in Ramallah, all the areas under the control of
the Palestinian Authority had been designated hostile territory in
which it was necessary to operate with extreme caution and with the
support of large IDF forces. But entering with such a large force in
order to arrest or kill Abayat would give him time to flee to a hideout.
The only way to reach him, the Israelis concluded, was with a combined operation using an undercover commando force and an attack
from the air.

The air force commando unit Kingfisher (Shaldag in Hebrew),
which designated targets by laser deep behind enemy lines, was assigned to the operation. It was selected because at the time it was the
only available unit trained to act in close cooperation with the air
force.

On November 9, 2000, Abayat was seen by a Palestinian Shin Bet
source getting into his black Mercedes and leaving the village of Beit
Sahour, near Bethlehem, with some of his men. A Shin Bet operative
accompanying the source was in touch with the Joint War Room, and
the JWR was in touch with the air force and the land forces. Kingfisher spotters designated the vehicle with laser markers for two for-
mations of two Apache helicopters each, who were following at a
distance. The car stopped at a house, and a crowd gathered around
it. "We waited a few minutes until it moved off again and away from

the people," the deputy commander of the Apache squadron said. "Then we fired two missiles. I fired one, and the second was fired by the squadron commander, who was leading the other formation. They both hit the target. Until then, we had executed missions like this only in Lebanon. It was a strange feeling [doing this inside an Israeli-controlled area]."

The killing of Abayat was the first aerial assassination in the occupied territories. It was unusual also because the Shin Bet generally preferred low-signature killings: those without open involvement of Israeli forces, which was forbidden by the peace agreement of 1994. But now the orders were coming to take out specific targets in the territories, with or without the involvement of Israeli forces.

One of them was Iyad Haradan, a commander of the Islamic Jihad in the Jenin district. On April 5, 2001, Haradan picked up the handset of the pay phone he habitually used (many terrorists now realized that the Israelis were listening in on their cellphone conversations and had begun to use public pay phones instead), in downtown Jenin, when it rang. But instead of the call he was expecting, there was a loud explosion that killed him instantly. The device had been planted there the previous night by a Birds unit. The area had been under surveillance of two drones, and when Haradan's voice was identified on the phone, the signal activating the bomb was sent from the JWR. A similar operation on June 27 killed Osama al-Jawabra, a member of Fatah's Al-Aqsa Martyrs' Brigades in Nablus.

The Shin Bet also tried to eliminate the secretary general of the PFLP in Palestine, Abu Ali Mustafa, using various low-signature methods—poisoning, booby-trapping his cellphone, blowing up his car in a way that would make it look as if explosives that Mustafa himself was transporting had gone off by mistake. But when those plans failed, the Shin Bet gave up trying to be discreet. On August 27, an Apache helicopter fired rockets through the window of Mustafa's office in Ramallah. Israel claimed that its decision to hit Mustafa "was not because of his being a political leader, but in spite of this"—according to the Israelis, he was directly involved in terrorism.

Israel's assassination of Mustafa did not quell the suicide attacks at all. Furthermore, for the Palestinians, a line had been crossed. "I would like to remind Israel of the period of the early 1970s," a PFLP leader said. "We must respond in a manner that will deter the Israelis from further attacks on Palestinian leaders." In an act of retaliation two months later, on October 17, in the Hyatt Hotel in Jerusalem, members of the PFLP assassinated Rehavam Zeevi, a minister in Sharon's cabinet and a former IDF general, who held extreme nationalist views.

Zeevi had been an admired and prominent Israeli, a good friend of Sharon's since their army days. In truth, none of the other targeted killings or the other aggressive military operations carried out by Israel had accomplished anything, either, other than killing 454 Palestinians, wounding thousands more, and prolonging a bloody and asymmetrical conflict that left more Israelis dead.

Sharon grew even more frustrated with the defense establishment's impotence. One morning, his bureau chief and right-hand man, Dov Weissglass, asked the head of the Shin Bet's intelligence division, Barak Ben-Zur, to meet him at an unusual venue, the entrance to the international trading center of a Tel Aviv bank.

Weissglass had arranged for entry passes to the center's operations room.

He took Ben-Zur to the middle of the large space, surrounded by flickering screens that recorded the money flowing in and out of Israel, the oxygen of the country's economy.

"What do you hear, Ben-Zur?" Weissglass asked after a long minute of silence.

Ben-Zur was puzzled. "Nothing," he said. "I don't hear a thing."

"That is exactly it. There's nothing to hear. No action. Foreign investors won't come here, because they're scared something will happen to them, and they aren't bringing money because it's not clear what will happen tomorrow. If you—the Shin Bet, the IDF, the air force—don't do something, then on top of the blood and the grief and the mourning and the terrible sadness, this country will face economic collapse."

The Shin Bet got the message. If isolated killings didn't work—and they didn't—the agency needed a broader strategy to limit the capacity of Hamas and of the other terror organizations that used suicide bombers. While intelligence officers usually prefer to arrest adversaries, one of the agency's officials told the security cabinet that

when control of the territory is lacking, that isn't an option. Consequently, "you have no choice—you are both prosecutor and defense
counsel, both judge and executioner." No one dreamed of total victory, or was even sure what that would look like, but rather sought a
reasonable security situation that would ensure a relatively peaceful
life for the citizens of Israel.

Agency director Avi Dichter presented the new strategy to Sharon
and the government during a series of meetings toward the end of
2001. At first, the ministers were hesitant. But at a meeting after the
terror attack on a bus in Haifa, in which fifteen passengers were
killed, Sharon whispered to Dichter, "Go for it. Kill them all."

# "MORE SUICIDE BOMBERS THAN EXPLOSIVE VESTS"

UNTIL THE END OF 2001, the Shin Bet confined itself to targeting what were known as "ticking time bombs," people who either were working on planning an attack or about to carry out an attack, or who were directly involved in such behavior—the commander and recruiter of the suicide attackers, or the bomb maker, for example.

There were a number of problems with that approach. The first was identifying targets from among the seemingly endless supply of volunteers. There were "more suicide bombers than explosive vests," a Hamas spokesman boasted. These Palestinians fit no profile: They were young and elderly, educated and illiterate, those who had nothing to lose and those who had large families. At first they consisted only of adult males, but later on, Hamas leaders encouraged women and children to sacrifice themselves, too.

Successfully identifying an attacker, moreover, did not necessarily mean stopping an attack. The monitors, the desk officers, the interpreters, the intelligence analysts, and the technologists might all track an attack as it "rolled along"—in the agency's professional lingo—"almost until the bang." But they could not stop them, because Israel could not operate openly inside hostile Palestinian-controlled territory. And by the time the bomber reached Israel, it was generally too late.

There were several nervous breakdowns among these desk officers and monitors during this period. One desk officer detected a May 2001 attack on the Netanya mall and activated the entire system to try to stop it. But the bomber got into Israeli territory and could not be pinpointed until he had already killed himself and five civilians. "The desk officer sits there crying, with the TV sets around her showing the bodies being removed," Shin Bet director Dichter said, "but by then the next alert comes in and she has to wipe away her tears and carry on working."

Since picking off individual bombers was ineffectual, Dichter decided to shift focus. Starting at the end of 2001, Israel would target the "ticking infrastructure" behind the attacks. The person who blew himself up or planted the bomb or pulled the trigger was, after all, usually just the last link in a long chain. There were recruiters, couriers, and weapons procurers, as well as people who maintained safe houses and smuggled money—an entire organization overseen by commanders of regional cells, above whom were the main military commanders, themselves subordinate to the political leaders of the organizations.

They would all be targets. A potential death sentence was hung over the heads of all active members of the Hamas military wing, known as the Izz al-Din al-Qassam Brigades, and the Palestinian Islamic Jihad. "They would very quickly realize that not one of them—from the regional operations officer to the taxi driver to the photographer who shoots the suicide bomber's farewell video—was immune to getting hit," said Yitzhak Ilan, a senior Shin Bet operative at the time and later deputy head of the agency.

Targeting suicide attackers was futile, because they were, by definition, expendable and easily replaced. The people who groomed and organized and dispatched them, however, were not. Nor, as a rule, were they nearly as eager for martyrdom as those they recruited. Israeli intelligence figured that there were fewer than three hundred people actively involved in organizing the suicide bombings, and no more than five hundred active members of all the terrorist groups combined.

They would not all have to be killed. "Terror is a barrel with a bottom," Dichter explained to the Knesset's Foreign Affairs and Defense Committee. "You do not have to reach the last terrorist to neutralize it. It is enough to reach a critical mass, and in effect you bring it to a standstill."

The Administration for the Development of Weapons and Technological Infrastructure (DWTI) developed a mathematical model to determine the amount of "redundancy" or reserve manpower in Hamas. The results showed that taking out 20 to 25 percent of the organization would lead to its collapse. "A simple example is the automobile," said DWTI chief Ben-Yisrael:

> There are critical components, and you build it from the outset with a degree of redundancy. You have a spare wheel, not one hundred wheels. You're driving, *bang!*—puncture—you change the wheel. You drive on and *bang!*—another puncture. Can you go on driving? Less likely. Why don't they give you more wheels? Because it takes space and adds weight. Redundancy also has an optimal level.
>
> Suppose we want to stop a car and we stand facing it and begin to shoot. You fire one shot, completely random. Will the car go or not? Depends where it hits. It could hit a fender, it could hit the radio. The car won't stop. Fire again and then again. Will the car go or not? It's clear that at some stage the car will stop, even though most of it has not been hit. Why? Because you'll have hit one of the critical parts. And that is precisely our model.

Of course, the assassinated would quickly be replaced by those next in line, but over time, the average age dropped, as did the level of experience as younger and younger people filled the ranks. As Yitzhak Ilan said, "One day, when the commander of Islamic Jihad in Jenin was brought into the interrogation room, a man whom, by chance, we had captured and not killed, I was pleased to learn that he was nineteen years old. I realized that we were winning, that we had axed the entire chain that had preceded him."

Now that a coherent strategy had been developed, they had to figure out how to find and kill these targets. The Shin Bet informed Prime Minister Sharon that, with so many assassinations under consideration, all the relevant resources of the State of Israel would be required.

.   .   .

PALESTINIANS IN THE OCCUPIED territories had long been used to seeing drones buzzing across the sky. "They flew around there all the time," said Moshe Yaalon, the deputy chief of staff at that time. The unmanned aerial vehicles were gathering intelligence via their high-definition cameras. "Just like there's a sun and a moon," Yaalon said, "there was the noise and view of the UAVs."

But most civilians, Arab and Israeli alike, did not know how far drone technology had advanced in the decades since Israel first used them. They were now larger, they could stay in the air longer (up to forty-eight hours), and they carried more advanced optics and heavier payloads—up to a ton of precision-guided missiles.

In an August 2001 war game simulating combat with Syria, the IDF realized that it could effectively fight what was then seen as its most pressing military challenge—the Syrian Army's arsenal of tanks, which numbered in the thousands—using only drones. "We had more bombs than there were targets in the Middle East," said Yaalon.

As the United States had, in Operation Desert Storm and the Balkans, Israel could wage war from afar. But Israel's capabilities were even more advanced than those of the United States. Not only did they have precision weaponry, like guided missiles and rockets, but they also had aircraft that could get very close to their targets and had an exceptionally high probability of hitting them, because the drones could adjust themselves midflight in response to the moving targets.

The IDF and the air force both preferred to keep their capabilities secret until an all-out war. But when the military protested Sharon's demand to use the drones against human targets and thus expose them to the Palestinians, the prime minister banged his fist on his desk. "He decided that this weapons system, instead of snoozing on the shelf waiting for the war it was made for and that was not happening, should be used against the present enemy," said General Yoav Galant.

The air force set up a special squad to retrofit the drones, both in munitions and targeting technology. Identifying a Syrian tank on the battlefield is different from following a man on a donkey who is trying to evade Israeli assassins, and destroying an armored vehicle requires a different missile from the kind used to kill one or two people without annihilating a city block. The air force settled on a warhead that sprayed hundreds of three-millimeter tungsten blocks that could rip through thin metal and cement blocks but that, because of their density, would be contained to an area sixty feet in diameter.

With the proper weapons appropriated from the military, the Shin Bet now needed its intelligence as well. Sharon instructed AMAN, which was several times larger than the Shin Bet, and the Mossad, whose relations with the Shin Bet were patchy at best, to put themselves at the Shin Bet's disposal for as long as they required.

Unit 8200, the SIGINT arm of AMAN, underwent the biggest change. Previously, it had dealt mainly with Israel's external enemies, mainly Syria. Now, many of its powerful antennas, surveillance facilities, and code-breaking and computer-hacking departments were focused on the war against suicide terror. Turban, one of the unit's listening bases, which had been close to shutting down at the beginning of the peace process, was converted and put entirely at the disposal of the Shin Bet. It became Unit 8200's largest base, and effectively a production line for targeted killings.

AMAN and the air force put their fleet of observation aircraft—and, eventually, the spy satellites Israel placed in orbit—to work for the Shin Bet. That fleet, which had originally been built to provide real-time battlefield information to fighting units, was given responsibility for observing targets during an operation. "Very many Israeli citizens owe their lives to information derived from VISINT—visual intelligence—and, by the same token, very many terrorists owe their death to that same information," said Yitzhak Ilan.

The result of all of this was "intelligence fusion," Moshe Yaalon said, which was "far more than mere integration of the material." Putting all the people from all the agencies around the table in the JWR was a catalyst for the creation of more intelligence. "All of a sudden," said Dichter, "the 8200 representative, a man who does not work in the Yiddish language"—in other words, whose job, as a monitor of enemy phones, required a command of Arabic—"hears a Shin Bet case officer talking in Arabic to a Palestinian source, and chips in with a question of his own. And then the lookout on the ground reports that the bad guy has entered Abu Hassan's grocery store, and the question of who this Abu Hassan is comes up, and whether he shouldn't also be painted in the bad guys' colors on the computer, and so on. And that's how the JWR, by itself, in the course of the operations, began to be a source in which a very great amount of intelligence was created."

Real-time IT had become particularly vital, because the targets had learned their own lessons and were taking precautions to evade the assassins. They moved around rapidly, changing vehicles and sometimes wearing disguises. "Target shelf life" was the technical term for the time in which it was possible to identify a particular target and to zero in on him. It was becoming very short—never any more than a couple of hours, and often just a few minutes. Only very rapid transmission of data could enable successful assassinations of such quick-moving targets.

Beyond the JWR, the counterterror targeted killing system encompassed thousands of participants: case officers, systems analysts, camouflaged infantry soldiers conducting ground lookout duties, observation drone operators, killer drone operators, interpreters, explosives experts, and snipers.

This very large and complex system nevertheless had a clear and strict hierarchy, with the Shin Bet at the top, running the show. An internal Shin Bet document noted, "The General Security Service [the Shin Bet's official moniker] is in charge, inter alia, by the terms of the GSS Law, of preserving the security of the state. . . . [O]ne way in which this goal is achieved is the interdiction and prevention of terrorist attacks by means of preemptively striking the objective."

In general, a targeted killing operation began with field operatives gathering intelligence and pinpointing a target. Typically, the target would be a prominent figure in a terror organization—"someone who deserves his ticket on the train to elimination," as Dichter put it—or another individual worth the investment of resources required to kill him. An intelligence dossier on the target would be compiled, and that dossier would be handed to the deputy director, who would then decide whether the man was indeed a suitable candidate for elimination. If the deputy director and then the director both endorsed the assassination, a Red Page would be presented to the prime minister.

After the prime minister signed, the intelligence arms that dealt with the geographical area and terror organization in question would be instructed to pay special attention to information that would facilitate the hit. This information was different from intel about what the target was planning, for example, or who his accomplices were. It was confined specifically to intel that might help determine whether there was "operational feasibility" for the hit, and it had to be gathered around the clock.

The moment an opportunity to execute arose, the prime minister would be contacted again, to authorize the killing at that specific time. Once the second go-ahead was obtained, the IDF General Staff's Operations Directorate determined the "executing body and the method of execution and select[ed] the type of munitions." After the chief of staff approved the plan, the JWR needed positive identifications of the target from at least two separate sources—the framing stage.

The baton was then passed to the implementing body, usually the air force.

Schematically, much of the new targeted killing system wasn't fundamentally new at all: The intelligence echelon gathered information, the prime minister authorized, and the field forces executed the hit, just like in the 1970s and '80s in Europe and Lebanon. But there were important differences. As one seasoned intelligence officer said, paraphrasing Marshall McLuhan, "The scalability is the message," meaning that the use of advanced technology in itself created a completely new reality. Enlisting the entire intelligence community, assisted by the best communications and computer systems in the world, along with the most advanced military technology developments, drastically increased the number of assassinations that the system could carry out simultaneously. Until then, "it took the Mossad months, if not years, to plan and implement one hit," said a Shin Bet officer. But now, "from the Joint War Room, we could run four or five a day."

OPERATIONS RUN OUT OF the JWR killed twenty-four people in 2000, eighty-four in 2001, one hundred one in 2002, and one hundred thirty-five in 2003. Unlike sporadic Mossad killings abroad, it wasn't possible—or at least plausible—for Israel to deny that it was behind the assassinations.

"We could not claim that these operations were executed by the government of Finland," said Brigadier General Yossi Kuperwasser, head of AMAN's research division. Also, there was physical evidence: Palestinians had salvaged a number of missiles that hadn't exploded because of technical failures and found stamped on them the Hebrew word MIKHOLIT ("brushlet"), the antipersonnel variant of the Mikhol ("brush") antitank missile.

Criticism of the targeted killings inside and outside Israel had also made it necessary to justify each one, disclosing details of the victims' misdeeds to establish that Israel had sufficient cause to respond. Gradually, what had once been considered highly damaging—acknowledging responsibility for an assassination—eventually became official policy.

"Continuing to try not to take responsibility would have been ridiculous," Dov Weissglass explained. "Minutes after a hit, the Palestinians would be taking fragments of a missile bearing the name of an Israeli company out of the car. More than that, we wanted a deterrent effect. Every buzz in the sky over Gaza and you'd see thousands fleeing in all directions. They never had a minute's peace. The population of Gaza reached a state where anything that contained electronic radiation, from a cellphone to a toaster, looked to them like something that could attract Israeli missiles. Absolute panic."

The IDF began putting out statements after each hit. Simultaneously, the Shin Bet, which until the start of the intifada had been extremely reluctant to maintain contacts with the media, distributed excerpts of the relevant Red Page—summaries of material about the dead man's actions—to various news outlets. Israel was now completely rearranging its communications policy—fighting, in effect, a propaganda war.

Explaining, even highlighting, what had long been state secrets required new language and new euphemisms. "Intifada," with its overtones of a popular uprising, for instance, was replaced with "war of suicide bombers." The deaths of innocent civilians during an assassination operation became known as *nezek agavi*—"accidental damage"—which, over time, became the acronym NAZA.

"'Assassination' or 'elimination' or 'killing' or—perish the thought—'murder' were all very jarring, not appropriate for us to use," said a senior official in the prime minister's office. "So we looked around for terms that are one step removed, free of emotion, sterile, which expressed the evil that we were trying to prevent by doing what we did." At first they used "PAAMON," which means "bell" but also is an acronym for "preventive action," but that wasn't catchy enough. After that, a few more proposals were discarded, including the code words long used by the intelligence community, like "negative treatment." Finally, they picked the term *sikul memukad*—Hebrew for "targeted preventive acts." The phrase, which in Hebrew has a kind of high-tech, clean sound to it, communicated everything that the defense establishment wanted to signal to the outside world.

THOUGH THESE EUPHEMISMS MAY have been helpful for public relations, it was not clear whether Israel's new, open campaign of extrajudicial killings—be they "assassinations" or "targeted preventive acts"—was legal.

Not surprisingly, some of the families of the assassinated Palestinians and victims of "accidental damage" didn't believe so. They enlisted the help of human rights associations and experienced liberal left-wing Israeli attorneys to petition the Israeli Supreme Court to order the investigation and prosecution of those responsible, or at least to ban the use of assassinations and order that only the regular law enforcement legislation should be applied to the Israeli-Palestinian conflict.

Opposition to the policy was not limited to its targets, either. Major General Aharon Zeevi-Farkash, the head of AMAN, for instance, did not oppose assassination in principle, but he did think it was dangerously myopic. "Every decision, every consideration, every reference to every subject was examined by the cabinet only through the lens of the targeted killing policy," he said. "All of a sudden, the Shin Bet, which had acquired enormous power, was the first to be consulted about everything. I thought that was a problematic situation."

More surprisingly, the previous head of the Shin Bet, Ami Ayalon, whose overhaul of the intelligence and operational systems had allowed the new assassination program to begin, agreed. He argued that the Shin Bet was killing people without first considering relevant political and international events, and that they failed to understand when an assassination would quell the flames of conflict and when it would fan them.

On July 31, 2001, for instance, IDF drones fired several missiles into the office of Jamal Mansour, a member of the political arm of Hamas, a student leader at Al-Najah University in Nablus, and head of a Palestinian research institute.

He was killed, together with one of his helpers and six other Palestinian civilians, including two children. The IDF spokesman's statement said that although he was a political and media figure, he was involved in terrorism and organized suicide attacks. Ami Ayalon called up the Shin Bet command and asked a top-level official there if they had gone insane. "Why, this man just two weeks ago came out with a statement saying that he supported a halt to terror attacks and that the peace process should be given a chance!"

The official replied that they were not aware of such a statement. "What does that mean, you 'aren't aware'?" Ayalon fumed. "All the Palestinian newspapers covered it! The whole world is aware!"

Another assassination Ayalon disagreed with was that of Raed Karmi, one of the leaders of the Tanzim, Fatah's armed militia. Tanzim had begun to carry out terror attacks, and Karmi's Red Page was growing longer due to its murders of Israeli merchants, settlers, and soldiers in the occupied territories. Karmi had survived a number of assassination attempts, and he took extraordinary precautions as he went about his business.

Eventually, the Shin Bet found a weak spot. Karmi used to pay regular afternoon visits to a mistress of his, the wife of one of his subordinates, always taking the same footpath along the wall around the Nablus cemetery, hugging the wall, for fear that an Israeli drone might be hovering overhead. One night, Birds operatives replaced one of the stones of the wall on that path with a new one filled with a powerful explosive material. The next day, as Karmi headed for his lovers' tryst, the bomb was detonated by remote control, and he was killed outright.

Ayalon did not doubt that Karmi was involved in terror, but he said that the timing chosen—in the midst of an intensive U.S. initiative for a ceasefire, for which Arafat had declared his support—was a mistake and, in fact, made the act illegal. "The rules of war exist in order to make the end of wars possible, to ensure that they do not keep on escalating. It is forbidden to execute warlike acts when it is obvious that they will only make the end of the conflict more remote." Ayalon claimed that in the wake of the killing of Karmi, Fatah had become much more deeply involved in terrorism and had even begun to carry out suicide attacks.

Shin Bet chief Dichter told Ayalon that he, Ayalon, was not familiar with the intelligence, that Karmi was engaged in planning attacks, and that neither he nor Arafat had any sincere intent to cease the terror. In the absence of an understanding ear in the Shin Bet, Ayalon called up the minister of defense in the Sharon government, Benjamin "Fuad" Ben-Eliezer, and loudly scolded him: "[U.S. Secretary of State Colin] Powell is due to come on a visit, and Arafat is looking for an opportunity to resume the peace process. He has issued an order to all of his forces forbidding terror attacks." Ayalon quoted up-to-date intelligence that Arafat's order had had an impact on the internal debate in Fatah, in which Karmi himself had been involved. "So what if the Shin Bet wanted to kill him? Why was it necessary to kill one of Arafat's men precisely at this point in time? Just because there was an operational opportunity?"

Ben-Eliezer, according to Ayalon's account, said to him, "What do you want from me? It's that crazy Dichter." Ayalon responded, "You are the minister of defense, not Dichter. It's your call, not his."

"I call it the banality of evil," Ayalon said later, borrowing Hannah Arendt's observation about what happens when ordinary people are put into corrupt situations that encourage their conformity. "You get used to killing. Human life becomes something plain, easy to dispose of. You spend a quarter of an hour, twenty minutes, on who to kill. On how to kill him: two, three days. You're dealing with tactics, not the implications."

THOUGH THE ISRAELIS MIGHT not have given full consideration to the moral implications of the new program, they were aware that they needed to provide legal cover for officers and subordinates who might later face prosecution, either in Israel or abroad. In early December 2000, IDF chief of staff Shaul Mofaz summoned the chief of the Military Advocate General's Corps, Major General Menachem Finkelstein, to his office.

"I assume that you know that Israel sometimes has a policy of 'negative treatment,'" Mofaz told Finkelstein. "In the current legal situation, is it permitted for Israel to openly kill defined individuals who are involved in terrorism? Is it legal or illegal?"

Finkelstein was stunned. "Do you realize what you are asking me, Chief of Staff?" he replied. "That the IDF's advocate general will tell you when you can kill people without a trial?"

Mofaz fully realized that. He asked again: Was it legal to assassinate suspected Palestinian terrorists?

Finkelstein told him that it was a delicate and complex matter, one that required a comparative study of statutes all over the world, probably even the invention of an entirely new legal concept. *"Inter arma enim silent leges,"* he said finally, quoting Cicero. In times of war, the law falls silent.

Nevertheless, he ordered a team of bright young attorneys in the IDF to puzzle out a solution. On January 18, 2001, a top-secret legal opinion signed by Finkelstein was submitted to the prime minister, the attorney general, the chief of staff and his deputy, and the director of the Shin Bet. Under the title "Striking at Persons Involved Directly in Attacks against Israelis," the document opened with this statement: "In the framework of this opinion, we have for the first time set out to analyze the question of the legality of the initiated interdiction"—another euphemism—"actions taken by the IDF. . . . We have been told by IDF and Shin Bet that such actions are carried out in order to save the lives of Israeli civilians and members of the security forces. This is, therefore, in principle, an activity that leans on the moral basis of the rules concerning self-defense, a case of 'He who comes to kill you, rise up early and kill him first.'"

For the first time, a legal instrument had been proposed for endorsing extrajudicial execution by the security forces. The opinion noted that its authors had done their best to find "the balance between a person's right to life and the duty of the security authorities to protect the citizens of the state."

For Finkelstein, it was a difficult moment. A religious man, well versed in the Bible, he was painfully aware that God prevented King David from building the Temple because he had killed so many enemies on behalf of the people of Israel. Finkelstein wondered if he would be punished one day. "I submitted the opinion with trembling hands," he said. "It was clear that this was not a theoretical matter, and that they were going to make use of it."

The opinion fundamentally recalibrated the legal relationship between Israel and the Palestinians. No longer was the conflict a matter of law enforcement, of police arresting suspects so that they can face trial. Rather, the intifada was an "armed conflict short of war," but to which the laws of warfare applied. Those laws allowed striking at the enemy wherever he may be, as long as a distinction is drawn between combatants and civilians.

In classic wars, that distinction is relatively easy: Members of the adversary's armed forces, as long as they are in the service, are legitimate targets. In the confrontation between Israel and the Palestinians, however, the distinction was much harder to make. Who is the enemy? How can he be identified? When, if at all, does he cease being the enemy?

The opinion posited a new kind of participant in armed conflict: the "illegal combatant" who takes part in armed operations but is not a soldier in the full sense of the word. The term covered anyone active in a terrorist organization, even if his activity was marginal. As long as he is an active member in the organization, he could be considered a combatant—even when he is asleep in his bed—unlike a soldier on leave who has taken off his uniform.

This expansive interpretation of "combatants" led, in marathon discussions in the International Law Department (ILD) of the IDF Military Advocate General's Corps, to an issue called "the Syrian Cook Question": If Israel were in a normal state of war with Syria, any Syrian combatant could be killed legitimately, even an army cook in a rear echelon. By that standard, then, given the broad definition of "illegal combatant" in the Israeli-Palestinian conflict, it could be presumed that any person assisting Hamas would qualify as a target, too. This might potentially include a woman who washed a suicide bomber's clothes before he set out on his mission or a taxi driver who knowingly took activists from one place to another.

That, according to the opinion, was too extreme. The opinion stipulated that only those about whom there is "accurate and reliable information that the person concerned carried out attacks or dispatched attackers" could be targeted. Moreover, assassination could not be used as punishment for past acts, nor as a deterrent to other combatants. It could be used only when "it is almost certain that the target will in the future continue carrying out actions such as this."

The opinion also stressed that, whenever possible, it was preferable to make an arrest than to kill someone, especially in areas controlled by the IDF. Unlike professional soldiers in a regular war, illegal combatants did not enjoy criminal immunity or prisoner-of-war status, so they could still be arrested and tried in regular criminal proceedings.

When killing was necessary, a principle of "proportionality" must still apply. The opinion stipulated that any killing should be as contained as possible, so that "the loss of life and damage to property collateral to the operational action" would not "immoderately exceed the military advantages expected from the action."

Finally, only the prime minister or the minister of defense could sign a Red Page.

The document was welcomed by Israeli officers, with a sigh of relief. "It was a stamp of confirmation that we're working in accordance with the criteria of international law," said Shin Bet deputy director Diskin. In 2003, the state submitted a non-classified version of the opinion to the Supreme Court, which it affirmed in 2006.

But while Finkelstein might have reasoned Israel into compliance with international law, international opinion was another matter altogether.

IN HIS DESK, PRIME Minister Sharon kept a booklet he'd occasionally pull out to share with visiting diplomats. He'd received it from the Israel Police, and it contained color photographs of a bus minutes after a suicide terrorist had blown himself up inside it. Decapitated bodies and human limbs were scattered in every corner. The fire had scorched the clothing off of victims and painted their skin with blotches of green and blue. "When one of those pesky diplomats came to talk to us once again about the elimination of this or that terrorist," said Dov Weissglass, Sharon's chief of staff and confidant, "Arik would force the person to look. He'd page through it, picture after picture, watching their eyes widen as they took in the atrocity of it. He didn't let them off even one contorted body or headless neck. When he was finished, he calmly asked, 'Now tell me: Would you be prepared for such a thing to happen in your country?'"

To provide Sharon with more material to show the diplomats, Weissglass's staff bought photographs from a Palestinian press agency showing Arabs being executed for suspected collaboration with Israel. Some of them were indeed Shin Bet agents and some merely victims of malevolent score settling. A few of the depicted executions were done by Muhammad Tabuah, a local gang leader nicknamed Hitler because of his cruelty. "He used to shoot them like dogs, with a murderous mob around him," Weissglass said. "The Palestinians looked like a chaotic maniacal mob."

Sharon did not, of course, share any reconnaissance of the aftermath of Israeli attacks. And, in any case, his visual aids ultimately were of little use: The rest of the world continued to criticize the targeted killing program, as well as Sharon's aggressive expansion of Jewish settlements in the occupied territories. Diplomats from scores of countries argued that there was a connection between those two policies and the Israeli bloodshed in the streets. Even the United States considered the targeted killing policy illegitimate, if not an outright war crime, and the settlements a needless provocation.

Sharon rejected such claims out of hand. "My problem," he proclaimed, "is that I was born long ago, long before all of you, yes? And I remember the thousands of Jews who were murdered by Arabs before the occupation. There's no connection between the two things."

Nevertheless, he realized that some agreement had to be made with the United States if he was to have any hope of placating the rest of the world. "If there was one lesson I learned from that period," Sharon said, referring to his term as defense minister in the 1980s, "it was never to get into a fight with the Americans."

Fortunately, Sharon already had a relationship with President George W. Bush, who had taken office at the same time as he had. Bush had come to Israel in November 1998, shortly after being re-elected governor of Texas, in a visit organized by Texas Jewish Republican businessmen as a stepping-stone toward the White House. At the time, Sharon was still a political pariah, but he and Governor Bush toured the country in a helicopter. Sharon lectured the governor on the security threats facing Israel and entertained him with tales of his own military exploits. By the end, Bush was convinced that "Sharon was a man he could trust," said Fred Zeidman, one of the men who'd organized the trip. The governor was profoundly affected by the tour and repeatedly stressed, "It's hard to believe as a Texan how small Israel is . . . how small the population was between, what has been over the course of history, enemy lines and population centers."

Two and a half years later, soon after his landslide victory, Sharon traveled to Washington. The aides who set up the visit told their American counterparts how suspicious Sharon was of the United States, and how he had been hurt by its attitude toward him personally over the preceding two decades. President Bush heard the reports and ordered that everything be done to make Sharon feel welcome: meetings with all the top administration officials, presidential hospitality at Blair House, an honor guard, and a twenty-one-gun salute. "Sharon was in the clouds," recalled his foreign affairs adviser, Shalom Turgeman. "Even he, skeptic and cynic that he was, could not but be affected by this treatment, and he realized that they really wanted to work with him."

Eventually, Weissglass proposed an idea to Sharon. "Arik," he said, "any warmth, support, and friendship that you may earn from the U.S. government in your role as an anti-terror warrior fades away when you put on your mega-settler cap. The more compliance you show toward the American demands to stop the settlement project, the more slack the Americans will cut you when it comes to taking out the bad guys."

With Sharon's go-ahead, Weissglass worked out a secret deal with U.S. National Security Adviser Condoleezza Rice and her deputy, Stephen Hadley: Israel would significantly reduce the construction of new settlements in exchange for American backing of the war with the Palestinians and of Israel's targeted killing policy.

"After that, there was a perfect disproportion," Weissglass said. "On the one hand, our severest measures against the Palestinians were never rebuked—silence, or sometimes an obligatory expression of regret if innocent people were hit. On the other hand, any publication, even on some marginal right-wing blog about a planned settlement, and I'd get a phone call at 3 A.M. from Condi [Rice], bawling me out."

The moment President Bush got confirmation from his representatives in Israel and the territories that Sharon was sticking to his word, operational and intelligence cooperation between the two countries deepened considerably. Though there was still a good deal of criticism leveled by countries in Europe, the United States continually used its veto power in the UN Security Council to block attempts to condemn Israel for the assassinations. Eventually, the Arab states simply gave up and stopped submitting petitions on the subject.

ON SEPTEMBER 11, JIHADIST hijackers flew two airliners into the World Trade Center and a third into the Pentagon. A fourth crashed in a Pennsylvania field after the hijackers were overpowered by passengers.

"In one swoop, the complaints against us ceased," said Major General Giora Eiland, head of Israel's National Security Council. "It simply dropped off the [international] agenda."

Decades of Israel trying to explain its drastic measures to the rest of the world were suddenly made unnecessary. Everyone, for a time, seemed to understand. Sharon immediately ordered the intelligence organizations to give the Americans all of the files for "Blue Troll," the code name for the development of Al Qaeda in Sudan, and other relevant intelligence. Later, he ordered the Shin Bet and the IDF to share their experience with guests who came from abroad to learn from the country with the world's best counterterror program.

"There was a stream of people arriving here," said Diskin, who hosted the senior guests. Sharon issued instructions, as part of his relationship with Bush, "to show them [the Americans] everything, to give them the lot, to allow access to everywhere, including the Joint War Room, even during interdiction operations." The Americans were most interested to find out how the integrated assassination system of all the intelligence arms worked, and how Israel had developed the capability to execute a number of operations simultaneously. The very system internationally condemned only weeks earlier was now a model to be copied.

"The attacks on 9/11 gave our own war absolute international legitimacy," Diskin said. "We were able to completely untie the ropes that had bound us."

# "THE TARGET HAS BEEN ELIMINATED, BUT THE OPERATION FAILED"

WHEN AVI DICHTER WAS a young case officer in the Shin Bet, he questioned a man named Salah Shehade, a social worker from the Gaza Strip. Shehade was twenty-four years old, from the northern Gaza town of Beit Hanoun, where he'd been a brilliant student, accepted for engineering and medical studies by universities in Turkey and the Soviet Union. But Shehade's family was poor, and he had to settle for studying social work in Alexandria, Egypt. When he graduated, he got a job in Al-Arish, on the Sinai Peninsula, close to the border with Gaza.

That was where Dichter first noticed him, in 1977. "He was different," Dichter said. "Well groomed, carrying a kind of James Bond briefcase. Altogether, he made a good impression." Dichter thought he might be able to recruit Shehade as an agent or collaborator.

Nothing came of their meeting.

After five years in the social services, Shehade joined the faculty of the Islamic University of Gaza, later becoming dean of students as well as serving as a preacher at one of the city's mosques. In the course of his activities, he met Sheikh Yassin, the founder of Hamas. The two became very close. Shehade was entranced by Yassin's charisma, his knowledge, and his vision of establishing a Muslim theocracy in all of Palestine. In Shehade, Yassin found a man with remarkable command and management skills.

Yassin revealed to Shehade the big secret: that beneath the cloak of welfare work and religious activity, he was planning to set up a military-terrorist apparatus to operate against Israel. Shehade was made head of this project. He was arrested in the Shin Bet's first campaign against Hamas (which was acting under another name at the time) in 1984, convicted, and released two years later. He was arrested again in 1988, convicted of a large number of terror-related offenses, and sentenced to ten years. But even from prison, he commanded the military wing of Hamas.

In September 1998, he completed his sentence, but he was held in administrative detention after that—a controversial measure similar to the United States' imprisonment of detainees without trial in Guantánamo; his release, according to the Shin Bet, would be "an immediate and certain danger to the security of the region." The long years in Israeli prisons gave him the status of a hero in Gaza.

In 2000, the Palestinian Authority appealed to Israel to release Shehade and some of his comrades, in a bid to appear concerned for all of the state's citizens in the eyes of the Palestinians, including those members of Hamas who enjoyed great popularity. Salah Shehade, the Palestinian Authority told the Israelis, was a pragmatic man, an administrator with a humanitarian background, unlike the more radical Sheikh Yassin.

It was a time of great hope, just before the Camp David Summit. Ehud Barak and Yasser Arafat were in close touch with each other, trying to speed the peace process along. Israel wanted to make gestures of good faith so that the Palestinian Authority might win over skeptics on their side, too. Hamas activity was also at an unprecedentedly low ebb, thanks to the Shin Bet's successes.

Israel agreed to the request. Shehade signed a pledge that he wouldn't go back to terrorist activity, which was customary for prisoners released by Israel, and the Palestinian Authority stood as guarantor.

In retrospect, the Israelis who agreed to the release might seem to have been naïve, "but our feeling then was that there was really hope," said a former Shin Bet operative.

For four months after his release, Shehade avoided illegal activities, but then the intifada erupted and he returned to the battlefield. "Since then," according to his Shin Bet file, "Shehade's positions have become more extreme and he has turned to activities of incitement, direction, guidance, and involvement in the planning and execution of murderous terrorist operations and in the militant leadership of the Hamas organization."

Almost thirty years after Avi Dichter tried to recruit Shehade, the Shin Bet was building a thick file on the man they code-named Flag Bearer. The two had met many times during Shehade's years of incarceration (during which, under various kinds of duress, he also informed on his fellow prisoners). Shehade was "the person who formed the principal threat to us, more than Yassin," Dichter said. "Unlike Yassin, he was educated and had experience in management, something that gave him extraordinary operational ability."

Shehade initiated and oversaw the development of new combat techniques, such as firing mortar rounds at armored vehicles in a flat trajectory and using explosive devices against tanks. He came up with novel ways to deploy suicide bombers, using boat bombs and tanker truck bombs. He was also responsible for the introduction of the high-trajectory Qassam rocket, which transformed the way Hamas fought Israel. The head of the Shin Bet in the southern region understood his importance: "He himself, with his own mouth, gives concrete orders for carrying out attacks, lays down terror policies, and issues instructions for when the attacks should take place. He is the driving force; he *is* the attacks."

According to the Shin Bet file, Shehade had direct involvement in attacks that killed 474 people and wounded 2,649 between July 2001 and July 2002. He was placed under intensive surveillance, but because Shehade operated out of Gaza, it wasn't possible for Israel to arrest him. Nor did the Palestinian Authority appear willing to enforce its guarantee that Shehade wouldn't attack Israelis.

So Shehade's name was put on a Red Page, and Operation Flag Bearer was put in motion.

IN ANY TARGETED KILLING mission, before the trigger was pulled, the identity of the person about to be killed had to be confirmed by two independent sources in real time. The process of "framing" was designed to ensure that the right person died, "and not his friend, his brother, his double, or some passerby," said Avi Dichter. The Shin

Bet, AMAN, and the air force invested huge efforts into ensuring that there would never be any errors. "We must not allow another Lillehammer to occur," Dichter repeated over and over again. On many occasions, JWR commanders aborted missions rather than risk hitting the wrong man.

In practice, "framing" a target was far more difficult than it might sound. In many cases, one of the two required sources was a Palestinian agent who knew the target and had to identify him from a concealed position at the final stages of the operation. The Shin Bet and AMAN's Unit 504 had many sources, but "these guys were not our chief rabbis," said Dichter, implying that their moral standards, as traitors to their people and their friends, left something to be desired. "We had to treat them with a great deal of skepticism."

The JWR also had a rule that if visual contact with a confirmed target was lost, the framing would be canceled and would have to begin again. If, for instance, a target got into a car after being positively identified but then ducked under the roof of a gas station where he couldn't be seen, the process had to restart. This sort of situation happened many times, often because of overcast skies, and frequently meant that the hit had to be scrapped entirely.

Due to these strict identification procedures, the Shin Bet had a sterling accuracy record. "One hundred percent accurate framings," Dichter said. "Regrettably, not in every case was the target destroyed, but in every case where we attacked the target that we wanted to attack." What's more, the targeted killings were having their intended effect. By the middle of 2002, Israel's war against suicide terrorism was beginning to show results: The number of Israelis being killed by suicide bombers was on the decline. After eighty-five Israeli deaths in March, there were only seven fatalities in July, seven in August, and six in September.

And yet, though enormous efforts were devoted to ensuring accurate framing of the target, much less effort was put into determining that the target was alone and that there were no innocent civilians nearby. Despite the rules, safeguards, and redundancy, Israel was now executing targeted killing operations at such a scale that mistakes were bound to be made, and though there were relatively few of them, when they did happen, innocent people died.

Sometimes, too, the decision-makers would deliberately consider whether it was permissible to kill people around the target if he could never be reached when he was alone. In such deliberations, the IDF and the Shin Bet would ask the International Law Department to send its representatives to sit with them in the Joint War Room. "It puts us ILD folks into a very complicated situation," said Daniel Reisner, chief of that unit. "For it's clear that if a lawyer was present and he didn't say no, it's as if he was saying yes."

The chief military advocate general was co-opted to the General Staff forum and was made a partner to top-secret security consultations. The Shin Bet made its dossiers on the targeted killing candidates available to the lawyers for as long as they wanted to study them. Reisner and the ILD were frequently present in the JWR when the hit was being executed. Their presence was "legal cover," in Finkelstein's words, that the security people felt they needed in case they were ever prosecuted, in Israel or abroad.

The ILD's main consideration was the practical application of "proportionality," which in theory demanded that the damage inflicted by Israel would not exceed the benefits. How many innocent lives, if any, is Israel permitted to place in jeopardy in order to kill a dangerous terrorist?

"The terrorists," said Reisner, "fully exploited our sensitivity about harming the innocent. They used to pick up children in their arms to cross the street, surround themselves with civilians. One time, I was present in the JWR when a missile was fired at a terrorist standing on a roof. Then, all of a sudden, we saw him pick up a kid. Of course, I immediately gave an order to divert the missile into open ground."

The lawyers found it hard to formulate a uniform rule on the question of collateral damage and casualties. "Judge every case on its own merits," said Reisner. "However, we had one clear rule: We were all parents; we could not approve of killing children. We never, ever signed off on an assassination operation like that."

Whenever intelligence showed in advance that there was "positive knowledge of the presence of children" in the hit zone, the operation was not authorized. However, the presence of a few adults who were connected in one way or another to the condemned man would not necessarily stop an operation, even if those adults had no links to terrorist organizations. The same went for wives, friends, and various kinds of transporters, like taxi drivers.

OPERATION FLAG BEARER WAS a particularly thorny case. At least twice, according to Shin Bet records, authorization for a hit on Flag Bearer was withheld for fear of harming innocents. The first time was on March 6, 2002. Shehade had been placed with a high degree of certainty in a south Gaza apartment, but because of the presence of a large number of civilians in the same building, along with the knowledge that his wife, Leila, and possibly also his fifteen-year-old daughter, Iman, were with him, the attack was called off.

Three days later, a suicide bomber sent by Shehade blew himself up in Café Moment, near the prime minister's residence in Jerusalem, killing eleven civilians.

On June 6, another attempt on Shehade was called off, for similar reasons. Twelve days after that, a suicide bomber from the Hamas military wing killed nineteen passengers on a bus in Jerusalem.

The frustration in the Israeli security establishment was palpable. As IDF chief of staff Moshe Yaalon said, "I told my American counterparts about this business, and it exasperated them. I told them that at first we held back because his wife was with him, that he never moved without her. From their angle, that was insane. 'What,' they asked me, 'because of his wife you didn't attack?' Their criteria regarding collateral damage was very different from the suspenders that we'd tied our own hands with."

In July 2002, the defense minister, Benjamin Ben-Eliezer, approved another plan to kill Shehade, this time by blowing up the apartment. However, in this case, the restrictions regarding civilian casualties were different.

Once again, "if there are women or children close to said apartment," Ben-Eliezer wrote, "the operation is not authorized." But Shehade's wife was now an exception. If she happened to be in the apartment at the time, the operation could still go forward. Men, whether they were neighbors or passersby, guilty or innocent, were also an exception. They would all be allowed to die.

"In the end, we had no choice," Yaalon said. "There was nothing else we could do. You saw more Jewish blood being spilled, again and again, as time went by. I did not delude myself that [Hamas] without him would stop carrying out terror attacks, but his ability to have terrible attacks executed—because of his experience, because of his know-how, because of his connections—was unparalleled."

Shehade moved often, but he was spotted on July 19 in a three-story building in the densely populated Al-Daraj neighborhood of northern Gaza City, populated mainly by refugees.

Intelligence from human sources indicated that the ground floor was made up of empty storerooms, which made it a perfect building on which to drop a bomb. It just had to be done quickly, before Shehade moved again.

Deputy director Yuval Diskin was not eager to go ahead. He demanded that the intelligence desk officers gather more information. Even if the target building was empty, it was surrounded by tin shanties that likely had entire families living in them. He wanted the feasibility of a ground operation—a sniper, for instance—to be gamed out. Performance research (the air force department responsible for forecasting the outcome of attacks) estimated that there would be "heavy damage" to the shanties.

Serious doubts had been raised in IDF discussions as well. The head of the General Staff Operations Directorate recommended waiting forty-eight hours, "to clear the tin shacks and make sure there's no one living there." Deputy chief of staff Gabriel "Gabi" Ashkenazi also expressed reservations about executing the operation before more information was known.

But the pressure to eliminate the elusive Shehade was too great. A Shin Bet southern region commander rejected Diskin's appraisal, because his own intelligence reports suggested that at night the tin shanties abutting Shehade's building were not inhabited. He appealed to Shin Bet chief Dichter, who approved the immediate assassination of Shehade by a bomb from an air force fighter.

AMAN chief Aharon Zeevi-Farkash supported this decision. "If we do not get rid of people like Salah Shehade, more and more Israelis will get hurt," he later said, recounting the decision. "In situations like this, Palestinian civilians are liable to get hurt." He added, "When you have to decide between two children, I prefer that the Jewish Israeli child won't weep."

THE PILOT CLIMBED INTO his F-16 fighter, sitting on the tarmac at Hatzor, the air force base in south-central Israel. His plane was armed with a one-ton bomb. Two half-ton bombs would have limited the damage and contained the blast area, but it was impossible to know exactly where in the house Shehade would be. There was no point in destroying just the second floor if he was sleeping near the door to the street. A bigger bomb would make sure he was dead.

The operation had been canceled three times already, first because the nineteenth was a Friday and the Muslim day of rest, when the streets would be crowded, and again on the next two nights, the twentieth and twenty-first, because Shehade's daughter was believed to be with him.

On the evening of July 22, however, the team was divided. Although everyone agreed that Shehade's wife was at the apartment, and that the orders permitted them to continue on with the operation anyway, only some of the team believed that the intelligence indicated that the daughter was not at home.

Yuval Diskin, who was directly in charge of the targeted killing operation, was not entirely convinced by the estimation that there was a low likelihood of Iman being in the apartment.

Diskin phoned Dichter and told him about his doubts, and recommended calling off the attack, but, according to an official inquiry, "the director of the Shin Bet weighed all of the data and estimations and reached the conclusion that there was a very high probability that Iman was not in the house, and accordingly he ordered that the operation be executed."

Dichter phoned Prime Minister Sharon's military secretary. He woke Sharon, who authorized "immediate execution" of the bombing raid.

The pilot started to close the canopy. His base commander came running up to his plane and climbed the ladder to his cockpit. "Do you want to know who it is?" he asked the pilot and the navigator. Who they were going to kill, he meant.

"Get off my plane," the pilot said. "We don't want to know. It means nothing."

In a way, it didn't. The men who did the actual killing, who flew the missions and released the bombs, often knew the least. At altitude, all they could see were small targets identified by the twelve numbers of the coordinates, and there was no need to look for anything more.

A siren sounded and the F-16 was cleared for takeoff. It was eleven o'clock on the night of July 22. Flying time from Hatzor to Gaza was two minutes, but the pilot was ordered to fly west, over the sea, far out into the dark. "Shehade, he smells planes, hears planes, and he runs away," the pilot said later. "We wait over the sea for fifty minutes. Then my flight controller tells me on the radio, 'Engage.'"

The plane streaked eastward, turned back to the west, and dropped the bomb. "You must have seen it in the movies," the pilot said. "That's what it looks like. We hit it, and the house collapses, falls down."

IN THE DAYS BEFORE the F-16 took off, air force intelligence had carried out a number of reconnaissance missions over the house where Shehade was hiding. Analysts studied aerial photographs and saw solar heaters, laundry hung out to dry, and satellite dishes bolted to shacks. People lived there. The Shin Bet case officer thought so, too. Because the entire area was densely populated, he noted, he presumed that the shacks were, too.

But the Shin Bet did not get "positive intelligence" from any source indicating with certainty that the shacks were inhabited. In other words, none of the sources walked in and explicitly said *that shack* was occupied by *this family*. As the operational plans grew more detailed and the time for execution approached, common sense was overwhelmed by excitement over the opportunity to eliminate a man involved in the murders of almost five hundred people, including thirty who were killed after two other assassination missions had been scrapped. At some point, according to Shin Bet personnel involved, "no positive intelligence" became "no civilians live there."

"The location of Shehade created a window of opportunity that was unlikely to be repeated at all or in the near future," an inquiry later concluded. "He constituted a ticking time bomb that had to be neutralized." The result was catastrophic. Shehade was killed outright, as was his assistant, Zaher Nassar, and his wife. But so were his daughter, Iman, and ten other civilians, including seven children, the youngest less than one year old. One hundred fifty people were wounded.

*Haaretz* journalist Gideon Levy, whose reports and columns reflect the concerns of liberal Israelis over the plight of the Palestinians, arrived at the scene a few hours after the disaster. He recalled:

> They said they thought there were uninhabited shacks there. Those were two- and three-story buildings—there's no such building in Gaza that isn't inhabited. The people who were out to eliminate Shehade knew this.
>
> I am not naïve or a bleeding heart. If I could rely on the establishment having restraints, I would certainly have been in favor of killing a man like Salah Shehade, as long as he was alone and it was possible to ensure that no one else would be hurt. But I know that it is impossible to rely on them to restrain themselves. There is no control, neither internal nor public, and ultimately, they do whatever they wish. The cost-benefit of assassinations is awful. Awful. This case is ample proof. Entire families were wiped out. In the hospital I saw a little boy about to die, his whole body full of shrapnel. Awful.

Avi Dichter immediately grasped the consequences. "The target has been eliminated," he said, "but the operation failed."

CURIOUSLY, THERE WAS LITTLE international condemnation of the attack. But in Israel, there was a storm of protest. The media, which generally repeated the statements put out by the IDF spokesperson and the Shin Bet, was harshly critical, amplifying anonymous leaks of mutual recrimination among those involved in the operation. More and more voices were heard in Israel questioning the wisdom of assassination as a weapon.

The commander of the air force, Major General Dan Halutz, who had not been directly involved in the operation because he was traveling abroad, was furious at the media and wanted to support his subordinates. He gave an interview to *Haaretz* in which he roundly condemned the critics, saying that some of them should be prosecuted for harming state security. Halutz stressed that he fully backed his pilots and completely condoned the elimination of Shehade, although he did express "sorrow over the loss of life among uninvolved persons."

He recounted that a short time after the operation, he met with the airmen involved in the bombing. "Guys, you can sleep well at night," he told them. "You did exactly what you were instructed to do. You did not deviate a millimeter to the left or the right. Let all those who have a problem with it come to me."

Halutz, a former pilot himself, added, "If you nevertheless want to know what I feel when I release a bomb, then I'll tell you: I feel a slight shudder in the wing as a result of the release of the bomb, after a second it passes and that's all. That's what I feel."

The interview, and particularly the phrase "a slight shudder in the wing," which has since become shorthand in Israel for indifference to the lives of innocents, only flared tempers further. Even other airmen were appalled. The pilot who dropped the bomb wasn't initially concerned with *whom* it was that he hit—"That's nice," he said when his commander told him it was Shehade—but whether it was a *good* hit. "But a few days after that," he said, "three guys came to the squadron. Three reservists. They said, 'What have you done? You went, you killed, you murdered.'"

A rebellion was rising among reservist pilots, who after their discharge do a day's duty every week in peacetime, and full-scale service in wartime. They were generally older, had lived as civilians, and saw the world more from a perspective of democratic governance than military dominance. Groups of them—airmen and Sayeret Matkal reservists—published (separately) letters in the media announcing their refusal to take part in aggressive actions against Palestinians, primarily targeted killings. The protesting airmen and soldiers knew they would pay a high price for signing the open letters. In a tense public atmosphere created by the bloodshed of the suicide terrorists, these statements were perceived by many Israelis as no less than treason, and by some of the top IDF officials as a refusal to carry out orders in wartime.

Particularly striking was the signature of former brigadier general Iftach Spector, a pilot with a world record of twelve enemy supersonic fighters shot down, who was considered by many to be the best combat pilot in the history of the Israeli Air Force. Another signatory was Lieutenant Colonel Yoel Peterberg, a renowned helicopter pilot who had been decorated for extreme bravery in rescuing a ground force pinned down by an ambush in Lebanon.

"Shalom, my name is Yoel," he said in a speech at a protest rally. "I have been the pilot of Cobra, Apache, and Blackhawk helicopters in the Israel Defense Forces, and today I am refusing to serve in the Israel occupation forces. . . . We are the soldiers of peace. We shall stop the war, the death, and the grieving. You are the leaders of the state, leaders of the army, and you will face the consequences. If not in Israeli courts, then in the court at The Hague, and if not in The Hague, then before your maker."

Before the intifada, targeted killings had been primarily the secret business of small, compartmentalized teams working for the Mossad, far from the borders of the country. They might have been carried out in the national interest, but any moral reckoning was confined to a handful of operatives and government ministers. Once those intimate operations were developed into a large-scale killing machine, however, thousands of people became complicit. IDF soldiers and airmen, Shin Bet personnel, the people who collected and filtered and analyzed and disseminated intelligence—they were all directly involved, often in more important ways than those who did the actual killing. And by the summer of 2002, no Israeli could claim ignorance of what was being done in his name.

The protests were greeted mostly by angry rebuttals. Ehud Yatom, the former Shin Bet operative who had killed the two Bus 300 prisoners, was at the time a politician in Benjamin Netanyahu's Likud party (and was to become a Knesset member in 2003). Those who refused to serve were "defeatists," he said. "They must be condemned, prosecuted, stripped of their unit's insignia, and thrown out of the army." The IDF announced that it would indeed oust those who did not withdraw their signatures from the protest letters.

Three days after the pilots' letter was published, Ariel Sharon's closest advisers gathered at his Sycamore Farm (*Havat Shikmim*), in southern Israel. One of them called the letter "the wailing of defeatists." Sharon raised his voice at him. "You are wrong," he snapped. "These are not those beatniks who report to the induction center with the earrings and the green curl. There are people on this list who have done the most daring of deeds for Israel."

Sharon looked at his advisers. He understood how dire the situation had become. "A fire," he said, "has taken hold among the cedars."

# THE REBELLION IN UNIT 8200

WHEN A PERSON DIES, the joke goes, he ascends to Heaven to stand before God, seated on his divine throne. God asks each of the newly dead whether he should remain in Heaven or be cast into Hell. Each one answers, God passes his judgment, and then the next steps forward.

In the joke, the last person is always a network intelligence officer. Within the larger military and intelligence communities, NIOs are the ones who pick which bits of intel among the massive flood arriving every day are worth pursuing. They decide what is important and what is not. They decide, in a way, which people will stand in line before God's throne.

The NIO steps forward. "And where should you go?" God asks.

"Nowhere," the NIO says, slightly annoyed. "You're sitting in my chair."

Amir (not his real name) was an NIO, a bright young man assigned to Unit 8200, one of the most prestigious outfits in the IDF. He worked, like all NIOs, at a base protected by reinforced concrete, monitoring information. Most of the incoming material couldn't be translated and processed, because there was simply too much of it and too little time. The NIOs' job, then, was to decide which channels of communication should be listened to and which broadcasts should be intercepted. Soldiers like Amir decided which bits of the intelligence sieved by his subordinates would be translated and disseminated. He was the final editor of the "article," as intelligence messages are called in 8200; he wrote the headline and decided who would read it. He had to decide, for example, whether the speaker in an intercepted conversation was a storekeeper ordering merchandise or a jihadist delivering coded instructions to prepare a bomb. If he made a mistake, innocent people—Israelis on one side, a hapless shop owner on the other—could die. And he needed to do all of this very quickly.

Officially, Amir and his colleagues at Unit 8200's Turban base were responsible for stopping terror attacks. Unofficially, they were deciding whom Israel killed. True, it was Sharon who authorized the targeted killings, and there was a long chain of command between them and the Prime Minister's Office. But the politicians merely approved the intelligence community's recommendations, which were ultimately conceived, to a large extent, by the NIO. "Our role in the selection of targets for assassination was dramatic," one NIO said. "I could decide if, in my estimation, someone was the coordinator of a cell, to 'sit on him' firmly and to collect enough info to zero in on him as a target for elimination. If the man actually was involved in terror, it was a process that would take a few weeks, no more."

Often, Unit 8200 also picked out buildings to bomb. Sharon, along with IDF chief of staff Moshe Yaalon, held the Palestinian Authority fully responsible for every attack, even if the actual perpetrators came from organizations—Hamas and the Palestinian Islamic Jihad—that opposed the Authority. As a result, Israel took punitive measures against the Palestinian Authority after each attack, bombing its facilities. Most of these facilities were offices of the civilian government, and the same ones were often bombed repeatedly, even after they had been destroyed and abandoned. The bombings were a way to send a message to the Palestinians, but also simply a way for Israel's leaders and soldiers to express their frustration and anger.

"The targets for reprisal bombardments were not chosen in order to achieve a concrete military goal," Amir said, "but were rather a political message that could be summed up simply as 'We'll show them.'"

At first, Israel would notify the Palestinian leadership that the air force was setting out to destroy a particular building, in order to give the people inside time to evacuate. But over time, this practice eroded to a certain extent, and later, toward the end of 2002, the air force often bombed at night, without advance warning, on the assumption that the buildings were empty at that time. It was, for the most part, a purely symbolic campaign.


ON JANUARY 5, 2003, two suicide bombers from Fatah's Al-Aqsa Martyrs' Brigades slipped into Tel Aviv and made their way toward the old central bus station. At 6:26 P.M., they blew themselves up near downtown Tel Aviv. The final death count was twenty-three, with more than a hundred wounded. Many were babies or children.

The Palestinian Authority condemned the attack and promised to make every effort to apprehend the men who had planned it. The Israelis were not convinced of the sincerity of this condemnation, however. After all, the bombers came from an organization affiliated with Fatah, which was under Arafat's command. Most of the top members of the Palestinian Authority were Fatah people.

Prime Minister Sharon immediately summoned the defense leadership for a consultation in his office, and they decided to step up action against the Palestinian Authority.

Following that meeting, less than three hours after the attack, chief of staff Yaalon decided to bomb Target 7068, the code name for the Fatah branch office in the Gaza Strip city of Khan Yunis. This time, there would be no warning, and the attack would not come at night. The IDF would instead wait, deliberately and patiently, until there were people in the building.

At 11:45 P.M., the Targets Department (Anaf Matarot) at AMAN HQ submitted a request to the 8200 Turban base to collect information on the Fatah building in Khan Yunis. At 12:31 A.M., Turban sent out its report on the chosen target.

According to the report, Target 7068 had no connection to terror activities. The sergeant who conducted the investigation of the site wrote, simply and directly, "Don't bomb them—they haven't done anything bad."

"It was a very informal way of putting it," Amir said, "and of course I had to change the wording to something more businesslike before sending out the cable. But his heading reflected the content of the report very well. No activity connected to terror took place there, just routine office work regarding local political activists, paying out welfare and salaries. It was the Gaza Strip equivalent of a labor union local."

Early the next morning, Amir, who assumed Target 7068 would be just another symbolic strike, told AMAN HQ that no one was in the building and that it was safe to start the bombardment.

"It's on hold," he was told by a representative of AMAN's Targets Department. "They're waiting for the office to open."

"What? Who are they expecting?"

"No one. It's not a particular person; just anyone. Let us know when someone goes inside."

That seemed strange. Amir thought it had to be a misunderstanding. The presence of civilians in a building was a reason to stand down, not to strike. Waiting for people—bureaucrats, cleaners, secretaries—went flatly against Finkelstein's 2001 legal memo. Targeting civilians, in fact, was an outright war crime.

But there was no misunderstanding. The Targets Department issued a written order so that everyone understood that they were waiting for "an indication" that the building was occupied: "Indication = an attempt to make a phone call or a phone conversation. Do not wait for the speaker to identify himself or for a conversation of any value to take place. Every indication of the habitation of the building is to be reported, without connection to who the speaker is or the content of the conversation." In other words, the intention was simply to kill someone—anyone.

The order bothered some of the NIOs, who dared speak of it only in the mess hall. "We sat there, three NIOs eating supper," Amir recalled. "And someone said, half in jest but actually serious, 'Say, isn't this precisely the definition of a manifestly illegal order?' He said it offhandedly, not in any heavy way, but it made us start thinking. Maybe we were really crossing a red line here? Maybe this was something improper? How would we know who we were killing? Maybe it would be a kid from a nearby school who went in to make a phone call. Maybe it would be a clerk who came to hand out UN aid money, or an office cleaner who came in early, before work hours."

. . .

THE FACT THAT SUCH a conversation would take place among members of Unit 8200 was fitting. This, after all, was the unit that had tried its hardest to warn AMAN in the days preceding the surprise attacks on Israel in October 1973, cautioning that Egypt and Syria were bent on going to war.

In the wake of that failure, "we intentionally chose opinionated people for the position of NIO, who think out of the box and who would not be afraid to say what they thought," said Professor Eyal Zisser, a prominent Tel Aviv University Middle East specialist who did his IDF reserves service as head of the NIO selection committee.

Because of their access to highly classified material at such a young age, the army tried to inculcate the NIOs with a sense of moral and legal responsibility during their lengthy training. One of their lessons, for example, dealt with civil rights, and the violation of those rights that sometimes occurs as a result of wiretaps. The trainees were told that they must not exploit the immense power they were given for any purpose other than obtaining information for the benefit of the security of the state. The case study that was used outlined an incident in 1997 in which some men from Unit 8200, attempting to locate calls concerning Osama bin Laden, accidentally picked up then purposely recorded some cellphone conversations between Tom Cruise, who was working in the Middle East at the time, and his then wife, Nicole Kidman. They then distributed the recordings to their pals and read the transcripts out loud.

"And if *that* eavesdropping was perceived as a forbidden and immoral act," said Amir, "then it's clear that bombing that building should be forbidden. The more I thought of it, the more I realized that it was forbidden to carry out such an order."

Amir raised the matter with the senior NIO and with the command of 8200. The command said they "understood there was a problem," and the operation was put on hold until further notice. "That satisfied me, and I could go back to my post, which I had closed down, at about 2 A.M., with the sense that the story was behind us."

However, the next morning, when he sat down at the NIO's work-station and began directing the shift, he got a call from the Targets Department notifying him that the bombing of the Fatah branch in Khan Yunis was about to get under way. Amir objected, but the offi-cer on the other side of the scrambled line got angry.

"Why does it seem manifestly illegal to you? They're all Arabs. They're all terrorists."

"In my unit," Amir told him, "we make a very clear distinction between terrorists and those who were not involved, such as people who routinely used the target building."

But he wasn't changing anyone's mind, and by then the operation was already in motion. Two armed F-16 fighter jets were circling over the Mediterranean, waiting for the order. A drone was photographing the building from a distance. As soon as Amir told them someone was in the building, two Hellfire missiles would be launched at the struc-ture.

Amir decided he would refuse to cooperate. The fire in the cedars was spreading.

Impatient calls started coming in to 8200 command from the air force and AMAN. "They were saying, 'Listen, your unit is refusing to give us such-and-such information,'" Brigadier General Yair Cohen, commander of Unit 8200 at the time, recalled. "I said that they must be mistaken, that there was no such thing in 8200 as not providing information, that it had never happened and never would happen."

At 10:05, Amir got a call from 8200 command. "Yair [Cohen] says this is no time to ask questions," he was told, "but a time to act." The operational order required the bombardment to be completed by 11:30, when children would be emptying into a nearby schoolyard.

"This is a manifestly illegal order, and I do not intend to obey it," Amir said. "The fact that the commander has declared it to be legal doesn't make it legal."

There was a pause on the line. "I have conveyed the message from the commander as it was issued," Amir was told. "I'm happy not to be in your position at this moment."

A few minutes later, one of Amir's soldiers told him that phone calls were being made inside the Fatah building. A man was dealing with wage payments, trying to get money to some employees, despite the hard times in the Palestinian Authority and the ongoing war. A secretary was gossiping about a local gigolo.

That was the go signal. The F-16 could fire. Israel could kill them both.

Amir sat in his chair as the on-duty NIO. "A certain serenity came over me," he said. "I felt that there was only one right thing to do. It was clear to me that this operation should not go forward, that it crossed a red line, that it was a manifestly illegal order over which a black flag flew, and that it was my responsibility, as a soldier and a human being, to refuse to carry it out."

He ordered the information not be passed on. He ordered all activity stopped.

At 10:50, just forty minutes before the operation's time window closed, Amir's direct commander, Y., arrived at the base, relieved Amir of his post, and took the NIO seat for himself. He ordered one of the soldiers to report that people were in the building. The bombing could go ahead.

But it was already too late: The planes had returned to base, at the Tel Nof airfield. Now the information was passed on to them and they took off again, but by the time they homed in on the target, the clock showed 11:25, and the school bell rang.

THAT EVENING, THE 8200 command sent an urgent message to the head of AMAN, expressing grave reservations about the operation. It was transmitted to the minister of defense, who ordered the cancellation of the attack on Target 7068.

This was a clear vindication of Amir's moral stand, but it was too late to silence the storm that the "mutiny in 8200" had unleashed in the military. Unit 8200's command came under heavy fire from all sides of the defense establishment—even Prime Minister Sharon let it be known that he took a very dim view of what had transpired. Brigadier General Cohen was summoned to an IDF General Staff meeting devoted entirely to Amir. He should face a court-martial, the officers argued, and go to jail for at least six months. One general went further: "That officer should have been convicted of treason and put in front of a firing squad."

The protests by airmen after the Shehade bombing, a few months earlier, and the refusal of Sayeret Matkal personnel to take part in targeted killing operations were still fresh in everyone's mind. Someone, possibly from one of 8200's rival units, leaked the story to the media. There were no details in the report, but, given the already tense public atmosphere, it was enough to get demonstrators from the left and from the right out onto the streets. Although it was only a few days before the Knesset elections, many of the headlines were about the "refusers."

The military and intelligence establishments were concerned that Amir could be the first of many soldiers to refuse to carry out orders. From the commanders' perspective, putting down a Palestinian uprising didn't leave a lot of room for squishy liberal objectors.

"Unit 8200 is the epitome of the culture of secrecy, always far out of sight, always alone, isolated from the rest of the army, high-quality and covert," a man who served in a senior position at the time said. "All of a sudden, it found itself under a spotlight inside the IDF, and in the most negative possible context. Everyone always says that the 8200's soldiers are pampered kids from the best part of Tel Aviv who go to the army and get the best training in the world and then cash in their skills for billions in high-tech startups, and that they must all be left-wingers and homos. The unit is constantly trying to fight that image, and suddenly it gets labeled as being full of anarchists who refuse to carry out orders."

Amir's contention that what amounted to an order to murder civilians was manifestly illegal was rejected out of hand by the military. For one thing, only someone actually pressing the trigger, and not anyone else involved in the operation, could refuse out of a belief that such a kill order was illegal, declared Major General Elazar Stern, the head of the IDF's Human Resources Directorate. Professor Asa Kasher, a philosopher, was invited by the commander of 8200 to discuss the issue. He believed that Amir's actions were morally incorrect. "I could not under any circumstances endorse the act of the NIO," he said. "In the situation that prevailed there, when he was an NIO at a distant base, he lacked the moral authority to determine that the order was manifestly illegal. He did not know the entire story. He did not see the entire picture, and he did not know about the broader tactics that the chief of staff had decided on. . . . I'm in favor of asking questions and raising doubts, but an order should not be refused at such moments."

Amir was quietly discharged without being indicted, preventing the courts from having an opportunity to determine whether the order to murder civilians in Target 7068 had been legal.

THE OPERATION ON TARGET 7068 had violated the guidelines set by the IDF military advocate general's International Law Department— that the target for elimination must be an individual directly linked to terrorism. But that wasn't the only guideline that was now breached all too regularly—part of a general decline in the prevailing moral and legal standards.

There was also a guideline that called for an investigation each time innocent civilians were killed along with the target. In fact, this protocol was almost never followed. The inquiry into the Shehade killings, which ultimately came to the conclusion that no one was to blame for the deaths of twelve civilians, was the exception, and it, too, was set up only after heavy public and international pressure on Israel.

Another guideline now frequently breached dictated that there should be no killings when there was a "reasonable arrest alternative"— when the terrorist could be detained without endangering the lives of soldiers or civilians. Alon Kastiel, a soldier in the Cherry unit's intelligence section, said, "Everything about my military service changed after the outbreak of the intifada. Before that, we made very great efforts to capture wanted men alive. After the outbreak, this modus operandi ended. It was clear that we were out to kill."

Operational orders from that period indicate that the expectation was that the wanted man would be killed the moment he was identified. In Operation Two Towers, for example, the operational order contradicts itself: "1. The objective is arrest; 2. If the 'framing' [positive identification] is of a senior PIJ [Palestinian Islamic Jihad] figure Walid Obeid, Ziad Malaisha, Adham Yunis, the force is authorized to execute interception." The term "interception" is a euphemism for "elimination" or "killing," and it came to be used frequently as a way to sidestep the ILD's guidelines. The operation unfolded accordingly: Malaisha was "framed" and "intercepted," shot dead.

Yet another violation of the ILD's protocol regularly occurred as a result of the provision that only the prime minister had the authority to approve targeted killing ops. AMAN officials resented the fact that Sharon had given the Shin Bet overall authority on assassinations.

In order to bypass the IDL guidelines, AMAN set up an identical parallel apparatus to carry out, without needing Sharon's approval, what it called "interception operations" against anyone linked to acquiring, developing, stockpiling, transporting, or using weapons on behalf of terrorist organizations. "Orders barred me from carrying out assassinations, but no one forbade us to shoot at anyone launching Qassams or transporting explosives," said a senior AMAN officer.

On some occasions, a shipment of weapons or a Qassam-launching squad was in fact identified in real time, so the killing was indeed justifiable. But often, "interception" was simply another word for a preplanned assassination, because AMAN wanted a certain person dead. "We called it interception, but of course it was assassination," said an AMAN official. "We ran one operation after another, without stopping." Some of these were legitimate military actions, some were assassinations of key terrorists, and many were in a gray area between the two.

Over time, the military and intelligence communities got better and better at inventing novel ways of gaming the official protocols. The IDF had greatly broadened the open-fire procedures, such that in terrorist-infested areas, soldiers were instructed to shoot at anyone holding any kind of firearm, Molotov cocktail, or explosive device, without any warning, and then confirm the kill. In order to create situations in which armed suspected terrorists would emerge from their hiding places and into the streets and alleys, where they would be exposed to Israeli gunfire, an operational procedure code-named Grass Widow was developed.

During the course of the conflict in the occupied territories, several variations of the Grass Widow technique were used, baiting gunmen out of their hiding places and exposing them to fire from a concealed sniping position. In one variation, an Israeli force would arrest a comrade of the terrorists out in the open on the street, prompting armed gunmen to come outside and attack the force. In another, an armored car would drive up and down a street, with a loudspeaker broadcasting an Arabic recording of shouted challenges like "So where are all the big heroes of Izz al-Din al-Qassam? Why don't you come out and fight? Let's see if you are men." Or, more provocatively, "All the Jihad are fags" or "Hamas are sons of whores. Your mothers work in the streets and give it out free to anyone who wants it." These are some of the more refined remarks—others are even less suitable for print. Perhaps surprisingly, this method has worked well. Gunmen come out to shoot at the offending vehicle and end up getting picked off by a sniper from Grass Widow concealed in a nearby apartment.

Grass Widow operations killed dozens of gunmen from all the Palestinian organizations. From the military's point of view, the system worked, and the IDF gained relative freedom of action in the streets of Palestinian cities. The legality of these operations, however, is debatable at best.

BY THE SUMMER OF 2002, the Shin Bet and its partners were able to stop more than 80 percent of attacks before they turned deadly. The targeted killings were clearly saving lives. But there was a disturbing trend in the data, too: The number of *attempted* attacks was increasing. Rather than being worn down, the Palestinians were spawning more and more attackers. That meant that Israel had to focus on more targets. But it also raised a fear that, over time, the terrorist groups would learn from each individual defeat and would adapt and get smarter and tougher, leading to a potentially endless escalation in a potentially endless war.

"We felt we had something like a year, perhaps a little more, to give them such a punch that would make the whole business not worth it, from their point of view," said a senior Shin Bet official from that period.

That concern led to a new plan, code-named Picking Anemones. Although Israel already had declared every member of those organizations part of the "ticking infrastructure," it had almost never touched the political leaders. But that reasoning had evolved. "In

Hamas, there was no distinction between the political and military echelons," said AMAN chief Major General Zeevi-Farkash. "The leaders who are called 'political' are involved in everything. They lay down the policy and issue orders about when to carry out attacks and when to hold back." Indeed, the argument went, the only point of declaring a political wing was to fabricate international status and give certain leaders immunity from assassination. "We had to build a clear-cut deterrent," Zeevi-Farkash said. "There's no such thing as a political echelon which we will not touch."

Every leader of Hamas and the Palestinian Islamic Jihad was now a target. The plan was to kill them all.

# PICKING ANEMONES

IBRAHIM AL-MAKADMEH KNEW THE Israelis were going to kill
him. He should have, anyway, considering that the Palestinian Authority's intelligence agencies told him as much. They'd heard it from
a Shin Bet double agent, who said he'd been asked by the Israelis to
monitor Makadmeh's routines. Why else would the Shin Bet want to
know his comings and goings, if not to kill him?

Maybe he didn't believe it. Makadmeh had published some books
and articles on religion, jihad, and Jewish immigration to Palestine,
and he was an Islamic theorist. An extreme Hamas strategist, he advocated a holy war to destroy the Jewish state, and he served as the
liaison between the organization's political and military wings. But he
was also a dentist and a popular lecturer at the Islamic University of
Gaza. He was a learned man of academia who spent most of his time
immersed in politics, rather than direct involvement in terror operations.

The PA operatives told him to lie low for a while and to wait until
the Israelis got tired of looking for him. Makadmeh ignored them and
continued lecturing at the university as usual. His assistant and two
bodyguards picked him up at his home, in the Gaza neighborhood of
Sheikh Radwan, at about 9:30 on the morning of March 8, 2003.

An Israeli drone watched.

The assistant called the dean's office at the university to let him
know Makadmeh would be there shortly and that he expected students to be waiting in the lecture hall. "Despite the risk to his life,"

the assistant added—a dramatic flourish he probably didn't really believe.

Makadmeh, the assistant, and the bodyguards made it a thousand feet down Al-Jalaa Street before four Hellfire missiles fired from two Apache helicopters destroyed the car.

They, along with a little child who was playing in the street nearby, were the first casualties of Operation Picking Anemones, approved by Sharon and his security cabinet in early 2003. The basic assumption was that what the leaders of the jihadist terror organizations wanted their followers to do—suicide attacks—would take on a different dimension when a price tag was attached, namely their own lives. Or, as Amos Gilad, head of the Defense Ministry's political-security staff, described it, "They all know that the seventy-two virgins in paradise is an option that cannot be proved, and they, the leaders, are simply not prepared to check it out for themselves."

Operation Picking Anemones was more nuanced than the wholesale assassination campaign against political leaders that AMAN chief General Zeevi-Farkash had advocated. The operation would not, in fact, go after *all* Hamas and PIJ leaders. Sheikh Yassin, the founder of Hamas, for instance, was left off the initial list of targets, for fear that more Palestinians would join the fighting if he were killed. But the point was the same: to let Hamas and the PIJ know that calling yourself a political functionary was no longer cover.

Defining the parameters had taken months of debate, as had agreeing on whether such killings were legal, moral, and, most important, strategically practical. "Drawing analogies between terrorism and a snake, which will stop functioning if you cut off its head, is such an oversimplification that it's alarming to think anyone believes it," argued Ami Ayalon, Avi Dichter's predecessor as Shin Bet director. "A terror organization is built like a matrix. Even if it does have a head, then it is an ideological head that hardly controls the operative head." In other words, there wasn't much of an operational point. But it did create a parallel precedent. If the political leaders of Hamas were legitimate targets, he said, what about "the [Israeli] defense minister who sits in his office and authorizes actions? Does this make *him* a legitimate target for elimination?"

Nonetheless, Operation Picking Anemones was eased into practice. Three months after Makadmeh was hit, an IDF drone fired at Abd al-Aziz Rantisi, the number-two man in Hamas, but only wounded him. Then, on August 12, Ismail Abu Shanab, a founder of Hamas, the leader of its political arm, and one of its main spokesmen in the Arabic and foreign media, was killed near the UN building in Gaza by five missiles fired from an Apache.

As senior Foreign Ministry officials had feared prior to embarking on Operation Picking Anemones, the international community did indeed make a distinction between attacking military operatives and political operatives. The Abu Shanab assassination sharpened the international debate about Israel's actions, despite the West's recognition that Israel was waging a tough battle against suicide bombers.

UN Secretary General Kofi Annan condemned the hit, declaring that Israel had no right to carry out an "extrajudicial killing" of a senior Hamas leader. The late Abu Shanab's boss, Sheikh Yassin, stated his intentions in starker terms: "All of the red lines have been crossed," he said in a statement to the Palestinian media. "And Israel will pay for it."

EXACTLY HOW ISRAEL WOULD pay for its latest escalation was unclear, perhaps even to Yassin. The old rules were bloody and savage, but at least they marked some semblance of a tactical boundary. The killing of Abu Shanab—someone who had been involved in the political part of Hamas and was seen by leaders of the organization as off-limits—deeply rattled Hamas. Yassin needed to figure out a response, and quickly.

Shortly after that assassination, Yassin ordered all of Hamas's military and political leadership to gather on September 6 at the home of Dr. Marwan Abu Ras, a leading religious figure in Gaza and a member of the Palestinian Legislative Council. That was an extraordinary risk—putting all of his senior men in one spot at one time created an enormous target. If the secret got out, Yassin's only hope would be that Israel might decide that killing everyone wouldn't be worth the potential collateral damage.

Avi Dichter, the Shin Bet director, who had learned of the meeting from both human and technological sources, thought it might be a fair trade. "In my entire career," he said, "never did such a serious adversary make such a serious mistake, a profound strategic mistake."

The meeting was supposed to begin at four o'clock. By 3:40 P.M., a pair of F-16s armed with one-ton bombs were in the air, circling above the Mediterranean Sea in order to avoid stirring suspicion among those gathered in the home. The Air Force analysis wing had calculated that a bomb that big was needed to destroy Abu Ras's three-story house.

At 3:45, chief of staff Yaalon called in the operations analysts with maps and aerial photographs.

"What's your estimate for collateral damage?" Yaalon asked.

There was a five-story apartment building close to the Abu Ras house. Nearly forty families lived there. "The men may not be home from work at 4 P.M.," AMAN chief Zeevi-Farkash said, "but it's clear that there must be dozens of women and children there."

"And what will happen to them if we use the one-ton bomb?"

"Dozens of casualties, possibly even more than that," another analyst answered.

The protests that followed the Shehade fiasco hadn't been forgotten. "There wasn't anyone among us who was obsessed with killing," said Dov Weissglass, Sharon's aide. "On the contrary, in time the air force realized that the damage that seven or eight civilian deaths caused was far greater than the benefits of eliminating one terrorist." The air force had even worked to develop munitions with a smaller blast radius, replacing up to 90 percent of the explosive material with cement. But a cement bomb wasn't going to take out a three-story building.

Yaalon joined a conference call with Sharon, Dichter, and three others. "Mr. Prime Minister," he said, "I recommend calling off the strike. The price of the operation will be dozens of civilians killed. We'll win the battle but lose the war in both the international and domestic arenas. The people of Israel will not tolerate another blow like this against women and children. We need internal and external legitimacy to carry on with our fight—and here we're liable to deal both a devastating blow."

Dichter argued that Israel would be missing a historic opportunity to cause "perhaps irreparable" damage to its principal enemy.

But Yaalon insisted. "Under no circumstances can we do this," he said. "We could wipe out the Hamas leadership, but we're also at risk of getting hundreds of thousands of protesters in Rabin Square, yelling that we are a brutal army that murders women and children. This we need to avoid. We'll get our chance. Their day will come."

Sharon called off the strike.

DICHTER STAYED BEHIND IN the Joint War Room, fuming and frustrated. Ironically, he'd been among the first to recognize what a disaster the Shehade fiasco had been, to realize that killing and wounding scores of civilians meant that "the target has been eliminated, but the operation failed."

But the Hamas gathering was historic. "The Dream Team gathering," he called it. He scrolled through all the intelligence information about the Hamas conclave and, after a few minutes, hit upon a solution. The *diwan,* the carpeted sitting room where meetings would be held, was on the top floor, where the drapes had been drawn. It was reasonable to assume the meeting would be held there, and he got an analyst in the JWR to say as much. Dichter called up operations analysts and asked if there was a way to destroy only that part of the house, ensuring that there would be no damage to adjoining structures. The reply was affirmative: If a small missile with a quarter-ton warhead was fired through a window, it would assure the destruction of everyone in the room while doing little or no damage outside of it.

Dichter got everyone back on the phone and told them the meeting would probably take place on the third floor. Zeevi-Farkash was doubtful. Yaalon was not convinced, either. "It seemed a little strange to me that they would carry Yassin up in his wheelchair," he said. "But that was the Shin Bet's assessment. A top floor I know how to wreck without causing casualties in the adjoining houses. It was possible to proceed." Again, there was a conference call with all of the top officials on the secure phone line. Sharon listened until Dichter and Yaalon finished speaking, and approved the operation.

The JWR put three drones into the air to keep an eye on the house. They watched the participants arriving and entering. The Shin Bet's information proved to be precise—the entire political and military leadership of Hamas was there, including Yassin in his wheelchair, Ahmed Jabari, who had replaced Shehade as field commander, and Mohammed Deif, commander of the Izz al-Din al-Qassam Brigades. The Israelis had been trying to kill Deif for more than seven years, ever since he replaced Yahya Ayyash in early 1996. "Each time, we took off an arm or a leg of his, but he survived it all," says a senior Shin Bet official who was present in the JWR that day.

At 4:35, an F-16 pilot launched a missile through the draped window on the third floor. "Alpha," reported the pilot, indicating a direct bull's-eye hit. The top of the building erupted in flames, and debris, including bricks and furniture, flew in all directions. JWR analysts tried to see whether the debris also included body parts. An enormous explosion shook the entire area.

But the meeting had been on the ground floor. "They just got up, brushed off the dust, and ran away from the house," Dichter said. "We watched them running for their lives. For a moment, I even thought that I saw Sheikh Yassin getting up on his feet from the wheelchair, out of panic, and starting to run."

Dichter wanted to send in a squadron of drones to blast all of the cars screeching out of the house's parking space, but he was overruled by Defense Minister Mofaz, because "civilians were likely to be hurt."

"I looked around the war room," said Dichter, "and I saw how everyone was going out of their mind at the missed chance. This was a classic example of the price you have to pay because of the problems that a story like the Shehade hit creates. I wouldn't dare to count up the number of Israelis who were killed and wounded due to the decision not to blast the whole house. Later on, we had to handle them one at a time. In some cases, we succeeded, after great efforts. Some of them, I'm sorry to say, are alive to this day."

THREE DAYS AFTER THE strike on Abu Ras's house, just before six o'clock, a man wearing an army uniform and carrying a large backpack joined a group of hundreds of IDF soldiers waiting outside the Tzrifin army base in the late-afternoon heat. The bus stop and hitch-hiking post had a high roof to provide shade from the blistering sun, and the men waited there for a bus or a lift from someone happy to offer a ride to the soldiers hurrying to begin their brief furloughs.

A few minutes later, an IDF patrol approached the stop. The man, a Hamas suicide bomber, apparently feared that he would be detected and pressed the button.

Nine soldiers were killed, and eighteen were wounded.

Hamas was flailing, lashing back at Israel for the strike on Abu Ras's house and the assassinations of its political figures. To retaliate, Hamas had returned to the same low-tech, high-terror tactics that had led to Israel's escalation in the first place: suicide bombers.

The mission had been assigned to the Hamas command center in Ramallah, which operated a cell already in contact with several potential suicide bombers from Beit Liqya, a Palestinian village northwest of Jerusalem. A day before the Tzrifin attack, a suicide bomber was dispatched to a restaurant in Jerusalem, but he retreated at the last minute, overcome by fear. Another bomber recruited for the mission, Ihab Abu Salim, was the young man who blew himself up the next day at the Tzrifin hitchhiking post.

Prime Minister Sharon received news of the attack while meeting in New Delhi with his Indian counterpart, Atal Bihari Vajpayee. In his absence, he authorized Foreign Minister Silvan Shalom to take "the necessary response actions." Shalom convened an urgent meeting of the heads of the IDF and the intelligence community at the Ministry of Defense.

At 10 P.M., four hours after the soldiers at Tzrifin were murdered, Shalom asked the Shin Bet and AMAN representatives present at the meeting whom in Hamas they could kill, immediately. A suicide attack would not go unanswered. "We have quite good surveillance on Mahmoud al-Zahar," a Shin Bet official said. Al-Zahar was a surgeon, but also one of the founders of Hamas, and he was seen as the leader of the extreme faction in the organization.

"Maybe we could take him out, but it would have implications as far as hurting uninvolved persons is concerned."

An hour passed. Part of the discussion also revolved around the

question of what to do with Yasser Arafat. Silvan Shalom had long
been calling for Arafat to be killed, or at least expelled. "He orches-
trates terror, he stands behind attacks, and as long as he's around,
there's no chance of stopping the bloodbath and reaching an accord
with the Palestinians." Shalom said that a very senior official in the
U.S. administration had telephoned him after hearing about the attack and asked, "Do you intend to assassinate the bastard?"

Opinions on how to handle Arafat were divided. In any case, it
was clear that this was a major decision that only the prime minister
could make.

At 11:20 P.M., aides came into the room. Their faces were grave.
Another suicide bomber had attacked, this time in Café Hillel, in
Jerusalem's German Colony. Seven people were dead, fifty-seven
wounded. The casualties included Dr. David Appelbaum, the director of the emergency unit at Shaare Zedek Medical Center, and his
daughter Nava, who was to be married the next day.

Al-Zahar was a dead man.

Shalom used the satellite phone to call Yoav Galant, the former
commander of Flotilla 13, who had participated in many targeted
killing operations and was now serving as the prime minister's military secretary. Galant woke up Sharon (India is two and a half hours
ahead of Israel), who immediately approved a missile strike on al-
Zahar's home, but only after 8:30 the next morning—once the adults
had gone to work, the schoolchildren were in class, and the streets
were quiet.

And what about al-Zahar's family? In the atmosphere following
two gruesome attacks in six hours that had horrified Israel, no one
really paid much attention to this question.

In the morning, Turban's sensors detected al-Zahar making a call
from his home, using the line in his office on the second floor.

The JWR notified Shalom. Seconds later, another report came in
from Turban: The call was an interview al-Zahar was giving to the
BBC Arabic service. Shalom was worried about the impact of a hit
during a live broadcast—"God forbid the boom would be heard"—
and ordered it postponed until the interview was over. The JWR personnel listened in until they heard al-Zahar hang up.

Since it was a landline phone with a single outlet, and since al-

Zahar's voice was clearly identified by Turban's skilled listeners and by the BBC interviewer, al-Zahar's "death warrant" was approved—even though no Shin Bet agent or camera had actually seen al-Zahar in his office. Two Apaches fired a total of three missiles, demolishing the house, killing al-Zahar's son Khaled, twenty-nine years old, and a bodyguard, and badly injuring his wife. But al-Zahar was only scratched: He'd been out in the garden with a cup of coffee, a cigarette, and a cordless phone.

OPERATION PICKING ANEMONES WASN'T working nearly as well in practice as it had in theory. Israel had missed several important targets, while Hamas had retaliated with two suicide bombers, sixteen dead, and seventy-five wounded. And although various anti-terror measures adopted by Israel, including the targeted killings of Hamas operatives, had led to some decrease in the number of Israelis killed and injured, Operation Picking Anemones wasn't having the desired effect on the number of terror attempts. Hamas political figures might have been spooked, but the organization did not run out of people willing to become a *shahid*.

The debate in the defense establishment intensified—what should be done about Sheikh Yassin? Ayalon's musings about snakes and cutting off heads notwithstanding, it seemed increasingly clear that Hamas's leader would have to be neutralized.

The Shin Bet and Sayeret Matkal collaborated on a complicated plan to abduct and imprison him. But that idea was dropped, because any such operation would almost certainly require a gunfight, and a gunfight meant that soldiers, civilian bystanders, or the sheikh himself could be hit. It also wasn't at all clear that Sheikh Yassin's return to prison would even stop the suicide bombings. Israeli officials remembered that his long period of incarceration (which ended in the humiliating deal with King Hussein following the failed attempt to kill Khaled Mashal) had been rife with acts of murder and abductions by Hamas aimed at freeing him, along with waves of suicide bombings.

The only effective way to deal with Yassin, many argued, was to kill him.

But Israeli decision-makers were much more hesitant about pulling the trigger when it came to Yassin, despite the fact that everyone agreed that he was actively involved in directing and planning Hamas terror. True, Israel had nearly killed him the previous year during the "Dream Team" meeting, but that meeting included military operatives, too. Assassinating him, and him alone, was a completely different matter. Sheikh Yassin was a founder of the Hamas movement, a political leader of world renown, and a religious figure accepted throughout the Middle East.

In a discussion in November, Avi Dichter argued, "Assassinating this particular individual is liable to set the Middle East ablaze and bring upon us waves of terror from outside our borders." Major General Amos Gilad, director of policy and political-military affairs at the Ministry of Defense, was known for his hawkish views, but he also objected. "Sheikh Yassin is the exact paradigm of an ideologue of death, an architect of endless murder," he said. But he concurred with those who feared a conflagration across the entire Islamic world in response to the slaying of someone perceived as a Muslim spiritual leader.

Yaalon countered that Yassin was not seen as a spiritual leader, and killing him would not cause any response, beyond angry condemnation. "It's inconceivable that we should go in circles around him, killing everyone else," he said, "and not strike at him."

Defense Minister Mofaz adopted an even harsher approach: "Not only must we hit him, but I also have no problem doing it with a 'high signature'"—that is, leaving no doubt that Israel had carried out the assassination.

Although Sharon agreed in principle with Yaalon and Mofaz, Dichter was his senior adviser on terrorism and targeted killings, and even the assertive Sharon seemed to have lost a bit of his confidence in light of the opposition from Dichter and others.

Major General Giora Eiland raised an additional cause for worry: bad PR. Was it not a problem for Israel to kill "an elderly, pitiable, half-blind cripple in a wheelchair? Won't we look like the Wild West?" Sharon was not really concerned, but he did ask to hear additional opinions.

The IDF's philosopher in chief, Asa Kasher, supported Yaalon:

"The distinction between political and military echelons fostered by international human rights organizations would also have left Hitler immune to attack for a significant period of time. The distinction between the echelons is particularly dubious when it comes to terrorist organizations." On the other hand, the military advocate general was emphatically opposed. Since Finkelstein and Daniel Reisner formulated the rules for targeting killings three years earlier, Reisner and his staff had been present for many of the actions, providing legal backing for them. In some cases, they ordered the postponement of an operation out of fear of injuring innocents. In the case of Yassin, for the first time, their strong opposition stemmed from the identity of the targeted person. The growing importance accorded to Reisner's opinion was due partly to the establishment of the International Criminal Court during that period. Senior officials in Israel began to worry about being indicted for targeted killings and sought legal support.

Nevertheless, Yaalon persisted, and the matter was taken up with the attorney general's office, the highest professional legal authority in Israel. It was the first time that the targeted killing of a specific person had come before this forum for discussion.

AMAN and Shin Bet officials brought with them the Red Page—all the evidence that had accumulated against Yassin: the founding of Hamas, virulent preaching against the existence of Israel, establishment of the terrorist apparatus, prior convictions on charges of ordering the abduction and murder of Israeli soldiers in the 1980s, acquisition of weaponry, fundraising for military activities, advocacy of suicide terror, and more.

Finkelstein and Reisner argued that, with all due respect to the Red Page, targeted killings were not meant to be carried out as revenge or punishment, but only in order to prevent a future attack.

There was no recent indication in the intelligence material that Yassin was involved directly in terror. "But that's because he knows we are keeping close track of him," argued an AMAN representative. "Therefore, he's being very careful not to say anything on the telephone or via any other electronic means."

Attorney General Elyakim Rubinstein endorsed the military advocate general's position and stated that he would not approve the assassination until clear-cut evidence was provided that linked Yassin directly to terror and "that would stand up in court."

SHORTLY THEREAFTER, ON JANUARY 14, 2004, a young woman from the Gaza Strip, twenty-one years old, tried to enter into Israel at the Erez Crossing. She had to pass through a metal detector, like all Palestinians. There was a high, pinging *beep-beep-beep-beep* when she went through the detector. *"Platin, platin,"* she told the border guards, pointing at her leg—a platinum implant.

The guards sent her through again, then a third time. The detector kept beeping. A female guard was summoned to frisk her. She then detonated a bomb that killed four examiners and wounded ten other people.

The woman's name was Reem Saleh Riyashi. She had two children, one three years old, the other only eighteen months.

A day later, Sheikh Yassin called a press conference at the home of one of his followers. He sat in his wheelchair, wrapped in a brown blanket, with a large wreath in the form of a heart carrying the inscription HAMAS in the background. He was smiling. "For the first time," he said, "we have used a woman fighter instead of a man. This is a new development in the struggle against the enemy." The sheikh, who in the past had issued several fatwas (religious edicts) against the use of female suicide bombers, said he had changed his mind. "The holy war obligates all Muslims, men and women. This is proof that the resistance will continue until the enemy is driven out of our homeland."

For Israel, such a shift in tactics was menacing. "We asked ourselves: How will we be able to cope with waves of female suicide bombers coming into the country?" Defense Minister Mofaz said. There are standards of decorum, even in a dirty war. "It is much harder to examine women and prevent explosives from being brought in."

In addition to Yassin's statement, AMAN was able to present Attorney General Rubinstein with transcripts of secret recordings made by 8200's Turban base, of Yassin telling his operational staff that women could be used as suicide bombers. "We had clear intelligence-based evidence of the direct link between the political leadership of Hamas, headed by Sheikh Yassin, and the planners and executors of the terror attacks," said Farkash.

Rubinstein was persuaded: Yassin could legally be killed. The security cabinet convened to decide. Shimon Peres was still opposed: "I feared that they would start trying to kill Israeli leaders," he later said. "I thought that it was precisely with him that we would be able to reach a peace agreement."

But by a majority of one, the ministers determined that he was a terrorist leader. "I was not impressed by the warnings that the earth would tremble or the skies fall in because of this assassination," said Ehud Olmert, then the minister for trade, industry, and communications, who was part of the majority.

In a procedure that had already become routine, the cabinet left it up to Sharon and Mofaz to approve the proposals of the IDF and Shin Bet concerning when and how to carry out the hit. Sharon's aides told U.S. National Security Adviser Condoleezza Rice that Yassin had become a legitimate target from Israel's point of view. "A pretty tough argument ensued," Weissglass said. "They were worried there'd be a general flare-up in the Middle East."

In public appearances, Sharon also dropped hints that he now saw Yassin as a target. This only led to a tightening of the security around the Hamas leader. He stayed home, emerging only to visit a mosque and his sister's home, both of which were near his house. Movement between the three points was in two vans, one equipped with a lift for Yassin's wheelchair, while his armed bodyguards traveled in the second. His life was confined to this triangle, and he and his people assumed that Israel would not dare strike at any of its vertices, each of which was crowded with women and children and, in the case of the mosque, innocent civilians.

But there were spaces in between those three points. On the evening of March 21, Yassin was driven to prayers at the mosque, his bodyguards following in a second van.

Mofaz ordered that both vehicles be destroyed on their way back. There were choppers in the air and UAVs buzzing overhead, and Yassin's son, Abd al-Hamid, had been around long enough to sense the danger. He raced to the mosque.

"Father, do not leave here," he warned. "They [the Israelis] will not attack a mosque."

The sheikh and his bodyguards decided to be cautious and remain in the mosque.

Hours went by. The JWR and all the forces remained on alert, with the air force keeping shifts of drones and attack helicopters in the air, relieving them when they ran out of fuel. The sheikh went to sleep on a mattress on the floor of the mosque, waking up early because it was uncomfortable. After the dawn prayers, he wanted to go home. "Helicopters could not be heard above," his son said. "Everyone was sure the danger had passed."

Still, it was a risk. To confuse the trackers, they decided to bundle the sheikh in his wheelchair and then run to his home. The van would only draw attention. "To tell the truth, I did not think they'd fire at a cripple's wheelchair," Hamid said.

The trackers were still there, of course, the drones still watching through thermal-imaging cameras. People came out the front door, moving quickly past the vans parked by the entrance, pushing a wheelchair.

Air force commander Halutz could not authorize opening fire, because Defense Minister Mofaz's orders allowed him to fire only at the two vans.

"Mr. Minister," Halutz said, "we do not have framing of the vans, but we do see a group of bodyguards running with a wheelchair and someone wearing a kaffiyeh in it. Do we have authorization?"

Mofaz asked him to speak to the Apache pilot and ask him if he could clearly see the wheelchair and whether he could hit it.

"I see them very clearly," the pilot said. "I can take them out."

"I authorize," said Mofaz.

"*Rashai,*" Halutz radioed the pilot.

On the video feed, there was a flash, then a fraction of a second of blank screen. Then parts of the wheelchair flew in all directions, one wheel soaring upward and landing outside the frame, and people lying or crawling on the ground.

"Request permission for supplements," the pilot said.

"Permission granted," Mofaz answered.

Another missile hit the ground, killing anyone who was still alive.

Mofaz called Sharon, who was waiting tensely at his home on Sycamore Farm for the outcome of the operation. "We have video," he said. "Judging by the pictures, it looks good. We hit the bull's-eye, but let's wait for reports from additional sources."

Within a few minutes, the duty monitors at Turban reported that Hamas's communications channels were bursting with traffic. "Sheikh Yassin has become a *shahid,* along with a number of his bodyguards," the organization's members were telling one another. His son, Abd al-Hamid, was badly wounded. Sharon ordered that his staff be woken up to prepare to handle the fallout.

News of the assassination was received with deep concern in Washington. "They're on the verge of hysteria," Weissglass reported to Sharon. He told Rice not to worry, that Israel expected the Arab world's response to be condemnation and nothing more. "Condi," he said, in his calm and persuasive voice, "even in the Palestinian Authority, we do not anticipate anything unusual. They have declared three days of national mourning, but all the stores are open. It's going to be all right."

ONCE THE DAYS OF national mourning ended, Hamas's supreme leadership body, the Shura Council, appointed Abd al-Aziz Rantisi to succeed Yassin. He was sworn in on a soccer field in one of the Gaza refugee camps. Sitting on a dais before a large crowd, the entire leadership of the organization watched a parade of uniformed militiamen and kissed the new leader's hand. "We'll fight the enemy everywhere, we'll teach it the meaning of resistance," Rantisi declared in his maiden speech, and he vowed to avenge the slaying of Yassin.

The Israelis were aware of the plans for the parade and ceremony, but Sharon ordered the Shin Bet and the air force to hold their fire, for fear of hitting civilians and because it was clear that foreign TV networks would be there and would broadcast any Israeli attack live.

Nevertheless, by that point, Sharon had already authorized the new leader's assassination. This decision was much easier. Rantisi lacked Yassin's religious authority, and he wasn't an internationally recognized Arab political figure. His involvement in terror was indisputable, and, most important, the precedent had been set—now any Hamas leader could be liquidated.

Rantisi was cautious and tried to be deceptive, squirreling from one hideout to another, wearing wigs and using different code names on his cellphones. But Turban had no difficulty keeping tabs on him. On April 17, only a couple of weeks after being placed in charge of Hamas, he went home to make the final arrangements for the marriage of his son, Ahmed. It was a brief visit: He gave his wife the cash she needed to complete the preparations, then he left.

He was driving down Al-Jalaa Street when a Brushlet missile exploded into his Subaru.

A crowd of hundreds gathered around the charred remnants of the vehicle. A first-aid team tried in vain to save the lives of Rantisi and the two aides who were with him. A photograph distributed by the Reuters agency showed the screaming and weeping crowd, with one man holding his hands, smeared with the blood of the dead leader, up to the sky.

"He was a pediatrician who dealt mainly with the murder of children," Mofaz told the press. Associates of Sharon's made the implied warning explicit. "Arafat should take note," one said, "that anyone whose business is terror should be very wary of his fate."

The killing of Rantisi was the 168th targeted killing operation since the beginning of the intifada, in late 2000. By that point, Operation Picking Anemones had successfully thrown Hamas into a state of shock and confusion. The Shura Council immediately appointed a successor to Rantisi, but he was a minor figure whose name was kept classified so that he wouldn't end up dead, too. All of the senior Hamas officials took extreme measures to remain under Israel's radar, effectively spending most of their time just trying to stay alive.

"The Zionist enemy has succeeded in assassinating many of the fighting brothers, and this at a time when we badly need each and every pure fighter," a declaration on the Hamas website stated. "There is no doubt at all that negligence is one of the main reasons for the enemy's success, because the electronic spy planes never leave the skies of Gaza. The many eyes assigned this task do not know sleep, and the Apache helicopters are ready and available with their missiles and waiting for the opportunity. You are a target for assassination every day, even every hour of the day."

Two weeks after Rantisi was killed, General Omar Suleiman, the Egyptian intelligence minister and the most powerful man in the Cairo regime after President Mubarak, went to Israel for an urgent meeting with Mofaz, Yaalon, and Dichter. "I come with a message of conciliation," Suleiman said. He presented Hamas's proposal for a ceasefire, the gist of which was "no assassinations, no terror attacks."

Mofaz thanked Suleiman for coming. He told him that, as always, Egypt's efforts to bring about conciliation in the region were appreciated. But there was nothing more to discuss. Israel, he said, would not stop the targeted killings in general or the campaign to kill Hamas leadership in particular.

Suleiman grew angry. "I came all the way from Cairo and bring you an offer to stop the attacks. This is what you wanted. Why are you persisting?"

"Hamas wants a truce so it can grow stronger," Mofaz said. "We have to defeat them, not allow them to breathe."

Suleiman appealed to Sharon, who greeted him warmly but yielded no ground. "Our defense establishment's position is that we must not agree to a ceasefire," he said. "I cannot oppose my own generals." He offered only that Israel would carefully monitor Hamas's conduct.

Hamas activists tried to make it difficult for the Israeli drones and Apaches to find them. They moved only when necessary, used motorcycles, and tried to keep to narrow streets. It didn't matter: Two were killed by missiles in Gaza on May 30, and another was killed in the Balata refugee camp two weeks later. On that same day, Suleiman came to see Sharon in person again, after intensive phone communications that had taken place since the previous visit. "Mr. Prime Minister, now you know their offer is serious and they have ceased attacking."

Grudgingly, Sharon agreed to stop the targeted killings. Hamas ordered an absolute and immediate cessation of suicide attacks.

·　·　·

ARIEL SHARON NOW HAD the upper hand in the fight against terror. During that period, when the security situation became a bit calmer, he even began to consider a political solution to the historic conflict in the Middle East. His close affinity to President Bush and the deep relationship he developed with the entire American administration—predicated upon the trade-off of freezing settlements in exchange for carte blanche in targeted killings—made Sharon come to feel that the Americans sincerely wanted to help the State of Israel, and gave him some new realizations.

"Sharon reached the conclusion that it doesn't matter who is sitting in the White House—they will always view the settlements as a significant problem," said Weissglass.

And for Sharon, the settlements—which he had wholeheartedly promoted in his previous positions—were not a religious, ideological issue; rather, they were a security consideration. "The moment he understood that they're a burden and not an advantage, he had no problem evacuating them and turning his back on the settlers." Sharon, the sworn hawk, who had built his career on his aggressive policy toward the Arabs in general and the Palestinians in particular, "underwent a dramatic change," Weissglass said. "He wanted to exit the stage as a battle-worn general who became a great peacemaker."

However, Sharon still believed that there was one key obstacle to achieving this vision: Yasser Arafat. The prime minister had come to accept that there was no way to preclude the creation of an independent Palestinian state, but this didn't decrease his loathing for their leader. He regarded Arafat as someone who "had established a regime of terror in the territories he ruled, training terrorists in an organized and state-sponsored way, inciting, funding, equipping, and arming them, and dispatching them to kill throughout Israel." In a telephone conversation with Russian defense minister Sergei Ivanov, Sharon described Arafat as "a pathological liar, a murderer who ordered the killing of children, women, and infants."

Israeli intelligence received a large portion of Yasser Arafat's archives when IDF forces captured part of his headquarters near Ramallah, and this material provided hundreds of footnotes to Sharon's accusations. Arafat had ordered, in his own handwriting, the transfer of huge sums to support Fatah's terror activities. The Palestinian president and his circle were also involved in an unprecedented amount of corruption. The documents indicated that Arafat repeatedly reneged on his promises to Israel and the international community to build a true democratic state with a modern economy and a single armed force. He failed to make the transition from the head of a guerrilla organization to the leader of a democratic state, and continued to manage the Palestinian Authority with the same methods of manipulation, corruption, and divide-and-conquer he employed in managing the PLO—all with the goal of ensuring his survival as the Palestinian leader.

As part of a plan to delegitimize Arafat, Sharon gave a few journalists (me and, subsequently, several non-Israeli journalists) access to these archives in order for them to be published throughout the world. He also gave a directive to transfer money from the Mossad director's secret fund in order to help with the overseas publication of a book about these documents.

Sharon even considered disseminating a videotape filmed by Romanian intelligence in the late 1970s. General Ion Mihai Pacepa, the former head of DIE (the Soviet-Romanian intelligence organization)—who said of Arafat, "I have never seen so much cleverness, blood, and abomination combined in one man"—recalled that his men had installed hidden cameras in the official guesthouse where Arafat stayed after meeting with President Nicolae Ceauşescu, and that these cameras documented Arafat engaging in homosexual relations with his bodyguards. Sharon told his aides that this documentation had reached the hands of Israeli intelligence and that he considered disseminating it anonymously on the Internet.

Sharon dropped this distasteful idea when Israel achieved its objective through other means—by convincing the American administration that Arafat was incorrigible. Israel acquired unequivocal proof of Arafat's involvement in smuggling weaponry on the *Karine A* ship from Iran to terror groups in the Palestinian Authority. After Flotilla 13, in Operation Noah's Ark, seized control of the ship at sea, and its crew was arrested and interrogated, implicating a close associate of Arafat's, the president of the Palestinian Authority denied that he or any of his staff were involved in a special letter to President Bush. However, intelligence information—including wiretaps, documents, and interrogation transcripts—taken to the White House by a senior AMAN officer, in a briefcase chained to his wrist, was much more convincing. When Bush learned that Arafat had brazenly lied to him, he declared the Palestinian president irrelevant and on June 24, 2002, called upon the Palestinian people to elect a new leader.

In November 2002, in the wake of several horrific attacks against Israelis, Sharon gave an order to encircle the Mukataa, Arafat's headquarters, and to leave Arafat and some of his men besieged inside. His instructions were to make life miserable for "the dog from the Mukataa," as he called him—sometimes cutting off electricity, sometimes cutting off the water supply. Sharon then ordered a company of armored D9 bulldozers to demolish another wall of the compound every few days.

Even still, there were disagreements about what, finally, should be done with Arafat. Some thought he should be made a target for liquidation and that Israel should strike against him. Some thought he should be hit covertly, without connecting the action to Israel. Others were in favor of exiling him, while some said he should be left alone "to rot" in the Mukataa.

After a grave attack in April 2002, Sharon and chief of staff Mofaz were overheard conducting a private conversation. They sat near microphones at a public event, unaware that a television crew was already connected to the microphones and was filming them from afar.

MOFAZ: We've got to get rid of him.

SHARON: What?

MOFAZ: To get rid of him.

SHARON: I know.

MOFAZ: To take advantage of the opportunity now. There won't be another opportunity. I want to talk with you now.

SHARON: When we act . . . I don't know what method you use for this (*chuckles*). But you put everyone to sleep . . . (*becomes serious*). We have to be careful!

It is unclear precisely which "act" Sharon was referring to here, but the IDF and the intelligence community did prepare contingency plans for each potential Arafat strategy. The commander of the air force, Dan Halutz, who was an enthusiastic proponent of exiling Arafat, picked out two small islands—one near the coast of Lebanon and the other near Sudan—as potential new homes for the president. In his view, Arafat should be dispatched there with two aides and a little food and water for the trip, and then Israel would announce his whereabouts to the world. Special infantry units were slated to seize the Mukataa and proceed to Arafat's room. Israel considered launching sleeping gas into the compound prior to the raid in order to spare lives.

Ultimately, the operation was canceled, because "we couldn't ensure that Arafat would come out of all this alive," recalled the head of the trauma unit of the Medical Corps, Lieutenant Colonel Dr. Amir Blumenfeld. "After all, we were dealing with an old man who had lots of medical problems, and with the possibility of a battle erupting with the soldiers who came to abduct him."

The deliberations surrounding Arafat eventually reached Washington. Bush administration officials feared that, just as Sharon had decided to liquidate Yassin, he would also order the assassination of Arafat. In a meeting at the White House on April 14, 2004, Bush demanded that Sharon promise not to harm Arafat. According to one of the participants in the meeting, Sharon told the president that he understood his request ("I see your point"). Bush saw that the prime minister was prevaricating, and he pressed on until Sharon explicitly promised not to kill Arafat.

Even before this promise, Sharon, in consultation with the heads of the IDF and the intelligence community, had reached the conclusion that Israel must not be seen as being involved in the death of Yasser Arafat in any way. This became even more important after he made the promise to President Bush.


AND THEN, SUDDENLY, THE man who had managed to elude death so many times succumbed to a mysterious intestinal disease and died. Laboratory tests conducted at the initiative of various parties came to different conclusions. According to some tests, there were traces of polonium, a radioactive material used in assassinations, on Arafat's clothes and remains. Other experts determined that he had died a natural death. Arafat's medical file from the French military hospital near Paris, where Sharon permitted him to be flown so that he wouldn't die in an area under Israeli control, raises many questions and does not rule out the possibility that he died from AIDS.

Israeli spokespersons categorically denied that Israel was in any way involved in Arafat's death. "We didn't kill Arafat," senior members of the intelligence community and political echelon have solemnly repeated.

On the other hand, there is no doubt that the timing of Arafat's death was quite peculiar, coming so soon after the assassination of Yassin. In his book *Ariel Sharon: An Intimate Portrait,* Uri Dan, Sharon's loyal spokesman, claimed that in a later meeting with Bush, Sharon said that he no longer considered himself bound to his earlier promise not to kill Arafat, and that the president offered no response. During that period, Dan complained to Sharon, asking why he didn't exile Arafat or put him on trial: "So, Arafat has complete immunity?"

Sharon responded tersely: "Let me do things my way." Dan then noted, "Suddenly, he cut off our conversation, something unusual in the relations between us." Dan went on to say that Arafat's condition began to deteriorate after that meeting with the president, and concluded by stating, "Ariel Sharon will appear in the history books as the one who wiped out Arafat without killing him."

If I knew the answer to the question of what killed Yasser Arafat, I wouldn't be able to write it here in this book, or even be able to write that I know the answer. The military censor in Israel forbids me from discussing this subject.

One can say with certainty that Sharon wanted to get rid of Arafat, whom he saw as a "two-legged beast" and whom he had failed to kill twenty years earlier. If Sharon indeed ordered Arafat's liquidation, it was done in utmost secrecy, in much smaller forums than with any other targeted killing. Sharon himself defined the goal of such an operation, without admitting it: "Recent events are likely to be a historical turning point," he said in a special statement following Arafat's death. "If, after the Arafat era, a different, serious, responsible leadership emerges, one that carries out its undertakings . . . a fair opportunity will arise to coordinate various moves with that leadership, and even to resume diplomatic negotiations with it."

Without acknowledging direct involvement in Arafat's death, all of the senior echelon during that period agreed that the removal of Arafat improved Israel's security. Mahmoud Abbas (Abu Mazen), who was appointed to replace him as president, and the new Palestinian prime minister, Salam Fayyad, who had close ties to the American administration, launched a determined campaign against terror. Even the skeptical heads of the Shin Bet admit that the Palestinians became serious about stopping terrorism after the arrival of Abbas and Fayyad, and that the quiet achieved since Arafat's death is due largely to the close security cooperation with the two of them.

The war between Israel and the Palestinians that broke out in September 2000—a war of continual retaliations of suicide bombings and targeted killings—gradually subsided until it stopped altogether.

ISRAEL DEPLOYED A NUMBER of measures in its war against Palestinian terror in the Second Intifada, including IDF ground forays to conduct extensive arrests and the construction of a barrier between the West Bank and Israel that made it more difficult for suicide terrorists to enter into Israel. But while these measures somewhat hampered the terror organizations, statistics clearly show that they continued their attempts to execute murderous terror attacks after those measures were initiated, and that the terror attacks ceased only after a massive number of targeted killings of terrorist operatives and—in Operation Picking Anemones—the assassination of terrorist leaders.

Thanks to its streamlined targeted killing apparatus, the Israeli intelligence community triumphed over something that for many years had been considered unbeatable: suicide terrorism. By investing the resources of an entire country, through dogged persistence and cooperation between the intelligence and operational arms, and under the decisive leadership of Ariel Sharon, Israel proved that a murderous and seemingly uncompromising terror network can be brought to its knees.

The use of targeted killings, however, had heavy concomitant costs. The price was paid, first and foremost, by the innocent Palestinians who became the "coincidental damage" of the assassinations. Many innocent people were killed, and thousands, including many children, were wounded and left disabled for life. Others were mentally scarred or homeless.

A high-ranking Shin Bet officer said, "In the past when it was all secret and of dubious legality, we could carry out very few hits. How many of these can be done without getting exposed? The minute the IDF advocate general made these actions kosher, legal, and overt, we opened up an assembly line for assassinations. So now our consciences are cleaner, but a lot more folks ended up dead."

Gabriella Blum, as of 2018 a law professor at Harvard, was an officer in the IDF Military Advocate General's Corps and one of the authors of the memorandum that legalized assassinations. Commenting in 2017, she expressed her serious regrets: "I am deeply concerned that what was originally authorized as an exceptional act to be taken in exceptional cases became a regular practice."

The targeted killing campaign also did a great deal to further marginalize and delegitimize Israel in the eyes of the world. David was once again behaving like Goliath.

Chief of Staff Dan Halutz tried to explain why Israel adopted its targeted killing policy: "This is the basic code of conduct in the Middle East: They realized that we are insane, that we are ready to go all the way, that we would not be prepared to swallow any more."

Yet although the deaths of two high-ranking figures, Yassin and Arafat, certainly had a dramatic impact on the region, Ami Ayalon was right when he said that while assassinating leaders was likely to divert history onto a new course, it would not necessarily be a better one than the previous path—it might very well be one that ends up prolonging the amount of time before peace is attained.

As it turned out, Arafat was the only person able to keep the Palestinian people united, more or less, under the PA's control. After his demise, President Abbas failed in this regard, and Hamas took over Gaza and established a second Palestinian entity there. This new arrangement constituted a grave threat to Israel, a threat much greater than Arafat ever was.

Hamas succeeded in gaining control of Gaza thanks to the enormous assistance it received from Iran. Paradoxically, it is hard to believe that Hamas would ever have succeeded in establishing a state of its own in the Gaza Strip if Sheikh Yassin were still alive. Yassin strongly opposed any cooperation or ties with Iran, and he imposed his view on the organization.

Undoubtedly, the killing of Sheikh Yassin was the harshest blow suffered by Hamas in its entire history, and the single biggest factor in its desire to reach a ceasefire with Israel. But it also led to another unlikely twist in the course of Middle East history: Thanks to Yassin's removal from the scene, Iran, Israel's most dangerous enemy, forged the last link in its plan to become a regional power.

# THE RADICAL FRONT

LEADERSHIP CAME UNEXPECTEDLY TO Bashar al-Assad.

Hafez al-Assad, who seized control of Syria in November 1970, had expected his eldest son, Bassel, to succeed him, but he was killed in a car crash. Assad's second choice was his youngest son, Maher, who had chosen a military career. But he proved too hot-headed, inclined to fits of rage and violent outbursts. A third son, Majd, suffered from a congenital disease, which later killed him. That left Bashar, who was twenty-nine years old and in London, doing postgraduate training in ophthalmology, when his father summoned him back to Damascus right after Bassel's fatal accident, in 1994.

Bashar had always been considered the weakest of the Assad sons, somewhat aloof and dreamy, appearing a little intimidated. His father may have been aware of Bashar's weaknesses, but his concern about the family's continued rule was his top priority. He sent Bashar to the military, where he quickly rose to the rank of colonel, then appointed him commander of the Syrian forces in Lebanon for seasoning. By the end of the 1990s, Bashar was well groomed for the presidency. Hafez al-Assad died in June 2000. Bashar was elected president the next month.

But Assad's inheritance was, at that precise moment, a problematic one. The Soviet Union had dissolved a decade earlier, the Cold War was over, and Russia at that time wasn't nearly as influential in the Middle East as it had been. The global stage was being reset, and Bashar al-Assad had to find Syria's place on it.

The Syrian economy, however, was in worse shape than ever. The state's coffers were empty, and its army, though one of the largest in the region, was partly outdated and in urgent need of modern weaponry. Most important, Israel still held the Golan Heights, captured from Syria in 1967. It was a deep and open wound, and national pride would not allow it to clot.

In the middle of 2000, Assad had a choice: to align Syria with the United States, the last remaining superpower, or with Iran, the emerging regional power. This was not a difficult decision. Ten years before he died, President Hafez al-Assad had stunned the world by agreeing to join the alliance the United States forged against another Arab state—to expel Saddam Hussein from Kuwait. He hoped for something in return—economic benefits, removal of Syria from the list of states involved in terrorism and the drug trade, and pressure on Israel to completely withdraw from the Golan Heights. He received none of these.

Three months before he died, Hafez al-Assad met with President Bill Clinton in Geneva, the climax of an American diplomatic effort to broker a peace accord between Syria and Israel. Clinton brought a message to Assad from Prime Minister Ehud Barak that included the best offer he had ever received from Israel: a nearly complete withdrawal from the Golan Heights, except that no "Syrian soldiers would splash their feet in the waters of the Sea of Galilee"—that is, there would be no permanent Syrian presence on the shore. Assad heard Clinton and torpedoed the summit shortly after it started.

For Israel and the United States, this was proof of Hafez al-Assad's illogical intransigence, perhaps attributable to the stomach ailments and dementia from which he suffered. In the eyes of Assad, a great devotee of conspiracy theories, the summit was additional proof that the United States was just a satellite of Israel, not the other way around, and that he would never receive all of the Golan Heights or any other significant benefit from his connection with the United States.

And Israel seemed weakened.

Ehud Barak pulled out unconditionally from Lebanon in May 2000, which, from Assad's perspective, amounted to a humiliating defeat. To him, it proved that effective use of guerrilla warfare could force even the most powerful military force in the region to surrender.

Hafez al-Assad exhorted his son Bashar to retrieve the occupied Golan Heights. But he also advised him to avoid head-on military confrontation with Israel, from which Syria almost certainly would emerge the loser. Iran, however, already had proxy terror groups—Hezbollah chief among them—waging an asymmetrical war against the Jews. Bashar al-Assad believed it was better, then, to let the radicals fight a dirty war that might force Israel into concessions. Why shed Syrian blood when the jihadists were so willing to spill their own?

Assad accordingly made the link with Hezbollah and its patrons in Tehran the central component of his security doctrine. Syria and Iran signed a series of agreements on mutual defense, arms supplies, and weapons development, and Tehran gave Assad $1.5 billion to rebuild his army.

MANY OF THE TOP theocratic Iranians considered Assad and his Alawite brethren to be heretics, traitors to holy tradition, infidels who offended Allah. On the other hand, Syria had a strong military, a border with Israel, and more international credibility than Tehran.

The Iranian government also had some problems of its own. The state was in the throes of a severe economic crisis, and there were acute rifts in Persian society and growing resentment toward the ayatollahs. Along with North Korea and Iraq, Iran had become among the most isolated and ostracized countries in the world. In his State of the Union address in January 2002, President Bush would describe these three countries as the "axis of evil." Thereafter, the American administration tightened sanctions against Iran.

Bush did not include Syria in the "axis of evil" because the Americans still hoped it could be pulled toward the West, in part because Syria maintained friendly relations with many Western states—France and Germany, in particular. "We tried to cooperate with him

[Assad] against the terrorists who were fighting us in Iraq," said Michael Hayden, chief of the NSA and the CIA during the first decade of the twenty-first century, adding that such hopes were soon dashed.

An alliance with Syria was in Iran's best interests. Tehran could offer cash, which Damascus desperately needed, and advanced military technology, such as solid-fuel rocket engines for long-range missiles. In return, Syria could provide direct access to Iran's principal adversary and, more important, a bridge to the wider world. Iranian imports and exports could be filtered through Syrian seaports and airports, lessening Iran's international isolation.

At the same time, Iran was running a proxy militia in Lebanon, where Syria maintained large military and intelligence operations. To keep Hezbollah supplied and functioning, the Iranians required freedom of movement, which the Syrians could not only allow but also facilitate.

But the young Assad did more than merely choose a side.

For decades, his father had been allowing the Iranians to fly shipments of arms into Damascus and then truck them overland to Hezbollah. But Hafez al-Assad assisted the Iranians only by letting them operate unencumbered—he carefully and cautiously avoided any close ties with the jihadists themselves. Bashar al-Assad, however, saw an opportunity. Hezbollah's victory over Israel and the doctrine of Hassan Nasrallah, the organization's secretary general, who likened Israel to a "spiderweb"—strong from afar but soft up close—made an impact on him.

The younger Assad decided to wholeheartedly throw his lot in with both the theocrats and the jihadists, and put all of Syria's resources at their disposal. Starting in early 2002, Assad opened his own army's armories to Hezbollah, providing the organization with modern Soviet weaponry that even Iran lacked, and long-range surface-to-surface missiles. He also opened the gates of his palace to Nasrallah, whom he regarded as a role model.

Syria had practical motives for wanting to strengthen Hezbollah as well. Lebanon was an economic lifeline for Syria and for Assad's generals, who enjoyed generous commissions from deals in which the state was involved. Recently, however, a number of powerful figures in Lebanon had risen and demanded that the Syrians leave. In response, Imad Mughniyeh, the Hezbollah chief of staff, began to assassinate those figures, one after another, on behalf of the Iranians and the Syrians. The assassination campaign peaked when Mughniyeh's men killed Rafik Hariri, the most important politician in the Middle East, who had twice served as prime minister of Lebanon and had tried to mobilize the world to expel the Syrians from his country.

It became clear that there was a confluence of interests among Iran, Hezbollah, and Syria, and that the three of them were uniquely suited to work together and help one another in their times of need. Thus, an alliance—which Israel's intelligence community called "the Radical Front"—was born.

THE ALLIANCE OF A terrorist organization, a pariah theocracy, and a modernized nation-state allowed a sprawling network of guerrillas, self-styled revolutionaries, and criminal thugs to operate with an unusually robust level of military efficiency. The leaders of the countries and the organization developed strategy and supplied matériel for an otherwise disparate collection of operatives, spread across the length and breadth of the Middle East.

At the network's highest operational level were three men: Qassem Suleimani of the Iranian Revolutionary Guards, Imad Mughniyeh of Hezbollah, and General Muhammad Suleiman of Syria. Islamic Jihad leader Ramadan Shalah, who operated in Damascus under the auspices of Iran and Syria, was also brought into the alliance and invited to some of the discussions.

Their lieutenants included Hassan al-Laqqis, Hezbollah's R&D chief, and Mahmud al-Majzub, the head of Palestinian Islamic Jihad in Lebanon. Hamas had no official role in the Radical Front—Sheikh Yassin, a Sunni, despised the Shiite Iranians—but Khaled Mashal, the leader of Hamas outside of Palestine, thought otherwise and instructed one of the organization's operational commanders in Damascus, Izz al-Din al-Sheikh Khalil, to be in close contact with the other members of the front.

With a web of connections and transport lines, the Radical Front began channeling more and deadlier aid for the struggle against Israel. From Beirut, Hezbollah supported and armed Palestinian terrorists, paying bonuses for each Israeli killed in suicide bombings. Rockets were dismantled in Syria or Iran, smuggled, in pieces, over land or by sea into the Gaza Strip, and then reassembled by Palestinian Islamic Jihad fighters. Majzub arranged to have the Revolutionary Guard ship missiles in the same manner to PIJ guerrillas in Lebanon. Mashal and Sheikh Khalil received substantial monetary assistance from Iran (perhaps without Yassin's knowledge), as well as considerable know-how that was transferred to Gaza and helped in the production of homemade rockets.

Hezbollah's Laqqis, meanwhile, began constructing an enormous array of bunkers and missile silos in southern Lebanon that could confront an Israeli invasion or help launch an offensive. They were camouflaged so expertly that Israeli intelligence never saw them being built. Nor was Israel fully aware of the amount of lethal hardware being assembled. By 2003, according to one assessment, Hezbollah possessed the largest arsenal ever held by a guerrilla force.

Having enemies at the borders and in the occupied territories was not new for Israel, of course. But now it was surrounded by what was basically a single coordinated force—Hezbollah in Lebanon, the PIJ in the territories, Syria to the north—all funded with Iranian money and supplied with Iranian weapons.

THE ISRAELI AGENCY RESPONSIBLE for gaining intel and countering such an external threat was the Mossad. But its efforts had been far from adequate, largely because it had not adapted itself to changing times. The Mossad's inability to penetrate the jihadist organizations, its lack of technological capabilities in a world where everyone has access to a cellular device and encryption software, and a series of severe operational failures, led by the botched assassination of Mashal, were all indications that the Mossad had become deficient and ineffectual. Iran was a more sophisticated and original rival than any Arab state the Mossad had tried to penetrate, and Bashar al-Assad instituted strict field security measures in Syria as well.

Here and there, the Mossad tried to thwart dangerous projects undertaken by members of the Radical Front. It learned, for example, that General Anatoly Kuntsevich, a veteran of the Russian military industries, was helping Syria produce the deadliest chemical weapon, the nerve agent VX. Official protests to Moscow were ignored. So, in April 2002, Kuntsevich mysteriously dropped dead on a flight from Aleppo to Moscow.

But that was an isolated success. There was no consistent and steady strategy against the Radical Front, and the Israelis remained dangerously unaware of many of their adversary's plans and actions. Compared with the successes of the Shin Bet and AMAN in the occupied territories, the Mossad was considered the weak link in the intelligence community.

Prime Minister Sharon was exasperated by the agency. The Mossad was too sleepy and effete for his liking, and too reluctant to take risks, after its earlier operational mishaps. Mossad chief Efraim Halevy's approach was the exact opposite of Sharon's, who always wanted to take the initiative and attack. As Dov Weissglass explained, "At a time when Israel found itself in one of the most difficult battles of its life, the Second Intifada, we could never understand why that magnificent body known as the Mossad was simply nonexistent. With Halevy, the diplomatic aspect was infinitely developed. The operational aspect was like an appendix to him, superfluous tissue that was dispensable."

THIS PERIOD COINCIDED WITH the peak of the intifada, and the initial and most urgent targets on the liquidation list were those who encouraged Palestinian terrorism.

Hezbollah, under Iranian control, had set up its Unit 1800 to provide the Tanzim terrorist group (established under the auspices of Arafat's Fatah) with money and training for more suicide attacks. Palestinian Islamic Jihad, in Lebanon, also supported the suicide terror activities of its members in the West Bank and Gaza with money, training, and guidance.

In the absence of any strong counterinitiative on the part of the Mossad, AMAN tried to fill the gap. "The Mossad was not an operational partner," said AMAN chief Aharon Zeevi-Farkash. "On the other hand, we in AMAN marked fifty Palestinians in the West Bank who, with the funding and support of Hezbollah Unit 1800, in Lebanon, were toiling all the time to produce suicide attacks. The situation had become intolerable." The idea was, therefore, "to hit a number of targets in Hezbollah in order to explain to its leaders that there was a price to be paid for these actions."

Colonel Ronen Cohen, the head of counterterrorism in AMAN, drew up a list of targets (dubbed the Twelve Musketeers) that included operatives of Unit 1800 in Hezbollah, along with a number of names from Islamic Jihad and Hamas.

One of the names on the list was Kais Obeid, who once was an agent for the Shin Bet but had defected to Hezbollah's Unit 1800. Obeid managed to lure a senior IDF reserve officer to Dubai. The officer had become enmeshed in debt, and Obeid promised to get him out of his financial troubles. He walked into a trap and was drugged, placed in a crate, and sent by diplomatic mail from the Iranian embassy in Dubai to Beirut. During his interrogation, he revealed important military secrets to Hezbollah and the Syrians. After that, Obeid, who knew a lot of Israeli Arabs and spoke fluent Hebrew, began to recruit suicide bombers.

Obeid was an Israeli citizen, and there was an unwritten rule among the country's intelligence agencies that forbade killing fellow Israelis. But under the grave menace of suicide terror, this rule was suspended. Nevertheless, Cohen's list of "Musketeers" did not include the top Hezbollah officials, Mughniyeh and his two deputies, or Secretary General Nasrallah. "We feared that this might start an all-out war," said one of the men involved in the operation.

In Zeevi-Farkash and Cohen's meeting with Sharon to discuss the operation, they argued that, while the Shin Bet was doing excellent work in eliminating the highest-ranking terrorists in the West Bank and Gaza, no one was acting against the heads of the organizations providing support from outside Israel's borders. Sharon hardly needed persuasion. "It's a pity that there are no initiatives like this coming from your friends," he said sourly, referring to the Mossad.

The first target was Ramzi Nahara, a drug dealer and Israeli intelligence agent who had switched allegiances when Israel withdrew from Lebanon, and who was one of Obeid's colleagues in the abduction of the Israeli officer. On December 6, 2002, he was traveling with his nephew Elie Issa to their home village of Ain Ebel, in southern Lebanon. At the entrance to the village, a large explosive device camouflaged as a rock blew up as their car passed by. They were both killed.

Next in line was Ali Hussein Salah, registered at the Lebanese Interior Ministry as a driver for the Iranian embassy in Beirut, but actually an operative of Unit 1800. On August 2, 2003, he was in his black BMW luxury sedan with its diplomatic license plates, on his way to work at Unit 1800 headquarters, in the Dahiya neighborhood of Beirut. At 8:32 A.M., a large explosive device that had been concealed in the backseat of the car detonated, ripping the car in two and hurling it fifty feet from the large crater the blast made in the road. "The explosion tore Salah's body into two, one in each part of the car," AMAN's report on the incident stated.

After the death of Salah, Hezbollah no longer concealed his true occupation, and Al-Manar, the movement's TV station, reported, "Hezbollah mourns the death of one of the greatest mujahideen [holy warriors]."

On July 12, 2004, Ghaleb Awali, who had replaced the slain Salah in Unit 1800, left his home in the Haret Hreik Shiite neighborhood of Beirut. He entered his Mercedes and turned the key in the ignition. Seconds later, the car exploded. He was severely wounded and rushed to the hospital, but pronounced dead on arrival.

A new group, making its first and last appearance in Lebanon, took responsibility for the killing. Calling itself Jund al-Sham ("Soldiers of the Levant"), the Sunni group declared, "We have executed one of the symbols of treachery, the Shiite Ghaleb Awali."

Hezbollah had no doubt that this was an Israeli disinformation stunt and that Israel was behind the assassination. In his eulogy at the magnificent funeral staged for Awali, Hassan Nasrallah noted that the deceased had belonged to a special unit dedicated to supporting the Palestinians' struggle. "He is a *shahid* on our way to Palestine, a *shahid* for Jerusalem and the Al-Aqsa Mosque in the confrontation with the Zionist entity," Nasrallah declared over Awali's coffin, draped in the yellow Hezbollah flag. He accused AMAN commander Zeevi-Farkash of being responsible for the killing.

.   .   .

SHARON WAS APPRECIATIVE OF Zeevi-Farkash's efforts, but he realized that more was needed to counter the Radical Front, and that radical change within the Mossad was necessary.

Sharon wanted Halevy replaced, and several names, including Mossad veterans and IDF generals, were suggested. But Sharon really had only one person in mind: Meir Dagan, his good friend who had served under him in the army. Dagan was tough and aggressive, exactly the kind of person Sharon needed to fight back against the Radical Front.

Dagan had left the IDF in 1995 and later became the head of the Counter-Terrorism Bureau at the prime minister's office. In that capacity, he'd set up a clandestine body called Spear, aimed at disrupting the enemy's financial resources. "I attributed great importance to the economic warfare that had to be an integral part of our campaign against our main adversary," said Dagan.

Spear's investigations led Israel to outlaw all organizations that held funds on behalf of Hamas, some of them coming from wealthy Muslims abroad. (Spear also urged the FBI and its European counterparts to do the same in their respective countries, but this was before 9/11, and their warnings fell upon deaf ears.) At one meeting, the contrast in style between Dagan's and Halevy's Mossad was apparent. The Mossad presented information indicating that some of the money provided by Iran to Hamas was channeled through a European bank headquartered in Zurich.

"No problem," said Dagan. "Let's burn it."

"Burn what?"

"The bank, of course," Dagan replied. "We have the address, no?"

The participants explained that it wasn't a matter of cash, but of electronic transfers through SWIFT, which were backed up elsewhere.

"So what?" Dagan said. "Let's burn it anyway. The bank's managers realize that this is not legitimate money. It won't do any harm."

Dagan ultimately accepted the counsel of his advisers and did not order the burning of the bank. In general, however, that was the approach Sharon sought: "a Mossad chief with a dagger between his teeth," as the premier told some of his aides.

This did not mean, however, that he was eager to engage in a large-scale confrontation with the enemy. On the contrary, Dagan continued to argue that Israel should do everything to avoid a general military conflict with all of the states in the region, a conflict that would be impossible to win comprehensively.

"It's the job of the Israeli defense establishment," Dagan used to lecture his new subordinates at the Mossad, "to do whatever it can to put off the next war for as long as possible, using covert means to strike at the enemy in a focused manner."

DAGAN TOOK OVER THE Mossad in September 2002. Shortly afterward, Sharon put him in charge of covert efforts to stymie Iran's nuclear program. Since the late 1990s, Iran had poured huge resources into its plan to acquire a nuclear weapon capability as rapidly as possible, buying equipment and expertise wherever it could. Both men saw a nuclear Iran as an existential danger to Israel.

Dagan was told that he would receive whatever he wanted—money, personnel, endless resources—as long as he stopped the ayatollahs from building an atomic bomb. He took it all and got down to work.

"Sharon was right to appoint him," Weissglass said. "Meir arrived and began to work wonders."

Dagan moved into his new office in the Mossad's main building and hung a picture of his grandfather, kneeling, staring in terror at the German troops around him, minutes before he was murdered. "Look at this photograph," Dagan would say to Mossad operatives before sending them off on missions. "I'm here—we, the men and women of the Mossad, are here—to make sure it doesn't happen again."

Dagan decided to dismantle the Mossad and reassemble it in a way that suited him. First, he sharply focused the Mossad's intelligence-gathering objective. Information was not to be collected for its own sake, catalogued, and filed into an impotent library— Dagan wanted intelligence that could be directly put to use against the enemy. He wanted information that led quickly to preemptive and preventive operations, to sabotage, ambushes, targeted killings, and assassinations. The Mossad, under the new director, would be a warrior agency.

"I told Arik [Sharon] that in my opinion, a deep change had to be made in the organization," Dagan said. "'But you have to decide,' I warned him, 'whether you're ready to pay the price. Journalists will climb all over me and you and the Mossad. It won't be easy. Are you ready to pay the price?' He said that he was. Arik knew how to back someone up."

Dagan frequently met in private with Sharon to get approval for covert operations. A former senior Mossad officer described the mood: "Those were days of hysteria. Dagan would arrive early in the morning, and until nightfall he never stopped yelling at everyone that they weren't delivering the goods and that they were worthless."

In Dagan's view, it was particularly important "to straighten out" the personnel in the Junction division, which was in charge of recruiting and operating agents. This was "the real heart of the Mossad," in his eyes. "Underlying every operation, however you put it together, there is HUMINT."

Junction's core personnel were "collection officers" (*katsa*), case officers who recruited and ran the agents. They were sophisticated professionals, skilled in manipulation.

According to Dagan, however, the collection officers also manipulated the Mossad itself. Dagan described the Junction division he encountered upon assuming his position as "a complete system of falsehood, which deceives itself and feeds itself lies" in order to convince itself and the entire Mossad of its success. "For years, they did whatever they wanted. They recruit a guy who serves tea in some office near a nuclear facility and say they have someone inside the Iranian atom project. They needed to be grabbed by the collar and given a boot in the ass."

Dagan changed Junction's procedures and demanded that all agents undergo a polygraph test in order to prove that they were reliable sources. Junction's collection officers strongly protested subjecting their agents to polygraph testing. "It will express lack of trust; they'll be insulted and won't want to work with us again."

The director harshly dismissed these objections. "Are you an idiot?" he asked one of them. "The man betrays his country, everything that is dear to him. You think that he won't be willing to undergo a polygraph in exchange for money?"

Dagan said that the resistance to the polygraph was, in effect, an attempt by Junction personnel to avoid "exposing their bluff," because they had recruited unreliable agents. He made an effort to meet each of the Mossad's hundreds of case officers throughout the world on a frequent basis: "The agent handler, who had never seen the Mossad director, suddenly sees him every three months, and he takes an interest in him not only on the theoretical level but also in his operations, and asks him where he succeeded and why he failed. This severely hampered the ability of the man's bosses to later pull the wool over my eyes."

Once Dagan had put the Mossad on an effective war footing, he also narrowed its mission. He declared that the agency would have only two broad targets. One was any hostile country attempting to attain a nuclear weapon, and Iran's nuclear project in particular. Importation of equipment and raw materials would be disrupted, stalled, and stopped, facilities already in operation would be seriously sabotaged, and nuclear scientists would be harassed, co-opted, and, if necessary, killed.

The second target was the Radical Front. There were no plans for an all-out war with Iran or Syria, but the Mossad could break the supply lines that funneled weapons to Hezbollah and Hamas and the PIJ. It could also go after individual terrorists, and it could take out the Radical Front's senior figures, even if they were Syrian generals.

Under orders from Sharon, AMAN chief Zeevi-Farkash agreed to let his military intelligence operation cooperate fully with the Mossad, creating a joint "intelligence pool" in which all intelligence could be shared—an enormous expansion of the Mossad's practical resources.

To coordinate this vast interorganizational effort, and to head up the Mossad's hundreds of operations, Dagan appointed Tamir Pardo, the commander of the agency's operational unit, Rainbow. Formerly an officer in Sayeret Matkal, he had stood next to Yonatan Netanyahu when he was hit by a bullet during the Entebbe hostage operation.

Pardo was a courageous operations man with strategic vision and an irrepressible drive. Dagan named him his deputy.

In May 2003, in front of Dagan and the senior command forum of the Mossad, Pardo presented a top-secret plan—the product of an intensive four-month effort—for stopping the Iranian nuclear project. "The starting assumption is that a technologically advanced state with a wealth of resources like Iran, which seeks to attain an atomic bomb, will succeed in doing so at the end of the day," Pardo began. "In other words, an immediate halt to the project can only be the result of a change of mind or a change in the identity of the political echelon in Iran."

Some sighs and mumbles were heard in the room, but Pardo continued. "In this situation, Israel has three options. One: to conquer Iran. The second: to bring about a change in the regime in Iran. The third: to convince the current political echelon that the price they'll pay to continue the nuclear project is greater than what they can gain by stopping it."

Since the first and second options were unrealistic, only the third option remained—to take overt and covert action that would put so much pressure on the ayatollahs that they would decide to simply give up. "In the meantime, until they reach the conclusion that it's not worth it for them," Dagan said in summary, "we must employ a number of means to delay again and again their attainment of a bomb so that at the breaking point, they will not yet be armed with the weapon."

Dagan had a bold idea for how this could be done: by asking for help from Israel's friends, even the ones that were ostensibly enemies. He knew that while most of the countries in the Middle East were publicly anti-Israel, in private they were more accommodating and practical. "There is an intersection of interests, not a small one, between us and many of the Arab states," he said. The interests of most of those states—Jordan, Egypt, Saudi Arabia, the Gulf emirates, Morocco, and so on—did not correspond with those of radical Shiite revolutionaries or their allies in Damascus, let alone their heavily armed proxy militias. Those Arab states mostly feared the thought of Iran with a nuclear weapon, maybe more so than Israel.

From an operational standpoint, the intelligence services of those states had a number of advantages over the Mossad: Their operatives were Arabs who spoke the language perfectly, they maintained diplomatic relations with countries hostile to Israel (sometimes quite good relations, at least on the surface), and they could travel in those hostile countries relatively unimpeded. In many cases, they'd also already had spies in Syria, Iran, and Lebanon for many years, due to internal Arab power struggles.

Dagan ordered the Mossad to ramp up its secret liaisons with foreign intelligence bodies. Many of the signal achievements of Israeli intelligence during the following years—the ability to identify, monitor, and strike against terrorists in Lebanon and Syria; the intel about which Iranian embassies were dispatching terrorist cells throughout the world; the information about the ayatollahs' nuclear project—were a result of this cooperation. While these Arab countries condemned Israel at the United Nations, they were also collaborating with the Jewish state in the most secret of missions.

Dagan's reforms led to sharp internal opposition and, later, to the resignation of many senior Mossad officials. The Mossad is a closed, tight-lipped organization fanatically committed to keeping its secrets— any cooperation that might require divulging methods and sources to foreign agencies, especially Arab ones, was considered sacrilege. But to Dagan, this was all nonsense, merely an excuse for intellectual and operational decline.

"I thought they were wrong, that it was idiocy to oppose collaboration with other factors [Middle East intelligence agencies] who saw things the way we did," he said. "The Mossad was obligated to mobilize whatever it could—any resource, any ally—in order to achieve its objectives. I told them to stop talking crap—let's accumulate our own assets, blue and white, in order to do business with other intelligence agencies. I decided that anything that did not endanger ourselves or our sources could be traded, or otherwise no one would take us seriously.

"Three hundred people quit when I came to the Mossad, a massive exodus," he said. "Incidentally, I'm glad that some of them left."

In light of the demand for more and more operations, Dagan also abolished some of the Mossad's operational security protocols that had been in place for a long time, some of them for decades. Before he took over, if there weren't enough passports, credit cards, and secure means of communication for an operation, it was aborted, to stay on the safe side. A large number of operations were canceled due to these security protocols.

Not under Dagan. "He would call in the person in charge of the passports unit who had warned that the documentation was insufficiently safe and would not stand up to scrutiny," said someone who attended many discussions in the Mossad chief's office, "and tell him that if, by the next morning, there were not another five passports ready on his desk, he should have a letter of resignation there instead."

Dagan confirmed the facts but brushed away any of the concern. "Nonsense. If you dig deep enough, you'll always get to the shit. It's all *meises* [Yiddish for "tales"], excuses for not taking action."

DAGAN BELIEVED IN TARGETED killings as an important and necessary weapon, but only if used consistently and as part of a broad arsenal that included other measures—clandestine, diplomatic, and financial. Any single killing could be rationalized by the enemy as a unique, one-time misfortune, and even intermittent assassinations could be dismissed as products of circumstance, a fatal result for the unguarded and sloppy. In order for targeted killings to be strategically effective, they needed to be an ongoing threat.

"Sporadic eliminations are worth nothing," Dagan said. "Eliminations of senior operational personnel, along with striking at the leadership level as a permanent and ongoing policy, are a very good thing. When I say 'leadership,' I mean, of course, in the widest sense. Would I always choose to kill the number one? Not necessarily. I look for the supreme operative echelon, the one that really runs things, that has the most dominant influence on the ground."

AMAN and the Mossad drew up a list of candidates from the Radical Front for negative treatment. The problem was, they were all in so-called target countries where, as a rule, the Mossad did not carry out such missions. But Dagan decided to change this rule, too.

"When I came to the Mossad, there weren't real operational capabilities in the target countries," said Dagan. In order to rectify this, he first had the Mossad create documentation systems (passports, cover stories, etc.) that would allow the operatives to withstand long interrogation if suspicions arose.

Dagan also reversed the long-standing policy of conducting only blue-and-white assassinations—those involving only its own personnel. Dagan preferred to use proxies, based on his experience from the countless liquidations he was involved in during his military service in Gaza and Lebanon. "I'm prepared to cry over the coffin of any such agent or proxy who dies and returns his soul [to his maker]. Believe me, I would shed real tears over him. But I also prefer to see them dead than my [Israeli/Jewish] operatives dead."

Dagan also pushed the Mossad to update its technology. He didn't personally understand much of that world, but he realized that it had become indispensable and that the Mossad lagged far behind other countries' intelligence services, and even other agencies in Israel. He appointed "N.," a senior operational officer who understood the needs of agents in the field, to head the Technology Division.

The changes Dagan instituted soon began to show their effects. Dagan believed that the time had come for the agency to begin operations and argued that from now on, all targeted assassinations abroad should be under his command, and that they should be run by his deputy, Tamir Pardo.

AMAN opposed this plan, and a vociferous quarrel broke out between the Mossad and AMAN's Aharon Zeevi-Farkash and Ronen Cohen. Ultimately, Sharon made the decision: Syria was transferred to Dagan's jurisdiction, and hits in Lebanon were to remain under AMAN's authority.

In parallel to this secret bureaucratic process, Israel identified a troubling change in the enemy's bureaucratic structure. The assassination of Sheikh Yassin, in March 2004, effectively removed all of the restrictions he had placed on relations with Iran. "The moment Yassin was taken out of the game, Hamas's center of gravity was transferred out of the Israeli-controlled territories to the leadership in Syria and Lebanon, and Khaled Mashal became the organization's strongman," said the Shin Bet's Yitzhak Ilan.

Mashal instructed his men, led by Izz al-Din al-Sheikh Khalil, to inform the Iranians that Hamas was now ready to receive any and all assistance from them. The Iranians were pleased: With Hamas becoming a full member, the "resistance" front was now complete. Under Khalil's supervision, the Iranians began to send missile parts to the Gaza Strip in an effort to increase the range and lethality of the organization's arsenal. Instructors from the Revolutionary Guard came to Gaza as well.

On September 26, 2004, Khalil got into his car next to his home, in southern Damascus. Just as he sat down, his mobile phone rang. *"Ya, Abu Rami, hada Ramzi min Tubas"* ("Abu Rami, this is Ramzi from Tubas," a village in the West Bank). "Yes," said Khalil, "how can I help you?" The line went dead. A second later, the car blew up and Khalil was dead.

Next on the hit list was Mahmud al-Majzub, the Palestinian Islamic Jihad's top man in Lebanon. On May 26, 2006, at 10:30 A.M., he left the PIJ's office in the port city of Sidon, in southern Lebanon, accompanied by his brother Nidal, who served as his bodyguard. As Nidal opened the driver's door, a bomb concealed in the door was detonated via remote control by a lookout standing nearby, killing the two men.

"Of course, I don't take responsibility for these events," Dagan said of this string of killings, following Israel's official policy of not claiming responsibility for targeted killings outside its borders. "But as a concept," he added, "if the State of Israel is dealing with a challenge like Hamas, the PIJ, and suicide terrorism, it's inconceivable that the Mossad wouldn't put its shoulder to the wheel."

The hits against the personnel of Unit 1800, Islamic Jihad, and Hamas constituted a grave loss to those organizations, but they did not change the overall picture. The Radical Front continued to present a serious threat and was still coordinating its actions against Israel.

THE ISRAELI PUBLIC HAS always been particularly affected by abductions of IDF soldiers. Nasrallah, who well understood this particular sensitivity, ordered his men to conduct as many abduction operations as possible, and he advised his partners in the front to do the same. Some attempts failed. Those that succeeded caused great damage to Israeli morale.

In October 2000, under Mughniyeh's orders, a special Hezbollah unit abducted three Israeli soldiers patrolling the Israel-Lebanon border. In order to secure the return of the abducted soldiers, Israel consented to a humiliating prisoner-exchange deal with Hezbollah.

The Islamic Jihad prisoners released in the deal resumed terrorist activity immediately upon their return to Gaza, launching a horrific campaign of suicide bombings. These freed prisoners managed to direct eight suicide attacks, in which thirty-nine civilians were killed, before the Shin Bet and the IDF were able to kill them or arrest them once again.

On June 25, 2006, seven Hamas fighters climbed out of a tunnel. They had spent long months digging it in secret, all the way from a well inside the Gaza Strip, under the border fence, and up to a nearby Israeli village. In a daring operation, they crept up behind an IDF encampment, killing two of the soldiers there, wounding others, and dragging one soldier, Gilad Shalit, on the road with them toward Gaza. They hung Shalit's flak jacket on the fence between Israel and Gaza, sending a message of defiance.

The Shin Bet and the IDF were completely unable to locate the imprisoned Shalit. Though the Shin Bet and AMAN were usually exceptionally effective at both intelligence gathering and operations within Gaza, the guidance Hamas received from Iranian intelligence proved itself. Throughout the entire five years of Shalit's captivity, Israel had no idea where he was being held.

By the time of the raid, Hamas had already matured into a governing institution: Six months earlier, with Iranian backing, the political wing had won the elections in the Palestinian Authority. Ismail Haniyeh, the elected prime minister—who had survived a number of Israeli attempts on his life, including the 2003 bombing of the conclave of the Hamas leadership (the Dream Team)—traveled to Tehran, where he was promised $250 million in aid. "Iran is the Palestinians' strategic depth," he declared during that visit. "We will never recognize the Zionist regime. We will continue the jihad until Jerusalem is liberated." He returned to Gaza with $35 million in cash, packed into a number of large suitcases.

Israel responded to the killing of its soldiers and the kidnapping of Shalit with a heavy bombardment on Gaza, killing more than two hundred Palestinians. It also conducted raids in the West Bank, abducting a number of Hamas government ministers. But the organization did not blink: It demanded that Israel release one thousand Palestinian prisoners in exchange for the one Israeli soldier.

Two weeks after Shalit was captured, on July 12, the Radical Front turned up the heat. Hezbollah guerrillas abducted two soldiers patrolling Israel's northern border. For the Israelis, this was one attack too many, and the new prime minister, Ehud Olmert (the successor of Sharon, who had suffered a stroke), told his associates that he was going "to fuck" Hezbollah once and for all. Arik Sharon had never hesitated to use force, but he had been skeptical of the IDF's capability to win such a war against Hezbollah's guerrillas. Olmert was sucked in by the assurances of the chief of staff, Lieutenant General Dan Halutz, who was certain that Hezbollah could be defeated from the air, without endangering ground troops. "Except for a donkey carrying a Katyusha here or there," he believed the air force's fighter-bombers could cripple the organization's capacity to strike at Israel.

This was a fatal error, which cost Israel dearly and ended Halutz's military career. Although the aerial bombardment of Hezbollah's positions did cause significant damage, its array of bunkers, launchers, and concealed communications systems held up. Israel knew very little about this array, which it called "the nature preserves," set up under the supervision of Hassan al-Laqqis, on orders from Imad Mughniyeh, using advanced equipment obtained from Iran and Syria. Hezbollah rockets continued to rain down on northern Israel. Eventually, on July 29, the IDF launched a hesitant and ineffectual land invasion. It destroyed some of Hezbollah's positions, but the IDF also suffered heavy losses before shamefacedly withdrawing two weeks later.

The entire campaign (known in Israel as the Second Lebanon War) was a humiliating defeat that achieved almost none of its aims. The most powerful military force in the Middle East had been beaten twice in six years by the same guerrilla army. "It was something like the North Vietnamese Army after the Tet Offensive," Dagan said.

"Although the offensive failed and they took some heavy blows, they won the war."

After the ceasefire was signed, Nasrallah became the most popular leader in the Arab world, the only one in many years to have faced Israel in a military confrontation and won.

Israel tried to compensate for its failure on the battlefield with attempts on the lives of Hezbollah leaders, primarily Nasrallah. "If we had succeeded in killing Nasrallah, it would have changed the picture," said Halutz. "We tried, but without success." Three times, specific intelligence information was obtained regarding Nasrallah's whereabouts. Once, a building was bombed shortly after he left it. Twice, the bombs actually hit his location but failed to penetrate the thick layers of reinforced concrete above the underground bunkers where he was hiding. "It's incredible what they built down there," said Halutz. "You hit one spot and all of a sudden you see the smoke coming out of some hole at the end of the street, and you realize that there's some tunnel down there that you never knew about."

Other efforts to take out high-ranking Hezbollah officials ended the same way. On July 20, Israel tried to zero in on Laqqis by pinpointing his cellphone. An F-16 fired a missile into the apartment in Beirut where the phone was located, but it turned out that Laqqis had left it there and gone out. His son was killed. "We did not approach this business [the assassinations] as prepared as we should have been," Halutz admitted.

IN JUNE 2007, A year after killing four IDF soldiers and touching off another war, Hamas forces—angry that Abu Mazen's Fatah members still controlled Palestinian Authority institutions despite the Hamas election victory—massacred a large number of Fatah officials in Gaza and seized the Strip by force, effectively setting up an independent Hamas state.

The situation could not have been worse for Israel. From the north and south, it was surrounded by states and organizations with military power and enormous budgets, controlled by the Radical Front, while Israel itself was bruised and hesitant after the capture of its soldiers and the defeat in the 2006 war.

A month after the takeover in Gaza, the Radical Front's senior commanders held a secret summit in Damascus to discuss future joint activity against the enemy.

The atmosphere was festive. The front had succeeded in re-launching a campaign of suicide bombings within the State of Israel; an array of tens of thousands of rockets and missiles in Lebanon and the Gaza Strip had the entire territory of Israel covered; Hezbollah had defeated Israel's attempt to destroy it the previous summer; Hamas had won the elections in the Palestinian Authority and built its own state in Gaza; Iran and Syria, each on its own, were making significant progress toward completing production of a nuclear weapon. The situation, they all agreed, was the best the "resistance" axis could have hoped for.

Israeli officials watched the conference from a distance. And planned. Dagan knew this war would have to be fought in the shadows, replete with risks and without limits.

# KILLING MAURICE

IBRAHIM OTHMAN SAT DOWN next to a pretty stranger at the bar of a Vienna hotel. He was a middle-aged man, balding and droopy-eyed, but the woman next to him seemed interested, at least in having a conversation. She spoke French—Othman spoke French!—and loved Paris and dogs. Othman bought her a drink and told her about the poodles he raised at his home in Damascus.

Othman was the director of the Syrian Atomic Energy Commission. The woman was a Mossad operative. The Israelis weren't exactly sure what kinds of secrets Othman held, but they knew he would be in Vienna in January 2007, and it was comparatively easy to run an operation there. They did not consider the operation to be an especially important one—it was being run concurrently with several that were deemed more significant.

Nevertheless, while the female agent indulged Othman's stories of poodles at the bar, a team of Rainbow operatives searched his room. A preliminary inspection didn't produce anything of value, and they began trying, without success, to open a heavy, locked case that Othman had left in the room. To do so without leaving any trace required a special effort, and in the meantime a surveillance detail had noticed that Othman was showing signs of weariness and would soon be going back to his room.

"I am going in. Give me the timing," whispered the commander, abandoning his lookout position and entering the room to take charge. Othman signed the check. "You have about four minutes," radioed one of the lookouts. The Syrian thanked his new friend, and the two arranged to speak in the morning and perhaps meet up. Othman began walking to the elevator. "Two minutes," radioed the lookout. "Get out of there."

In the room, the Rainbow team had just opened the bag and begun copying the pictures inside it as quickly as possible, without paying attention to what they were. Othman was inside the elevator. "One minute to contact," said the tense voice on the radio. By now everything had been shot, and the bag repacked and locked. "The elevator's there. Get out now!"

Othman was now in the hallway, only thirty seconds away, almost within sight of his room. One member of the team was preparing to execute a diversionary trick, by acting drunk and spilling a glass of whisky on him. But with seconds to spare, the rest of the team exited the room and walked rapidly down the corridor in the opposite direction. "We're out. All's okay. Disengage," came the calm and confident voice of the commander.

The material the Mossad team copied there that day was not immediately deciphered. It took some two weeks after the break-in at Othman's room in Vienna until someone looked at it.

That was when they first saw the pictures of the reactor.

Syria was trying to build a bomb. It was, in fact, making dramatic progress toward building a bomb, yet it had managed to keep the entire enterprise a complete secret. And this was one situation that could not be resolved by rubbing out a few key people. Drastic action of a different kind was called for.

Strangely enough, Bashar al-Assad had enormous respect for Israeli intelligence, which was why he worked so hard to deceive it. He was convinced that every message in Syria transmitted by electromagnetic means—telephone, cellphone, fax, text, email—was being intercepted by Israeli intelligence. "He truly believed that every time Mustafa called Mohammed, Moishele was listening in," an officer from Unit 8200 said. "And that was not necessarily a drastic mistake."

To minimize the risk, Assad instructed General Muhammad Suleiman—his liaison to the Radical Front—to set up a shadow army, one separate and independent from the rest of the Syrian defense establishment. Even the highest-ranking officials and officers, including the military chief of staff and the minister of defense, were kept ignorant. Suleiman ordered that all important communications be passed only on paper, in envelopes sealed with wax, by a network of motorcycle couriers. This retreat from the electronic age worked. Suleiman's organization remained totally invisible to Israeli intelligence for years.

Suleiman's biggest secret was hidden away in the arid district of Deir al-Zor, inside a deep canyon a few miles from the banks of the Euphrates in northeastern Syria. Since 2001, he'd been overseeing the construction of a building to house a nuclear reactor that Syria had purchased from North Korea, with Iranian funding. The reactor would enable the Syrians to produce plutonium for an atomic bomb, which, Assad believed, would give him strategic parity with Israel.

Suleiman had spared no effort to conceal the site—but Othman was one of the few people Suleiman trusted. He knew about the reactor, and he'd left files concerning it in his bag. And now the Israelis knew, too.

WHEN THE MOSSAD GOT its hands on the material in January 2007, Mossad director Dagan was in the midst of becoming the chief defense and strategy adviser to Ehud Olmert. When Olmert decided to go to war against Hezbollah in July 2006, Dagan fiercely opposed chief of staff Dan Halutz's plan to defeat the Shiite militia through air attacks, and he told the cabinet, "I know Lebanon, and I know Hezbollah, and without boots on the ground, on a large scale, it won't work." The more time went by and Dagan's concerns were validated, the more attentive Olmert became to his opinions.

Dagan was someone who could see into the souls of others, and he was a talented PR man as well. He shared the juiciest tidbits of operations with Olmert, who was captivated by Dagan and his world of espionage and special ops. After losing his faith in the IDF and extensive all-out military campaigns, he gave more and more power to his spymaster to wage his war of shadows against the Radical Front. "I believed in Meir," said Olmert. "He needed my support in order to approve the crazy ideas that his agency came up with."

The discovery of the reactor was yet another feather in Dagan's cap—especially since no other intelligence agency, including those in the United States, had been able to find it—but mostly it was a cause for serious concern. The news that the country's top enemy was at an advanced stage in a nuclear weapons program, about which they knew absolutely nothing, swept through the length and breadth of the Israeli intelligence community instantaneously. "Meir came to me with this material [the pictures taken from Othman's room]," recalled Ehud Olmert, "and it was like an earthquake. I realized that from now on, everything would be different."

Shortly afterward, Olmert dispatched Dagan to brief U.S. National Security Adviser Stephen Hadley and CIA chief Michael Hayden.

By this time, as he rode the elevator up to the seventh floor of CIA headquarters, at Langley, he was already a familiar and welcome guest. Dagan got along famously with Hayden: "He was to the point, an intelligence officer in every bone of his body, and he listened to what I proposed." In turn, Hayden believed that Dagan was "straightforward, plainspoken, bluntly honest, unpretentious, sincere, and very knowledgeable."

The two men established the closest levels of trust in history between the intelligence agencies of the two countries, initiating an era of deep cooperation. Hayden described the relationship between the agencies as complementary: "We're big, we're rich, technologically sophisticated, and we're global," while the Israelis are "small, focused, culturally and linguistically smart, and relevant to the targets," by which he meant jihadist terrorism and attempts by Middle Eastern countries to develop weapons of mass destruction.

Each time Dagan visited the CIA, he brought with him sensitive information and suggestions, some of them quite imaginative, for joint operations. But at that April meeting, not even the experienced Hayden anticipated the bombshell. "Dagan sat down, opened his briefcase, and took out color copies of the pictures of the reactor at Deir al-Zor."

For a long while, Dagan went over the material with Hayden, asking whether his experts saw eye to eye with the Israelis' analysis. Dagan was also well aware that, despite the Mossad's capabilities in

Syria, his agency had almost no information about what was happening on the other end of the nuclear deal. So he asked Hayden to take the intel he had brought "and plug it into the CIA's broader knowledge of North Korea."

The next morning, Hayden went to the White House to meet with President George W. Bush. While he and the other participants were sitting and waiting for the president to arrive, Hayden leaned over to Vice President Dick Cheney, who had long opined that the Syrians were trying to get their hands on nuclear weapons, and whispered, "You were right, Mr. Vice President."

Bush ended the meeting with two clear-cut but practically contradictory orders: "Number one: Be sure. Number two: This can't leak." Hayden went back to Langley wondering how to confirm the Israeli information without spreading the word around. "To be sure, you want to get more people involved, but that increases the risks of spilling the secret."

While trying to balance these two directives, the CIA and other U.S. agencies started "an intensive, months-long effort to confirm and corroborate the information Israel provided us on the reactor and to gather more details from our own sources and methods." The conclusions of the joint Pentagon-CIA-NSA team came in June, and they were just as worrying as the Israelis'. "Our intelligence experts are confident," the team wrote, "that the facility is in fact a nuclear reactor of the same type North Korea built indigenously at its Yongbyon nuclear facility. . . . We have good reason to believe this reactor was not intended for peaceful purposes."

The United States had committed to Israel's security, and Olmert wanted that commitment honored—he wanted U.S. forces to destroy the reactor. Timing was an issue as well. Experts at Israel's nuclear facility in Dimona said that according to what they saw in the pictures, the Syrian plant was very close to completion. They estimated that it would be hot within half a year, and that if they waited until then to bomb it, it would cause radioactive pollution and an environmental disaster.

Operationally, it was a relatively simple mission for the U.S. Air Force. A squadron of B-2 stealth bombers could have destroyed the installation without any special problems. But CIA Middle East experts reckoned that an American bombing mission in the region would be fraught with danger.

"My analysts are very conservative," Hayden said to Dagan, in what he called "one of the most candid conversations I ever had with him." The Assad family, Hayden said, reminded him of the Corleone family in *The Godfather*. But when Sonny was rubbed out, the don had the gifted Michael to replace him. When Basel Assad was killed in an accident, "Hafez had to settle for Fredo/Bashar," who was known in the CIA as a "serial miscalculator."

"Assad could not stand another embarrassment after the [2005] withdrawal from Lebanon," Hayden said. "Out of weakness, he would have to show his strength and retaliate with war."

Dagan had the exact opposite opinion: "You had to look at it from Assad's point of view," he said. "On the one hand, he had always wanted to reach strategic equality with Israel and, therefore, to get his hands on nuclear weapons. On the other hand, Bashar al-Assad always preferred not to confront us directly. Furthermore, if he went to war after the bombing, this would expose the existence of the nuclear installation—that he had built an atomic facility in violation of his signature on the NPT [Non-Proliferation Treaty], which even the Russians, his allies, don't know about, and for sure would not be happy to know of. If we were to attack covertly and keep it totally under wraps, without publicizing it and embarrassing him, Assad would not do anything."

The final decision was made in a meeting with the president that, due to the high degree of secrecy, was held not in the West Wing of the White House but in the Yellow Oval Room of the residential wing, so that the meeting would not even be listed on the public presidential appointments register.

Only Vice President Cheney was in favor of an American attack, claiming that the United States should do it to send a strong message not only to Syria and North Korea but also to Iran.

Secretary of State Rice acknowledged that the reactor in Syria was "an existential threat" to Israel, but she did not think that the United States should get involved. Hayden made it clear that the reactor was in an advanced stage of construction, but Syria was still a long way away from getting a nuclear bomb.

Already bogged down in two wars in Muslim countries, Bush concluded, "What Mike [Hayden] just told me is this is not an imminent danger, and therefore, we will not do this."

Israel could rely only on itself.

NUCLEAR WEAPONS IN SYRIAN hands would undoubtedly be an existential threat to Israel. But AMAN analysts agreed with Hayden and warned Olmert that attacking Syria without direct prior provocation could lead to a strong military reaction by Assad. Dagan, on the other hand, recommended bombing the site immediately, before the reactor was activated. "The State of Israel cannot tolerate a country with which it is at war having nuclear weapons," he said.

Dagan had made a significant wager. If he was wrong, open warfare with Syria probably still would have ended in an Israeli victory, but it would cost thousands of lives. Yet despite the enormous risks, thanks to his charisma, self-confidence, and past successes, Dagan's opinion carried the day.

At 3 A.M. on the morning of Thursday, September 6, scores of fighter planes took off from the Ramat David air force base, in northern Israel, fifteen miles southeast of Haifa. They wheeled westward, in the direction of the Mediterranean, and then southward. It was part of a routine base evacuation drill, familiar to the Arab intelligence services that monitored the Israeli Air Force. Nothing special. But this time, the planners of the exercise were out to deliberately confuse those men watching the proceedings on radar screens in Damascus.

Somewhere over the sea, a formation of seven F-15I fighters broke away from the others and headed in the opposite direction—northward. The crews knew the exact location of the targets they had to destroy, and the exact nature of those targets. The importance of their mission had been divulged to them by their commander just before takeoff. They flew very low, along the Mediterranean coast and then over Turkey, before entering Syrian airspace. At a range of thirty miles, they launched twenty-two missiles at the three sites within the nuclear complex.

The Syrians were taken completely by surprise. Their air defense systems detected nothing until the missiles were already fired, leaving no time for the sites to be evacuated. A few antiaircraft missiles were dispatched, but only after the planes were long gone.

Shortly afterward, American and Israeli satellites hovering above Syria documented the total destruction of the site. Olmert sent a secret message to Assad via Turkish prime minister Recep Tayyip Erdoğan, saying that if Assad acted with restraint, Israel would refrain from publicizing the attack. This would save Syria the embarrassment of being exposed as having acted in gross violation of the Non-Proliferation Treaty, to which it was a signatory. The world also wouldn't have to know that Syria had just gotten years' worth of expensive military research and technology blown up by the Jewish state—a situation that would almost necessitate some sort of face-saving retaliation. Keeping the whole thing quiet was better for all involved.

The big winner in Operation Out of the Box, as it was code-named, was Dagan, whose agency had produced the information that exposed the Syrian project and who, said CIA director Hayden, "turned out to be right, while my analysts turned out to be wrong."

After the success of Out of the Box, Olmert loosened the government's purse strings still further, granting the Mossad the biggest budgetary allocations it had ever received. One senior Mossad official said, "There wasn't a single activity that was postponed or canceled for financial reasons. The organization grew incredibly. Whatever we asked for, we got."

"Arik [Sharon] and Rabin were far more hesitant than I was in approving missions," said Olmert with a satisfied smile, adding, "I okayed three hundred [Mossad] operations during my term as prime minister, and only one of them failed, and we kept the lid on that one, too."


FROM THE TIME HE took over the Mossad, one of Dagan's top priorities was killing Imad Mughniyeh, the Hezbollah chief of staff. This goal was not unique to Dagan: Israeli intelligence and defense had been trying to kill Mughniyeh for almost thirty years. The enemy that had caused Israel the most damage operationally and politically in the preceding decades was Hezbollah, and Dagan thought that one man was the primary driving force responsible for its achievements. "Mughniyeh," he said, "is a combination of chief of staff and defense minister. [Secretary General] Nasrallah may be the political leader, but he is neither a military commander nor the man who does all the real deals with the Syrians and with the Iranians. Nasrallah, at the most, says yes."

Mughniyeh was, in fact, an international fugitive, high on the most-wanted lists of forty-two countries. Dozens of nations had issued warrants for his arrest, and the FBI offered a $25 million reward for information leading to his capture. In Lebanon in the 1980s, Mughniyeh had killed hundreds of Americans in car bombings, and he'd kidnapped and tortured to death several high-ranking U.S. officials. "The Americans remember," Dagan said. "They appear to be liberals"—in Israel, "liberal" also means forgiving and merciful—"but they are far from that."

The problem was, no one could find him. Mughniyeh was a phantom. He was aware that Western intelligence agencies were investing immense resources to locate him, so he devoted equally immense effort to eluding capture—using fake documentation even inside Lebanon, limiting his contacts to only a small, close circle of family members and trusted associates, and employing a number of extreme measures to secure his communication.

But in July 2004, after a senior Hezbollah commander, Ghaleb Awali, was killed when his Mercedes exploded, the organization made a memorial film about him that was screened at internal gatherings. The Mossad got hold of a copy, and it was shown in December to a group of experts from Unit 8200 and the Mossad. During an all-night session, they scrutinized it in the hope of learning new details about the shadowy group.

Late in the night, while everyone was sitting together in a room in Mossad headquarters with their eyes glued to the screen, one of the 8200 officers yelled out, "That's him. That's Maurice."

Maurice was the code name for Mughniyeh.

The picture on the screen showed Hezbollah's Hassan Nasrallah, in his brown cleric's robe and black turban, looking at an enormous tabletop computer monitor upon which a map was displayed. Opposite him stood a man, his face mostly concealed, but revealed for fractions of a second as he moved: bearded, bespectacled, in camouflage uniform and a cap, pointing out different spots on the map for Nasrallah. This man was Imad Mughniyeh.

Finally, they had at least some sort of lead. In the days that followed, various ideas were tossed around, including trying to trace the videographer in order to recruit him as an agent, or setting up a straw company for the supply of items like the tabletop computer their target was using, which could be booby-trapped and detonated when Mughniyeh was nearby.

Dagan shot them all down. The Mossad wasn't ready yet. "Don't worry," he told the staff. "His day will come."

THE BREAKTHROUGH CAME THANKS to the persistence and inventiveness of Aharon Zeevi-Farkash, in AMAN. The former commander of 8200 had spurred the development of more and more methods to deepen the SIGINT penetration of the enemy. Together, Zeevi-Farkash's AMAN and Dagan's Mossad jointly devised a new operating system called HUGINT, a combination of HUMINT and SIGINT—in other words, a way of using the Mossad's agents in order to improve the capability of 8200 to intercept the enemies' messages, and vice versa.

One of the developers of the HUGINT method was Yossi Cohen (the director of the Mossad at the time of this writing), who is known by his colleagues as "the Model" because of the care he takes with his grooming and appearance. In 2002, Cohen was appointed head of the special-ops department of Junction, the Mossad's agent-recruitment division. Cohen was considered one of the most brilliant recruiters in the agency's history, one of the few who ever managed to break into Hezbollah and the Islamic Revolutionary Guard Corps and recruit Mossad agents from among their numbers. While under cover as various European businessmen, he was able to use his vast general knowledge and insights into human nature to enlist a huge number of agents, perfecting the Mossad's HUGINT methodology in the process. In recognition of these achievements, Cohen was awarded the Israel Security Prize, the country's highest decoration for defense-related achievements.

In 2004, Dagan nominated Cohen to be chief of the Mossad's Iranian operations. Thanks to Cohen's agents and HUGINT, 8200 succeeded in cracking parts of the Iranian government communication systems, allowing Israel to penetrate deeper into the dense network of communications between commanders of the Radical Front. This generated more information about Mughniyeh: more clues, more eavesdropped computer communications and cellphone calls, more agents who had heard or seen something relevant.

The top men of the Radical Front, the Israelis eventually learned, preferred to hold their meetings in Damascus, where, under the protection of the Syrian secret services, they felt secure. After Hezbollah's victory in the 2006 war, Mughniyeh believed that Israel would greatly increase its efforts to kill him and Nasrallah. So he surrounded the secretary general with an elite crew of bodyguards and persuaded him not to make public appearances or to appear live on television, and also to spend as much time as possible in Hezbollah's command bunker, underneath Beirut's Dahiya quarter.

As for himself, he relocated from Beirut to Damascus, both for security reasons—he felt safer in a city that was under the control of the Syrian intelligence services, which were considered tough and professional—and because much of his business was conducted in the Syrian capital.

Although the protection of Suleiman's "shadow army" was very strong, "Mughniyeh did not suddenly become any less cautious in Damascus," Dagan said. He allowed only a close circle of people to know that he had moved to Damascus, and even fewer knew where he lived, how he moved around, and what name was written in his fake passport.

Nevertheless, Israel managed to get an agent inside that close circle around Suleiman, and "it was in Damascus that we knew more about him than when he was in Beirut," Dagan recalled.

Damascus was, however, the capital city of a target country and, along with Tehran, the most dangerous place for the Mossad to operate. It was clear that the numerous arrivals and departures of Mossad operatives in and out of the country, necessary for them to plan and prepare for an operation, would expose them to too much scrutiny, whatever their cover. And because of the extremely sensitive nature of the information, Dagan decided that this time he could not use Arab informants.

So once again, Dagan decided to ignore a long-held, ironclad rule of the Mossad—he turned to another country to assist with an assassination. He invited himself to another meeting with Hayden.

The CIA, however, is forbidden to carry out or support assassinations, under Executive Order 12333. While both countries believed it was permissible to kill people, they had somewhat different legal perspectives. The United States would not normally participate in the execution of someone in a country with which America was not at war or involved in an armed conflict.

Ultimately, the CIA legal advisers came up with a solution whereby it would be legal to strike Mughniyeh in Syria, based on the principle of self-defense, since Mughniyeh was sending his men from Syria to Iraq to spur the Shiite militias to carry out terror attacks against American personnel.

President Bush then granted Dagan's request for assistance, but only on the condition that it be kept a secret, that Mughniyeh alone would be killed, and that Americans would not be the ones to do the actual killing. Prime Minister Olmert himself guaranteed this to the president. (Even years after the event, Hayden refused to say anything about the American involvement.)

The United States still had an active embassy in Damascus, and American businessmen could enter and exit Syria relatively freely. This enabled the CIA, with assistance from the NSA, to send in its own people and use its local agents for the mission.

As one of the commanders of the operation put it, "This was a gigantic, multi-force operation, with crazy resources invested by both countries and, to the best of my knowledge, the most ever invested to kill a lone individual."

With help provided by the Americans, Mughniyeh was eventually located. They discovered that he often met with his comrades from the Radical Front at various intelligence installations: office buildings heavily guarded by Syrian police officers and soldiers, and safe houses with undercover plainclothes guards. They also found out that Mughniyeh regularly visited three good-looking local women whom Suleiman had supplied for his rest and relaxation.

Mughniyeh never took his bodyguards along on these visits to the women, which exposed him to surveillance and to his adversary's operational activities in a place that wasn't under his control. They were "a significant field security error," said one of the commanders of the operation. "At the end, after so many years, even the most careful of men becomes full of confidence that nothing can happen to him."

But an operation in any one of these places would make it very difficult for the Israelis to keep their promise to the Americans not to harm anyone else but Mughniyeh, not to mention the enormous risks that would have to be taken by the actual operatives.

Mossad planners came up with a number of ideas, but all were ruled out. There was only one real possibility: to strike Mughniyeh on his way from one of the sites to another. There were still a number of serious difficulties, though. It was unclear how they would be able to follow him and eliminate him while he was riding or walking, since he was almost constantly accompanied by bodyguards and traveled on different routes and at different times, which the Mossad could not predict in advance. It was also unclear how the operators would be able to make their getaway before the airfields and ports were alerted and shut down.

The deliberations dragged on for months, as Dagan rejected plan after plan. Then, in November 2007, the head of the Mossad's technological division, N., came into Dagan's office with a proposal for an operation that would eliminate Mughniyeh using a bomb detonated by remote control. This bomb would ostensibly kill only Mughniyeh, with no collateral damage, and would also give the operatives on the ground enough time to escape the scene. Dagan said he was prepared to give the plan the go-ahead, though he believed that the chances of its succeeding were very slim.

The basic assumption of N.'s plan was that it would be impossible to follow Mughniyeh around Damascus, so instead they would have to find a way to place the explosive device into something that was frequently physically close to him. A cellphone, like the one that killed Yahya "the Engineer" Ayyash in 1995, was always an option, but that was ruled out because Mughniyeh kept changing them regularly. The one item he used consistently was his vehicle, at the time a luxurious silver Mitsubishi Pajero SUV.

The Mossad knew that both Mughniyeh and his bodyguards frequently examined the inside and the bottom of the car to see if it had been tampered with. But there was one place they never checked: the spare tire cover clamped onto the back of the vehicle. With American aid, the components of a sophisticated explosive device were smuggled into Syria, as well as a tire cover identical to the one on Mughniyeh's car.

After months of preparations and meticulous surveillance, in early January 2008, Mossad operatives managed to get close to the parked SUV while Mughniyeh was paying a nocturnal visit to one of his paramours. They took out the spare tire and replaced the cover with a new one, with the bomb inside. They also planted a number of miniature cameras and a transmitter so that Mossad operatives in Damascus could see what was happening just outside the car.

The Mossad's explosives experts promised that if the bomb was detonated right when Mughniyeh was about to enter the car, the explosion would kill him. But in order to be completely sure, they suggested that the bomb be detonated when the car was parked alongside other vehicles, so that the blast would bounce off them and cause considerably more damage.

For six long weeks, the hit team followed Mughniyeh, reporting to a special war room isolated from the rest of the Mossad, where only a select few were permitted to enter. Again and again—thirty-two times in total—the circumstances were almost right, but each time the operation was called off at the last second, either because Mughniyeh was accompanied by someone else or because there were other people nearby or because he got in the car too quickly—the bomb was effective only if he was outside the car.

On the morning of February 12, Mossad operatives watched Mughniyeh approach the car with another man. "Hey, look, it's Suleimani," one of the operatives yelled out. Suleimani, the Islamic Revolutionary Guard strongman, was leaning on the Pajero, standing very close to Mughniyeh. It was clear from watching them talk (there was no audio feed) that the two were very friendly with each other.

Excitement about the opportunity to kill both men ran through the war room. But first they had to get approval. Dagan was at his home, in Rosh Pina, mourning the death of his mother, who had died two days earlier. But I, the Mossad official commanding the operation, called Dagan, who in turn called Prime Minister Olmert. Olmert, however, refused to let them proceed. The explicit promise given to the president of the United States had been unequivocal—to kill Mughniyeh, and Mughniyeh alone.

That same day, at around 8:30 P.M., Mughniyeh arrived at a safe house in the upscale Kafr Sousa neighborhood of Damascus, just a few hundred yards from one of the most important headquarters of Syrian intelligence. He met with several aides of General Suleiman and two Hezbollah officers and, at about 10:45, left the meeting before it had ended. He exited the building, alone this time, and walked up to his Pajero in the parking lot. As he moved between his vehicle and another car parked alongside it, right before he opened the door, the order to execute was given.

The bomb exploded. Imad Mughniyeh, thirty years a phantom, was finally dead.


THE SYRIANS WERE IN shock. A guerrilla fighter and tactical master who for three decades had managed to evade the intelligence and military resources of Israel, the United States, and forty other countries had been assassinated literally right beneath their intelligence headquarters—some of the building's windows were shattered by the explosion.

"Just think what this does to the Syrians," said Dagan. "Right in the heart of the most guarded place in Damascus. Think of what it does to Assad, what it does to Hezbollah, when they grasp that they're not safe even in Damascus."

"You give the adversary a sense of total intelligence penetration, a sense that you know everything, both about the organization and about the host country," he added.

President Assad realized the magnitude of the disaster and wanted to keep as far away as possible from the whole affair. He sent condolences to Nasrallah but suggested that no mention of the attack be made in Syria. He even suggested that the wrecked Pajero, with the body placed in it, be transferred under cover of night to Beirut, to make it look as if Mughniyeh had died there.

Nasrallah refused. He was furious with the Syrians for failing to look after his comrade. Some Hezbollah members—as well as Mughniyeh's wife—even accused the Syrians, wrongly, of being involved in the killing. Assad was forced to deny and apologize over and over again. Nasrallah issued orders that no Syrian representatives be invited to the funeral in Beirut.

Mughniyeh's funeral was held in pouring rain. The procession of Shiite mourners encountered Sunnis who had just taken part in a memorial for their beloved leader, Rafik Hariri, who had been murdered on Mughniyeh's orders exactly three years before. Such is life in Lebanon.

Thousands managed to cram into the enormous hangar in south Beirut where Hezbollah occasionally held its larger rallies. Tens of thousands were left outside. Mughniyeh's casket was carried to the podium while the mourners reached out and tried to touch it, to be blessed by his honor and holiness on his final journey. An honor guard of Hezbollah militiamen in khaki uniforms flanked the casket on the podium, together with the sober-faced leaders of the organization, dressed in their black robes. On the walls, and in the hands of the mourners, were thousands of posters bearing the last photograph of Mughniyeh, which only now, after his death, was allowed to be revealed. The caption read, "The great martyred hero." The crowd cried out in grief for revenge.

Faithful to the wishes of his departed comrade, Nasrallah remained in his bunker and did not appear at the funeral. Giant screens transmitted his eulogy to the masses, inside and outside the hangar. In solemn words, he eulogized his top fighter, "who devoted his life to martyrdom, but waited many years to become a martyr himself."

He mentioned the assassination of his predecessor as secretary general, Abbas Mussawi, which had only strengthened the resistance and led to more and more humiliation for Israel. "The Israelis do not realize what the blood of Sheikh Abbas did for Hezbollah, the emotional and spiritual uniqueness that it gave us," he said. "Let the world write down, and upon my responsibility, that [with Mughniyeh becoming a *shahid*] we have to historically mark the beginning of the fall of the State of Israel."

The crowd responded, "We are at your service, O Nasrallah."

Nasrallah ended with a threat. "You crossed the borders, Zionists. If you want an open war"—a war outside of the borders of Israel and Lebanon—"let it be an open war anywhere."

Nasrallah and the Iranians appointed at least four people to take over Mughniyeh's duties. But the open war never came to pass. The same intelligence penetration that had allowed a bomb to be planted in Mughniyeh's Pajero also allowed Israel to stop all of Hezbollah's planned attacks. Only one succeeded, a suicide terrorist who blew himself up next to a busload of Israeli tourists in Bulgaria, killing six and wounding thirty.

In his death, the legends about Mughniyeh proved to have been true. "His operational capabilities were greater than those of the entire quartet that replaced him taken together," said Dagan. Mughniyeh's absence was made especially conspicuous by the organization's inability to respond to the assassination. "If Mughniyeh was around to avenge his own death," an AMAN officer said, "the situation would likely have been completely different. Lucky for us, he wasn't."

IN LESS THAN SIX months, General Suleiman had lost a nuclear facility he'd managed to keep secret for five years, and a close confidant and ally who'd cheated death for decades. Humiliated and furious, he ordered Scud missiles, some armed with chemical warheads, prepared for launch into Israel. He demanded that Assad strike back with aggression.

Assad refused. He understood his general's rage, but he also understood that an open attack on Israel—to say nothing of a chemical attack—was not in Syria's best interests. This behavior "took discipline," Olmert observed in a meeting with House Minority Leader John Boehner. "Bashar is no dummy." Olmert told his close advisers that "Assad, the man we all love to hate, is displaying moderation and pragmatism in his response."

Like Assad, Olmert was forced to moderate his underlings, many of whom believed Assad should be killed, too. After all, he had aligned himself with terrorists and Iranians. "All the stories about the progressive Western eye doctor had turned out to be wishful thinking," one high-ranking AMAN officer said. "We have here an extremist leader. And unlike his father, he's unstable, with a tendency for dangerous adventures."

But Olmert rejected the idea. "It is precisely with this man," he said, "that a peace agreement can be reached."

Suleiman was a different case. "Suleiman was a real shit, with a remarkable capability for organization and maneuvering," Olmert said. In many respects, Suleiman was the second-strongest man in Syria, with an office across the hall from Assad's in the presidential palace and, as a top-secret NSA memo noted, "a hand in three primary areas: internal Syrian issues connected to the regime and the party; sensitive military issues; and Lebanon-related issues through which he was apparently connected both to Hizbollah and to others in the Lebanese political arena."

This time, though, the Israelis knew there was no chance the United States would get involved. Mughniyeh, who had killed hundreds of Americans, was one thing. A Syrian general, the high-ranking official of a sovereign state, was something entirely different. On their own, then, the Israelis began planning a way to dispose of Suleiman.

After the Mughniyeh operation, security arrangements in Damascus had been stepped up, and any idea of conducting the operation there was ruled out. Suleiman was closely guarded and constantly escorted by a convoy of armored vehicles, so the possibility of using an explosive device was also rejected. Meir Dagan reached the conclusion that the Mossad would need assistance, and, as it happened, the IDF was eager to take on the job. The glory bestowed on the Mossad after Mughniyeh's killing had stoked the military leaders' desire to carry out the assassination of a key figure themselves, so that "the finger on the trigger would be of a soldier, not a Mossad man."

On Friday, August 1, 2008, at about 4 P.M., Suleiman ended his day's work at the palace earlier than usual and set out northward in his secure convoy. He was heading to the summer residence he had built on the Mediterranean coast, near the port city of Tartus. It was a spacious villa with a large patio of polished stone, overlooking the sea. That evening, the general invited a number of local dignitaries to dine with him and his wife, Rahab, and his close advisers. They were attended by a staff of servants and, of course, bodyguards.

The party was sitting at a round table, with a magnificent view of the sun setting into the sea. Suleiman's wife sat to his left, his *chef de bureau* on his right. Two men smoked fat Cuban cigars.

Suddenly the general lurched back in his chair, then hurled forward and fell facedown onto his plate. His skull was split open, fragments of bone and flecks of brain matter and blood splattering all over Rahab. He'd been shot six times, first in the chest, the throat, and the center of his forehead, then three times in the back. Only Suleiman was hit. He was dead before his face hit the plate.

Within thirty seconds, the two Flotilla 13 snipers who had fired the shots from two different spots on the beach were already on rubber dinghies, headed to a navy vessel. Back on the beach, they had left behind some cheap Syrian cigarettes, part of a disinformation campaign to make the assassination look like an internal Syrian affair.

As a frantic search for the shooters got under way in the villa, the commander of Suleiman's bodyguards called the presidential palace to notify Assad that his closest adviser had been killed. Six bullets, from two directions, and no one ever saw the assassins. Assad listened, and remained silent for a minute. "What has happened has happened," he said firmly. "This is a military secret of the highest level. Bury him now, straight away, without telling anyone. And that is that." The funeral was held the next day, in utmost secrecy.

"This was the first known instance of Israel targeting a legitimate government official," the NSA concluded.


MEIR DAGAN WAS NOW the head of a completely different Mossad from the one he had inherited six years earlier. No longer the timid institution unnerved by its own failed and sloppy operations, Dagan's Mossad had infiltrated Hezbollah and Suleiman's shadow army, disrupted the transfer of weapons and advanced technologies between members of the Radical Front, killed Radical Front activists, and even assassinated the long-sought Imad Mughniyeh.

Dagan had also developed a plan to stall Iran's nuclear ambitions, which thus far had proven remarkably successful. It was a five-pronged approach: heavy international diplomatic pressure, economic sanctions, support to Iranian minorities and opposition groups to help them topple the regime, the disruption of consignments of equipment and raw materials for the nuclear program, and, finally, covert ops, including the sabotage of installations and targeted killings of key figures in the program.

The idea behind this integrated effort, "a series of pinpoint operations meant to change reality," in Dagan's words, was to delay the project as much as possible so that before Iran could build an atom bomb, either the sanctions would cause a grave economic crisis that would force Iran's leaders to drop the project or the opposition parties would be strong enough to overthrow the government.

In support of these efforts, the quadrilateral collaboration between the CIA, the NSA, the Mossad, and AMAN was finally formalized by way of a cooperation pact between Bush and Olmert that included revealing sources and methods ("total mutual striptease," in the words of one of the prime minister's aides).

American intelligence agencies and the Department of the Treasury, together with the Mossad's Spear unit, launched a comprehensive campaign of economic measures to impair the Iranian nuclear project. The two countries also embarked on an effort to identify Iranian purchases of equipment for the project, particularly items that Iran could not manufacture itself, and to stop the shipments from reaching their destination. This continued for years, through the Bush administration and into that of Barack Obama.

But the Iranians were tenacious. In June 2009, the Mossad, together with U.S. and French intelligence, discovered that they had built another secret uranium enrichment facility, this one at Qom. Publicly, three months later, President Obama made a dramatic announcement and condemnation, and the economic sanctions were tightened further. Covertly, joint sabotage operations also managed to produce a series of breakdowns in Iranian equipment supplied to the nuclear project—computers stopped working, transformers burned out, centrifuges simply didn't work properly. In the largest and most important joint operation by the Americans and the Israelis against Iran, dubbed "Olympic Games," computer viruses, one of which became known as Stuxnet, caused severe damage to the nuclear project's uranium enrichment machinery.

The last component of Dagan's plan—the targeted killing of scientists—was implemented by the Mossad on its own, since Dagan was aware that the United States would not agree to participate. The Mossad compiled a list of fifteen key researchers, mostly members of the "weapons group" that was responsible for developing a detonation device for the weapons, as targets for elimination.

On January 14, 2007, Dr. Ardeshir Hosseinpour, a forty-four-year-old nuclear scientist working at the Isfahan uranium plant, died under mysterious circumstances. The official announcement of his death noted that he had been asphyxiated "following a gas leak," but Iranian intelligence is convinced that he was a victim of the Israelis.

On January 12, 2010, at 8:10 A.M., Masoud Alimohammadi left his home in an affluent North Tehran neighborhood and walked toward his car. He had been awarded a doctorate in the field of elementary particle physics in 1992 by Sharif University of Technology, and became a senior lecturer there. Later, he joined the nuclear project, where he was one of the top scientists. As he opened his car door, a booby-trapped motorcycle that was parked nearby exploded, killing him.

The slaying of scientists—people working in government positions for a sovereign state, who were not involved in terrorism in any way—did not go without an internal debate in the Mossad. At one of the operational approval meetings in Dagan's office, an intelligence officer working under the deputy director, Tamir Pardo, stood up and said that her father was a top scientist in Israel's nuclear program. "Going by the way of thinking prevalent here," she asserted, "my father would be a legitimate target for elimination. I think that this is neither moral nor legal." But all such objections were rebuffed.

The Iranians, for their part, realized that someone was killing their scientists and began guarding them closely, especially the chief of the weapons group, Mohsen Fakhrizadeh, who was considered the brains behind the project. The Iranians posted cars full of cops around their homes, making their lives a nightmare and pitching them and their families into profound anxiety.

The series of successful operations also had an additional effect, one that Israel did not initiate but that ended up working to its great benefit: Each member of the Radical Front began to fear that Israel had penetrated their ranks, and thus started devoting huge efforts to locating their leaks and trying to protect their personnel against the Mossad. The Iranians also became paranoid about the possibility that all the equipment and materials they'd acquired on the black market for their nuclear project—for very large sums of money—were infected, and they examined and reexamined each item over and over. These efforts greatly slowed down other aspects of the nuclear project, even bringing some to a standstill.

Dagan's Mossad was now once again the Mossad of legend, the agency that historically had been either feared or admired, but never dismissed. The staff were proud to be serving there. Dagan had introduced a boldness to the agency that would have been bravado had it not been so completely and utterly effective.

# IMPRESSIVE TACTICAL SUCCESS, DISASTROUS STRATEGIC FAILURE

MAHMOUD AL-MABHOUH ENTERED THE lobby of the Al-Bustan Rotana Hotel just before 8:30 in the evening, one of many guests coming and going at the hotel. Like them, he was captured by the closed-circuit camera over the entrance. He had black hair, a slightly receding hairline, and a thick black mustache. He wore a black shirt and a coat a little too large for him. It was a relatively cold night in Dubai, which is usually very warm.

He'd been in Dubai for less than six hours, but already he'd met with a banker who was helping him arrange various international financial transactions required to purchase special surveillance equipment for Hamas in Gaza. He'd also met with his regular contact from the Iranian Revolutionary Guards, who flew in to coordinate the delivery of two large shipments of weapons to the extremist Islamic organization.

Al-Mabhouh did a lot of business in Dubai. When he flew into the little city-state on January 19, 2010, it was at least his fifth visit in a little less than a year. He traveled on a Palestinian passport—the emirate was one of the few places that recognized papers issued by the Palestinian Authority—which listed a fake name and a fake occupation. In reality, he was a top Hamas operative and had been for decades: Twenty years earlier, he'd kidnapped and murdered two Israeli soldiers, and more recently, after his predecessor, Izz al-Din al-Sheikh Khalil, had been disposed of by the Mossad in Damascus, he'd been in charge of stocking Hamas armories.

A step or two behind al-Mabhouh, there was a man with a cell-phone, following him into the elevator. "Coming now," the man said into his phone. Al-Mabhouh might have overheard, but he didn't seem to notice. There was nothing unusual about a tourist in Dubai telling a friend he was on his way.

Al-Mabhouh was by nature an extremely cautious man. He knew that the Israelis wanted to kill him. "You have to be alert," he'd told Al Jazeera in an interview the previous spring. "And me, praise Allah, they call me 'the fox' because I can sense what is behind me, even what is behind that wall. Praise God, I have a highly developed sense of security. But we know what the price of our path is, and we have no problem with it. I hope that I get to die a martyr's death."

The elevator stopped at the second floor. Al-Mabhouh stepped off. The man with the phone stayed on, going to a higher floor. Definitely a tourist.

Al-Mabhouh turned left and walked toward his room, 230. The hallway was empty. Out of habit, he quickly scanned the frame of his door and the lock mechanism, looking for nicks, scratches, any hint of tampering. There was nothing.

He entered the room, closed the door behind him.

He heard a noise and turned to see what it was.

Too late.


THE PLAN FOR THE assassination of Mahmoud al-Mabhouh had been approved four days earlier, on January 15, during a hastily arranged meeting in the large conference room near Meir Dagan's office, after Israeli military intelligence had hacked into the email server used by al-Mabhouh and discovered that he'd reserved a flight from Damascus to Dubai on January 19.

In that meeting, there were some fifteen people seated around a long table, including representatives of the Mossad's intelligence, technology, and logistics wings. The most important person at the conference, after Dagan, was "Holiday," the head of Caesarea. Holiday, who is bald and stocky, had taken it upon himself to personally command Operation Plasma Screen.

Al-Mabhouh had long been on the Israelis' kill list. A year earlier, the situation on the Gaza Strip border had deteriorated so badly that on December 27, 2008, Israel launched Operation Cast Lead, a large-scale attack to stop Hamas from raining Qassam and Katyusha rockets down on Israeli communities. Hamas was able to fire a great deal of ordnance from the Gaza Strip, thanks to al-Mabhouh's weapons acquisition and transportation network, and the assistance it received from the Iranian Revolutionary Guards.

Israel's intelligence about Hamas had improved greatly in recent years, and the operation began with the air force's huge aerial bombardment, code-named Birds of Prey, on the silos where Hamas's rockets were concealed. The Mossad had learned that the network al-Mabhouh managed had been replenishing the Hamas weapons stockpiles. The weapons were shipped from Iran to Port Sudan, on the Red Sea, and from there smuggled via Egypt and Sinai into the Gaza Strip via the multiple tunnels used to avoid the Egyptian border guards and patrols. The Mossad kept track of the shipments at sea and when the trucks left Port Sudan. In January 2009, the Israeli Air Force carried out four long-range raids and destroyed the convoys and the men escorting them.

"Activities like these did a lot of damage to the smuggling routes from Iran to Hamas," Dagan said. "Not an absolute impact, not enough to win outright, but a significant reduction."

For some reason, however, al-Mabhouh did not travel that day with the trucks, but instead left Sudan by another route. To rectify this, Dagan requested and obtained approval from Olmert for a negative treatment operation against al-Mabhouh. When Benjamin Netanyahu took over from Olmert, in March 2009, he renewed the approval.

Dubai was the most convenient place to kill al-Mabhouh. The other areas where he spent time—Tehran, Damascus, Sudan, and China—had efficient secret services and posed far more problems for a Mossad hit team. Dubai, on the other hand, was teeming with tourists and foreign businessmen and had, the Mossad believed, much weaker enforcement and intelligence forces. Dubai was still a target country, officially hostile to Israel, but by this point the Mossad had killed a man in downtown Damascus, and a Syrian general in his own villa. By comparison, a Hamas operative in touristy Dubai would be a relatively easy target.

Still, the operation called for a large team, divided into smaller squads, which would be able to spot the target when he arrived in Dubai and keep him under surveillance while others set up and executed the actual hit in the hotel room, making sure it would appear that al-Mabhouh had died a natural death. They would then need to remove all evidence and leave the country before the body was found, just in case foul play was suspected anyway.

Not everyone thought that al-Mabhouh was important enough to justify the effort and risk. Some even told Dagan that he did not meet the basic conditions required for negative treatment. Everybody in the Mossad agreed that al-Mabhouh deserved to die, but in order to carry out an operation in a target country, he also had to be a serious danger to Israel, one whose elimination would have a profoundly disruptive effect on the enemy's equilibrium. In truth, al-Mabhouh did not fit either criterion. But after all of their previous success, Dagan and other Mossad officials were so full of self-confidence that they went forward anyway.

A team of Caesarea operatives had first trailed al-Mabhouh in Dubai in 2009, not to kill him but to study his movements and, mostly, to be certain that he was their man. Four months later, in November, the Plasma Screen crew went to Dubai again, this time to eliminate him. They poisoned a drink that was brought to his hotel room, but either they got the dose wrong or he didn't swallow enough: Al-Mabhouh only fainted. When he came to, he cut short his visit and returned to Damascus, where a doctor attributed his fainting spell to mononucleosis. He accepted this diagnosis and didn't suspect that an attempt on his life had been made.

This turn of events caused profound frustration within the Mossad. People and resources had been risked, and still the job had not been finished. Holiday insisted that there would be no mistakes this time: The hit squad would not leave Dubai before they saw with their own eyes that al-Mabhouh was dead.

One objection arose at the January 15 meeting near Meir Dagan's office. The documentation department would have trouble preparing credible new fake passports for the entire team. There were more than two dozen people going to Dubai, and some would be entering the same country with the same identities and cover stories for the third time in barely six months. In the Mossad's more timid days under Halevy, the operation would have been canceled for that reason alone. But Dagan and Holiday decided to take the risk. They would send the team in with the existing papers.

Holiday didn't expect any problems anyway. The discovery of the body was liable to arouse suspicion, and an investigation might ensue, he acknowledged, but that would happen only long after the team had returned to Israel. Zero evidence would be left for the police to work with. No secret of the Mossad would be given away. No one would be caught. The whole thing would be forgotten quickly.

Dagan dictated the final decision to his chief assistant: "Plasma Screen—authorized for execution." As the participants left, he added, in his deep voice, "And the best of luck to all."


THE FIRST THREE MEMBERS of the Plasma Screen team landed in Dubai at 6:45 on the morning of January 18. Over the next nineteen hours, the rest of the team—at least twenty-seven members altogether—arrived on flights from Zurich, Rome, Paris, and Frankfurt. Twelve of their passports were British, six Irish, four French, four Australian, and one German. All were genuine, but none actually belonged to the person using it. Some were borrowed from their owners, residents of Israel with dual citizenship, some were obtained under false identities, some were stolen, and others belonged to the deceased.

At 2:09 A.M. on the 19th, "Gail Folliard" and "Kevin Daveron" landed. They were to be the main pivots for the operation—controlling the forward command room, the communications personnel, the guards, and the lookouts. They checked into separate rooms at the Jumeirah hotel. Both paid cash, though many of the other team members used debit cards issued by a company called Payoneer, the CEO of which was a veteran of an IDF commando unit.

The reception clerk Sri Rahayu took their money and gave Folliard room number 1102 and Daveron 3308. Before going to sleep,

Folliard ordered a light meal from room service. Daveron took a soft drink from his minibar.

"Peter Elvinger," the commander of the mission, landed at the airport twenty-one minutes after Folliard and Daveron, carrying a French passport. After clearing passport control, Elvinger pulled a countersurveillance maneuver (*maslul* in Hebrew), exiting through the terminal door, waiting three minutes, then turning around and going back inside for a predetermined meeting with another team member who had come to the airport earlier by car. All members of a hit team, as a standard procedure, constantly used *maslul*, frequently changing clothing and disguises, such as wigs and false mustaches. This is to make sure that one is not being followed and to enable a switch of identities between various stages of an operation.

Elvinger and his contact spoke for less than a minute before the commander took a cab to his hotel.

By early afternoon, the entire team was waiting tensely for the arrival of al-Mabhouh. He was expected to fly in at three o'clock, but there were still some gaps in the intelligence. The Plasma Screen team did not know where he would be staying, when and where he would be having meetings, or how he would move from place to place. The team, which couldn't cover the whole city, might lose him, and it was impossible to plan in advance how to get close enough to kill him. "It's the kind of hit," a veteran operative said, "where the target dictates how and when he is to be made dead."

Some of the team members had deployed to three hotels where al-Mabhouh had stayed in his previous visits. Another surveillance squad was at the airport, passing time with what appeared to be idle telephone chatter. The remaining personnel, seven people, remained with Elvinger in another hotel, waiting.

Al-Mabhouh arrived at 3:35. A team tailed him to the Al-Bustan Rotana Hotel, and a message was sent to the operatives at the other hotels, telling them they were clear to leave their posts. The team members made extensive use of cellphones, but in order to avoid direct links between their numbers, they dialed a number in Austria, where a simple switchboard installed in advance put the call through, either to another phone in Dubai or to the command post in Israel.

The crew members already in the lobby of the Al-Bustan Rotana were wearing tennis clothes and carrying rackets, though, curiously, without the usual accompanying covers. After al-Mabhouh got his room key, two of them entered the elevator after him. When he got out on the second floor, they followed at a discreet distance and noted that he was staying in room 230. One of the two men reported this, by way of a cellphone call routed through Austria, before the two returned to the lobby.

Once Elvinger knew al-Mabhouh's room number, he made two phone calls. The first was to the Al-Bustan Rotana, to book a room. He asked for 237, directly across the corridor from 230. Then he called an airline to reserve a seat on a flight to Munich via Qatar later that evening.

A little after 4 P.M., al-Mabhouh left the hotel. The team trailing him noticed he was taking precautionary measures, doing his own kind of *maslul*. He had good reason to do this: Almost all of his comrades in Hamas since the late 1980s had died unnatural deaths. But his moves were simple and unsophisticated, and the team had no trouble keeping eyes on him.

KEVIN DAVERON WAITED IN the Al-Bustan lobby for Elvinger, who arrived at 4:25, handed Daveron a suitcase without a word, and then went to the registration desk. The security camera clearly captured his red-covered European Union passport. After checking in to room 237, he gave the key to Daveron, again without a word, and left the hotel without his suitcase.

Two hours later, four men came to the hotel, in two pairs. All wore baseball caps that hid their faces. They carried two large bags. Three of them were Caesarea "executioners." The fourth was an expert at picking locks. They went directly to the elevators and to room 237. An hour after that, at 7:43, the surveillance team in the lobby was relieved, replaced with fresh eyes—four hours after they'd first arrived, the fake tennis players finally left the lobby.

At ten o'clock, the crew tailing al-Mabhouh reported that he was heading back to the hotel. Daveron and Folliard kept watch in the corridor while the lock picker began working the lock on the door to 230. The idea was to reprogram it so a Mossad master key would open the door without being logged, but at the same time not disrupt the normal functioning of the proper key. A tourist stepped off the elevator, but Daveron quickly engaged him in some innocent, distracting conversation. The tourist saw nothing, the lock was picked, and the team entered the room.

Then they waited.

AL-MABHOUH TRIED TO ESCAPE back into the corridor. But two pairs of strong arms gripped him. A third man gagged him with one hand and, with the other, pressed to al-Mabhouh's neck an instrument that uses ultrasound waves to inject medication without breaking the skin. The instrument was loaded with suxamethonium chloride, an anesthetic known commercially as Scoline that is used in combination with other drugs in surgery. On its own, it induces paralysis and, because it causes the muscles used in breathing to stop working, asphyxiation.

The men maintained their grip until al-Mabhouh stopped struggling. As the paralysis spread through his body, they laid him on the floor. Al-Mabhouh was wide awake, thinking clearly, seeing and hearing everything. He just couldn't move. Foam formed at the corners of his mouth. He gurgled.

Three strangers stared at him dispassionately, still lightly holding his arms, just in case.

That was the last thing he saw.

The executioners checked his pulse in two places, as they had been instructed to do by a Mossad doctor, making sure that this time he was really dead. They removed his shoes, shirt, and trousers, placed them neatly in the closet, and put the body into the bed, under the covers.

The entire episode took twenty minutes. Using a technique developed by the Mossad for such occasions, the team closed the door in such a way that it seemed to have been locked from the inside, with the chain slid into place. They hung a DO NOT DISTURB sign on the door handle, knocked twice on the door of 237 as a mission-accomplished signal, and then disappeared into the elevators.

Folliard left one minute later, Daveron four minutes after that, then the surveillance team in the lobby. Within four hours, most of the team was out of Dubai, and none were left twenty-four hours later.

In Tel Aviv, a mood of self-satisfaction reigned, an atmosphere that was later described as "the euphoria of a historic success." Everyone involved—Meir Dagan, Holiday, the hit team—believed another mission had been expertly accomplished. Dagan reported the kill to Netanyahu. "Al-Mabhouh," he said, "won't bother us anymore."

HOTEL SECURITY FOUND THE body the next afternoon, after no one answered the maid's repeated knocks throughout the day. There did not seem to be any cause for alarm, however. A middle-aged merchant dead in bed in a locked room with no signs of struggle or trauma was likely indicative of nothing more than a heart attack or maybe a stroke. Al-Mabhouh's body was taken to the morgue, his death recorded and catalogued under the bogus name on his passport. The matter was given no more or less attention than any other dead middle-class foreigner in Dubai.

In Damascus, however, Hamas officials were beginning to wonder why the man they'd sent to broker several arms deals hadn't reported back as scheduled. A day later, on January 21, a local envoy asked around at police stations and morgues until he found al-Mabhouh's unclaimed body in a refrigerated drawer.

A Hamas official contacted the Dubai police chief, Lieutenant General Dhahi Khalfan Tamim, and told him that the dead man with the Palestinian passport was, in fact, a top member of their organization. He told Khalfan that the death almost certainly had not been from natural causes and that, more likely than not, the Mossad had been behind it.

Khalfan, fifty-nine years old and highly decorated, had made it his personal mission to rid his country of criminals and foreign agents who used Dubai as a base for carrying out illegal activity. "Take yourselves," he yelled into the phone, "*and* your bank accounts *and* your arms *and* your fucking counterfeit passports and get the hell out of my country!"

Still, he couldn't have the Mossad wandering around killing people, either. Khalfan pulled the body out of the morgue for an autopsy. The results were not definitive, and it was not possible to determine whether al-Mabhouh had been murdered, but Khalfan's basic assumption was that the Hamas official had been right.

ONE DISADVANTAGE ISRAELI OPERATIVES have, in comparison with their American or British counterparts, is that they have to use fake passports. A CIA squad can easily be outfitted with legitimate U.S. State Department passports, albeit under assumed names, and they essentially have an endless supply—one identity just buried under the next as needed. American and British passports are accepted everywhere in the world and rarely draw undue attention.

Israeli passports are not. They are useless for getting into many Asian and African countries—countries where the Mossad is occasionally interested in killing someone or conducting some other covert op. The Mossad commonly forges copies from other, less suspicious countries. In the post-9/11 world, however, counterfeiting passports had become a more complicated business.

Documents that were sloppily made or have been used too often could endanger a mission and operatives' lives. So when Halevy scrubbed missions for lack of enough proper papers, it wasn't solely out of timidity. And when Dagan bullied rushed passports and identities from reluctant technicians, that was bold leadership only until it went horribly wrong.

Dagan had allowed the Plasma Screen team to use the same identities four times in Dubai. It was not difficult for Khalfan to get a list of everyone who entered the UAE shortly before al-Mabhouh and then left right after he died. Nor was it difficult to narrow that list down by comparing it with those who came and went the previous three times al-Mabhouh visited. That gave Khalfan names, which could then be cross-referenced with hotel registries, which almost always have cameras recording the front desk. Soon the police knew who came when, where they stayed, and what they looked like.

Assassins prefer cash, because it is anonymous; it generally cannot be traced. Credit cards—or prepaid Payoneer debit cards—can be. A cluster of calls to an Austrian switchboard will be logged and, if someone is looking, noticed. So, too, will the numbers that the switchboard calls. Reconstructing the movement of every Mossad operative in Plasma Screen and the connections among them, therefore, was not terribly difficult. It only required sifting through a lot of data.

From multiple CCTV cameras, Khalfan assembled a video narrative of the entire operation. It included bits of clumsy *maslul* for good measure. For instance, the camera above the door to one hotel's bathroom showed Daveron entering bald and coming out with a full head of hair, without even noticing that he was on camera, although it was not hidden. This was not something that would have given the team away in real time, but the sloppy execution of the identity switch certainly made things easier for the investigators.

Khalfan then held a press conference and put the entire video on the Internet for the world to see. He called on Dagan to "be a man" and own up to the hit. He demanded international arrest warrants for Netanyahu and Dagan, and Interpol actually did issue arrest warrants for all twenty-seven members, though under their assumed names.

The countries whose passports Israel had used were furious. Many of them quietly cooperated with the Mossad, but not to the point of allowing their citizens, fictitious or not, to be dragged into assassination plots. Some governments ordered the Mossad representatives in their countries to leave immediately and would not allow the agency to replace them for several years. All of them cut back on their collaboration with the Israeli agency.

It was a calamity born of hubris. "I love Israel and love the Israelis," said one of the former chiefs of German intelligence. "But your problem has always been that you disparage everyone—the Arabs, the Iranians, Hamas. You're always the smartest and think that you can fool everyone all of the time. A little more respect for the other side, even if you think that he's an ignorant Arab or an unimaginative German, and a little more modesty would have saved all of us from this awkward mess."

On one level, none of that mattered in Israel. The harsh condemnations it was subjected to on the international stage—combined with similar condemnations the nation regularly received for its treatment of the Palestinians—produced an upsurge of patriotism. On Israel's carnival holiday, Purim, which fell a few weeks after the story broke, a popular costume was that of a pistol-packing tennis player. Hundreds of Israelis with dual citizenship volunteered their passports to the Mossad for use in future operations. The organization's website was flooded with inquiries about joining up.

Things were different, however, inside the agency. The exposure and the negative attention the Mossad got was terribly damaging on an operational level, despite the fact that Khalfan never managed to prosecute any of the perpetrators. Whole sections of the Mossad's operations were shut down, both because so many operatives had had their cover blown and because of the need to develop new procedures and methodologies, after the old ones had been all over the media.

Early in July 2010, realizing that the Dubai affair had blocked his run to become head of the Mossad, Caesarea chief Holiday quit.

Meanwhile, Meir Dagan adopted a business-as-usual attitude. In general, Dagan definitely believed that "in certain cases the Mossad's director has to hand over the keys if he's got a mishap that harms the state, because that would ease the pressure on the country." But from Dagan's point of view, nothing had happened—no foul-up, no mistakes. "We hit an important target, he's dead, and all the troops got home," he summed up after the operation.

Only in 2013, in an interview for this book, would Dagan admit, for the first time, that "I was wrong in sending the team in with those passports. It was my decision and only my decision. I bear the full responsibility for what happened."

AS THE DUBAI FIASCO unfolded, Netanyahu "felt a sense of déjà vu," one of his close aides said, as if 1997 was happening all over again. Back then, the Mossad had assured him it could go into a "soft target" country, Jordan, and cleanly eliminate Khaled Mashal. That ended in humiliation and capitulation. There was no telling how long the fallout from Dubai would last. He had to restrain the Mossad, he decided, and green-light fewer dangerous missions.

In addition, Dagan had to be reined in.

The two men had never gotten along. Indeed, Netanyahu's relations with all of the intelligence community chiefs were problematic. "Netanyahu doesn't rely on anyone, and so he made covert diplomatic moves without informing the heads of the community," said Netanyahu's national security adviser, Uzi Arad. "From one moment to the next, I watched the rift of distrust opening up between him and them."

Dagan, for his part, thought the prime minister was too hesitant to approve operations, and yet also fearful of being seen as hesitant—a bundle of neuroses unfit for keeping a nation secure.

But Dagan remained at the Mossad. The campaign against Iran, multipronged and interconnected and complicated, was still in play. In fact, after the successful hit on Masoud Alimohammadi, earlier in January, Dagan asked Netanyahu for approval to intensify the campaign and to continue killing the remaining thirteen scientists of the weapons group. Netanyahu, apprehensive about another imbroglio, was in no hurry. It wasn't until October that he gave the green light for another hit. On November 29, 2010, two motorcyclists blew up the cars of two senior figures in the Iranian nuclear project by attaching limpet mines to them and speeding away. Dr. Majid Shahriari was killed by the blast in his Peugeot 206; Fereydoon Abbasi-Davani and his wife, who was also in the car, managed to escape his Peugeot 206 before it exploded just outside Shahid Beheshti University.

By this point, however, it had become evident that the targeted killing campaign, along with the economic sanctions and the computer sabotage, had slowed but not stopped the Iranian nuclear program. The program "reached a point far beyond what I had hoped for," Defense Minister Ehud Barak said. He and Netanyahu both concluded that Iran was nearing the moment when the project's installations would be indestructible, and they agreed that Israel should act to destroy the facilities before that happened. They ordered the IDF and the intelligence arms to prepare for Operation Deep Waters: an all-out air attack, supported by commando forces, in the heart of Iran. Some $2 billion was spent on preparations for the attack and for the anticipated ensuing war against the Radical Front.

Dagan, among others, thought the plan was insane. He saw it as a cynical move by two politicians who wanted to exploit the wide-spread public support that the attack would provide them in the next elections, not a levelheaded decision based on national interest. "Bibi learned a technique, the essence of which was to convey messages in a short time. He reached a remarkable level of mastery and control on this. But he is also the worst manager that I know. He has a certain trait, similar to Ehud Barak: Each of them imagines that he is the world's greatest genius. Netanyahu is the only prime minister [in the country's history] who reached the situation where the entire defense establishment failed to accept his position."

"I've known a lot of prime ministers," Dagan said. "Not one of them was a saint, believe me, but they all had one thing in common: When they reached the point where the personal interest came up against the national interest, it was the national interest that always won. There was absolutely no question. Only about these two I cannot say it—Bibi and Ehud."

The enmity between Dagan and Netanyahu reached a boiling point in September 2010. Dagan claimed that Netanyahu had taken advantage of a meeting, purportedly about Hamas, with him, the head of the Shin Bet, and the chief of staff, in order to illegally order preparations for an attack: "As we were leaving the room, he says, 'Just one moment, Director of the Mossad and Chief of Staff. I have decided to place the IDF and you at O plus 30.'"

"O plus 30" was short for "thirty days from an operation," which meant that Netanyahu was calling a full-scale attack on Iran an "operation," rather than the more appropriate term, an "act of war." Wars needed a vote in the cabinet, but prime ministers could simply order an operation.

Dagan was stunned by the recklessness: "The use of [military] violence would have intolerable consequences. The working assumption that it is possible to fully halt the Iranian nuclear project by means of a military offensive is incorrect. . . . If Israel were to attack, [Iranian Supreme Leader] Khamenei would thank Allah: It would unite the Iranian people behind the project and enable Khamenei to say that he must get himself an atom bomb to defend Iran against Israeli aggression."

Even the mere act of putting the Israeli forces on attack alert could lead to an inexorable slide into war, Dagan argued, because the Syrians and the Iranians would see the mobilization and could take preemptive action.

Barak had a different version of that dispute—he said that he and the prime minister were only examining the feasibility of an attack—but that hardly mattered. The breakdown in relations between Dagan and Netanyahu was irreparable. Dagan had run the Mossad for eight years, longer than anyone else in history except Isser Harel. He had re-created it in his image, had revived a moribund and timid agency and restored it to the historical glory it had enjoyed for decades. He'd penetrated Israel's adversaries more deeply than anyone believed possible, had eliminated targets who'd evaded death or capture for decades, had stalled for years an existential threat to the Jewish state.

None of that mattered. Dubai was an embarrassment, or maybe just an excuse. In September 2010, Netanyahu told Dagan his appointment would not be renewed.

Or maybe Dagan quit. "I decided by myself that it's enough," he said. "I want to do other things. And also, the truth is that I was sick of him."

TAMIR PARDO, WHO SUCCEEDED Dagan as director, had to rehabilitate a large part of the operations teams and procedures, which were wrecked in the aftermath of the Dubai hit. He appointed N., a man who had been instrumental in planning the hit on Mughniyeh, to conduct a comprehensive evaluation of the damage, and later made him his deputy. The reconstruction of the operational units did not stop the agency's activities, though, especially not those aimed at the Iranian nuclear project. After a few months in the job, Pardo went back to the targeted killing policy his predecessor had laid down.

In July 2011, a motorcyclist followed Darioush Rezaeinejad, a doctor of nuclear physics and a senior researcher for Iran's Atomic Energy Organization, until he reached a point close to the Imam Ali Camp, one of the most fortified bases of the Revolutionary Guard, which contains an experimental uranium enrichment area. The biker drew a pistol and shot Rezaeinejad dead.

In November 2011, a huge explosion occurred in another Revolutionary Guard base, thirty miles west of Tehran. The cloud of smoke was visible from the city, windows rattled, and satellite photos showed that almost the entire base had been obliterated. General Hassan Tehrani Moghaddam, head of the Revolutionary Guard's missile development division, was killed in the blast, as were sixteen of his personnel.

Despite the demise of al-Mabhouh, arms shipments continued to flow into Gaza from Iran via Sudan. The Mossad maintained surveillance, and the Israeli Air Force kept up attacks on the convoys. The biggest success came after the Mossad discovered that three hundred tons of advanced weaponry and explosives, which were disguised as civilian goods and stored at a military compound in the south of Khartoum, were awaiting shipment to Gaza. The arms cache included short- and medium-range rockets and advanced antiaircraft and antitank missiles and was defined by Israel as something that would "upset the equilibrium." If it were to reach Gaza, said one of the AMAN officers who briefed Prime Minister Netanyahu, "we would recommend attacking Hamas even without prior provocation, to prevent them from deploying it."

But the arms never went anywhere. At 4 A.M. on October 24, 2012, IAF F-15 fighters attacked the site and destroyed the weapons, as well as the Hamas and Islamic Revolutionary Guard Corps personnel who were there at the time. The skies over Khartoum were illuminated by the explosions. Roofs were blown off and windows shattered by the blast. The residents of Khartoum suffered because of their government's decision to allow the country to be part of the terrorist weapons-smuggling pipeline. After this incident, the Sudanese authorities told the IRCG that they would no longer permit it.

Like his predecessors, Pardo refrained from risking Israeli operatives in killings undertaken in target countries, particularly in places as dangerous as Tehran. All the hits on Iranian soil were, in fact, implemented by members of that country's underground opposition movements and/or members of the Kurdish, Baluchi, and Azerbaijani ethnic minorities who were hostile to the regime.

These targeted killings were effective. Information reaching the Mossad indicated that they brought about "white defection"—

meaning that the Iranian scientists were so frightened that many requested to be transferred to civilian projects. "There's a limit to an
organization's ability to coerce a scientist to work on a project when
he does not want to," Dagan said.

In order to intensify the fears of the scientists, the Mossad looked
for targets that were not necessarily very high up in the nuclear program, but whose elimination would cause as much apprehension as
possible among the greatest numbers of their colleagues at the same
level. On January 12, 2012, Mostafa Ahmadi-Roshan, a chemical
engineer at the Natanz uranium enrichment facility, left his home
and headed for a laboratory in downtown Tehran. A few months earlier, a photograph of him accompanying Iranian president Mahmoud
Ahmadinejad on a tour of nuclear installations had appeared in media
across the globe. Once again, a motorcyclist drove up to his car and
attached a limpet mine that killed him on the spot. His wife, who
was sitting next to him, was not hurt, but she saw everything and told
his colleagues, horrified at what had happened.

Assassinating scientists, whatever they are working on, is an illegal act under American law, and the United States never knew, and
did not want to know, about these actions. The Israelis never told the
Americans their plans, "not even with a wink and a smile," said the
CIA's Michael Hayden. That said, Hayden had no doubt about which
measure undertaken to stop the Iranian nuclear project was most effective: "It was that somebody was killing their scientists."

At the first session of the National Security Council with the new
president, Barack Obama, in 2009, Obama asked the CIA director
how much fissile material Iran had stockpiled at Natanz.

Hayden replied, "Mr. President, I actually know the answer to
that question, and I'm going to give it to you in a minute. But can I
give you another way of looking at this? It doesn't matter.

"There isn't an electron or a neutron at Natanz that's ever going to
show up in a nuclear weapon. What they're building at Natanz is
knowledge. What they're building at Natanz is confidence, and then
they will take that knowledge and that confidence and they'll go
somewhere else and enrich uranium. That knowledge, Mr. President, is stored in the brains of the scientists."

Hayden made it abundantly clear that "this program has no American relationship whatsoever. It is illegal, and we [the CIA] never would have recommended it or advocated such a thing. However, my broad intelligence judgment is that the death of those human beings had a great impact on their nuclear program."

THE AYATOLLAHS' REGIME IN Tehran had wanted an atomic bomb to make Iran a regional power and to ensure their continued grip on the country. Instead, Israeli and American actions, particularly Israel's targeted killing operations and the virus infections of Operation Olympic Games, had slowed the program's progress considerably. In addition, international sanctions had flung Iran into a grave economic crisis that threatened to bring down the regime entirely.

These sanctions, particularly the ones imposed by the Obama administration (including the detachment of Iran from the international money transfer system, SWIFT), were so harsh that in August 2012, the head of Spear, E.L., estimated that if he could persuade the United States to take just a few more economic measures, the Iranian economy would be bankrupt by the end of the year. "And that situation would bring the masses out into the streets again and would likely lead to toppling the regime," he said.

Nevertheless, this did not stop Benjamin Netanyahu from making preparations for an open military assault on Iran. It's not entirely clear whether he ever really intended to execute the plan: His defense minister, Ehud Barak, maintained that, "if it depended on me, Israel would have attacked," but there are others who believe that Netanyahu—who had the last word—only wanted to make Obama believe that he intended to attack, in order to force Obama's hand, to steer him to the conclusion that America would inevitably get embroiled in the war anyway, so it would be better for the United States to carry out the attack itself, first, in order to be able to control the timing.

The Obama administration feared that an Israeli attack would send the price of oil soaring and that chaos would ensue in the Middle East, harming the president's chances of reelection in November 2012. The administration also estimated that Israel was likely to attack soon and worriedly watched Israel's every move—even regular army brigade maneuvers became a source of apprehension that an Israeli attack on Iran was imminent. In January, Senator Dianne Feinstein met with Mossad director Pardo in her Senate office, demanding that he explain the reason for movements by Israel's 35th Brigade, as captured by a U.S. satellite. Pardo didn't know anything about the routine drill, but he later warned Netanyahu that continued pressure on the United States would lead to a dramatic measure, and likely not the one that Netanyahu hoped for. Pardo himself believed that another two years of economic and political pressure would probably make Iran surrender under favorable conditions and give up its nuclear project entirely.

But Netanyahu refused to listen to him, ordering Pardo to continue with the assassinations, and the IDF to continue its preparations for an attack.

In December, the Mossad was ready to eliminate another scientist, but just before it went ahead, Obama, fearing Israeli action, agreed to an Iranian proposal to hold secret negotiations in Muscat, the capital of Oman. "The Americans never told us about those talks, but they did everything to make sure we would learn about them," said a Mossad intelligence officer who discovered the Muscat meetings. She recommended to Pardo that he immediately drop the assassination plan. "We must not do this when a political process is under way," she said. Pardo agreed with her and asked Netanyahu for permission to cease the entire assassination campaign as long as the talks were ongoing.

It is reasonable to assume that if the talks had begun two years later, Iran would have come to them in a considerably weaker state, but even the deal that was eventually struck was an Iranian capitulation to a number of demands that the ayatollahs had been rejecting for years. Iran agreed to dismantle the nuclear project almost entirely and to be subject to strict limits and supervision for many years into the future.

For Dagan, the agreement marked a double triumph: His five-front strategy against Iran had achieved many of its objectives. At the same time, Netanyahu had grasped that launching an attack while negotiations with Iran were under way would be an intolerable slap in the Americans' faces. He postponed the attack again and again, and when the final agreement was signed, he canceled it altogether, at least for the near future.

But Dagan was not satisfied. He was bitter and frustrated over the manner in which Netanyahu had shown him the way out, and he did not intend to take it lying down. In January 2011, on the last day of his tenure, he invited a group of journalists to Mossad headquarters and, in an unprecedented move—and to the journalists' astonishment—lashed out fiercely at the prime minister and the minister of defense. After his address, the chief military censor, a woman with the rank of brigadier general, stood up and announced that everything Dagan had said about Israeli plans to attack Iran was in the top-secret category and could not be published in the media.

When he saw that the military censor had barred the publication of his remarks, Dagan simply repeated them at a conference at Tel Aviv University in June, before hundreds of participants, knowing that someone of his stature would not be prosecuted.

Dagan's criticism of Netanyahu was trenchant and personal, but it also sprang from a profound change in attitude that Dagan underwent in his later years as director of the Mossad, a change that was of far greater importance than his ferocious fight with the prime minister over the Iranian nuclear project.

Dagan, along with Sharon and most of their colleagues in Israel's defense establishment and intelligence community, believed for many years that force could solve everything, that the right way to confront the Israeli-Arab dispute was by "separating the Arab from his head." But this was a delusion, and a dangerously common one at that.

Throughout their successive histories, the Mossad, AMAN, and the Shin Bet—arguably the best intelligence community in the world—provided Israel's leaders sooner or later with operational responses to every focused problem they were asked to solve. But the intelligence community's very success fostered the illusion among most of the nation's leaders that covert operations could be a strategic and not just a tactical tool—that they could be used in place of real diplomacy to end the geographic, ethnic, religious, and national disputes in which Israel is mired. Because of the phenomenal successes of Israel's covert operations, at this stage in its history the majority of its leaders have elevated and sanctified the tactical method of combating terror and existential threats at the expense of the true vision, statesmanship, and genuine desire to reach a political solution that is necessary for peace to be attained.

Indeed, in many respects the story of Israel's intelligence community as recounted in this book has been one of a long string of impressive tactical successes, but also disastrous strategic failures.

Toward the end of his life, Dagan, like Sharon, understood this. He came to the conclusion that only a political solution with the Palestinians—the two-state solution—could end the 150-year conflict, and that the result of Netanyahu's policies would be a binational state with parity between Arabs and Jews and a concomitant danger of constant repression and internal strife, replacing the Zionist dream of a democratic Jewish state with a large Jewish majority. He was anxious that the calls for an economic and cultural boycott of Israel because of the occupation would become bitter reality, "just like the boycott that was imposed against South Africa," and even more anxious about the internal division in Israel and the threat to democracy and civil rights.

At a rally in central Tel Aviv before the March 2015 elections, calling for Netanyahu to be voted out, he addressed the prime minister: "How can you be responsible for our fate if you are so frightened of taking responsibility?

"Why does a man seek the leadership if he does not want to lead? How did it happen that this country, several times stronger than all the countries in the region, is not capable of carrying out a strategic move that would improve our situation? The answer is simple: We have a leader who has fought only one fight—the fight for his own political survival. For the sake of that war he has cast us down into becoming a binational state—the end of the Zionist dream."

Dagan cried out to the tens of thousands in the crowd: "I do not want a binational state. I do not want an apartheid state. I do not want to rule over three million Arabs. I do not want us to be hostages of fear, despair, and deadlock. I believe that the hour has come for us to wake up, and I hope that Israeli citizens will stop being hostages of the fears and the anxieties that menace us morning and night."

With the signs of his cancer evident, he ended his speech with tears in his eyes: "This is the greatest leadership crisis in the history of the state. We deserve a leadership that will define a new order of priorities. A leadership that will serve the people and not itself."

But his efforts were to no avail. Despite the enormous adulation he enjoyed as the ultimate Israeli master spy, Dagan's speech, as well as the calls of many other former heads of the intelligence and military establishments for a compromise agreement with the Palestinians and for other adjustments in Israel's relations with the outside world, have all fallen on deaf ears.

There were times when the words of the generals were taken as sacred by most Israelis. But their campaigns against Netanyahu have thus far failed to topple him, and some say they have even bolstered him. Israel has undergone drastic changes in recent decades: The strength of the old elites, including the generals and their influence over the public agenda, has ebbed. New elites—Jews from Arab lands, the Orthodox, the right wing—are in ascendancy. "I thought I would be able to make a difference, to persuade," Dagan told me sorrowfully in the last phone conversation we had, a few weeks before he died, in mid-March 2016. "I was surprised and disappointed."

The divide between the combat-sated generals, who once had "a knife between their teeth" but later grasped the limits of force, and the majority of the people of Israel, is the sad reality in which Meir Dagan's life came to its end.

# ACKNOWLEDGMENTS

Over the past seven and a half years of work on this book, I have had the good fortune and the honor to encounter a number of amazing, talented, wise, and warmhearted people who gave me their support and good advice along the way.

I owe profound thanks to Joel Lovell and Andy Ward, who, on March 11, 2010, sent me the email that started everything off, asking if I would like to write a book about the Mossad. It was Shachar Alterman, a close friend and the editor of my books in Hebrew, who suggested that we focus on the history of Israel's use of assassinations and targeted killings. Joel became an editor at *The New York Times Magazine,* where I have worked closely with him. He is someone who takes manuscripts and makes them smooth and tightly stretched to the level of perfection of the sheets on the bed in a first-class hotel room, to borrow a metaphor once used by David Remnick. Andy Ward never abandoned me or my book-in-the-making, even after he became editor in chief at Random House, and even as deadlines came and went. In his quiet, confident, and determined way, Andy guided the project through to the end.

I also wish to thank other members of the Random House team for their immense contributions and assistance, especially Sean Flynn for editing the first draft and Samuel Nicholson for his work on the final manuscript. They are both fine examples of a rare breed of outstanding editors, who many times put exactly what I wanted to say into words far better than I could find myself.

Special thanks to my agent in the United States, Raphael (Rafe) Sagalyn, who watched over each stage of my work carefully and responsibly, a little like a father caring for a difficult child with serious disciplinary problems. Whenever necessary, he was able to get me back on track and soothe all those I'd managed to irritate with missed deadlines and endless departures from the originally agreed-upon length.

Four people worked closely with me through substantial parts of the time I spent on the book:

Ronnie Hope was far more than an able translator from the Hebrew. He was also a friend and professional colleague whose advice on structure, form, and content was invaluable. He labored with consistent devotion on the various raw versions of the book, often at cruel and unusual hours of the day and night. I also have Ronnie to thank for coming up with the book's title.

The tact and wisdom of Yael Sass, project manager for the book in Israel, was unparalleled. Her toil on the endnotes and bibliography was an unenviable task, but Yael undertook it with poise and great skill, and she ensured the quiet, pleasant, and businesslike atmosphere that enabled me to finish the job.

Dr. Nadav Kedem served as fact-checker and academic adviser. In a book as full of secret details as this one, it's nearly impossible to reach a state of flawlessness, but the work done by Nadav and the Random House copy editors, Will Palmer and Emily DeHuff, has made it as free of errors as was conceivably possible.

Adi Engel's exceptionally bright mind, knowledge, original thinking, and vision were invaluable in shaping the book's structure. I believe that the uncompromising spirit of Adi's commitment to human rights pervades the pages of this book.

I feel deeply grateful to these four—their mark on the book cannot be overstated.

Kim Cooper and Adam Vital helped me in my first efforts to work in the United States. Their excellent counsel and their early faith in the project entitle them to a big share of the credit for the end product. Richard Plepler encouraged my work on the book and taught me that very important word in Yiddish, at just the right time. Thanks to Dan Margalit and Ehud (Udi) Eiran, both so knowledgeable and wise, for reading the manuscript and offering valuable insights; to Dr. Chen Kugel, for his help in deciphering the writing of Professor Otto Prokop (who carried out an autopsy on Wadie Haddad); and to Vanessa Schlesier, who helped us both with translation from German and also assisted me with the reconstruction of the attempt on the life of Khaled Mashal in Amman. This is the place, too, to express my gratitude to the Jordanian royal family's physician, Dr. Sami Rababa, for helping me in Jordan.

A number of journalists, historians, and photographers were extremely collegial toward me and helped with advice and with archival material: Ilana Dayan, Itai Vered, Yarin Kimor, Yoram Meital, Shlomo Nakdimon, Dov Alfon, Klaus Wiegrefe, Zeev Drori, Motti Golani, Benny Morris, Nir Mann, Shachar Bar-On, Yoav Gelber, Ehud Yaari, Ziv Koren, Alex Levac, and the late Aaron Klein. Thanks are also due to Tal Miller and Lior Yaakovi for their research in the early stages and to Haim Watzman, Ira Moskowitz, and Deborah Cher for translation and editing during that period.

Attorneys Eitan Maoz, Jack Chen, and Dvorah Chen gave me good and important advice on various legal matters.

My travels in pursuit of information about secret Israeli operations now provide me with the pleasant duty of extending my thanks to various people around the world: to Gunther Latsch, for picking through the Stasi files; to Robert Baer and the late Stanley Bedlington, for helping me to better understand the nooks and crannies of the CIA; to Crispin Thorold and Marianne El Hajj of the Special Tribunal on the murder of Rafik Hariri in The Hague, for the astonishing material about Hezbollah's death squads; to the Israel Defense Forces' 202 Paratroop Battalion, for protection against Hamas's attempts to blow up the house in the Nablus casbah we were in; to Aql al-Hashem, who extricated us from an exchange of fire in southern Lebanon (and who was sure he was bulletproof until he was killed by a Hezbollah IED); to the Argentinean special prosecutor, the late Alberto Nisman, who allowed me to witness his struggle to discover the truth about the explosion of the AMIA Jewish center in Buenos Aires without knowing that he would be that incident's next victim; to "J.," who accompanied me to the Triple Frontier zone at Ciudad del Este and insisted that we immediately leave the mosque of the cousin of the Hezbollah secretary general; to Calder Walton, who shared his groundbreaking research on British intelligence and the Jewish underground militias in Mandatory Palestine; to my mentor at Cambridge University, Professor Christopher Andrew, for the road map to the KGB documents in the Mitrokhin Archive, which he was the first to reveal; to "Ethan," "Iftach," and "Advantage," who provided much advice and guidance and helped me establish the intricate web of connections that was the foundation of much of the information that appears in this book.

Special, heartfelt thanks to my friend and colleague Holger Stark, for his assistance vis-à-vis the German intelligence and defense establishment, as well as the support, joint projects, friendship, and many secrets we have shared and trusted no one but each other with. My agent in Germany, Hannah Leitgeb, and the journalist and editor Georg Mascolo contributed greatly to the publication of the German translation of the book by DVA/Spiegel. Many thanks to both of them, as well as to DVA's staff, especially Julia Hoffmann and Karen Guddas.

The Zen scholar Professor Jacob Raz, a truly enlightened person, tried to teach me the art of brevity. The book's size, half the length of the original manuscript, is proof that he at least partially succeeded.

Finally, I thank my interviewees and sources for the time, the effort, the willingness, and—in some cases—the great risks they took upon themselves. This includes those whom I have sharply criticized and those whose descriptions of their deeds made my blood curdle. They all opened their memories and their hearts to me, so I could see and tell my readers about the inevitable, violent, and sometimes irreconcilable clash between a nation's need to defend itself and the fundamental principles of democracy and morality.

The best parts of the book are due to all the people I have listed above. The errors are all mine, and my responsibility.

# NOTES

## A NOTE ON THE SOURCES

xiii    **Efforts to persuade the Israeli defense establishment**   The IDF and Defense Ministry Archive (which includes the archive of AMAN) allowed access to only a small number of files, and in them only materials that originated in open media—in other words, zero relevant original documents. The Shin Bet agreed only to send a number of tables regarding terror attacks and data about a few specific terrorists, but refused to reveal any facts about its own actions. The Mossad does not maintain any relations with the media. Efforts to secure the cooperation of its special operations division, Caesarea, also failed. Responding to my request for an interview, the unit's historian, Y., told me, "Even if I were the last person in the intelligence establishment who has not yet made the pilgrimage to you, I would by no means cooperate with you. I despise whoever it was who gave you my phone number, just as I despise you." (Exchange of text messages with Y., August 15, 2015.)

xiii    **A petition to the Supreme Court**   Supreme Court HCOJ [Bagatz] 4801/07, *Dr. Ronen Bergman and Yedioth Ahronoth v. the Prime Minister's Office, the Defense Ministry Director General, the Mossad and Director of the Mossad, the Shin Bet and Director of the Shin Bet, and the Atomic Energy Commission.*

xiii    **The defense establishment did not merely sit**   The research led to the uncovering of spying activity by people close to the chief of staff against the minister of defense, Ehud Barak, which were described later in my book *The Pit* (written with journalist Dan Margalit). Uri Misgav, "Ex-CoS Gabi Ashkenazi Pressed the Shin Bet to Open an Investigation Against a Journalist," *Haaretz,* November 29, 2013. Richard Silverstein, "IDF Chief Threatened Journalist with Espionage for Exposing Rampant Military Corruption," *Tikun Olam,* December 20, 2013, https://www.richardsilverstein.com/2013/12/20/idf-chief-threatened-journalist-with-espionage-for-exposing-rampant-military-corruption/.

xiv    **None of the thousand interviews**   Most of the interviews were held after work on the book began in 2010, and a smaller number were conducted as part of research for other projects in the two preceding decades. None of them were officially sanctioned.

## PROLOGUE

xvii    **Dagan had no love for the media**   Interview with Meir Dagan, May 29, 2013.

xviii    **making him very angry**   Because of these published reports of mine, Dagan got Prime Minister Ehud Olmert to order the Shin Bet to conduct comprehensive surveillance to find the source of the leaks, including tapping the phones of the heads of various Mossad divisions. In the wake of this investigation, Dagan ousted his then deputy, whom he accused of leaking information despite his vigorous denials. Ronen Bergman, "Dismissal at Mossad's High Command," *Yedioth Ahronoth,* July 10, 2007.

xx    **The tension between the two men**   Interview with "Eldy," June 2014, and "Nietzsche," July 2007.

xxii **The numbers speak for themselves** These figures relate to all of the assassination operations about which information was gathered in the research conducted for this book, most of which are mentioned in it. However, calculating the numbers is a complex matter, because sometimes the target of an operation is a mixed one—both enemy offices and compounds and specific persons. The number here includes the actions of the Front for the Liberation of Lebanon from Foreigners, a terrorist organization that Israel ran in Lebanon in the years 1980–83, and which on its own attacked many PLO members and Palestinian civilians, as well as the unsuccessful attempts by Operation Salt Fish to kill Arafat, which cost the lives of many civilians. Because much of the material locked away in the intelligence community's safes cannot be accessed, the estimate here is a conservative one. The actual numbers are probably significantly higher.

xxii **During the Second Intifada** Sources in the Shin Bet say that during the period of the Second Intifada, for each assassination operation that succeeded, there were five to seven earlier attempts at the same target that failed. Some of these were aborted before fire was opened, while some failed because the missile was diverted when civilians were spotted in the target zone, and others because the target was missed. During Operation Birds of Prey, which began the hostilities between Israel and Hamas in Gaza in 2008 by attempting to sow "shock and awe" in the Strip, there were more than a thousand bombing missions, some aimed at personnel and others at structures and storage facilities. Interviews with Ehud Barak, July 1, 2013, Yoav Galant, June 1, 2011, and "Amazonas," June 2017.

xxii **By contrast, during the presidency of George W. Bush** In an interview with the author (June 12, 2016), Tim Weiner, author of *Legacy of Ashes*, the authoritative history of the CIA, argued that no CIA-attempted assassinations against political leaders such as Fidel Castro of Cuba were successful. Furthermore, these attempts all came to a halt after the murder of John F. Kennedy. However, Weiner also said that the CIA continued afterward to be involved in providing intelligence and operational assistance to United States proxies throughout the world, and that many thousands of people were killed by these proxies as a result of the CIA's direct and indirect support—some during torture, others during paramilitary activity in the shadow war the agency conducted until the end of the Cold War. The total number killed by U.S. proxies is very difficult to establish, but Weiner said that in the Vietnam War alone the number included more than twenty thousand suspected Vietcong. In the wake of various inquiry panels' investigations into CIA activities, Presidents Ford and Carter issued directives barring the intelligence community from conducting any direct or indirect targeted killings. After 9/11, however, targeted killing operations resumed, primarily by means of drones in Pakistan, Afghanistan, Somalia, and Yemen. The numbers cited in the text are taken from the D.C.-based think tank New America at https://www.newamerica.org/in-depth/americas-counterterrorism-wars/pakistan/.

## CHAPTER 1: IN BLOOD AND FIRE

3 **Wilkin was the commander of the Jewish unit** Interviews with David Shomron, May 26, 2011, and Yitzhak Shamir, January 1997.

3 **Thanks to the intelligence they provided** Harouvi, *Palestine Investigated*, 230 (Hebrew).

4 **campaign of "personal terror"** Interview with Yitzhak Shamir, January 1997.

4 **Wilkin knew he was a target** Harouvi, *Palestine Investigated*, 191 (Hebrew). Banai, *Anonymous Soldiers*, 243 (Hebrew). Fearing assassination, Morton was posted to the British colony of Trinidad, but Lehi tried to kill him there too. Yahav, *His Blood Be on His Own Head: Murders and Executions During the Era of the Yishuv*, 286 (Hebrew).

4 **None of those details** Harouvi, *Palestine Investigated*, 235.

4 **"We were too busy and hungry"** Interview with Shomron, May 26, 2011.

4 **Wilkin left the officers' lodgings** Ben-Tor, *The Lehi Lexicon*, 119–20 (Hebrew).

5 **"The only thing that hurt me"** Interview with Shomron, May 26, 2011.

5 **The roots of that strategy can be traced to eight men** There is a lack of clarity as to the date of the historic meeting. Most Hebrew sources give it as September 29, whereas the sources in English say September 28. All the sources say it was on the eve of the festival of Simhat Torah in 1907, but that occurred on September 30.

6 **Ben-Zvi and his seven comrades** There is also disagreement over the number of participants. Most sources say eight, but some say ten. It may be that after the fact, there were those who wanted to be associated with what turned out to be a historic event.

6 **Many were living in abject poverty** Hagai, *Yitzhak Ben-Zvi: Selected Documents*, 15–16 (Hebrew).

6 **Some were former members of Russian left-wing revolutionary movements** En-

listment of Jews in the revolutionary movements was no longer a rarity by the mid-1870s. Vital, *A People Apart: A Political History of the Jews in Europe 1789–1939,* 400–415.

7   **They all were desperately poor**   Particularly ardent was Manya Shochat, a woman who joined the group shortly afterward and who had taken part in a number of terrorist actions in Russia and had hidden some of the underground's weapons in her home in Odessa. After a student happened to inadvertently see the cache, Shochat didn't hesitate. She drew a miniature pistol with a silencer and shot the unfortunate student dead. Then she and a friend cut the legs off the corpse so it would fit into a trunk, which they dispatched to a made-up address. Lazar, *Six Singular Individuals,* 52–53 (Hebrew).

8   **Mounted on their horses**   Yahav, *His Blood Be on His Own Head,* 40 (Hebrew).

8   **Hashomer did not recoil**   Yahav, *His Blood Be on His Own Head,* 33–39 (Hebrew).

8   **Haganah in its early years was influenced**   It emerged later that Manya Shochat, one of Hashomer's founders, who sent the assassins, had based her decision on flawed information. Dalia Karpel, "The Untold Story About the Wrong Arab, Who Got Assassinated by Manya Shochat," *Haaretz,* June 5, 2009. Yahav, *His Blood Be on His Own Head,* 41 (Hebrew). Lazar, *Six Singular Individuals,* 78–93.

9   **On June 30, 1924—just a day before**   Nakdimon, *De-Han: The First Political Murder,* 171–82 (Hebrew). Interview with Shlomo Nakdimon, February 18, 2015. Email from Nakdimon, May 29, 2017.

9   **Ben-Gurion, however, took a dim view of such acts**   Israel Galili Testimony, Yad Tabenkin Archive (YTA), 5/7/1–2–15.

10   **targeted killings against . . . Jews**   Like any underground resistance, the Zionist cells were constantly threatened with infiltration and exposure. Jewish informants, confirmed or merely suspected, were swiftly eliminated—26 by the Irgun and 29 by Lehi. Ben-Gurion himself approved the elimination of many Jewish informants by Haganah, making sure the killings would receive wide publicity in order to deter others. Gelber, *A Budding Fleur-de-Lis: Israeli Intelligence Services During the War of Independence, 1948–1949,* 553 (Hebrew). The figures are from research by the journalist Shlomo Nakdimon.

10   **targeted killings would not be used as a weapon**   Ronen Bergman, "The Scorpion File," *Yedioth Ahronoth,* March 30, 2007.

11   **"The Jewish people had been humiliated, trampled, murdered"**   Interview with Mordecai Gichon, May 7, 2010.

11   **tried to draw out of them details**   The reports sent by the Brigade personnel, including Gichon, to the Haganah and Yishuv leadership in Palestine were the first information about the scale of the destruction of Europe's Jews, first from Italy and Austria, and in October 1945 also from Poland and the death camps themselves. The Jewish Brigade, Mission to Locate Relatives of Soldiers, Mission Diary, Pinhas Loebling, October 1956, in the collection of the Jewish Legion Museum, Museums Unit of the Ministry of Defense.

12   **"We thought we could not rest"**   Interview with Hanoch Bartov, June 6, 2010.

12   **"Revenge now is an act of no national value"**   Even the heads of the far-left Hashomer Hatzair movement were aware of the vengeance operations and gave their silent consent. Halamish, *Meir Yaari,* 283 (Hebrew).

12   **they sanctioned some types of reprisals against the Nazis**   Another vengeance initiative was launched by a group of Jews who had fought the Germans as partisans, under the command of Abba Kovner. They wanted to kill six million Germans by poisoning reservoirs. Later they changed their plan and tried to kill German POWs by poisoning their bread. Scientists in the Yishuv supplied them with arsenic, but to this day it is not known what the leaders in Palestine knew of this plan. The Partisans claim they managed to kill hundreds of Germans, but the American military who were in charge of the camp say only a few dozen went down with severe stomach poisoning. Interview with Dina Porat, October 2014. Porat, *Beyond the Corporeal: The Life and Times of Abba Kovner,* 224–48. Bar-Zohar, *The Avengers,* 40–47 (Hebrew).

12   **"revenge, but not a robber's revenge"**   Testimony of Kalman Kit, Haganah Historical Archives, 48.42.

12   **"We looked for big fish"**   Interview with Gichon, May 7, 2010.

13   **Coercion worked**   Testimony of Dov Gur, HHA, 12.36. Gelber, *Jewish Palestinian Volunteering in the British Army,* 307–308 (Hebrew).

13   **stark choice: cooperate or die**   Testimonies in the series *The Avengers,* directed by Yarin Kimor and broadcast on Israel's Channel 1 TV in 2015. Transcript of testimonies in author's archive, courtesy of Yarin Kimor.

13   **"The goy broke and said he was willing to cooperate"**   Testimony of Yisrael Karmi, HHA, 51.4.

13   **"No one suspected me"**   Interview with Gichon, May 7, 2010. Diary of the intelligence officer of the Brigade's First Battalion (author's archive, received from Gichon).

14   **teams of no more than five men**   In order to conceal their nighttime activities, the group of avengers, who during the daytime acted as regular soldiers in the British army, used the cover of an imaginary unit, the TTG Company, a name they used on the papers they presented to sentries at roadblocks on their way to carrying out their operations (as well as smuggling arms and Holocaust survivors). The letters TTG, which the British sentries may have thought was a top secret unit, so secret nobody had heard of it, actually stood for *tilhas tizi gesheftn,* a combination of Yiddish and Arabic meaning "lick-my-ass business." Eldar, *Soldiers of the Shadows,* 12, 17 (Hebrew).

15   **"In most cases we brought the Nazis to a small line"**   Shalom Giladi testimony, HAA, 150.004.

15   **The operation lasted only**   Bar-Zohar, *Avengers,* 37 (Hebrew).

15   **the methods used to identify targets were insufficient**   Interview with Yoav Gelber, May 16, 2011. Naor, *Laskov,* 141–43 (Hebrew). Gmul veterans admit to only one mistake: In June 1945 they were certain they'd located and disposed of Adolf Eichmann, the SS officer in charge of shipping millions of Jews to their death. Only years after the killing, when Israel received information that he was alive, did they realize they were wrong.

15   **Gmul was closed down**   Gelber, *Growing a Fleur-de-Lis,* 457–60 (Hebrew).

16   **The leader of the Templers in Palestine**   Mann, *Sarona: Years of Struggle, 1939–1948,* 111–13 (Hebrew).

16   **"I asked them if they knew there was a hell on earth"**   David Giladi, "With the Son of Wagner from Sarona, and with the Guest from the Monastery in Budapest," *Yedioth Ahronoth,* March 29, 1946. "The 'Palestinians' Were Supervising the Extermination," *Yedioth Ahronoth,* March 31, 1946.

16   **"Here come exultant Germans"**   Interview with Rafi Eitan, January 24, 2013.

16   **the Haganah's "special company"**   "German Shot Dead," *Palestine Post,* March 24, 1946. Mann, *Sarona,* 111–38 (Hebrew).

16   **Yitzhak Sadeh, realized that this was not a regular military operation**   Yahav, *His Blood Be on His Own Head,* 96 (Hebrew).

16   **To encourage them, he told them about a man he had shot**   Mann, *Sarona,* 124 (Hebrew).

16   **the hit squad lay in wait for Wagner**   Sauer, *The Story of the Temple Society,* 260. Interview with Eitan, January 24, 2013.

17   **"It had an immediate effect"**   In time, as part of the reparations agreement between West Germany and Israel arising from the Holocaust and World War II, the State of Israel agreed to compensate the Templers for the property they had abandoned in Palestine. Mann, *The Kirya in Tel-Aviv: 1948–1955,* 29–30 (Hebrew).

17   **Haganah units began assassinating Arabs**   For example, after four Jews were killed and seven wounded in a Tel Aviv café on August 10, 1947, a five-man Haganah squad set out to kill the man identified as the commander of that action. They did not find him at home, but they killed five passersby who tried to run away. Yahav, *His Blood Be on His Own Head,* 91 (Hebrew).

17   **"personal terror operations"**   Yahav, *His Blood Be on His Own Head,* 97 (Hebrew).

18   **Yitzhak Shamir, now in command of Lehi**   Yahav, *His Blood Be on His Own Head,* 25 (Hebrew). Banai, *Anonymous Soldiers,* 243. Frank, *Deed,* 20–21 (Hebrew).

18   **Walter Edward Guinness**   Ben-Tor, *Lehi Lexicon,* 198–200. Yalin-Mor, *Lohamey Herut Israel,* 210–21 (Hebrew).

18   **Shamir ordered Moyne killed**   Interview with Shamir, January 1997. Michael J. Cohen, "The Moyne Assassination, November 1944: A Political Assessment," *Middle Eastern Studies,* vol. 15, no. 3 (1979), 358–73.

19   **"a new group of gangsters"**   Porath, *In Search of Arab Unity, 1930–1945,* 134–48 (Hebrew). Wasserstein, *The Assassination of Lord Moyne,* 72–83.

19   **bombed the British embassy in Rome**   Arnaldo Cortesi, "Rome Hunts Clues in Embassy Blast," *New York Times,* November 1, 1946.

20   **Lehi mailed letter bombs**   "Stern Group," s.111z: Alex Kellar to Trafford Smith, Colonial Office (August 16, 1946). James Robertson to Leonard Burt, Special Branch (August 26, 1946), NA KV5/30.

20   **British intelligence sources warned of a wave of attacks**   "Appreciations of the Security Problems Arising from Jewish Terrorism, Jewish Illegal Immigration, and Arab Activities," August 28, 1946, UK NA KV3/41. Interview with Paul Kedar, June 15, 2011.

"Activities of the Stern Group," James Robertson to Trafford Smith, Colonial Office, February 5, 1946, UK NA FO 371/52584. Walton, *Empire of Secrets*, 78–80.

20 **"Only these actions, these executions"** Interview with Shomron, May 26, 2011.

## CHAPTER 2: A SECRET WORLD IS BORN

21 **ambushed two Israeli buses** *Davar*, December 1, 1947. Interview with Gelber, May 16, 2011.

21 **Civil war between Palestinian Arabs and Jews had begun** Gelber, *Independence Versus Nakbah*, 119 (Hebrew).

21 **a force of five hundred guerrillas** The number five hundred was taken from Kai Bird, *The Good Spy*, 87.

22 **its high command launched Operation Starling** Danin, *Tzioni in Every Condition*, 222–25 (Hebrew).

22 **poison Tel Aviv's water supply** The poison that was to be used in Operation Atlas was arsenious oxide, and its aim, according to the participants who were interrogated violently by British intelligence, was "to inflict maximum damage" on the common enemies of the Palestinians and the Nazis—Jews, British, and Americans (UK NA KV2/455).

22 **tried to locate the former and kill him** The account of the assassination attempts on the mufti was taken from Yahav, *His Blood Be on His Own Head*, 94 (Hebrew). Gelber, *Growing a Fleur-de-Lis*, 653.

23 **the first Haganah operation to integrate human and electronic intelligence** Pedahzur, *The Israeli Secret Services*, 18. Harel, *Security and Democracy*, 94 (Hebrew).

23 **Salameh survived multiple assassination attempts** Salameh was wounded by a mortar shell in the May 31, 1948, battle for Rosh HaAyin, the springs northeast of Tel Aviv that supply the city's drinking water. He died two days later. The Mufti Haj Amin al Husseini survived all the hits against him and died a natural death in Beirut in 1974. Gelber, *Israeli-Jordanian Dialogue, 1948–1953: Cooperation, Conspiracy, or Collusion?* 119 (Hebrew).

24 **"We focused on the Arab arms acquirers"** Interview with Avraham Dar, April 18, 2012.

24 **The Arab Platoon was established** Dror, *The "Arabist" of Palmach*, 56–58 (Hebrew).

24 **Cooperation between the two units produced an attempt on the life** HHA, Testimony of Yoseph Tabenkin, 199.6.

24 **In February 1948, they ambushed al-Khatib** HHA 100.100.61. Eldar, *Flotilla 13: The Story of Israel's Naval Commando*, 107–108 (Hebrew). Yahav, *His Blood Be on His Own Head*, 95 (Hebrew).

25 **killing the five Palestinians working on it** Not all of the Arab Platoon's actions succeeded. Some of its members were caught and executed. One such failure was an attempt to use them to carry out a massacre in Gaza by poisoning the water supply. This was done in response to the invasion by the Arab states after the declaration of independence. The two men sent on the mission were caught and killed. HHA 187.80.

25 **"the Arab states have decided finally to launch a simultaneous attack"** Political Department of the Agency to Zaslani, May 12, 1948, Central Zionist Archive, S25\9390.

25 **seven armies attacked** The regular armies of six Arab states invaded Israel: Egypt, Syria, Jordan, Iraq, Lebanon, and Saudi Arabia, along with the Palestine Liberation Army, all acting in conjunction with the internal Palestinian units operating from inside the country.

25 **They far outnumbered and were infinitely better equipped** Later research into the War of Independence, some written by a group known as the New or Post-Zionist historians, because of their innovative approach to the Israel-Arab conflict (which many of the "Old Historians" considered wrong), has concluded that from the start there was parity between the Jewish and Arab forces, and that in some of the battlefields the Jews even enjoyed an advantage because of the internal divisions, quarrels, and inferior planning of the Arab side. Morris, *Righteous Victims*, 209 (Hebrew).

26 **"This will be a war of great destruction and slaughter"** The interview with Azzam, which was first published in an Egyptian newspaper in October 1947, has been cited multiple times since then and became the subject of a sharp argument over what he actually meant. Morris, *Righteous Victims*, 208. Tom Segev, "The Makings of History: The Blind Misleading the Blind," *Haaretz*, October 21, 2011.

26 **Though Israel had repelled superior armies** Morris, *Israel's Border Wars, 1949–1956*, 3 (Hebrew).

26 **They vowed to destroy Israel** Golani, *Hetz Shachor*, 13 (Hebrew).

26 **Ben-Gurion did not need to be persuaded** An important intelligence success before the establishment of the state was the outcome of the huge intelligence effort Ben-Gurion

ordered to sway the opinions of the members of the United Nations Special Committee on Palestine (UNSCOP), which was appointed in May 1947 to recommend to the General Assembly what should be done with Palestine, to be in favor of an independent Jewish state. Ronen Bergman, "A State Is Born in Palestine," *New York Times Magazine*, October 7, 2011. Interview with Elad Ben Dror, November 12, 2003. Elad Ben Dror, "The Success of the Zionist Strategy Vis-à-vis UNSCOP," Ph.D. dissertation, Bar-Ilan University.

26   **That day, he ordered the establishment of three agencies**   The Bureau of the Minister of Defense to the heads of the defense establishment and the intelligence community, *Organization of Intelligence Services*, February 15, 1959, Ministry of Defense and IDF Archives, 870.22. Ben-Gurion Diary, vol. B. 494, 590. Shiloh, *One Man's Mossad*, 120–21 (Hebrew).

27   **Abandoned Templer homes in the Sarona neighborhood**   Sauer, *The Holy Land Called: The Story of the Temple Society*, 208.

27   **nothing in those first months and years was so tidy**   Interview with Isser Harel, March 1999. Siman Tov, "The Beginning of the Intelligence Community in Israel," *Iyunim*, vol. 23.

27   **The first challenge that Ben-Gurion's spies faced**   The Irgun leader, Menachem Begin, was an extremist in his opinions, but he acted firmly to prevent the outbreak of a civil war, and despite his anger at the sinking of the *Altalena* and his differences with Ben-Gurion, he ordered his men to accept the authority of the state and to integrate into the IDF.

28   **Lehi issued several public warnings**   Sheleg, *Desert's Wind: The Story of Yehoshua Cohen*, 88–95 (Hebrew).

28   **Three young men wearing peaked caps jumped out**   United Nations Department of Public Information, Press Release PAL/298, September 18, 1948, "General Lundstrom Gives Eyewitness Account of Bernadotte's Death."

28   **The whole attack was over in seconds**   Regev, *Prince of Jerusalem*, 13–17 (Hebrew).

29   **The perpetrators were never caught**   In the late 1950s, Ben-Gurion resigned and took up residence in Kibbutz Sdeh Boker in the Negev, in a move aimed at encouraging young people to settle in the desert. Yehoshua Cohen also moved there with his family, inspired by the same pioneering spirit. In time he became a close friend and companion to Ben-Gurion, and served as his bodyguard. On one of their walks together, Cohen admitted to Ben-Gurion that it was he who had fired the shots that killed Bernadotte and that he was the person who Ben-Gurion's spies had been searching for to no avail. Bar-Zohar, *Ben-Gurion*, 316–17 (Hebrew). Regev, *Prince of Jerusalem*, 100.

29   **The Security Council condemned it as "a cowardly act"**   "The U.N. Must Act," *New York Times*, September 19, 1948.

29   **Ben-Gurion saw Lehi's rogue operation as a serious challenge**   Bar-Zohar, *Ben-Gurion*, 317.

29   **Lehi ceased to exist as an organization**   Interviews with Amnon Dror, January 1997, and Menahem Navot, April 6, 2017. Navot, *One Man's Mossad*, 24–25 (Hebrew).

29   **for his vigorous action against the underground**   Harel saw the secessionist organizations as extreme rightists or extreme leftists, and he hated both. "Even back when I was a child [he was born in Russia] I saw manifestations of violence, and arbitrary brutality and the cruel visions of the Bolshevik revolution were deeply etched into my mind. These visions aroused in me a profound and uncompromising dislike." Harel, *Security and Democracy*, 78. Interview with Harel, April 6, 2001.

29   **conducted political espionage against Ben-Gurion's political opponents**   Harel would later claim this was surveillance of elements that he suspected of forming a new underground or other subversive acts, but he was actually using the Shin Bet as a political espionage agency on Ben-Gurion's behalf. The agency was keeping tabs on Ben-Gurion's rivals and critics, even if it was clear that they were not engaged in anything illegal. The agency even set up an ostensibly commercial pro-Ben-Gurion magazine with Shin Bet funds. Called *Rimon*, it competed with the racy news magazine *Haolam Hazeh*, which attacked Ben-Gurion. Interviews with Harel, April 6, 2001, Uri Avnery, July 19, 2013, and Arie Hadar, July 8, 2011. Ronen Bergman, "The Shin Bet Secrets," *Yedioth Ahronoth*, March 23, 2007.

30   **Those diplomatic overtures obviously were not effective**   Israel State Archive 3771/70. Sutton and Shushan, *People of Secret and Hide*, 144–46 (Hebrew). Erlich, *The Lebanon Tangle 1918–1958*, 262–65 (Hebrew). Interviews with Moshe Sasson, May 1996, Reuven Erlich, December 9, 1999, and Rafi Sutton, May 9, 2012.

30   **"Sharett was vehemently opposed to the idea"**   Interview with Arthur Ben-Natan, September 13, 2010.

30   **Israeli intelligence services coalesced into the three-pronged community**   The quarreling over the allocation of authority, resources, and territory between the services has never ended. Every decade or so, prime ministers have set up a secret panel to reformulate

a "Magna Carta" for the intelligence community delineating these matters. Those original three agencies would be later joined by four others: LAKAM (acronym for the Bureau of Scientific Relations), in the Defense Ministry, engaged in technological and nuclear espionage; the Israeli Atomic Energy Commission, which supervised the country's nuclear program; the Scientific Administration, which controls, inter alia, the Biological Institute in Ness Ziona, where biological weapons and countermeasures are developed; and Nativ, which was responsible for undercover contacts with Soviet Jewry.

30 **It was also a personal victory for Isser Harel** Harel enforced iron discipline in the Mossad as well as a strict adherence to secrecy. He ordered each of the Mossad operatives to adopt a pseudonym and to give code names to each unit, operation, and agent. These code names and pseudonyms had to be used at all times, even in internal correspondence and in internal discussions. This practice has been preserved to this day.

31 **Ben-Gurion kept all of the agencies under his direct control** Under the "Residual 32 Section" of "Israel's Basic Law: Government" (in the absence of a constitution, Israel's Basic Laws are the country's highest level of legislation, and the most difficult to amend), it says that the government may do "all it considers necessary" in order to carry out its duties. In effect, this vague phrasing gave the prime ministers of Israel the authority to order secret operations and assassinations with almost no oversight by Israel's democratic institutions or the press. In the wake of a series of exposés of illegal acts by Shin Bet personnel in the mid-1980s, and the consequent dismissal of the agency's top echelon, the new leadership requested the enactment of a law that would explicitly define what was permitted and what was not. Such a law was passed by the Knesset in 2002. Since then the Mossad has deliberated about the formulation of a similar law for itself, but these deliberations have always run into a fundamental contradiction: Unlike the Shin Bet, which operates inside Israel and the territories it controls, almost everything the Mossad does constitutes a breach, sometimes flagrant, of the laws of other countries. This type of activity is very difficult if not impossible to circumscribe within the framework of legislation, not to mention that it would be public and constitute a written parliamentary confirmation that the State of Israel allows grave violations of the sovereignty of foreign countries. In May 2017, Mossad director Yossi Cohen decided to put an end to the protracted deliberations and ruled that a Mossad law would not be enacted. Interviews with Dagan, May 26, 2013, "Iftach," March 2017, "Advantage," July 2017, "Sasha," June 2015, and "Serenity," September 2017.

32 **In Israeli law, there is no death penalty** With the exception of Nazi war criminals and their abettors (applied only once, in the case of Adolf Eichmann) and the theoretical power that courts-martial have, which was exercised a few times against terrorists, only to be annulled by the Supreme Court.

33 **Duvall's real name was Shlomo Cohen-Abarbanel** Interviews with Yuval Cohen-Abarbanel, July 1997, and Haim Cohen, July 1997. Ronen Bergman, "Under the Layers of Paint," *Haaretz,* August 29, 1997.

34 **To this end, AMAN set up a unit called Intelligence Service 13** This was not the only special operations unit given this number—the marine commandos were called Shayetet (Flotilla) 13. The air force also planned to set up a Tayeset (Squadron) 13, with the mission of transporting Israeli personnel to their targets. The number appeared elsewhere as well—the official date of the Mossad's founding is December 13, 1949.

34 **"no dog, no rabies"** Interviews with Dar, January 5, 2015, and Arie Krishak, March 12, 2007.

35 **"aiming to undermine · Western confidence . . . by causing public insecurity"** Unit 131, Mordechai Ben Tzur to head of AMAN, "Events in Egypt, July–September 1954," October 5, 1954, MODA 4.768.2005.

35 **AMAN's recruits were amateurish and sloppy** Avraham Dar to AMAN director, "Report on Conversation with Defense Minister 29.12.54," January 10, 1954; and in the years that followed: Dar to AMAN Director and commander of Unit 131, "The Reasons for Leaving Unit 131," September 30, 1955; Dar to Mossad Director Meir Amit, August 29, 1967; Dar to Prime Minister Eshkol, "Prisoners in Egypt," September 27, 1967 (author's archive, received from Dar).

36 **"'We don't kill Jews,' he said"** Interview with Eitan, September 19, 2011.

36 **Harel himself said, "It never occurred to me"** Interview with Harel, March 1999.

37 **The plan unfolded perfectly at first** Interviews with Harel, April 6, 2001, Imanuel Talmor, May 1, 2013, and "Victor," September 2013.

37 **Harel's people fed the Israeli press false information** The son born to Yisraeli's wife a few months later grew up thinking his father had abandoned him and his country. Only fifty years later did he learn the truth, from the writer of this book. In my home, in May

2006, the man, Moshe Tsipper, met with Raphi Medan, one of the Mossad men who participated in the abduction. Tsipper sued the state and demanded that he be recognized as a war orphan—his father was on active service when the incident occurred—and that he be shown the relevant documentation. After a years-long process, the Mossad agreed to compensate him financially, but not to reveal the documents. Interviews with Raphi Medan and Moshe Tsipper, May 2, 2006, and Eitan, February 19, 2006. Tel Aviv District Court (in camera), *Tsipper v. Ministry of Defense,* December 11, 2013. Ronen Bergman, "Throw Away," *Yedioth Ahronoth,* May 26, 2006.

38    **were invited to Harel's home in north Tel Aviv and sworn in**    Interviews with "Patriot," August 2011, Harel, April 6, 2001, Shomron, May 26, 2011, and Shamir, January 1997. Shamir, *As a Solid Rock,* 122–24 (Hebrew). Shlomo Nakdimon, "Yitzhak Shamir: Top Secret," *Yedioth Ahronoth,* April 25, 2000.

## CHAPTER 3: THE BUREAU FOR ARRANGING MEETINGS WITH GOD

39    **Some of those infiltrators were refugees**    Morris, *Israel's Border Wars, 1949–1956,* 3–5, 28–68 (Hebrew).

39    **A young captain in Egyptian military intelligence, Mustafa Hafez**    Argaman, *It Was Top Secret,* 18 (Hebrew).

40    **altogether some one thousand civilians between 1951 and 1955**    Gilbert, *The Routledge Atlas of the Arab-Israeli Conflict,* 58. The Jewish Agency for Israel website, Fedayeen Raids 1951–56, https://web.archive.org/web/20090623224146/http:/www.jafi.org .il/education/100/maps/fed.html.

40    **"one of the three Ps—praise, payment or pussy"**    Interview with Rehavia Vardi, August 19, 1997.

40    **in ten to fifteen of those cases**    The numbers cited for agents and killings that Unit 504 was involved in at that time are estimates based on interviews. Unit 504 burned most of its records in the 1980s. Interviews with Sutton, May 9, 2012, Yaakov Nimrodi, December 14, 2010, and "Sheldon," February 1999.

40    **"It was all very, very secret"**    Interview with Natan Rotberg, July 13, 2015.

42    **"We had our limitations"**    Interview with Yigal Simon, July 29, 2012.

42    **At a secret meeting on June 11, 1953**    Cabinet Secretariat, Cabinet Decision no. 426 of June 11,1953 (author's archive, received from Gilad Livneh).

42    **"He was confident that with seven or eight good men"**    Gilad Sharon, *Sharon: The Life of a Leader,* 82 (Hebrew).

43    **Unit 101 came into being**    Unit 101 was given the same number as the special force to which the famed British officer Orde Charles Wingate had belonged in Ethiopia and Eritrea during World War II. Prior to that war, Wingate had been posted in Palestine, where he had headed the joint British-Jewish Night Squads. He was considered a hero by many IDF senior figures who had served under him in the Night Squads. The date of the formation of the unit is taken from a lecture given by Ariel Sharon in Sderot on March 20, 2003.

43    **"This unit was set up for the purpose of operations across the border"**    Sharon, *Life of a Leader,* 552.

43    **the first to try out the new and still secret Israeli-made Uzi**    Interview with Uzi Gal, November 2002.

44    **Sharon, craving action, drew up plans**    Interview with Uzi Eilam, December 2, 2009.

44    **The government vowed to retaliate**    Morris, *Israel's Border Wars, 1949–1956,* 274–76 (Hebrew).

44    **"In the Qibya operation"**    Ilil Blum, "Father's Great Spirit," *Yedioth Jerusalem,* May 1, 2009.

45    **The death toll was sixfold higher**    Oddly, the number of the resolution condemning Israel for the raid was 101. Security Council Resolution 101 (1953), November 24, 1953 (S/3139/Rev.2).

45    **Unit 101 "proved . . . that there was no mission it could not carry out"**    From a lecture given by Sharon in Sderot on March 20, 2003.

45    **Dayan merged it with the Paratroopers Brigade**    Dayan, *Story of My Life,* 113–15 (Hebrew).

46    **Sharett wrote in his diary**    Sharett, "Personal Diary," vol. C, 823 (Hebrew). Gratitude to Yaakov Sharett, son of Moshe, who called my attention to this entry.

47    **In the middle of the 1950s, Hafez was winning**    Morris, *Israel's Border Wars, 1949–1956,* 81, 101, 343–45 (Hebrew).

47　**Yet he was a vague figure, cloaked in shadows**　Interview with Nimrodi, December 14, 2010. Thanks to Ofer Nimrodi and Shimon Shapira for their help in setting up the interview.

48　**the seminal formulation of Israeli militarism**　Aluf Benn, "Militaristic and Post-Zionist," *Haaretz*, May 9, 2011.

49　**"This is our generation's destiny"**　Bar-On, *Moshe Dayan*, 128–29 (Hebrew).

49　**Natan promised his uncle, Shmaryahu, that he would avenge Roi, his son**　Interview with Rotberg, August 3, 2015.

50　**"which sets off the bomb, and—*kaboom!*"**　Interview with Rotberg, August 3, 2015.

51　**"When he pulled the book out of the package"**　Egyptian Military Intelligence, *Inquiry into the Death of Colonel Hafez*, July 16, 1956 (author's archive, received from Nimrodi).

51　**The same day Hafez was killed**　Dar, encouraged by his success, suggested to Dayan that he go a step further and use a double agent to assassinate a Syrian general, the chief of Military Intelligence. Dayan approved the detailed operational order and passed it on to Ben-Gurion but he demurred. The Israeli PM was afraid that repeated assassinations of senior government officials would motivate the Arabs to retaliate against their counterparts in Israel, perhaps even against himself, and did not approve the operation. Interview with Dar, October 8, 2015.

## CHAPTER 4: THE ENTIRE SUPREME COMMAND, WITH ONE BLOW

53　**try to make it look as if the plane had crashed because of a technical fault**　Israeli military censors barred publication of details about the operation until 1989. Recording of Mordechai Bar-On about Dayan, from the seminar "Operation Rooster 56," March 5, 2015.

53　**AMAN assigned the task of identifying and tracking the air convoy**　Interview with Gelber, May 16, 2011. Uri Dromi, "Urgent Message to the CoS: The Egyptian Code Has Been Decrypted," *Haaretz*, August 29, 2011.

53　**Days passed slowly, radio operators patiently waiting**　Interview with Yom-Tov Eini, January 19, 1999. Argaman, *It Was Top Secret*, 39–60.

54　**Mattias "Chatto" Birger, commander of the air force's 119 Squadron**　Tsiddon-Chatto, *By Day, By Night, Through Haze and Fog*, 220–21 (Hebrew).

55　**"the downing of the Egyptian General Staff"**　Nevertheless, it's difficult to find grounds for the claim about its immediate effect. In Egypt, nothing has ever been published about the incident. In Israel as well—as far as the research for this book has managed to discover—no specific information has been registered regarding the identity of the people on board the Ilyushin that blew up, or about any problems faced by the Egyptian high command in the wake of the interception. Interviews with David Siman Tov and Shai Herschkowitz, February 12, 2017, Yoram Meital, October 18, 2013, and Motti Golani, January 15, 2013.

57　**ordered that it be leaked to *The New York Times***　On Monday, June 4, 1956, *The New York Times* published the news that the text of the speech was in American hands, and the next day it ran lengthy excerpts from it, under a heavy bank of headlines: KHRUSHCHEV TALK ON STALIN BARES DETAILS OF RULE BASED ON TERROR. CHARGES PLOT FOR KREMLIN PURGES. DEAD DICTATOR PAINTED AS SAVAGE, HALF-MAD AND POWER-CRAZED. The publication sent shock waves around the world, exactly what the CIA was looking for.

57　**The secret alliance between American and Israeli intelligence was born**　Other Israeli and American intelligence organizations besides the Mossad and the CIA have forged links with each other as well. Particularly important was the relationship between the American NSA and its Israeli counterpart, Unit 8200 of AMAN. Among the documents that Edward Snowden leaked, there were several historical surveys of these relations, dating back to the early 1960s and documenting deep cooperation in espionage against common adversaries in the Middle East. Perusal of Snowden documents in a vault of *The Intercept*, New York, May 2016, made possible through assistance and cooperation of that website's staff, with special thanks to Henrik Moltke.

57　**Israel's Sinai Campaign of 1956**　Interview with Harel, April 6, 2001. The most detailed report on the Suez Campaign and Israeli gains and losses may be found in Golani, *There Will Be War Next Summer*, 597–620 (Hebrew).

57　**"the periphery doctrine"**　David Kimche, a senior Mossad commander in Africa, explained: "It cost us the same amount of money to send over to Africa an expert on henhouses or an instructor on intelligence gathering. The latter would end up meeting the emperor. The former would end up in a henhouse. It's obvious what our first choice was. Intelligence liaisons were the fastest way to foster an intimate relationship." Interviews with David Kimche, August 18, 1998, Harel, April 6, 2001, Reuven Merhav, April 22, 2014, Ben-Natan, September 13, 2010, Tamar Golan, September 24, 2007, Hannan Bar-On, December 30, 1997, Yoav Biran, April 22, 1999, Lubrani, December 26, 1997, and Arie Oded, September 16, 1998. *Pilpul in Addis Ababa to the MFA—Report on meeting with Ethiopian Emperor and chief of staff,* August 25, 1957, ISA 3740/9. Black and Morris, *Israel's Secret Wars,* 186.

58    **the CIA provided funds for its activities**    Ben-Gurion explained the nature of this alliance in a letter he sent to President Dwight Eisenhower: "With the goal of erecting a high dam to stem the Nasserite-Soviet tidal wave, we have begun tightening our links with several states on the outside perimeter of the Middle East. . . . Our goal is to organize a group of countries, not necessarily an official alliance, that would be able to resist Soviet expansion by proxy, such as Nasser." Eshed, *One Man's Mossad,* 277. The C'LIL agreement called for periodic meetings between the heads of the intelligence bodies of the three states, with a different country serving as host each time. The three nations also set up a complex mechanism for intelligence coordination and information exchange on various issues. Israel considered C'LIL an unprecedented strategic achievement, as Israel had positioned itself as the central axis in a military-intelligence pact. In regional disputes that arose between Turkey and Iran, C'LIL served as a platform and Israel as arbitrator. "At the time," explained Reuven Merhav, a Mossad official who was involved in planning the C'LIL meetings, "all the heads of intelligence in Turkey, Iran, and Ethiopia had a direct link to the boss, whether it was the shah or emperor Haile Selassie. Through C'LIL, it was possible to pass messages and ideas directly to the ruler. [The original triple alliance] gave us a triple orgasm, and with the inclusion of Ethiopia, a quadruple orgasm." The CIA wanted to express its appreciation for the establishment of Trident, and it financed the construction of a two-story building on a hilltop outside Tel Aviv to serve as the alliance's HQ. Interviews with Reuven Merhav, April 22, 2014, Harel, March 1999, and Yossi Alpher, May 18, 2015. Ronen Bergman, "Israel and Africa: Military and Intelligence Liaisons," Ph.D. dissertation, Cambridge University, 53–78. Bureau of Minister of Defense, report on meeting between Lt. Col. Vardi and Emperor of Ethiopia, February 24, 1958, Ministry of Defense and IDF Archives (MODA) 63-10-2013.

58    **Bauer left him alone, with the classified documents lying on the desktop**    Interviews with Zvi Aharoni, July 1998, Medan, June 30, 2015, and "Lexicon," March 2016. Mossad, *Report Regarding Dybbuk,* Zvi Aharoni, March 4, 1960. Mossad, *Operation Eichmann: A Report on Stage A,* Zvi Aharoni, undated (both in author's archive, received from "Lexicon").

58    **Ben-Gurion authorized Harel to go to Buenos Aires**    Interviews with Zvi Aharoni, July 1998, Amram Aharoni, October 21, 2012, and "Ethan," May 2016. Neal Bascomb, *Hunting Eichmann,* 208–18 (Hebrew).

60    **Harel was considered the strongman**    An expression of Harel's unprecedented power can be found in the way he himself described, to Mossad historians in the early 1980s, his relationship with the prime minister, apparently unaware of the grave flaws in his understanding of democracy. "Ben-Gurion never gave us operational orders. He would express some concern or wish for something. He did not know how to translate his ideas into the language of operations, and indeed he did not need to know. The prime minister should deal with setting policy and not with details, on the basis of certain principles, of course." The Mossad summed it up, "Isser [Harel] generally did not report to the prime minister precisely what he was doing and how he was operating." Mossad, History Department, "The German Scientists Affair," 1982, 14, henceforth Mossad German Scientists Dossier (author's archive, received from "Toblerone").

## CHAPTER 5: "AS IF THE SKY WERE FALLING ON OUR HEADS"

61    **the new Al-Zafer (the Victor) model**    Central Intelligence Agency, Scientific Intelligence Memorandum, "The United Arab Republic Missile Program," February 26, 1963, https://www.cia.gov/library/readingroom/docs/DOC_0001173825.pdf.

61    **the Egyptian military was now capable of hitting any point**    Jay Walz, "Nasser Exhibits Military Might," *New York Times,* July 24, 1962.

62    **"Former German Nazis are now helping Nasser"**    Edwin Eitan, *Canadian Jewish Chronicle,* May 10, 1963.

62 **a humiliating failure for Harel's Mossad** Later examination revealed that Mossad personnel in Europe had in fact garnered various items of information in the years prior to the parade indicating that Nasser was recruiting German scientists. The Mossad tried to blame Military Intelligence and the Defense Ministry for the failure, claiming it had conveyed the information to them but they had made light of it. Mossad German Scientists Dossier, 8–10.

62 **the German scientists developing the Egyptian missiles** Harel allocated the task of uncovering the conspiracies that he was sure veterans of the Wehrmacht, the Gestapo, and the SS were plotting to a group of German-speaking Mossad personnel. This unit, code-named Amal, did not discover anything, because there were no such plots. Embarrassingly, the one case in which former figures in Hitler's advanced weaponry program were in fact involved, the Egyptian missile project, remained undetected. Yossi Chen, the Mossad, History Department, "Staff Organization, Amal-Meser," May 2007.

62 **"I felt helpless"** Many Mossad and AMAN staffers interviewed for this book recall a similar sense of shock and anxiety when the first details about the German scientists and their project came out. Moti Kfir of AMAN's Unit 188 said: "I had a big fear, a real sense of existential danger." Interviews with Moti Kfir, June 9, 2011, and Ben-Natan, September 13, 2010.

62 **"It was one of the most important and traumatic events"** Mossad German Scientists Dossier, 2.

64 **The document was an order written in 1962 by Pilz** Mossad German Scientists Dossier, 17.

64 **Harel's plan, then, was to kidnap or to eliminate the Germans** Interview with Eitan, September 1, 2013.

64 **Harel decided to act against Krug** Interview with Harel, April 6, 2001. Mossad German Scientists Dossier, 39.

64 **On Monday, September 10, at 5:30 P.M.** Mossad German Scientists Dossier, 40–41.

65 **Krug met Oded in the lobby** Eyewitnesses at the Ambassador Hotel, including the reception clerks, and at the Intra offices who were questioned later by the police said Saleh was "of Levantine appearance." An identikit reconstruction of his likeness was printed prominently in the press with reports of Krug's disappearance. "The truth is that the identikit was quite like me," Oded says with a smile. It meant that he'd been burned, and he was told not to travel to Germany for ten years. Oded says that from the moment the door closed behind Krug he "disengaged from the entire operation" and that "he has no idea what happened to the German." Interview with Oded, August 3, 2015.

65 **"Do exactly what we say or we'll finish you off"** Mossad German Scientists Dossier, 43–44.

66 **the Mossad launched a wide-ranging disinformation operation** Mossad German Scientists Dossier, 44–45. Interview with "Patriot," September 2013.

66 **"yielded much fruit"** Mossad German Scientists Dossier, 45.

66 **to take Krug to a deserted spot north of Tel Aviv and shoot him** The execution of Krug really angered some of the few Mossad people who knew about it. Zvi Aharoni (who later on was to become a bitter opponent of Harel) said, "This was an unforgivable act, a stain on all of us." Rafi Eitan observed: "That was Isser's way. I don't think he got Ben-Gurion's okay." Interviews with "Patriot," August 2011, Zvi Aharoni, July 1998, and Amram Aharoni, May 3, 2016.

67 **Isser Harel resented Unit 188** Head of AMAN Chaim Herzog to chief of staff, January 2, 1962. Shaul Avigur, Report of the Committee for Examining the Intelligence Community, July 31, 1963, 3, MODA 7-64-2012.

67 **188 had a veteran operative under deep cover in Egypt** Mossad German Scientists Dossier, 45.

67 **Yariv ordered Natan Rotberg to start preparing the bombs** Interview with Rotberg, August 3, 2015.

68 **Unit 188 also helped the French smuggle explosives into Cairo** Yosef Yariv, commander of Unit 188, coordinated these activities in Paris, together with deputy AMAN chief Prof. Yuval Neeman (a prominent physicist and one of the founders of the Israeli nuclear project), who said that "If I saw that the French wanted something from us, a murder for example, that if it came out later, would really embarrass the State of Israel, I decided that I would make the decision, and if there was a fiasco, I would bear full responsibility." Interviews with Yuval Neeman, August 2011, Harel, August 1998, Meir Amit, July 12, 2005. Bar-Zohar, *Phoenix: Shimon Peres—A Political Biography*, 344 (Hebrew). Harel, *Security and Democracy*, 295.

68    **Brunner received a large envelope in Damascus**   In July 1980, this time with the enthusiastic authorization of Prime Minister Begin, the Mossad sent another letter bomb to Brunner. The ostensible sender was the "Association of Friends of Medicinal Plants" because Brunner was known to be a firm believer in this form of medicine. He opened it and it exploded, causing the loss of several fingers. Interview with Rotberg, August 3, 2015, and "the Pilot," March 2015. Adam Chandler, "Eichmann's Best Man Lived and Died in Syria," *Atlantic,* December 1, 2014.

68    **"I oppose any action that I don't control"**   Interview with Eitan, December 1, 2012.

68    **getting to the Germans in Egypt turned out to be a very complicated matter**   Mossad German Scientists Dossier, 52.

70    **The next target on Harel's hit list was Dr. Hans Kleinwächter**   Interviews with Harel, August 1998, and Zvi Aharoni, July 1998. Mossad German Scientists Dossier, 74.

70    **"We needed to wait a bit and create a trap of our own"**   Interview with Eitan, December 1, 2012. Mossad German Scientists Dossier, 61.

70    **Vallentin had grasped that Kleinwächter would be the Mossad's next target**   Interview with Zvi Aharoni, July 1998.

71    **Aharoni got out of the car and went up to Kleinwächter**   Mossad German Scientists Dossier, 62–64. Interviews with Nehemia Meiri, June 12, 2012, and Harel, April 6, 2001.

71    **These operations also failed dismally**   Bar-Zohar, *Issar Harel and Israel's Security Services,* 237–38 (Hebrew).

72    **information gathered in Cairo about a Dr. Hans Eisele**   Mossad German Scientists Dossier, 66.

72    **three journalists, whom he subsequently recruited into the Mossad**   His new recruits were Shmuel Segev of *Maariv,* Naftali Lavie of *Haaretz,* and Yeshayahu Ben-Porat of *Yedioth Ahronoth.* "Disenchik [Aryeh Disenchik, *Maariv's* editor in chief] supported Golda and Isser," Segev said. "He wanted to make use of my materials to demolish Ben-Gurion and Peres, and then prevented me from speaking about the subject because he knew that my position was different." Interview with Shmuel Segev, June 6, 2010.

73    **Harel's stories generated a media frenzy**   Bar-Zohar, *Ben-Gurion,* 534–35.

73    **Ben-Gurion tried to calm Harel down**   Meir Amit to Aharon Yariv (handwritten), Office of the Chief of AMAN, March 28, 1964 (author's archive, received from Amos Gilboa).

73    **"He was not, in my opinion, quite sane"**   Bar-Zohar, *Phoenix,* 362 (Hebrew).

73    **It ended, as most obsessions do, in Harel's own destruction**   Harel later gave his version to a number of journalists and writers, and this was reflected in their writings, which were very supportive of Harel. Among these writings were Kotler, *Joe Returns to the Limelight,* 34–38; Bar-Zohar, *Isser Harel and Israel's Security Services,* 239–49 (Hebrew), and Caroz (Harel's deputy), *The Man with Two Hats,* 160–63 (Hebrew).

73    **Ben-Gurion summoned Harel to his office**   Bar-Zohar, *Ben-Gurion,* 537–38. Bar-Zohar, *Phoenix,* 361 (Hebrew).

73    **replaced by Meir Amit, the chief of AMAN**   Yossi Melman and Dan Raviv, *The Imperfect Spies,* 122. Amit, *Head On,* 102–103 (Hebrew). Amit to Yariv (handwritten), March 28, 1964.

74    **Ben-Gurion squabbled ceaselessly with Golda Meir**   The clash between Ben-Gurion and Meir over the German scientists was one of several sharp confrontations between Labor Party leaders, most of which can be seen as a steady process of a decline in support for "the Old Man," as Ben-Gurion was called, and the intergenerational struggle to succeed him. Meir and her allies in the old guard feared Ben-Gurion was going to go over their heads and pass the baton of leadership directly to the younger generation, led by Dayan and Peres. Bar-Zohar, *Ben-Gurion,* 542–47.

74    **took over a Mossad in disarray**   Interview with Amit, April 2006. AMAN head and acting Mossad director Amit to Defense Minister, "Preliminary thoughts on reorganization of the intelligence community," May 20, 1963, MODA 24-64-2012.

74    **As Israeli diplomats reported to the Foreign Ministry**   Israeli Mission in Cologne to Foreign Ministry, September 20, 1963 (author's archive, received from "Paul").

74    **a drastic reduction of the resources being devoted to the hunt for Nazi criminals**   Among the beneficiaries of that edict was a fifty-three-year-old German doctor named Josef Mengele, Auschwitz's "Angel of Death." In mid-1962, in the wake of the successful abduction of Eichmann, Harel ordered Operation Encore to examine the information gathered about "Meltzer," the code name for Mengele. On July 23, 1962, at the same time as the missile tests in Egypt, Zvi Aharoni and Zvi Malchin identified a person closely resembling the description of Mengele in a farm in Brazil, but Amit ordered that activity on the subject of Vipers (Tzif'onim in Hebrew), the Mossad code name for the hunt for the

Nazis, be cut down and in October 1963 instructed Junction to "handle the subject only to the degree that it was able, in addition to its main missions." Mengele lived for another decade before drowning while swimming in the sea off the Brazilian coast in 1979. Mossad, History Department, *Looking for the Needle in the Haystack: Following the Footsteps of Josef Mengele,* 2007, 65–78 (author's archive, received from "Midburn"). Interviews with Zvi Aharoni, July 1998, Amram Aharoni, October 21, 2011, Eitan, November 1, 2012, Medan, June 30, 2015, and Amit, May 2005. Ronen Bergman, "Why Did Israel Let Mengele Go?" *New York Times,* September 6, 2017.

75　**there was a blast in the post office**　Interviews with Samir Raafat, September 1995, and Rotberg, March 5, 2012. Samir Raafat, "The Nazi Next Door," *Egyptian Mail,* January 28, 1995.

75　**convinced Amit that targeted killings should only be used very sparingly**　Mossad German Scientists Dossier, 80. Interviews with Amit, April 2006, and Eitan, November 1, 2012.

77　**"the most dangerous man in Europe"**　UK NA, KV 2\403\86109.

77　**The Mossad file on the countess**　Mossad German Scientists Dossier, 88.

77　**"She was involved in everything"**　Interview with Medan, July 10, 2007.

79　**though written in dry professional language**　Mossad German Scientists Dossier, 136.

79　**"Skorzeny was a giant. A hulk of a man"**　Ahituv to Eitan and to the Mossad headquarters, September 14, 1964 (shown to the author by "Raphael").

80　**He pointed to an X inked next to his name**　Raphi Medan, unpublished manuscript, 113.

80　**"An exchange of views"**　There was another request: Skorzeny noted that the head of the Jewish community in Frankfurt had asked a German court to ban distribution of the books in Germany, because he was a fugitive from justice. He wanted the Mossad to make public that the books were being used in the training of IDF officers so he could use that as evidence in the trial. Mossad German Scientists Dossier, 92.

80　**Skorzeny's conditions sparked a sharp argument in the Mossad**　Interviews with Amit, May 2005, Eitan, November 1, 2012, Medan, June 30, 2015, Avner Barnea (Shin Bet director Ahituv's bureau chief, who heard much from his boss about the recruitment of Skorzeny), May 30, 2011, and "Milen," August 2015. Very partial but accurate reporting on the recruitment of Skorzeny appears in the book by Argaman, *The Shadow War,* 22–38 (Hebrew).

81　**"To my astonishment"**　Interview with Medan, June 30, 2015.

83　**Skorzeny invited other former Wehrmacht officers**　Skorzeny remained connected to the Mossad until his death in 1975 (when ex-comrades from the Wehrmacht attended his funeral and gave the Heil Hitler salute) and helped the organization a great deal even after the scientists affair was over. Vallentin also continued serving for many years. In 1969, Harry Barak asked him to agree to be "transferred" from MI6 to the Mossad although he had actually been run only by the Mossad all along. After that he was aware that he was functioning as an Israeli agent. Mossad German Scientists Dossier, 95–96. Interviews with Medan, June 30, 2015, "Toblerone," January 2014, and "Patriot," July 2015.

83　**Thanks to the new wealth of information from this operation**　Mossad German Scientists Dossier, 100.

83　**carried a locked case containing a number of documents**　Copy of dossier handed to Strauss (author's archive, received from "Paul"). Mossad German Scientists Dossier, 109.

84　**Peres and Strauss were architects of the restitution agreement**　Medan, unpublished manuscript, 116. Interviews with Medan, June 30, 2015, and Shimon Peres, August 4, 2015.

## CHAPTER 6: A SERIES OF CATASTROPHES

86　**Amit wanted to establish a single operations division in the Mossad**　Interviews with Shamir, January 1997, and Amit, April 2006.

87　**Operation Diamond**　The dossier on Operation Diamond was shown to the author by Amit, May 23, 2005. Black and Morris, *Israel's Secret Wars,* 206–10.

87　**the Mossad received the right to establish a permanent station**　Mossad Director Bureau, "The Ben Barka Affair," memorandum submitted to the inquiry panel on the subject, February 21, 1966 (author's archive, received from "Alen"). Caroz, *The Man with Two Hats,* 164–65 (Hebrew).

87　**The height of the cooperation**　Interviews with Eitan, September 19, 2011, Shlomo

Gazit, November 29, 2016, Amit, April 2006, and Navot, April 6, 2017. Meeting protocol between the PM Levi Eshkol and head of the Mossad, Meir Amit, April 2006 (author's archive, received from "Alen").

87    **"This sensational material"**   Mossad Director Bureau, "Ben Barka Affair," February 21, 1966, 4.

88    **Eli Cohen, who'd penetrated the ruling circles in Damascus**   Segev, *Alone in Damascus*, 16–18 (Hebrew).

88    **under pressure from his operators**   Segev, *Alone in Damascus*, 262. Interview with Shumel Segev, June 6, 2010.

88    **was a serious and unprofessional error**   Segev, *Alone in Damascus*, 13–39.

88    **"Eli Cohen was one of the people who went through life walking sideways"**   Interview with Kfir, June 9, 2011.

88    **The letter bomb sent to Brunner**   This account was supplied by Lt. Col. Ahmed Suedani, in charge of internal security in Syria, who was the first to suspect Cohen, in an interview with *Al Usbua al Arabi*, London, March 1, 1965, translated into Hebrew by AMAN's Unit 550, MODA 1093/04/638.

89    **Cohen was arrested, brutally tortured**   Protocol of the trial of Eli Cohen, MODA 1093/04/636.

89    **"I looked at him, at my Eli, on Syrian television"**   Interview with Gedaliah Khalaf, July 12, 1996.

89    **Amit's Mossad, so freshly confident, was humiliated**   The story of Eli Cohen has been told in numerous books and movies, and many streets and public buildings are named after him in Israel. He is considered one of the most prominent models and heroes in the country's history. The Mossad Academy at Glilot, a building erected with CIA funds, bears his name.

90    **another hard blow for the Mossad**   Ronen Bergman, "Gone in the Smoke," *Yedioth Ahronoth*, September 19, 2003.

90    **regarded the downfall of the two spies as a national disaster**   Interview with Kfir, June 9, 2011.

90    **Cukurs, it emerged, had burned alive some of Yariv's relatives and friends**   Medan, unpublished manuscript, 92. Interviews with Medan, June 30, 2015, and Amos Gilboa, March 18, 2015.

90    **received permission to have Cukurs eliminated**   Some Mossad veterans from this period, among them Mike Harari, claim that Amit was envious of Isser Harel's success in catching Eichmann, and that he also wanted to go down in history as having eliminated a Nazi criminal. Interview with Mike Harari, March 29, 2014.

91    **Then the third assassin**   Sodit-Sharon, a leading Etzel fighter, had a reputation for being especially daring and wild. In 1952 he tried to assassinate the West German chancellor, Konrad Adenauer, by means of a letter bomb he mailed from France—an attempt to torpedo the reparations agreement with Israel. A German security man was killed trying to defuse it. Sodit-Sharon was caught with explosives in France and sentenced to four months, after which he was deported to Israel. Later, he claimed he had made the attempt on Adenauer under orders from Menachem Begin. Back in Israel, on June 16, 1960, he was recruited by Harel to the Mossad's Mifratz special-ops unit.

92    **"Those Who Will Never Forget"**   Interview with Gad Shimron, August 16, 2015. An exhaustive description of the operation can be found in Shimron's book *The Execution of the Hangman of Riga*.

92    **Inside the Mossad**   Interviews with Medan, June 30, 2015, Harari, April 11, 2014, and Amit, April 2006.

92    **one of the commanders of the Moroccan intelligence service**   Mossad Director Bureau, "Ben Barka Affair," February 21, 1966, 3.

92    **"On the one hand they've given us these tapes"**   Protocol of meeting between Prime Minister Levi Eshkol and General M. Amit, Dan Hotel, Tel Aviv, October 4, 1965, 2 (author's archive, received from "Alen").

92    **The opposition leader Mehdi Ben Barka**   Bergman and Nakdimon, "The Ghosts of Saint-Germain Forest," *Yedioth Ahronoth*, March 20, 2015.

92    **"We faced a dilemma"**   Interview with Amit, May 2005.

93    **they took it upon themselves to handle the corpse**   Mossad, Aterna File, Junction, Colossus, 325 various cables and memos, September–November 1965 (author's archive, received from "Alen").

93    **"I won't take any steps without telling you"**   Meeting between Eshkol and Amit, October 4, 1965, 2.

94 **"The Mossad, and through it the state"** Isser Harel, intelligence adviser to Prime Minister Levi Eshkol, "Head of the Mossad and the Adviser" (undated, apparently late October 1965) and attached memo in Harel's handwriting titled "Notes on the report itself" (author's archive, received from "Alen").

94 **he informed high-ranking party members of the details** Ronen Bergman and Shlomo Nakdimon, "The Ghosts of Saint-Germain Forest," *Yedioth Ahronoth,* March 20, 2015. Interview with David Golomb, March 13, 2015.

94 **"I should topple Eshkol, and take his place?"** From transcripts of interviews conducted by the journalist Shlomo Nakdimon (author's archive, courtesy of Shlomo Nakdimon).

94 **When Harel's vitriolic attacks did not subside** Ronen Bergman and Shlomo Nakdimon, "The Ghosts of Saint-Germain Forest," *Yedioth Ahronoth,* March 20, 2015.

95 **And, indeed, there was enough material** Interviews with "Thunder," February 2013, and "Ross," January 2015.

95 **Amit gave Yisraeli's file to a veteran of the Mossad** Interviews with Dar, January 28, 2015, Harel, March 1999, Amit, April 2006, David Vital, December 22, 2010, and "Hurkenus," June 2012.

95 **"we must never get involved"** Interview with Amit, April 2006.

95 **The predominant figure conducting these inquiries was Michael "Mike" Harari** Ronen Bergman, "Harari Code," *Yedioth Ahronoth,* April 4, 2014.

96 **Harari was born in Tel Aviv in 1927** Interview with Harari, March 23, 2014.

96 **he was sent to Europe** Interviews with Harari, March 23, 2014, and Aaron Klein, October 6, 2014.

97 **he submitted his doctrine to the heads of the Mossad** Interview with Harari, March 10, 2014. At one of our meetings, Harari showed me the documentation of the founding of the new Caesarea, as presented to the heads of the Mossad, and signed with his code name, Shvat (the name of a month in the Hebrew calendar).

98 **"This phenomenal record"** Interview with "Ethan," May 2015.

98 **The perfect candidate was of European appearance** Interview with Kfir, June 9, 2011.

99 **From those pools of potential recruits** Interview with Harari, February 12, 2014.

100 **"The desired warrior has to be a Zionist"** Interview with Kfir, June 9, 2011.

100 **Harari also initiated one other particularly ambitious recruitment program** Interviews with Harari, April 11, 2014, and Aaron Klein, October 6, 2014.

101 **the Mossad actually became an early pioneer in gender equality** Vered Ramon Rivlin, "There Is Nothing to Stop a Woman from Becoming the Director of the Mossad," *Lady Globes,* September 12, 2012.

101 **"A team made up of members of both sexes"** Interview with "Ethan," January 2015.

101 **Skills are honed in a series of practice missions** The natural wariness that is part of the Israeli character makes the country a nearly ideal training ground, without any need to send Mossad cadets overseas until the very end of their course. Long years of Palestinian terrorism have made the average Israeli cautious in the extreme. Often these exercises are carried out "against" former Mossad employees, who agree to be the targets of surveillance, burglaries, or attempts to establish contact with them under false identities.

102 **The cover story, molded over time** Interview with "Emerald," June 2015.

102 **simulating arrest and brutal interrogation** Interview with "Kurtz," October 2005.

103 **Harari introduced iron discipline into Caesarea** Interview with "Ethan," May 2015.

103 **the unit needed a civilian shipping vessel** The missions were part of operations Sauce (*Rotev* in Hebrew) and Porcupine (*Dorban*), in which Israel provided massive military aid for the royalists of North Yemen, in cooperation with the British MI6 and Saudi Arabian intelligence, against revolutionaries who had seized power with Egyptian assistance. Alpher, *Periphery,* 67–69. Interviews with Harari, March 23, 2014, Klein, May 28, 2014, Alpher, May 18, 2015, and "Shaul," July 2011.

104 **"We were not ready for this new menace"** Interview with Harari, March 23, 2014.

## CHAPTER 7: "ARMED STRUGGLE IS THE ONLY WAY TO LIBERATE PALESTINE"

105 **Refugees were settled into Gaza** On the eve of the war, the population of the Gaza Strip was a little over 70,000, and in a census taken in 1967, it was 350,000. Kabha, *The Palestinian People: Seeking Sovereignty and State,* 157–58. CIA World FactBook, https://www.cia.gov/library/publications/the-world-factbook/geos/gz.html; United States Census Bureau, International Programs, International Data Base, https://www.census.gov/population

/international/data/idb/region.php?N=%20Results%20&T=13&A=separate&RT=0&Y
=1967&R=-1&C=GZ.

106   **Among them was a boy named Khalil al-Wazir**   Zelkovitz, *The Fatah: Islam, Nationality, and the Politics of an Armed Struggle*, 25–26 (Hebrew).

106   **"sought out mujahideen"**   The literal meaning of *mujahideen* is "people engaged in
jihad." It is used to describe guerrilla fighters or—in Israeli and Western parlance—
terrorists. The quote from al-Wazir is taken from Sayigh, *Armed Struggle and the Search for
State*, 81.

106   **Arafat's place of birth is disputed**   Cobban, *The Palestinian Liberation Organization:
People, Power and Politics*, 6–7. Yaari, *Fatah*, 9–17 (Hebrew). Zelkovitz, *The Fatah*, 25–26
(Hebrew).

107   **decided the Palestinians could end their plight only by engaging in independent
operations**   Sayigh, *Armed Struggle*, 84, 85n.

107   **Arafat and Abu Jihad relocated to Kuwait**   Sayigh, *Armed Struggle*, 85.

108   **expressed in the Palestinian National Convenant**   On the early founding documents
of the Fatah, see Sayigh, *Armed Struggle*, 88–89.

108   **two Israeli spies filed the first field reports on the organization**   Mossad, History
Department, *Ladiyyah: The Mistarev and the Warrior*, 1989, 42 (author's archive, received
from "Lindt"). The Shin Bet, *The Mistaravim Affair*, undated (author's archive, received
from "Twins"). Interviews with Harel, April 6, 2001, Sami Moriah, August 12, 2013, Shay
Yisrael, October 13, 2016, and Hadar, September 1, 2013. Ronen Bergman, "Double Identity," *Yedioth Ahronoth*, August 30, 2013.

109   **Fatah was "something entirely different"**   Mossad, History Department, *Ladiyyah:
The Mistarev and the Warrior*, 1989, 54.

109   **an attempt to bomb Israel's National Water Carrier**   Yaari, *Fatah*, 40–41 (Hebrew).

109   **"an unyielding campaign to prevent [Israel] from realizing its dream"**   Interview
with Salah Bitar, September 11, 1963, quoted in Segev, *Alone in Damascus*, 223.

109   **arrested in Gaza a whole week before the launch date**   Cobban, *Palestinian Liberation Organization*, 33.

109   **Another group was also arrested in Lebanon**   Yaari, *Fatah*, 40–41 (Hebrew).

109   **failed to go off and were discovered by a security patrol**   Yaari, *Fatah*, 9 (Hebrew).
Cobban, *Palestinian Liberation Organization*, 33. Sayigh, *Armed Struggle*, 107–8.

110   **planted microphones in the apartment**   Mossad, History Department, *Uri Yisrael
("Ladiyyah")—a Unique Operational Figure*, 1995 (author's archive, received from "Lindt").

110   **"Arafat's true nature was apparent even back then"**   Interview with Eitan, January
24, 2013.

110   **Fatah carried out more and more guerrilla attacks**   Pedahzur, *The Israeli Secret Services and the Struggle Against Terrorism*, 30.

111   **"Too bad they didn't listen to me"**   Interview with Eitan, January 24, 2013.

111   **there were more attacks**   Cobban, *Palestinian Liberation Organization*, 33.

111   **"We have three targets"**   "Meeting Between Eshkol and Amit," October 8, 1965, 5.

112   **Arafat and Abu Jihad were in Damascus**   Segev, *Alone in Damascus*, 29.

113   **"We didn't want to give Fatah credit"**   Interview with Shlomo Gazit, September 12,
2016.

113   **In early 1967, the situation worsened rapidly**   "Operation Tophet," *Maarakhot*, April
1984, 18–32. Sayigh, *Armed Struggle*, 211–12.

113   **Many Arabs believed that at last the time had come for the liquidation of the
State of Israel**   A large part of the deterioration in the situation between Israel and the
Arab states stemmed from the malevolent interference of Soviet intelligence. Ronen Berg-
man, "How the KGB Started the War That Changed the Middle East," *New York Times*,
June 7, 2017. Interviews with Shimon Shamir, April 6, 2017, Michael Oren, April 6, 2017,
and Ami Gluska, April 6, 2017.

113   **gave a speech . . . that only made things worse**   Eshkol was very hesitant about going
to war without American approval, and he was even more hesitant when, at a meeting between Mossad chief Amit and the CIA station head in Israel, John Hadden, the latter
threatened, "If you attack, the United States will land forces on Egypt's side to defend it."
Amit responded: "I do not believe [what I am hearing]." Mossad, report on the meeting with
John Hadden, May 25, 1967 (author's archive, received from Amit). Interviews with John
Hadden, June 2006, Navot, April 6, 2017, and Yeshayahu Gavish, April 6, 2017.

114   **were sure of their own capabilities**   Mossad Chief Amir to PM Eshkol, "Report on
U.S. Visit 31.5–2.6.1967," June 4, 1966 (author's archive, received from Amit).

114   **"flashing green light"**   Interview with Amit, April 2006. Central Intelligence Agency,

"Office of the Director, Richard Helms, to the President," with the attachment of "Views of General Meir Amit, Head of the Israeli Intelligence Service, on the Crisis in the Middle East," June 2, 1967 (author's archive, received from Amit).

114 **Gazit composed a special top-secret paper** AMAN Research Division, *Israel and the Arabs: A New Situation,* June 8, 1967 (author's archive, received from Gazit). Interview with Gazit, September 12, 2016.

115 **"What's happening now is a disappointment"** Personal diary of Meir Amit, July 1967 (author's archive, received from Amit).

115 **Fatah would continue its struggle** Yaari, *Fatah,* 92–94 (Hebrew).

116 **"Israel must strike at the heart of the terror organizations"** Arbel's Diary is quoted in Perry, *Strike First,* 42 (Hebrew).

116 **"Short, 155–160 cm; dark-skinned"** Shin Bet, Wanted poster for Yasser Arafat, June 1967 (author's archive, courtesy of Shlomo Nakdimon).

116 **Israeli forces tried to kill Arafat a few times** Interview with Sutton, May 9, 2012. Bechor, *PLO Lexicon,* 266 (Hebrew). Rubinstein, *The Mystery of Arafat,* 98 (Hebrew).

117 **urged Eshkol to approve a massive military operation** "Meeting of the IDF General Staff 38-341," April 1968, 17–18 (author's archive, received from "Sheeran").

117 **The Mossad was frustrated** Interview with Zvi Aharoni, July 1998.

117 **The plan they came up with in January 1968** Klein, *The Master of Operation: The Story of Mike Harari,* 100–101 (Hebrew). Interviews with Harari, March 29, 2014, and Klein, October 6, 2014.

117 **Eshkol gave in to the pressure** Supreme Command Secretariat, Bureau of the Chief of the General Staff, General Staff debriefings on Operations Tophet and Assuta, MODA, 236/72. Interviews with Hadar, March 25, 2013, Immanuel Shaked, May 14, 2013, and Sutton, May 9, 2012.

118 **This showed who the real victors were** Zeev Maoz, *Defending the Holy Land,* 244–46 (Hebrew).

118 **Transcripts of general staff meetings** For example, see the protocol of meeting, number 341-5, the first General Staff meeting with the newly appointed PM Golda Meir in March 1969, reviewing all the threats Israel faced at the time (author's archive, received from "Sheeran").

118 **they were even willing to adopt a particularly bizarre plan** Interviews with Sutton, May 9, 2012, "Steve," March 2013, and Zvi Aharoni, July 1998.

119 **he could brainwash and hypnotize him into becoming a programmed killer** At that time, other espionage agencies, including those of the United States and the Soviet Union, were also experimenting with using hypnosis and drugs to create highly trained and fearless operatives. One of these plans, which apparently examined the various effects of psychosis-inducing drugs and the possibility of using them in order to create the perfect soldier or to extract information in interrogations, was a CIA project called MKULTRA. Frank Olson, one of the staffers on the project, either committed suicide or was murdered. Interview with Eric Olson, September 2000. Ronen Bergman, "Vertigo," *Yedioth Ahronoth,* October 6, 2000.

119 **went several times to observe Shalit's work** Interview with Aharon Levran, May 31, 2011.

120 **Fatkhi waved goodbye to his operators** Interviews with Sutton, May 9, 2012, and "Steve," January 2013.

120 **Fatkhi had been handed over to the organization** Thirty years later, when Rafi Sutton was on a visit to Jordan in the 1990s—after that country signed a peace treaty with Israel—he was approached by a man who identified himself as Fatkhi. "I'm the Fatah prisoner that an Israeli officer tried to hypnotize and sent to kill Arafat," he said. He expressed his gratitude to Sutton for treating him well and respectfully, and to his driver for saving his life in the river. He smiled and said, "*Inshallah* [God willing] that there be peace and no more need for hypnosis." Interviews with Sutton, May 9, 2012, and Zvi Aharoni, July 1998. Sutton, *The Orchid Salesman,* 162–65 (Hebrew).

## CHAPTER 8: MEIR DAGAN AND HIS EXPERTISE

122 **countering Palestinian terrorism became the principal objective** Melman and Raviv, *Imperfect Spies,* 154–58 (Hebrew).

122 **The peak came in 1970** IDF, History Department, *Security, Summer of 1969–1970,* September 1970 (author's archive, received from "Sheeran").

122 **The intelligence for these activities**  Interview with Yaakov Peri, May 21, 2011.

123 **"Saber-rattling and killing for the sake of killing"**  Interview with Yitzhak Pundak, June 6, 2017. Some of what was said was also included in Pundak's book *Five Missions,* 322–54 (Hebrew).

123 **Sharon's mind immediately turned to Meir Dagan**  Interview with Ariel Sharon, May 2003. I interviewed Dagan several times in 2013 and 2014 in his home in one of Tel Aviv's new upscale apartment towers, after his retirement as the director of the Mossad, a post he held for nine years. By the time I spoke with him, Dagan was something of a medical miracle. A year before, he had been diagnosed with liver cancer. Only a transplant could save his life, but at the age of sixty-seven he was too old to qualify under Israeli regulations. With the Mossad's support, friends and colleagues all over the world rallied to assist him. In the end, Alexander Lukashenko, the autocrat of Belarus who knew Dagan from his Mossad days, ordered his doctors to find a liver for Dagan. "I'm afraid that I had to disappoint everyone who was looking forward to my imminent demise," Dagan told me. He was still heavily guarded by the Shin Bet, because of warnings that someone—the Syrian or Iranian secret services, Hamas, Hezbollah, Palestinian Islamic Jihad, the list goes on—would target him to avenge assassinations of their top personnel. "Nothing to do about it," he said, smiling. "This is what happens when you get into scraps against everyone." The cancer returned in late 2015 and Dagan succumbed to it in March 2016. He was buried with all the honors of a national symbol, at a funeral attended by thousands.

124 **"My parents never spoke of that period"**  Interview with Dagan, May 26, 2013.

124 **"Let's admit the truth"**  Interview with Dagan, May 29, 2013.

125 **"behaved as if he was born to be a soldier"**  Anat Talshir and Igal Sarna, "I Love to Put On a Costume and Go Act in Enemy Territory," *Yedioth Ahronoth,* October 24, 1997.

125 **That was what he remembered: the fruit in his hand**  Interview with Dagan, July 20, 2013.

125 **Yatom remembered being alarmed**  Yatom, *The Confidant,* 83 (Hebrew).

126 **Yatom made the cut, but Dagan didn't**  Interview with Dagan, May 26, 2013.

126 **Dagan would emerge, bare-chested, from his bedroom**  Interview with "the Cube," March 2004.

127 **Dagan began to develop his battle doctrine**  Interview with Dagan, January 8, 2011.

127 **a file of wanted men in the Gaza Strip**  Interview with Avigdor (Azulay) Eldan, April 20, 2016.

127 **"Red" targets, on the other hand**  The Shin Bet's Wanted list (author's archive, received from "Jedi").

128 **"we didn't know what they were training us for"**  Moshe Rubin from Sayeret Matkal was brought in to teach the techniques and methods used by that unit deep inside enemy territory. Along with firearms practice and orientation, the training also included a technique known as "dancing," aimed at reducing the size of one's silhouette when entering a house so as to minimize the danger of being hit by gunfire from inside. Trainees also practiced operational driving in various vehicles, including those used by the inhabitants of the Gaza Strip, and walking around alone, disguised as Arabs, all over the Strip, "simply in order to raise our confidence that we would not be identified," said Meir Teichner, one of the first "Chameleons." Interviews with Eldan, Moshe Rubin, and Meir Teichner, April 20, 2016.

128 **The Chameleons**  There are a number of competing stories about the founding of Chameleon/Rimon Rangers. It is certain, however, that at a certain stage the unit was placed under Dagan's command with the backing of Arik Sharon. Interviews with Dagan, May 29, 2013, and Rubin, Teichner, Eldan, and Dani Perl, April 20, 2016.

128 **"We exploited the main weak point of these terror cells"**  Interview with Dagan, May 29, 2013.

129 **"They were scared of us"**  Interviews with "Neta," July 2013, and "the Cube," March 2004.

129 **In a staged operation to establish credibility**  Interviews with Rubin, Teichner, and Eldan, April 20, 2016.

129 **After a day, the terrorists showed up**  Interview with Dagan, June 19, 2013.

130 **they were stopped at a makeshift roadblock**  "Suddenly There Was an Explosion in the Car," *Yedioth Ahronoth,* January 3, 1972.

131 **"We decided that things could not go on this way"**  Interview with Dagan, June 19, 2013.

131 **"There is no other way to describe this act than ethnic cleansing"**  Interview with Gazit, September 12, 2016.

132   **Dagan pretended to be a corpse**   Interview with Dagan, June 19, 2013.

132   **A month after the Aroyo killings**   Interviews with Dagan, June 19, 2013, and Sharon, May 2003. Certificate of award of Medal of Valor to Capt. Meir Huberman (Dagan's original last name) by the chief of the General Staff, Lt. Gen. David Elazar, April 1973.

132   **the effectiveness of Dagan's chosen methods**   Gazit, *Trapped Fools*, 61–63. Interviews with Dagan and Peri. Letter from David Ronen to *Haaretz*, October 2002. Archival material summarizing operations of Grenade Rangers shown to the author by "Emilia."

133   **Pundak took this story to Southern Command chief Sharon**   Interview with Pundak, June 6, 2017. After Pundak's death in August 2017 and the publication of what he had told me about the document, Sharon's son Gilad responded on behalf of the family: "This is a collection of lies and fantasies from a man whose salient achievement was the great old age that he reached" (WhatsApp message from Gilad Sharon, August 30, 2017).

133   **they shot people after they surrendered**   On August 12, 1997, Daniel Okev, who'd been one of Dagan's fighters, picked up two young British hitchhikers, Jeffery Max Hunter and Charlotte Gibb, while driving through the Negev on his way to the casino in Taba, just over the Egyptian border in Sinai. On the way he took his 9 mm gun and shot them. Hunter was killed immediately. Gibb was wounded and played dead. On trial Okev claimed that he did it because "I heard a foreign language and suddenly I felt as if I was in a Mercedes [the cars the Grenade Rangers used], in Gaza, disguised as an Arab." He was sentenced to twenty years. The court rejected the prosecution demand for a life sentence, recognizing that at the time of the killings Okev was "in a state of deep mental derangement." He was paroled after thirteen years in prison. Another Grenade Ranger, Jean Elraz, confirmed accounts of the unit's killings. "I personally killed more than twenty people," he wrote from prison, where he's locked up for murdering a kibbutz armory guard in March 2001, stealing the weapons, and selling them to terrorists. Anat Talshir and Igal Sarna, "I Love to Put On a Costume," *Yedioth Ahronoth*, October 24, 1997. Interview with Jean-Pierre Elraz, January 1993. Letters from jailed Elraz, August 2002. Ronen Bergman and four other reporters, "Killer," *Yedioth Ahronoth*, September 6, 2002.

134   **Dagan confirms this but says it was justified**   Interview with Dagan, June 19, 2013.

134   **"And what exactly would you want me to do?"**   Interview with Shmuel Paz, March 31, 2017.

## CHAPTER 9: THE PLO GOES INTERNATIONAL

136   **At 11:07, the control tower in Rome received a message**   Announcement by transportation minister on the hijacking of the El Al plane, the Knesset, session 312, July 23, 1968.

137   **The seizure of Flight 426**   Interview with Eitan Haber, June 21, 2009. Bergman, *By Any Means Necessary: Israel's Covert War for Its POW and MIAs*, 28–29 (Hebrew).

137   **the world offered a much bigger stage**   Yaari, *Strike Terror*, 242. Merari and Elad, *The International Dimension of Palestinian Terrorism*, 29–41 (Hebrew).

137   **TWA Flight 840 took off from Los Angeles for Tel Aviv**   "No Response from El Al Flights: The Hijack of an Airplane to Algeria," Israeli Air Force website.

138   **saying it was her birthplace**   *Leila Khaled: Hijacker*, a 2006 documentary on Leila Khaled, directed by Lina Makboul.

138   **fatally wounding the copilot**   Yoram Peres was a pilot in training with El Al. He was very badly injured in the attack and taken to a hospital, where he died six weeks later. Letter from Tami Inbar, Peres's sister, to the author, December 5, 2008.

138   **Khaled, meanwhile, became a symbol of the era**   *Guardian*, January 26, 2001. Merari and Elad, *International Dimension of Palestinian Terrorism*, 95 (Hebrew).

139   **put the plane into a sudden dive**   Interview with Uri Bar-Lev, June 19, 2017.

139   **hijacking Pan Am, Swissair, and TWA planes that day**   Even before the spectacular operation, Habash admitted openly that the goal of his actions was to implicate the Arab states. "That is exactly what we want. These actions are meant to limit the prospects for a peaceful solution that we are not ready to accept." *Jerusalem Post*, June 10, 1969, as quoted in Merari and Elad, *International Dimension of Palestinian Terrorism*, 28 (Hebrew).

139   **launch a brutal attack against Arafat's people**   Syria sent forces to aid the Palestinians, but Israel, at America's request, moved forces to the border and declared that if Damascus did not withdraw its armored column, it would find itself under attack. The Syrians retreated, and Hussein regained full control of Jordan. A detailed account of the events of Black September is to be found in Sayigh, *Armed Struggle*, 261–81. Interview with Shlomo Gazit, November 29, 2016.

140 **Black September was another of the ever-evolving Fatah factions** "Protocol of a meeting between PM Meir and Mossad Director Zamir," January 5, 1972 (presented to the author by "Paul"). Abu Iyad admitted years later in his memoirs that Black September was indeed part of the PLO. Abu Iyad, as quoted in Merari and Elad, *International Dimension of Palestinian Terrorism,* 33 (Hebrew).

140 **Khalaf redefined the enemies of the Palestinian people** Abu Iyad interview to *Jeune Afrique,* October 19, 1971. Sayigh, *Armed Struggle,* 309.

140 **Meir Dagan and members of the Chameleon unit suggested** Interview with Dagan, May 29, 2013.

141 **the Palestinians' main strategic aim was achieved** Sayigh, *Armed Struggle,* 308, note 207.

141 **Many of those revolutionaries soon rallied to the Palestinian cause** Ibid., 309, note 210.

141 **three members of the Japanese Red Army** The Red Army leader, Fusako Shigenobu, who sent her husband on the suicide mission, said, "Because of my organizational responsibilities, and because I was his wife, I was the last person to meet the commandos before they boarded the plane which took them to Lod." Farrell, *Blood and Rage,* 138.

141 **The three Japanese men pulled AK-47s** *New York Times,* June 1, 1972. Interview with Eilam, an eyewitness to the events at the airport, December 2, 2009.

142 **The sounds of ambulances filled the streets** One of the Japanese, Kozo Okamoto, survived, to his regret. He refused to talk under interrogation and, unlike Arab terror suspects, he was not tortured. He agreed to open up only after an Israeli general offered to give him a pistol with one bullet so he could commit suicide if he cooperated. The general, Rehavam Zeevi, did not fulfill his part of the deal. Steinhoff, unpublished manuscript, 55, as referred to in *Blood and Rage,* 141.

142 **defended the massacre of the pilgrims** *New York Times,* June 4, 1972.

142 **Levi Eshkol ordered a punitive operation** Operation Gift (Tshura) on the Israeli Air Force website, http://iaf.org.il/4694-32941-HE/IAF.aspx.

142 **de Gaulle tightened his country's weapons embargo** Henry Tanner, "France Pledges to Aid Lebanon If Her Existence Is Threatened," *New York Times,* January 15, 1969.

142 **Further failures would follow** Interviews with Harari, March 23, 2014, Klein, May 28, 2014, and "Black," November 2015.

143 **"Haddad behaved like the lord of the manor"** Interviews with Zvi Aharoni, July 1998, Amram Aharoni, May 14, 2016, and "Darren," September 2014.

143 **"But what can you do"** Interview with Harari, March 10, 2014.

143 **an Israeli agent in Lebanon located George Habash's villa** Interview with Clovis Francis, February 2005.

143 **Operation White Desert** Interview with Harari, March 23, 2014.

144 **Everything was ready to go** Harari received Zamir's okay for a rehearsal operation in real time during the ceremony to get to the apartment from which the shots were supposed to be fired, to simulate the shooting, and to get away—all to show the prime minister what Caesarea was capable of. Everything worked perfectly, except that the Mossad operative designated to "kill" Arafat in the rehearsal was not carrying a gun, and so could do nothing more than point his finger at Arafat's head.

144 **These bombs "had two clear advantages"** Interview with Kfir, June 9, 2011.

144 **The Israelis did manage to maim a couple of militants** Bassam Abu Sharif, the spokesman for the PFLP, for example, sustained facial wounds and lost several fingers when he opened a copy of Che Guevara's memoirs. Merari and Elad, *International Dimension of Palestinian Terrorism,* 119. Bechor, *PLO Lexicon,* 25.

144 **fingers were pointed at the intelligence community** On one occasion during that period, the Mossad decided to take direct action in Beirut. Another PFLP spokesman, a well-known writer and poet named Ghassan Kanafani, made the Mossad hit list after he was identified in photographs taken with the Japanese Red Army militants shortly before they set out. On July 8, 1972, six weeks after the slaughter at Lod, Kanafani and his seventeen-year-old niece, Lamees Najim, got into his Austin 1100, which blew up when he turned the ignition. The fact that the Mossad killed an innocent young girl whose only sin was getting into the wrong car with the wrong man was never discussed or investigated. Interviews with Harari, March 23, 2014, and "Ethan," July 2014.

144 **In order to do that** Interviews with Harari, March 23, 2014, and "Kurtz," October 2005.

145 **at a secret meeting of the Knesset's Foreign Affairs and Defense Committee** Knesset Committee on Foreign Affairs and Security, October 9, 1972 (author's archive, received from "Paul").

145    **"'the land shall have rest for forty years'"**   Quotation as recalled in November 2012 by "Dark Chocolate," a member of Caesarea in the 1970s.

146    **The nucleus of Bayonet**   Interview with "Shaul," June 2017.

146    **"All of this is not simple. It's not our country"**   Knesset Committee on Foreign Affairs and Security, protocol of session on October 9, 1972, 10.

146    **"We respected the prime minister's policy"**   Zamir, *With Open Eyes,* 67 (Hebrew).

146    **speedy movement from rest to a firing position**   Beckerman's instinct shooting is also used by undercover Shin Bet air marshals who fly on El Al flights. Beckerman's technique is now taught in the secret Shin Bet firing range east of Tel Aviv. The range is built like a series of mazes, separated into rooms and staircases with nooks and crannies where cardboard enemies are hidden. It's covered with a reinforced glass ceiling through which instructors can view trainees while they give commands over loudspeakers. The mazes are constructed so trainees can fire live ammunition in any direction, and sensors and cameras record every shot. Author's visit to the Shin Bet firing range, May 2005.

147    **Then recruits needed training in one more skill: makeup**   Interview with Yarin Shahaf, January 22, 2013. During the high time of fighting terror, in mid-1972, Harari changed the name of Caesarea to Masada, after the isolated mountaintop fortress in the Judean desert overlooking the Dead Sea. This was where the last of the Jewish rebels against the Roman Empire in the first century C.E. took refuge and held the besieging Roman legions at bay, ultimately choosing to commit suicide, together with their women and children, rather than surrender and become slaves. Masada is a symbol of heroism that is an important part of the Israelis' ethos of independence, signifying a readiness to sacrifice through which "Masada shall not fall again." Down the road, the unit's name would be changed several times. To avoid confusion, it is called Caesarea throughout this book.

147    **eight members of Black September arrived at a training camp**   Sayigh, *Armed Struggle,* 309.

147    **chosen for a variety of reasons**   Personal details of the Black September operatives taken from the great reporting about the Munich attack by Shai Fogelman, "Back to the Black September," *Haaretz Weekly Magazine,* August 31, 2012.

148    **Palestinian agent code-named Lucifer**   Interview with "Ethan," July 2014.

149    **As she had done in every case during her term as prime minister**   Goldstein, *Golda: A Biography,* 525 (Hebrew).

149    **"In the Sabena affair, they let me work properly"**   Interview with Victor Cohen, May 27, 2015.

150    **left a deep impression in Zamir's mind**   Zamir, *With Open Eyes,* 69.

150    **Cohen took the megaphone**   Interview with Victor Cohen, May 27, 2015.

151    **one of the German pilots crying out for help**   Security Cabinet meeting, September 6, 1972 (author's archive, received from "Paul").

152    **"on a mountaintop visible from all corners of the globe"**   *Al-Sayyid,* September 13, 1972, as quoted in Merari and Elad, *International Dimension of Palestinian Terrorism,* 35.

152    **Meir also ordered air strikes**   Secret annex to cabinet decision following the Munich attack, Michael Arnon to Defense Minister, September 11, 1972 (author's archive, received from "Paul"). The Palestinians claimed that two hundred civilians were killed in these attacks, among them women and children. Israel denied this. Fogelman, *Haaretz Weekly Magazine,* August 21, 2012.

152    **"The German disgrace is immeasurable"**   Security Cabinet meeting, September 6, 1972, 5 (author's archive, received from "Paul").

152    **At a secret meeting of the Knesset panel**   Meeting of Knesset Foreign Affairs and Security Committee, protocol no. 243, November 3, 1972 (author's archive, received from "Paul").

152    **Meir, heavily criticized for the failure of the intelligence organizations**   Meeting of Knesset Foreign Affairs and Security Committee, protocol no. 243, November 3, 1972 (author's archive, received from "Paul").

## CHAPTER 10: "I HAVE NO PROBLEM WITH ANYONE THAT I'VE KILLED"

154    **"The Beautiful Sarah"**   Interview with "Black," November 2015. An account that is similar in some of the details appears in Klein, *Striking Back,* 117–18.

154    **he had spent the evening at the home of his friend**   Letter from Peter Manning, a biographer of Janet Venn-Brown, to the author, October 20, 2015. Interview with Peter Manning, December 24, 2015.

155    **The Mossad also suspected Zwaiter**   Although the attempt was foiled (the booby-trapped record player taken onto the plane exploded in midair, but the pilot managed to land safely) and the two Palestinian terrorists who persuaded the two European tourists to take it aboard were captured and tried, Prime Minister Golda Meir was certain that the Italians would surrender to pressure and release them. "The Italians are sitting and shivering," she said. She was proved correct shortly afterward when the Italian government, under pressure from the PLO, released them. Protocol of cabinet meeting, November 5, 1972 (author's archive, received from "Paul").

155    **None of them had been caught**   Since its inception, the Mossad has stirred great interest from around the world and a seemingly insatiable thirst for stories about its exploits. Films, books, and television dramas purportedly offering an insider's look at the organization regularly top bestseller lists. One story in particular seems to hold an enduring fascination—the one behind Golda Meir's order to target and assassinate Palestinian terrorist operatives in Europe in the early 1970s. Perhaps the best-known portrayal of this story is Steven Spielberg's 2005 feature *Munich,* starring Eric Bana and Daniel Craig, which was nominated for five Academy Awards. The connection between the movie—as well as most of the other accounts of the operations, which all lack references and footnotes (except for the great reporting in Aaron Klein's *Striking Back*)—and reality is very slim. The movie is based on the outcome of a book written by George Jonas, who reportedly relied on the account of one Juval Aviv, supposedly the lead assassin of the group. Aviv's credentials as a former Mossad agent have been the subject of much skepticism. Even the code name of the operation that has been given in the various publications—"God's Wrath"—is incorrect, according to all those who actually took part in it and who spoke about it for this book and for Klein's books. Interviews with Yuval Aviv, December 1995, November 6, 2005. Letter from Aviv to the author, November 7, 2005, about his connections with Spielberg and Dream-Works. Most of Yuval Aviv's material is discussed in Ronen Bergman, "Living in a Movie," *Yedioth Ahronoth,* December 2, 2005. Spielberg responded by saying that the film was based on the best information that could be obtained publicly. Ofer Shelah, "Save Munich," *Yedioth Ahronoth,* February 17, 2006. More details appeared in Chris Thompson, "Secret Agent Schmuck," *Village Voice,* October 16, 2007.

155    **"Those who harm the Jews first"**   *Yedioth Ahronoth,* March 6, 1973.

156    **This policy change had a significant effect on Caesarea's operations**   Interviews with Harari, March 10, 2014, Klein, October 6, 2014, Kurtz, October 2005, and "Black," November 2015.

156    **in Europe it was a lot easier to kill a man**   Interview with "Salvador," May 2012.

157    **anyone suspected of belonging to the PLO . . . became a legitimate target**   Mossad chief Zamir would claim later that the assassinations were not motivated by a desire for vengeance, but were meant to prevent future terrorist attacks. However, this is difficult to reconcile with what Zamir's subordinates say. Most of them stated explicitly that revenge was on their minds when they set out on a hit operation. One of them observed drily, "It had to be made clear that anyone who kills Jews becomes a legitimate target." The heads of the Mossad who replaced Zamir, Nahum Admoni and Meir Dagan, said that revenge was one of the motives for the assassinations in the 1970s. Interviews with "Black," June 2015, Nahum Admoni, May 29, 2011, and Dagan, May 29, 2013. Interview with Zvi Zamir in Yossi Melman, "Golda Gave No Order," *Haaretz,* February 17, 2006.

157    **"We wanted to create a noisy effect"**   Interviews with "Black," November 2015, and Harari, April 11, 2014.

157    **"Those words . . . roused a sense of pride in us"**   Interview with "Kurtz," October 2005.

157    **The leader of the hit teams**   There are contradictory indications as to whether Meiri was ever officially appointed to head Bayonet as he himself and some Mossad sources asserted, or was rather named field commander of some of the team's ops, as claimed by Harari. Certain differences and disagreements between the two men emerged over the years. Interviews with "Shaul," June 2017, Nehemia Meiri, June 12, 2012, and Harari, March 10, 2014.

157    **He was twelve years old**   Interviews with Nehemia Meiri, June 12, 2012, and Haber, June 21, 2009. Recording of conversation between Nehemia Meiri and journalist Eitan Haber (author's archive, conveyed by Moshe Meiri).

158    **"with a knife between his teeth"**   Interview with "Shaul," June 2017.

158    **"in order to create a killing machine"**   Interview with Haber, June 21, 2009.

158    **"I dream at night about my family"**   Interview with Nehemia Meiri, June 12, 2012.

158    **Meiri was one of the men who shot Zwaiter**   After Harari resigned from his post as

head of Caesarea in 1980, the unit presented him with a special parting gift—the Beretta pistol with which Meiri had dispatched Zwaiter, set on a framed plaque with a dedication from his operatives. Harari kept it on a prominent shelf in his living room.

158   **The Mossad blamed him for a conspiracy**   Aaron Klein, *Striking Back*, 130–31.

159   **She invited Harari to her home**   Interview with Harari, March 10, 2014.

159   **her minister for religious affairs, Zerach Warhaftig**   The final go-ahead for the Hamshari hit was pushed forward when on November 29, Black September hijacked a Lufthansa plane en route from Beirut to Frankfurt. The Germans immediately freed the three Munich Olympic terrorists still in prison; they were flown to Libya, where they received a royal welcome. The circumstances of the hijacking roused suspicions that it had been coordinated with the Germans to provide a pretext to release the athletes' murderers. The level of anger in Israel soared, with ministers especially furious over the German government spokesman's statement that "Germany didn't cause the Middle East conflict." Minister Warhaftig stated, "The murder of six million Jews did have an effect on the Middle East conflict." After that cabinet meeting, Warhaftig approached Meir and urged her to approve more targets for assassinations. Interview with "Toblerone," January 2014. "Germany's Secret Contacts with Palestinian Terrorists," *Der Spiegel*, August 28, 2012.

159   **broke into Hamshari's apartment**   In an era when miniature communications devices were not yet available, in order to warn of dangers from the outside without making a noise, the commander of the unit, Zvi Malchin, contrived a small box that could be hung on the belt, and which vibrated when a radio signal was sent on a certain wavelength. This, in fact, may have been the first beeper.

160   **Hamshari was "almost cut in half"**   Interview with "Kurtz," October 2005. The day after Hamshari was killed, someone made an anonymous phone call to Ankie Spitzer, the widow of Andre Spitzer, a fencing coach who was among the Munich victims. "Listen to the news at ten," said the caller. "It's for Andre." Interview with Ankie Spitzer, February 22, 2012. Klein, *Striking Back*, 129–33.

160   **"In Caesarea there were no born killers"**   Interview with Harari, March 10, 2014.

160   **Mossad chief Zamir also knew that having Meir's backing was important**   From accounts given by Director Zvi Zamir to the Mossad's history department, quoted in Zamir, *With Open Eyes*, 76–80.

160   **"I sit facing them . . . full of wonder at their courage"**   Knesset Committee on Foreign Affairs and Security, protocol of session on November 3, 1972 (author's archive, received from "Paul").

161   **"we didn't know why we were killing them"**   Interview with "Black," June 2015.

161   **"it was a terrible mistake"**   Interview with "Iftach," May 22, 2011.

161   **insisted that Zwaiter was a peaceable intellectual**   Some additional bolstering for the Palestinian claims came in a surprising 1993 interview of Aharon Yariv, Meir's adviser on counterterrorism, by the BBC. Yariv admitted for the first time that the Mossad was behind the assassinations and contradicted the Mossad's claims regarding Zwaiter when he said, "He had a certain connection to terror. Not on the operational side." Similar doubts were also raised by Aaron Klein in his book *Striking Back*, 119.

161   **But for some, that didn't matter**   Interview with "Select," April 2011.

161   **The problem inherent in this approach**   It was clear that during the first months of the Mossad's assassinations in Europe, the Palestinians remained unfazed and continued to step up terrorism in Europe and elsewhere. They staged attacks against El Al offices, sent out explosive packages, ambushed Israeli representatives and, at their height, seized the Israeli embassy in Bangkok and its staff. Merari and Elad, *International Dimension of Palestinian Terrorism*, 17 (Hebrew).

161   **it had not damaged the top echelons of the PLO**   Fatah also fought back against the Mossad, and in January 1973 managed to turn two Palestinian agents whom Junction was running. One of them drew a pistol during a meeting with his controller, Tzadok Ofir, and shot and wounded him; the other killed his Mossad case officer, Baruch Cohen, during a meeting in Madrid. In Israel, these incidents only served to prove that the assassination campaign had to be intensified. Interviews with Gideon Ezra, February 4, 1999, Sutton, May 9, 2012, and Alpher, May 18, 2015. Klein, *Striking Back*, 142–47.

162   **Three days after his message requesting a meeting**   Interview with Francis, February 2005.

163   **crafted a cover story**   Yael was given a brief training course in the ways a writer lives and works by Shabtai Tevet, senior journalist for the *Haaretz* newspaper, the biographer of Ben-Gurion, and a friend of Harari's.

164   **carrying a handbag with a camera inside it**   Caesarea file of intelligence gathered

before Operation Spring of Youth, including photographs that Yael took while in Beirut, is in author's archive (received from "Gustav").

164   **"Every detail was important"**   Mass, *Yael, the Mossad Warrior in Beirut,* 66 (Hebrew) (uncensored draft manuscript in author's archive, received from "Maurice").

164   **Romi and Harari came to an unavoidable conclusion**   Interview with Harari, March 23, 2014. Klein, *Striking Back,* 157–61.

165   **Sayeret Matkal was set up in the late 1950s**   Dar to CoS, Chief of AMAN and Commander of Unit 131, "Setting the Ground of the Establishment of Undercover Mista'ravim Unit," October 2, 1955 (author's archive, received from Avraham Dar).

165   **install highly sophisticated listening and observation devices**   The listening devices were operated for lengthy periods thanks to nuclear batteries that were supplied by the Jewish American scientist Zalman Shapiro, owner of the NUMAC company of Pennsylvania. Interviews with Amit, June 6, 2005, and Amiram Levin, July 16, 2017. Ronen Bergman, "The Nuclear Batteries and the Secret Listening Devices," *Yedioth Ahronoth,* June 6, 2017.

165   **Barak pushed for Sayeret Matkal to be a bigger part of IDF operations**   Barak was right to exert this aggressive push to be integrated into IDF operations. In the course of time, Sayeret Matkal became synonymous with excellence, determination, and originality. Unit veterans went on to top positions in the military and became part of the Israeli elite after their release. Ehud Barak, who later served as chief of the General Staff (CoG), went into politics and became defense minister and prime minister. Uzi Dayan became deputy CoS, and as a civilian, head of the National Security Council. Danny Yatom became director of the Mossad. Shaul Mofaz became CoS and defense minister. Moshe Yaalon became CoS, minister of defense, and vice premier to Benjamin Netanyahu, himself another veteran of the Sayeret. A report compiled by the daily newspaper *Yedioth Ahronoth* in late 2012 revealed that substantial parts of the centers of economic, social, security, and political power in Israel were manned by former soldiers of the Sayeret Matkal, which is no bigger than a single battalion.

165   **"a look of satisfaction spread across Barak's face"**   Betser, *Secret Soldier,* 143 (Hebrew).

166   **Elazar smiled and gave Barak the green light**   Interviews with Amnon Biran, June 5, 2011, and Barak, November 24, 2013.

166   **The plan for Operation Spring of Youth**   This wasn't the first time the IDF was operating against PLO targets in Lebanon, but it had never done so on such a large scale, requiring combined forces, including the Mossad. For information on previous attacks in Lebanon (Operation Bardas) see Nadel, *Who Dares Wins,* 198–235 (Hebrew). On the planning of Spring of Youth, see Betser, *Secret Soldier,* 109–14 (Hebrew). Operations Division, Spring of Youth, April 9, 1973, MODA 580-75-401. Interview with Barak, July 1, 2013.

166   **a complex exercise, involving the coordination and integration of different units**   The landing and the car ride to the destination were practiced on the beach near a new upscale neighborhood in north Tel Aviv, Ramat Aviv, which had skeletons of high-rise apartment blocks under construction that were somewhat similar to the luxurious buildings where the targets lived. Interviews with Shaked, May 1, 2013, and Barak, January 13, 2012.

167   **Yael and Model continued gathering intelligence**   Harari decided not to tell Yael about the details of the operation or its timing. "The possibility, even the very slightest, that she would be exposed without our knowing, and be forced to tell what she knew, would have endangered our forces," he told me. Mossad, intelligence summary for Operation Spring of Youth, April 6, 1973 (author's archive, received from "Gustav"). Interview with Amnon Biran, June 5, 2011.

168   **Shaked exploded in anger and turned to Zamir**   Reconstruction of the meeting from interviews with Shaked, May 14, 2013, Harari, March 29, 2014, and Ammon Biran, June 5, 2011.

168   **"after you make sure that he won't get up again"**   Various notes in the handwriting of the operation's commander, made close to the force's departure, and notes for the last briefing by Brig. Gen. Immanuel Shaked on April 4, 1973 (author's archive, received from "Stark").

169   **"an operation for which there was no rescue option"**   Interview with Eli Zeira, June 29, 2010.

169   **Barak thought he was either sick or injured**   Interview with Barak, November 24, 2013.

169   **"It reminds me of Rome"**   Interview with Muki Betser, June 10, 2016.

170   **One bullet hit the car and set off its horn**   Betser, *Secret Soldier,* 163.

170  **"More proof that there's always some new surprise"**  Interview with Betser, June 10, 2016.

171  **"Shoot him, Muki"**  Chief Infantry and Paratroops Officer headquarters, operations report for Operation Spring of Youth, May 11, 1973 (author's archive, received from "Stark"). Amnon Biran, "Spring of the Elite Forces," *Mabat Malam*, April 2011 (Hebrew). Interviews with Barak, November 24, 2013, "Dark Chocolate," November 2012, "Black," January 2013, and Aviram Halevi, October 12, 2010. Betser, *Secret Soldier*, 164–66.

171  **Pressler thought he'd been left alone**  Interview with Yigal Pressler, July 6, 2017.

172  **"My hardest moment . . . was not during the actual combat"**  Interview with Amnon Lipkin-Shahak, May 26, 2011. Klein, *Striking Back*, 168–69.

172  **they found the Caesarea man sitting in his car**  Interview with Lipkin-Shahak, April 3, 2012.

172  **Two of the paratroopers couldn't restrain themselves**  Interview with "Sinbad," October 2013.

173  **When she woke up she was surprised to find her husband**  Interview with Barak, November 24, 2013.

173  **Yael had written a letter to her case officer**  Copy of the letter in author's archive, obtained from "Midburn."

173  **"When the plane took off . . . I relaxed in my seat"**  Mass, *Yael, the Mossad Warrior in Beirut* (uncensored draft manuscript in author's archive, received from "Maurice"), 117 (Hebrew).

174  **shortly before the raid he left one of the targeted apartments**  He and his aide, Tawfiq Tirawi, were visiting with the three terrorists who took part in the Munich massacre and had been freed by the Germans. At about 1 A.M., Tirawi recounts, they heard shooting and one of the bodyguards who'd been waiting outside burst in and yelled, "Al-Mossad, al-Mossad, they are here." Interview with Tawfiq Tirawi, June 2002.

174  **details about PLO cells in the occupied territories**  Additional documents pointed at the links between the PLO and left-wing organizations in Europe, strengthening the standing of the Mossad as a body that could be useful to Western states in *their* battle against local terrorism, as well as Israel's argument that only cooperation would be able to block the phenomenon. Interviews with Shimshon Issaki, September 2, 2015, and Reuven Hazak, February 1, 1999. Sayigh, *Armed Struggle*, 311.

174  **no attention was paid in Israel**  A few days after the operation, Brig. Gen. Shaked demanded that the director of the Mossad fire the Caesarea operative, and when he refused, Shaked urged chief of staff Elazar to ask the prime minister to order that it be done, but "In the euphoric atmosphere after the operation, no one would listen to me." Interview with Shaked, May 1, 2013.

174  **The operation left Lebanon in shock**  Quoted in *Haaretz*, March 12, 1973.

## CHAPTER 11: "WRONG IDENTIFICATION OF A TARGET IS NOT A FAILURE. IT'S A MISTAKE."

175  **before they shot him dead**  The Mossad suspected al-Kubaisi of planning an attempt on Golda Meir's life by detonating a car bomb as her convoy passed by during a visit to New York. Al-Kubaisi arrived in Paris in February and checked in to a small hotel near the Place de la Madeleine. He soon began visiting bars frequented by young Arabs. Nehemia Meiri felt that he was too old to mingle with them, so he took the extremely unorthodox measure of sending his son, Moshe, to keep an eye on al-Kubaisi. The boy lacked any formal training in spycraft, but Moshe says Nehemia was convinced he had passed some of it on in his genes. "I used to go in to the bar, order something to drink and start talking to one of the Arabs. I had a bag with a concealed camera and while I was sitting there I snapped the people in the bar." From these photographs as well as documentation from other surveillance teams, the Mossad identified meetings between al-Kubaisi and Fatah members. Interviews with Moshe and Nehemia Meiri, June 12, 2012.

175  **only hours after the Spring of Youth forces returned**  "To our regret, they don't just croak on their own. They have to be helped," explained Kurtz, who participated in the killing of Hussein Abd al-Chir. Interview with "Kurtz," October 2005. Klein, *Striking Back*, 137–38.

175  **"an outstanding source with excellent and exclusive access"**  Mossad, History Department, *Report on Operation Heartburn*, 1996, 17, quoting from AMAN's Annual Report for 1978–79 (author's archive, received from "Lexicon").

176  **A few seconds later . . . the button was pressed**  Interview with Harari, April 11,

2014. An account similar in certain aspects appears in Klein, *The Master of Operations,* 17–19. "Two Bomb-Carrying Arabs Injured in Explosion," *JTA,* June 18, 1973.

176   **"Sadness" also reported on the activities of Mohammed Boudia**   Interview with Hadar, February 7, 2012.

176   **During June 1973, Sadness reported**   Interviews with Harari, February 12, 2014, "Dark Chocolate," November 2, 2012, and Klein, May 28, 2014.

177   **Bayonet's string of triumphs instilled a sense of euphoria**   Boudia was a major loss for the PFLP. Two days later, the organization announced that it had avenged Boudia by killing the Israeli military attaché in Washington, D.C., Col. Yosef "Joe" Alon, who had been shot dead in the driveway of his Maryland home on July 1. The actual circumstances of Alon's death remain a mystery and at the center of many conspiracy theories. The investigation has recently been reopened, after evidence surfaced that Ilich Ramírez Sánchez—Carlos "the Jackal"—was involved in, or at least knew about, the affair. Adam Goldman, "I Wrote to Carlos the Jackal, and an Israeli's Assassination Case Was Revived," *New York Times,* January 8, 2017. Email correspondence with Sophie Bonnet, director of a future documentary about "Carlos the Jackal," May 2017.

177   **"there was nothing the Mossad couldn't do"**   Interview with "Kurtz," October 2005.

178   **Ali gave in and presented himself at the Fatah recruitment office**   Nadia Salti Stephan, "Abu Hassan by Abu Hassan," *Monday Morning,* April 1976.

178   **"raised eyebrows in Fatah"**   AMAN Research Department, "Terror Activity Abroad" May 1, 1969 (shown to author by "Lexicon").

178   **Documents seized in al-Najjar's apartment**   Interview with Issaki, September 2, 2015. Bird, *Good Spy,* 90.

178   **maintained that Salameh wasn't involved**   Bird, *Good Spy,* 133–34. Klein, *Striking Back,* 192.

178   **"The fact that Abu Daoud . . . wanted to take all the credit"**   Interview with Issaki, September 2, 2015.

179   **Salameh was a marked man**   Harari quote from Yarin Kimor, *Sealed Lips,* Channel 1, September 20, 2014.

179   **The Caesarea men trailing Benamene**   Klein, *Striking Back,* 186–87. Interviews with Harari, March 10, 2014, Ilan Mizrahi, October 22, 2014, "Kurtz," October 2005, "Dark Chocolate," November 2012.

179   **two Bayonet teams engaged in missions elsewhere in Europe**   In another version, Benamene embarked in Milan on a train to Oslo, followed by a Mossad team, and there, according to one of the followers, "The error occurred when we confused him with another passenger on the train." Interview with "Shaul," June 2017.

180   **"like two brothers look like each other"**   Gen. Aharon Yariv, BBC interview, November 23, 1993.

181   **She was not the only one**   Meiri, on the other hand, did believe that the man apparently leading a quiet life in Lillehammer was indeed Salameh. Interviews with Harari, March 10, 2014, Nehemia and Moshe Meiri, June 12, 2012, and "Shaul," June 2017.

181   **"Seven operatives make a positive identification"**   Interview with Harari, March 23, 2014.

181   **Harari told the logistics man, Arbel, to park the car**   They abandoned the car in the parking garage of a prestigious Danish hotel, where it remained for three years before an attendant realized that there was something wrong and it was returned to the car rental company.

182   **Harari's climb to the directorship of the Mossad**   Interviews with Harari, March 29, 2014, and "Shaul," July 2011. Y. turned down a request for an interview conveyed to him via a relative, a former commander of the Israeli Air Force, on March 20, 2017.

182   **a Moroccan working as a waiter**   Bouchiki was also the brother of Chico Bouchikhi, co-founder of the Gipsy Kings. Interview with Uli Weidenbach, February 26, 2017.

182   **"All of a sudden, my husband fell"**   Moshe Zonder, "I Was Sure They'd Kill Me Too," *Maariv,* September 13, 1995.

182   **Zamir tried to dismiss the disaster**   Yarin Kimor, *Sealed Lips,* Channel 1, September 20, 2014.

183   **Bayonet's problems were just beginning**   Interviews with "Shaul," July 2011, and Harari, March 23, 2014.

183   **The police were waiting at the rental car return**   In the Norwegian police records, however, there's a slightly different account of the circumstances under which Arbel was detained, crediting themselves and not the alert neighbor who'd taken the number down.

Either way, the end result was a disaster for the Mossad. Yossi Melman, "Protocols of Lillehammer Failure Revealed," *Maariv,* July 2, 2013.

183 **"A man writes an honest report and no one reads it"** Reacting to "Shaul's" words, Harari said, "Until Lillehammer, we didn't know he [Arbel] suffered from claustrophobia. On the contrary, in all his previous missions he had functioned superbly." The question is whether they should have known. Harari, when confronted with this question, interrupted me in a distinctly sarcastic tone: "You're a serious person, right? So look, let's say you're an operative and you're in Norway, the end of the world, next to the North Pole, and you don't know the language or the alphabet. So you can't read the street names, or the nameplate outside an apartment or a headline in a newspaper that could be relevant to your mission. Which is to say that my trained people can't speak the language, so I take the half-trained, including 'quasi-operatives' by which I mean people in the middle of the course, but who do know Norwegian, because that's what I've got, and I need someone who can translate." Interview with Harari, March 23, 2014.

183 **Documents found on the detainees** Many questions around the performance of the heads of Caesarea in the Lillehammer affair and harsh criticism of them are to be found in an anonymous letter written by one of Harari's subordinates in April 2014, which contains thitherto unpublished information and which is in the author's archive.

183 **Israel did not admit that it was responsible for killing Bouchiki** Only in the mid-1990s did Israel decide to own up to the killing, after legal proceedings were instituted against Harari and Zamir in Norway. Israel paid Torill Larsen Bouchiki and her daughter, Malika, twenty-two, the sum of $283,000, while Mr. Bouchiki's son by a previous marriage, Jamal Terje Rutgersen, won a separate settlement of $118,000. "Israelis to Compensate Family of Slain Waiter," *New York Times,* January 28, 1996.

184 **a secret agreement was reached between the governments of Israel and Norway** Israel's diplomatic and legal entanglement in Lillehammer is well described in Palmor, *The Lillehammer Affair,* a report by a Foreign Ministry official who was appointed to coordinate the efforts on the subject.

184 **"Lillehammer was a real failure"** Interview with Kfir, June 9, 2011.

184 **That miracle was Golda Meir, the Mossad's greatest fan** Interview with Harari, March 23, 2014.

184 **planning to shoot down an El Al airliner** Gaddafi had his own reasons for wanting to bring down an Israeli aircraft. On February 21, 1973, the Israeli Air Force shot down a Libyan Airlines passenger plane en route from Tripoli to Cairo that had lost its way and entered Israeli-controlled airspace over Sinai and was heading toward the secret nuclear facility at Dimona. Of the 113 people on board, 108 were killed.

184 **"a catapult shot from the runway"** Interview with Harari, March 23, 2014. Zamir, *With Open Eyes,* 142–46. Klein, *Master of Operations,* 28–35.

185 **"Don't worry, Nehemia"** Interviews with Harari, March 23, 2014, Nehemia Meiri and Moshe Meiri, June 12, 2012, and "Black," November 2015.

185 **arrested all the members of al-Hindi's squad** Most of the Palestinian prisoners were loaded onto an Italian Air Force cargo plane, which took off for Libya but exploded in mid-air over the Mediterranean. Everyone aboard was killed. Some Italian officials blamed the Mossad for the mysterious technical failure that caused the explosion. Israel denies the allegations, and as far as I was able to ascertain, they are telling the truth.

## CHAPTER 12: HUBRIS

186 **the general mood in the defense establishment remained euphoric** Spring of Youth wasn't the only success of the intelligence community in 1973. The Mossad had been running, with what it believed to be great results, a spy in the top echelons of the Egyptian government—a man by the name of Ashraf Marwan, who was the chef de bureau of President Anwar Sadat and the son-in-law of the late President Nasser. In addition, Sayeret Matkal placed surveillance devices deep inside Sinai in Operation Consulate, hooking up to the main communications cables of the Egyptian military and making parts of their top secret conversations accessible to AMAN. Interviews with "Constantine," November 2011, Ehud Barak, January 13, 2012, and Levin, May 10, 2017. On the matter of Ashraf Marwan's recruitment and handling and his possible involvement in the Egyptian deception prior to the Yom Kippur War, see Bergman and Meltzer, *The Yom Kippur War: Moment of Truth,* 31–41, 470–522 (Hebrew).

186 **Dayan climbed to the top of the mountain fortress of Masada** *Davar,* April 17, 1973.

186 **Chief of staff Elazar, in a letter to Zamir** Quotes from scanned documents printed in Zamir, *With Open Eyes,* photo insert after 128.

186 **confidence can too easily slip into overconfidence** Interview with Barak, January 13, 2012.

187 **Kissinger launched a secret diplomatic initiative** Kissinger to President Nixon, Washington, February 25–26, 1973. National Archives, Nixon Presidential Materials, NSC Files, Kissinger Office Files, Box 131.

188 **"I prefer Sharm el-Sheikh without peace"** Kipnis, *1973: The Way to War,* 89 (Hebrew).

188 **would be able to give Israel at least forty-eight hours' warning** Testimony of CoS David Elazar before the Agranat Commission, January 31, 1974, February 17, 1974, February 21, 1974 (author's archive, received from "Picasso").

188 **On October 6, at 2 p.m., the Egyptian and Syrian armies launched** Harari and Caesarea had several contingency plans for the outbreak of war, including the consignment and detonation of a container full of explosives in the harbor at Port Said, and the placing of explosive charges in various military HQs and government offices in Cairo. Harari offered them to Prime Minister Meir, but, shocked and appalled by the events, she did not want to take additional risks and declined. Bergman and Meltzer, *The Yom Kippur War: Moment of Truth,* 23–97 (Hebrew). Interview with Harari, March 29, 2014.

189 **three members of the Democratic Front for the Liberation of Palestine** *Yedioth Ahronoth,* May 16, 1974.

190 **The normally aggressive Golda Meir . . . was prepared to concede** *The Truth Behind the Maalot Massacre,* documentary film by Orly Vilnai and Guy Meroz, Channel 10, March 2014.

191 **the Sayeret proved inadequate to the task** Zonder, *Sayeret Matkal,* 119 (Hebrew).

191 **the operation had had a chilling effect** Interview with Issaki, September 2, 2015.

191 **"It obliged them to hide and run"** Interview with Harari, March 29, 2014.

192 **strengthened the hand of Abu Jihad** Sayigh, *Armed Struggle,* 310–11.

192 **a secret military report** IDF General Staff Branch, History Department, *The Terror Attack at the Savoy Hotel,* August 1975 (author's archive, received from "Gomez").

193 **The terrorists were so close to the Kirya compound** Interview with Gazit, September 12, 2016.

193 **This was seen as yet another significant failure** Interview with Omer Bar-Lev, November 15, 2012.

194 **a Mossad mole inside Fatah reported** Interviews with "Greco," October 2014, and "Jacob," August 2015.

194 **the head of AMAN . . . vigorously opposed it** Interview with Gazit, September 12, 2016.

195 **His objections were overruled** The operation was code-named Operation B'nei Mazor (Sons of Relief). Interview with Aviem Sella, July 10, 2013. (The report on the occurrence in the air force archives was shown to the author by "Roi.")

195 **murderous attacks against Jewish and Israeli targets abroad** In the period between December 1973 and May 1978, the Popular Front perpetrated twenty acts of international terrorism. Merari and Elad, *International Dimension of Palestinian Terrorism,* 170–74 (Hebrew).

196 **the organization's most brilliant operational mind** Interview with Mizrahi, April 22, 2014.

196 **"He preferred quality operations"** Interview with Issaki, September 2, 2015.

196 **Others admired Haddad's professionalism as well** The Mitrokhin Archive, K-24, 365, Churchill College, Cambridge University. Ronen Bergman, "The KGB's Middle East Files: Palestinians in the Service of Mother Russia," *Yedioth Ahronoth,* November 4, 2016. Andrew and Mitrokhin, *The Mitrokhin Archive II,* 244. Interview with Christopher Andrew, February 21, 2016.

196 **Haddad was independent and resolute** Interview with Issaki, September 2, 2015. Mossad, *Operation Heartburn,* 7.

196 **The PLO had excellent ties** Ravid, *Window to the Backyard,* 49.

196 **Haddad was on especially good terms** The link between Haddad and Baader Meinhof was forged by his deputy, Taysir Kubeh, who was in charge of the organization's secret foreign relations, via Palestinian faculty and students in Germany. Interview with Issaki, September 2, 2015.

197 **Three of the PFLP's own men** Some other Palestinian and German personnel were dispatched to Nairobi to aid with the logistics. The operational order written by Haddad is to be found in Mossad, *Report on Operation Heartburn*, 68–80.

197 **In the two months before the operation** Ibid., 73.

197 **An argument broke out inside the agency** Ibid., 30.

198 **There were also operational considerations** Interview with Eliezer Tsafrir, October 2, 2015.

198 **"The principle had not changed"** Interview with Issaki, September 2, 2015.

198 **enlisted the help of Kenya's security forces** The Mossad had a rich and very positive history of cooperation with the Kenyan security services. Ronen Bergman, "Israel and Africa," 112–16.

198 **seventeen Israelis flew out** Mossad, *Report on Operation Heartburn*, 30–31.

198 **"There was great anxiety"** Interview with Tsafrir, October 2, 2015.

199 **A combined Mossad-Kenyan team** Mossad, *Report on Operation Heartburn*, 36–37.

199 **El Al Flight LY512** Tsafrir, one of the Mossad operatives sent to Nairobi, faced a unique dilemma: He had learned that his niece, Gilat Yarden, was taking this flight. "I didn't know whether to warn her not to take the flight or to let her take it without warning her," he told me. "On the one hand absolute secrecy was particularly important. Any leak of information was liable to scare the terrorists off. I was quite sure we would stop them before they could fire the missile. On the other hand—this was my sister's daughter, and in an operation like this anything could happen. What if we couldn't find the terrorists? What's more important, loyalty to the Mossad or to my family?" In the end, Tsafrir decided that the Mossad came first and he let Gilat board the plane, taking responsibility for her life. Interview with Tsafrir, October 2, 2015.

199 **the Kenyans had been completely cooperative** Interview with Tsafrir, July 14, 2015, Mossad, *Report on Operation Heartburn*, 59.

200 **reconsidering the wisdom of bringing the prisoners to Israeli land** Interviews with "Eleanor," September 2014, "Mark," March 2011, and "Ringo," July 2013. Mossad, *Report on Operation Heartburn*, 59–60.

200 **the proposal to dump the perpetrators into the sea** As soon as he left the room, Barak summoned a consultation on the subject with senior Justice Ministry officials, headed by State Attorney Gabriel Bach, who was also "shocked to the depths of his soul" when he heard Zeevi's suggestion. Interviews with Dorit Beinish, September 28, 2014, and "Ringo," July 2013.

200 **"we decided to play ghost games with them"** Interview with Hadar, May 14, 2017.

201 **The senior 504 interrogator, Y.** Interview with "Mark," March 2011.

201 **"Y. didn't kill him"** Interview with Yigal Simon, July 29, 2012.

201 **"The lady [Schulz] made a remarkable impression"** Interview with Gazit, July 19, 2017.

202 **"I was pleased"** Interview with Hadar, May 14, 2017. Schulz also left a strong impression on John le Carré (David Cornwell), for whom his friend AMAN chief Gazit arranged a visit to the secret detention installation that was nicknamed at the time Villa Brigitta after the German terrorist. The female Mossad staffer who translated the interrogations for Hadar was introduced to le Carré under a false name and title—"prison director Capt. Kaufman." Le Carré, *The Pigeon Tunnel*, 109–15 (Hebrew).

202 **entered the room and handed Rabin a note** Protocol of cabinet meeting, June 27, 1976 (author's archive, received from "Paul"). The note handed by Poran is in the author's archive (received from Avner Avraham). Interview with Amos Eiran, February 11, 2009.

202 **There were four hijackers** IDF, History Department, *Operation Thunder Ball*, November 1977, MODA, 107.79.18, 3–11.

203 **Amin, an ex-boxer and a sergeant in the British Army** Ronen Bergman, "Israel and Africa," 121–39.

203 **Haddad believed that Israel would have no alternative** Interviews with Avner Avraham, October 14, 2015, Akiva Lakser, April 1, 2016, and Ido Netanyahu, June 29, 2016. Netanyahu (ed.), *Sayeret Matkal at Antebbe*, 25–28 (Hebrew).

203 **demanded the release of fifty-three "freedom fighters"** Report by Shin Bet director Avraham Ahituv, meeting of Security Cabinet, June 30, 1976 (author's archive, given by "Paul").

203 **"They want the five? With pleasure"** Interviews with Tsafrir, October 2, 2015.

204 **Rabin listened to the plan, growing angrier by the minute** Eventually, it emerged from a recon patrol conducted by the naval commandos along the shore of Lake Victoria that the plan was not feasible because the lake was teeming with crocodiles. Halevy,

Reicher, and Reisman, eds., *Operation Yonatan in First Person*, 38–39 (Hebrew). Interview with Eiran, February 11, 2009.

204 **"with blood on their hands"**   Interview with Eiran, July 2013. Ronen Bergman, "Gilad Shalit and the Rising Price of an Israeli Life," *New York Times Magazine*, November 9, 2011.

204 **"take a military correspondent and lock him up and grill him"**   Rabin was speaking at an emergency meeting of heads of the defense establishment that he had called on the afternoon of June 30. Chief of staff Mordechai Gur agreed with Rabin that the journalist should be grilled by the Shin Bet. "I think this has to be done, and agree with it one hundred percent. It's not too late to do it today." But no such interrogation took place, after Attorney General Barak told Rabin that it would be illegal and forbade it. "Meeting Between Prime Minister and Minister of Defense with Heads of the Defense Establishment," June 30, 1976 (author's archive, received from "Paul").

205 **David rented a plane in Kenya**   While speaking to them, he was able to take photographs of the control tower from the ground and even to get the information that the air force needed so badly—the diameter of the fueling nozzles at the airport. Interviews with Harari, March 10, 2014, Klein, October 6, 2014, and Avi Weiss Livne, September 12, 2016. Copies of the pictures that "David" took of the Entebbe Airport are in the author's archive (received from "Ethan").

206 **the prime minister gave the green light for the raid**   "Protocol of Cabinet Meetings on July 3, 1976, and July 4, 1976" (author's archive, received from "Paul"). Interview with Peres, August 4, 2015.

206 **The first Hercules landed as planned**   Interviews with Yiftach Reicher, November 25, 2013, and Weiss Livne, May 16, 2016. Ronen Bergman, "Operation Entebbe as Told by the Commandos: Planning the Mission," *Yedioth Ahronoth*, June 27, 2016. Halevy, Reicher, and Reisman, eds., *Operation Yonatan in First Person*, 19–32 (Hebrew).

206 **The element of surprise was almost lost**   Ronen Bergman and Lior Ben Ami, "Back from Africa," *Yedioth Ahronoth*, June 17, 2016.

207 **The sound of the rifle brought other Ugandan troops**   Interviews with Reicher Atir, November 25, 2013, Weiss Livne, May 16, 2016, Amir Ofer, April 1, 2016, Giora Zussman, May 2016, Dani Arditi, June 13, 2011, Omer Bar-Lev, November 15, 2012, Pinchas Buchris, May 2016, Rami Sherman, July 6, 2016, Shlomi Reisman, July 6, 2016, Shaul Mofaz, June 14, 2011, and Betser, June 10, 2016.

207 **the man who'd ordered the hijacking**   Interviews with "Greco," March 2015, and "Jacob," August 2015.

## CHAPTER 13: DEATH IN THE TOOTHPASTE

209 **"It was very strange for us"**   Interview with Yitzhak Hofi, Begin Center, January 11, 2002.

209 **Begin gave the military and intelligence agencies carte blanche**   Interview with Admoni, May 29, 2011.

209 **wanted the Mossad to launch a large-scale targeted killing campaign**   Begin annulled the decisions by preceding prime ministers (Eshkol signed the order on December 31, 1968, and Meir and Rabin ratified it) to place the hunt for Nazi criminals lower on the Mossad's order of priorities, and with his vigorous backing, the Cabinet's security committee resolved on July 23, 1977, "to order the Mossad to resume the search for Nazi war criminals, in particular Josef Mengele. If there is no way of bringing them to justice, to kill them." From that point on, the Mossad did act with the intent of finding and eliminating Mengele, but these efforts were to no avail. Caesarea did locate Klaus Barbie, "the Butcher of Lyon," commander of the Gestapo in that city who was responsible for sending thousands of Jews to death camps, in Bolivia. Caesarea director Harari traveled to La Paz to supervise the preparations for the assassination, but in the end he decided to cancel it due to uncertainties about the escape route. In retrospect, he thought that he had been overly cautious: "I think that more should have been done [against the Nazis]. As long as a single Nazi was still breathing in any corner of the world, we should have helped him to stop breathing. Today, when I know the territory where these Nazis were living, Central and South America, and how easy it would have been for us to turn the world upside down there, I think what idiots we were." Instead of killing him, Israel conveyed the information it had collected about Barbie to France, which extradited him and put him on trial in 1983. In 1987 he was sentenced to life, and he died of cancer in prison in 1991. Interviews with Medan, June 30, 2015, Harari, March 10, 2011, Klein, May 28, 2014, and Yossi Chen, September 11, 2017.

Mossad, Caesarea, Revav, commander of Messer, to Mike Harari, April 11, 1978. Mossad, History Department, *Looking for the Needle in the Haystack,* 2007, 117–220 (author's archive, received from "Midburn"). Ronen Bergman, "Why Did Israel Let Mengele Go?" *New York Times,* September 6, 2017. Interview with Hofi, Begin Center, January 11, 2002. Klein, *Master of Operations,* 236–39.

209 **"Unlike other Israelis"** Interview with Nakdimon, February 18, 2015.

210 **diplomatic recognition for the PLO** Merari and Elad, *International Dimension of Palestinian Terrorism,* 130–31 (Hebrew).

210 **Arafat appeared before the UN General Assembly** United Nations General Assembly, Twenty-Ninth Session, Official Records, A/PV.2282.

210 **A December 1974 paper prepared by AMAN** Intelligence Branch, Research Division, Special Report 12/906, December 25, 1974 (author's archive, received from "the Biologist").

211 **"Arafat was the complete opposite"** Interview with Amos Gilad, July 31, 2012.

211 **a sharp debate between the Mossad and AMAN** Interview with Pressler, July 6, 2017.

211 **"After Arafat's speech at the UN"** Interview with Issaki, September 2, 2015.

211 **Arafat's name was removed from the kill list** Mossad, *Operation Heartburn,* 105–8.

212 **Sadness switched Haddad's toothpaste** Interviews with Dagan, July 20, 2013, "Bertie," June 2009, "Eldy," August 2016, and "Ethan," June 2015.

212 **Haddad began feeling sick** In Aaron Klein's book *Striking Back,* a slightly different account appears, according to which the poison was concealed in Belgian chocolate, which Haddad particularly liked, and was given to him by one of his men who was a Mossad agent. Klein, *Striking Back,* 179–81.

212 **He was first diagnosed** A report on the patient "Ahmed," written by Dr. O. Prokop, Humboldt University, April 21, 1978 (author's archive, received from Gunther Latsch).

212 **Arafat instructed an aide to approach the Stasi** The internal correspondence of East German intelligence about the Palestinians is not devoid of blatantly racist references to the Palestinians, who are called "camel fuckers" in these memos. Stasi provided training and weapons to the Palestinian organizations and together with the KGB urged it to act against Israeli and American targets while also making sure that they would not operate within the Communist Bloc. Information courtesy of journalist Gunther Latsch. Ronen Bergman, "KGB's Middle East Files," *Yedioth Ahronoth,* November 4, 2016.

213 **Wadie Haddad died in great agony** "Maj. Gen. Dr. Fister to the 'Great Minister' [identity undisclosed, probably Erich Mielke] with the Following Documents on 22.4.78: A Report on the Patient 'Ahmed,' Written by Dr. Prokop 21.4.78; Institute of Forensic Medicine at the Humboldt University, *Corpse of Ahmed Doukli,* 20.4.1978; An Expert Medical Report, number 258/78, by Dr. Geserick, Designated for the Military District and State Attorney, on the Corpse of Doukli, Ahmed. 29.3.78" (author's archive, received from Gunther Latsch).

214 **"I was very happy when I heard Haddad was dead"** I read to Issaki the German doctors' reports on the horrendous suffering that Haddad went through before dying. He smiled: "These stories of suffering have an effect of their own. They spread out and reach the ears of other terrorists, get into their minds, cause them awe and terror, disrupt their judgment, change their behavior, make them make mistakes." Interview with Issaki, September 2, 2015.

214 **"When they killed Bouchiki, I was in Europe"** Bird, *Good Spy,* 152.

215 **This interview was distributed to the heads of the intelligence community** Interview with "Black," September 2016.

215 **"Killing Salameh was first and foremost"** Interview with Ravid, January 17, 2013.

215 **insisted that Salameh remained a threat** Interview with "Ethan," June 2015.

215 **said that his CIA counterparts had hinted** In *The Good Spy,* Kai Bird describes a similar scene in which the issue of the relations between Salameh and American intelligence was discussed by Alan Wolfe of the CIA and the Mossad in the summer of 1978. Bird, *Good Spy,* 207–208. Interview with "Legend," May 2011.

215 **"This man has Jewish blood on his hands"** Interview with Issaki, September 2, 2015.

216 **The PLO was officially considered a terrorist organization** Memorandum of Conversation: Kissinger, Helms, Saunders, July 23, 1973, and attachment Ames to Helms, July 18, 1973. NA, RN, NSC Files Box 1027.

216 **Ames did all he could to persuade Salameh** Bird, *Good Spy,* 145.

217 **The only point over which Ames saw fit to admonish Salameh** Ibid., 126.

217 **Through the Ames-Salameh middleman** Ibid., 151.

217 **he organized the visit and arranged meetings** Interview with "Jacob," August 2015.

217 **A deep friendship had formed between Ames and Salameh** Bird, *Good Spy*, 176–78.

218 **The Israelis looked on and ground their teeth** Interviews with Harari, March 10, 2014, Klein, October 6, 2014, and Issaki, September 2, 2015.

218 **The CIA escort, Charles Waverly, recalled the visit** Bird, *Good Spy*, 181–83.

218 **Ames and his CIA colleague were not impressed** Ibid., 179–80.

219 **The CIA even supplied Salameh with encrypted communications equipment** Ibid., 208.

219 **there was only one way this relationship could be interpreted** Interview with "Jacob," August 2015.

219 **"cutting this channel was very important"** Interview with "Legend," May 2011.

219 **"a blue-and-white job"** Interview with Harari, March 10, 2014.

220 **Al-Hajj used his network of sources** Interview with Amin al-Hajj (in the presence of his former Mossad Case Officer, "Kobi"), August 14, 2014. Ronen Bergman, "Waltz with Amin," *Yedioth Ahronoth*, November 14, 2014.

220 **Harari was pleased** Interview with Harari, March 29, 2014.

220 **"The idea in encounters like these"** Interview with "Black," June 2015.

221 **Another alternative, placing an explosive device in Salameh's locker** Interviews with Harari, March 29, 2014, Klein, May 28, 2014, and "Tuna," August 2015.

222 **Rinah's real name was Erika Chambers** Dietl, *Die Agentin des Mossad*, 85–96, 112, 147.

222 **Rinah and two men were selected for the assassination** In addition to practicing the actual killing, the three also trained to evacuate by sea. It was assumed the Beirut airport would be closed, or at least under tightened security, after a car-bombing downtown. David Shiek, then a young officer and later deputy commander of Flotilla 13, drilled them in coping with emergency situations in which they might be required to swim or to use weapons in the course of evacuation to the sea. Interview with David Shiek, April 11, 2013.

223 **a team from Sayeret Matkal crossed the border** Interview with "Lychee," November 2011.

223 **He could not allow himself another failure** Interview with Harari, March 23, 2014.

223 **The operative muttered through his teeth, "Die, motherfucker!"** Interview with "Black," September 2016.

223 **Abu Daoud . . . ran up and tried to help** Bird, *Good Spy*, 215–16.

224 **Rinah and the two other operatives waited on a beach** Interview with Shiek, April 11, 2013.

224 **"At your age, I lost my father"** Bird, *Good Spy*, 217.

## CHAPTER 14: A PACK OF WILD DOGS

225 **left the meeting feeling very worried** Interviews with Gilad, August 4, 2015, and Gadi Zohar, January 2, 2013.

225 **Gilad wanted to strike first** Interviews with Gilad, July 31, 2012, and Galant, August 19, 2011.

227 **the police managed to stop the bus** IDF General Staff, History Department, *Terror Attack on the Coastal Road*, December 1, 1983 (author's archive, received from "Paul").

227 **most were burned alive** In some later media reports it has been claimed that Israeli panic and misunderstanding of the situation caused excessive shooting that caused most of the deaths, whereas the aim of the attackers was to conduct negotiations for the release of prisoners. Even if this claim is correct, everyone agrees that Abu Jihad ordered his men to kill the hostages if the negotiations didn't succeed. *Uvda*, Channel 2, May 26, 2013, "The Terrorist Who Carried Out the Attack on the Bloodbath Bus: I Apologize and I Regret It," October 31, 2011.

228 **Israeli soldiers also committed a few acts of killing prisoners** Most of these cases never reached the courts, including grave actions carried out on March 15 and April 16, among them the murder of "a terrorist, aged about 13." "Treatment of Prisoners," Y. Einstein, head of the IDF inspection in the State Comptrollers Office, to the Chief of the General Staff, November 9, 1978 (author's archive, received from "Bell").

228 **"believed in taking the war against the PLO to the enemy's rear"** Interview with Galant, September 4, 2014.

229 **was to pardon two convicted IDF criminals** Military Court file no. 313/78, IDF Prosecutor v. First Lt. Daniel Pinto, judgment (in camera) of February 9, 1979 (author's

archive, received from "Snow"). Eitan, *A Soldier's Story: The Life and Times of an Israeli War Hero,* 163–65 (Hebrew).

229 **"You, Flotilla 13, are like a priest's balls"** Interview with Shiek, April 11, 2013.

229 **Flotilla 13 carried out twenty-three raids** Facts courtesy of Mike Eldar. Eldar, *Flotilla 13,* 572–83 (Hebrew).

230 **"He didn't even try to justify his order"** Interviews with Ami Ayalon, January 21, 2013, Galant, September 4, 2014, and Eldar, September 18, 2011. Eldar, *Flotilla 13,* 583 (Hebrew).

230 **no one went to the port for coffee** Zrair remained one of the top activists in PLO activities against Israel and also played a role in the fighting after Israel's June 1982 invasion of southern Lebanon. During that year, Unit 504 recruited one Ibrahim Firan, a senior official at Tyre port who was close to Zrair. The two shared an attraction to young boys. Unit 504 paid Firan a tidy sum, some of which was used to finance their partying. In exchange, Firan came up with the location of Zrair's hideout—a villa on the beach between the mouths of the Zahrani and Litani rivers, north of Tyre. On August 5, 1982, a force from the Israel Police's YAMAM special counterterrorism squad raided the house, supported by troops from Division 91. The raiders reported that Zrair had gone for his pistol and they shot him dead. Fatah intelligence suspected Firan of informing on Zrair and liquidated him two weeks later, near the café that Flotilla 13 assassins had in their sights just over two years before. Zvika Bandori of the Shin Bet says that Zrair was not armed and did not resist, and that he was killed in line with a Shin Bet execution procedure known as "Krenk" ("sickness" in Yiddish). The hunger to avenge him on the part of his comrades led to their joining up with elements in Hezbollah, which had just been formed, to blow up the Israeli HQ in Tyre not long afterward, according to Bandori. Interviews with Ravid, January 17, 2013, Yitzhak Mordechai, March 22, 2015, and Zvika Bandori, September 11, 2017.

231 **"made no difference which Palestinians we killed"** Interview with Shiek, April 11, 2013.

231 **"asked him how we were supposed to identify the terrorists"** Interview with "Olive," May 2013.

231 **"unanimously sentenced him to death, without the right of appeal"** Interview with Ravid, January 17, 2013.

232 **Israeli intelligence was establishing a permanent presence** Schiff and Yaari, *Israel's Lebanon War,* 50–75 (Hebrew).

232 **The Phalangists were exceptionally brutal** Interview with Uzi Dayan, April 18, 2013.

232 **an Israeli-trained Maronite militant named Robert Hatem** Hatem has been living in Paris under the aegis of the French security services since the mid-1990s. This is where I conducted a series of interviews with him in February 2005. Ronen Bergman, "The Cobra," *Yedioth Ahronoth,* March 4, 2005.

233 **"At the outset of our relationship with them"** Interview with Merhav, October 5, 2011.

233 **"Begin saw himself as the savior of the oppressed"** Interview with Mordechai Tzipori, March 11, 2015.

233 **"we must not be the Phalangists' patrons"** Ronen Bergman, "Dismissal in the Mossad Leadership," *Haaretz,* January 3, 1997.

234 **"So I kept my hand over her mouth"** Smadar Haran Kaiser, "The World Should Know What He Did to My Family," *Washington Post,* May 18, 2003.

234 **The horrendous murder in Nahariya** Interview with Avigdor Ben-Gal, November 6, 2013.

235 **"We had a lot of disagreements"** Eitan, *Soldier's Story,* 182.

235 **With Eitan's blessing, Ben-Gal appointed the man** Interviews with Ben-Gal, November 6, 2013, and Dagan, May 26, 2013.

235 **"I gave his secret operations complete freedom"** Interview with Ben-Gal, November 6, 2013.

235 **"the aim . . . was to cause chaos"** Interview with David Agmon, October 28, 2015.

236 **"Raful and I used to okay missions with a wink"** Interview with Ben-Gal, November 6, 2013.

236 **ordered by Eitan to cooperate without knowing what the purpose was** The conscience of one member of this unit was troubled by its activities, calling them "not less than war crimes." He left the army and emigrated to the United States, cutting off most of his ties with Israel. Interviews with "Rupert," March 2016, Ben-Gal, November 6, 2013, Dagan, May 29, 2013, Agmon, May 8, 2016, and Gadi Aviran, April 16, 2012.

236 **"We'd come there at night"** Interviews with Ben-Gal, November 6, 2013, and Aql al-Hashem, December 1999. Sayigh, *Armed Struggle,* 513–21.

237  **"Ben-Gal even tried to bar me"**  Interview with Yehoshua Saguy, November 20, 2015.

237  **"There was a constant struggle with the Northern Command"**  Interview with Gilboa, March 18, 2015.

237  **"realized that something irregular was going on"**  Interview with Ben-Gal, November 6, 2013.

238  **Ben-Gal had an encrypted connection set up**  Interview with Ephraim Sneh, October 20, 2015.

238  **AMAN had apparently managed to tap his encrypted phone**  Interview with Ben-Gal, November 6, 2013.

238  **"They tell me about the explosions in Lebanon"**  Interview with Tzipori, March 11, 2015.

238  **"Raful had not submitted it upstairs"**  Interview with Ben-Gal, November 6, 2013.

239  **Ben-Gal was summoned to the defense minister's bureau**  Account of the meeting taken from interviews with Tzipori, March 11, 2015, and Ben-Gal, November 6, 2013. Aside from a few minor differences, their accounts are identical.

240  **"'Let the young men arise and play before us'"**  Interview with Gilboa, December 30, 2013.

240  **"the activities took place in a gray area"**  Interview with Ben-Gal, November 6, 2013.

242  **Sharon thought, correctly, that every day that went by peacefully**  Schiff and Yaari, *Israel's Lebanon War*, 125–26.

242  **"The aim . . . was to sow such chaos"**  Interview with Sneh, October 26, 2015.

242  **car bombs were exploding regularly**  Sayigh, *Armed Struggle*, 513–21. Al-Hurriyya, July 9, 1981. List of incidents involving the FLLF on the Global Terrorism Database (GTD): http://www.start.umd.edu/gtd/search/Results.aspx?perpetrator=2991.

243  **"With Sharon's backing . . . terrible things were done"**  Interview with "Sally," February 2015.

243  **"I saw from a distance one of the cars blowing up"**  Interview with "Eldy," January 2015.

243  **"The targets were always military targets"**  Interview with Ben-Gal, November 6, 2013.

243  **"You can give him explosives"**  Interview with Dagan, May 26, 2013.

244  **Sharon had Arafat returned to the wanted list**  Interviews with Ben-Gal, November 6, 2013, Dagan, May 26, 2013, Agmon, October 28, 2015, Sneh, October 20, 2015, and Azriel Nevo, January 5, 2016.

245  **The death and destruction**  Zvika Bandori, who was acting head of the Arab division of the Shin Bet at the time, says that Rafi Eitan, the prime minister's adviser on terrorism, and Meir Dagan presented him with the plan and rejected his opposition, which was based on the presence of large numbers of civilians. They argued that there would not be many civilians there. At Eitan's request, Bandori says, he arranged a meeting between Eitan and Shin Bet director Avraham Shalom, who also expressed his strong opposition to the operation. Interviews with Bandori, September 11, 2017, and "Henry," October 2015.

245  **This was written not in fear**  Interview with Sneh, October 20, 2015.

245  **someone leaked the plan to Saguy**  Interviews with Saguy, November 20, 2015, and Dagan, May 26, 2013.

245  **"It was a very rainy day"**  "I hadn't been so scared in a long time as on that flight to Jerusalem," Dagan recalls. Eitan had a military pilot's license and took a practice flight every now and again when he visited Air Force bases. Regular airmen tried to avoid accompanying him. "It was really a danger to life and limb," one of them recalls. Sometimes Eitan would prepare bags of salt and drop them on couples making out on the beach. Ben-Gal remembers these flights with horror. Once, he relates, Eitan saw a ship out at sea "and he shouted 'there's a terrorists' boat, let's buzz it.'" He swung the Cessna away from the coastline and headed for the vessel, which turned out to be a destroyer from the U.S. Sixth Fleet. Eitan, in his playful mood, kept up the joke, as if it were a terrorists' boat, although Ben-Gal yelled at him, "Look at the cannons and the flag!" But the CoS enjoyed Ben-Gal's nervousness and he began flying passes over the destroyer at mast height until its crew got teed off and sprayed the Cessna with foam. Interviews with Dagan, May 29, 2013, Ravid, November 13, 2012, and Ben-Gal, November 6, 2013.

246  **"If something happens to him"**  Interview with Saguy, November 20, 2015.

246  **"there was no Soviet ambassador"**  Interview with Dagan, May 26, 2013.

247  **Everything went well until dawn**  Interviews with Dagan, May 26, 2013, and "Sally," February 2015.

## CHAPTER 15: "ABU NIDAL, ABU *SHMIDAL*"

248 **Argov shook hands with the press mogul Robert Maxwell** Interview with Yoav Biran (Argov's number 2 at the embassy at the time, who was also at the Dorchester that night), April 22, 1999.

248 **waiting, watching the front door of the Dorchester** Telephone interviews with Hussein Said, April-May 1999.

249 **Carrying a Polish-made WZ-63 miniature submachine gun** Hussein Said to the author, April 20, 1999 (author's archive). Telephone interviews with Hussein Said, April-May 1999.

249 **Said's companions were caught** The incident led to serious friction between British and Israeli intelligence, with Mossad officials alleging that the British could have done more to prevent the assassination attempt. Five years later, Israel was running a double agent inside an operational Fatah cell in London, without the knowledge of the British. Cell members assassinated Naji al-Ali, a Palestinian caricaturist with British citizenship, who had ridiculed Arafat in his cartoons. Arafat had ordered him liquidated. The British authorities claimed that Israel could have averted the slaying and that it had not done so as revenge for the attack on the ambassador or simply because it didn't care about the killing of an Arab. The British expelled most of the members of the Mossad station in London. Interviews with Ravid, January 17, 2013, and "Gelato," February 1999. Sharon Sade and Ronen Bergman, "I Shot Shlomo Argov," *Haaretz*, June 11, 1999.

249 **Shortly after the assassination attempt, Israeli intelligence learned** Interview with Simon, July 29, 2012.

249 **hoped that the assassination would bring about a large-scale military clash** Saddam also wanted to take revenge on Israel for its attack on the Iraqi nuclear reactor Tamuz Osirak a year earlier. Amatzia Baram and Pesach Malovany, "The Revenge of Saddam Hussein," *Yedioth Ahronoth*, June 14, 2012.

250 **"Abu Nidal, Abu *Shmidal*. We've got to whack the PLO"** Schiff and Yaari, *Israel's Lebanon War*, 12 (Hebrew).

250 **Arafat could not let this pass without reacting** Ibid., 16.

250 **he didn't believe his shot had started the Israeli war** Letter from Hussein Said to the author, April 20, 1999 (author's archive). Telephone interviews with Said, April-May 1999.

250 **It would be a limited incursion, Sharon told the cabinet** Minister of Defense at the Foreign Affairs and Defense Committee, Knesset, June 7, 1982, 1 (author's archive, received from "Dorris").

250 **The only minister who opposed the plan was Mordechai Zippori** Schiff and Yaari, *Israel's Lebanon War*, 146.

251 **This was indeed only the beginning of Sharon's actual plan** Landau, *Arik*, 140–41, 196–98 (Hebrew). Interview with Nevo, January 14, 2016.

251 **"I knew that they had not given up their ambition"** Begin Center, interview with Hofi, January 11, 2002. Author's interview with Saguy, November 20, 2015.

252 **The beginning was promising** Bergman, *Authority Granted*, 170–80 (Hebrew).

252 **The militiamen performed even worse than AMAN had predicted** Description of the invasion in Schiff and Yaari, *Israel's Lebanon War*, 163–82 (Hebrew), and Sayigh, *Armed Struggle*, 508–31.

252 **took advantage of the opportunity to settle the score** The combat arena between Israel and Syria became the first testing ground for the most advanced weaponry developed in the United States and Israel against the front line of the Red Army laboratories. The outcome was clear-cut. On June 9, the biggest aerial battle of the jet age took place over Lebanon. In Operation Mole Cricket (Arzsav) 19, the Israeli Air Force knocked out almost all of Syria's Russian-made surface-to-air missile batteries in Lebanon. On the same day, in aerial combat, the Israelis shot down 26 Syrian Russian-made front-line fighters. In all, a total of 82 Syrian warplanes were destroyed in 46 hours, for the loss of one Israeli plane. Interviews with Sella, July 10, 2013, David Ivri, April 18, 2013, Yitzhak Ben-Yisrael, June 5, 2011, and "Amit," April 2013. Schiff and Yaari, *Israel's Lebanon War*, 183–222 (Hebrew).

252 **"the forty-kilometer plan was melting away"** Interview with Nevo, January 5, 2016.

253 **"The Mossad . . . was absolutely wrong"** Interview with Nevo, January 14, 2016.

253 **In a meeting with chief of staff Eitan** Mossad, "Notes on Meeting Between Johni Abdu, Bashir Gemayel and the CoS," June 16, 1982 (author's archive, received from "Dorris").

253  **in a combined operation code-named the Spark**  "Summary of Course of Events in West Beirut," document submitted to Inquiry Commission on behalf of Defense Minister Sharon (author's archive, received from "Dorris").

253  **During a meeting at Sharon's home**  Defense Minister's Bureau, "Meeting Between Bashir Gemayel, Johni Abdu, and the Minister of Defense," August 1, 1982 (author's archive, received from "Dorris").

253  **"there is no intention to enter Beirut"**  "Meeting of Knesset Foreign Affairs and Security Committee," June 13, 1982, 10, and "Statement of Defense Minister at Cabinet Meeting," July 7, 1982 (author's archive, received from "Dorris").

254  **"to destroy whatever can be destroyed"**  Schiff and Yaari, *Israel's Lebanon War*, 259–60 (Hebrew).

254  **"You are causing a holocaust in Beirut"**  Interview with Nevo, January 14, 2016.

254  **by leaking to the London *Observer* documents**  *Yedioth Ahronoth*, July 18, 1982. Interview with "Miguel," July 2012. "Arrow," January 1999.

254  **were being made without the approval of the cabinet**  Schiff and Yaari, *Israel's Lebanon War*, 116 (Hebrew).

255  **Sharon would sue a journalist who wrote**  Sharon sued the journalist Uzi Benziman, who later recounted the story of the trial in a book titled *I Told the Truth* (Hebrew). An extensive, gripping, sometimes amusing, and of course very subjective account of the trial appears in the book by Dov Weissglass (who was also the lead counsel for Sharon in the lawsuit against *Time* magazine), *Ariel Sharon: A Prime Minister*, 38–75 (Hebrew).

255  **the plan to do away with Yasser Arafat**  In a long interview Begin gave to Israel TV in late June 1982, he flatly denied that one of the aims of the campaign was to kill Arafat, but only to put an end to his command and the two "Abu somethings," a contemptuous reference to Arafat's two deputies. He declared that "the IDF is not only a humane army, but also a democratic army. It's wonderful to see [the IDF's commanders] doing their job." An indication of the highly sensitive nature of the matter can be found in research into the Lebanon War carried out by the IDF's History Department, which includes extensive references to Operation Salt Fish. But the project was abruptly shut down when it seemed as though the researcher, Prof. Motti Golani, was displaying too much independence. The work, which includes highly sensitive material, was never completed, and all of Golani's material was confiscated. Interview with Golani, January 15, 2013.

255  **In a letter to Reagan on August 2**  *Yedioth Ahronoth*, August 3, 1982. Schiff and Yaari, *Israel's Lebanon War*, 274 (Hebrew).

255  **In a speech in the Knesset the same week**  *Yedioth Ahronoth*, June 30, 1982.

255  **"But without causing too much collateral damage"**  Interview with Dayan, June 4, 2012.

255  **was summoned to Beirut in June**  Interview with "Vivaldi," August 2011.

255  **the Salt Fish teams had an abundance of information**  The Salt Fish team wanted to add Abu Jihad to the hit list. The Mossad knew where to find his wife, Intisar, and the team planned to poison her, making her very ill. Abu Jihad, a devoted family man, would come to see her, and the assassins would be waiting. "But Begin heard about the plan and he thought it was too diabolical and ruled it out," said a senior member of the Salt Fish team. Interview with Dayan, April 18, 2013, and "Yoav," December 2016.

256  **Once they even heard Arafat himself on the phone**  Interview with Dayan, June 4, 2012.

256  **He scattered disinformation around among his aides**  A Mossad document from July 1, 1982, shown to the author by "Matias," said, "Salt Fish is taking extreme safety precautions and according to Junction sources, he gives his own people disinformation out of fear that some of them may be serving us."

256  **"Arafat kept on breaking his routine"**  Interview with Moshe Yaalon, August 16, 2011. "He changes places all the time. . . . From command post to command post, with all their communications systems, and their international communications . . ." Sharon report to cabinet, July 18, 1982. Arafat himself claimed to have counted thirteen Israeli attempts to kill him during the siege. Rubin and Colp-Rubin, *Yasir Arafat*, 98–99, 102.

256  **"My goal was to begin paving a path"**  Interview with Avnery, July 19, 2013.

256  **decided to take advantage of the opportunity**  Interview with Yaalon, August 16, 2011.

257  **Among the Salt Fish team members, a discussion took place**  Interview with Avner Azulay, July 6, 2015.

257  **"I thought that it was messy"**  Interview with Ivri, May 30, 2011.

257  **"Raful used to blow up with anger"**  Interview with Dayan, June 4, 2012.

258 **chief of staff Eitan was obsessive about killing Arafat** Interview with Sella, April 7, 2013.

259 **Eitan took a helicopter ride to Beirut** Later that evening, Eitan flew back to report to a cabinet meeting. and Sharon told the ministers proudly about how chief of staff Eitan "took part in a bombing raid in Beirut" that morning. Transcript of cabinet meeting, August 4, 1982, 7 (author's archive, received from "Eric").

259 **now an object of global sympathy** Schiff and Yaari, *Israel's Lebanon War*, 273–76 (Hebrew).

260 **"someone should go and kill Sharon"** Interview with Dayan, May 15, 2012. While I was working on this book, some of the men from the Paratroop Recon unit, one of the elite IDF infantry units that spearheaded the invasion forces, sent me a copy of a letter they had written to Prof. Amnon Rubinstein, a liberal member of parliament, in September 1982. "Today the situation no longer allows for silence," they wrote, followed by a grave indictment of Sharon for dragging Israel into a war with his lies and deceptions—an unnecessary war that allowed for the perpetration of grievous war crimes.

260 **"the famous kaffiyeh on the famous head"** Interview with "Simon," April 1994.

260 **It would have been so easy to kill him** Interview with Yaalon, August 16, 2011.

260 **One of the commanders was in radio contact** Interview with Gilboa, August 4, 2015.

261 **Arafat was already in Athens** "Arafat in Greece in Snub to Arabs," *New York Times*, September 2, 1982.


### CHAPTER 16: BLACK FLAG

262 **the Lebanese parliament voted** IDF and Mossad personnel including Meir Dagan and Rehavia Vardi oversaw the armed "escorting" of members of parliament who refused to attend the vote out of fear of the Syrians and the PLO. Mossad, "Minutes of Meeting Between Maj. Gen. Amir Drori and Gemayel," July 27, 1982. Interview with Rehavia Vardi, August 19, 1997. Menachem Navot, deputy Mossad director responsible for activities in Lebanon, claims these were merely "persuasive conversations." Interview with Navot, April 6, 2017. Navot's typed personal diary, copied by the author and located in his archive, 99–103.

262 **"How will we be able to take care of the terrorists"** Notes of Sharon's meeting with heads of Shin Bet and Mossad and Sharon's account of cabinet meeting, August 21, 1982 (author's archive, received from "Dorris").

262 **suggested that the Phalangists go into west Beirut** Foreign Affairs and Security Committee, Protocol No.118, September 24, 1982, 22 (author's archive, received from "Eric").

262 **Begin liked this idea** Protocol of cabinet meeting, June 15, 1982 (author's archive, received from "Dorris").

263 **The Mossad embellished this proposition** Interview with Azulay, July 6, 2015.

263 **Gemayel was instead murdered** Sharon report to cabinet, September 16, 1982, 9 (author's archive, received from "Dorris").

263 **"I saw the boys of Elie . . . sharpening their knives"** Interview with Ravid, January 17, 2013.

263 **a group commanded by Marom Mashalani** Interview with Robert Hatem, February 2005.

263 **a horrific massacre**: Sayigh, *Armed Struggle*, 539.

263 **Sharon would later claim** "Main Points of Defense Minister's Version at the Inquiry Commission," document submitted to the Kahan Commission, par. 34 (author's archive, received from "Eric").

264 **the barbaric behavior pattern of the Phalange** "AMAN's References to Phalange Characteristics, Dec. 1981–September 1982," document submitted to Kahan Commission, par. 29 (author's archive, received from "Dorris").

264 **"they will rape and loot and kill"** Sharon was speaking half a year before Israel invaded Lebanon, as part of the preparation for the campaign, which makes his subsequent conduct all the more grave. Ministry of Defense, "Minister's Visit to the Northern Command," January 14, 1982 (author's archive, received from "Dorris").

264 **began counseling the Maronite militia** Interviews with Yuval Diskin, October 18, 2011, Gilad, July 31, 2012, Nevo, January 5, 2016, Gilboa, January 8, 2014, Amir Drori, May 1996, and Ron Ben-Yishai, March 30, 2014. Mossad, *Summary of Meeting Between the CoS and CoS of Lebanese Forces*, September 19, 1982. Schiff and Yaari, *Israel's Lebanon War*, 334 (Hebrew).

264    **Testifying behind closed doors**    "Minister of Defense at the Foreign Affairs and Defense Committee," September 24, 1982, 11 (author's archive, received from "Eric").

265    **"He realized that Sharon had hoodwinked him"**    Interview with Nevo, January 5, 2016.

265    **His condition deteriorated so much**    Police Minister Yosef Burg suggested sending police in to move the demonstrators out of hearing, but Begin, the heart-and-soul democrat, responded: "By no means. It is their right to protest." Interview with Nevo, January 5, 2016.

266    **"A very embarrassing situation"**    Interview with Nahum Admoni, July 23, 2006, Begin Center. Thanks to Rami Shahar of the Begin Center for assistance in locating the material.

266    **his aides worked to conceal his true condition**    Shilon, *Begin,* 411–37 (Hebrew).

266    **"I told them to classify the schedule 'Top Secret'"**    Interview with Nevo, January 5, 2016.

266    **"giving orders over chief of staff Eitan's head"**    Interview with Sella, May 31, 2011.

266    **"Sharon dominated the meetings"**    Interview with Admoni, July 23, 2006, Begin Center Archive.

267    **Operation Salt Fish morphed into Operation Goldfish**    Interview with Gilboa, December 30, 2013.

267    **Arafat was traveling frenetically**    Interview with "Sally," May 2016, and "Tavor," June 2011.

268    **There was no question of shooting it down**    Interview with Gilad, December 30, 2013.

268    **AMAN saw no possibility of assassinating him**    Interview with Gilboa, January 17, 2016.

268    **demanded that a number of operational steps be taken**    Interview with Gilboa, March 1, 2016.

269    **they found their opening in Greece**    Interview with Admoni, May 29, 2011.

269    **Sharon kept up constant pressure**    Interview with Ivri, April 18, 2011.

269    **one of the Caesarea operatives in Athens**    Documentation of the operation was shown to the author by "Dvir."

271    **He was still stalling for time**    Interview with Ivri, April 18, 2011.

271    **a phone jangled in Canary**    Interview with "Eldy," August 2014.

271    **another report came in to Canary**    Interviews with Ivri, April 18, 2011, and "Tavor," June 2011.

272    **Aviem Sella couldn't believe his ears**    Interview with Sella, April 9, 2014.

273    **General Gilboa expressed his sharp opposition**    Interview with Gilboa, January 17, 2016.

273    **Gilboa could feel his heart thumping in his chest**    Interview with Gilboa, January 17, 2016.

274    **"The distinguishing mark of a manifestly illegal order"**    Military prosecution against Captain Malinki, 3/57, 213–14.

274    **refusing to obey orders that they believed to be manifestly illegal**    Interview with Sella, April 9, 2014.

274    **On each of the five occasions**    One of the pilots on the alert for intercepting Goldfish was "Amit," a twenty-four-year-old airman who had already acquired a reputation for being one of the Israeli Air Force's aces. "To this day I am plagued by the question of what I would have done if the moment had come when I was ordered to shoot the plane down. Would I have opened fire? Would I have disobeyed the order? In many conversations that I've had with trainees over the years, I have raised these questions, asked them what they would do. I would of course like to hope that all of us would refuse to shoot and fly back to base." Interview with "Amit," April 2013.

275    **"we simply drew the time out"**    Interview with Sella, May 31, 2011.

275    **after heavy international criticism**    In February 1983, *Time* magazine ran a story by the journalist David Halevy saying that Sharon knew in advance of the planned revenge. Sharon sued *Time* for libel in a New York court. Halevy said *Time* paid a senior officer, an associate of Sharon, for the classified documents about the affair. The judge, however, did not allow the submission of the documents as evidence. A jury found that Sharon indeed had been libeled, but as the magazine had not been motivated by malice, he was not entitled to damages. Interviews with David Halevy, September 20, 2016, and Dov Weissglass, December 23, 2014. *Ariel Sharon, Plaintiff, v. Time, Inc., Defendant,* United States District Court, S.D. New York, 599 F.Supp. 538 (1984).

275    **made the first cracks in Sharon's monolithic power**    While the commission was hearing its witnesses, the Front for the Liberation of Lebanon from Foreigners struck again.

On January 29, 1983, it detonated a car bomb close to the Fatah HQ at Shtura, in Lebanon's Bekaa Valley, and another in West Beirut, close to the HQ of the left-wing Mourabitoun, which was close to Fatah. Some sixty people were killed and hundreds wounded. This was the Front's last act.

275 **The commission recommended that Sharon be dismissed immediately** A summary of the activities of the Kahan Commission from *Cabinet Discussions of Establishment of Kahan Commission and Its Conclusions,* February 10, 1983, published by Israel State Archives on February 1, 2013.

## CHAPTER 17: THE SHIN BET COUP

277 **acts of Jewish terrorism against Arabs** The details come from Rachum, *The Israeli General Security Service Affair,* 44–45 (Hebrew).

279 **Conducting the negotiation was the Shin Bet's senior expert** Interview with Nahman Tal, November 24, 2016.

279 **got the impression that if the Shin Bet managed** Interview with Barak, March 8, 2013.

279 **when he realized they were not dangerous** Interview with Shai Avital, December 2010.

279 **was questioning both of them** Interview with Micha Kubi, September 8, 2013.

280 **"Shalom became the most important person in the security establishment"** Interview with Carmi Gillon, January 27, 2016.

280 **subordinates considered him a manipulative and ruthless dictator** Dror Moreh, *The Gatekeepers,* 33. Shalom used to ambush latecomers at the Shin Bet HQ in north Tel Aviv and penalize them by, for instance, confiscating their vehicles. Once, an operative nicknamed Spartacus because of his massive size came a half hour late after a tiring night's work in the field. Shalom told him that for a month he would have to travel to and from work by bus. The gigantic Spartacus loomed over Shalom, who was quite short, and roared that he was not prepared to accept the penalty. Shalom didn't flinch and said he saw Spartacus's conduct as "an act of treason." Then he confiscated his car for *two* months. Interview with "Avishag," May 2008.

280 **"Avrum [Shalom] was holding a pistol"** Interview with Kubi, June 11, 2013.

280 **Shalom signaled to the unit's commander** Moreh, *Gatekeepers,* 37 (Hebrew).

281 **the beating they had supposedly received from civilians and soldiers** Interview with Kubi, June 11, 2013.

282 **Every now and again, a PLO activist would simply disappear** Interview with Weissglass, recounting his conversations with Ginossar, December 23, 2014.

283 **"there are times when it's not worthwhile to take prisoners"** Interview with "Raphael," March 2006.

283 **summary executions of suspects** Interview with "Elvin," January 2013, and "Yan," August 2017.

283 **Some of the detonations in Weights operations** Interview with "Edgar," January 2013.

283 **"More than a few innocent people were killed"** Interview with "Raphael," May 2011.

283 **The Shin Bet implemented a strict policy of telling the truth** Maiberg, *The Patriot,* 66–67 (Hebrew).

284 **"We never invented facts we did not believe to be true"** Hadar also admitted that on at least one occasion a man's confession turned out to be false, but Hadar insists that the moment this became evident he himself informed the Justice Ministry what had happened. Interview with Hadar, October 9, 2011. Report of committee of inquiry into interrogation means used by the General Security Services (Landau Commission), part 1, paragraph 2.27.

284 **after a flawed bomb killed a Shin Bet operative** Before that, an IDF officer was killed on the outskirts of Raffah when he approached a pit in which he suspected weapons had been hidden, but which had been booby-trapped by the Shin Bet and exploded as he lifted the cover. Interviews with Hadar, October 9, 2011, Bandori, September 11, 2017, and "Edgar," January 2013. The Shin Bet posted a page dedicated to Moshe Goldfarb, the operative killed that day, https://www.shabak.gov.il/memorial/Pages/110.aspx.

284 **"All we did was control the war"** Moreh, *Gatekeepers,* 28–29 (Hebrew).

284 **Almost all the heads of the intelligence community** Interviews with Peri, May 21,

2011, Gillon, January 27, 2016, Ayalon, January 21, 2013, Avi Dichter, November 4, 2010, Uri Sagie, June 3, 2012, Amos Yadlin, January 15, 2012, Aharon Zeevi Farkash, November 7, 2016, and Danny Yatom, April 7, 2011.

285 **That freedom of action affected Avraham Shalom**   Maiberg, *Patriot,* 108.

285 **"When I snapped that shot, I didn't know who he was"**   Gidi Weitz, "The Bus 300 Affair," *Haaretz,* February 28, 2013.

285 **he quickly switched the rolls in his camera**   Interview with Alex Levac, October 1998.

286 **"terrorists had died when troops attacked the bus"**   David K. Shipler, "News of Hijacking Denied to Israelis," *New York Times,* April 14, 1984.

286 ***Hadashot* defied the censor and ran the story anyway**   David K. Shipler, "Israel Said to Name Panel on 4 Hijackers," *New York Times,* April 28, 1984.

286 **The publication of the photographs**   The *Hadashot* daily broke censorship and reported on one of the panels. It was penalized for this: shut down for four days, while its editors were prosecuted. The editors were convicted by the District Court but acquitted on appeal by the Supreme Court. Criminal Appeals 93/1127, *State of Israel v. Yossi Klein and Others,* Judgment *mem-het* (3) 485.

286 **Shalom and his men took an oath**   Ministry of Justice, *Opinion in the Matter of the Investigation of the Terrorists on Bus 300,* December 20, 1986, 31 (author's archive, received from "Liran").

287 **They knew that if they told the truth**   *Kill Them!* a documentary film by Levi Zeini and Gidi Weitz, Channel 10, October 2011.

287 **"a preplanned campaign against the institutions of law"**   Interview with Hazak, June 21, 2012.

287 **Shalom's Trojan horse**   The term "Trojan horse" regarding Ginossar is taken from the report of the commission of inquiry into the Shin Bet methods, part 1, paragraph 2.4.

287 **"so many actors outside of the Shin Bet were there"**   Maiberg, *Patriot,* 65.

287 **"Not telling the truth is an integral part of removing the problem"**   Interview with Yossi Ginossar (thanks for arranging the meeting to journalist Rami Tal, September 2002).

287 **the commission sat in a Defense Ministry meeting room**   Ministry of Justice, *Opinion in the matter of the investigation of the terrorists on bus 300,* December 20, 1986, 33, 34.

288 **framing innocent Israeli soldiers for the two murders**   Interviews with Mordechai, March 22, 2015, and Ginossar, July 22, 1999. Maiberg, *Patriot,* 95.

289 **"Who did you see doing the hitting?"**   Gidi Weitz, "The Bus 300 Affair," *Haaretz,* February 28, 2013.

290 **The commission did not determine who had killed the prisoners**   A number of Shin Bet operatives, meanwhile, including Yatom and Kubi, were tried by an internal disciplinary tribunal and cleared. Interviews with Kubi, September 20, 2017, and Peri, May 21, 2011.

290 **but almost no one believed him**   Interview with Barak, April 2, 2014.

290 **"I and my family went through hell"**   Interview with Mordechai, August 28, 2015.

290 **examined the evidence and felt that something was wrong**   Interview with Menachem Finkelstein, July 18, 2012.

291 **Finkelstein fought against the Shin Bet**   "Lethal Blow and Blow of a Lethal Nature," Opinion of Judge IDF Advocate General's HQ (author's archive, received from "Bell").

291 **his meticulous legal work was instrumental in the trial**   Additional help had come in the form of an anonymous phone call received the night before the trial, at the home of Maj. Gen. Haim Nadel, who had been appointed the head of the special court-martial. The voice on the other end told Nadel he was being led astray and that Mordechai did not kill the terrorists. The voice belonged to Kubi, whose conscience was bothering him. Interview with Kubi, June 11, 2013.

291 **the court acquitted Mordechai**   Mordechai went on to become a general and after retiring from the IDF, he went into politics and became minister of defense in Benjamin Netanyahu's first government, in 1997.

291 **"because of the cover-up"**   Interview with Peleg Raday, April 1, 1998.

292 **"The moral basis . . . has collapsed"**   Interview with Nevo, January 14, 2016. *Kill Them!* Zeini and Weitz, Channel 10, October 2011.

292 **With Peres's full backing, Shalom dismissed the three whistleblowers**   Black and Morris, *Israel's Secret Wars,* 406.

292 **"I felt as if the sky had fallen down"**   Interview with Yehudit Karp, January 7, 2016.

293 **"the untrammeled powers of the Shin Bet"**   Shin Bet conference on "Bus 300 Affair," Beinish speech, Kibbutz Tzuba, June 2004.

293 **Eventually, Shalom resorted to simply lying under oath**  Ministry of Justice, *Opinion in the Matter of the Investigation of the Terrorists on Bus 300*, 22.

294 **on charges of murder**  Rachum, *General Security Service Affair*, 101.

294 **writing down the names, places, and dates**  Interview with Weissglass, December 23, 2014. Maiberg, *Patriot*, 223–29.

294 **"You can choose how to die"**  *New York Times*, July 10, 1984. Black and Morris, *Israel's Secret Wars*, 397.

295 **called it the Skulls Dossier**  Interview with "Elvin," January 2013.

295 **"He told me, 'Don't you dare'"**  Moreh, *The Gatekeepers: A Documentary*, 2012.

295 **a stenographer who would record the proceedings**  Interview with Danny Yatom, July 7, 2011.

295 **"a junta in some remote Latin American state"**  In 1992, when Rabin was elected prime minister, Ginossar asked to be appointed director general of the Housing Ministry. Rabin said it would be difficult because of his past. Ginossar did not give up. He turned to "Amos," a senior Shin Bet official, and offered him a deal: "He promised me that if I assisted him in getting the appointment as D.G. of the Housing Ministry he would give me a top job in the ministry. He wanted me to come with him to Rabin and extort him by saying that if he didn't name Ginossar, we'd expose assassination operations that he'd approved in the 1970s." Amos threw Ginossar out of his house. Ginossar made a similar threat in a meeting with the journalist Dan Margalit, apparently intending for it to get to Rabin's ears. Margalit left the meeting in anger, and he wouldn't speak to Ginossar after that for a very long time. Rabin, however, gave in to Ginossar's pressure and granted him the post he was so eager to get. But after a petition was lodged with the Supreme Court, the court ruled in a sharply worded judgment, "An offender who committed perjury and perverted the course of justice and in so doing violated individual freedom, how could such a person direct a government ministry?" In the end, Rabin did give Ginossar a senior post with regard to which the Supreme Court could not intervene: to serve as his liaison with Yasser Arafat, a position that Ginossar, without Rabin's knowledge, parlayed into large-scale private business deals with leaders of the corrupt Palestinian Authority, making him a very rich man before he died in 2004. Interviews with "Amos," July 2013, and Dan Margalit, January 17, 2017. Interview with Yossi Ginossar, May 1999. Ronen Bergman, "The Man Who Swallowed Gaza," *Haaretz*, March 4, 1997. Margalit, *I Have Seen Them All*, 180 (Hebrew). Yoel Eisenberg v. Minister for Construction and Housing, High Court of Justice 6163/92.

296 **"uncovering the modus operandi of the Shin Bet"**  Chaim Herzog, interview in *Yedioth Ahronoth*, June 27, 1986.

## CHAPTER 18: THEN CAME A SPARK

298 **Abu Jihad spread out a map**  The film of Abu Jihad briefing his fighters was shot in 1985 and released by Fatah on the anniversary of the formation of the organization, January 1, 2012.

299 **"I used to call it 'sharpening the sword'"**  Interview with Harari, March 23, 2014.

299 **The stars were now graduates of IDF combat units**  The new Bayonet executed its first mission on July 25, 1979, in an apartment house in Cannes on the French Riviera. When Zuheir Mohsen, the leader of the Palestinian pro-Syrian Al-Saiqa organization, arrived, "Berry" pumped four bullets into him and the team drove off. Mohsen expired later in the hospital. With his demise, Al-Saiqa ceased terror operations. The Mossad marked the hit down as a success. Interviews with Issaki, September 2, 2015, Pressler, July 6, 2017, and "Sally," February 2015.

299 **As he was on his way to close the deal in Athens**  Interviews with "Sally," February 2015, and Shmuel Ettinger, February 11, 2013. "Palestinian Shot Dead by Gunmen in Athens," *New York Times*, August 21, 1983.

300 **enlisted him for one of his planned operations in Europe**  The mid-1980s were a peak period of Palestinian international terrorist acts. In 1985 alone, 105 men, women, and children were killed and 433 wounded in these acts. Merari and Elad, *International Dimension of Palestinian Terrorism*, 29–41 (Hebrew).

300 **Munzer Abu Ghazala . . . had been the object**  Prime Ministers Shamir and Peres approved the series of targeted killings. However, "the selection of targets came from below, from the field, from the operational echelons, via the head of the Mossad, to the prime minister," says Nahum Admoni, the chief of Mossad from 1982 to 1989. "I don't remember

a single case where the political echelon instructed me to act against anyone." Interview with Admoni, May 29, 2011.

300    **other PLO operations in Europe**    The Mossad also tried with all its might to find Muhammad Zaidan (Abu al-Abbas), a leader of the Palestinian Liberation Front. The Israelis kept him on their radar, but he took extreme precautionary measures and an opportunity to strike at him never arose. Nevertheless, thanks to this close surveillance, on October 7, 1985, AMAN's Unit 8200 intercepted a phone call between Zaidan and a team of his men who hijacked the Italian cruise ship *Achille Lauro*, off the Egyptian coast. The terrorists murdered an elderly Jewish American man in a wheelchair, Leon Klinghoffer, and threw his body overboard. Later on, they agreed to leave the ship in Egypt in exchange for safe conduct to Tunisia. Israel tracked the plane they were on and informed the Americans, who sent fighters to intercept it and force it to land in a NATO base in Sicily. But the Italians freed Zaidan, who was on the plane, over the objections of the United States. Zaidan denied being connected to the ship hijack, but the then head of AMAN, Ehud Barak, making his first appearance on Israel TV, exposed the 8200 intercept and the terrorist's lies. Barak's polished and charismatic performance, at a time when Israel still had only one TV channel, made a huge impression and, some say, set him on course for his political career. Interviews with Barak, August 26, 2015, and "Cinema," October 2014.

300    **Israel had known that an attack of some kind was planned**    Interviews with Ettinger, January 21, 2013, and "Ethan," January 2015.

300    **four missile boats and Flotilla 13 commandos**    Interview with Ayalon, March 14, 2016. "Operation Hawk's Way: How the Navy Operated in Algeria," *Israel Defense*, August 8. 2015.

301    **refused the Israeli call to surrender**    Interview with Oded Raz, January 20, 2013. Michal Yaakov Itzhaki, "The Terrorists Planned to Arrive at the Kirya Base in Tel Aviv," *Maariv,* April 12, 2013.

301    **Loud music blared in their cells**    A state inquiry commission headed by former Supreme Court justice Moshe Landau was set up following the revelations about the culture of lies and torture in the Shin Bet. In a secret annex to its report, the commission ruled that it was permissible to use "moderate physical pressure" while interrogating terror suspects. This phrase was very broadly interpreted in the internal regulations compiled by the legal advisers of the Shin Bet and AMAN Unit 504, in a way that made possible the use of "special measures," a euphemism for torture. Shin Bet and 504 interrogators then proceeded to go a few steps further, torturing suspects with measures that were several times more aggressive and ignoring the new regulations. Again, suspects were being physically injured, subjected to severe trauma. Some died because of the torture. Unit 504, "Order on the Use of Auxiliary Interrogation Methods," updated file, July 1994 (author's archive, received from "Bell").

301    **Were it not for AMAN's precise intelligence**    Interview with Raz, January 20, 2013.

301    **These men would all land on the Tunisian shore**    Interviews with Mordechai, March 22, 2015, and "Nano," March 2012.

302    **worried about the repercussions of an Israeli attack**    Interview with "David," October 2015.

302    **Israel simply stole it**    Director of Central Intelligence, Foreign Denial and Deception Analysis Committee, October 1987, *The Jonathan Jay Pollard Espionage Case: A Damage Assessment,* 4 (author's archive, received from "Patriot").

302    **"anti-Israeli attitudes among his colleagues"**    Director of Central Intelligence, *Jonathan Jay Pollard Espionage Case,* 5.

302    **"I could not resist the temptation"**    Interview with Eitan, January 24, 2013.

303    **knew about the situation but turned a blind eye**    The prime minister's military secretary under Peres and Shamir, Brig. Gen. Azriel Nevo, firmly denies that he, as the recipient of all intelligence material addressed to the prime minister, knew about Pollard or that Israel was running a spy in the United States. Interview with Nevo, January 5, 2016.

303    **sneaking huge quantities of documents out of his workplace**    Interview with Shlomo Brom, October 27, 2015.

303    **asked his spy for all available information**    Interview with Eliot Lauer, October 20, 2015. Director of Central Intelligence, *Jonathan Jay Pollard Espionage Case,* 40.

303    **tried to persuade Rabin to back the sea-land proposal**    Interview with Mordechai, January 24, 2013.

303    **they are often driven by political concerns**    Three years later, Abu Jihad almost died as a result of exactly the same electoral strategy, when the Likud-led government was pressuring the IDF to kill him in Amman, the capital of Jordan. "It was totally transparent," says

Omer Bar-Lev, who commanded Sayeret Matkal at the time. "The Likud wanted it [the assassination of Abu Jihad] executed before the elections in July, so they would win. I was facing a difficult personal and political conflict." Bar-Lev's father, Haim, a former chief of the General Staff, was now a prominent politician in the Labor Party. The success of his son in killing al-Wazir would likely have a significant effect on his career. As it happened, those earlier plans were repeatedly postponed for operational, rather than political, reasons. Interview with Omer Bar-Lev, November 15, 2012.

304   **"waited for the Palestinians to arrive"**   Interview with Yoni Koren, March 22, 2013.

304   **on a ship named *Opportunity***   The information was conveyed to the Mossad by the agent Amin al-Hajj, "Rumminegge," who had relocated, at the Mossad's request, to Cyprus and set up a network of drivers, customs agents, and prostitutes, which provided a great deal of information about the PLO to the Mossad. Interview with Amin al-Hajj, November 5, 2013.

305   **planning to use a shipping container**   Junction's chief agent recruiter, Yehuda Gil, went to Piraeus, located the customs agent who was code-named Golden Earrings by the Mossad, and conned her into giving him information about the Palestinians who were transporting the containers of raisins via her agency. Abu Jihad, suspecting Golden Earrings of collaborating with the Mossad, dispatched two of his men to kill her. Yehuda Gil, who was running Golden Earrings, was credited with being a man "who could get a telephone pole to talk." But later on it emerged that Gil had been one of the great failures of the Mossad's apparatus for recruiting and overseeing its personnel. In 1974 he enlisted "Red Falcon," a Syrian army general, and ran him as an agent for many years. In 1996 it turned out that Gil had been making up the information ostensibly provided by his agent, because he feared having to admit that the recruitment had been a dud and he wanted to go on being relevant. This fake information twice almost led to wars breaking out between Israel and Syria. Gil was not the only Junction dramatic fiasco. Ben Zygier, an Australian Jew and a committed Zionist, immigrated to Israel and was recruited by the Mossad in 2003. These were the frenetic days of Meir Dagan's directorship, when vast budgets were made available for the expansion of the organization. This entailed a reduction in the meticulousness with which recruits were selected. Zygier, who was born and grew up in a foreign country, was considered an ideal candidate. However, after finishing the Junction course, and while trying to penetrate firms doing business in Iran and the Arab states in order to recruit sources, it turned out Zygier could not do what the Mossad expected of him. He was called back to Israel with a deep sense of failure that he apparently could not cope with. He tried to initiate a rogue operation of his own, and without informing his superiors he met and tried to recruit a Hezbollah member, to prove that he could do it. However, his target was more cunning than he was and deceived Zygier into inadvertently disclosing information about the communication system used by Mossad agents and burning two of them. A joint Mossad–Shin Bet investigation cracked the case open, and Zygier was secretly arrested and imprisoned. He was indicted but committed suicide before the trial. Bergman, *Operation Red Falcon*, https://magazine.atavist.com/operation-red-falcon. Interviews with Yehuda Gil, March 30, 2015, Dvora Chen, March 21, 2012, Haim Tomer, March 3, 2015, "Oktoberfest," March 2013, and "Loacker," December 2016. Ronen Bergman, Julia Amalia Heyer, Jason Koutsoukis, Ulrike Putz, and Holger Stark, "The Real Story Behind Israel's 'Prisoner X,'" *Der Spiegel*, March 26, 2013.

305   **According to medical documents submitted to the court**   Supreme Court, 861/87, *Abu Sharah v. Lod Military Court*, vol. 42(1), 810. Interview with Adv. Amnon Zichroni, January 27, 2011.

305   **raided an Israeli yacht**   Interviews with Eran Ron, August 1995, Talia Avner, August 1995, and David Avner, August 1995. Ronen Bergman, "Pilot's Fate," *Haaretz*, September 8, 1995.

306   **Preparations for the attack began immediately**   Erele Weissberg and Lior Yacovi, "'Alpha,' the Pilots Reported. 'Terror Fortress Destroyed,'" *Yisrael Hayom*, September 18, 2015.

306   **All the targets were hit**   "Tunisia's Leader Bitter at the U.S.," *New York Times*, October 3, 1985.

306   **"I was filled with elation that I'd never felt before"**   "Remembering Wooden Leg, the longest-range attack," Israeli Air Force website, http://www.iaf.org.il/4373-37989-he/IAF .aspx, September 27, 2011.

307   **the legend that his life was always saved by miracles**   "'Alpha,' the Pilots Reported," *Yisrael Hayom*, September 18, 2015.

307   **"we decided he wasn't a target"**   Interview with Koren, December 22, 2013.

307   **Only one senior official, Nur Ali, was killed**   Nur Ali was related to Princess Dina,

King Hussein's former wife and at that time the wife of Salah Tamari, a senior Fatah commander, who was imprisoned in an Israeli detention facility in South Lebanon. Dina and Ali were busy setting up a big prisoner exchange deal between the PLO and Israel, and afterward remained at the center of secret communication channels between the two sides. Interview with Gadi Zohar, July 8, 2017. Bergman, *By Any Means Necessary*, 83–84 (Hebrew).

307 **The failure to eliminate more of the PLO leadership** There were some in the Mossad who supported killing a less famous but much more important target from an operational standpoint—the deputy chief of the Western Sector, Mustafa Liftawi (Abu Firas). The latter was seen as the brains behind the terror attacks, a man who "bathed in a tub of Jewish blood" according to Yisrael Hasson, the Shin Bet operative who was in charge of combating his activities. But in the end, the heads of the Mossad, and later the prime minister, preferred to go for a more emblematic figure, someone known to the public, and not the clandestine, anonymous Abu Firas. Interviews with Yisrael Hasson, November 17, 2010, Shimon Shapira, January 31, 2015, "Sally," September 2016, and Raz, January 20, 2013.

308 **the Mossad could and should execute the mission itself** Interview with Lipkin-Shahak, April 3, 2012.

309 **Israeli intelligence had also overlooked another dramatic development** Schiff and Yaari, *Intifada: The Palestinian Uprising*, 44–70 (Hebrew).

310 **"From an operational point of view"** Interview with David Tzur, May 30, 2011.

311 **the Palestinian uprising against Israeli rule, the Intifada** Interview with Nevo, January 14, 2016.

311 **rioting mobs hurled rocks** "Fatalities in the First Intifada," B'Tselem website (Hebrew), http://www.btselem.org/hebrew/statistics/first_intifada_tables.

311 **Israel was now Goliath** Shalev, *The Intifada: Causes and Effects*, 19–36.

311 **"The Intifada"** Interview with Admoni, May 29, 2011.

312 **If it was all a PLO plot** Interviews with Shamir, January 1997, and Moshe Nisim, February 21, 2013.

312 **Rabin ordered the IDF** Interview with "Sally," September 2016.

313 **thwarting the plan** Interview with "Elvin," January 2013.

313 **the local police almost caught the Israelis** Interview with "Pegasus," February 2011.

313 **"Listen, history plays strange games"** Interview with Galant, August 19, 2011.

313 **to discuss the killing of Abu Jihad** The cabinet had been convened following the infiltration of a squad of three Western Sector terrorists into Israel from Egypt on March 7. They happened to run into a bus carrying civilians, many of them working mothers, to the Negev Nuclear Research Center in Dimona. They opened fire on the bus, killing two of the women, and hijacked it. "Abu Jihad sent us!" one of the hijackers yelled from the bus. Then they executed one more of the passengers. Moments later, police SWAT team snipers killed them. "As far as I was concerned," said Lipkin-Shahak, "the attack on the 'mothers' bus sealed Abu Jihad's fate." Interviews with Tzur, May 30, 2011, and Lipkin-Shahak, April 3, 2012.

314 **"Shamir could have made do with his own order"** Interview with Nevo, January 14, 2016.

314 **"My information was that Abu Jihad was a moderate"** Interview with Peres, September 17, 2012.

314 **"for the sake of the national morale"** Interview with Nisim, February 21, 2013.

315 **"'If a man comes to kill you, rise early and kill him first'"** Interview with Nisim, February 21, 2013.

315 **"but never in Tunisia"** Interview with Nahum Lev, August 2000.

315 **"I came to know and respect the man"** The Israelis monitoring al-Wazir's telephone calls heard a sharp argument between him and his eldest son, Jihad, who was studying business administration. Jihad wanted to join in the armed struggle, but his father wouldn't hear of it and told him to stay in school and to go on studying. "When our state is established," he told his son, "it won't need people like me, but rather people like you." In 2012, I accompanied a group of senior German civil servants on a tour of the West Bank, where they met Palestinian Authority officials. One of them, the head of the Palestinian Monetary Authority, was introduced as "our most important young economist." He made a powerful impression on me. He spoke articulately and sensibly in fluent English, and unlike some of his colleagues, refrained from blaming Israel for everything bad that had ever happened or was happening then to the Palestinian people. As he spoke I realized that this was the young business administration student. He had done what his father had told him to do, kept up

his studies, and had actually become one of the builders of the economy in the embryonic Palestinian state. Dr. Jihad al-Wazir had added "Khalil" to his name after the assassination of his father. I approached him after his talk and told him about the book I was writing, and about the recording of the conversation with his father that was preserved in the archives of Israeli military intelligence. He said that he remembered the conversation very well, and then he began sobbing. Interview with Raz, October 13, 2014.

316 **Rabin was satisfied** Interview with "Sally," February 2015.

317 **The convoy halted twenty-five miles from the Tunisian coast** The entire operation was planned and managed by "Steven," Caesarea's intelligence officer. Interviews with Yaalon, December 21, 2016, Barak, March 8, 2013, Yiftah Reicher, November 28, 2013, Lev, August 2000, "Sally," February 2015, Ettinger, January 21, 2015, Galant, September 4, 2014, and Ayalon, January 21, 2013.

319 **called Sayeret commander Moshe Yaalon on the radio** A recording of the conversation was first aired on Channel 2's *Uvda* program on May 27, 2013.

320 **The technicians played crowd noises** The previous day, the Shin Bet had indeed arrested Faiz Abu-Rahma, a lawyer and Abu Jihad's cousin. He'd been arrested before, but always for questioning after a terror attack. This time, it was merely a pretext for the call that followed hours later.

321 **the family's Tunisian gardener** The question whether it was necessary or permissible to kill the gardener remained open and was a subject for argument in the Sayeret even after the operation was over. Sayeret Matkal operatives were permitted by their commanders to kill civilians who might report their presence inside enemy territory—a modified license to kill. Earlier on, in late 1978, a Sayeret force under the command of an officer named Shai Avital embarked on a mission deep inside a very hostile Arab country. They came across a shepherd tending his flock. The squad stopped moving and tied up the shepherd, effectively neutralizing him. But then an argument broke out between Avital and his superiors in the rear command post. Chief of staff Eitan ordered Avital to kill the shepherd, while Avital insisted he be spared. "How can I kill him?" pleaded Avital, who was born in a farming community and had studied at an agricultural college. "He's a farmer, like us." Eitan insisted. Eventually, one of the soldiers got up and shot the shepherd in the head, dumped his body into a nearby well, and told the stunned Avital: "That's it. The argument is over. We can get on with the mission." Doron Avital, a soldier and officer in the Sayeret, with a doctorate in philosophy, made Shai Avital's plea into a doctrinal tenet. In 1994, when he was commanding the Sayeret, while plans were being developed to abduct a Hezbollah man named Mustafa Dirani, he decreed, "If we take the lives of Lebanese civilians in this operation we will have lost the moral justification for carrying it out." Interviews with "Lenin," December 2016, Avital, December 29, 2010, and Halevi, October 12, 2010. Bergman, *By Any Means Necessary,* 381 (Hebrew).

321 **They shot him, too** Interview with Lev, August 2000.

321 **Then Lev fired a long burst** Interviews with Lev, August 2000, Reicher, November 28, 2013, "Sally," February 2015, and Yaalon, December 21, 2016. According to some testimonies, Lev did not fire at Abu Jihad but stayed outside the house during the operation, securing it. *Uvda,* Channel 2, May 27, 2013.

322 **He called the operation "the perfect hit"** Interview with Yaalon, December 21, 2016.

322 **All of the Israelis escaped Tunisia unharmed** In the submarine that escorted the force to and from Tunisia, the *Gal,* relations between the crew and the deputy commander were not particularly friendly. On the way home someone posted the following anonymous message on the notice board: "Top Secret / To: Yasser Arafat / Dear Sir, / We have killed your deputy! Now you kill our deputy! / Greetings, The crew of the Israel Navy Vessel *Gal.*"

322 **"I heard about it . . . on the radio"** That official silence continued for decades. In 2012, while writing this book, after I threatened to bring a Supreme Court petition against military censors, the Censor permitted me to publish some of the details about the assassination in *Yedioth Ahronoth* (http://www.theguardian.com/world/2012/nov/01/israel-acknowledges-killing-palestinian-deputy). Following the publication, the commander of Sayeret Matkal wrote a letter to all the veterans of the unit, demanding that "The cloak of secrecy around the classified operational activity of the unit be restored, and that unit be left outside of the doings of the media." *WallaNews,* December 2, 2012, https://news.walla.co.il/item/2592534.

322 **"What joy it has brought to the nation!"** Interview with Nisim, February 21, 2013.

323 **"He could have made a significant contribution"** Interview with Lipkin-Shahak, April 3, 2012.

325    **"to ascertain who authorized such an action"**    Interviews with Uri Bar-Lev, December 17, 2015, Avital, December 2010, Nevo, January 5, 2016, and Avraham Pazner, March 19, 2016. "Israel Mounts Inquiry into a Charge by ABC," *New York Times,* July 7, 1988.

325    **a highly secretive unit, Duvdevan**    Interviews with Barak, August 26, 2015, and Dagan, July 20, 2013.

326    **The nucleus of Duvdevan**    Interview with Galant, July 7, 2011.

326    **the ABC News ruse**    Interviews with Uri Bar-Lev, December 17, 2015, and Nevo, January 5, 2016.

327    **"to carry out low-signature killings"**    Interview with Koren, December 22, 2013.

327    **to perform "dead checking"**    Interview with "Santa," May 2016.

327    **An IDF Criminal Investigation Division probe**    Final Report of Military Police Investigation (CID) 92/0450/06 of MP Central Unit, July, 9 1992 (author's archive, received from "Bell").

328    **and suddenly drawn a concealed weapon**    The large numbers of dogs, which would bark at the slightest provocation, were a serious problem for Cherry fighters trying to silently approach Arab villages at night. Many solutions were tried, including instruments that produced sounds at wavelengths audible only to canines and were supposed to calm them down. In the end, they found that bags of lion dung, collected at the Safari Park in Ramat Gan, worked best. When the dogs smelled the odor given off by the king of beasts, they would quiet down and slink off.

328    **"put the members of the terror cells into absolute uncertainty"**    Interview with Uri Bar-Lev, December 17, 2015.

329    **eliminate former members of Black September**    The Mossad failed to kill the remaining terrorists implicated in the Munich operation. Only two of them, Yusuf al-Najar and Ali Salameh, were eliminated during Harari's time. Especially painful was the failure of the hunt for the commander of the Munich attack, Mohammad Oudeh (Abu Daoud). In 1985 the Mossad obtained information on the whereabouts of Jamal al-Gashey, one of three Palestinians who actually killed Israelis in Munich. He had left Libya, where he settled after the Germans released him, and had taken refuge in Spain, under a false identity. He was suffering from cancer and receiving chemotherapy. Inside the Mossad a debate arose as to whether resources should be devoted to taking him out or he should be left for the cancer to kill him. In the end, Shavit decided that if al-Gashey could be reached, he should be killed. A lethal dose was slipped by a Caesarea operative into a cup of coffee he was drinking at a restaurant near his home. The poison didn't kill him, apparently because the dosage was incorrect, or because of the effects of the heavy chemotherapy he was undergoing at that time. Indeed, shortly after swallowing the poison, al-Gashey recovered and returned to his pleasant previous life. In 2000, he was interviewed for Arthur Cohn's Academy Award–winning documentary on the Munich massacre, *One Day in September.* Interviews with Harari, March 10, 2014, and "Sally," January 2015.

331    **"We are talking about innumerable delicate nuances"**    Interviews with "Oktoberfest," February 2013, and "Alfred," February 2013. Mossad director Shavit would say only, "It was a very nice operation, wasn't it?"

333    **The plan was to kill Yitzhak Shamir and Ariel Sharon**    Interview with "Oktoberfest," February 2013.

333    **"Just got off the plane and hop! He was captured"**    Interview with Jibril Rajoub, August 23, 2002.

334    **Mossad leaked the scandalous news of his visit**    The affair led to the resignations of high-ranking officials in the Foreign Ministry and the Interior Ministry and of the director of the French Red Cross, who was also a key adviser to President François Mitterrand. *Los Angeles Times,* February 4, 1992. Interview with Judge Jean-Louis Bruguière, May 2000. Miscellaneous correspondence between Foreign Ministry and the Israeli embassy in Paris (author's archive, received from "Paul").

334    **"the Red Pages were open-ended"**    Interview with "Polly," March 2016.

334    **Shamir re-endorsed the Red Page for Bseiso**    Interview with "the Pilot," November 2015.

334    **"I arrived in Paris on that day"**    Interview with Robert Baer (in the presence of Seymour Hersh), August 2001. Email from Robert Baer, February 1, 2016.

334    **According to a number of sources**    Interviews with "Polly," March 2016, and "the Pilot," November 2015.

336 **A judicial inquiry into the murder remains open**  Interview with Judge Jean-Louis Bruguière, May 2000.

336 **The targeted killing . . . badly weakened the PLO**  Bergman, *Authority Granted*, 178–79 (Hebrew).

336 **they refused to join an Arab League resolution**  Agence France-Presse, February 26, 1991.

337 **make genuine efforts to achieve peace with the Palestinians**  Interviews with Dalia Rabin, October 2005, Amos Eran, February 11, 2009, Haber, June 21, 2009, and Shimon Sheves, August 25, 2010.

338 **his tried and tested survival technique**  Interview with Yezid Sayigh, October 2001.

338 **Arafat permitted his people to open a secret back channel**  Interviews with Peres, September 17, 2012, Yossi Beilin, October 14, 2002, Ron Pundak, August 2002, and Alpher, May 18, 2015.

338 **When Peres informed Rabin about the contact**  Pundak, *Secret Channel*, 100–105, 122, 146–49, 172 (Hebrew).

338 **The negotiations, however, were kept secret**  Interviews with "Noah," January 2016, and "Polly," March 2016.

339 **the country's intelligence agencies continued fighting a covert war**  Interviews with Haber, June 21, 2009, and "Polly," March 2016.

340 **Shavit realized what an achievement this was**  One thing that came up often was Abbas's burning hatred for Arafat. Sometimes he called him "that bastard," sometimes "the little whore."

340 **conducting advanced negotiations with the PLO behind his back**  Interviews with "Oktoberfest," December 2015, "Polly," March 2016, and "Jango," October 2016.

340 **"We couldn't understand . . . how it was possible"**  Interview with "Oktoberfest," February 2013.

341 **"This aroused the suspicion of eavesdropping"**  Interview with Rajoub, August 23, 2002.

341 **He was undeniably a traitor**  "Top PLO Security Official Accused of Being Mossad Spy: Arafat Orders Inquiry," *Independent*, November 4, 1993.

342 **a series of agreements that became known as the Oslo Accords**  Interview with Ron Pundak, August 2002. Beilin, *Touching Peace*, 61–164 (Hebrew). Pundak, *Secret Channel*, 129–90.

342 **The Oslo Accords engendered security coordination committees**  Interviews with David Meidan, August 2, 2015, Dichter, June 2012, and Hasson, November 17, 2010.

342 **to request clemency for Yassin**  Interview with "Oktoberfest," February 2013.

## CHAPTER 20: NEBUCHADNEZZAR

343 **The hangar belonged to the CNIM Group**  Interview with Raphael Ofek, January 24, 2016.

343 **five Bayonet operatives hustled over the fence**  Interviews with "April," November 2016, Harari, March 29, 2014, and Benny Zeevi, February 12, 1999. A partially similar account appears in Victor Ostrovsky, *By Way of Deception: The Making of a Mossad Officer*, 19–20.

345 **the enemy of my enemy is my friend**  As part of the Periphery doctrine, the Mossad extended aid to liberation movements and underground militias in a number of hostile nations, including, for example, the Anyanya, Christian separatist rebels in southern Sudan. Interviews with Alpher, May 18, 2015, and Amit, July 12, 2005. Alpher, *Periphery*, 57–71 (Hebrew). Ben Uziel, *On a Mossad Mission to South Sudan*, 9–36 (Hebrew). Ronen Bergman, "Israel and Africa," 234–46.

345 **"the Butcher of Baghdad"**  Interview with Rotberg, March 5, 2012.

345 **Meir refused to sign the Red Page**  But as the booby-trapped Koran was ready for use, "They [the Kurds] sent it to some governor who had abused them, and he was killed along with his entire staff," Rothenberg recalls.

346 **Saddam thought that Jews were "a mixture of the garbage"**  He went to the trouble of publishing a luxurious edition of his admired Uncle Tulpah's thoughts, including the contention that "There are three things Allah should not have created: The Persians, the Jews, and flies." Karsh Efraim and Rautsi Inari, *Saddam Hussein*, 19 (Hebrew).

346 **"budgets of billions, practically unlimited"**  Interview with Amatzia Baram, October 28, 2015.

347    **"The Franco-Iraqi agreement is the first Arab step"**   Nakdimon, *Tammuz in Flames*, 50 (Hebrew).

347    **The Iraqis paid very generously**   Ibid., 75–76 (Hebrew).

348    **"to zero in on Iraq's intention to obtain nuclear weapons"**   Interview with Admoni, May 29, 2011, and Gazit, September 12, 2016.

348    **might potentially become informants**   Interview with Yehuda Gil, May 15, 2011. Koren Yehuda, "My Shadow and I," *Yedioth Ahronoth*, July 6, 2001.

348    **"It was a terrifying tape"**   Interview with Dr. Khidir Hamza by Hoda Kotb, NBC *Dateline* research material transcript, "Iraq 1981," (author's archive, courtesy of Shachar Bar-On).

348    **the Mossad obtained the "project book"**   Interview with "Elmo," August 2010. "Oktoberfest," January 2013.

348    **"From that book . . . we learned a lot"**   Interview with Ofek, January 24, 2016.

349    **the security cabinet authorized the prime minister**   "Decision of the Cabinet Security Committee," November 4, 1978, shown to author by "Paul."

349    **the Israelis believed they'd set back Saddam's nuclear ambitions**   Interviews with Harari, February 12, 2014, and "Black," September 2016.

349    **"the brains of the project"**   Interview with Ofek, January 17, 2016.

349    **He was a graduate of Birmingham University**   A detailed biography of Jafar Jafar appears in Windrom, *Critical Mass*, 35–40.

350    **Mashad traveled frequently**   Interview with "April," December 2016.

351    **Hotel security found Mashad's body**   Interview with "Black," June 2015. A partly similar description appears in Ostrovsky, *By Way of Deception*, 22–25.

351    **"I thought we were all targeted"**   Interview with Dr. Khidir Hamza by Hoda Kotb, NBC *Dateline* research material.

352    **The Mossad had poisoned him**   Interviews with "Black," June 2015, and "Amir," February 2016. Claire, *Raid on the Sun*, 76–77.

352    **he came down with what seemed to be food poisoning**   For obvious reasons—the use of toxins and the fact that explosions and assassinations were carried out on French soil—Israel maintained tight secrecy about its acts. In 1990, there was a serious leak. A Mossad washout named Victor Ostrovsky announced that he would publish *By Way of Deception: The Making of a Mossad Officer*, his memoirs, in Canada, a major violation of Mossad rules and Israeli Security. The agency tried to persuade Ostrovsky to withdraw his book. He refused. Agents broke into his publisher's office and stole the galleys, which turned out to contain a huge amount of information about the agency, some of it accurate, including many pages about the actions taken against Iraq's nuclear project and Iraqi scientists. The galleys raised no small panic within the Mossad. "I was called to the director's office and shown the pages referring to me," said Ami Yaar, who had Ostrovsky as a trainee for some time and is mentioned in the book. "It was very unpleasant." Yossi Cohen, who was a young officer and a rising star in the Mossad, and met Ostrovsky when they were both trainees, submitted a detailed plan to Mossad chief Shavit for the elimination of Ostrovsky. Shavit liked it and went to Prime Minister Shamir, who vetoed the idea, under the "We don't kill Jews" rule. Instead, the Mossad asked the courts in Canada and the United States to bar publication of the book based on the confidentiality oath taken by Ostrovsky when he joined the organization. The courts ruled against it, and the entire exercise only gave the book credibility and boosted its sales. Interviews with Ami Yaar, December 3, 2012, "Advantage," April 2017, "Toblerone," May 2014, and "Lexicon," January 2017.

352    **received a letter containing a blunt warning**   Nakdimon, *Tammuz in Flames*, 309 (Hebrew).

352    **received training in personal security and self-defense**   The East German Stasi and the KGB, who were in touch with Saddam's secret services, had learned lessons from the way Wadie Haddad had been eliminated. Interview with "Ilay," June 2010.

353    **"The only way still open is bombing from the air"**   Interview with Hofi, Begin Center, January 11, 2002.

353    **There was so much tension**   Interview with Eilam, December 2, 2009.

353    **leaked the plan for the anticipated attack**   Interview with Uzi Even, December 2, 2009.

353    **wrote a memo in his own handwriting to Begin**   There was great alarm in the defense establishment in the wake of the leak to Peres and his memo to Begin. The attack was postponed and the code names were changed. CoS Eitan ordered a large-scale wiretap of the General Staff and other senior officers who had security clearance for the operation.

But the actual whistleblower, Prof. Even, was not identified, and he confessed his role for the first time in an interview with me in 1996. Interview with Even, May 1996. Ronen Bergman, "The First Iraqi Bomb," *Haaretz,* May 31, 1996.

354    **The pilots flew very low**    By chance, the planes flew right above King Hussein, who was aboard his royal yacht in the Gulf of Aqaba. He must have seen the planes and grasped the direction they were flying, but any warning to the Saudis and Iraqis either got stuck on the way or wasn't transmitted at all. Nakdimon, *Tammuz in Flames,* 15–16 (Hebrew).

354    **The planes reached the target toward sundown**    Interview with Aviem Sella, May 31, 2011. Nakdimon, *Tammuz in Flames,* 188–203.

355    **"the reactor has been totally destroyed"**    Interview with Ofek, January 24, 2016.

355    **"This country and its people would have been annihilated"**    International press conference with Menachem Begin, June 9, 1981. The Israeli action evoked admiration for its execution, but also harsh international political condemnation. It seems that only *The Wall Street Journal* supported the raid, in an editorial that to this day hangs proudly in that paper's meeting room.

355    **Saddam delivered a speech of his own**    Recordings of Baath Party Supreme Council, Pentagon Archives, CRRC SH.SHTP.A.001.039, courtesy of Prof. Amatzia Baram.

356    **the bottom of the list of intelligence priorities**    Interview with Gilad, July 31, 2012.

356    **a joint Iraqi, Egyptian, and Argentinean effort to develop missiles**    Interview with "Gauguin," the agent the Mossad ran in the scientific section of the Condor project in Argentina, June 2016. Director of Central Intelligence, *Jonathan Jay Pollard Espionage Case,* October 30, 1987, 39.

357    **They received anonymous phone calls**    Interview with "Sally," September 2016. Burrows and Windrem, *Critical Mass,* 442, 461, 466–80.

357    **a Canadian rocket scientist, formerly employed by NASA**    The Mossad file on Bull includes much of his contracts and correspondence with Iraq, mainly with General Hussein Kamel, Saddam's brother-in-law and head of Iraq's arms acquisition organization (author's archive, received from "Bogart").

357    **erected the cannon at Jabal Hamrayn**    AMAN sent all the material it and the Mossad had collected about Bull to the Ministry of Defense's Administration for the Development of Weapons and Technological Infrastructure (known by its Hebrew acronym Maf'at), and to the IDF's artillery corps. These units examined Bull's computations and ran a few computer models. The surprising result was that the super-cannon was scientifically feasible and that Bull was not hallucinating. Interview with Gilad, July 31, 2012.

357    **Bull never took seriously the threatening anonymous phone calls**    Bayonet's intelligence officer Moshe "Mishka" Ben-David said, "In the few cases in which we concluded that the local authorities did not intend to do anything about it, there were shipments that caught fire or exploded, and there are a few gentlemen who are no longer among us today." Interview with "Romeo," January 2013. Cockburn, *Dangerous Liaison,* 306.

357    **they leapt out from behind the door**    Interview with "Romeo," one of the heads of Caesarea who coordinated the hit against Bull, May 2000.

358    **"If you go to work tomorrow . . . you'll end up like this"**    During the same period in which they were contending with the problem of the Condor and the super-cannon, Israel's security chiefs also had to debate the possibility of eliminating an Israeli Jew: In 1986 a low-ranking technician at Israel's nuclear reactor in Dimona, Mordechai Vanunu, who felt discriminated against because of his Moroccan, non-European origins and had espoused extreme left-wing ideas, smuggled a camera into Israel's most secret facility and photographed, among other things, a hydrogen bomb. He sold his photographs and a trove of other information to the *Sunday Times* in Britain, which planned to publish the material. The Mossad heard about it from one of its oldest sources, press magnate Robert Maxwell. "You have to get Vanunu," a leading Israeli journalist named Dan Margalit told Prime Minister Shimon Peres, during the off-the-record talk, just before he was about to interview him. "Dead or alive." Peres firmly objected: "We don't kill Jews," he said. Peres told me that the Mossad had asked him for permission to eliminate the man, but he had flatly refused: "I prevented his slaying. I ordered that he be brought back to stand trial in Israel." Margalit, a prominent commentator on current affairs, is convinced to this day that Peres was wrong: "They should have killed Vanunu abroad, or simply left him alone. 'We don't kill Jews' is a racist expression. Either Israel strikes at people who are a grave danger to its national security or it does not, without considerations of race or religion." Vanunu eventually was lured by a female Mossad operative to fly from London—where the organization was reluctant to act—with her to Rome, where he was seized, drugged, and smuggled onto an Israeli merchant ship. He was tried and sentenced to eighteen years in prison. Interviews with "Sally,"

February 2015, "Raphael," May 2011, Yechiel Horev, July 2004, Benny Zeevi, February 12, 1999, Peres, January 30, 2005, and Margalit, November 17, 2016.

358　**No one turned up at the office the next day**　Ronen Bergman, "Killing the Killers," *Newsweek*, December 13, 2019. "The Man Who Made the Supergun," *Frontline* (PBS), February 12, 1992. Burrows and Windrem, *Critical Mass*, 164–77.

358　**"make the fire eat up half of Israel"**　"Iraq Chief, Boasting of Poison Gas, Warns of Disaster if Israelis Strike," *New York Times*, April 2, 1990.

358　**"This huge and very sophisticated network"**　Interview with Shapira, January 31, 2015.

358　**"had more luck than sense"**　On January 16, 1990, the night after the United States and its allies launched Operation Desert Storm, Saddam ordered a barrage of missiles fired at Israel—the same missiles Israeli intelligence hadn't known were being developed, and later on were sure would "fall into the sea like stones." The defense chiefs proposed attacking Iraq, but under American pressure, this was ruled out, as President Bush feared for the integrity of his international coalition if Israel were to intervene. For many years, Saddam looked like the only leader in the Arab world who had dared attack Israel and had proved that its threats against him were empty. Israel's humiliation profoundly influenced the subsequent discussion about whether plans should be made to assassinate Saddam.

358　**UN inspectors then found what the Mossad had missed**　Interviews with Rolf Ekeus, September 1996, and Hans Blix, August 2000.

359　**Saddam remained a clear and present danger to Israel**　Barak was relying on a psychiatric profile of Saddam Hussein drawn up by a team of psychologists and psychiatrists in AMAN, in which they stated, "Saddam perceives the world as a brutal, cold place of constant deathly danger. In this system, there is no room for moral laws and there are no behavioral codes that cannot be violated because of social norms. . . . Saddam is not daunted by war, even a war against strong forces. On the contrary, he is likely to view a war against strong forces as proof of Iraq's importance and power. . . . Saddam's aspiration to obtain nuclear arms . . . is connected to his psychological need to create for himself an unassailable sense of power. . . . He never forgets and never forgives anyone who hurts him . . . Saddam will not hesitate to use non-conventional weapons against Israel . . . other costs and moral compunctions will not stand in his way." (AMAN, Research Department, *Psychological Portrait of Saddam Hussein*, Special Intelligence Survey 74/90, November 1990.) Interview with Barak, July 1, 2013.

359　**"the formation of a team to examine the possibility"**　CoS Barak Bureau to Amiram Levin, Deputy CoS, head of AMAN, head of Mossad, "Sheikh Atad" (Thorn Bush) [the operation's code name], January 20, 1992 (author's archive, received from "Julius").

359　**preparations be made for execution of the plan**　CoS Bureau to Deputy CoS, head of AMAN, director of Mossad, Commander of Air Force, and Amiran Levin, *Thorn Bush*, March 17, 1992 (author's archive, received from "Julius").

359　**"we could have saved the world an entire decade"**　Interview with Barak, January 13, 2012.

359　**Many ideas were put forward**　Interview with Nadav Zeevi, October 15, 2012.

360　**The Israelis closely followed the treatment Tulfah was receiving**　Interview with "Zolphi," September 2012.

360　**they would launch the missiles and kill him**　On October 8, Prime Minister Rabin asked once more, "Should the State of Israel kill the incumbent leader of another country?" Amiram Levin answered: "Imagine that someone had killed Hitler in 1939." Eventually Rabin was convinced and told the CoS, and the heads of AMAN and the Mossad, that he "approves of the target." Azriel Nevo to CoS, head of AMAN, and head of Mossad, *Computer Workshop* (one of the code names for the operation), October 13, 1992 (author's archive, received from "Julius").

361　**the man playing Saddam was among the . . . wounded**　Interviews with Nadav Zeevi and Eyal Katvan, the soldier playing Saddam, October 15, 2012.

361　**a fierce political storm and an ugly quarrel**　Interviews with Barak, May 10, 2013, Sagie, June 3, 2012, Lipkin-Shahak, April 3, 2012, Avital, December 29, 2010, and Nadav Zeevi, October 15, 2012. A detailed account of the wars waged in the upper echelons of Israel following the accident may be found in the book by Omri Assenheim, *Zeelim*, 221–304 (Hebrew).

## CHAPTER 21: GREEN STORM RISING

362 **on their way to meet His Imperial Majesty** Part of the story of that meeting was first published in Bergman, *Secret War with Iran*, 15–18.

362 **The shah's foreign policy was based on close . . . links with the United States** Ibid.

362 **intimate intelligence alliance with Israel** Ibid.

363 **"seemed to us to have significant potential dangers"** Interview with Merhav, April 22, 2014.

363 **convinced that he had been visited by the Archangel Gabriel** Menashri, *Iran Between Islam and the West*, 134 (Hebrew).

364 **Khomeini reshaped Shiite Islam** Taheri, *The Spirit of Allah*, 27–28, 131 (Hebrew). Menashri, *Iran Between Islam and the West*, 131 (Hebrew).

364 **"Please kill us"** Taheri, *Spirit of Allah*, 132–33 (Hebrew). Interviews with Uri Lubarni, December 26, 1997, and Tsafrir, October 2, 2015.

365 **attracted more and more students** Bergman, *Secret War with Iran*, 13–14.

365 **"Who do you think you are?"** Bergman, *Point of No Return*, 50 (Hebrew).

365 **The distribution of the Khomeini cassettes was observed** Ibid., 51–52.

365 **Only Lubrani was granted an audience** Interview with Merhav, October 5, 2011.

366 **Iran would remain an ally of Israel and the United States** Bergman, *Secret War with Iran*, 17.

366 **Would the Mossad please kill Khomeini?** Interview with Tsafrir, October 2, 2015.

367 **"I cannot accurately evaluate whether the risk is justified"** Interview with Alpher, May 18, 2015.

367 **This episode was another demonstration** Bakhtiar himself went into exile in Paris, where a decade later he was killed by assassins sent by Iranian intelligence. Bergman, *By Any Means Necessary*, 316–17 (Hebrew).

367 **The dream of an Islamic republic became reality** Interview with Itzhak Segev, January 5, 2007. Bergman, *Point of No Return*, 74 (Hebrew). Taheri, *The Spirit of Allah*, 273–94 (Hebrew).

368 **But Khomeini's rise was the culmination of years of foment** Israel also tried to exploit the Iran-Iraq war in order to preserve military relations with Iran, supplying it with a lot of weaponry (Operation Seashell is described in detail in Bergman, *Secret War with Iran*, 40–50). Still later, Israel and the United States became embroiled in the Iran-Contra affair, a shameful and abortive effort to get Iran to trade Western hostages taken by Hezbollah in exchange for weapons, all behind the back of Congress. Bergman, *Secret War with Iran*, 110–22. Prime Minister Shimon Peres's adviser on terrorism, Amiram Nir, ran the Israeli side of the operation. He briefed Vice President Bush on the affair, and his account was liable to cast a shadow over Bush's 1987 presidential campaign. Nir died under mysterious circumstances in Mexico in 1988 (Hungarian Octagon file in author's archive, received from "Cherry").

368 **"We felt helpless in the face of this new threat"** Interview with Robert Gates, November 7, 2012.

368 **was now their bitterest enemy** The failure of the bid to free the hostages in Tehran made a deep impact on the American establishment and was one of the reasons for Defense Secretary Robert Gates's opposition to the operation to capture or eliminate Osama bin Laden in May 2011. When Gates, by then the defense secretary, was in the White House situation room and saw one of the U.S. helicopters crash in Abbottabad, he remembers, "I said to myself, there you go, the catastrophe is beginning again." Interview with Gates, November 7, 2012.

368 **one of Khomeini's closest allies** Bergman, *Point of No Return*, 147, 162 (Hebrew).

369 **to eventually extend the Islamic revolution . . . to Lebanon** Kramer, *Fadlallah: The Moral Logic of Hizballah*, 29 (Hebrew).

369 **Almost three years after the fall of the shah** Shapira, *Hizbullah: Between Iran and Lebanon*, 134–37.

370 **Assad concluded from the Israeli invasion** Bergman, *Secret War with Iran*, 58–59. Shapira, *Hizbullah*, 135–39.

370 **"He built up an apparatus for squeezing blood out of Israel"** Interview with Dagan, May 19, 2011.

370 **Iran and Syria signed a military alliance** Shapira, *Hizbullah*, 144–60 (Hebrew).

371 **He was one of the Shiites swept up in the fervor of Hezbollah** Taken from the interview with the parents conducted by a Hezbollah historian and broadcast on Al-Manar in a film on the life of Qassir in 2008, http://insidehezbollah.com/Ahmad%20Jaafar%20 Qassir.pdf.

372    **This secrecy was convenient for Israel's defense establishment**    Only in 2012, and following my publication on the matter (*By Any Means Necessary,* 160–62), was a secret inquiry committee set up in the Shin Bet. The committee's report determined that there was indeed high probability that this was an act of suicide terrorism perpetrated by Qassir. Despite all of this, the Shin Bet left the report's top-secret classification in force and turned down my request to hand it over. Interviews with Tal, November 24, 2016, and Bandori, September 11, 2017.

372    **the new militant force rising from the smoking ruins of Lebanon**    Interview with Raz, January 20, 2013.

372    **"We missed the process"**    Interview with Yekutiel Mor, January 12, 2009.

372    **"coming out of the office of Mohtashamipur"**    Interview with David Barkai, July 18, 2013. The CIA was no less surprised or uninformed about the new movement. Weiner, *Legacy of Ashes,* 390.

373    **"joined a training camp of Force 17"**    Interview with al-Hajj, August 14, 2014.

373    **Mughniyeh wanted to belong to something larger**    Thanks to Dr. Shimon Shapira for material on the boyhood of Imad Mughniyeh.

373    **"an extremist, uninhibited psychopath"**    Interview with "Eldy," January 2015.

373    **"Hezbollah's spiritual compass"**    This epithet was coined by Martin Kramer in his book on Fadlallah, *The Moral Logic of Hizballah.*

373    **the Syrians and Iranians wanted the occupiers driven out**    Jaber, *Hezbollah,* 82.

374    **"We believe that the future has surprises in store"**    Fadlallah, *Taamolat Islamia,* 11–12.

374    **By "sacrifice oneself," Fadlallah was referring**    The earliest precedent may well have been the biblical figure Samson, who took his own life to wreak vengeance upon the Philistines by pulling down the pillars of the house in Gaza. And, according to legend, a fanatical Muslim sect on the shores of the Caspian Sea in the eleventh and twelfth centuries, the Hashashiyoun ("hashish users," from which the word "assassin" derives) would drug young men and persuade them to go on murderous missions from which they would not return. The Japanese also had their kamikazes in World War II, and the Peruvian terrorist organization Shining Path employed suicide tactics as well.

374    **detonating the ton of explosives stuffed inside**    Kenneth Katzman, *Terrorism: Middle Eastern Groups and State Sponsors,* Congressional Research Service, Library of Congress, August 9, 1995.

374    **drove trucks packed with huge quantities of explosives**    Hala Jaber, *Hezbollah,* 77, 83.

374    **241 peacekeepers were killed**    Robert Baer said that the CIA had evidence that Yasser Arafat was involved in the planning of the three 1983 Beirut attacks. This information, Baer says, was never published because of the agency's desire to maintain a working relationship with the PLO. In addition, the KGB station chief in Beirut at the time, Yuri Perfilyev, said that Arafat's moves were coordinated with Mughniyeh. Interviews with Robert Baer, August 2001, Yuri Perfilyev, October 2001 (with the help of Isabella Ginor). Bergman, *Point of No Return,* 164–65 (Hebrew).

374    **body parts fell on the Shin Bet HQ in Beirut**    Interview with Dov Biran, January 28, 2013.

375    **facing a new type of enemy**    In mid-1983, the ambassador ordered Mughniyeh to begin wielding a new and highly effective weapon: He and his Hezbollah men began hijacking planes and abducting individuals in order to achieve political and symbolic goals. The United States failed to secure the release of most of the abductees. Two high-ranking Americans were kidnapped as well—Col. William Higgins, who was serving with the UN, and William Buckley, head of the CIA station in Beirut. Later on it was learned that they had both been tortured and murdered. The frustration and sense of impotence in the United States swelled. Two Mossad sources told me that at the end of 1983, they were informally told by the CIA that "our friends in Washington would welcome" severe measures against Iran and Hezbollah leaders. "It was clear that they were urging us to carry out assassinations," one source told me. At that time the CIA's hands were tied by presidential executive order number 12333, but there were those in the government who were, according to these sources, asking Israel to act on their behalf. Bergman, *By Any Means Necessary,* 163–80 (Hebrew). Interviews with Barkai, July 18, 2013, and "Salvador," May 2012.

376    **"that they chose a modus operandi"**    Interview with "Sally," June 2015.

377    **Mohtashamipur opened the book**    Wright, *Sacred Rage,* 89.

377    **"I hope that your health will soon return"**    Shahryar Sadr, "How Hezbollah Founder Fell Foul of Iranian Regime," Institute for War and Peace Reporting, July 8, 2010.

377 **Hezbollah wasn't one man's guerrilla force—it was a movement** Nada al-Watan, "Interview with Hassan Nasrallah," Beirut, August 31, 1993.

378 **Dagan dispatched two Lebanese agents** A few months later, Hezbollah arrested two Shiites from the village of Tibneen and accused them of shooting Harb. Under torture they confessed that they had been working for years for Israeli intelligence and had carried out the assassination mission. Shortly afterward, they were executed by a firing squad. Dagan said that Hezbollah caught the wrong men: "It's no problem to nab someone and force him to confess. The people that did it were never captured." In 2008, a Lebanese criminal living in Denmark, Danny Abdallah, admitted that it was he who shot Harb. Since then he has been on Hezbollah's hit list and his extradition has been requested by the government of Lebanon.

378 **sent a cable of condolences** *Tehran Times*, February 20, 1984.

379 **eighty people were killed and two hundred injured** In his book *Veil*, Bob Woodward claims that the Saudi Arabians helped William Casey carry out the operation, as revenge for the suicide bombing of the U.S. embassy and the Marine barracks that Mughniyeh organized. On the other hand, Tim Weiner said that the United States was not involved in the incident and that he believes Israel was responsible. This version is supported by several other sources. A senior Mossad official said that the Front for the Liberation of Lebanon from Foreigners, a terrorist movement established by Meir Dagan in Lebanon, was responsible. Interviews with Tim Weiner, June 12, 2016, "Pier," December 2012, and Kai Bird, October 11, 2012. Bergman, *Secret War with Iran*, 73. Woodward, *Veil*, 407–9 (Hebrew).

379 **try to solve its Lebanon problem through targeted killings** Interview with Barkai, July 18, 2013.

380 **Ahmed Jibril wasn't even there that night** On May 20, 2002, Israeli agents planted two kilos of TNT under the driver's seat of the car used by Jihad Jibril, Ahmed's son and heir, while it was parked in the Mar Elias neighborhood of Beirut. He was killed instantly.

380 **difficult for Israel to recruit live agents** Interviews with Barkai, July 18, 2013, Yitzhak Tidhar, April 2011, Mor, February 23, 2009, and Danny Rothschild, December 15, 2008.

380 **Between 1984 and 1991, there were 3,425 operations** Figures from *Israel Government Statistical Yearbooks* 1984–1991. Ronen Bergman, "Like Blind Ducks," *Haaretz*, May 14, 1999.

## CHAPTER 22: THE AGE OF THE DRONE

383 **"We've got him"** AMAN Research Division, *Night Time: The Elimination of Hezbollah's Secretary General, Abbas Mussawi, in February '92*, by Brig. Gen. Amos Gilboa, January 20, 1999, 25 (author's archive, received from "Robin").

384 **The IAF had lost more than a quarter of its warplanes** Interviews with Sella, April 7, 2013, Eitan Ben Eliyahu, April 28, 2011, and Yitzhak Yaakov, January 5, 2007.

384 **to introduce drones into the air force** Israeli Air Force, *The History of Squadron 200*, 7–14 (author's archive, received from "Hilton").

384 **Hours elapsed between taking the pictures** Interviews with Ivri, April 18, 2013, and Eitan Ben Eliyahu, April 24, 2011. Israeli Air Force, *History of Squadron 200*, 20–22 (Hebrew).

384 **a new type of drone was developed** Interview with Alon Unger, April 21, 2013. Israeli Air Force, *History of Squadron 200*, 24–26.

385 **Weinberger didn't much appreciate the surveillance** Interview with Sella, October 26, 2015. Israeli Air Force, *History of Squadron 200*, 27–29.

386 **Combining and synchronizing both systems** Interview with "Onyx," May 2013.

386 **the whole team would practice "passing the baton"** Interview with Unger, April 21, 2013. Israeli Air Force, *History of Squadron 200*, 42–43.

387 **The navigator, Ron Arad, could not be located** Bergman, *By Any Means Necessary*, 197–206 (Hebrew).

387 **to do everything and more to get MIAs and POWs home** This topic was covered in detail in Ronen Bergman, "Gilad Shalit and the Rising Price of an Israeli Life," *New York Times Magazine*, November 9, 2011.

387 **"the biggest search operation ever conducted"** Interviews with "Mark," April 2005, and Lior Lotan, May 2009.

387 **Israel abducted two relatively minor Hezbollah officials** Interviews with Israel Perlov, October 15, 2000, Rami Igra, February 2008, and "Amazonas," October 2011. Bergman, *By Any Means Necessary*, 279–90 (Hebrew).

387    **"an emblematic operation"**   Interview with Mor, January 12, 2009.

388    **"The future will be for the Resistance"**   Zolfiqar Daher, "From Lebanon to Afghani-
       stan, Sayyed Abbas: The Leader, the Fighter, the Martyr," Al-Manar, February 18, 2015,
       http://archive.almanar.com.lb/english/article.php?id=196205. Shapira, *Hezbollah: Between
       Iran and Lebanon*, 110–11.

388    **Hezbollah would hold a large political rally**   AMAN Research Division, *Night Time*, 5.

389    **no one in the room knew even the basics of Shiite memorial rites**   Interview with
       Shapira, January 31, 2015. AMAN Research Division, *Night Time*, 15.

389    **no way he could recommend an immediate abduction mission**   Arditi claimed that
       he wasn't invited to further discussions that day, including those held with Defense Minis-
       ter Moshe Arens, because it was clear he would speak out sharply against the operation.
       Interview with Arditi, June 13, 2011.

389    **"SOE does not want to do it"**   AMAN, *Night Time*, 9.

389    **a critical misunderstanding crept in**   Interviews with Mor, January 12, 2009, and Yosi
       Dimenstein, January 26, 2016.

390    **two parallel plans had thus been created**   The CoS's counterterrorism adviser, Meir
       Dagan, proposed his own plan: to replace the monument for Gharib Harb, whose slaying he
       had been behind in 1984, with an identical, booby-trapped one to be exploded when Mus-
       sawi appeared. AMAN, however, saw Dagan as a competitor and asked CoS Barak to rule
       his plan out, as it would endanger the lives of women and children. "I told the CoS that was
       bullshit," said Dagan. "According to Shi'ite mourning customs, only male dignitaries would
       stand in the front row. The women would wait in the *husaniyeh* . . . but they [AMAN] man-
       aged to persuade Ehud [Barak]." Interview with Dagan, June 19, 2013.

390    **"Mussawi's convoy of cars"**   AMAN, *Night Time*, 11.

390    **This was a dangerous contradiction**   AMAN, *Night Time*, 15. Interview with Moshe
       Arens, August 25, 2009.

391    **On Sunday, the day of the operation**   Interviews with Arditi, June 13, 2011, Barak,
       March 8, 2013, Sagie, November 20, 2015, Ofer Elad, January 12, 2015, and Unger, May
       21, 2013.

391    **"We've got him!"**   AMAN, *Night Time*, 16.

392    **Barak told an aide to update the defense minister's military secretary**   Ibid., 17.

392    **"we'll be moving up a level in fighting Hezbollah"**   Ibid., 15.

392    **unanimous in their opposition to killing Mussawi**   Interview with Mor, January 12,
       2009.

393    **he would go in the third car**   AMAN, *Night Time*, 22.

395    **"They are all yours"**   Ibid., 23.

395    **"Positive identification of target"**   Israeli Air Force, *History of Squadron 200*, 43–45.

396    **"The claim that AMAN didn't know"**   Interview with Dagan, June 19, 2013.

397    **"that account will be closed by us"**   On May 3, 1992, Barak Ben-Tzur of AMAN and
       Uri Chen, the head of the Mossad's delegation in the United States, briefed members of the
       CIA on Operation Night Time, describing it as "the first integrated aerial assassination."
       They brought with them video footage shot by the drones. The briefing opened with chuck-
       les when a technician screened the start of the movie *Prizzi's Honor* by mistake, but it
       continued on a more serious note. The Americans were impressed. Robert Gates, CIA di-
       rector at the time, told me that the footage would influence his insistence on the continued
       development of the Predator attack drone over the stubborn resistance of the U.S. Air
       Force. Jim Woolsey, who replaced Gates as head of the CIA, said similar things about the
       Israeli contribution to the development of the U.S. drones. Interviews with Gates, Novem-
       ber 7, 2012, James Woolsey, December 2001, and Barak Ben-Tzur, April 2010.

## CHAPTER 23: MUGHNIYEH'S REVENGE

398    **did not hasten to carry out the burial**   AMAN, *Night Time*, 24.

399    **there had been no serious discussion before the hit took place**   Interview with
       "Roni," November 2008.

399    **to appoint a pious thirty-two-year-old cleric**   "New Hezbollah Leader a Disciple of
       Iran's Revolution," Associated Press, February 12, 1992.

400    **Israel was a "cancerous growth, this contaminating germ"**   Interview with Hassan
       Nasrallah, Al-Manar, December 27, 1997.

401    **"He was responsible for building Hezbollah's military strength"**   Interview with
       Dagan, July 20, 2013.

401 **preferable to a full-scale confrontation with the Hezbollah forces** Eiran, *The Essence of Longing*, 97.

402 **He struck first in Turkey** Interview with "the Pilot," June 2015. Bergman, *Point of No Return*, 249–50 (Hebrew). Email exchange and phone conversations with Rachel Sadan, January 2007.

402 **exploded a car bomb outside the Israeli embassy in Buenos Aires** American intelligence gave the Israelis clear-cut proof—"not a smoking gun, but a muzzle-flashing gun," one AMAN man said—that Imad Mughniyeh and his lieutenant, Talal Hamia, were behind the attack. The Americans had tapped in to a telephone call with Hamia in which Mughniyeh was heard mocking the Shin Bet's failure to protect the embassy. Interviews with "Lenin," April 2013, and Alberto Nisman, December 18, 2007. Bergman, *Point of No Return*, 210–22 (Hebrew).

403 **"The aim of the cells is to provide an immediate response"** Interviews with Stanley Bedlington, October 31, 2011, Hugo Anzorgi, September 2001, Alberto Nisman, December 18, 2007, and Daniel Carmon, February 24, 2016.

403 **"A town called Hell"** Interview with "the Pilot," June 2015.

404 **Hezbollah's performance improved and its daring increased** Tamir, *Undeclared War*, 133–36 (Hebrew). Bergman, *Point of No Return*, 335–39 (Hebrew).

404 **Israel had crossed a red line** Interview with "the Pilot," June 2015.

405 **the Israelis decided a response was necessary** Interview with "Advantage," February 2016.

405 **no one in Israeli intelligence knew where Asgari was** He remained high up in the Iranian regime and was involved in a large number of attacks targeting Israel and the United States. In February 2007, he vanished without a trace from his hotel room in Istanbul. According to some sources, he defected to Israel or the United States. The Iranians and his family, however, say that he was abducted, and possibly killed. Interviews with Dagan, May 19, 2011, Sagie, March 6, 2012, and "Herods," September 2017. Mail exchange with Robert Baer, September 2017.

405 **Fifty of them were killed and another fifty wounded** Interview with "Lenin," July 2016.

405 **"the same as someone bombing Eton College"** Interview with Ben-Tzur, April 2010.

405 **Mughniyeh struck in Buenos Aires once again** The criminal investigation in Argentina concerning the two bombings dragged on for years and in fact has never ended at all. The special prosecutor appointed to investigate the affair, Alberto Nisman, gathered a large amount of information that led to the issuance of Interpol international arrest warrants against a number of high-ranking Iranians and Hezbollah officials. Nisman also filed indictments "against all of the Argentinean individuals involved in the cover-up" and declared war against the heads of the country's intelligence community, legal system, and the political echelon. A short time before he was to disclose the documents and recordings he had collected to prove this grave allegation to a parliamentary committee, Alberto Nisman was found shot to death in his apartment, in mysterious circumstances. Interview with Nisman, December 18, 2007. Ronen Bergman, "Holding Iran Accountable," *Majalla*, November 24, 2016.

406 **finally woke Israeli intelligence to the full reality** Interviews with Mizrahi, March 22, 2015, and "the Pilot," September 2016.

407 **killing him and three passersby** Interviews with "Oktoberfest," January 2013, "the Pilot," September 2016, Francis, July 15, 2003, and "Eldy," September 2014.

407 **an Israeli double agent working for Hezbollah** It was Ramzi Nahara, a drug dealer who was activated for many years by Unit 504 as part of a network of drug dealers who assisted Israel with a large amount of information in exchange for the freedom to continue conducting their business. Interview with Ravid, November 13, 2012.

407 **"I did not accurately foresee Hezbollah's reaction"** Interviews with Sagie, June 24, 2007, and Arens, May 25, 2009.

408 **he admitted the facts, but not the error** Interview with Barak, June 7, 2011.

## CHAPTER 24: "JUST ONE SWITCH, OFF AND ON"

409 **tried to understand where they had erred** Interview with Hasson, November 17, 2010.

410 **Yassin set up mosques and Islamic educational institutes** Aviad, *Lexicon of the Hamas Movement*, 150–54 (Hebrew).

411 **"He was so different from the PLO terrorists"** Interview with "Aristo," June 2013.

411   **"the Shin Bet grew the jihadist"**   Interview with Lipkin-Shahak, May 26, 2011.

411   **"The agency was one of the factors"**   Interview with Ayalon, March 29, 2012.

411   **"The apologetics . . . began to disappear"**   Interview with Diskin, October 23, 2011.

412   **gave an open palm slap to the man's face**   Interview with Kubi, September 8, 2013.

412   **whose leader was a Palestinian, Abdallah Azam**   Lawrence Wright, *The Looming Tower: Al-Qaeda and the Road to 9/11,* 120–30 (Hebrew).

413   **place him in a very embarrassing situation**   Interview with "Aristo," October 2013.

414   **Yassin . . . had secretly set up a small military unit**   Roni Shaked and Aviva Shabi, *Hamas: Palestinian Islamic Fundamentalist Movement,* 88–97 (Hebrew).

414   **"very smart, a little better educated than the average"**   Interview with Kubi, May 29, 2013.

414   **"the whole Shin Bet missed it completely"**   Interview with "Aristo," June 2013.

414   **Yassin was sentenced to thirteen years**   Bergman, *By Any Means Necessary,* 101 (Hebrew). Interview with Micha Kubi, May 29, 2013. Ronen Bergman, "Oops, How Did We Miss the Birth of Hamas?" *Yedioth Ahronoth,* October 18, 2013.

415   **the dying person is not acting out of personal motives**   Nachman Tal, "Suicide Attacks: Israel and Islamic Terrorism," *Strategic Assessment,* vol. 5, no. 1, June 2002, Jaffee Center for Strategic Studies, Tel Aviv.

415   **"Hamas," which also means "enthusiasm"**   Shaked and Shabi, *Hamas,* 92–107 (Hebrew).

415   **Salah Shehade, the most senior member detained**   Interviews with Dichter, November 4, 2010, and Kubi, May 29, 2013.

416   **Izz al-Din al-Qassam Brigades**   Gelber, *Growing a Fleur-de-Lis,* 104–37.

416   **Shehade continued to command the military wing**   Ronen Bergman, "The Dubai Job," *GQ,* January 4, 2011.

416   **"We disguised ourselves as religious Jews"**   " 'To Israel I Am Stained with Blood,' " Al Jazeera, February 7, 2010, http://www.aljazeera.com/focus/2010/02/2010271441269105 .html.

417   **Al-Mabhouh and Nasr fled to Egypt**   Interview with "Aristo," June 2013.

417   **Nissim Toledano of the border police**   MOD, Office of the Chief Coordinator for Judea and Samaria, *Hamas announcement on the kidnapping to The Soldier,* October 11, 1994 (author's archive, received from "Bell").

418   **"you will be wiped off the face of the earth"**   Interview with Ben-Tzur, March 26, 2011.

418   **"We are sorry that we have to kill you"**   Shaked and Shabi, *Hamas,* 11–21.

418   **"We had tried a lot of methods against Hamas"**   Interview with Yatom, April 7, 2011.

419   **news about the operation had leaked out anyway**   Supreme Court File 5973/92, *Association for Civil Rights in Israel v. Minister of Defense.*

419   **the expulsion was in fact a serious blow to Hamas**   AMAN Research Division, *Brief on Saudi Money Funneled to HAMAS,* May 6, 2002 (author's archive, received from "Chili").

420   **Hezbollah could and should use the opportunity**   Interview with "Leon," July 2013. Aviad, *Lexicon of the Hamas Movement,* 199–201.

420   **Militant Shiites did not . . . make alliances with Sunni Muslim Palestinians**   *Globe and Mail* (Canada), December 28, 1993.

421   **hundreds of thousands of dollars in cash**   Though they received an abundance of information from the Shin Bet, and they collected a fair amount of information themselves, the FBI refrained from taking any action until after the Twin Towers fell. The FBI, Holy Land Foundation for Relief and Development, International Emergency Economic Powers Act, Dale Watson, Assistant Director, Counterterrorism Division to Richard Newcomb, Director, Office of Foreign Assets Control, Department of the Treasury, November 5, 2001. Bergman, *Follow the Money: The Modus Operandi and Mindset of HAMAS Fundraising in the USA and the PA Using American and Saudi Donations,* Cambridge University, Centre of International Studies, October 2004.

422   **"The power of the terrorists had grown exponentially"**   Interview with Dichter, November 4, 2010.

423   **"his blood boiling with fury"**   Interview with Eitan Haber, June 21, 2009.

## CHAPTER 25: "BRING US THE HEAD OF AYYASH"

425   **controversy followed Rabin**   Goldstein, *Rabin: A Biography,* 415–24 (Hebrew).

425   **"Neither of the sides grasped the meaning"**   Interview with Ayalon, September 4, 2002.

425 **Efforts to resolve the conflicts on Israel's northern borders**  "Grey File" (preparation for the secret talks with Syria) documents, author's archive, received from "Bell." Ronen Bergman, "The Secret of the Grey File," *Yedioth Ahronoth,* January 26, 2007.

426 **"We sit in the fortresses scratching our balls"**  Interviews with Erez Gerstein, April 1996, and Ehud Eiran, May 13, 2013.

426 **pleaded with Israel to at least target Hezbollah officers**  Interview with Aql al-Hashem, December 1999.

426 **quickly organized a new commando unit, known as Egoz**  Tamir, *Undeclared War,* 116.

426 **"the experience of the Americans in Vietnam"**  Raviv Shechter, interview with Moshe Tamir, *Yisrael Hayom,* May 14, 2010.

427 **he saw great importance in targeted strikes**  Interview with Levin, July 16, 2017.

427 **"we, the IDF, would have to do it on our own"**  Interview with Ronen Cohen, July 5, 2015.

428 **Hezbollah's radio networks exploded with transmissions about the killing**  Interview with Ronen Cohen, September 1, 2016.

428 **Operation Golden Beehive was the model for additional attacks**  The IDF needed to develop new devices and capabilities for these assassinations. The bombs, for instance, were problematic. The batteries of the firing devices had to last the sometimes protracted period between the planting and the detonating, long-range wireless communication was required for the detonation, and the devices had to be small and camouflaged. The IDF's weapons development blew up a few dozen old Mercedeses, the most popular cars in Lebanon, with store-window mannequins belted inside, trying to figure out how much of what material placed where was most effective. In one important experiment, anesthetized pigs were used, as their skin and tissues are similar to those of human beings. The bombs that killed them were nicknamed "oink-oink." Interviews with "Leo," February 2016, and "Pie," November 2011.

429 **this workaround of the system was not seen as troublesome**  Interview with Sheves, August 25, 2010.

429 **"a precedent was created"**  Interview with "Leo," February 2016.

430 **PIJ's Beit Lid bombings were the climax of this campaign**  Kurtz, *Islamic Terrorism and Israel,* 139–48.

430 **Shaqaqi gave an interview**  Lara Marlowe, "Interview with a Fanatic," *Time,* February 6, 1995.

430 **signature on Shaqaqi's death**  Interview with "the Pilot," May 2016.

431 **"making a sovereign government change its decisions"**  Interview with Gillon, January 27, 2016. Carmi Gillon, *Shin-Beth Between the Schisms,* 201 (Hebrew).

431 **executing the Red Page on Shaqaqi**  Interview with Sagie, March 6, 2012.

432 **A car bomb driven by a PIJ suicide terrorist**  In 1998 a federal district judge ordered the Iranian government to pay $247.5 million in damages to Flatow's family, and in June 2014, BNP Paribas was ordered to pay huge compensation to the family for processing forbidden Iranian financial transactions.

432 **he silenced them and decided in Shavit's favor**  Interview with Lipkin-Shahak, April 3, 2012.

432 **Surveillance had shown that Shaqaqi was in regular contact**  Interview with "Diamond," August 2011.

433 **"Almost no one ever uses this road"**  Interview with "the Pilot," May 2016.

433 **The assassination operation began**  Interviews with Galant, August 19, 2011, and Ayalon, June 22, 2011.

434 **"we heard on our headsets 'Cease advance now!'"**  Interview with "Fred," September 2015.

434 **Ayalon ordered the commandos to withdraw**  Interview with Ayalon, March 14, 2016.

434 **"If Abu Mussa goes, our client won't be able to stay away"**  Interview with Moshe Ben-David, January 23, 2013.

435 **One of the Israelis followed him**  Interview with "Lego," May 2000.

436 **the Malta police found the motorcycle on the beach**  Interview with "the Pilot," May 2016. Bergman, *Secret War with Iran,* 213–16.

437 **Rabin "was red in the face"**  Interview with Gillon, January 27, 2016.

437 **"A secret Israeli organization by the name of OAS"**  Interview with Yasser Arafat, April 1995.

438 **"Get going, and bring us the head of Ayyash"**  Interview with Hasson, November 17, 2010.

438   **Hasson was taking a new approach to Ayyash**   Interview with Amit Forlit, January 4, 2010.

439   **he seemed to never trust anyone**   Interview with Itzhak Ilan, January 26, 2016.

439   **the efforts to locate Crystal bore fruit**   Interview with Gillon, January 27, 2016.

440   **"we had decided to go ahead with it nevertheless"**   Interview with Hasson, November 17, 2010.

440   **he had managed to slip away to Gaza**   Interview with Ilan, November 5, 2014.

440   **"That, too, was a failure of ours"**   Interview with Gillon, January 27, 2016.

440   **"'First of all, let's eliminate him, and then see what happens'"**   Interview with Hasson, November 17, 2010.

441   **"But here's the dilemma"**   Interview with Dichter, November 4, 2010.

442   **"but the coffee stays in the machine"**   Interview with Dichter, November 4, 2010.

442   **a senior member of the VIP protection unit**   Interview with Ilan, November 5, 2014.

442   **The peace rally was organized by left-wing groups**   Gillon, *Shin-Beth Between the Schisms,* 267–76.

443   **was the first to receive Yigal Amir**   Interview with Lior Akerman, October 15, 2015.

444   **"Suddenly the line went dead"**   "The Phone Rang, Yihyeh Ayyash Answered, and the Instrument Blew Up," *Haaretz,* January 7, 1996.


## CHAPTER 26: "SLY AS A SNAKE, NAÏVE AS A LITTLE CHILD"

446   **"I didn't have the men"**   Interview with Rajoub, May 3, 2010.

446   **"Jibril's a liar"**   Interview with Diskin, October 15, 2011.

447   **"Mohammed *shu?*"**   Interview with Yaalon, August 16, 2011.

447   **"We sat together, and I ate from his hand"**   Interview with Peres, September 17, 2012.

447   **"derailed the peace process"**   Interview with Hasson, November 17, 2010.

449   **he forced him out in 2016**   Ronen Bergman, "For Israel, Frightening New Truths," *New York Times,* January 7, 2017.

449   **"The Shin Bet is used to collecting evidence"**   Interview with Yaalon, August 16, 2011.

449   **backed up his boss's words**   Interview with Yassi Kuperwasser, May 21, 2004.

450   **so Shin Bet investigators wouldn't be able to trace them**   Interview with "Disco," August 1997.

451   **Netanyahu called in Mossad director General Danny Yatom and demanded a hit list**   Interview with Yatom, July 7, 2011.

452   **"you can't survive your second operation"**   Interview with Ben-David, January 23, 2013.

452   **"I want leaders, not merchants"**   Interview with Benjamin Netanyahu, July 3, 2007.

453   **"'I cannot allow more suicide bombings'"**   Interview with Ben-David, May 6, 2002.

453   **"No risks, nothing that could go wrong"**   Interview with Shapira, October 27, 2013.

453   **Netanyahu's eyes lit up**   Interview with Ben-David, January 15, 2013. Request for the Extradition of Abu Marzook, Israeli Ministry of Justice, U.S. District Court for the Southern District of New York—924 F. Supp. 565 (S.D.N.Y. 1996) (author's archive, received from "Mocha").

453   **Marzook also was an American citizen**   Interview with "Lego," May 2000.

454   **far from sufficient information to act against the other three**   When I told Netanyahu what I had heard from the Mossad operatives, Netanyahu said that no one manipulated him and that he himself selected Mashal as the target for assassination. "I sensed that Mashal was a very problematic character, and very dangerous. Even then we identified his terrible passion for killing us. In retrospect, when you look at where the man got to and what he has done and how he became the engine of Hamas, it is clear to all that I was right when I thought that his vanishing off the map was likely to significantly damage Hamas's capabilities." Interview with Netanyahu, July 3, 2007.

454   **"Potion of the gods"**   Interview with "the Pilot," May 2016.

455   **The assassins were still practicing their technique**   Doron Meiri, "The Terrorist Entered the Street Dressed as a Drag Queen," *Yedioth Ahronoth,* September 7, 1997.

455   **Yatom once again tried to persuade Netanyahu**   Interview with Yatom, July 7, 2011.

455   **the moment the Mossad agreed to immediately carry out the hit on Mashal**   This was because Caesarea's documentation department did not have other, more suitable pass-

ports ready for the whole team. In other instances, in the past, such a situation was liable to lead to a postponement of the entire operation until a solution was found.

456 **"not to allow . . . bad luck to screw things up"**   Interview with "the Pilot," May 2016.

456 **he simply didn't know about it**   Interview with Mordechai, August 28, 2015.

456 **"didn't give me correct estimations of the risks"**   Interview with Yatom, July 7, 2011.

456 **"I have to rely on them"**   Interview with Netanyahu, July 3, 2007.

457 **carrying the antidote to levofentanyl**   A request for a reaction from Dr. Platinum elicited the following response: "Hi Ronen, It would be an honor for me to talk to you, but I do not understand how I am connected or would be able to help you. Platinum." Attempts to arrange a phone conversation with her did not succeed. Email, Ronen Bergman to Dr. Platinum, December 25, 2013, and her reply, December 26, 2013.

457 **"Amman is a very interesting city"**   Interview with Ben-David, January 23, 2013.

458 **"that clearly indicated that there should not be execution"**   When I told Yatom that the operatives claimed they didn't see the little girl or the driver and that Jerry hadn't been able to warn them, he was contemptuously dismissive: "That's all blabber. They were simply overmotivated to execute, after all the days that they had not been able to. That's why they took it upon themselves to do something that was in total contradiction to my basic orders."

459 **Ideally, a second Caesarea team would have been posted nearby**   Contrary to this testimony, Hamas and Jordanian intelligence personnel I met in Amman said that Abu Seif was Mashal's bodyguard and not a random passerby. If this is true, it makes the Bayonet team's failure much graver, because the operatives never even knew of his existence, not to mention his training, and therefore didn't foresee what would happen.

459 **"I jumped on him, threw him down"**   Interview with Saad al-Khatib, December 2013.

460 **someone loaned him a cellphone**   There is a significant discrepancy between al-Khatib's version of the incident and that of the two operatives, but there's no argument about how it ended up.

461 **Ben-David called Mossad headquarters**   Interview with Ben-David, January 23, 2013.

461 **"Batihi started complaining to me"**   Interview with Yatom, July 7, 2011.

462 **The doctors had Mashal get to his feet and walk around**   Interview with Sami Rababa, December 2013.

462 **King Hussein wanted to make it clear that he took the incident very seriously**   Interviews with "the Pilot," May 2016, and Yatom, July 7, 2013.

463 **Ben-David went to the lobby**   Interview with Ben-David, January 15, 2013.

463 **Platinum was taken to Rababa's office**   Interview with Rababa, December 2013. Email exchange with Rababa, December 2013.

463 **Rababa maintained his professional decorum toward Platinum**   How was Mashal's life saved? The Jordanian doctors claim they did it themselves, without any help and without injecting him with the antidote. "When the results of the chemical analysis of the substance that we received from the woman doctor arrived," said Rababa, "we saw that it was exactly the same medication we had already given him. The formula of the poison itself we received after Mashal had recovered totally." The Israelis contend that this is an empty boast, because it is impossible that their secret toxin could be recognized by Jordanian doctors and it was only thanks to the Mossad giving the Jordanians the antidote, as well as the formulas for both the antidote and the poison, that Mashal's life was saved. Interviews with Ben-David, January 15, 2013, Yatom, April 7, 2011, "Jeffery," November 2013, and Rababa, December 2013.

464 **"wall-to-wall opposition"**   Halevy refused to be interviewed for this book. However, at a July 13, 2011, meeting with the German defense minister, in the presence of Gen. Amos Gilad and the author, Halevy spoke freely about the Mashal affair, praised (justly) his own contribution to the solution, and several times mentioned that Gilad, who was then head of the AMAN Research Division, was one of the main opponents of his suggestion that Yassin be freed, graciously adding "and this was indeed one of the small mistakes you made in your career." See also Halevy, *Man in the Shadows,* 132–42 (Hebrew).

464 **Netanyahu consulted with Shin Bet director Ami Ayalon**   Interview with Kubi, September 8, 2013.

464 **Ayalon conveyed this message to Netanyahu**   Halevy, *Man in the Shadows,* 138–40 (Hebrew).

465 **An official reconciliation between Hussein and Netanyahu**   Interview with Yoram Ben Zeev, April 17, 2012.

465 **The internal and external inquiry panels**   Interviews with Joseph Ciechanover, April

28, 2017, and "the Pilot," May 2016. Ciechanover came to the conclusion that, in general, Netanyahu acted reasonably and properly.

465    **all claimed they had not known about the operation**    Interviews with Mordechai, August 28, 2015, and Yaalon, August 16, 2011.

465    **Ayalon was severely critical of the entire operation**    Interview with Ayalon, September 4, 2002.

466    **An internal Mossad investigation**    Interview with "the Pilot," May 2016.


## CHAPTER 27: A LOW POINT

467    **the two Northern Command officers believed the mission was unnecessary**    Rami Michaela, the intelligence officer for Flotilla 13's Operation Poplar's Song, claims that he has no recollection of any opposition from Northern Command to hitting the target of the operation. In any case, all agree that command of the operation was removed from Northern Command and transferred to the General Staff. Interviews with Ronen Cohen, February 18, 2016, and Rami Michaela, March 15, 2016.

468    **When the force reached the point marked on their coded map**    Interviews with Michaela, March 15, 2016, Galant, September 4, 2014, Shay Brosh, May 2013, and Oren Maor, January 2013.

468    **That may have been the most convenient explanation**    Bergman, *By Any Means Necessary*, 428 (Hebrew).

469    **the mission would probably have been postponed**    Intel personnel who were concerned about the operation, from Michaela through Navy intelligence chief Brosh all the way up to then CoS Yaalon, all claim that it was not a leak of information that led to the disaster, but a problem with the explosives, that fire was never opened at the force, and that all the men were killed by the blasts. Interviews with Brosh, May 2013, Michaela, March 15, 2016, Galant, September 4, 2014, Mordechai, August 28, 2015, and Lipkin-Shahak, April 3, 2012.

469    **called them the "four dishrags"**    "The Four Mothers Are Four Dishrags," Nana 10 website, February 16, 2000, http://news.nana10.co.il/Article/?ArticleID=6764.

470    **Mossad chief . . . resigned**    The three operatives Swiss police found in the basement tried to pretend they were tourists who'd sneaked in for a quickie threesome. They were caught, literally, with their pants down. The police believed them, too, until one of them claimed the bag of tools and cables he was carrying was "diplomatic baggage."

470    **"the protective shield that they deserved"**    Speech by Shin Bet director Avi Dichter at Herzliyah Conference, December 16, 2003.

471    **"The organization is not attuned to the environment"**    Interview with Diskin, June 1, 2017.

471    **analyze it in the briefest of time spans**    Interview with Ayalon, January 21, 2013.

472    **more emphasis on the network**    One of the fathers of the technological revolution in the Shin Bet was Jerusalem-born Gadi Goldstein. He was at that time deepening his knowledge of various philosophical concepts ranging from the Judaic to the oriental religions. In the mid-1990s, and especially in the macho environment of the Shin Bet, Goldstein's preoccupation with such matters seemed odd, to say the least. Goldstein based his innovative operational concept on the words attributed to the biblical Moses, alongside principles of Zen philosophy. He stressed the doctrine of the *anatta,* or "no-self," which says that the I of each of us does not stand alone and is not defined by itself. Zen teaches that the I is in constant conversation with everything in the environment, influencing it and influenced by it. Thus there is no independent existence for any individual or any animal or object; everything exists only as part of a much wider array, which defines it. "Let's say ten people live in a building," he said at one of the discussions that were held as the new system was being developed, "and we, the Shin Bet, want to know if and what they are plotting, and we have *x* amount of energy for investigating that building. We have to invest our energy in what is under way between them, the synergy they are creating together, the 'range' within which each of them influences and is influenced." At that meeting, Goldstein quoted from the book *Zen and the Art of Motorcycle Maintenance* by Robert Pirsig, which elevates, almost sanctifies, the no-self concept. One of the participants suggested with a smile that Goldstein's new intelligence doctrine should be named "Zen and the Art of Assassination." Interview with Gadi Goldstein, November 2012.

472    **"We set up an entire division of Q's"**    Interview with Diskin, June 1, 2017.

473    **thereby preventing a major disaster**   Details about Sharif supplied by "Twins," March 2016.

473    **escaped from a Palestinian Authority prison**   According to Shin Bet records, the brothers were connected to a number of terror attacks in which dozens of Israelis were killed and hundreds wounded, including the attack at Café Apropos in Tel Aviv on March 21, 1997, where 3 people were killed and 47 injured, two suicide attacks in Jerusalem in 1997, one on July 30, when 15 were killed and 170 wounded, and one on September 4 with 5 dead and 169 wounded. They were also responsible for gunfire attacks in the Hebron area and Jerusalem, in which 7 Israelis were killed, as well as the abduction and murder of the soldier Sharon Edry on September 9, 1996, among others. Shin Bet, "Elimination of the Awadallah Brothers and Deciphering the Archive of the Military Arm of Hamas in Judea and Samaria," March 2014 (author's archive, received from "Twins").

474    **"the best operational chief the agency had ever had"**   Interview with Ayalon, January 21, 2013.

474    **That man was Yuval Diskin**   Diskin introduced a new conceptual framework into the Shin Bet: Most terror attacks, especially suicide attacks, are preceded by a number of actions by the terrorist organizations that are largely similar from one attack to the next. These actions, Diskin argued, leave a trail behind them in both the digital and the physical world. If they can be defined and identified, it's possible to stop a future attack in its early stages. The system Diskin developed saved the lives of countless Israelis in the decades to follow.

474    **"Adel was very suspicious"**   Interview with Diskin, June 1, 2017.

474    **seeing the fate of Mohi al-Dinh Sharif**   Interview with "Amazonas," October 2011.

476    **not eager to assassinate another Hamas official**   Interviews with Mofaz, June 14, 2011, and Ayalon, June 22, 2011.

477    **"I will resign as head of the Shin Bet"**   Interview with Ayalon, January 21, 2013.

478    **and soon found the archive**   Shin Bet, "Elimination of the Awadallah Brothers," 2.

478    **"including an absolute stop to the peace process"**   Interview with Ayalon, January 21, 2013.

478    **began poring over the Hamas military archives**   Shin Bet, "Elimination of the Awadallah Brothers," 3.

479    **"I come from another place, another culture"**   Interview with Yaalon, August 16, 2011.

480    **In theory, the solution was simple**   Interview with Diskin, June 1, 2017.

481    **"The whole force identified him and opened fire"**   The hit on Batat had a jarring end from Cherry's point of view. The bodies of Batat and Nader Masalma were taken to the unit's HQ, and there the soldiers who took part in the operation began posing for photographs with them. "Very soon there was a big demand for pictures," Cherry soldier Alon Kastiel said. "There are a lot of cameras in the unit, and there was a crazy demand for photos. Everyone wanted photos. It went on for maybe two hours. I didn't say a word, I didn't think of morality, it's a dead corpse, not a live person, and your officer is posing for pictures with them and you never rebuke your officer. . . . You look at the pictures and later on you put them in the most remote corner of the house, making sure you won't come up against them for years. They disgusted me. I don't know what disgusted me more, the bodies or my own conduct. I used to see the bag with the pictures once a year from a distance and never opened them. They were buried in a drawer in the end." An IDF spokesman claimed that the military had conducted an incisive investigation and prosecuted those involved in these bizarre proceedings. Interview with Alon Kastiel, May 29, 2016. Gideon Levi, "A Nightmare Reunion Photo," *Haaretz*, December 25, 2004.

482    **"This intelligence superiority"**   Interview with Yaalon, August 16, 2011.

482    **This part was termed "framing"**   Interview with Dichter, November 4, 2010.

482    **The timing was fortuitous**   Interview with Diskin, June 28, 2017.

## CHAPTER 28: ALL-OUT WAR

483    **"Peace is a common interest"**   Statement by the prime minister, protocol of Knesset session no. 59, December 13, 1999.

484    **Barak had to keep his promise and pull out of Lebanon**   Gilboa, *Morning Twilight*, 25–28 (Hebrew). Ronen Bergman, "AMAN Chief to PM Barak," *Yedioth Ahronoth*, February 12, 2016.

484    **They planned to have him assassinated**   A Unit 8200 communications monitor by the

name of Mor, a fluent Arabic speaker, was the expert on identifying Mughniyeh's voice. Out of respect for Mor's ability, experience, and dedication, the code name given to Mughniyeh in those years, "Maurice," echoed her name. However, for many years, Imad Mughniyeh had seemingly vanished, and Unit 8200 could find no trace of him in Hezbollah's communications traffic. On May 21, 2000, Mor, stationed at a Unit 8200 Grizim base in northern Israel, identified his voice while listening in to the communications of a tour by Hezbollah leaders along the border of Israel's security zone in Lebanon, probably in preparation for Israel's anticipated withdrawal. "It's him! I'm sure. It's him. That's 'Maurice' talking," Mor exclaimed joyfully. Based on the surveillance and the location of the source of the conversation, AMAN and the Air Force began plotting to kill Mughniyeh. Summary of meeting on May 22 in handwriting of prime minister's military secretary, Gen. Moshe Kaplinsky, shown to the author by "Ben," April 2014.

485 **Nasrallah celebrated the withdrawal as a complete victory** Nasrallah speech, Bint Jebail, May 26, 2000.

485 **"that there was no other option"** Interview with Barak, April 2, 2014.

485 **ferment among the Palestinians had reached new heights** Interview with Yaalon, December 21, 2016.

485 **"We were not preparing, and we did not intend to start"** Interview with Rajoub, May 3, 2010.

485 **"We're on a giant ship that's about to collide with an iceberg"** Interview with Margalit, November 17, 2016.

486 **No Israeli leader had ever agreed to give away so much** Landau, *Arik,* 263 (Hebrew).

486 **Barak hadn't done enough in advance** Members of the American delegation, notably Robert Malley in his book *Camp David: The Tragedy of Errors,* blamed Ehud Barak for his condescending and insensitive behavior. Barak conducted the bulk of the negotiations via Yossi Ginossar, who was now a secret conduit to Arafat and—it later emerged—his business partner. Uzrad Lew, *Inside Arafat's Pocket,* 163 (Hebrew). Interviews with Barak, August 26, 2015, and Merhav, December 20, 2016.

486 **"If Clinton had adopted Carter's strategy"** Interview with Itamar Rabinovich, July 2013.

486 **attempts were made to bridge the gaps** Landau, *Arik,* 262–65 (Hebrew).

486 **"we were breathing gunpowder"** Interview with "Hendrix," August 2013.

487 **"to remove the abomination"** Interviews with Alexander Pantik, November 2003, and Gillon, January 27, 2016. Gillon, *Shin-Beth Between the Schisms,* 100–36 (Hebrew). Documents from military police investigation of the "Jewish Underground" that plotted to blow up the Temple Mount mosques in author's archive, received from "Bell."

487 **soon they clashed with the police** Landau, *Arik,* 269 (Hebrew). Anat Roeh and Ali Waked, "Sharon Visits the Temple Mount: Riots and Injuries," *Ynet,* September 28, 2000, http://www.ynet.co.il/articles/0,7340,L-140848,00.html.

487 **By the time of the next morning's prayers** Interviews with Ahmed Tibi, August 23, 2002, and Tirawi, June 2002. Bergman, *Authority Granted,* 106–10 (Hebrew).

487 **Inside Israeli intelligence, the argument** Interviews with Aharon Zeevi Farkash, April 10, 2013, Mofaz, June 14, 2011, Yaalon, August 16, 2011, Dan Halutz, July 5, 2011, Dichter, November 4, 2010, Diskin, October 18, 2011, Ben-Yisrael, June 5, 2011, Giora Eiland, June 5, 2011, Ayalon, June 22, 2011, Gilad, June 25, 2012, and Kuperwasser, January 2011.

488 **"trying to attain diplomatic achievements by means of spilling Israeli blood"** Interview with Mofaz, June 14, 2011.

488 **Arafat . . . was being dragged along by the tide of events** Interview with Diskin, June 1, 2017.

489 **"I slaughtered your husband a few minutes ago"** Amos Harel and Avi Issacharoff, *The Seventh War,* 37–39 (Hebrew). Mark Seager, "'I'll Have Nightmares for the Rest of My Life,'" *Daily Telegraph,* October 15, 2000, http://www.jr.co.il/articles/politics/lynch.txt.

489 **The Shin Bet designated the lynching an "emblematic attack"** Interview with Dichter, November 4, 2010.

489 **In the wake of the Ramallah lynch mob** Figures from the human rights NGO B'Tselem, http://www.btselem.org/hebrew/statistics/fatalities/before-cast-lead/by-date-of -event.

490 **Sharon had been a political pariah for almost two decades** Gad Barzilai, *Wars, Internal Conflicts, and Political Order: A Jewish Democracy in the Middle East,* SUNY series in Israeli Studies, 1996, 148. Michael Karpin, *Imperfect Compromise: A New Consensus Among Israelis and Palestinians,* 94.

490   **Large crowds of Israelis protesting in the streets**   Landau, *Arik*, 171–75, 207–11 (Hebrew).

490   **The contrast was immediately evident**   Interviews with Shalom Turgeman, June 28, 2011, Assaf Shariv, January 28, 2007, Danny Ayalon, June 22, 2011, and Weissglass, June 11, 2012.

490   **felt it deeply whenever Israelis or Jews anywhere were killed**   Interview with Galant, June 1, 2011. Sharon at first tried, or at least wanted to look as if he was trying, to speak with Arafat, and in April 2001 he sent his son Omri to a secret meeting with the Palestinian leader in Ramallah, but it ended quickly. "It was clear that relations between the two [Ariel Sharon and Arafat] could lead only to a blowup," said one of the participants. Interview with "Date Palm," August 2017.

491   **"lost its fortitude over the years"**   Interviews with Galant, June 1, 2011, and Weissglass, June 11, 2012.

492   **"support for Hamas grew in direct proportion"**   Interview with Diskin, June 1, 2017.

492   **"this was the worst thing I had seen in my life"**   Interview with Shlomo Cohen, March 28, 2012.

492   **"We are facing an all-out offensive"**   Shuli Zuaretz and Sharon Rofeh, "Haifa: 14 of 15 Dead in Attack Are Identified," *Ynet*, December 2, 2001, http://www.ynet.co.il /articles/0,7340,L-1373989,00.html.

493   **138 men, women, and children were killed by suicide bombers**   State of Israel, "Special Committee for Examining the Targeted Killing of Salah Shehadeh," February 2011, 21 (author's archive, received from "Ellis").

493   **"the worst year for terror attacks against us"**   Interview with Dichter, November 4, 2010.

493   **"This was a national trauma"**   Interview with Mofaz, June 14, 2011.

493   **"we did not realize that it could be done in such huge numbers"**   Interview with Ben-Yisrael, June 5, 2011.

493   **"The frustration was huge"**   Interview with Eiland, June 5, 2011.

494   **shooting attacks on the roads in the West Bank**   "He was killing us," said Uri Halperin, AMAN's top officer for the northern West Bank. Interview with Uri Halperin, May 27, 2014.

495   **"Then we fired two missiles"**   Anat Waschler, "The Drone Pilots' War," *Air Force Journal*, December 1, 2000.

495   **instead of the call he was expecting**   Interview with "Matan," June 2012.

495   **tried to eliminate the secretary general of the PFLP**   Ali Wakad, "The Funeral of Abu Ali Mustafa Is Held in Ramallah," *Ynet*, August 28, 2001, http://www.ynet.co.il /articles/1,7340,L-1058108,00.html.

496   **Sharon grew even more frustrated with the defense establishment's impotence**   Ben-Tzur, recounting the meeting to me in April 2010, asked that the name of the bank not be mentioned.

496   **"Foreign investors won't come here"**   An analysis of the destructive effect that the Suicide Bombers Intifada had on the economies of Israel and the Palestinian Authority can be found in Ben-Yisrael, "Facing Suicide Terrorists: The Israeli Case Study," in Golan and Shay, *A Ticking Bomb*, 19–21.

497   **"both judge and executioner"**   Interview with Hasson, November 17, 2010.

497   **Dichter presented the new strategy to Sharon**   The Shin Bet also proposed two other measures that the cabinet approved only at a later stage—limited land incursions into Palestinian Authority territory in order to carry out arrests (Operation Defensive Shield), and the construction of a separation barrier (the West Bank Barrier) between Israel and the Palestinian areas. Interview with Dichter, November 4, 2010.

497   **"Go for it. Kill them all"**   In an interview with David Landau, the defense minister at the time, Benjamin Ben-Eliezer recalled a similar statement by Sharon when he ordered the IDF and the Shin Bet to "kill the dogs," which Ben-Eliezer said was "his most moderate demand." Landau, *Arik*, 291 (Hebrew).

## CHAPTER 29: "MORE SUICIDE BOMBERS THAN EXPLOSIVE VESTS"

498   **by the time the bomber reached Israel, it was generally too late**   Interview with Ben-Yisrael, June 5, 2011.

499   **the "ticking infrastructure" behind the attacks**   Interview with Dichter, November 4, 2010.

499   **They would all be targets**   Interview with Ilan, November 5, 2014.

499   **"Terror is a barrel with a bottom"**   Interview with Dichter, November 4, 2010.

500   **"A simple example is the automobile"**   Interview with Ben-Yisrael, June 5, 2011. Ben-Yisrael, "Facing Suicide Terrorists," 25–26.

500   **"I realized that we were winning"**   Interview with Ilan, November 5, 2014.

501   **"They flew around there all the time"**   Interview with Yaalon, December 21, 2016.

501   **most civilians . . . did not know how**   The most important of these was a UAV capable of delivering missiles, Hermes 450, informally known as Zik ("spark" in Hebrew), manufactured by Haifa-based Elbit Systems Ltd. and Israel Aircraft Industries' Heron and Heron TP.

501   **As the United States had, in Operation Desert Storm**   Interview with Wesley Clark, January 23, 2012. (Thanks to Eytan Stibbe for help in arranging the meeting.)

501   **the prime minister banged his fist on his desk**   Interview with Galant, September 4, 2014.

501   **set up a special squad to retrofit the drones**   *Precisely Wrong: Gaza Civilians Killed by Israeli Drone-Launched Missiles*, Human Rights Watch, June 2009.

502   **to put themselves at the Shin Bet's disposal**   Interviews with Galant, September 4, 2014, Dichter, November 4, 2010, and Farkash, November 7, 2016.

502   **Unit 8200 . . . underwent the biggest change**   Interview with "Fidel," April 2014.

502   **put their fleet of observation aircraft**   Yitzhak Ilan Lecture, Herzlia IDC, May 2013.

502   **The result of all this was "intelligence fusion"**   Interview with Yaalon, December 21, 2016.

502   **"a man who does not work in the Yiddish language"**   Interview with Dichter, November 4, 2010.

503   **"The General Security Service . . . is in charge"**   Shin Bet, *Preventive Strike Procedure*, paragraph 1, January 3, 2008 (author's archive, received from "Ellis").

504   **the framing stage**   State of Israel, *Special Committee for Examining the Targeted Killing of Salah Shehadeh*, 26.

504   **"The scalability is the message"**   Interviews with "Leila," March 2013, and "Amazonas," October 2011.

504   **"we could run four or five a day"**   Interview with "Amazonas," June 2017.

504   **Operations run out of the JWR killed twenty-four people in 2000**   Data from NGO B'Tselem, http://www.btselem.org/hebrew/statistics/fatalities/before-cast-lead/by -date-of-event.

505   **"that these operations were executed by the government of Finland"**   Interview with Kuperwasser, December 24, 2014.

505   **"Absolute panic"**   Interview with Weissglass, June 11, 2012.

505   **The IDF began putting out statements after each hit**   Interview with "Pixie," August 2016.

506   **Hebrew for "targeted preventive acts"**   After the first wave of assassinations (before 9/11), Sharon began receiving complaints from the United States. He decided to send Dichter to Washington to meet American intelligence chiefs and explain to them how the assassinations policy was saving lives. Dichter asked his aides to translate the PowerPoint presentation into English. Like most Israelis, these aides were sure that their passing grades in high school English were enough to qualify them for the job. They repeatedly used the phrase "focused preventions," which, Dichter realized later, "sounds more like a kind of condom than killing terrorists." Dichter met his counterparts at the Pentagon and enthusiastically began lecturing them on "focused preventions," careful not to use more explicit terms, but his sharp eye soon picked up that "they didn't have any idea what I was talking about." Eventually, according to Dichter, CIA director George Tenet raised his hand and said, "Ah, now I understand you, Dichter, you mean targeted killings." "Then I realized," he says, "that it was enough already of the laundered language and it was fine to say 'killing' and that's that." Interview with Dichter, November 4, 2010.

506   **"I thought that was a problematic situation"**   Interview with Farkash, March 14, 2011.

507   **"What does that mean, you 'aren't aware'?"**   Interview with Ayalon, March 14, 2016.

507   **Eventually, the Shin Bet found a weak spot**   Interview with Ilan, January 26, 2016. Harel and Issacharoff, *Seventh War*, 181–88 (Hebrew).

508   **"It's that crazy Dichter"**   Dichter and his people flatly deny Ayalon's allegations and argue that Arafat, and certainly Karmi, had no intention of stopping the fighting. Yitzhak Ilan, who was in charge of the assassination operation against Karmi, says, "The claim that it was only after Karmi's elimination that the Tanzim began carrying out suicide terror at-

tacks is an outright lie. He had dispatched two suicide bombers previously, but it simply didn't work. We located one of them, and the other lit a cigarette while on his way, detonated the bomb, and his body was blown to pieces in a deserted place. Karmi was in the midst of preparing a third terror attack when we killed him." Interviews with Dichter, November 4, 2010, and Ilan, January 26, 2016.

508 **"I call it the banality of evil"** Interview with Ayalon, March 14, 2016.

509 **In times of war, the law falls silent** Interview with Menachem Finkelstein, July 18, 2012. Among those young officers was Dr. Roi Scheindorff, a New York lawyer who became one of the youngest ever appointed a deputy attorney general in charge of Israel's fight to avoid having its officials prosecuted in international tribunals because of their involvement in assassinations and targeted killings.

509 **a top-secret legal opinion signed by Finkelstein** IDF Advocate General, "Striking Against Persons Directly Involved in Attacking Israelis in the Framework of Events in the Warfare in Judea and Samaria and the Gaza District, January 18, 2001 (author's archive, received from "Ellis").

509 **For the first time, a legal instrument had been proposed** Ibid., page 1, paragraph 1.

510 **"I submitted the opinion with trembling hands"** Interview with Finkelstein, July 18, 2012.

511 **a principle of "proportionality" must still apply** IDF Advocate General, "Striking Against Persons," 8.

511 **"It was a stamp of confirmation"** Chief Justice Aharon Barak wrote the court's detailed judgment on assassinations. In a masterpiece of jurisprudence, the Supreme Court had ruled that the assassinations were legal in principle, as long as they met certain conditions, similar to those required in the advocate general's opinion. Many of the principles in this judgment were adopted by the legal advisers of the American intelligence community and are today a cornerstone of the concept that permits targeted killings. Interview with Diskin, October 18, 2011. Supreme Court 769/02, *Public Committee Against Torture v. State of Israel and Others*, December 14, 2006. Comprehensive analysis of judgment in Scharia, *Judicial Review of National Security*, 58–66. Interview with Diskin, October 23, 2011.

511 **In his desk, Prime Minister Sharon kept a booklet** Interview with Weissglass, June 11, 2012. The foreign minister of Canada, Bill Graham, visited Sharon at his bureau on May 26, 2002, to plead with him to stop the assassinations. "These are illegal acts," the minister insisted. In the middle of his heated speech, military secretary Galant brought in a note. Sharon read it to himself, and then out loud, in English so the Canadian would understand. A Hamas member, according to a Shin Bet report, had just left Jenin for Israel, carrying a backpack with nine kilograms of explosives, screws, and nails. The Shin Bet and the air force were requesting permission to kill him. "Mr. Minister," Sharon asked with the hint of a smile, "you tell me, yes, what would you do in my place? Authorize? But you've said it's illegal. Not authorize? And have the blood of the victims as your responsibility, and in your worst nightmares?"

512 **"never to get into a fight with the Americans"** Interview with Ariel Sharon, May 2002.

513 **"It's hard to believe as a Texan how small Israel is"** Michael Abramowitz, "Bush Recalls 1998 Trip to Israel," *Washington Post*, January 10, 2008.

513 **"Sharon was in the clouds"** Interview with Turgeman, June 28, 2011.

514 **"After that, there was a perfect disproportion"** In order to improve coordination between the countries, deputy assistant to the president Elliott Abrams ordered that a direct encrypted phone line be set up between the White House and Sharon's office. "Our aim," says Danny Ayalon, then the Israeli ambassador in Washington, "was to be certain that when the president woke up in the morning he would get the same intelligence picture in the Presidential Daily Briefing that Israel was seeing." Interviews with Weissglass, June 11, 2012, and Ayalon, October 9, 2012.

514 **operational and intelligence cooperation . . . deepened considerably** On a visit to Paris on July 5, 2001, Sharon tried to get President Jacques Chirac to change his mind about targeted killings. He had Shin Bet deputy director Diskin describe an operation that had taken place three days before, when an Israeli Air Force helicopter fired four missiles that killed three Hamas operatives, including Muhammad Bisharat, who had been involved in a number of terrorist attacks. He reviewed Bisharat's history of involvement in suicide terrorism and detailed the requests to the Palestinian Authority to arrest him, without response. Chirac was silent for a moment. Then he cleared his throat and said, "I have to say that at a distance of four thousand kilometers, things look totally different." From that day,

France moderated its criticism toward Israel on this point, though it did not cease entirely. Not long after that, Sharon asked Diskin to accompany him on a visit to the Kremlin to give Vladimir Putin the same talk. Diskin began speaking, but Putin cut him short after three sentences: "I really do not care. From my point of view, you can kill them all," he said. Then he turned to Sharon and said, "Come, let's go and eat and drink something." The attitude toward Israel of French president Nicolas Sarkozy, who replaced Chirac, was much more positive than his predecessor's, and tolerant of the use of targeted killing. Interviews with Diskin, June 1, 2017, and Nicolas Sarkozy, November 7, 2012.

514  **"In one swoop, the complaints against us ceased"**  Interview with Eiland, June 5, 2011. The American approach toward targeted killings has changed from one end to the other. When I asked former secretary of homeland security Michael Chertoff what he thinks of targeted killings he replied: "I think they are much better than nontargeted killings." Interview with Michael Chertoff, May 27, 2017.

514  **to give the Americans all of the files for "Blue Troll"**  Israeli intelligence's surveillance of Hamas, Palestinian Islamic Jihad, and Hezbollah led, among other places, to Sudan, which was ruled in the 1990s by Dr. Hassan al-Turabi, a British-educated, well-mannered, extremist Islamist cleric. Khartoum had become a willing host for many terrorist organizations and a friend to the states that aided them, such as Iran. In October 1993, Imad Mughniyeh went to Khartoum to meet with two of the most prominent leaders who had found asylum there. One was Ayman al-Zawahiri, the leader of Egyptian Islamic Jihad, who had been involved in the assassination of Egyptian president Anwar al-Sadat in 1981. The other was Osama bin Laden, who had harnessed his construction concern to the Islamist holy war. On July 7, 1995, a terrorist squad tried to kill Egyptian president Hosni Mubarak, an ally of Israel, by attacking his motorcade between Addis Ababa, the capital of Ethiopia, and the city's airport. Mubarak made a miraculous escape. Thanks to its activities in Sudan, Israel was able to discover that Ayman al-Zawahiri and Osama bin Laden had sent in the hit team. Israeli intelligence was the first to recognize the menace of what is known today as the "global jihad," and a special desk was set up in the Mossad to handle the phenomenon. The Mossad planned a complex assassination operation against bin Laden, and Rabin signed a Red Page for him. Bin Laden's secretary was recruited, there was cooperation with the intelligence service of the moderate Sunni Muslim state whence the secretary hailed, and later on there was even surveillance of bin Laden and some preliminary intelligence gathering. But before the final step, which called for the secretary to poison him, the aforementioned Muslim state froze relations with Israel because of the deadlock in the peace process with the Palestinians, and the operation could go no further. Interviews with "Joseph," January 2015, Ehud Olmert, August 2011, Dan Meridor, August 30, 2006, Nathan Adams, August 21, 1996, and Farkash, March 14, 2011. Bergman, *Secret War with Iran*, 217–23.

515  **"The attacks on 9/11 gave our own war absolute international legitimacy"**  Danny Ayalon, the Israeli ambassador to Washington at the time, recalls one of the first meetings after 9/11, when he accompanied some senior Israeli Air Force officers to a meeting with Defense Secretary Donald Rumsfeld and his deputy Paul Wolfowitz: "Rumsfeld began by saying, 'We need your help. We want to know how you convert intelligence into a rocket that hits a terrorist.'" Interviews with Diskin, June 1, 2017, Paul Wolfowitz, July 2008 (thanks to Mark Gerson for help in arranging the meeting), and Danny Ayalon, August 24, 2017.


## CHAPTER 30: "THE TARGET HAS BEEN ELIMINATED, BUT THE OPERATION FAILED"

516  **"He was different"**  Interview with Dichter, November 4, 2010.

517  **He was arrested again in 1988**  Israel Defense Forces, indictment, *Military Prosecutor v. Salah Mustafa Mahmud Shehadeh*, 11524/89, September 17, 1989 (author's archive, received from "Twins").

517  **long years in Israeli prisons gave him the status of a hero**  Shin Bet, *Condensed Summary on Salah Shehadeh*, June 25, 2001 (author's archive, received from "Ellis").

517  **"our feeling . . . was really hope"**  Interview with "Goldi," January 2010.

517  **"Shehade's positions have become more extreme"**  Shin Bet, *Salah Shehadeh— Military Head of Hamas in the Gaza Strip*, November 23, 2003 (shown to the author by "Ellis").

518  **killed 474 people and wounded 2,649**  Special Committee for Examining the Targeted Killing of Salah Shehadeh, "Testimony of A.L.," 45.

519    **"these guys were not our chief rabbis"**   Interview with Dichter, November 4, 2010.

520    **"It puts us ILD folks into a very complicated situation"**   Interview with Daniel Reisner, July 6, 2011.

520    **"we could not approve of killing children"**   The other half of Reisner's description was given with a smile. "On the other hand, we were also married to women and we know what wives are like. With women it was easier to authorize opening fire." Interview with Reisner, July 6, 2011.

520    **the presence of a few adults**   State of Israel, *Special Committee for Examining the Targeted Killing of Salah Shehadeh,* 67.

521    **They would all be allowed to die**   Minister of Defense, *Sorties and Operations Discussion,* July 17, 2002 (shown to the author by "Ellis").

521    **"In the end, we had no choice"**   Interview with Yaalon, December 21, 2016.

522    **Diskin was not eager to go ahead**   Shin Bet, Deputy Head of Service, *Flag Bearer,* appendix, *Framing/Activation,* July 19, 2002 (shown to the author by "Ellis").

523    **"between two children"**   Interview with Farkash, March 14, 2011.

523    **intelligence indicated that the daughter was not at home**   Shin Bet, *The Flag Bearer—Head of Service's Orders Regarding His Framing,* July 21, 2002 (shown to the author by "Ellis").

523    **"he ordered that the operation be executed"**   State of Israel, *Special Committee for Examining the Targeted Killing of Salah Shehadeh,* 69.

524    **"We hit it, and the house collapses, falls down"**   The pilot was speaking on December 19, 2010, at the Binah Center in Tel Aviv. The transcript was published first by Amira Haas in *Haaretz,* January 7, 2011.

525    **"The people who were out to eliminate Shehade knew this"**   Interview with Gideon Levy, March 30, 2011.

525    **"The target has been eliminated"**   Interview with Dichter, November 4, 2010.

526    **"I feel a slight shudder in the wing"**   Vered Barzilai, interview with Dan Halutz, *Haaretz,* August 23, 2002.

527    **considered by many to be the best combat pilot**   Spector took part in the attack on the USS *Liberty* on June 8, 1967, in which thirty-four American seamen were killed. Israel claimed the ship was not flying the American flag and that it believed the *Liberty* was an Egyptian warship, but the reason for the attack has not been clearly established. Some believe that Spector's signature on the protest letter was his way of atoning for what happened then.

527    **"Shalom, my name is Yoel"**   "You, Opponents of Peace," interview with Yoel Peterburg, *Anashim,* June 27, 2006.

528    **"has taken hold among the cedars"**   Interview with Weissglass, December 23, 2014.

## CHAPTER 31: THE REBELLION IN UNIT 8200

529    **Amir (not his real name) was an NIO**   Interview with "Amir," March 2011. He asked to remain anonymous for fear that revealing his identity could cause him harm where he is working and studying now.

530    **"Our role in the selection of targets for assassination was dramatic"**   Interview with "Globus," April 2011.

532    **the intention was simply to kill someone—anyone**   Unit 8200, Center 7143, *Reaction of Unit 8200 to Information Request Regarding the Bombing of Fatah Facility in Khan Yunis,* March 4, 2003 (author's archive, received from "Globus").

532    **"isn't this precisely the definition of a manifestly illegal order?'"**   Interview with "Amir," March 2011.

533    **"we intentionally chose opinionated people"**   Interview with Eyal Zisser, April 1, 2011.

533    **recorded some cellphone conversations between Tom Cruise . . . and . . . Nicole Kidman**   When the commander of the unit heard about it, he had the officer, "Janek," tossed into military prison, a highly infrequent occurrence in 8200, and he announced that the next soldier caught doing something similar would be ejected from the unit. It turned out, however, that the commanders of the unit were a lot less concerned when it came to the right to privacy of Arabs. In 2014, a group of officers and soldiers from 8200 signed a sharp letter of protest over allegations that some of the signatories had been ordered to listen in to conversations of Palestinians and to note intimate information. This information was then handed over to the Shin Bet so it could pressure and blackmail those Palestinians

into agreeing to become agency informants. This information and recordings of the compromising conversations, the letter stated, were also distributed around the unit for the officers' enjoyment. The IDF never investigated the complaints of these protesters, and they were all thrown out of the unit's reserves. Interview with "Leila," December 2015. "Janek" and the IDF media office declined to comment.

534  **"it had never happened and never would happen"**  Interview with Yair Cohen, August 18, 2011.

534  **"I'm happy not to be in your position at this moment"**  Reconstruction of events from documents for attack on objective 7068, including operation orders, debriefings, and exchange of internal emails between participants via 8200's secured server (author's archive, received from "Globus").

535  **forty minutes before the operation's time window closed**  Interview with Dani Harari, August 18, 2011.

536  **"Unit 8200 is the epitome of the culture of secrecy"**  Interview with "Roman," March 2011.

536  **only someone actually pressing the trigger**  Interview with Elazar Stern, August 18, 2011.

536  **"I could not under any circumstances endorse the act of the NIO"**  Interview with Asa Kasher, June 5, 2011. A short time after the incident, chief of staff Yaalon said that he had never given an order to kill anyone in the Khan Yunis building. These claims, however, do not accord with written orders and top-secret internal 8200 documents. And in 2012, in an interview for this book, Yaalon, by then serving as deputy prime minister, in effect confirmed that he had ordered the killing, but argued that the order was legal. Yaalon's statements, however, starkly contradict the position of the ILD of the IDF's advocate general on the subject of assassinations, which states that only persons "directly linked" to terror are legitimate targets.

537  **"It was clear that we were out to kill"**  Interview with Kastiel, December 31, 2013.

538  **Malaisha was "framed" and "intercepted," shot dead**  The Two Towers case was first published by Uri Blau in *Haaretz*, November 28, 2008, and caused much consternation in the defense establishment. The Shin Bet immediately launched an inquiry to find Uri Blau's sources. The discovery came fairly quickly—Anat Kam, a junior officer serving in the Central Command. She was prosecuted and sent to prison. This was followed by a brutal assault on the journalist Blau. Out of fear of arrest, detention, and prosecution, Blau, who was on a trip abroad at the time, delayed his return for an extended period. The Israeli police declared him a fugitive from justice and issued an international arrest warrant for him. When he eventually returned, he was forced to hand over his entire archive to the Shin Bet for destruction. He was charged with aggravated espionage, convicted, and sentenced to four months of community service.

538  **what it called "interception operations"**  Interview with "Oscar," May 2014.

538  **"We ran one operation after another, without stopping"**  According to AMAN's count, for example, in just one four-month period, between the beginning of July and the end of October 2005, more than seventy terrorists were killed in interception operations.

538  **several variations of the Grass Widow technique were used**  In 2004, I persuaded the IDF spokesman to allow me to observe one of these Grass Widow operations, codenamed "Swamp King," the aim of which was to flush out and kill Hamas and Islamic Jihad terrorists in the heart of the casbah of the city of Nablus in the West Bank. The operation was carried out by Paratroop Battalion 890, whose commander, Amir Baram, dealt a lot with Grass Widow techniques, and adopted as his unit's motto the United States Marines slogan "Patience, perseverance, and sometimes a bullet between the eyes." At the pre-op briefing he said: "Fire at the center of the body and a little higher, that's the best. If one falls, take another shot to confirm the kill. Don't forget, we want him to come out of this dead!" Ronen Bergman, "Code Name Grass Widow," *Yedioth Ahronoth*, April 26, 2004. Interview with Amir Baram, March 2004.

539  **the Palestinians were spawning more and more attackers**  Shin Bet, *Survey of Characteristics of Salient Terror Attacks in the Current Confrontation. Analysis of Characteristics of Terror Attacks in Last Decade*, 2–5. Ben-Yisrael, "Facing Suicide Terrorists," 16.

539  **"We felt we had something like a year"**  Interview with "Guy," November 2012.

540  **"We had to build a clear-cut deterrent"**  Interview with Farkash, November 7, 2016.

## CHAPTER 32: PICKING ANEMONES

541   **Ibrahim al-Makadmeh knew the Israelis were going to kill him**   Interview with "Guy," November 2012.

542   **"the seventy-two virgins in paradise is an option that cannot be proved"**   Interview with Gilad, August 4, 2015.

542   **calling yourself a political functionary was no longer cover**   Interview with Farkash, November 7, 2016.

542   **"Drawing analogies between terrorism and a snake . . . is such an oversimplification"**   Interview with Ayalon, March 14, 2016.

542   **Operation Picking Anemones was eased into practice**   Eldar, *Getting to Know Hamas*, 51 (Hebrew).

544   **"never did such a serious adversary make such a serious mistake"**   Yassin still wasn't a target, but what did that matter? If Hamas political and military leaders could all be killed at once, if their bodies could all be found in the rubble of the same building, it would prove what Israel had long contended—that there was no practical difference between the so-called political arm and those who killed Jews. Interviews with Dichter, November 4, 2010, and Ofer Dekel, February 2009.

544   **"We need internal and external legitimacy to carry on with our fight"**   Reconstruction of the events from interviews with Dichter, November 4, 2010, Yaalon, June 12, 2011, Mofaz, June 14, 2011, Farkash, April 10, 2013, Galant, August 19, 2011, and Eiland, June 5, 2011.

545   **But Yaalon insisted**   I decided to play devil's advocate with Yaalon. "What would you have done," I asked, "if there wasn't an apartment block next door, only the building where the Dream Team was meeting, and there were three children there too?" Yaalon: "I'd have no problem. I'd authorize it. What's the problem?" "And five children?" I ask. "Also authorize. Look, we knew in advance that there were likely to be members of the host's family in the house. We didn't know how to keep it perfectly clean. From my perspective, there was a distinction between the chances of harming members of the same family and the many dozens who were likely to be hurt in an adjacent building."

546   **"I saw Sheikh Yassin getting up on his feet from the wheelchair"**   Dichter was kidding, of course. Actually, Yassin was carried. "We heard the boom above us," Yassin's son said. "Abu al-Abed said, 'We've been bombed, *ya sheikh*, we have to leave here quickly.'" So as not to waste precious time on the wheelchair, al-Abed took the sheikh's legs, his son took his arms, and together they ran with him to the car outside. Eldar, *Getting to Know Hamas*, 39.

546   **"civilians were likely to be hurt"**   Interview with Mofaz, June 14, 2011.

546   **"I looked around the war room"**   Interview with Dichter, November 4, 2010.

547   **to take "the necessary response actions"**   Interviews with Shalom, March 1, 2011, and "Guy," November 2012.

550   **"is liable to set the Middle East ablaze"**   Interviews with Dichter, June 2012, Gilad, July 31, 2012, and Farkash, March 14, 2011.

550   **"killing everyone else . . . and not strike at him"**   Interview with Yaalon, June 12, 2011.

550   **"I also have no problem doing it with a 'high signature'"**   Interview with Mofaz, June 14, 2011.

550   **"Won't we look like the Wild West?"**   Interview with Eiland, June 5, 2011.

551   **"would also have left Hitler immune to attack"**   Interview with Kasher, June 5, 2011.

551   **the military advocate general was emphatically opposed**   Interview with Reisner, July 6, 2011.

551   **"he knows we are keeping close track of him"**   Interview with "Terminal," November 2015.

552   **She then detonated a bomb**   Ali Wakad, "Suicide Bomber: 'I Always Wanted Parts of My Body to Fly Through the Air,'" *Ynet*, January 14, 2004. Riyashi was the eighth female suicide bomber but the first from Hamas. http://www.ynet.co.il/articles/0,7340,L-2859046,00.html.

552   **"It is much harder to examine women"**   Interview with Mofaz, June 14, 2011.

552   **AMAN was able to present Attorney General Rubinstein**   Interview with Yair Cohen, December 4, 2014.

552   **"We had clear intelligence-based evidence"**   Interview with Farkash, March 14, 2011.

553   **"that we would be able to reach a peace agreement"**   Interview with Peres, September 17, 2012.

553 **"I was not impressed by the warnings"** Interview with Olmert, August 29, 2011.

553 **"A pretty tough argument ensued"** Interview with Weissglass, October 11, 2012.

553 **But there were spaces in between those three points** The final decision to kill Yassin was made following another attack: On March 15, 2004, two Hamas suicide bombers blew themselves up at the Ashdod Port, after being smuggled in in a double-wall container. Ten people were killed, thirteen wounded. That night, chief of staff Mofaz scratched an entry in his diary. "Decision: To up the ante against Hamas leadership," he wrote. "Gear Handle"— that was Yassin's code name—"to raise for approval tomorrow." Interview with Mofaz, June 14, 2011.

554 **"I did not think they'd fire at a cripple's wheelchair"** Eldar, *Getting to Know Hamas*, 55.

554 **people lying or crawling on the ground** A video of the hit against Yassin, like all of the videos of Operation Picking Anemones, is stored in the digital archive of the Air Force's internal system, shown to the author by "Hilton."

555 **"We hit the bull's-eye"** Interview with Mofaz, June 14, 2011.

555 **Sharon ordered that his staff be woken up** Interview with Assaf Shariv, June 9, 2011. After it became clear that Yassin had indeed been killed in the attack, one of the officers in the Turban bunker that had handled the operation printed out a small notice and stuck it on the door: "Only God forgives. We set up the meeting."

555 **"They're on the verge of hysteria"** Interview with Weissglass, June 11, 2012.

556 **Turban had no difficulty keeping tabs on him** Interview with "Diamond," August 2011.

556 **a Brushlet missile exploded into his Subaru** The video of "Electronic Erase," the assassination of Rantisi, was shown to the author by "Hilton."

556 **"Arafat should take note . . . that anyone whose business is terror"** Itamar Eichner, "Not the Last Killing," *Yedioth Ahronoth*, April 18, 2006.

557 **"We have to defeat them, not allow them to breathe"** Conversation reconstructed from my interview with Mofaz, June 14, 2011, and a synopsis that Mofaz wrote in his notebook at the time.

557 **Suleiman appealed to Sharon** Interview with Galant, August 19, 2011.

557 **"now you know their offer is serious"** Interview with Mofaz, June 14, 2011. Eldar, *Getting to Know Hamas*, 62–63.

558 **Sharon, the sworn hawk . . . "underwent a dramatic change"** Interview with Weissglass, December 23, 2014.

558 **"dispatching them to kill throughout Israel"** Sharon's speech in the Knesset, April 8, 2002.

558 **Sharon described Arafat as "a pathological liar, a murderer"** Sharon, *Sharon: The Life of a Leader*, 363 (Hebrew).

559 **ensuring his survival as the Palestinian leader** Bergman, *Authority Granted*, 17–28, 165–77 (Hebrew).

559 **the overseas publication of a book about these documents** A high-ranking representative of Sharon, accompanied by a representative of Meir Dagan, offered to finance translation of my book about the Palestinian Authority, *Authority Granted,* into English and to assist with any other expenses involved. "Money is not an issue," he said, "the most important thing being that the world gets to know the truth about this despicable man." I declined the offer. Meeting with "the Prince" and "Leonid," September 2002.

559 **"I have never seen so much cleverness, blood, and abomination"** Pacepa, *Red Horizons*, 44–45 (Hebrew).

559 **Sharon dropped this distasteful idea** Interviews with Kuperwasser, May 21, 2004, Mofaz, June 14, 2011, and Gilboa, April 9, 2014.

560 **a company of armored D9 bulldozers** The company had a female commanding officer named Tali. Sharon was obsessive in regard to Arafat and would go into precise details with chief of staff Yaalon about where the bulldozers were advancing. "He would call me every day," Yaalon recalls, "and ask: 'So, what did Tali *hahoreset* do today?' (*Hahoreset* is a double entendre here, meaning "destroy" and, in Hebrew slang, "the gorgeous woman.") He enjoyed this so much, he really watered at the mouth." Interview with Yaalon, December 21, 2016.

561 **and then Israel would announce his whereabouts to the world** Interview with Halutz, July 5, 2011.

561 **"we couldn't ensure that Arafat would come out of all this alive"** Interview with Blumenfeld, May 28, 2010.

561 **("I see your point")** Interview with Eiland, January 19, 2015.

561 **Laboratory tests . . . came to different conclusions** "Swiss Study: Polonium Found in Arafat's Bones," Al Jazeera, November 7, 2013.

562 **the possibility that he died from AIDS** Harel and Issacharoff, "What Killed Him?" *Haaretz,* September 6, 2005.

562 **categorically denied** Here's what some top Israeli officials said when I asked them what caused the Palestinian leader's death: Chief of staff (at the time of Arafat's death) Moshe Yaalon (August 16, 2011) said with a smile: "What do you mean? Arafat died of sorrow." Deputy Prime Minister Shimon Peres (September 17, 2012): "I didn't think we should kill him. I thought we would ultimately need him to make peace." Deputy chief of staff Dan Halutz (July 5, 2011): "Ah, I understand that now is that part of the interview when you try to decipher my body language." AMAN chief Zeevi-Farkash (April 10, 2013): "I was torn— sometimes I thought we needed to strike against him, and sometimes I thought we mustn't, that there was a difference between him and Nasrallah or Yassin."

562 **Sharon himself defined the goal of such an operation** Aluf Ben, "A Responsible Leadership Will Enable Resumption of Negotiations," *Haaretz,* November 12, 2004.

563 **close security cooperation with the two of them** Interviews with Diskin, October 23, 2011, Gad Goldstein, September 2012, and "Hoover," December 2015.

564 **"I am deeply concerned"** Email exchange with Prof. Gabriella Blum, August 2017. For further reading see Gabriella Blum and Phillip B. Heymann, "Law and the Policy of Targeted Killing," *Harvard National Security Journal,* vol. 1, no. 145, 2010.

## CHAPTER 33: THE RADICAL FRONT

568 **Syria and Iran signed a series of agreements** Bergman, *Secret War with Iran,* 350–58.

568 **Bush did not include Syria in the "axis of evil"** Interview with Hayden, August 20, 2014.

569 **An alliance with Syria was in Iran's best interests** Ronen Bergman, "The Secret Syrian Chemical Agent and Missile City," *Yedioth Ahronoth,* September 6, 2002.

569 **Syria had practical motives for wanting to strengthen Hezbollah** Ronen Bergman, "They Are All 'the Hezbollah Connection,'" *New York Times Magazine,* February 10, 2015.

570 **developed strategy and supplied matériel** Interviews with "Terminal," September 2014, and "Iftach," November 2016.

571 **They were camouflaged so expertly** Interviews with Dagan, May 26, 2013, and "Advantage," January 2016.

571 **it had not adapted itself to changing times** Interview with "Loacker," August 2015.

571 **the Mossad tried to thwart dangerous projects** Bergman, *Secret War with Iran,* 352.

572 **"The operational aspect was like an appendix to him"** Interview with Weissglass, December 23, 2014.

572 **the initial and most urgent targets on the liquidation list** Bergman, *Authority Granted,* 269–96 (Hebrew).

573 **"there was a price to be paid"** Interview with Farkash, April 10, 2013.

573 **drew up a list of targets (dubbed the Twelve Musketeers)** Interview with Ronen Cohen, November 17, 2015.

573 **Obeid managed to lure a senior IDF reserve officer to Dubai** Bergman, *By Any Means Necessary,* 462–63 (Hebrew).

573 **"We feared that this might start an all-out war"** Interview with "Leo," September 2016.

573 **no one was acting against the heads of the organizations** Interview with Ronen Cohen, November 17, 2015.

573 **The first target was Ramzi Nahara** He helped Imad Mughniyeh kidnap Ahmad Halak, the Mossad agent who had killed Mughniyeh's brother (see chapter 23), he was at the center of Iran's and Hezbollah's espionage efforts in Israel, and he dispatched money and instructions to the organizers of suicide terror.

574 **"The explosion tore Salah's body into two"** Interview with "Bourbon," October 2016.

575 **the head of the Counter-Terrorism Bureau at the prime minister's office** Dagan was appointed deputy director of the Counter-Terrorism Bureau in 1997 and also engaged in political activity, including the movement against withdrawal from the Golan Heights. He managed Sharon's Election Day operations in 2001 as well.

575 **"No problem," said Dagan. "Let's burn it"** Interview with "Mozart," May 2016.

576 **"a Mossad chief with a dagger between his teeth"** Just after he appointed Meir Dagan as director of the Mossad in 2002, I asked Prime Minister Ariel Sharon if he thought

that this man, with the reputation of an impetuous, bellicose, trigger-happy officer, averse to the regular chain of command, could restore the agency to its former glory. Sharon, with his sly grin and half-chuckle, shot back, "No doubt about it. Do you know what Meir's great specialty is?" I shook my head, and Sharon answered his own question with his characteristically cynical black humor: "Meir's great specialty is separating a terrorist from his head." Interviews with Sharon, April 2004.

576 **Both men saw a nuclear Iran as an existential danger to Israel** Interviews with "Eldy," August 2014, and Galant, July 7, 2011.

577 **"Journalists will climb all over me and you"** Dagan mentioned two journalists from whom he expected critical coverage—Amir Oren of *Haaretz* and Ronen Bergman. On both counts, Dagan was correct in his prediction. Interview with Dagan, May 29, 2013.

577 **"never stopped yelling at everyone that they weren't delivering the goods"** Interview with "Salvador," May 2012.

578 **"to later pull the wool over my eyes"** Interview with Dagan, June 19, 2013.

578 **the agency would have only two broad targets** Originally, the list included another objective: the war against global jihad, which had been a priority ever since Al Qaeda's attempt in November 2002 to down an Israeli aircraft with shoulder-launched missiles in Mombasa. This goal was later set aside when Dagan reached the conclusion that any contribution the Mossad might make in the global battle against Al Qaeda would be insignificant next to the enormous efforts being made by the United States.

578 **creating a joint "intelligence pool"** Interview with Farkash, January 31, 2016.

579 **Since the first and second options were unrealistic** Interviews with "Eldy," September 2014, and "Iftach," November 2016.

580 **Dagan ordered the Mossad to ramp up its secret liaisons** Dagan named David Meidan, of Mossad's Universe (Tevel) division, responsible for the secret liaisons with foreign intelligence bodies, to head up this effort. Both Dagan and Meidan would travel secretly to meet the heads of the governments and intelligence services of many Middle Eastern countries to persuade them to do the inconceivable—to collaborate with the Israeli Mossad against other Arab and Islamic countries. Meidan's fluent Arabic and intimate understanding of the Arab world and culture greatly helped in breaking the ice. Interviews with Meidan, July 16, 2015, Dagan, June 19, 2013, and Turki bin Faisal al Saud, February 2014.

580 **Dagan's reforms led . . . to the resignation of many senior Mossad officials** Ronen Bergman, "A Wave of Resignations at the Mossad Command," *Yedioth Ahronoth*, October 7, 2005.

580 **"I thought they were wrong, that it was idiocy"** Interview with Dagan, May 29, 2013.

581 **"if, by the next morning, there were not another five passports ready"** Interview with "Eldy," January 2015.

581 **"Sporadic eliminations are worth nothing"** Interview with Dagan, June 19, 2013.

582 **a vociferous quarrel broke out** Interview with Ronen Cohen, February 18, 2016.

582 **"The moment Yassin was taken out of the game"** Interview with Ilan, October 22, 2014.

583 **The line went dead** Interview with "Iftach," March 2017.

583 **"I don't take responsibility for these events"** Interview with Dagan, June 19, 2013.

584 **Israel consented to a humiliating prisoner-exchange deal** The deal also included Col. (Res.) Elhanan Tannenbaum, the artillery officer who'd been lured into a drug deal in Dubai and was abducted to Beirut. Interviews with Elhanan Tannenbaum, August 2004, Lotan, January 13, 2009, and Aharon Haliva, November 17, 2002. Bergman, *By Any Means Necessary*, 440–56, 475–88 (Hebrew).

584 **These freed prisoners managed to direct eight suicide attacks** Interview with "Amazonas," October 2011.

584 **They hung Shalit's flak jacket on the fence** Bergman, *By Any Means Necessary*, 563–71 (Hebrew).

584 **the guidance Hamas received from Iranian intelligence** Interviews with Barak, November 22, 2011, and "Fanta," December 2016.

585 **It demanded that Israel release one thousand Palestinian prisoners** Netanyahu had launched his international career by presenting himself as an expert on terrorism who had continually preached that one should never succumb to demands for the release of prisoners in exchange for hostages. And yet he was the one who ordered the release of 1,027 Palestinian prisoners, including countless Hamas members who had been directly involved in murdering Israelis, in exchange for Shalit. This was the highest price ever paid for a deal of this kind. Ronen Bergman, "The Human Swap," *New York Times Magazine*, November

13, 2011. A few of the terrorists who were released during that deal were targeted and killed by Israel in the following years. One of them was Mazen Fuqaha, who was involved in suicide bombings and sentenced in 2003 to nine life imprisonments and an additional fifty years. He was shot several times in his head, near his house in Gaza, by Israeli-run assassins on April 24, 2017.

585 **This was a fatal error, which cost Israel dearly**  Interviews with Dagan, May 29, 2013, Barak, November 22, 2011, and "Iftach," November 2011.

585 **the IDF launched a hesitant and ineffectual land invasion**  Interviews with Ehud Adam, August 9, 2006, and Mordechai Kidor, August 4, 2006. Bergman, *Secret War with Iran,* 364–78.

585 **"It was something like the North Vietnamese Army after the Tet Offensive"**  Interview with Dagan, May 29, 2013.

586 **"We did not approach this business . . . as prepared as we should have been"**  Interview with Halutz, July 5, 2011.

587 **the best the "resistance" axis could have hoped for**  Interviews with Dagan, March 19, 2013, "Eldy," January 2014, "Iftach," March 2017, and "Advantage," December 2016.

## CHAPTER 34: KILLING MAURICE

588 **"I am going in. Give me the timing"**  Interviews with "Charles," April 2012, and "Iftach," December 2016.

589 **"every time Mustafa called Mohammed, Moishele was listening in"**  Interview with "Leila," March 2013.

590 **remained totally invisible to Israeli intelligence**  Interview with Shahar Argaman, March 17, 2013.

590 **the construction of a building to house a nuclear reactor**  Israeli intelligence received contradictory reports about whether the Iranians were aware that part of the money was being used to finance the North Korean–Syrian nuclear project. Bergman, *Secret War with Iran,* 257–58.

590 **The more time went by and Dagan's concerns were validated**  Interview with Shariv, August 10, 2006.

590 **"the crazy ideas that his agency came up with"**  Interview with Olmert, August 29, 2011.

591 **mostly it was a cause for serious concern**  Hayden, *Playing to the Edge,* 255.

591 **"Meir came to me with this material . . . and it was like an earthquake"**  Olmert set up a special panel, headed by Yaakov Amidror and with the participation of an AMAN research division expert, to carry out a critical examination of the Mossad's material. The panel reached the same conclusion: Syria was building a reactor with the aim of making nuclear weapons. Interviews with "Charles," April 2012, and Olmert, August 29, 2011.

591 **he was already a familiar and welcome guest**  Interviews with Dagan, June 19, 2013, and Hayden, August 20, 2014.

591 **The two men established the closest levels of trust**  Interview with Hayden, February 1, 2014.

591 **not even the experienced Hayden anticipated the bombshell**  Ibid.

592 **Hayden leaned over to Vice President Dick Cheney**  Hayden, *Playing to the Edge,* 256.

592 **"this reactor was not intended for peaceful purposes"**  Secretary of State Rice, "Syria's Clandestine Nuclear Program," April 25, 2008 (taken from the Wikileaks archive, as given to the author by Julian Assange, March 4, 2011).

592 **he wanted U.S. forces to destroy the reactor**  Interview with "Oscar," April 2014.

593 **The Assad family . . . reminded him of the Corleone family**  Interview with Hayden, July 20, 2016.

593 **"Assad could not stand another embarrassment"**  That retreat was forced on Assad by the international community, led by the United States and France, for his involvement in the assassination of Rafik Hariri.

593 **Dagan had the exact opposite opinion**  Interviews with Dagan, May 29, 2013, and "Ed," October 2016.

593 **The final decision was made in a meeting with the president**  Hayden, *Playing to the Edge,* 261–63.

593 **she did not think that the United States should get involved**  Rice's view was supported by Hayden and the rest of the U.S. intelligence community. Hayden reminded Bush

of the agency's well-known slogan, "No Core No War," and said that he had no evidence of the construction of a plutonium extraction plant, without which there could be no bomb. Interview with Hayden, August 20, 2014.

594    **"this is not an imminent danger"**    Hayden recalled, "I was quite calm about the matter of the Syrian reactor because it was clear to me that if we didn't attack, the Israelis would." Interview with Hayden, August 20, 2014. Hayden, *Playing to the Edge,* 263–64.

594    **Israel could rely only on itself**    In an interview for this book in 2011, when Olmert wanted to explain the gravity of the dilemma over the Syrian reactor and his decision to act, he pointed to a photograph on his office wall that he had taken with him when he left the Prime Minister's Office. An identical picture can be seen on the walls of many of the offices of top-ranking Israelis. It was taken during Israeli Air Force flight 301, which took off from Radom in Poland on September 4, 2003. Three IAF F-15 fighters are seen flying over what may be the best-known gate and strip of rail track in the world, those of the Nazi death camp at Auschwitz. On the photo, which Air Force commander Eliezer Shkedi distributed to a number of top-level Israeli officials, he wrote: "The Israeli Air Force over Auschwitz, in the name of the Jewish people, the State of Israel, and the IDF: To remember and not to forget, to rely only upon ourselves."

595    **This would save Syria the embarrassment of being exposed**    On June 9, 2011, the IAEA announced that Syria had failed to report the construction of a nuclear reactor, a gross violation of the NPT. IAEA Board of Governors, *Implementation of the NPT Safeguards Agreement in the Syrian Arab Republic,* June 9, 2011. Interview with "Charles," April 2012.

595    **"turned out to be right, while my analysts turned out to be wrong"**    Interview with Hayden, August 20, 2014.

595    **"Whatever we asked for, we got"**    Interview with "Eldy," August 2014.

595    **"I okayed three hundred [Mossad] operations"**    Interview with Olmert, August 29, 2011.

596    **one man was the primary driving force**    Interview with Dagan, May 26, 2013.

596    **"That's him. That's Maurice"**    Interview with "Leila," March 2013.

598    **This generated more information about Mughniyeh**    Interview with "Leila," March 2013.

598    **he relocated from Beirut to Damascus**    Interviews with "Iftach," May 2011, "Leila," March 2013, and Richard Kemp, March 2007.

598    **the most dangerous place for the Mossad to operate**    Interview with Dagan, May 29, 2013.

599    **he turned to another country to assist with an assassination**    Interview with "Neta," July 2013.

599    **The United States would not normally participate in the execution**    Asked to explain the United States' targeted killings against Al Qaeda, Hayden noted that "assassination" was defined as forbidden lethal acts "against political enemies," whereas "U.S. targeted killings against Al Qaeda are against members of an opposing armed enemy force. This is war. This is under the laws of armed conflict." He added, "Israel is probably the only other country in the world who thinks like the United States—that what we do there is legal." Interview with Hayden, August 20, 2014.

599    **the CIA legal advisers came up with a solution**    Interview with "Neta," July 2013.

599    **President Bush then granted Dagan's request for assistance**    According to a *Newsweek* report it took Bush about thirty seconds to reply to Hayden's question on hitting Mughniyeh by saying, "Yes, and why haven't you done this already? You have my blessing. Go with God." Jeff Stein, "How the CIA Took Down Hezbollah's Top Terrorist, Imad Mugniyah," *Newsweek,* January 31, 2015.

599    **but only on the condition that it be kept a secret**    President Bush ordered total secrecy about all aspects of Mughniyeh's killing. Only in January 2015 did *The Washington Post*'s Adam Goldman and *Newsweek*'s Jeff Stein publish, on exactly the same day, reports about the collaboration between the Mossad and the CIA in this operation. At least parts of these two reports seem to have come from the same sources, described there as senior American intelligence officials who were involved in the killing. According to these sources (unlike what is described in this book), the CIA and not the Mossad was the main actor, while Michael Hayden was the supreme commander of the operation. In an interview with Hayden in the D.C. offices of the Chertoff Group, where he serves as principal, in July 2016, I read him the section of this book dealing with the collaboration between Israel and the United States in the hit on Mughniyeh. When I finished, Hayden smiled and said: "Interesting story. I have nothing to say."

599    **"This was a gigantic, multi-force operation"**    Interview with "Iftach," May 2011.

600    **"even the most careful of men becomes full of confidence"**   Interview with "Iftach,"
       May 2011.

600    **using a bomb detonated by remote control**   "If we succeed, just promise me you'll let
       me be the one giving the okay (*rashai*) order," said N., and went back to the drawing board.
       Interview with Dagan, May 29, 2013.

601    **The Mossad's explosives experts promised**   Faithful to his undertaking to Bush, Ol-
       mert called in N, who was in charge of the technological aspects of the operation, and I, the
       supreme commander of the hunt for Maurice, and repeatedly demanded that the Mossad
       assure him that it was capable of ensuring Mughniyeh and Mughniyeh alone would be
       killed—in other words, that it would be able to ascertain that there was no one else nearby
       and that the blast would be pinpointed at him alone. The Americans insisted on witnessing
       trial runs of the hit to satisfy them that the Mossad had this capability.

601    **each time the operation was called off at the last second**   Interviews with "Loacker,"
       February 2015, and "Lexicon," January 2017.

602    **Olmert, however, refused to let them proceed**   Interviews with "Shimshon," August
       2011, "Iftach," May 2011, and "Lexicon," January 2017.

602    **right before he opened the door, the order to execute was given**   Dagan had kept
       his promise to let N. issue the order to kill Mughniyeh, but N. had passed the privilege on
       to an electronics engineer who had played a central role in the operation. Interview with
       "Loacker," January 2015.

602    **The bomb exploded. Imad Mughniyeh . . . was finally dead**   In June 2008, Prime
       Minister Olmert visited the White House. Vice President Cheney was waiting outside to
       welcome him as the motorcade of limousines drew up under the portico. As Olmert walked
       up, Cheney, instead of shaking Olmert's outstretched hand, came to attention and saluted
       the Israeli prime minister. Only the two men and their close aides understood the meaning
       of the gesture. Inside the Oval Office, President Bush thanked Olmert dearly for doing
       away with Mughniyeh. He then showed him Saddam Hussein's pistol, kept in a special box
       inscribed "To Our President," given by the Delta Force team that captured the Iraqi tyrant.
       Interview with "Shimshon," August 2011.

602    **"Just think what this does to the Syrians"**   Interview with Dagan, May 29, 2013.

603    **He was furious with the Syrians for failing to look after his comrade**   Interviews
       with "Shimshon," August 2011, and "Diamond," March 2014.

603    **Mughniyeh's funeral was held in pouring rain**   Description of the funeral and pic-
       tures of it courtesy of the *Der Spiegel* correspondent in Beirut, Ulrike Putz, who attended it.

604    **"You crossed the borders, Zionists"**   The Revolutionary Guards and Mughniyeh's suc-
       cessors concocted a number of daring schemes to abduct Israelis who had served in the
       intelligence community, to blow up Israeli diplomatic missions and Zionist institutions
       across the globe, to attack the members of the Chabad Hasidic sect who maintain centers
       for Israeli travelers all over the world, and to strike at Israeli tourists wherever they could lay
       their hands on them. Almost all of these plans were thwarted thanks to precise warnings
       issued by Israeli intelligence. In one case, the police in Thailand, after getting a hot tip from
       the Mossad, chased a group of Iranian and Lebanese terrorists. One of them had a sophis-
       ticated time-fused bomb that he was planning to attach to an Israeli diplomat's car. Instead,
       he threw it at the police as they came after him. But it hit a tree and bounced back to the
       terrorist's feet before it went off, ripping off both his legs. The cops left the rest of him sit-
       ting against the tree so that press photographers could record the horrific moment for pos-
       terity.

604    **"His operational capabilities were greater"**   Interview with Dagan, June 19, 2013.

604    **"Lucky for us, he wasn't"**   Interview with "Terminal," September 2014.

604    **This behavior "took discipline," Olmert observed**   "Boehner's Meeting with Prime
       Minister Olmert," March 23, 2008, Tel Aviv 000738 (author's archive, received from Julian
       Assange).

605    **But Olmert rejected the idea**   Interview with "Shimshon," November 2012.

605    **"Suleiman was a real shit"**   Interview with Olmert, August 29, 2011.

605    **"a hand in three primary areas"**   "Manhunting Timeline 2008," Intellipedia, NSA
       (Snowden archive), www.documentcloud.org/documents/2165140-manhunting-redacted
       .html#document/p1.

605    **the Israelis knew there was no chance the United States would get involved**   By
       April 2008, the CIA had reached the conclusion that Assad would not start a war over the
       bombing of the reactor, that there was no more need for secrecy, and that it was possible to
       use the materials on the affair for other purposes. Israel was firmly opposed to the publica-
       tion of the pictures, but Hayden thought otherwise: "We needed to make it [the Syrian reac-

tor affair] more public because we were about to enter into an agreement with North Korea, which was guilty of the greatest proliferation crime in history. We had to inform Congress." The affair had been a major intelligence victory, and after suffering from a lot of negative publicity over the years, the agency was only too happy to show off a success. The CIA included a picture of General Suleiman with the head of the North Korean nuclear program. The Mossad and AMAN fumed, fearing that the photo would be leaked and alert Suleiman that he was a marked man. It didn't happen. "Background Briefing with Senior U.S. Officials on Syria's Covert Nuclear Reactor and North Korea's Involvement," April 24, 2008. Interviews with Dagan, July 20, 2013, and Hayden, July 20, 2016. Hayden, *Playing to the Edge,* 267–68.

605  **the Mossad would need assistance**  There were some in the Mossad who were adamantly opposed to killing Suleiman. A very high-ranking Mossad source said, "This is the execution of a uniformed officer of a sovereign state. Suleiman serves his country to the best of his ability, by his own lights. He is not a terrorist. Indeed, he is involved in very dark deeds, but we also have officers who are involved in acts that the other side deems problematic." Interviews with "Iftach," March 2017, and "Dominick," April 2013.

606  **His skull was split open**  This description of the assassination is based on a video taken by Flotilla 13 commandos and interviews with "Shimshon," November 2012, and "Dominick," May 2011.

606  **"the first known instance of Israel targeting a legitimate government official"**  According to documents delivered by Edward Snowden and published on the First Look website, American intelligence intercepted Flotilla 13's communications prior to the attack and knew exactly who was behind it. Matthew Cole, "Israeli Special Forces Assassinated Senior Syrian Official," *First Look,* July 15, 2015.

607  **"total mutual striptease"**  Interview with "Oscar," May 2014.

607  **launched a comprehensive campaign of economic measures**  Interviews with Dagan, June 19, 2013, and "the Prince," March 2012.

608  **computer viruses, one of which became known as Stuxnet**  Even in the conservative estimate of the German BND, Stuxnet alone delayed the Iranian nuclear project by at least two years. Interview, together with Holger Stark, with "Alfred," a high-ranking German intelligence official, February 2012.

608  **the targeted killing of scientists**  Interviews with Dagan, May 29, 2013, "Iftach," March 2017, "Eldy," September 2014, and "Luka," November 2016.

608  **On January 12, 2010, at 8:10 A.M., Masoud Alimohammadi left his home**  Interview with "Leila," December 2015.

608  **did not go without an internal debate in the Mossad**  Interview with "Iftach," March 2017.

608  **realized that someone was killing their scientists**  Interviews with "Iftach," March 2017, "Leila," December 2015, and "Advantage," March 2017.

609  **These efforts greatly slowed down other aspects of the nuclear project**  Interview with Dagan, January 8, 2011.

## CHAPTER 35: IMPRESSIVE TACTICAL SUCCESS, DISASTROUS STRATEGIC FAILURE

611  **Al-Mabhouh was by nature an extremely cautious man**  Interview with "Ethan," November 2011.

614  **"Plasma Screen—authorized for execution"**  Interview with "Eldy," April 2014.

614  **All were genuine, but none actually belonged to the person using it**  Ronen Bergman, "The Dubai Job," *GQ,* January 4, 2011.

615  **Folliard ordered a light meal from room service**  The receipts the two received when paying for the meal and drinks are in the author's archive, received from "Junior."

615  **"It's the kind of hit . . . where the target dictates"**  Interview with "Loacker," February 2015.

620  **"A little more respect for the other side"**  Interview with "Ilay," June 2010.

621  **Whole sections of the Mossad's operations were shut down**  Interview with "Iftach," March 2017.

621  **from Dagan's point of view, nothing had happened**  Netanyahu initially ordered Dagan to set up an internal inquiry team, and Dagan agreed but later told Netanyahu that the man he wanted to head the panel, a high-ranking recent retiree from the Mossad, had refused to take the job. According to a source close to Netanyahu, the prime minister sub-

sequently heard a different story from that man. Either way, an inquiry panel was not set up. Interview with "Nietzsche," May 2017.

621 **Only in 2013 . . . would Dagan admit, for the first time** Interview with Dagan, June 19, 2013.

621 **the Mossad had assured him it could go into a "soft target" country** Interview with "Nietzsche," May 2017.

622 **"Netanyahu doesn't rely on anyone"** Interview with Uzi Arad, December 20, 2011.

622 **fearful of being seen as hesitant** In order to intensify Netanyahu's fear of appearing hesitant or weak, Dagan increased the size of the delegations that he took to see the prime minister about operations, sometimes appearing on Netanyahu's doorstep with as many as fifteen Mossad officials. He reckoned the prime minister would not refuse approval because with so many witnesses there, the danger that his hesitancy would leak out was much greater. When he came out of such meetings, Dagan says, he would think, "Now his balls will shrink and he'll regret having given the okay." Dagan added, "I love falafel, very much. Because I knew he would soon call me back, I'd drive to the Mahaneh Yehuda market [a few minutes away from the prime minister's office] to have a falafel, and wait for the phone call, and not start the trip back to Tel Aviv. When I was not so sure, I'd go to the Kurds' restaurant in Mevaseret Zion [ten minutes away] or a hummus place in Abu Ghosh [fifteen minutes] and wait there. The main thing was not to be too far from Jerusalem. Believe me, I'm telling you, looking back, I was never wrong. He always called me back." Interview with Dagan, June 19, 2013.

622 **The program "reached a point far beyond what I had hoped for"** Interview with Barak, January 13, 2012.

623 **Dagan was stunned by the recklessness** Interview with Dagan, June 19, 2013.

624 **only examining the feasibility of an attack** Commenting on Dagan's remarks about him, Barak wrote to me, "Despite what Dagan said, there's never been any person in the Israeli leadership who didn't realize that it was not possible to completely stop the Iranian nuclear program in a surgical strike. At most, it was a matter of delaying it for a number of years. Both the opponents and the supporters of the need to weigh it were united in an awareness that [military] action was feasible only as a last resort. And only if and when operational capability, international legitimacy, and supreme necessity were present." Barak's email to the author, March 30, 2016.

624 **"the truth is that I was sick of him"** Interview with Dagan, June 19, 2013.

624 **especially not those aimed at the Iranian nuclear project** Interview with "Iftach," November 2011.

625 **"we would recommend attacking Hamas"** Interview with "Terminal," September 2014.

625 **The skies over Khartoum were illuminated by the explosions** Interview with "Iftach," May 2017.

626 **"to coerce a scientist to work on a project"** Interview with Dagan, June 19, 2013.

626 **In order to intensify the fears of the scientists** It appears that following the operations against Moghaddam and Ahmadi-Roshan, Israel departed from its policy of silence. Ehud Barak stated, regarding the deaths of these scientists, "May there be many more to come." The chief of the IDF General Staff, Lt. Gen. Benny Gantz, remarked, "In Iran some things happen in an unnatural way," while the IDF spokesman said he "wouldn't shed a tear" for Ahmadi-Roshan. The daily newspaper *Haaretz* ran a jubilant cartoon showing Ahmadi-Roshan in heaven with a somewhat irritated God grumbling, "Another one," while a little cherub next to him quips, "We already have enough to open a nuclear reactor."

626 **would cause as much apprehension as possible among the greatest numbers of their colleagues** The assassinations continued, against others in the Radical Front as well. The highest-ranking target, whom the Mossad had been hunting since 1996, was Hassan Laqqis, who headed Hezbollah's weapons development department. He was taken out on December 3, 2013, when hit men armed with pistols fitted with silencers pumped bullets into him in the parking lot of his residence in a Beirut suburb. Hassan Laqqis was working intensively with Mohammad al-Zawahri, a Tunisian-born aviation engineer who joined the opposition in his country and was obliged to live in exile for a number of years, joining forces with Hezbollah and Hamas. Upon returning to his country, al-Zawahri worked to establish a fleet of unmanned aircraft and submarines for Hamas, to be used to strike at the oil and gas rigs Israel was building in the Mediterranean. The Mossad, now under the command of Yossi Cohen, intercepted communications between al-Zawahri and his cohorts in Gaza and Lebanon, and killed him on December 16. Interviews with "Charles," April 2012, "Advantage," December 2016, and "Iftach," May 2017.

627    **"the death of those human beings had a great impact on their nuclear pro-
        gram"**  Interview with Hayden, July 20, 2016.

627    **if he could persuade the United States to take just a few more economic mea-
        sures**  Interview with "the Prince," March 2012.

627    **"if it depended on me, Israel would have attacked"**  At a certain stage, Netanyahu
        and Barak stopped concealing their intentions, and in a *New York Times Magazine* cover
        story in January 2012, Barak implied that the attack would take place soon. In light of the
        harsh criticism from defense and intelligence personnel, Barak said, "We, Bibi and myself,
        are responsible, in a very direct and concrete way, for the existence of the State of Israel—
        indeed, for the future of the Jewish people. . . . [A]t the end of the day, when the military
        and intelligence command looks up, it sees us—the minister of defense and the prime
        minister. When we look up, we see nothing but the sky above us." Ronen Bergman, "Israel
        vs. Iran: When Will It Erupt?" *New York Times Magazine,* January 29, 2012.

627    **harming the president's chances of reelection in November 2012**  Obama and his
        team were also under pressure from elements of the American media who believed Obama
        was being too soft on Iran. Meeting with Roger Ailes, January 4, 2012.

628    **if the talks had begun two years later**  Tamir Pardo thought that the JCPOA had both
        positive and negative aspects, and that in any case Israel had to try to work in tandem with
        the Obama administration in order to improve its terms, because there was no chance of
        blocking its passage. Netanyahu thought otherwise and made desperate efforts to use his
        considerable political clout with the Republicans in Washington to thwart the agreement,
        including a controversial speech before a joint session of Congress in March 2015. Netan-
        yahu was wrong.

628    **Iran agreed to dismantle the nuclear project almost entirely**  This agreement goes
        much farther than anything the Tehran regime had ever agreed to in the past. But it also
        reflects significant concessions on the part of the international community, including the
        crossing of red lines that the United States had promised Israel would not be crossed, as
        well as almost full permission for Iran's military industries to press forward with their mis-
        sile development. Ronen Bergman, "What Information Collected by Israeli Intelligence
        Reveals About the Iran Talks," *Tablet,* July 29, 2015.

629    **Dagan simply repeated them at a conference**  Memorial gathering for Yosef Harel,
        commander of AMAN's assassination unit, 188. Dagan was interviewed by the journalist Ari
        Shavit.

631    **Israel has undergone drastic changes in recent decades**  Ronen Bergman, "Israel's
        Army Goes to War with Its Politicians," *New York Times,* May 21, 2016.

More archival references, sources, and pictures used in the research for this book will be posted at
www.ronenbergman.com.

# BIBLIOGRAPHY

## INTERVIEWS

Aharon Abramovich, Worko Abuhi, Ehud (Udi) Adam, Nathan Adams, Avraham Adan, Nahum Admoni, Gadi Afriat, Shlomi Afriat, David Agmon, Amram Aharoni, Zvi Aharoni, Wanda Akale, Lior Akerman, Fereda Aklum, Aql Al-Hashem, Kanatjan Alibekov, Doron Almog, Ze'ev Alon, Yossi Alpher, Hamdi Aman, Yaakov Amidror, Meir Amit, Frank Anderson, Christopher Andrew, Hugo Anzorreguy, Uzi Arad, Dror Arad-Ayalon, Yasser Arafat, David Arbel, Dani Arditi, Moshe Arens, Anna Aroch, Julian Assange, Rojer Auqe, Gad Aviran, Shai Avital, Juval Aviv, Pinchas Avivi, David Avner, Talia Avner, Uri Avnery, Avner Avraham, Haim Avraham, Aharon Avramovich, Ami Ayalon, Danny Ayalon, Avner Azoulai, Robert Baer, Yossi Baidatz, Ehud Barak, Amatzia Baram, Miki Barel, Aharon Barnea, Avner Barnea, Itamar Barnea, Omer Bar-Lev, Uri Bar-Lev, Hannan Bar-On, David Barkai, Hanoch Bartov, Mehereta Baruch, Yona Baumel, Stanley Bedlington, Benjamin Begin, Yossi Beilin, Dorit Beinisch, Ilan Ben David, Moshe Ben David, Zvika Bendori, Gilad Ben Dror, Benjamin Ben-Eliezer, Eliyahu Ben-Elissar, Eitan Ben Eliyahu, Avigdor "Yanosh" Ben-Gal, Isaac Ben Israel, Arthur (Asher) Ben-Natan, Eyal Ben Reuven, Eitan Ben Tsur, Barak Ben Tzur, David Ben Uziel, Ron Ben-Yishai, Yoran Ben Ze'ev, Ronnie (Aharon) Bergman, Muki Betser, Avino Biber, Amnon Biran, Dov Biran, Ilan Biran, Yoav Biran, Kai Bird, Uri Blau, Hans Blix, Gabriella Blum, Naftali Blumenthal, Yossef Bodansky, Joyce Boim, Ze'ev Boim, Chaim Boru, Avraham Botzer, Eitan Braun, Shlomo Brom, Shay Brosh, Jean-Louis Bruguière, Pinchas Buchris, Haim Buzaglo, Zvi Caftori, Haim Carmon, Igal Carmon, Aharon Chelouche, Dvora Chen, Uri Chen, Michael Chertoff, Itamar Chizik, Joseph Ciechanover, Wesley Clark, Avner Cohen, Haim Cohen, Moshe Cohen, Ronen Cohen (scholar), Dr. Ronen Cohen (AMAN Officer), Yair Cohen, Yuval Cohen-Abarbanel, Reuven Dafni, Meir Dagan, Avraham Dar, Yossi Daskal, Ruth Dayan, Uzi Dayan, Puyya Dayanim, Ofer Dekel, Avi Dichter, Yuval Diskin, Amnon Dror, Moshe Efrat, Dov Eichenwald, Uzi Eilam, Giora Eiland, Robert Einhorn, Yom Tov (Yomi) Eini, Amos Eiran, Ehud Eiran, Elad Eisenberg, Miri Eisin, Rafael Eitan, Rolf Ekeus, Ofer Elad, Avigdor Eldan (Azulay), Mike Eldar, Jean-Pierre Elraz, Haggai Erlich, Reuven Erlich, Dror Eshel, Shmuel Ettinger, Uzi Even, Gideon Ezra, Meir Ezri, Aharon Zeevi Farkash, Menachem Finkelstein, Amit Forlit, Moti Friedman, Uzi Gal, Yehoar Gal, Yoav Galant, Yoram Galin, Robert Gates, Karmit Gatmon, Yeshayahu Gavish, Shlomo Gazit, Yoav Gelber, Reuel Gerecht, Dieter Gerhardt, Erez Gerstein, Binyamin Gibli, Mordechai Gichon, Gideon Gideon, Yehuda Gil, Amos Gilad, Amos Gilboa, Carmi Gillon, Yossi Ginat, Isabella Ginor, Yossi Ginossar, Caroline Glick, Tamar Golan, Motti Golani, Ralph Goldman, Gadi Goldstein, Karnit Goldwasser, David Golomb, Sarit Gomez, Oleg Gordievsky, Ran Goren, Uri Goren, Eitan Haber, Arie Hadar, Amin al-Hajj, Asher Hakaini, Eli Halachmi, Aharon Halevi, Aliza Magen Halevi, Aviram Halevi, David Halevi, Amnon Halivni, Uri Halperin, Dan Halutz, August Hanning, Alouph Hareven, Elkana Har Nof, Dani Harari, Shalom Harari, Isser Harel, Hani al-Hassan, Yisrael Hasson, Robert Hatem, Shai Herschkovich, Seymour Hersh, Robin Higgins, Shlomo Hillel, Gal Hirsch, Yair Hirschfeld, Yitzhak Hofi, Lior Horev, Yehiel Horev, Rami Igra, Yitzhak Ilan, Shimshon Issaki, David Ivri, Aryeh Ivtzan, Yehiel Kadishai, Oleg Kalugin, Anat Kamm, Tsvi Kantor, Yehudit Karp, Asa Kasher, Eugene Kaspersky, Samy Katsav, Kassa Kebede, Paul Kedar, Ruth Kedar, Moti Kfir, Gedaliah Khalaf, Moti Kidor, David Kimche, Yarin Kimor, Ephraim Kleiman, David Klein, Yoni Koren, Joseph Kostiner, Aryeh Krishak, Itzhak Kruizer, David Kubi, Chen Kugel, David Kulitz, Yossi Kuperwasser, Anat Kurz, Gunther Latsch, Eliot Lauer, Nachum Lev, Shimon Lev, Alex Levac, Amihai Levi, Nathan Levin, Nathaniel Levitt, Aharon Levran, Avi Levy, Gideon Levy, Udi Levy, Bernard Lewis, Rami Liber, Avi Lichter, Alon Liel, Danny Limor, Amnon Lipkin-Shahak, Dror Livne, Tzipi Livni, Lior Lotan, Uri Lubrani, Uzi Mahnaimi, Nir Man, Francine Manbar, Nahum Manbar, Victor Marchetti, Dan Margalit, David Meidan, Gideon Meir, Moshe Meiri, Nehemia Meiri, Yoram Meital, David Menashri, Ariel Merari, Reuven Merhav, Dan Meridor, Joy Kid Merkham, Gidi Meron, Hezi Meshita, Benny Michelson, Amram Mitzna, Ilan Mizrahi, Shaul Mofaz, Yekutiel Mor, Yitzhak Mordechai, Shmuel (Sami) Moriah, Benny Morris, Shlomo Nakdimon, Hamid Nasrallah, David Nataf, Yair Naveh, Yoni Navon, Menahem Navot, Ori Neeman, Yuval Ne'eman, Jack Neria, Benjamin Netanyahu, Yaakov Nimrodi, Nimrod Nir, Alberto Nisman, Moshe Nissim, Tzila Noiman, Rafi Noy, Oded (last name confidential), Arye Oded, Raphael Ofek, Amir Ofer, Ehud Olmert, Reza Pahlavi Shah, Gabriel Pasquini, Alexander Patnic, Shmuel Paz, Avi Peled, Yossi Peled, Gustavo Perednik, Shimon Peres, Amir Peretz, Yuri Perfilyev, Yaakov Peri, Richard Perle, Israel Perlov, Giandomenico Picco, Zvi Poleg, Eli Pollak, Yigal Pressler, Avi Primor, Ron Pundak, Yitzhak Pundak, Ahmed Qrea, Rona Raanan Shafrir, Dalia Rabin, Itamar Rabinovich, Gideon Rafael, Rani Rahav, Jibril Rajoub, Natan Rotberg (Rahav), Haggai Ram, Haim Ramon, Muhammad Rashid, Yair Ravid-Ravitz, Oded Raz, Benny Regev, Yiftach Reicher Atir, Shlomi Reisman, Daniel Reisner, Bill Rois, Dafna Ron, Eran Ron, Yiftah Ron-Tal, Avraham Rotem, Danny Rothschild, Elyakim Rubinstein, Joseph Saba, Dov Sadan, Ezra Sadan, Rachel Sadan, Jehan Sadat, Uri Sagie, Ori Salonim, Wafiq al-Samarrai, Yom Tov Samia, Eli Sanderovich, Yossi Sarid, Nicolas Sarkozy, Igal Sarna, Moshe Sasson, Uri Savir, Oded Savoray, Yezid Sayigh, David Scharia, Otniel Schneller, Yoram Schweitzer, Patrick Seale, Itzhak Segev, Samuel Segev, Dror Sela, Aviem Sella, David Senesh, Michael Sfard, Oren Shachor, Yarin Shahaf, Moshe Shahal, Hezi Shai, Emmanuel Shaked, Arik Shalev, Noam Shalit, Silvan Shalom, Yitzhak Shamir, Shimon Shapira, Yaakov Shapira, Assaf Shariv, Shabtai Shavit, Gideon Sheffer, Rami Sherman, Shimon Sheves, David Shiek, Dov Shilansky, Dubi Shiloah, Gad Shimron, Amir Shoham, Dan Shomron, David Shomron, Eliad Shraga, Zvi Shtauber, Yigal Simon, Efraim Sneh, Ovadia Sofer, Sami Sokol, Ali Soufan, Yuval Steinitz, Elazar Stern, Rafi Sutton, Rami Tal, Anat Talshir, Dov Tamari, Avraham Tamir, Elhanan Tannenbaum, Benjamin Telem, Ahmad Tibi, Izhak Tidhar, Rafi Tidhar, Yona Tilman, Tawfiq Tirawi, Haim Tomer, Richard Tomlinson, Eliezer (Geize) Tsafrir, Moshe Tsipper, Yoram Turbowicz, Shalom Turgeman, David Tzur, Ernst Uhrlau, Alon Unger, Rehavia Vardi, Matan Vilnai, David Vital, Ali Waked, Tim Weiner, Anita Weinstein, Avi Weiss Livne, Dov Weissglass, Robert Windrem, Paul Wolfowitz, James Woolsey, Yitzhak Ya'akov, Moshe Ya'alon, Amos Yadlin, Yoram Yair, Amos Yaron, Danny Yatom, Ehud Yatom, Eli Yossef, Dov Zakheim, Zvi Zamir, Benny Zeevi, Dror Ze'evi, Nadav Zeevi, Doron Zehavi, Eli Zeira, Amnon Zichroni, Eyal Zisser, Eli Ziv, Shabtai Ziv, Eli Zohar, Gadi Zohar, and Giora Zussman, as well as 350 interviewees who cannot be named; the initials or code names of 163 of them appear in the endnotes.

## BOOKS IN ENGLISH

Abrahamian, Ervand. *Khomeinism: Essays on the Islamic Republic.* London: University of California Press, 1993.

Adams, James. *The Unnatural Alliance.* London: Quartet, 1984.

Agee, Philip. *Inside the Company: CIA Diary.* Harmondsworth, UK: Penguin, 1975.

Andrew, Christopher. *The Defence of the Realm: The Authorized History of the MI5.* London: Penguin, 2009.

———. *For the President's Eyes Only.* London: HarperCollins, 1995.

Andrew, Christopher, and Vasili Mitrokhin. *The Mitrokhin Archive II.* London: Penguin, 2005.

———. *The Sword and the Shield: The Mitrokhin Archive and the Secret History of the KGB.* New York: Basic Books, 1999.

Angel, Anita. *The Nili Spies.* London: Frank Cass & Co., 1997.

Arnon, Arie, Israel Luski, Avia Spivak, and Jimmy Weinblatt. *The Palestinian Economy: Between Imposed Integration and Voluntary Separation.* New York: Brill, 1997.

Asculai, Ephraim. *Rethinking the Nuclear Non-Proliferation Regime.* Tel Aviv: Jaffee Center for Strategic Studies, TAU, 2004.

Avi-Ran, Reuven [Erlich]. *The Syrian Involvement in Lebanon since 1975.* Boulder, Colo.: Westview, 1991.

Bakhash, Shaul. *The Reign of the Ayatollahs: Iran and the Islamic Revolution.* New York: Basic Books, 1984.

Baram, Amatzia. *Building Towards Crisis: Saddam Husayn's Strategy for Survival*. Washington, D.C.: Washington Institute for Near East Policy, 1998.

Barnaby, Frank. *The Indivisible Bomb*. London: I.B. Tauris, 1989.

Ben-Menashe, Ari. *Profits of War: Inside the Secret U.S.-Israeli Arms Network*. New York: Sheridan Square, 1992.

Bergen, Peter L. *Holy War Inc.: Inside the Secret World of Osama Bin Laden*. London: Weidenfeld and Nicolson, 2003.

Bergman, Ronen. *Israel and Africa: Military and Intelligence Liaisons*. PhD diss., University of Cambridge, November 2006.

———. *The Secret War with Iran: The 30-Year Clandestine Struggle Against the World's Most Dangerous Terrorist Power*. New York: Free Press, 2008.

Bird, Kai. *The Good Spy*. New York: Crown, 2014.

Black, Ian, and Benny Morris. *Israel's Secret Wars: A History of Israel's Intelligence Services*. London: Hamish Hamilton, 1991.

Blum, Gabriella. *Islands of Agreement: Managing Enduring Rivalries*. Cambridge, Mass.: Harvard University Press, 2007.

Bobbitt, Philip. *Terror and Consent: The Wars for the Twenty-first Century*. London: Penguin, 2008.

Bolker, Joan. *Writing Your Dissertation in Fifteen Minutes a Day: A Guide to Starting, Revising, and Finishing Your Doctoral Thesis*. New York: Henry Holt and Co., 1998.

Boroumand, Ladan. *Iran: In Defense of Human Rights*. Paris: National Movement of the Iranian Resistance, 1983.

Brecher, Michael. *Decisions in Israel's Foreign Policy*. London: Oxford University Press, 1974.

Burrows, William E., and Robert Windrem. *Critical Mass*. London: Simon & Schuster, 1994.

Butler, Richard. *Saddam Defiant*. London: Weidenfeld and Nicolson, 2000.

Calvocoressi, Peter. *World Politics, 1945–2000*. 9th ed. Harlow, UK: Pearson Education, 2001.

Carew, Tom. *Jihad: The Secret War in Afghanistan*. Edinburgh: Mainstream, 2000.

Carré, Olivier. *L'Utopie islamique dans l'Orient arabe*. Paris: Fondation Nationale des Sciences Politiques, 1991 (in French).

Cline, Ray S., and Yonah Alexander. *Terrorism as State-Sponsored Covert Warfare*. Fairfax, Va.: Hero, 1986.

Cobban, Helena. *The Palestinian Liberation Organisation*. Cambridge, UK: Cambridge University Press, 1984.

Cockburn, Andrew, and Leslie Cockburn. *Dangerous Liaisons: The Inside Story of the U.S.–Israeli Covert Relationship*. New York: HarperCollins, 1991.

Cohen, Avner. *Israel and the Bomb*. New York: Columbia University Press, 1998.

Cookridge, E. H. *Gehlen: Spy of the Century*. London: Hodder and Stoughton, 1971.

Dan, Ben, Uri Dan, and Y. Ben-Porat. *The Secret War: The Spy Game in the Middle East*. New York: Sabra, 1970.

Deacon, Richard. *The Israeli Secret Service*. London: Hamish Hamilton, 1977.

Dekmejian, R. Hrair. *Islam in Revolution: Fundamentalism in the Arab World*. 2nd ed. Syracuse, N.Y.: Syracuse University Press, 1995.

Drogin, Bob. *Curveball*. New York: Random House, 2007.

Edward, Shirley. *Know Thine Enemy*. New York: Farrar, Straus and Giroux, 1997.

Eisenberg, Dennis, Uri Dan, and Eli Landau. *The Mossad: Israel's Secret Intelligence Service: Inside Stories*. New York: Paddington, 1978.

Eisenstadt, Michael. *Iranian Military Power: Capabilities and Intentions*. Washington, D.C.: Washington Institute for Near East Policy, 1996.

Eveland, Wilbur Crane. *Ropes of Sand: America's Failure in the Middle East*. New York: W. W. Norton, 1980.

Farrell, William R. *Blood and Rage: The Story of the Japanese Red Army*. Toronto: Lexington, 1990.

Freedman, Robert O. *World Politics and the Arab-Israeli Conflict*. New York: Pergamon, 1979.

Gabriel, Richard A. *Operation Peace for Galilee: The Israeli-PLO War in Lebanon*. New York: Hill and Wang, 1984.

Gates, Robert M. *From the Shadows*. New York: Simon & Schuster Paperbacks, 1996.

Gazit, Shlomo. *Trapped Fools: Thirty Years of Israeli Policy in the Territories*. London and Portland, Ore.: Frank Cass, 2003.

Gilbert, Martin. *The Routledge Atlas of the Arab-Israeli Conflict*. New York: Routledge, 2005.

Ginor, Isabella, and Gideon Remez. *Foxbats over Dimona*. New Haven, Conn.: Yale University Press, 2007.

Halkin, Hillel. *A Strange Death*. New York: PublicAffairs, 2005.

Harclerode, Peter. *Secret Soldiers: Special Forces in the War Against Terrorism*. London: Sterling, 2000.

Hatem, Robert M. *From Israel to Damascus: The Painful Road of Blood, Betrayal, and Deception*. La Mesa, Calif.: Pride International Press, 1999.

Hayden, Michael. *Playing to the Edge*. New York: Penguin Press, 2016.

Hersh, Seymour. *The Samson Option*. New York: Random House, 1991.

Hoffman, Bruce. *Recent Trends and Future Prospects of Iranian Sponsored International Terrorism*. Santa Monica, Calif.: Rand, 1990.

Hollis, Martin, and Steve Smith. *Explaining and Understanding International Relations*. Oxford, UK: Clarendon, 1990.

Hurwitz, Harry, and Yisrael Medad, eds. *Peace in the Making*. Jerusalem: Gefen, 2011.

Jaber, Hala. *Hezbollah: Born with a Vengeance*. New York: Columbia University Press, 1997.

Jonas, George. *Vengeance: The True Story of a Counter-Terrorist Mission*. London: Collins, 1984.

Juergensmeyer, Mark. *Terror in the Mind of God: The Global Rise of Religious Violence*. Berkeley: University of California Press, 2000.

Keddie, Nikki R., ed. *Religion and Politics in Iran: Shi'ism from Quietism to Revolution*. New Haven, Conn.: Yale University Press, 1983.

Kenyatta, Jomo. *Facing Mount Kenya*. Nairobi: Heinemann Kenya, 1938.

Klein, Aaron J. *Striking Back: The 1972 Munich Olympics Massacre and Israel's Deadly Response*. New York: Random House, 2005.

Kurginyan, Sergey. *The Weakness of Power: The Analytics of Closed Elite Games and Its Basic Concepts*. Moscow: ECC, 2007.

Kwintny, Jonathan. *Endless Enemies: The Making of an Unfriendly World*. New York: Penguin, 1984.

Landler, Mark. *Alter Egos*. New York: Random House, 2016.

Laqueur, Walter. *The New Terrorism: Fanaticism and the Arms of Mass Destruction*. London: Phoenix Press, 1999.

Livingstone, Neil C., and David Halevy. *Inside the PLO*. New York: Quill/William Morrow, 1990.

Marchetti, Victor, and John D. Marks. *The CIA and the Cult of Intelligence*. New York: Dell, 1980.

McGeough, Paul. *Kill Khalid*. New York: New Press, 2009.

Mearsheimer, John, and Stephen Walt. *The Israeli Lobby and U.S. Foreign Policy*. New York: Farrar, Straus and Giroux, 2007.

Melman, Yossi. *The Master Terrorist: The True Story Behind Abu-Nidal*. London: Sidgwick & Jackson, 1987.

Menashri, David, ed. *Islamic Fundamentalism: A Challenge to Regional Stability*. Tel Aviv: Moshe Dayan Center for Middle Eastern and African Studies, 1993.

Mishal, Shaul. *The PLO Under Arafat*. New Haven, Conn.: Yale University Press, 1986.

Mitrokhin, Vasiliy. *KGB Lexicon*. London: Frank Cass & Co., 2002.

Mohadessin, Mohammad. *Islamic Fundamentalism: The New Global Threat*. Washington, D.C.: Seven Locks Press, 1993.

Morris, Benny, and Ian Black. *Israel's Secret Wars*. London: Warner, 1992.

Norton, Augustus Richard. *Amal and the Shia: Struggle for the Soul of Lebanon*. Austin: University of Texas Press, 1987.

Oded, Arye. *Africa and the Middle East Conflict*. Boulder, Colo.: Westview, 1988.

Oliphant, Laurence. *The Land of Gilead*. London: William Blackwood and Sons, 1880.

Ostrovsky, Victor, and Claire Hoy. *By Way of Deception: The Making and Unmaking of a Mossad Officer*. New York: St. Martin's, 1990.

Pacepa, Ion Mihai. *Red Horizons*. Washington, D.C.: Regnery Gateway, 1990.

Parsi, Trita. *Treacherous Alliance: The Secret Dealings of Israel, Iran and the United States*. New Haven, Conn.: Yale University Press, 2007.

Payne, Ronald. *Mossad: Israel's Most Secret Service*. London and New York: Bantam, 1990.

Pedahzur, Ami. *The Israeli Secret Services and the Struggle Against Terrorism*. New York: Columbia University Press, 2009.

Picco, Giandomenico. *Man Without a Gun*. New York: Times Books, 1999.

Pipes, Daniel. *The Hidden Hand*. New York: St. Martin's, 1996.

Polakow-Suransky, Sasha. *The Unspoken Alliance: Israel's Secret Relationship with Apartheid South Africa*. New York: Pantheon, 2010.

Porath, Yehoshua. *In Search of Arab Unity, 1930–1945*. London: Frank Cass & Co., 1986.

Posner, Steve. *Israel Undercover: Secret Warfare and Hidden Diplomacy in the Middle East*. Syracuse, N.Y.: Syracuse University Press, 1987.

Qutb, Sayyid. *The Future Belongs to Islam: Our Battle with the Jews*. Tel Aviv: Moshe Dayan Center for Middle Eastern and African Studies, 2017.

Ranelagh, John. *The Agency: The Rise and Decline of the CIA*. New York: Simon & Schuster, 1986.

Rimington, Stella. *Open Secret: The Autobiography of the Former Director-General of MI5*. London: Hutchinson, 2002.

Rivlin, Paul. *The Russian Economy and Arms Exports to the Middle East*. Tel Aviv: Jaffee Center for Strategic Studies, 2005.

Ruwayha, Walid Amin. *Terrorism and Hostage-Taking in the Middle East*. France: publisher unknown, 1990.

Sadjadpour, Karim. *Reading Khamenei: The World View of Iran's Most Powerful Leader*. Washington, D.C.: Carnegie Endowment for International Peace, 2009.

Said, Edward. *The End of the Peace Process: Oslo and After*. London: Granta, 2000.

Sauer, Paul. *The Holy Land Called: The Story of the Temple Society*. English edition. Melbourne: Temple Society, 1991.

Sayigh, Yezid. *Armed Struggle and the Search for State*. Oxford, UK: Oxford University Press, 1997.

Schulz, Richard, and Andrea Dew. *Insurgents, Terrorists and Militias*. New York: Columbia University Press, 2006.

Schulze, Kirsten E. *Israel's Covert Diplomacy in Lebanon*. Basingstoke, UK: Macmillan, 1998.

Seale, Patrick. *Abu Nidal: A Gun for Hire*. London: Hutchinson, 1992.

Shirley, Edward. *Know Thine Enemy*. New York: Farrar, Straus and Giroux, 1997.

Shlaim, Avi. *The Iron Wall*. London: Penguin, 2000.

Skorzeny, Otto. *My Commando Operations*. Atglen, Pa.: Schiffer, 1995.

Smith, Steven, Ken Booth, and Marysia Zalewski. *International Theory: Positivism and Beyond*. Cambridge, UK: Cambridge University Press, 1996.

Steven, Stewart. *The Spymasters of Israel*. London: Hodder and Stoughton, 1981.

Sumaida, Hussein, and Carole Jerome. *Circle of Fear*. London: Robert Hale, 1992.

Taheri, Amir. *The Spirit of Allah*. London: Hutchinson, 1985.

Tenet, George. *At the Center of the Storm*. New York: HarperCollins, 2007.

Teveth, Shabtai. *Ben-Gurion's Spy: The Story of the Political Scandal That Shaped Modern Israel*. New York: Columbia University Press, 1996.

Theroux, Peter. *The Strange Disappearance of Imam Moussa Sadr*. London: Weidenfeld and Nicolson, 1987.

Thomas, Gordon. *Gideon's Spies: The Secret History of the Mossad*. London: Pan Books, 2000.

Transparency International. *Global Corruption Report 2004*. London: Pluto Press, 2004.

Trento, Joseph J. *The Secret History of the CIA*. New York: MJF Books, 2001.

Trevan, Tim. *Saddam's Secrets: The Hunt for Iraq's Hidden Weapons*. London: HarperCollins, 1999.

Treverton, Gregory F. *Covert Action*. London: I.B. Tauris & Co., 1988.

Urban, Mark. *UK Eyes Alpha: The Inside Story of British Intelligence*. London: Faber and Faber, 1996.

Venter, Al J. *How South Africa Built Six Atom Bombs*. Cape Town: Ashanti, 2008.

Verrier, Antony, ed. *Agent of Empire*. London: Brassey's, 1995.

Walsh, Lawrence E. *Firewall: The Iran-Contra Conspiracy and Cover-up*. New York: W. W. Norton & Co., 1997.

Walton, Calder. *Empire of Secrets*. London: HarperPress, 2013.

Wardlaw, Grant. *Political Terrorism: Theory, Tactics and Counter-Measures*. Cambridge, UK: Cambridge University Press, 1982.

Wasserstein, Bernard. *The Assassination of Lord Moyne, Transactions & Miscellanies,* vol. 27. London: Jewish Historical Society of England, 1978–80.

Webman, Esther. *Anti-Semitic Motifs in the Ideology of Hizballah and Hamas*. Tel Aviv: Project for the Study of Anti-Semitism, 1994.

Weiner, Tim. *Enemies: A History of the FBI*. New York: Random House, 2012.

———. *Legacy of Ashes: The History of the CIA*. New York: Doubleday, 2007.

Wright, Robin. *Sacred Rage: The Wrath of Militant Islam*. New York: Simon & Schuster, 1986.

Ya'ari, Ehud. *Strike Terror: The Story of Fatah*. New York: Sabra, 1970.

## BOOKS IN HEBREW

Adam, Kfir. *Closure*. Oranit, Israel: Adam Kfir Technologies, 2009.

Almog, Ze'ev. *Bats in the Red Sea*. Haqirya, Israel: Ministry of Defense, 2007.

Alpher, Yossi. *Periphery: Israel's Search for Middle East Allies*. Tel Aviv: Matar, 2015.

Amidror, Yaakov. *The Art of Intelligence*. Haqirya, Israel: Ministry of Defense, 2006.

Amit, Meir. *Head On: The Memoirs of a Former Mossad Director*. Or Yehuda, Israel: Hed Arzi, 1999.

Argaman, Josef. *It Was Top Secret*. Haqirya, Israel: Ministry of Defense, 1990.

———. *The Shadow War*. Haqirya, Israel: Ministry of Defense, 2007.

Assenheim, Omri. *Ze'elim*. Or Yehuda, Israel: Kinneret Zmora-Bitan Dvir, 2011.

Aviad, Guy. *Lexicon of the Hamas Movement*. Ben Shemen, Israel: Modan, 2014.

Avi-Ran, Reuven. *The Lebanon War—Arab Documents and Sources: The Road to the "Peace for Galilee" War*. Vols. 1 and 2. Tel Aviv: Ma'arakhot, 1978.

Avnery, Uri. *My Friend, the Enemy*. London: Zed, 1986.

Banai, Yaakov. *Anonymous Soldiers*. Tel Aviv: Yair, 1974.

Bango-Moldavsky, Olena, and Yehuda Ben Meir. *The Voice of the People: Israel Public Opinion on National Security*. Tel Aviv: INSS, 2013.

Bar-Joseph, Uri. *The Angel: Ashraf Marwan, the Mossad and the Yom Kippur War*. Or Yehuda, Israel: Kinneret Zmora-Bitan Dvir, 2010.

Bar-On, Mordechai. *Moshe Dayan*. Tel Aviv: Am Oved, 2014.

Bar-Zohar, Michael. *The Avengers*. Ganey Tikva, Israel: Teper Magal, 1991.

———. *Ben Gurion*. Tel Aviv: Miskal, 2013.

———. *Issar Harel and Israel's Security Services*. London: Weidenfeld and Nicolson, 1970.

———. *Phoenix: Shimon Peres—a Political Biography*. Tel Aviv: Miskal, 2006.

Bar-Zohar, Michael, and Eitan Haber. *Massacre in Munich*. Or Yehuda, Israel: Kinneret Zmora-Bitan Dvir, 2005.

———. *The Quest for the Red Prince*. Or Yehuda, Israel: Zmora-Bitan, 1984.

Barda, Yael. *The Bureaucracy of the Occupation*. Bnei Brak, Israel: Van Leer Jerusalem Institute and Hakibbutz Hameuchad, 2012.

Bartov, Hanoch. *Dado: 48 Years and 20 More Days*. Or Yehuda, Israel: Dvir, 2002.

Bascomb, Neal. *Hunting Eichmann*. Tel Aviv: Miskal, 2009.

Bechor, Guy. *PLO Lexicon*. Haqirya, Israel: Ministry of Defense, 1991.

Beilin, Yossi. *Manual for a Wounded Dove*. Jerusalem: Yedioth Ahronoth, 2001.

———. *Touching Peace*. Tel Aviv: Miskal–Yedioth Ahronoth and Chemed, 1997.

Ben Dror, Elad. *The Mediator*. Sde Boker, Israel: Ben-Gurion Research Institute for the Study of Israel and Zionism, 2012.

Ben Israel, Isaac. *Israel Defence Doctrine*. Ben Shemen, Israel: Modan, 2013.

Ben-Natan, Asher. *Memoirs*. Haqirya, Israel: Ministry of Defense, 2002.

Ben Porat, Yoel. *Ne'ilah*. Tel Aviv: Yedioth Ahronoth, 1991.

Ben-Tor, Nechemia. *The Lehi Lexicon*. Haqirya, Israel: Ministry of Defense, 2007.

Ben Uziel, David. *On a Mossad Mission to South Sudan: 1969–1971*. Herzliya, Israel: Teva Ha'Dvarim, 2015.

Benziman, Uzi. *I Told the Truth*. Jerusalem: Keter, 2002.

Ben-Zvi, Yitzhak. *Sefer Hashomer*. Or Yehuda, Israel: Dvir, 1957.

Bergman, Ronen. *Authority Granted*. Tel Aviv: Yedioth Ahronoth, 2002.

———. *By Any Means Necessary: Israel's Covert War for Its POWs and MIAs*. Or Yehuda, Israel: Kinneret Zmora-Bitan Dvir, 2009.

———. *Point of No Return: Israeli Intelligence Against Iran and Hizballah*. Or Yehuda, Israel: Kinneret Zmora-Bitan Dvir, 2007.

Bergman, Ronen, and Dan Margalit. *The Pit*. Or Yehuda, Israel: Kinneret Zmora-Bitan Dvir, 2011.

Bergman, Ronen, and Gil Meltzer. *The Yom Kippur War: Moment of Truth*. Tel Aviv: Yedioth Ahronoth, 2003.

Betser, Muki (Moshe). *Secret Soldier*. Jerusalem: Keter, 2015.

Blanford Nicholas. *Killing Mr. Lebanon*. Translated by Michal Sela. Tel Aviv: Ma'ariv, 2007.

Bloom, Gadi, and Nir Hefez. *Ariel Sharon: A Life*. Tel Aviv: Miskal, 2005.

Boaz, Arieh. *The Origins of the Ministry of Defense*. Ben Shemen, Israel: Modan, 2013.

Bowden, Mark. *The Finish*. Or Yehuda, Israel: Kinneret Zmora-Bitan Dvir, 2012.

Brom, Shlomo, and Anat Kurz, eds. *Strategic Assessment for Israel 2010*. Tel Aviv: INSS, 2010.

Burgin, Maskit, David Tal, and Anat Kurz, eds. *Islamic Terrorism and Israel*. Tel Aviv: Papyrus, 1993.

Burton, Fred. *Chasing Shadows*. Or Yehuda, Israel: Kinneret Zmora-Bitan Dvir, 2011.

Caroz, Ya'acov. *The Man with Two Hats*. Haqirya, Israel: Ministry of Defense, 2002.

Cesarani, David. *Major Farran's Hat*. Or Yehuda, Israel: Kinneret Zmora-Bitan Dvir, 2015.

Claire, Rodger W. *Raid on the Sun*. Petah Tikva, Israel: Aryeh Nir, 2005.

Cohen, Avner. *Israel and the Bomb*. New York: Schocken, 1990.

Cohen, Gamliel. *Under Cover*. Haqirya, Israel: Ministry of Defense, 2002.

Cohen, Hillel. *An Army of Shadows: Palestinian Collaborators in the Service of Zionism*. Jerusalem: Ivrit, 2004.

———. *Good Arabs*. Jerusalem: Ivrit, 2006.

Cohen-Levinovsky, Nurit. *Jewish Refugees in Israel's War of Independence*. Tel Aviv: Am Oved, 2014.

Danin, Ezra. *Always Zionist*. Jerusalem: Kidum, 1987.

Dayan, Moshe. *Shall the Sword Devour Forever?* Tel Aviv: Edanim/Yedioth Ahronoth, 1981.

———. *Story of My Life*. Jerusalem: Idanim and Dvir, 1976.

Dekel, Efraim. *Shai: The Exploits of Hagana Intelligence*. Tel Aviv: IDF-Ma'archot, 1953.

Dekel-Dolitzky, Elliyahu. *Groundless Intelligence*. Elkana, Israel: Ely Dekel, 2010.

Dietl, Wilhelm. *Die Agentin des Mossad*. Tel Aviv: Zmora-Bitan, 1997.

Dor, Danny, and Ilan Kfir. *Barak: Wars of My Life*. Or Yehuda, Israel: Kinneret Zmora-Bitan Dvir, 2015.

Dror, Zvika. *The "Arabist" of the Palmach*. Bnei Brak, Israel: Hakibbutz Hameuchad, 1986.

Drucker, Raviv. *Harakiri—Ehud Barak: The Failure*. Tel Aviv: Miskal, 2002.

Edelist, Ran. *The Man Who Rode the Tiger*. Or Yehuda, Israel: Zmora-Bitan, 1995.

Edelist, Ran, and Ilan Kfir. *Ron Arad: The Mystery*. Tel Aviv: Miskal–Yedioth Ahronoth, 2000.

Eilam, Uzi. *The Eilam Bow*. Tel Aviv: Miskal–Yedioth Ahronoth and Chemed, 2013.

Eiran, Ehud. *The Essence of Longing: General Erez Gerstein and the War in Lebanon*. Tel Aviv: Miskal–Yedioth Ahronoth, 2007.

Eitan, Rafael. *A Soldier's Story: The Life and Times of an Israeli War Hero*. Tel Aviv: Ma'ariv, 1985.

Eldar, Mike. *Flotilla 11: The Battle for Citation*. Tel Aviv: Ma'ariv, 1996.

———. *Flotilla 13: The Story of Israel's Naval Commando*. Tel Aviv: Ma'ariv, 1993.

———. *Soldiers of the Shadows*. Haqirya, Israel: Ministry of Defense, 1997.

Eldar, Shlomi. *Getting to Know Hamas*. Jerusalem: Keter, 2012.

Elpeleg, Zvi. *Grand Mufti*. Haqirya, Israel: Ministry of Defense, 1989.

Elran, Meir, and Shlomo Brom. *The Second Lebanon War: Strategic Dimensions*. Tel Aviv: Miskal–Yedioth Ahronoth, 2007.

Erel, Nitza. *Without Fear and Prejudice*. Jerusalem: Magnes, 2006.

Erlich, Haggai. *Alliance and Alienation: Ethiopia and Israel in the Days of Haile Selassie*. Tel Aviv: Moshe Dayan Center for Middle Eastern and African Studies, 2013.

Erlich, Reuven. *The Lebanon Tangle: The Policy of the Zionist Movement and the State of Israel Towards Lebanon, 1918–1958*. Tel Aviv: Ma'arakhot, 2000.

Eshed, Haggai. *One Man's Mossad—Reuven Shiloah: Father of Israeli Intelligence*. Tel Aviv: Edanim/Yedioth Ahronoth, 1988.

———. *Who Gave the Order?* Tel Aviv: Edanim, 1979.

Ezri, Meir. *Who Among You from All the People: Memoir of His Years as the Israeli Envoy in Tehran*. Or Yehuda, Israel: Hed Arzi, 2001.

Farman Farmaian, Sattareh, and Dona Munker. *Daughter of Persia*. Rishon LeZion, Israel: Barkai, 2003.

Feldman, Shai. *Israeli Nuclear Deterrence: A Strategy for the 1980s*. Bnei Brak, Israel: Hakibbutz Hameuchad, 1983.

Finkelstein, Menachem. *The Seventh Column and the Purity of Arms: Natan Alterman on Security, Morality and Law*. Bnei Brak, Israel: Hakibbutz Hameuchad, 2011.

Friedman, Thomas L. *From Beirut to Jerusalem*. Tel Aviv: Ma'ariv, 1990.

Gazit, Shlomo. *At Key Points of Time*. Tel Aviv: Miskal, 2016.

Gelber, Yoav. *A Budding Fleur-de-Lis: Israeli Intelligence Services During the War of Independence, 1948–1949*. Haqirya, Israel: Ministry of Defense, 2000.

———. *Growing a Fleur-de-Lis: The Intelligence Services of the Jewish Yishuv in Palestine, 1918–1947*. Haqirya, Israel: Ministry of Defense, 1992.

———. *Independence Versus Nakbah: The Arab–Israeli War of 1948*. Or Yehuda, Israel: Zmora-Bitan, 2004.

———. *Israeli-Jordanian Dialogue, 1948–1953: Cooperation, Conspiracy, or Collusion?* Brighton, UK: Sussex Academic Press, 2004.

———. *Jewish Palestinian Volunteering in the British Army During the Second World War*. Vol. III, *The Standard Bearers: The Mission of the Volunteers to the Jewish People*. Jerusalem: Yad Izhak Ben-Zvi, 1983.

Gilboa, Amos. *Mr. Intelligence: Ahrale Yariv*. Tel Aviv: Miskal–Yedioth Ahronoth and Chemed, 2013.

Gilboa, Amos, and Ephraim Lapid. *Masterpiece: An Inside Look at Sixty Years of Israeli Intelligence*. Tel Aviv: Miskal, 2006.

Gillon, Carmi. *Shin-Beth Between the Schisms*. Tel Aviv: Miskal, 2000.

Givati, Moshe. *Abir 21*. Jerusalem: Reut, 2003.

Golani, Motti, ed. *Hetz Shachor: Gaza Raid & the Israeli Policy of Retaliation During the Fifties*. Haqirya, Israel: Ministry of Defense, 1994.

Goldstein, Yossi. *Rabin: Biography*. New York: Schocken, 2006.

———. *Golda: Biography*. Sde Boker, Israel: Ben-Gurion Research Institute for the Study of Israel and Zionism, 2012.

Goodman, Micha. *The Secrets of the Guide to the Perplexed*. Or Yehuda, Israel: Kinneret Zmora-Bitan Dvir, 2010.

Goren, Uri. *On the Two Sides of the Crypto*. Self-published, 2008.

Gourevitch, Philip, and Errol Morris. *The Ballad of Abu Ghraib*. Tel Aviv: Am Oved, 2010.

Gutman, Yechiel. *A Storm in the G.S.S.* Tel Aviv: Yedioth Ahronoth, 1995.

Halamish, Aviva. *Meir Yaari: The Rebbe from Merhavia*. Tel Aviv: Am Oved, 2009.

Halevy, Aviram, Yiftach Reicher Atir, and Shlomi Reisman, eds. *Operation Yonatan in First Person*. Modi'in, Israel: Efi Melzer, 2016.

Halevy, Efraim. *Man in the Shadows*. Tel Aviv: Matar, 2006.

Haloutz, Dani. *Straight Forward*. Tel Aviv: Miskal, 2010.

Harel, Amos, and Avi Issacharoff. *The Seventh War*. Tel Aviv: Miskal, 2004.

———. *Spider Webs (34 Days)*. Tel Aviv: Miskal, 2008.

Harel, Isser. *Anatomy of Treason*. Jerusalem: Idanim, 1980.

———. *Security and Democracy*. Jerusalem: Idanim, 1989.

———. *When Man Rose Against Men*. Jerusalem: Keter, 1982.

———. *Yossele Operation*. Tel Aviv: Yedioth Ahronoth, 1982.

Harouvi, Eldad. *Palestine Investigated*. Kokhav Ya'ir, Israel: Porat, 2010.

Hass, Amira. *Drinking the Sea of Gaza*. Bnei Brak, Israel: Hakibbutz Hameuchad, 1996.

Hendel, Yoaz, and Shalom Zaki. *Let the IDF Win: The Self-Fulfilling Slogan*. Tel Aviv: Yedioth Ahronoth, 2010.

Hendel, Yoaz, and Yaakov Katz. *Israel vs. Iran*. Or Yehuda, Israel: Kinneret Zmora-Bitan Dvir, 2011.

Herrera, Ephraim, and Gideon M. Kressel. *Jihad: Fundamentals and Fundamentalism*. Haqirya, Israel: Ministry of Defense, 2009.

Herschovitch, Shay, and David Simantov. *Aman Unclassified*. Tel Aviv: Ma'archot MOD, 2013.

Hounam, Peter. *The Woman from the Mossad*. Tel Aviv–Yafo: Or'Am, 2001.

Jackont, Amnon. *Meir Amit: A Man of the Mossad*. Tel Aviv: Miskal, 2012.

Kabha, Mustafa. *The Palestinian People: Seeking Sovereignty and State*. Tel Aviv: Matach, 2013.

Kam, Ephraim. *From Terror to Nuclear Bombs: The Significance of the Iranian Threat*. Haqirya, Israel: Ministry of Defense, 2004.

Kampf, Zohar, and Tamar Liebes. *Media at Times of War and Terror*. Ben Shemen, Israel: Modan, 2012.

Karsh, Efraim, and Inari Rautsi. *Saddam Hussein: A Political Biography*. Haqirya, Israel: Ministry of Defense, 1991.

Kfir, Ilan. *The Earth Has Trembled*. Tel Aviv: Ma'ariv, 2006.

Kimche, David. *The Last Option*. Tel Aviv: Miskal–Yedioth Ahronoth, 1991.

Kipnis, Yigal. *1973: The Way to War*. Or Yehuda, Israel: Kinneret Zmora-Bitan Dvir, 2012.

Klein, Aaron J. *The Master of Operation: The Story of Mike Harari*. Jerusalem: Keter, 2014.

———. *Striking Back: The 1972 Munich Olympics Massacre and Israel's Deadly Response*. Tel Aviv: Miskal–Yedioth Ahronoth, 2006.

Klieman, Ahron. *Double Edged Sword*. Tel Aviv: Am Oved, 1992.

Klingberg, Marcus, and Michael Sfard. *The Last Spy*. Tel Aviv: Ma'ariv, 2007.

Knopp, Guido. *Göring: Eine Karriere*. Tel Aviv: Ma'ariv, 2005.

Kotler, Yair. *Joe Returns to the Limelight*. Ben Shemen, Israel: Modan, 1988.

Kramer, Martin. *Fadlallah: The Moral Logic of Hizballah*. Tel Aviv: Moshe Dayan Center for Middle Eastern and African Studies, 1998.

Kramer, Martin, ed. *Protest and Revolution in Shi'i Islam*. Tel Aviv: Moshe Dayan Center for Middle Eastern and African Studies, 1987.

Kupperman, Robert H., and Darrell M. Trent. *Terrorism: Threat, Reality, Response*. Haqirya, Israel: Ministry of Defense, 1979.

Kurtz, Anat. *Islamic Terrorism and Israel: Hizballah, Palestinian Islamic Jihad and Hamas*. Tel Aviv: Papyrus, 1993.

Kurtz, Anat, and Pnina Sharvit Baruch, eds. *Law and National Security*. Tel Aviv: INSS, 2014.

Lahad, Antoine. *In the Eye of the Storm: Fifty Years of Serving My Homeland Lebanon: An Autobiography*. Tel Aviv: Miskal, 2004.

Landau, David. *Arik: The Life of Ariel Sharon*. Or Yehuda, Israel: Kinneret Zmora-Bitan Dvir, 2013.

Lazar, Hadara. *Six Singular Individuals*. Bnei Brak, Israel: Hakibbutz Hameuchad, 2012.

le Carré, John. *The Pigeon Tunnel*. Or Yehuda, Israel: Kinneret Zmora-Bitan Dvir, 2017.

Levi, Nissim. *One Birdless Year*. Tel Aviv: Am Oved, 2006.

Lew, Uzrad. *Inside Arafat's Pocket*. Or Yehuda, Israel: Kinneret Zmora-Bitan Dvir, 2005.

Livneh, Eliezer, Yosef Nedava, and Yoram Efrati. *Nili: The History of Political Daring*. New York: Schocken, 1980.

Lotz, Wolfgang. *Mission to Cairo*. Tel Aviv: Ma'ariv, 1970.

Lowther, William. *Arms and the Man*. Tel Aviv: Ma'ariv, 1991.

Macintyre, Ben. *Double Cross: The True Story of the D-Day Spies*. Translated by Yossi Millo. Tel Aviv: Am Oved, 2013.

Maiberg, Ron. *The Patriot*. Or Yehuda, Israel: Kinneret Zmora-Bitan Dvir, 2014.

Mann, Nir. *The Kirya in Tel Aviv, 1948–1955*. Jerusalem: Carmel, 2012.

———. *Sarona: Years of Struggle, 1939–1948*. 2nd ed. Jerusalem: Yad Izhak Ben Zvi, 2009.

Mann, Rafi. *The Leader and the Media*. Tel Aviv: Am Oved, 2012.

Maoz, Moshe. *The Sphinx of Damascus*. Or Yehuda, Israel: Dvir, 1988.

Margalit, Dan. *Disillusionment*. Or Yehuda, Israel: Kinneret Zmora-Bitan Dvir, 2009.

———. *I Have Seen Them All*. Or Yehuda, Israel: Kinneret Zmora-Bitan Dvir, 1997.

———. *Paratroopers in the Syrian Jail*. Tel Aviv: Moked, 1968.

Marinsky, Arieh. *In Light and in Darkness*. Jerusalem: Idanim, 1992.

Mass, Efrat. *Yael: The Mossad Combatant in Beiruth*. Bnei Brak, Israel: Hakibbutz Hameuchad, 2015.

Medan, Raphi. unpublished manuscript, 2010.

Melman, Yossi. *Israel Foreign Intelligence and Security Services Survey*. Or Yehuda, Israel: Kinneret Zmora-Bitan Dvir, 1982.

Melman, Yossi, and Eitan Haber. *The Spies: Israel's Counter-Espionage Wars*. Tel Aviv: Miskal–Yedioth Ahronoth and Chemed, 2002.

Melman, Yossi, and Dan Raviv. *The Imperfect Spies*. Tel Aviv: Ma'ariv, 1990.

———. *Spies Against Armageddon*. Tel Aviv: Miskal, 2012.

Menashri, David. *Iran After Khomeini: Revolutionary Ideology Versus National Interests*. Tel Aviv: Moshe Dayan Center for Middle Eastern and African Studies, 1999.

———. *Iran Between Islam and the West*. Haqirya, Israel: Ministry of Defense, 1996.

Merari, Ariel, and Shlomi Elad. *The International Dimension of Palestinian Terrorism*. Bnei Brak, Israel: Hakibbutz Hameuchad, 1986.

Moreh, Dror. *The Gatekeepers: Inside Israel's Internal Security Agency*. Tel Aviv: Miskal, 2014.

Morris, Benny. *Israel's Border Wars, 1949–1956*. Tel Aviv: Am Oved, 1996.

Nachman Tepper, Noam. *Eli Cohen: Open Case*. Modi'in, Israel: Efi Melzer, 2017.

Nadel, Chaim. *Who Dares Wins*. Ben Shemen, Israel: Modan, 2015.

Nafisi, Azar. *Reading Lolita in Tehran*. Tel Aviv: Miskal–Yedioth Ahronoth, 2005.

Nakdimon, Shlomo. *Tammuz in Flames*. Tel Aviv: Yedioth Ahronoth, 1986.

Naor, Mordecai. *Laskov*. Haqirya, Israel: Ministry of Defense, 1988.

———. *Ya'akov Dori: I.D.F. First Chief of Staff*. Ben Shemen, Israel: Modan, 2011.

Nasr, Vali. *The Shia Revival*. Tel Aviv: Miskal, 2011.

Naveh, Dan. *Executive Secrets*. Tel Aviv: Miskal–Yedioth Ahronoth, 1999.

Navot, Menachem. *One Man's Mossad*. Or Yehuda, Israel: Kinneret Zmora-Bitan Dvir, 2015.

Netanyahu, Iddo, ed. *Sayeret Matkal at Antebbe*. Tel Aviv: Miskal, 2006.

Nevo, Azriel. *Military Secretary*. Tel Aviv: Contento, 2015.

Nimrodi, Yaakov. *Irangate: A Hope Shattered*. Tel Aviv: Ma'ariv, 2004.

Oren, Ram. *Sylvia*. Jerusalem: Keshet, 2010.

Oufkir, Malika, and Michele Fitoussi. *The Prisoner*. Or Yehuda, Israel: Kinneret, 2001.

Pacepa, Ion Mihai. *Red Horizons*. Tel Aviv: Ma'ariv, 1989.

Pail, Meir, and Avraham Zohar. *Palmach*. Haqirya, Israel: Ministry of Defense, 2008.

Palmor, Eliezer. *The Lillehammer Affair*. Israel: Carmel, 2000.

Paz, Reuven. *Suicide and Jihad in Palestinian Radical Islam: The Ideological Aspect*. Tel Aviv: Tel Aviv University Press, 1998.

Perry, Yaakov. *Strike First*. Jerusalem: Keshet, 1999.

Pirsig, Robert M. *Zen and the Art of Motorcycle Maintenance*. Or Yehuda, Israel: Kinneret Zmora-Bitan Dvir, 1974.

Porat, Dina. *Beyond the Corporeal: The Life and Times of Abba Kovner*. Tel Aviv: Am Oved and Yad Vashem, 2000.

Pressfield, Steven. *Killing Rommel*. Petah Tikva, Israel: Aryeh Nir, 2009.

Pundak, Ron. *Secret Channel*. Tel Aviv: Sifrey Aliyat Hagag–Miskal–Yedioth Ahronoth and Chemed, 2013.

Pundak, Yitzhak. *Five Missions*. Tel Aviv: Yaron Golan, 2000.

Rabinovich, Itamar. *The Brink of Peace: Israel & Syria, 1992–1996*. Tel Aviv: Miskal, 1998.

———. *Waging Peace*. Or Yehuda, Israel: Kinneret Zmora-Bitan Dvir, 1999.

———. *Yitzhak Rabin: Soldier, Leader, Statesman*. Or Yehuda, Israel: Kinneret Zmora-Bitan Dvir, 2017.

Rachum, Ilan. *The Israeli General Security Service Affair*. Jerusalem: Carmel, 1990.

Ram, Haggai. *Reading Iran in Israel: The Self and the Other, Religion, and Modernity*. Bnei Brak, Israel: Van Leer Jerusalem Institute and Hakibbutz Hameuchad, 2006.

Raphael, Eitan. *A Soldier's Story: The Life and Times of an Israeli War Hero*. Tel Aviv: Ma'ariv, 1985.

Ravid, Yair. *Window to the Backyard: The History of Israel-Lebanon Relations—Facts & Illusions*. Yehud, Israel: Ofir Bikurim, 2013.

Regev, Ofer. *Prince of Jerusalem*. Kokhav Ya'ir, Israel: Porat, 2006.

Rika, Eliahu. *Breakthrough*. Haqirya, Israel: Ministry of Defense, 1991.

Ronen, David. *The Years of Shabak*. Haqirya, Israel: Ministry of Defense, 1989.

Ronen, Yehudit. *Sudan in a Civil War: Between Africanism, Arabism and Islam*. Tel Aviv: Tel Aviv University Press, 1995.

Rosenbach, Marcel, and Holger Stark. *WikiLeaks: Enemy of the State*. Or Yehuda, Israel: Kinneret Zmora-Bitan Dvir, 2011.

Ross, Michael. *The Volunteer: A Canadian's Secret Life in the Mossad*. Tel Aviv: Miskal, 2007.

Rubin, Barry, and Judith Colp-Rubin. *Yasir Arafat: A Political Biography*. Tel Aviv: Miskal, 2006.

Rubinstein, Danny. *The Mystery of Arafat*. Or Yehuda, Israel: Kinneret Zmora-Bitan Dvir, 2001.

Sagie, Uri. *Lights Within the Fog*. Tel Aviv: Miskal–Yedioth Ahronoth, 1998.

Scharia, David. *The Pure Sound of the Piccolo: The Supreme Court of Israel, Dialogue and the Fight Against Terrorism*. Srigim, Israel: Nevo, 2012.

Schiff, Ze'ev, and Ehud Ya'ari. *Israel's Lebanon War*. New York: Schocken, 1984.

Seale, Patrick. *Assad*. Tel Aviv: Ma'arakhot, 1993.

Segev, Shmuel. *Alone in Damascus: The Life and Death of Eli Cohen*. Jerusalem: Keter, 2012. First published 1986.

———. *The Iranian Triangle: The Secret Relation Between Israel-Iran-U.S.A.* Tel Aviv: Ma'ariv, 1981.

———. *The Moroccan Connection*. Tel Aviv: Matar, 2008.

Segev, Tom. *Simon Wiesenthal: The Life and Legends*. Jerusalem: Keter, 2010.

Senor, Dan, and Saul Singer. *Start Up Nation*. Tel Aviv: Matar, 2009.

Shabi, Aviva, and Ronni Shaked. *Hamas: Palestinian Islamic Fundamentalist Movement*. Jerusalem: Keter, 1994.

Shai, Nachman. *Media War: Reaching for the Hearts and Minds*. Tel Aviv: Miskal–Yedioth Ahronoth and Chemed, 2013.

Shalev, Aryeh. *The Intifada: Causes and Effects*. Tel Aviv: Papyrus, 1990.

Shalom, Zaki, and Yoaz Hendel. *Defeating Terror*. Tel Aviv: Miskal, 2010.

Shamir, Yitzhak. *As a Solid Rock*. Tel Aviv: Yedioth Ahronoth, 2008.

Shapira, Shimon. *Hezbollah: Between Iran and Lebanon*. Bnei Brak, Israel: Hakibbutz Hameuchad, 2000.

Sharon, Gilad. *Sharon: The Life of a Leader*. Tel Aviv: Matar, 2011.

Shay, Shaul. *The Axis of Evil: Iran, Hezbollah, and Palestinian Terror*. Herzliya, Israel: Interdisciplinary Center, 2003.

———. *The Islamic Terror and the Balkans*. Herzliya, Israel: Interdisciplinary Center, 2006.

———. *The Never-Ending Jihad*. Herzliya, Israel: Interdisciplinary Center, 2002.

———. *The Shahids: Islam and Suicide Attacks*. Herzliya, Israel: Interdisciplinary Center, 2003.

Sheleg, Yair. *Desert's Wind: The Story of Yehoshua Cohen*. Haqirya, Israel: Ministry of Defense, 1998.

Sher, Gilad. *Just Beyond Reach*. Tel Aviv: Miskal, 2001.

Shilon, Avi. *Menachem Begin: A Life*. Tel Aviv: Am Oved, 2007.

Shimron, Gad. *The Execution of the Hangman of Riga*. Jerusalem: Keter, 2004.

———. *The Mossad and Its Myth*. Jerusalem: Keter, 1996.

Shomron, David. *Imposed Underground*. Tel Aviv: Yair, 1991.

Shur, Avner. *Crossing Borders*. Or Yehuda, Israel: Kinneret Zmora-Bitan Dvir, 2008.

———. *Itamar's Squad*. Jerusalem: Keter, 2003.

Sivan, Emmanuel. *The Fanatics of Islam*. Tel Aviv: Am Oved, 1986.

Sobelman, Daniel. *New Rules of the Game: Israel and Hizbollah After the Withdrawal from Lebanon Memorandum No. 65*. Tel Aviv: INSS, March 2003.

Stav, Arie, ed. *Ballistic Missiles, Threat and Response: The Main Points of Ballistic Missile Defense*. Jerusalem: Yedioth Ahronoth, 1998.

Sutton, Rafi. *The Sahlav Vendor: Autobiography and Operations in the Israeli Intelligence and Mossad Service*. Jerusalem: Lavie, 2012.

Sutton, Rafi, and Yitzhak Shoshan. *Men of Secrets, Men of Mystery*. Tel Aviv: Edanim/Yedioth Ahronoth, 1990.

Sykes, Christopher. *Cross Roads to Israel*. Tel Aviv: Ma'arakhot, 1987.

Tal, Nahman. *Confrontation at Home: Egypt and Jordan Against Radical Islam*. Tel Aviv: Papyrus, 1999.

Tamir, Moshe. *Undeclared War*. Haqirya, Israel: Ministry of Defense, 2006.

Tehari, Amir. *The Spirit of Allah*. Tel Aviv: Am Oved, 1985.

Tepper, Noam Nachman. *Eli Cohen: Open Case*. Modi'in, Israel: Efi Melzer, 2017.

Teveth, Shabtai. *Shearing Time: Firing Squad at Beth-Jiz*. Tel Aviv: Ish Dor, 1992.

Tsafrir, Eliezer (Geizi). *Big Satan, Small Satan: Revolution and Escape in Iran.* Tel Aviv: Ma'ariv, 2002.

———. *Labyrinth in Lebanon.* Tel Aviv: Miskal–Yedioth Ahronoth, 2006.

Tsiddon-Chatto, Yoash. *By Day, by Night, Through Haze and Fog.* Tel Aviv: Ma'ariv, 1995.

Tsoref, Hagai, ed. *Izhak Ben-Zvi, the Second President: Selected Documents (1884–1963).* Jerusalem: Israel State Archives, 1998.

Tzipori, Mordechai. *In a Straight Line.* Tel Aviv: Miskal–Yedioth Ahronoth and Chemed, 1997.

Tzipori, Shlomi. *Justice in Disguise.* Tel Aviv: Agam, 2004.

Weissbrod, Amir. *Turabi, Spokesman for Radical Islam.* Tel Aviv: Moshe Dayan Center for Middle Eastern and African Studies, 1999.

Weissglass, Dov. *Ariel Sharon: A Prime Minister.* Tel Aviv: Miskal, 2012.

Wolf, Markus. *Man Without a Face.* Or Yehuda, Israel: Hed Arzi, 2000.

Woodward, Bob. *Veil: The Secret Wars of the CIA, 1981–1987.* Or Yehuda, Israel: Kinneret, 1990.

Wright, Lawrence. *The Looming Tower: Al-Qaeda and the Road to 9/11.* Or Yehuda, Israel: Kinneret Zmora-Bitan Dvir, 2007.

Ya'alon, Moshe. *The Longer Shorter Way.* Tel Aviv: Miskal, 2008.

Yahav, Dan. *His Blood Be on His Own Head: Murders and Executions During the Era of the Yishuv, 1917–1948.* Self-published, 2010.

Yakar, Rephael. *The Sultan Yakov Battle.* Tel Aviv: IDF, History Department, 1999.

Yalin-Mor, Nathan. *Lohamey Herut Israel.* Jerusalem: Shikmona, 1974.

Yatom, Danny. *The Confidant.* Tel Aviv: Miskal, 2009.

Yeger, Moshe. *The History of the Political Department of the Jewish Agency.* Tel Aviv: Zionist Library, 2011.

Zahavi, Leon. *Apart and Together.* Jerusalem: Keter, 2005.

Zamir, Zvi, and Efrat Mass. *With Open Eyes.* Or Yehuda, Israel: Kinneret Zmora-Bitan Dvir, 2011.

Zichrony, Amnon. *1 Against 119: Uri Avnery in the Sixth Knesset.* Tel Aviv: Mozes, 1969.

Zonder, Moshe. *Sayeret Matkal: The Story of the Israeli SAS.* Jerusalem: Keter, 2000.

# INDEX

RONEN BERGMAN is the senior correspondent for military and intelligence affairs for *Yedioth Ahronoth,* Israel's largest daily paid newspaper, and a contributing writer for *The New York Times Magazine,* where he reports on intelligence, national security, terrorism, and nuclear issues. Bergman is the author of five bestselling Hebrew-language nonfiction books and *The Secret War with Iran,* which was published in the United States by Free Press. Bergman is the recipient of the Sokolow Prize, Israel's most esteemed award for journalism, and the B'nai B'rith International Press Award, among other honors. A member of the Israeli bar, he graduated with honors from the University of Haifa Faculty of Law and clerked in the attorney general's office. A winner of a Chevening Scholarship from the British Foreign Office, he received a master's in international relations from Cambridge University, where he was also awarded his PhD in history.

ronenbergman.com
Facebook.com/bergmanronen
Twitter: @ronenbergman

## ABOUT THE TYPE

This book was set in Fairfield, the first typeface from the hand of the distinguished American artist and engraver Rudolph Ruzicka (1883–1978). Ruzicka was born in Bohemia (in the present-day Czech Republic) and came to America in 1894. He set up his own shop, devoted to wood engraving and printing, in New York in 1913 after a varied career working as a wood engraver, in photoengraving and banknote printing plants, and as an art director and freelance artist. He designed and illustrated many books, and was the creator of a considerable list of individual prints—wood engravings, line engravings on copper, and aquatints.